HISTORICAL DICTIONARIES
OF LATIN AMERICA
Edited by Laurence Hallewell

1. *Guatemala*, by Richard E. Moore, rev. ed. 1973.
2. *Panama*, by Basil C. Hedrick and Anne K. Hedrick. 1970.
3. *Venezuela*, by Donna Keyse Rudolph and G. A. Rudolph. 1971.
4. *Bolivia*, by Dwight B. Heath. 1972.
5. *El Salvador*, by Philip F. Flemion. 1972.
6. *Nicaragua*, by Harvey K. Meyer. 1972.
7. *Chile*, 2nd ed., by Salvatore Bizzarro. 1987. Out of print. See No. 28.
8. *Paraguay*, by Charles J. Kolinski. 1973. Out of print. See No. 24.
9. *Puerto Rico and the U.S. Virgin Islands*, by Kenneth R. Farr. 1973.
10. *Ecuador*, by Albert W. Bork and Georg Maier. 1973.
11. *Uruguay*, by Jean L. Willis. 1974.
12. *British Caribbean*, by William Lux. 1975.
13. *Honduras*, by Harvey K. Meyer. 1976. Out of print. See No. 25.
14. *Colombia*, by Robert H. Davis. 1977. Out of print. See No. 23.
15. *Haiti*, by Roland I. Perusse. 1977.
16. *Costa Rica*, 2nd ed., by Theodore S. Creedman. 1991.
17. *Argentina*, by Ione Wright and Lisa M. Nekhom. 1978.
18. *French and Netherlands Antilles*, by Albert Gastmann. 1978.
19. *Brazil*, by Robert M. Levine. 1979.
20. *Peru*, by Marvin Alisky. 1979.
21. *Mexico*, by Donald C. Briggs and Marvin Alisky. 1981.
22. *Cuba*, by Jaime Suchlicki. 1988. Out of print. See No. 27.
23. *Colombia*, 2nd ed., by Robert H. Davis. 1993.
24. *Paraguay*, 2nd ed., by R. Andrew Nickson. 1993.
25. *Honduras*, 2nd ed., by Harvey K. Meyer and Jessie H. Meyer. 1994.
26. *Trinidad and Tobago*, by Michael Anthony. 1997.
27. *Cuba*, 2nd ed., by Jaime Suchlicki. 2001.
28. *Chile*, 3rd ed., by Salvatore Bizzarro. 2005.
29. *Mexico*, 2nd ed., by Marvin Alisky. 2008.

Historical Dictionary of Mexico

Second Edition

Marvin Alisky

*Historical Dictionaries
of Latin America, No. 29*

The Scarecrow Press, Inc.
Lanham, Maryland • Toronto • Plymouth, UK
2008

SCARECROW PRESS, INC.

Published in the United States of America
by Scarecrow Press, Inc.
A wholly owned subsidiary of
The Rowman & Littlefield Publishing Group, Inc.
4501 Forbes Boulevard, Suite 200
Lanham, Maryland 20706
www.scarecrowpress.com

Estover Road
Plymouth PL6 7PY
United Kingdom

British Library Cataloguing in Publication Information Available

Library of Congress Cataloging-in-Publication Data

Alisky, Marvin.
   Historical dictionary of Mexico / Marvin Alisky.— 2nd ed.
      p. cm. — (Historical dictionaries of Latin America ; no. 29)
   Statement of responsibility in previous edition includes Donald C. Briggs.
   Includes bibliographical references.
   ISBN-13: 978-0-8108-5995-1 (hardcover : alk. paper)
   ISBN-10: 0-8108-5995-5 (hardcover : alk. paper)
   1. Mexico—Encyclopedias. I. Title. II. Series.

F1204.B74 2007
972.003—dc22
                                                    2007024644

Contents

Editor's Foreword

The first edition of *Historical Dictionary of Mexico* appeared in 1981, prepared by two scholars familiar with Mexico from having lived, studied, and carried out research there. Professor Donald Briggs has had a long interest in the Mexican Indians. His wife and eldest son were born in Mexico. His mother-in-law grew up in a small native village. On his many visits to this community, he lived with the Indians, concerning himself mostly with their language and culture. At home with family groups, he came to understand their present-day problems and the larger problems of Mexico itself. Between 1956 and 1974 he visited the country almost yearly, residing there for about four years altogether. He is a graduate of Ohio State University, has a master's in Spanish literature from the University of the Americas in Mexico City, and wrote his dissertation on how Hidalgo is presented in Mexican primary and secondary school textbooks. He has taught Latin American studies at Broward Community College, Barry College, Florida State University at Tallahassee, and Miami Dade Community College.

Unfortunately, it has not proved possible for Professor Biggs to continue his collaboration in this new edition. Although all revision and new material have been the work of Marvin Alisky, much of the original text has been incorporated into this new edition. As editor I also have had some input (431 entries, generally quite brief, indicated by "L. H." at the end of each such contribution). I first visited Mexico in 1970 and have been back several times since, including a prolonged stay in the fall of 2005.

The earlier edition of this dictionary was weighted toward the present century. The two decades since the first edition have seen enormous changes in Mexico, beginning with the debt moratorium of 1982 and the subsequent retreat from the *dirigiste* approach to the economy that had been perhaps the most far-reaching inheritance of the Revolution.

During the 1980s and 1990s the two major opposition parties gradually began to gain seats at all levels of government, but the benchmark dividing the "old" from the "new" in Mexican politics came with the elections of July 6, 1997. By losing its majority in the lower house of Congress, the Partido Revolucionario Institucional lost control of the federal budget. For the first time since the Constitution of 1917 was promulgated, there was a genuine tug-of-war over many fiscal and economic policies. In Sonora, a new PRI governor found himself with a state legislature divided among all three parties.

The updating of this book has naturally been concerned with the events of these last two momentous decades. Besides covering such recent developments, this new edition also has extended its coverage to such socially significant concepts as *compadrazgo* (the godfather system) and the *camarilla* (political clique).

At the same time the detail provided for the colonial period has been greatly expanded. There are now, for instance, entries for all Spanish viceroys and an accompanying chronological listing of such office holders. Transport and communications have received special attention. There are also entries for the 31 states and the Federal District, the state capitals and other major cities, ports, and border communities, along with much on Mexico's older administrative divisions. The criterion for inclusion of smaller towns and communities has been their having been mentioned in one or more of the dictionary's other entries. Although the entries include a few individual books and other artistic creations, most information of this type will be found in the articles on the writers or artists responsible.

In sum, this updated, expanded, and largely rewritten edition should prove a wide-ranging aid in studying this fascinating history of the world's most populous Spanish-speaking country and the United States' southern partner in the North American Free Trade Association.

The work has also undergone a change in basic conception. While the first edition had 1,006 articles, plus 62 "see" references, much specific information was "buried" within wider topics. This second edition has 2,390 generally briefer entries, plus 356 "see" references. In accord with the pattern established by the other volumes in the series, much such specific information has been extracted and entered under new, more "targeted," headings. Much tabular material has also been incorporated (thus the chronological list of presidents of the republic will be found under PRESIDENTS and of the chief executives of the colonial period under VICEROYS). The bibliography has also been enlarged, updated, and arranged by subject, with the main section, on general history, subarranged by period.

Dynamic and modernizing, Mexico demands a handy one-volume reference guide, in compact but readable prose, to its political, social, economic, industrial, technological, medical, military, cultural, literary, legal, and ecclesiastical development, from the earliest human settlement to the challenges of its participation in today's globalized economy. This work hopes to fulfill this objective.

The editor owes a special debt of gratitude to the University of the Americas in Cholula, and particularly to the director and staff of its Biblioteca Franciscana for facilitating his use of that fine collection during his stay there in the fall of 2005 to research a number of aspects of the work.

ARRANGEMENT

Historical Dictionary of Mexico: Second Edition follows the pattern of its sister volumes in the series. Between an outline chronology and a concluding selective subject-arranged bibliography, the bulk of the work is a dictionary arranged by wordy-by-word alphabetization (SAN LUIS POTOSÌ *before* SÁNCHEZ DE TAGLE), according to the English (not the Spanish) alphabet (Ñ is treated as N, CH precedes CI), but initial prefixes and articles are disregarded (thus MADRID, MIGUEL DE LA), with the now conventional exceptions of French personal names (LE BRIS, MICHEL) and the country EL SALVADOR.

Hispanic personal names are generally entered under the second of their three elements (the paternal *apellido*), but the last element (the maternal or marital surname) is included in the heading as a piece of information, whenever known, although its actual employment depends on individual custom and the formality of the occasion. This does however require the user to be prepared to find (e.g.) Mexico's great patriot Hidalgo under HIDALGO Y COSTILLA, MIGUEL. Occasional exceptions have been made for those Mexicans better known by their more distinctive or distinguished second *apellido*, thus: ALARCÓN Y MENDOZA, JUAN RUIZ DE, but in all such cases reference has been provided from the alternative form.

The abbreviations "Mc" and "St." are filed as if spelled out (McLANE as if "MACLANE"; ST. PATRICK BATTALION as if "SAINT PATRICK BATTALION"). Initials pronounced as such file at the head of their alphabetic section (C.T.M. before CABEZA DE VACA), but acronyms (abbreviations pronounced as words—increasingly the modern preference in Spanish as in English) are interfiled (e.g., PRI—*Partido Revolucionaria Institucional*—between PRESIDENCIAL and PRIETO). Spanish geographical names are entered under their particularizing element, e.g., MADRE, SIERRA; MEXICO, GULF OF; TEHUANTEPEC ISTHMUS (but RIO GRANDE, as this is treated as an anglicization).

In a work like this dealing with a foreign culture, the author finds himself playing a guessing game with the reader as to whether the English or the native form of a term will be the one looked up. Our principle throughout the series has been to use English for generic terms (e.g., TITHES, not *diezmos*), but Spanish for the names of specific institutions (e.g., FERROCARRILES NACIONALES DE MEXICO), unless the English is, or was, the official title (e.g., UNIVERSITY OF THE AMERICAS) or if we judged that the English form would spring much more readily to the reader's mind (e.g., ARMY, not *Ejército*; MEXICO CITY, not *Ciudad de México;* NATIONAL LIBRARY, not *Biblioteca Nacional*). In all these cases the other form has normally been included in the heading and as a cross reference at its appropriate place in the dictionary. The Spanish word *pronunciamiento* has however been preferred to its normal English form (*pronunciamento*). Traditional, archaic, or British forms of English (e.g., *The Havannah*, or *traveller*) have been retained where such phrase or spelling represents actual usage in (e.g.) titles of books or institutions.

As we have implied above, information is given as far as possible just once, under the most specific heading. This saves space at some cost to the user's convenience, and it is important to follow up on any cross-references. These are most often indicated by the use of boldface for the first mention in any section of a word or phrase used elsewhere for a heading in the dictionary.

Readers should also seek titles for further reading in the 1,660-item bibliography at the back of the book. Where an item is cited in the bibliography with no indication of its pagination or number of volumes, such omission may be taken as an indication that, although the item is believed to exist, it has not been possible to inspect a copy.

Measurements are metric (°C = degrees Celsius, cm = centimeter, g = gram, ha = hectare, kg = kilogram, km² = square kilometer, l = liter, m³ = cubic meter, mm = millimeter, t = metric ton/tonne/*tonelada* of 1,000 kg)—although the Anglo-American, or traditional Spanish, equivalents are usually also given. Dates are Gregorian from 1583.

Laurence Hallewell
Series Editor

Acronyms and Abbreviations

This list includes non-Mexican abbreviations if used in the Dictionary.

A.B.C. HOSPITAL	American-British Cowdray Hospital
A.F.I.	Agencia Federal de Investigación
A.G.N.	*Archivo General de la Nación*
Ags.	Aguascalientes
ALALC	Asociación Latinoamericana de Libre Comercio
AMIS	Asociación Mexicana de Instituciones de Seguros
AMLO	Andrés Manuel López Obrador
ANDA	*Asociación Nacional de Actores*
ANIERM	Asociación Nacional de Importadores y Exportadores de la República Mexicana
ANUIES	*Asociación Nacional de Universidades y Instituciones de Educación Superior* (National Association of Universities and Institutions of Higher Education)
APPO	Asamblea Popular de los Pueblos de Oaxaca
BANAMEX	Banco Nacional de México
BANCOMEXT	*Banco de Comercio Exterior* (Foreign Trade Bank)
BANCOMER	Banco de Comercio
BANOBRAS	Banco Nacional de Obras y Servicios Públicos
BANXICO	Banco de México
B.B.V.A.	*Banco Bilbao Vizcaya Argentino*
B.C.	Baja California
B.C.N.	Baja California del Norte
B.C.S.	Baja California del Sur
B.I.D.	*Banco Interamericano de Desarrollo*
BIMSA	*Buro de Investigaciones de Mercado S.A.*

B.M.V.	*Bolsa Mexicana de Valores*
BUAP	*Benemérita Universidad Autónoma de Puebla*
Camp	Campeche
CANACINTRA	Cámara Nacional de las Industrias de Transformación
C.C.I.	Confederación Campesina Independiente
C.D.I.	*Comisión Nacional para el Desarrollo de los Pueblos Indígenas*
CEDLA	*Centro de Estudios y Documentación Latinoamericanos*
CEIMSA	Compañía Exportadora Importadora Mexicana S.A.
C.E.N.	Comité Executivo Nacional of the PRI
CEPAL	*Comisión Económica para América Latina* (United Nations' Economic Commission for Latin America)
CERLAL	*Centro Regional para el Fomento del Libro en América Latina (y el Caribe)*
CESNAV	Centro de Estudios Superiores Navales
C.F.E.	Comisión Federal Electoral; Comisión Federal de Electricidad
C.F.R.A.I.	Coordenación de Fuerzas de Reacción y Apoyo Inmediato
C.F.T.	alternative to COFETEL
C.G.T.	Confederación General de Trabajadores
Chih.	Chihuahua
Chis.	Chiapas
CIESAS	*Centro de Investigaciones y Estudios Superiores en Antropología Social* (Research Center for Higher-level Studies in Social Anthropology)
CIICH	*Centro de Investigaciones Interdisciplinarias en Ciencias y Humanidades* (Center for Interdisciplinary Research in the Sciences and Humanities)
CISEN	Centro de Investigación y Seguridad Nacional
C.M.A.	Compañía Mexicana de Aviación
C.M.H.	Contadoría Mayor de Hacienda
C.M.T.	Confederación de Trabajadores Mexicanos; *Compañía Mexicana de Transportes*

C.N.A.	Comisión Nacional del Agua
C.N.B.V.	Comisión Nacional Bancaria y de Valores
C.N.C.	Confederación Nacional Campesina
C.N.C.A.	*Consejo Nacional para la Cultura y las Artes* (CONACULTA)
C.N.O.P.	Confederación Nacional de Organizaciones Populares
C.N.S.M.	*Comisión Nacional de Salarios Mínimos* (National Minimum Wage Commission)
C.N.T.	Cámara Nacional de las Industrias de Transformación
Coah.	Coahuila
COFETEL	*Compañía Federal de Teléfonos*; *Comisión Federal de Telecomunicaciones* (Federal Telecommunication Commission)
Col.	Colima
COLMEX	Colegio de México
COMPITE	Comité Nacional de Productividad e Innovación Tecnológica, A.C.
CONACINE	*Corporación Nacional Cinematográfica*
CONACULTA	*Consejo Nacional para la Cultura y las Artes* (National Council for Culture and the Arts)
CONACYT	Consejo Nacional de Ciencia y Tecnología
CONAFILM	*Comisión Nacional de Filmaciones México* (National Film Commission)
CONAINTA	*Consejo Nacional de la Industria Tabacalera* (National Council of the Tobacco Industry)
CONALEP	Colegio Nacional de Educación Profesional Técnica
CONASUPO	Compañía Nacional de Subsistencias Populares
CONCAMIN	Confederación de Cámaras Industriales
CONCANACO	*Confederación de Cámaras Nacionales de Comercio* (National Confederation of Chambers of Commerce)
CONDUMEX	Centro de Estudios de Historia de México
CONMUJER	*Comisión Nacional de la Mujer* (National Women's Committee)
COPARMEX	Confederación Patronal de la República de México

C.P.F.	Centro de Planificación Familiar
C.P.N.	Consejo Político Nacional
C.R.O.C.	Confederación Revolucionario de Obreros y Campesinos
CROM	Confederación Regional Obrera Mexicana
C.T.A.L.	*Confederación de Trabajadores de América Latina*
C.T.M.	Confederación de Trabajadores Mexicanos
DAAC	Department of Agrarian Affairs and Colonization (*Departamento de Asuntos Agrarios y Colonización*)
D.E.A.	United States Drug Enforcement Administration
D.F.	*Distrito Federal* (the Federal District)
D.F.S.N.	*Dirección Federal de Seguridad Nacional*
Dgo.	Durango
DINA	Diesel Nacional
DISEN	*Dirección de Inteligencia y Seguridad Nacional*
ECLA	United Nations' Economic Commission for Latin America
E.E.Z.	Economic Exploitation Zone
E.N.P.	Escuela Nacional Preparatoria
E.U.M.	*Estados Unidos Mexicanos* ("The United Mexican States")
E.Z.L.N.	Ejército Zapatista de Liberación Nacional
F.A.M.	*Fuerza Aérea Mexicana* (Air Force)
F.B.I.	United States' Federal Bureau of Investigation
F.C.C.M.	*Ferrocarril* (railroad) *Chiapas-Mayar S.A.*
F.C.E.	Fondo de Cultura Económica
F.C.N.M.	Ferrocarriles Nacionales de México
F.D.N.	Frente Democrático Nacional
FERROMEX	*Ferrocarril* (railroad) *Mexicano S.A.*
FERRONALES	Ferrocarriles Nacionales de México
FERROSUR	*Ferrocarril* (railroad) *del Sureste*
FINA	Financiera Nacional Azucarera, S.A.
FIT	*Ferrocarril* (railroad) *del Istmo de Tehyuatepec*
F.M.V.Z.	*Facultad de Medicina Veterinaria y Zootecnia* (UNAM's Veterinary Medicine and Animal Science Faculty)

FOBAPROA	Fondo Bancario de Protección al Ahorro
FONACOT	Fondo Nacional del Consumo de los Trabajadores
FONATUR	*Fondo Nacional de Fomento al Tourismo* (National Foundation to Encourage Tourism)
F.P.P.M.	Federación de Partidos del Pueblo de México
F.S.T.S.E.	Federación de Sindicatos de los Trabajadores en Servicio del Estado
GATT	General Agreement on Tariffs and Trade
G.D.P.	gross domestic product
Gro.	Guerrero
Gto.	Guanajuato
Hgo.	Hidalgo
H.V.	Hora de verano
HYLSA	Hojalata y Lámina, S.A.
I.E.P.S.	Impuesto especial sobre producción y servicios
I.B.D.	*Inter-American Development Bank* ("B.I.D")
I.E.P.E.S.	Instituto de Estudios Políticos, Económicos e Sociales
I.F.E.	Instituto Federal Electoral
I.L.O.	International Labour Organisation
IMCE	*Instituto Mexicano de Comercio Exterior* (Mexican Institute of Foreign Trade)
I.M.F.	International Monetary Fund
I.M.P.	*Instituto Mexicano del Petróleo* (Mexican Petroleum Institute)
I.M.S.S.	Instituto Mexicano del Seguro Social
INAH.	*Instituto Nacional de Antropología e Historia* (National Anthropology and History Institute)
INBA	Instituto Nacional de Bellas Artes
INE	*Instituto Nacional de Ecología*
INEGI	Instituto Nacional de Estadística, Geografía e Informática
INFONAVIT	Instituto del Fondo Nacional de la Vivienda para los Trabajadores
INFRATUR	Fondo de Promoción de Infraestrucutra Turística
INI	*Instituto Nacional Indigenista*
I.N.S.P.	*Instituto Nacional de Salud Pública* (National Institute of Public Health)

INTAL	Institute for the Integration of Latin America and the Caribbean (*Instituto para la Integración de América Latina y el Caribe*)
I.P.G.H.	*Instituto Panamericano de Geografía e Historia* (Pan American Institute of Geography and History)
I.P.N.	Instituto Politécnico Nacional
I.S.S.S.T.E.	Instituto de Seguridad y Servicios Sociales de los Trabajadores del Estado
ITAM	Instituto Tecnológico Autónomo de México
ITESM	Instituto Tecnológico y de Etudios Superiores de Monterrey
I.V.A.	*Impuesto al valor agregado* (value-added tax)
Jal.	Jalisco
J.F.C.A.	*Junta Federal de Conciliación y Arbitraje* (Federal Conciliation and Arbitration Board)
LADA	*Larga Distancia Automática* (direct distance dialing)
LAFTA	Asociación Latinoamericana de Libre Comercio
LAGDA	Latin American Government Documents Archive
LAGRA	Acronym of the Latin American Government Reports Archive
LANIC	University of Texas Latin American Network Information Center
L.C.D.	*Linea Coahuila a Durango*
L.S.M.	*Liga Socialista Mexicana*
M.A.T.T.	Mexicanos y Americanos Todos Trabajando
MAPFRE	*Agrupación de Proprietarios de Fincas Rústicas de España*
Méx.	*Estado de México* (Mexico State)
Mich.	Michoacán
M.L.N.	Movimiento de Liberación Nacional
M.I.T.	Massachusetts Institute of Technology
Mor.	Morelos
M.P.F.	*Ministerio Público Federal*
NAFIN	Nacional Financiera (Industrial Development Bank)

NAFTA	North American Free Trade Association
Nay.	Nayarit
N.G.O.	nongovernmental organization
N.L.	Nuevo León
NOM	*Norma Oficial Mexicana*
NOTIMEX	Noticias Mexicanas
N.S.	*Nuestra Señora* ("Our Lady," the Virgin Mary); *Nuestro Señor* ("Our Lord," Jesus Christ)
O.A.S.	Organization of American States
Oax.	Oaxaca
OCEZ	*Organización Campesina Emiliano Zapata* (the Emiliano Zapata Peasants' Organization)
O.E.C.D.	*Organization for Economic Cooperation and Development*
O.N.G.	*Organización no Gobernamental* (nongovernmental organization)
OPEC	Organization of Petroleum Exporting Countries
O.S.N.M.	Orquesta Sinfónica Nacional de México (National Synphony Orchestra of Mexico)
PAIGH	Pan American Institute of Geography and History
PAN	Partido de Acción Nacional
PANAL	Partido Nueva Alianza
PARM	Partido Auténtico de la Revolución Mexicana
PASC	*Partido Alternativo Socialdemócrata y Campesina* (Alternative Party of Social Democrats and Peasants)
P.C.G.	*Partido Cívico Guerrerense* (Party of Local Guerrero Patriotism)
P.C.M.	Partido Comunista Mexicano
P.D.F.	Partido de Fórum Democrático
P.D.M.	Partido Democrático Mexicano
Pemex	*Petróleos Mexicanos*
P.F.C.	*Policia Federal de Caminos* (Highway Police)
P.F.C.R.N.	Partido del Frente Cardenista de Reconstrucción Nacional
P.F.F.	*Policia Federal Fiscal* (Fiscal Police)
P.F.P.	Policia Federal Preventativa

P.G.R.	*Procuraduría General de la República* (office of the Procurador General, the Mexican attorney general)
P.J.E.	state police force
P.M.F.	*Policia Migratoria Federal* (Immigration Police)
P.M.T.	Partido Mexicano de los Trabajadores
P.N.R.	Partido Nacional Revolucionario
P.P.S.	Partido Popular Socialista
P.R.D.	Partido de la Revolución Democrática
PRI	Partido Revolucionario Institucional
P.R.M.	Partido Revolucionario Mexicano
PROFMEX	Consortium for Research on Mexico (*Consorcio Mundial para la Investigación sobre México*)
P.R.T.	Partido Revolucionario de los Trabjadores
PRUN	Partido Revolucionario de Unificación Nacional
P.S.E.	Pacto de Solidaridad Económica
P.S.T.	Partido Socialista de los Trabajadores
PSUM	Partido Socialista Unificado de México
P.T.	Partido del Trabajo
Pue.	Puebla
P.V.E.M.	Partido Verde Ecologista Mexicano
Q.R.	Quintana Roo
Qro.	Querétaro
RENAVE	*Registro Nacional de Vehículos*
RFC	*Registro Federal de Contibuyentes*
S.A.	*Sociedad Anónima*
S.A. de C.V.	*Sociedad Anónima de Capital Variabl*
SAGAR	*Secretaría de Agricultura, Ganadaría y Desarrollo Rural* (Agriculture and Rural Development Ministry)
SAGARPA	*Secretaria de Agricultura, Ganadería, Desarrollo Rural, Pesca y Alimentación*
SAHOP	*Secretaría de Asentimientos Humanos y Obras Públicas* (Human Settlements Ministry)
SARH	*Secretaría de Agricultura y Recursos Hidráulicos* (title of the Agriculture Ministry, 1976–1995)
S.C.H.P.	*Secretaría de Hacienda y Crédito Público* (Finance Ministry)

S.C.J.N.	*Suprema Corte de Justicia de la Nación* (Mexican Supreme Court)
S.C.T.	*Secretaría de Comunicaciones y Transportes* (Transport Ministry)
S.D.N.	*Secretaría de la Defensa Nacional*
S.E.	*Secretaría de Economía* (Economics Ministry)
SECODAM	*Secretaría de la Contraloría y Desarrollo Administrativo* (Ministry of the Comptrollership General)
SECOFI	*Secretaría de Comercio y Fomento Industrial* (former Trade Ministry)
SECOGEF	*Secretaría de la Contraloría de la Federación*
SECTUR	*Secretaría de Turismo* (Tourism Ministry)
SEDENA	*Secretaría de la Defensa Nacional* (Defense Ministry)
SEDESOL	*Secretaría de Desarrollo Social*
SEDUE	*Secretaría de Desarrollo Urbano y Ecología*
SEDUVI	*Secretaría de Desarrollo Urbano y Vivienda, Distrito Federal* (Department of Urban Development and Housing)
SEGOB	*Secretaría de Gobernación* (Interior Ministry)
SEIT	*Subsecretaría de Educación y Investigación Tecnológica* (Department of Technological Education and Research, Education Ministry)
SEMAR	*Secretaría de Marina* (Naval Ministry)
SEMARNAP	*Secretaría de Medio Ambiente, Recursos Naturales y Pesca* (now SEMARNAT)
SEMARNAT	*Secretaría de Medio Ambiente y Recursos Naturales* (current title of the Environment Ministry; the former SEMARNAP)
SEMATUR	Servicios Marítimos de Turismo
SENER	*Secretaría de Energía* (Energy Ministry)
SEMIP	*Secretaria de Energía, Minas y Industria Paraestatal* (former title of Environment Ministry)
S.E.P.	*Secretaría de Educación Pública* (post-1920 title of Education Ministry)
SEPANAL	*Secretaría de Patrimonio Nacional* (former ministry of natural resources)

SEPESCA	*Secretaría de Pesca* (former Fishery Ministry, now a department of the Agriculture Ministry)
SEPOMEX	*Servicio Postal Mexicano* (Mexican Postal Service)
SES	*Sistema de Educación Superior* (higher education system)
S.F.P.	*Secretaría de la Función Pública* (Public Administration Ministry)
S.G.	*Secretaría de Gobernación* (Interior Ministry)
S.H.C.P.	*Secretaría de Hacienda y Crédito Público* (Ministry of Finance and Public Credit)
SICARTSA	Siderúrgica Lázaro Cárdenas Las Truchas, S.A.
SIL	former *Summer Institute of Linguistics* (now *SIL International*)
Sin.	Sinaloa
S.L.P.	San Luis Potosí
S.M.A.	*Sociedad Mexicana de Antropología* (Mexican Anthropological Society)
S.M.N.	Servicio Meteorológico Nacional
S.N.T.E.	Sindicato Nacional de Trabajadores de la Educación. Son. Sonoa
SPP	*Secretaría de Programación y Presupuesto* (Planning Ministry)
S.R.A.	Agrarian Reform Ministry (*Secretaría de la Reforma Agraria*)
S.R.E.	Foreign Ministry (*Secretaría de Relaciones Exteriores*)
SSA	Health Ministry (*Secretaría de Salud*; also S.S.)
S.S.P.	*Secretaría de Seguridad Pública* (Public Security Ministry)
S.T.F.R.M.	*Sindicato de Trabajadores Ferrocarrileros de la República Mexicana* (Railroad Workers' Union)
S.T.M.M.R.M.	*Sindicato de Trabajadores Mineros y Metalúrgicos de la República Mexicana* (Mexican miners and steel workers' union)
S.T.P.R.M.	*Sindicato de Trabajadores Petroleros de la República Mexicana* (Mexican oil workers' union)

S.T.P.S.	*Secretaría de Trabajo y Previsión Social* (Labor Ministry)
STUNAM	*Sindicato de Trabajadores de la Universidad Nacional Autónoma de México* (Union of Employees of UNAM)
SUTERM	*Sindicato Único de Trabajadores Elecricistas de la Repúblic Mexicana* (official electrical workers union created in 1972 to replace STERM)
Tab.	Tabasco
TABAMEX	Tabacos Mexicanos S.A. de C.V. (tobacco firm)
TAESA	Transportes Aéreos Ejecutivos S.A. (air-taxi firm)
Tams.	Tamaulipas (also Tamps.)
TAMSA	Tubos de Acero de México, S.A.
TELECOMM	*Telecomunicaciones de México* (Federal Telecommunication Commission)
TELEMEX	*Teléfonos de México*
TELMEX	Former acronym and now legal name of the privatized *Teléfonos de México*
T.F.M.	*Transportación Ferroviaria Mexicana* (Mexican Railroad Transportation)
T.I.A.R.	Spanish abbreviation for the Inter-American Treaty of Mutual Assistance (*Tratado interamericano de asistencia recíproca*)
Tlax.	Tlaxcala
T.L.C.	*See* TLCAN
TLCAN	*Tratado de Libre Comercio de América del Norte*
UAA	Universidad Autónoma de Aguascalientes
UACh	Universidad Autónoma Chapingo
UADY	Universidad Autónoma de Yucatán
UAG	Universidad Autónoma de Guadalajara
UAM	Universidad Autónoma Metropolitana
U.A.N.L.	Universidad Autónoma de Nuevo León
U.C.P.	*Unión Cívica de Potosí* (San Luis Potosí Civic Union)
U.D.G.	Universidad de Guadalajara
UdeM	Universidad de Monterrey (also UDEM)

U.D.L.A.	*Universidad de las Américas* (University of the Americas, Cholula)
U.G.O.C.M.	Unión General de Obreros y Campesinos de México (General Union of Mexican Workers and Peasants)
U.I.	Universidad Iberoamericana (also U.I.A.)
U.K.	United Kingdom
U.J.E.D.	Universidad Juárez del Estado de Durango
U.M.S.N.H.	Universidad Michoacana de San Nicolás de Hidalgo
UNAM	*Universidad Nacional Autónomo de México* (Autonomous National University of Mexico)
U.N.T.	Unión Nacional de Trabajadores
U.P.N.	Universidad Padagógica Nacional
UPREZ	*Unión Popular Revolucionaria Emiliano Zapata* (Emiliano Zapata People's Revolutionary Union)
U.S.S.	*United States Ship*
USAER	*Servicio de Apoyo a la Educación Regular*
UV	Universidad Veracruzana
Ver.	Veracruz
W.T.C.	*World Trade Center*
W.T.O.	*World Trade Organization*
Yuc.	Yucatán
Zac.	Zacatecas
Z.M.V.M.	*Zona Metropolitana del Valle de México* (Mexico City Conurbation)

Chronology

BC

40,000   First humans arrive in the Americas, from Siberia.

38,000   First evidence of human presence in what is now Mexico.

10,000   End of the last Ice Age, long supposed to be the time when humans first arrived in North America, from Siberia.

8,000   The extermination of mammoths stimulates the beginnings of plant cultivation.

5,000   Corn growing in the valleys of Tehuacán and Oaxaca.

3,000   Farming villages in much of Meso-America.

1,500   Beginnings of Maya culture.

1,400   Beginnings of Olmec culture.

600   Construction of the round pyramid at Cuicuilco.

200   Earliest Meso-American (Zapotec) writing.

c.100   Teotihucán founded.

AD

c.300   Beginning of the "classic" period of Mayan civilization.

535 February: Explosion of Krakatoa (in Indonesia) so affects world climate as to be a likely explanation for the prolonged famine in Meso-America that caused the decline of its early civilizations.

c.900 Collapse of Mayan civilization.

950 Rise of Toltec civilization in Yucatán.

1111 The Aztecs leave their mythical homeland of Aztlan.

1194 Dissolution of the Mayan Mazapán Confederation.

1325 Tenochtitlán founded on an island in Lake Texcoco.

1428 Tepanecs crushed: beginnings of Aztec imperial expansion.

1492 Isabel I, queen of Castile, sponsors Columbus' first expedition.

1502 Montezuma II becomes ruler of the Aztecs.

1504 Hernán Cortés arrives in Hispaniola.

1507 Vicente Yáñez Pinzón sails along the Yucatán coast.

1516 The future Holy Roman Emperor Charles V becomes first king of the united kingdom of "the Spains" (and Burgundy).

1517 First Spanish expedition to Yucatán.

1518 Juan de Grijalva explores the Mexican coast northward from Yucatán and calls the country "New Spain."

1519 Jerónimo de Aguilar is shipwrecked in Yucatán.

1520 Beginning of the Spanish conquest of Mexico, accompanied by a smallpox epidemic.

1521 Charles V appoints Cortés as Captain General of New Spain.

1525 Cuauhtémoc, last Aztec ruler, is hanged.

1530 Mexico has its first bishop. Mexico City becomes the capital of New Spain. A measles epidemic devastates the population.

1534 Antonio de Mendoza is appointed first viceroy of New Spain.

1536 Álvar Núñez Cabeza de Vaca reaches Sonora after his epic overland journey from Florida.

1540 Fernando Vázquez de Coronado sets out from Compostela in Nayarit in a vain search for the "Seven Cities of Cíbola."

1543 Guatemala becomes a captaincy general.

1545 Silver is discovered at Zacatecas. Plague and typhus cause further heavy loss of population.

1546 The diocese of Mexico City becomes an archbishopric.

1550 A mumps outbreak further reduces the Indian population.

1553 Founding of the University of Mexico.

1558 Influenza epidemic.

1560–1585 War of the Chichimecs.

1563 Second smallpox epidemic.

1571 Establishment of the Holy Inquisition in New Spain.

1572 Arrival of the Jesuits in New Spain.

1576 The second great outbreak of plague.

1578 Sir Frances Drake enters the Pacific on his circumnavigation, challenging Spanish supremacy along the west coast of the Americas from Chile to California.

1581 Cuba becomes a captaincy general.

1592 First planting of the Alameda Park. Establishment of the Consulado of Mexico.

1615 Third smallpox outbreak.

1629–1634 Great Five-Year Flood destroys much of Mexico City; 30,000 Indians die.

1631 Second typhus epidemic.

1647 The African slave trade brings urban yellow fever to the Caribbean coast.

1670 Spain, by the Treaty of Madrid acknowledges English occupancy of Jamaica and other territories in North America.

1680–1692   Pueblo Indian revolt.

1696–1697   Tarahumara revolt.

1700   Death of Charles II, the last Spanish Habsburg: Spain's throne is claimed for a grandson of the French king Louis XIV, resulting in the War of the Spanish succession.

1711   Performance in Mexico City of first opera in the Americas.

1713   Treaty of Utrecht ends War of the Spanish Succession. Spain loses the Spanish Netherlands to Austria and opens its slave trade to the British.

1718   San Antonio de Béjar founded.

1767   Expulsion of the Jesuits from all Spanish domains.

1780   The Great Hurricane: one of the strongest ever recorded. Fourth great smallpox epidemic.

1785   Academía de San Carlos founded.

1779   Ignacio Fernando de Arteaga y Bazán reaches Hinchinbrook Island, the most northerly point reached in exploration from New Spain.

1808   French attempt to impose a puppet regime in Madrid, producing a crisis of legitimacy throughout the Spanish Indies.

1810–1821   Mexican War of Independence.

1820   Spain, by its Treaty of Limits with the United States, surrenders Florida and accepts the Platte River as the northern boundary of New Mexico.

1821   Plan of Iguala.

1822–1823   First empire.

1824   Constitution of 1824 creates the Estados Unidos Mexicanos.

1833   Mexico's first epidemic of Asiatic cholera.

1836   Texas declares itself an independent republic.

1838   The Pastry War diverts Mexican attention from any chance of suppressing the Texan revolt.

1846–1848   United States–Mexican War.

1848   Discovery of alluvial gold leads to the Great Californian Gold Rush, almost immediately after the territory is lost to Mexico.

1857   Liberal Constitution of 1857.

1857–1863   Third Federal Republic.

1858   Gadsden purchase.

1858–1863   War of the Reforms.

1859   McLane-Ocampo Treaty.

1862   French intervention; Mexican victory of May the Fifth at Puebla.

1864–1867   Second empire.

1867   The execution of Maximilian, along with Russia's sale of Alaska, and Britain's concession of "dominion status" to Canada, mark the effective end of European colonialism in North America.

1910–1921   Mexican Revolution of 1910.

1913   Murder of Francisco I. Madero.

1917   Proclamation of the current Constitution of 1917.

1919   Murder of Emiliano Zapata.

1920   Murder of Venustiano Carranza.

1927–1230   Cristero Rebellion.

1928   Murder of Álvaro Obregón.

1929   Escobar rebellion; foundation of the Partido Nacional.

1938   Nationalization of Mexico's petroleum industry.

1946   The government party is renamed the Partido Revolucionario Institucional.

1953   Female suffrage granted.

1968   **October:** Student riots in the Plaza de Tlatelolco just before the Mexico City Olympics.

1970 World soccer cup championship held in Mexico.

1978 Visit of King Juan Carlos I of Spain; remains of Aztec "great temple" is found in Mexico City.

1979 On his first trip abroad, Pope John Paul II visits the Dominican Republic, Mexico, and the Bahamas.

1982 Mexico's foreign debt moratorium causes capital flight from all Latin America.

1985 Great Mexico City earthquake of 1985.

1986 World soccer cup championship is held in Mexico for the second time.

1990 Policy of general privatization adopted.

1993 **August:** John Paul II makes his second visit to Mexico.

1994 North American Free Trade Agreement signed. Luis Donaldo Colosio is assassinated.

1998 Rocio Robles is elected Mexico City's first woman mayor.

1999 February: Third visit to Mexico by Pope John Paul II.

2000 The PRI's monopoly of federal authority ends with the election of Vicente Fox Quesada to the presidency. John Paul II makes his fourth visit to Mexico.

2001 The Ejército Zapatista de Liberación Nacional leads a motorcade from Chiapas to Mexico City to further its campaign for an "indigenous rights" law. [L. H.]

2002 **July:** John Paul II makes his fifth papal visit to Mexico. **October:** Hurricane Kenna strikes north-eastern Mexico.

2003 A strong earthquakes strikes Colima.

2004 President Fox visits Switzerland, Hungary, Poland, and Brazil. The "dinosaur" wing of the PRI is greatly strengthened by its success in the election of 2004. A flash flood drowns 31 in Piedras Negras. Bodega Aurrerá, a subsidiary of Wal-Mart, secures official backing to build a new store in the archaeological zone of Teotihuacan despite strong local protest. [L. H.]

2005 Hurricanes Emily, Stan, and Wilma strike southern Mexico. [L. H.] June 9–October 9: President Fox visits Spain, Italy, Morocco, and Algeria. London's Tate Modern holds an exhibition celebrating Frida Kahlo.

2006 July: Election of 2006 gives official candidate a narrow victory. **August:** Lucio Rendón and companion fishermen return home after nine months adrift in an open boat to face accusations of cannibalism and drug running. **September:** A show of hands by his supporters in the Zócalo appoints López Obrador head of a "parallel government" to oppose that of the President Elect, while comments on the election by Venezuelan president Hugo Chávez are denounced by Fox as interfering in Mexican internal affairs. **October:** President Bush approves law to erect an effective wall along the US-Mexican border to deter illegal immigration. President Fox orders federal forces to restore order in Oaxaca. **November:** Three central Mexico City buildings are bombed in leftist political protest by a hitherto unknown *Coordinación Revolucionaria*. **December:** The new President takes the oath in a rushed ceremony after secretly entering a riotous Congress chamber by a rear door, to the embarrassment of visiting foreign dignitaries. His draft budget proposal for a thirty percent budget cut for culture, including INBA, I.N.A.H., and Conaculta, as making no contribution to the country's economic development, is rejected by Congress. Pollution from a burst American offshore oil pipeline, three km south of Galveston TX, threatens a major Mexican source of shellfish. [L. H.]

Introduction

To understand modern-day Mexico, it is necessary to observe how attitudes were shaped by occurrences predating the arrival of the Spaniards in the New World and continuing right up to the eve of the Mexican Revolution of 1910. The great Indian civilizations, notably the Aztec and Mayan, were in many ways more advanced than their European contemporaries in spheres such as astronomy, mathematics, and city organization. Bernal Díaz del Castillo, on first seeing the Aztec capital, Tenochtitlán, was awed by its beauty and confessed he had never seen a city in Spain that could match it. All the Indian civilizations of New Spain (as Mexico came to be known) were defeated, subjugated, and ultimately subjected to almost total assimilation. Today, the Mexican nation is predominately a *mestizo* one. But even this fact has yet to be accepted by the Indian side of the Mexican, even though the European side is apparently predominant.

Cortés, the Spanish conqueror, is not generally liked in Mexico, although there is little doubt that he is respected. The national hero is Cuauhtémoc, although this tragic monarch witnessed the destruction of an empire that was his responsibility to preserve and maintain. Only a small, unobtrusive plaque in Mexico City's Square of the Three Cultures, commemorating the final Spanish victory over the Aztecs in August, 1521, bears witness to the profound suffering inflicted by the Spanish conquest: "What happened here was not a defeat, but the painful birth of what today is the Mexican nation." The Indian was to be a second-class citizen in his own land, but nevertheless he was to serve as the most important link between the great pre-Columbian civilizations and the post-colonial independent nation-state of Mexico. It will always be as impossible for Mexico to ignore its indigenous past, as to abandon its European heritage. The dream of José Vasconcelos of a union of the Indian and white races evolving into what he referred to as a "cosmic race," continues to be an idealized concept in Mexico. The Revolution has also paid homage to the Indian, even though the wretched condition of so many of them continues to contrast starkly with so idyllic a portrayal.

Lack of capable leadership has plagued Mexico down the centuries. The superstitions of Montezuma played right into the hands of Cortéz and, in large part, resulted in Mexico's conquest by Spain. It was not necessary to be a successful leader to be remembered favorably in Mexico. No better illustration of this exists than the case of Miguel Hidalgo y Costilla, honored as the father of Mexican independence. His lack of military ability is acknowledged by many Mexicans, and just before his death he renounced the movement that he had led and pleaded with the Spaniards for forgiveness. Even when Mexico did become independent, the likes of Agustín de Iturbide and José Antonio López de Santa Anna did not augur well for their country.

A measure of presidential respectability was manifest in Benito Juárez, although his efforts at effective government were often too idealistic, as when he refused to prod the legislature to limit debate in passing important laws. The long rule of Porfirio Diaz benefited Mexico in reducing brigandry, encouraging foreign investment, and stabilizing the peso, but at the cost of lowering the living standard of the Indians and confiscating their lands. These factors led directly to the Mexican Revolution, the first great social upheaval of the twentieth century.

Foreign intervention has also shaped the present day attitudes of the Mexican. Many nations took their turn at confiscating Mexico's wealth, occupying its territory, or, in the case of the United States, annexing large areas. Spain tried to subjugate Mexico again in 1829. France controlled her Veracruz custom house in 1838, the United States annexed over half her territory in 1848, and France imposed the 1864–1867 puppet regime of Maximilian. As recently as 1914 the United States occupied Veracruz with a large contingent of marines. If Mexico tends to be suspicious, it is understandable in the light of such experiences.

These then are briefly some of the factors that have contributed to the forming of modern Mexico. To be ignorant of them is to have little or no understanding of the forces at work in that country today.

THE DICTIONARY

– A –

ABAD Y QUEIPO, MANUEL (1751?–1825). Bishop of **Michoacán**, born in Asturias, he was denounced to the **Inquisition** but later was exonerated. He attempted by sound economic ideas to prevent the loss of Spain's American colonies, while he excommunicated Ignacio **Allende**, Miguel **Hidalgo y Costilla**, and many other leaders of the **Independence** Movement of 1810.

ABANICAR ("fan a breeze"). In Mexican **sport** slang, this means to strike out, as by a batter in **baseball**.

ABARCA ALARCÓN, RAIMUNDO (1906–). Born March 4, in **Chilpancingo**, graduated in medicine from **Mexico City**'s *Escola Médica Militar*, served as **alcalde** of **Iguala** from 1949–1950 and as governor of **Guerrero** from 1963–1969. A leader of the popular wing of the **Partido Revolucionario Institucional**, he achieved national distinction in the 1970s as administrator of the medical services of the **Ferrocarriles Nacionales de México** and of the government employees' **social security** scheme.

ABASOLO, MARIANO (1783–1816). A patriot, born in **Dolores Hidalgo**, he accepted Ignacio **Allende**'s offer to join a conspiracy, supporting it with his sizable fortune to win **independence**. He was also responsible for giving the followers of Miguel **Hidalgo** guns and munitions from the Spanish garrison in Dolores. Captured at **Acatita de Baján**, he was imprisoned in Cádiz, Spain, where he died.

ABOLITION OF SLAVERY. *See* AFRICAN SLAVERY.

ABORTION. Induced abortion is illegal in Mexico, but "surgical procedures to save a mother's life endangered by pregnancy" have become more frequent in recent years, with the suggestion that many cases are not death-risk situations. *See also* FAMILY PLANNING.

ABSENTEE LANDLORDS. *See* AGRARIAN REFORM.

ABU-JAMAL, MUMIA (1954–). American Black Panther journalist, born Wesley Cook, has been on death row since 1981 for the murder of Philadelphia policeman Daniel Faulkner. (The defense blamed the murder on a Mafia hit to prevent Faulkner from revealing police **corruption**). Abu-Jamal's predicament (along with the suppression of the protests in Seattle against the **World Trade Organization**) led to a march on the **United States** embassy by striking **UNAM** students, which was later broken up by the **police** on December 11, 1999. [L. H.]

ABURTO, MARIO. Presumed assassin of Luis Donaldo **Colosio**. He was held in Almoloya de Juárez Maximum Security Prison, near **Toluca**.

ACADEMIA DE SAN CARLOS. Founded in 1783 by **Viceroy** Matías de **Gálvez** as the *Academia de las Tres Nobles Artes de San Carlos* to honor King **Charles III**, the school had the avowed aim of having Neoclassicism replace the Baroque. After a decline following **Independence**, the academy was reorganized in 1843 by López de **Santa Anna**. All the great Mexican **muralists** studied there, only to rebel later against its traditional aesthetics and methods. It is now the **Escuela Nacional de Artes Plásticas**.

ACADEMIA MEXICANA DE LA HISTORIA. The Mexican Academy of History dates from 1871 but was established in its present form on September 12, 1919.

ACADEMIA MEXICANA DE LA LENGUA CASTELLANA. Founded in 1875, one of the 22 national members of the *Asociación de Academias de la Lengua Española*. José María **Roa Barcena** was its first treasurer.

ACAMAPICHTLI ("tuft of grey hair") (1350?–1403?). The Chief (**tlatoani**) of the Aztecs from 1375–1396, he was succeeded by **Huitzilihuitl.**

ACAPULCO. This city, officially *Acapulco de Juárez*, on an oval bay with many beaches, was founded in 1530 on **Guerrero**'s Pacific coast, 420 km (260 miles) south of **Mexico City**, at 16°50'N, 99°55'W, with 687,292 inhabitants in 1995 and 638,000 in 2003. In 1601 it became the port for the yearly **Manila galleon** and is still Mexico's chief naval base on the Pacific. It fell to the patriots led by **Morelos** shortly before the summoning of the Congress of **Chilpancingo**. It was only linked to the capital by road in 1927, but it was developed under President Miguel **Alemán Valdes**, attracting a huge **foreign investment** in luxury hotels. It is now a world famous resort, attracting affluent American tourists for swimming, **sport fishing**, golf, tennis, and nightclubbing. Divers jumping from the high cliffs into the ocean are a special attraction. In the 1960s–1970s Mexican **cinema** and **television** producers often chose Acapulco for making romantic and comedy films. In the 1980s and 1990s it lost out as American and Mexican celebrities began to prefer **Cancún**, but since 1995 Acapulco has begun to recover, attracting top singers and bands to entertain at its larger hotels.

ACATITA DE BAJÁN. This site near **Monclova** in **Coahuila** was the scene of an ambush of patriot forces by Governor Manuel Salcedo of **Texas**, March 21, 1811. Miguel **Hidalgo y Costilla**, Ignacio **Allende**, and José Mariano **Jiménez** were among those captured.

ACATLÁN. (1) City of **Hidalgo** state at 20°06'N, 98°26'W, 12 km northeast of Tulancingo, notable for its sixteenth century convent of San Miguel Arcángel, with a municipal population of 17,914 in 2005.

(2) City of **Jalisco**, 37 km southwest of **Guadalajara**, at 1,393 m above sea level, settled in 1509, Hispanized as Santa Ana Acatlán in 1550, formally renamed Acatlán de Juárez in 1909, and made a **ciudad** in 1972, the **cabecera** of a **municipio** of 177 km².

(3) City of **Puebla**, formally Acatlán de Osorio, at 18°12'N, 98°03'W, 2,120 m above sea level, founded, as Tizaá, by Mixtecs in the twelfth century, annexed and renamed by the Aztecs in the mid-fifteenth century, conquered by Pedro de **Alvarado Contreras y Mesia** in

March 1522, levelled by an earthquake in 1711, refounded 1712, and made a **ciudad** in 1883. It became the **cabecera** of a **municipio** in 1869, with 34,765 inhabitants in 2000 population on 175 km². (4) City of **Veracruz Llave** located at 19°42'N, 96°50'W. [L.H.]

ACCIÓN NACIONAL. *See* PARTIDO DE ACCIÓN NACIONAL.

ACCIÓN POLÍTICA FEMINISTA. *See* CERVANTES HERNÁNEZ, MARÍA.

ACEVES PARRA, SALVADOR (1904–1978). Physician born April 4 in La Piedad, **Michoacán**, trained at **UNAM**, did graduate work in the US, and became Professor of Medicine at UNAM. He directed the National Cardiology Institute from 1961–1965, served as assistant **health** minister from 1964–1967, and served as Minister of Health and Welfare from 1968–1970.

ACOLHÚAS. Nahua tribe also known as Texcocans for living near Lake **Texcoco**. It was part of the **Aztec** confederation. *See also* NET-ZAHUALCÓYOTL; TRIPLE ALLIANCE.

ACORDADA REVOLT. Troops of the Acordada garrison in **Mexico City** revolted in 1828, forcing President-elect Manuel **Gómez Pedraza** into exile and securing his replacement by Vicente **Guerrero**.

ACORDADA, TRIBUNAL DEL. Court set up in 1710 to eliminate **banditry** in **New Spain**, an early example of the **Bourbon Reforms**. Originally there was no appeal of its harsh sentences. Later the **viceroy** and a special committee ruled on all sentences.

ACOSTA ROMO, FAUSTO (c.1917–). Tax attorney active in the **Partido Revolucionario Institucional**, born in **Sonora State**, serving as its **senator** from 1952–1958. He gained national prominence as a negotiator on **irrigation** and labor relation problems, acted as state governor in 1951, and became assistant **procurador general** of Mexico from 1964–1966. In the 1970s he was a director of the **Banco Nacional de Crédito Ejidal** in **Ciudad Obregón**. He lost the PRI nomination for state governor in 1961, 1967, 1973, and 1979.

ACTA DE INDEPENDENCIA. *See* INDEPENDENCE.

ACULCO ("twisted water," perhaps from its meandering river). Town of **Mexico State**, on the **Querétaro** state line, at 20°06'N, 99°50'W, founded by the **Otomí** Indians in 1110, conquered by the **Aztecs** c.1450, became a Franciscan parish in 1625, and a secular parish as San Jerónimo de Aculco in 1759. It was made the **cabecera** of a **municipio** in 1825, now officially Aculco de Espinosa, after a local benefactor. Aculco had 34,378 inhabitants in 1995, 38,827 in 2000, on 466 km². [L. H.]

ACULCO, BATTLE OF. Royalists led by Félix María **Calleja** were victorious over insurgents led by Miguel **Hidalgo y Costilla** at this central Mexico town, then a small village, on November 7, 1810.

ACUÑA. *See* CIUDAD ACUÑA.

ACUÑA [Y BEJARANO], JUAN DE, MARQUÉS DE ESCALONA Y CASAFUERTE (1658–1734). Viceroy of **New Spain** from 1722–1734, born in Lima. He proved to be an energetic administrator, expelling British interlopers from the Caribbean coast of Mexico, **Guatemala**, and Honduras, encouraged the colonization of **New Mexico** and **Arizona**, laid out **Mexico City's Alameda**, and built its Casa de la **Moneda** and **Aduana** (Custom House). He died in office, from a creeping paralysis. [L. H.]

ADMINISTRATIVE LAW. As in other Roman **Law** countries, Mexico has a separate codification of administrative law, one of whose most influential jurists was José **Aguilar y Maya**.

ADMIRALTY. *See* NAVAL MINISTRY.

AEROMEXICO. Mexico's formerly government-owned airline was founded on May 15, 1934, by Antonio Díaz Lombardo as *Aeronaves de México*, a private company, to fly between **Mexico City** and **Acapulco**. In 1941 services began to **Oaxaca** and **Veracruz** and in 1943 to **Chiapas**. In 1940 Pan American Airways acquired a 40 percent holding, but in 1959 the Mexican government bought out all shareholders, making it a wholly owned public entity. In 1961 Aeronaves bought Guest Airways to obtain routes to Europe. By 1964, 90 percent of its aircraft were jets. In the 1970s it shortened its name to Aeroméxico.

Under bureaucratic management, overmanning was practiced to please the **trade unions**, a mainstay of the ruling **Partido Revolucionario Institucional**. In the 1980s, Aeromexico was flying fifteen percent fewer international and twenty percent fewer domestic passengers than Mexico's other national airline, **Compañía Mexicana de Aviación (CMA)**, and in April 1988 it filed for bankruptcy but was allowed to continue. In the 1990s it still lagged a few percentage points behind CMA in passenger sales, but in 1997 the PRI lost control of the **Cámara de Diputados Federales** and the airline was again privatized. Its management improved and private sector norms were adopted. The operational waste that had produced continuous delays and flight cancellations was greatly reduced. Free travel for government officials was cut back to a token amount. *See also* AIR TRANSPORT.

AFRICAN SLAVERY. Although Mexico at the end of the 1600s was importing more African slaves than any other region of the Spanish **Indies**—some 200,000 slaves had been brought in by 1700, to work in the **silver** mines, **sugar** plantations, and **cattle** ranches—an early decline in the economic importance of slavery not only led to the virtual disappearance of the institution but also to its banishment from the national consciousness. Miguel **Hidalgo y Costilla** outlawed slavery on December 10, 1810. Its formal abolition was called for by the **Apatzingán Congress** and was definitively secured by a proclamation of President **Guerrero** in 1829, a move clearly directed at **Texas,** since African slavery was by then of no economic importance elsewhere. Abolition was reconfirmed by the **Constitution of 1857**. *See also* BLACKS; MAROONS. [L. H.]

AFRO-MEXICANS. *See* BLACKS.

AGAVE. American genus of amaryllis, a cactus called *maguey* in Spanish. Its sap is the source of **pulque** and whose leaves provide the fiber used to make **sisal**. [L. H.]

AGENCIA FEDERAL DE INVESTIGACIÓN (A.F.I.). Mexican police body created on November 1, 2001, in clear imitation of the F.B.I.

AGIOTISTA ("usurer," "profiteer"). This term was used, particularly during the Antonio López de **Santa Anna** period from 1829–1855, for a businessman speculating in short term, very high interest loans to the government.

AGRAMONT COTA, FÉLIX (1917–). Agricultural engineer, born in La Paz, **Baja California del Sur**, graduated in 1945 from the **Escuela Nacional de Agricultura** (now the **Universidad Autónoma Chapingo**), and became an administrator for the **Agriculture Ministry** in **Jalisco**.

AGRARIAN REFORM. At the close of Spanish rule, the best lands were owned by 5,000 large landowners (*See* HACIENDA) or the **Church**. Although some Church land had been expropriated in 1805–1809 by the Law of **Consolidation**, and much more was seized following the **Reform Laws** of 1859, the **Porfiriato**'s land policy favored large estates, leaving 90 percent of country folk as landless employees of **latifundia** (*See* LAND LAW OF 1883), while one percent of Mexicans owned 97 percent of the land. Breaking up these huge estates became one of the aims of the **Revolution of 1910**, and the **Constitution of 1917** required the restoration of each illegally expropriated **ejido**. Despite the early efforts of the revolutionaries, and especially of Emiliano **Zapata**, little was done. Álvaro **Obregon** redistributed a token 1,133,000 ha (2.8 million acres), fearful that any meaningful effort would disrupt the **economy**. Lázaro **Cárdenas**, however, believed very strongly in land reform and 18,211,000 ha (45 million acres) were redistributed during his administration. Adolfo **López Mateos** also emphasized it, redistributing a further 10,118,000 ha (27 million acres).

As elsewhere in Latin America, illegal land occupation is a chronic associated problem (*See* PARACAIDISTA). Activists, such as Rubén **Jaramillo** in 1960–1962, have encouraged direct action by squatters. By the late 1960s, however, it was officially declared that all agricultural land had been redistributed. Nevertheless, new lands are occasionally "discovered." All in all, land reform has probably been more successful in Mexico than in any other Latin American country. In 1991 Congress amended the Constitution (effective January 6, 1992) to allow the supervised breakup of **ejidos**. *See also* PEASANT ASSOCIATIONS.

AGRARIAN REFORM MINISTRY (*Secretaría de la Reforma Agraria—***SRA).** Created in 1975, with a cabinet-rank minister, gave full autonomy to the Department of Agrarian Affairs and Colonization (*Departamento de Asuntos Agrarios y Colonización—*DAAC). The DAAC had been a 1958 expansion of the Agriculture Ministry's Agrarian Department, which began in 1934, to administer **agrarian reform** and settle landless peasants on lands newly opened to farming and ranching through irrigation. After January 1992 it supervised the breaking up of **ejidos**.

AGRICULTURE. Mexico's principal crop has been **corn** since preconquest times. **Wheat** is grown by **irrigation** in the Northeast. **Rice** and **beans** are also important for the domestic market. The main export crops are **cotton**, tomatoes, and **sugar**. **Coffee** is less significant. **Sisal** is important in **Yucatán**. **Cacao** has lost the importance it had had prior to the Spanish **conquest**.

Mexican agriculture employs 26 percent of the national workforce, but loses 30 percent of the crop between harvest and processing, a result of the inadequacy of so much of its infrastructure. *See also* AGRARIAN REFORM; CHICLE; FOOD AND FOOD SUPPLY; LIVESTOCK; WINE. [L. H.]

AGRICULTURE MINISTRY. The *Dirección General de Industria*, was formed in 1842 as a department of the then *Ministerio de Relaciones Exteriores y Interiores*. It was Mexico's first government agency with responsibility for **agriculture**. In April, 1853, a separate *Ministerio de Fomento, Colonización, Industria y Comercio* was formed. In 1891 a *Secretaría de Fomento* was named, whose title was changed in 1917 to *Secretaría de Agricultura,* then to *Secretaría de Agricultura y Fomento*, and in December 1946 to *Secretaría de Agricultura y Ganadería*. A 1976 merger with the *Secretaría de Recursos Hidráulicos* created the *Secretaría de Agricultura y Recursos*

Hidráulicos (SARH) which in 1995 became the *Secretaría de Agricultura, Ganadería y Desarrollo Rural* (SAGAR), and then in 2000 became the *Secretaria de Agricultura, Ganadería, Desarrollo Rural, Pesca y Alimentación*—Ministry of Agriculture, Livestock Rearing, Rural Development, Fisheries, and Food (SAGARPA). [L. H.]

AGUA PRIETA ("dark water"). **Sonora** town on the **United States border,** opposite **Douglas,** had 56,300 inhabitants in 1995 on 3,632 km². Established in 1903, following the arrival of the railroad in 1897, it became a **ciudad** in 1942. It saw a defeat of Pancho **Villa** by the Constitutionalists. [L. H.]

AGUA PRIETA, PLAN OF. This election program was **Obregón**'s successful 1920 bid for the presidency.

AGUAS BLANCAS. In this locality in the **Guerrero municipio** of Coyuca de Benítez, on June 28, 1995, state **police** fired on a truckload of militants of the *Organización Campesina de la Sierra del Sur,* killing 17. Allegations that this had been a **police** ambush rather than an attempt by the victims to run a road block led to the resignation of state governor Rubén Figueroa Alcocer in early 1996.

AGUASCALIENTES ("hot waters"). City founded as an **army** post and bishopric of **Nueva Galicia,** October 22, 1575, on the *Ruta de la Plata* highway between **Mexico City** and **Zacatecas,** at 21°51'N, 102°18'W. Situated 1,890 m above sea level, on the left bank of its namesake river, its development as a town began in 1609 following the decimation of the local **Indians** in the War of the **Chichimecs** and by punitive action and **disease.** It became a **villa** in 1661, the Villa de N.S. de la Ascensión de las Aguas Calientes, for its mineral springs, which have made it a spa town. In 1857 it became the capital of the new **Aguascalientes State.** Its 1998 population was 440,000 (city) and 719,659 (**municipio**), but with the recent annexation of its suburb of Jesús María, the municipal population now exceeds one million. The chief industries are food processing and **textiles.**

AGUASCALIENTES, CONVENTION OF. An unsuccessful attempt in November 1914 by Venustiano **Carranza,** Pancho **Villa,** and

Emilio **Zapata** to iron out their differences. When, against his wishes, the Convention chose Eulalio **Gutiérrez** as provisional president, Carranza withdrew his delegates and moved his government to **Veracruz**. Villa and Zapata moved to **Mexico City**, ostensibly to install Gutiérrez, but once they arrived they took turns occupying the **National Palace** themselves.

AGUASCALIENTES STATE. Small inland state created in 1857 of 5,589 km² (2,158 sq. miles) and only 11 **muncipios**, bounded by **Jalisco** on the south, and elsewhere by **Zacatecas**. Mostly on a plateau, 1,890 m (6,200 ft.) above sea level, it enjoys a mild climate. Its major industries are **agriculture** and **livestock** ranching. Some of Mexico's busiest cattle, sheep, and horse wholesalers maintain offices in the capital, **Aguascalientes**. Its **population** was 86,329, in 1857, and 86,576, in 1869. At successive **censuses** its population was 104,000 in 1895; 102,000 in 1900; 120,000 in 1910; 108,000 in 1921; 133,000 in 1930; 162,000 in 1940; 188,000 in 1950; 243,000 in 1960; 338,000 in 1970; 519,000 in 1980; 719,659 in 1990 (having more than doubled in 20 years); 944,285 in 2000; and 1,065,416 in 2005, overwhelmingly living in the state capital.

AGUILAR, CANDIDO (1888–1960). Statesman, born in Palma, **Veracruz state**, on February 12, governed his home state from 1914–1917. Nationally known as the vice-president of the **Querétaro Convention**, he was a federal **senator** from 1934–1940. A son-in-law of Venustiano **Carranza**, he also served as foreign minister during 1918.

AGUILAR, JERÓNIMO DE (1489–1531). A Spanish **conquistador** from Murcia who survived a shipwreck off **Yucatán** and lived eight years among the **Maya**. Having learned their language, he served Hernán **Cortés** as an interpreter and in 1527 was rewarded with several **encomiendas** in the Valley of **Mexico**.

AGUILAR, MARTÍN. Master of a ship of Sebastián **Vizcaíno**'s 1602 expedition, separated from the rest in a storm and discovered the "Entrada de Martín Aguilar," a large river mouth around 43°N, long regarded as the entrance to the Strait of **Anián**.

AGUILAR ÁLVAREZ, ERNESTO (1910–). Jurist, born in **Mexico City** on January 25, he graduated from **UNAM**, where he was a **law** professor from 1938–1966. He was subsequently a justice of the **Supreme Court** from 1966–1979.

AGUILAR TALAMANTES, RAFAEL (1940–). Marxist politician, born in Santa Rosalía, **Baja California del Sur**, studied law and economics at **UNAM** from 1958–1964 and led the Marxist National Democratic Student Federation. Imprisoned from 1964–1970 for leading riots in **Michoacán**, in 1974 he became founder and secretary general of the **Partido Socialista de Trabajadores** (Socialist Workers' Party) and later president of the **Partido del Frente Cardenista de Reconstrucción Nacional**.

AGUILAR Y MAYA, JOSÉ (1897–1966). Jurist, born in **Guanajuato** on July 28, he graduated from **UNAM**, where he became a law professor for 10 years before governing his home state from 1949–1955 and serving as **Procurador General** of Mexico from 1940–1946 and from 1955–1958. His writings influenced Mexican public **law**, especially the development of regulatory law in the 1940s and 1950.

AGUILERA AZPEITIA, JUAN. One of the founders of the **Partido Demócrata Mexicano**.

AGUSTÍN, JOSÉ (1944–). Acapulco-born journalist in **Mexico City**, he has developed into a nationally known novelist, fine arts critic, and **television** and motion picture writer. His first novel, *La tumba* (1964) describes wealthy Mexican youths lacking parental guidance. His *De perfil* (1966) analyzes the rootlessness of modern urban life. *Abolición de la propiedad* (1969)—a novel and a **cinema** film script— focused on the generation gap and in 1975 became the basis for a **television** drama.

AGUSTÍN I, EMPEROR. Imperial title adopted by Agustín de **Iturbide**.

AHOME. River and **municipio** of **Sonora state** (until December 1916 part of El **Fuerte**) had 304,160 inhabitants in 1990, on 4,357 km². The town of Ahome, a pre-Hispanic settlement, became a Spanish mission in 1605 but ceased to be the **cabecera** when this was moved to the much faster growing Los **Mochis** in December 1935. The mangrove swamps between the city and the sea are home to the yellow crocodile (*crocodylus acutus*). [L. H.]

AHUÍTZOTL ("water dog") (14??–1502). This **Aztec** "emperor" (**tlatoani**) from 1487–1502 was brother of his predecessor, **Tizoc.** His conquests extended the empire almost to **Guatemala.** He is credited with having reduced the number of human sacrifices in an attempt to abolish the practice entirely.

AHUMADA Y VILLALÓN, AGUSTÍN, MARQUÉS DE LAS AMARILLAS (17??–1760). Viceroy of **New Spain** from 1755–1760, died suddenly in office. He was credited with administrative reforms, control of **mining**, and with making an unsuccessful attempt to drive British logwood cutters from **Belize.** [L. H.]

AIR FORCE. President **Madero** had five soldiers trained abroad to fly French Blériot monoplanes for army reconnaissance as the *Escuadrilla Aérea de la Milicia Auxiliar del Ejército*, and in 1915 Venustiano **Carranza** formally inaugurated the *Arma de Aviación Militar.* French aircraft were replaced by British designs in the 1920s, some built under licence in Mexico. American planes were preferred from the 1930s, beginning with twelve Vought 02U-2M "Corsairs" sent to help suppress the **Escobar rebellion.** The present name of *Fuerza Aérea Mexicana* was adopted February 10, 1944. In 1945 its *Esquadrón de Caza 201* flew Republic "Thunderbolt" fighters in the liberation of the **Philippines.** The force's current strength includes Russian helicopters, Brazilian reconnaissance planes, British "Hercules" transports, and aging American Northrop F-5 jet fighters, bought in 1981 and now in need of replacement.

The national wing and fuselage symbol is a triangle in three concentric bands of red around white, around green. *See also* ESCUELA DE AVIACIÓN MILITAR; FUERZA AERONAVAL. [L. H.]

AIR TRANSPORT. Albert **Braniff** in a Voison biplane made the first flights into and out of **Mexico City** on December 8, 1910, and in 1911 he flew President Francisco **Madero** over the capital. Mexico's largest airline, **Compañía Mexicana de Aviación (CMA)**, began flying in 1924, and **Aeroméxico** followed in 1934. In 1991 a third airline, **Transportes Aéreos Ejecutivos S.A. (TAESA)**, came into existence. Beginning in 1995, President Ernesto **Zedillo** directed the government to encourage the general public to invest in stocks of airline, telecommunication, steel, and insurance companies. Major **newspapers'** financial pages have been replete with background stories on the pros and cons of such investments. They have permitted both CMA and Aeroméxico to modernize their jetliner fleets.

On June 3, 1996, the **Transport Ministry** announced a partial merger of Aeroméxico and CMA, with many day-to-day functions to be gradually combined over a period of some years, but continuing their names and separate sales offices. Freed of some non-essential activities that Aeroméxico could supply for both airlines, CMA began to show improved profits and improved services.

In April 1997, after a decade of deregulated air travel, the ministry insisted that Mexico's domestic routes were as uncompetitive as ever, although CMA and Aeroméxico were both rated as having improved their standard of service after 1994. *See also* AVIATION PIONEERS.

AIRPORTS. By the 1970s Mexico had 105 airports, of which 15 are of international standard. The most important are **Mexico City**, **Guadalajara**, **Monterrey**, **Acapulco**, **Mérida**, **Matamoros**, **Ciudad Juárez**, **Puerto Vallarta**, and **Tapachula**.

ALAMÁN Y ESCALADA, LUCAS (1792–1853). Politician and historian, this rich **creole** mine owner in **Guadalajara**, and pioneer industrialist became the leader of the **conservadores**, serving as foreign minister in 1823–1825, 1830–1832, and 1853. He was the member from **Guanajuato** of the **triumvirate** that secured the presidency for Anastacio **Bustamante** in 1829 and subsequently connived in the judicial execution of Vicente **Guerrero**. After Bustamante's fall, Alamán retired from politics until 1853, when he helped José Antonio López de **Santa Anna** become President, hoping to persuade him to effect positive changes in Mexico's government. Alamán's own death ended all hopes of this. Regarded as Mexico's ablest conservative statesman, his 1849 *Historia de México* is probably the best work of its kind for that period.

ALAMEDA ("grove of poplars"). Many late 18th century tree-lined avenues for social promenading in Hispanic cities. The one in downtown **Mexico City** forms a green park in the central area, lying just west of the **Palacio de Bellas Artes**, between avenues Juárez and **Hidalgo**, surrounded by theaters, restaurants, and one block east of the Casa de **Tejas**. It was originally laid out by **Viceroy Acuña y Bejarano**. For many years the city government has sponsored free **music** concerts in the park, from traditional **Mariachis** to modern popular and soft-rock groups. Organ grinders, formerly found in various sites in the central city, still perform in the park every day of the week.

    Saltillo is another city with an Alameda Park.

ÁLAMO, El ("the poplar tree"). Spanish mission in downtown **San Antonio**, Texas, the scene in 1836 of the most famous battle in Texan history. After an early victory, 181 Texans, under General William Barrett Travis, faced José Antonio López de **Santa Anna**'s 3,000-strong force and held out for two weeks until, on March 9, to the trumpet call of *degüello* ("no quarter"), Santa Anna finally succeeded in overpowering them, killing all the defenders. This costly victory marked the beginning of **Texas'** independence from Mexico, and the cry "Remember the Alamo" became the rallying point for the independence fight. Davy **Crockett** is probably the best known of the mission house's defenders.

ALANIS FUENTES GARCÍA, AGUSTÍN (1930–). Lawyer-politician, born in **Mexico City** on February 19, taught at the **Escuela Nacional Preparatoria** in 1950, graduated in law from **UNAM** in 1953, was director of social work for the Labor Ministry from 1964–1970, became a UNAM **law** professor in 1968, assistant minister of labor from 1970–1976, and then **procurador de justicia** for the **Federal District** in December 1976.

ALARCÓN Y MENDOZA, JUAN RUIZ DE (1580–1639). Leading playwright of Spanish Literature's "Golden Age." born in Tlacho, Mexico, left for Spain when he was only twenty, staying there for life, with but one brief visit back to Mexico. A hunchback, he was derided for this deformity and suffered greatly. His plays are characterized by a perfection of style and by their moralizing tendencies. His most famous plays are *La verdad sospechosa* (*The Suspect Truth*) and *Las paredes oyen* (*Walls Have Ears*).

ALBA PÉREZ, PEDRO DEL (1887–1960). Ophthalmologist, politician, and the author of several books on medicine, politics, and diplomacy, he was born on December 17 in San Juan de los Lagos, **Jalisco**. He graduated in medicine from **UNAM** and took graduate studies as a surgeon at the **Army**'s Military Medical School in 1913, and gained a diploma in ophthalmology in Paris. He was a federal deputy from **Aguascalientes state** in 1920–1922. In 1933 he organized the University of **Monterrey**, now the **Universidad Autónoma de Nuevo León**. He served as senator from Aguascalientes from 1922–1926 and 1952–1956, as ambassador to Chile during 1947, and as ambassador to the **United Nations** from 1951.

ALBARRADA, LA. Conservative defeat of Liberal forces on December 24, 1859, in a battle on the highway between **Colima City** and **Guadalajara**.

ALBUQUERQUE. New Mexico. City at 35°06'N, 106°36'W, established as a staging post on the *camino real* and named *Alburquerque* in honor of **Viceroy** Francisco **Fernández de la Cueva**, duke of Alburquerque. It was not formally founded until 1706 by Provincial Governor Francisco Cuevo y Valdés. The town only began to grow with the 1880 arrival of the Atchison, Topeka, and Santa Fé Railroad. It then dropped the first *r* in its name. By 2005, 797,940 people were living in the metropolitan area.

ALCABALA. Roman sales tax, the *gabella,* kept by the Moors (whence the form of its name) and brought by Spain to her New World colonies, where it was collected by the **audiencia**. Originally two percent, the **Bourbon reforms** increased it to six percent. It was abolished by José Yves **Limantour** in the 1890s.

ALCALÁ QUINTERO, FRANCISCO (1913–). Certified Public Accountant who became an administrator at the **Banco Nacional de Comercio Exterior** in 1946 and its director general from 1970–1980.

In the 1970s he formulated policies for the **Instituto Mexicano de Comercio Exterior** to increase **exports**.

ALCALDE. Mayor, the chief officer of a **municipio**. Etymologically the term is Arabic and has consequently been replaced in many other Hispanic countries (by, e.g., *intendente* or *prefecto*).

ALDAMA. (1) A 6,825 km^2 municipio of **Chihuahua** with 17,169 inhabitants in 1998, of whom 12,191 live in the **cabecera**, the former San Jerónimo, renamed in honor of Juan **Aldama**, 1,262 m above sea level at 28°50'N, 105°53'W. "Juan Aldama" is both the county seat of Aldama and the name of another **municipio**, in **Zacatecas**.

(2) A 2,825 km^2 seaside municipio of southeast **Tamaulipas**, with 25,725 inhabitants in 1998, of whom only 9,725 live in the **cabecera**, 90 m above sea level, at 22°37'N, 97°46'W, founded in April 1790 as the *Divina Pastora de las Presas del Rey*.

ALDAMA, IGNACIO M. (1769?–1811). Hero of the **Independence** Movement, a lawyer who had grown wealthy through commercial ventures, he became active in the movement because of his brother, Juan **Aldama**, serving mainly as a legal advisor and non-military counsel to Miguel **Hidalgo y Costilla** and as Mexico's first minister to the **United States**. He was captured at **Acatita de Baján** and shot on June 20 at **Monclova**.

ALDAMA, JUAN (1744–1811). Patriot, brother of Ignacio **Aldama**, born in San Miguel el Grande, **Guanajuato state**. He was one of the inner circle of the **Independence** Movement of 1810. When the plot was discovered, it was he who notified Miguel **Hidalgo y Costilla**. He took part in many military campaigns until captured at **Acatita de Baján**, along with Hidalgo, his brother Ignacio, and others. He was executed by a firing squad on June 28, and his head was exhibited on a corner of the **Alhóndiga de Granaditas**. In 1823 he was declared a national hero, and localities in **Chihuahua**, **Nueva León**, **Tamaulipas**, and **Zacatecas** were renamed in his honor.

ALDANA IBARRA, MIGUEL (1945?–). A businessman son of a soldier in Pancho **Villa**'s army, his education benefited from a government scholarship granted for spying on left-wing fellow students. He entered the **police**, retiring in 1984 as head of Interpol in Mexico and heading a **law** firm. Arrested in 1990 for **narcotics** trading—which he characterized as "revenge" for some of his large drug busts—he spent four years in prison before being cleared. Then in 2001 he created the *Confederación Nacional de Seguridad y Justicia en México A.C.* (National Confederation on Security and Justice) to get business people to collaborate on security projects. Later he went into real estate and construction. To the charge that he had Canadian and American partners in his (successful) bid for the **Excelsior** newspaper, he argued that these were only partners in other branches of his businesses.

ALDRETE, ALBERTO V. (1881–1959). A large-scale **wheat** farmer, born in **Baja California del Norte**, he owned a flour mill in **Mexicali** and founded the Tecate brewery in Baja California which marketed beer throughout Mexico. He died in **Mexicali**.

ALEGRE, FRANCISCO JAVIER (1729–1788). A Jesuit priest and historian. As a youngster he already had a complete command of Latin, and by his ordination he knew Greek, Hebrew, and **Nahuatl**, preaching to the **Indians** in their native tongue. A true humanist, he rejected **African slavery**, stating that the authority of one man over others derived from the consent of the group. He wrote a history of the **Jesuits** in **New Spain**. After the expulsion of the order he lived out his remaining years in Italy.

ALEJO LÓPEZ, FRANCISCO JAVIER (1941–). Prominent business executive and politician of the 1960s, assistant finance minister in 1970–1974, minister of **natural resources** (*Secretario de Patrimonio Nacional*) in 1975–1976, and in December 1976 became director of the government's industrial complex, Ciudad Sahagún, manufacturing railroad cars and various types of heavy machinery.

ALEMÁN VALDÉS, MIGUEL (1902–1983). President of Mexico from 1946–1953, he was born in Sayula, **Veracruz**. He was the first popularly elected civilian president since the **Revolution of 1910**. His was an administration run by businessmen. The **economy** prospered, despite much alleged **corruption**. He did little for **agrarian**

reform but spent considerable amounts on **irrigation** projects. He maintained a vigorous foreign policy and took an active role in the **United Nations**. He advanced programs in **education** and science, including the setting up of Mexico's first **television** station.

ALEMÁN VELASCO, MIGUEL (1932?–). Lawyer-businessman son of Miguel **Alemán Valdés**, born in **Veracruz** on March 18. He became news director of **Televisa** and then its president from 1985–1989. In 1990 he sold his 17 percent interest in the network to Emilio **Azcárraga Milmo**. Inheriting his father's stock and property holdings had already made him one of Mexico's wealthiest men. His wife is an actress and former Miss Universe.

ALENCASTRE NOROÑA Y SILVA, FERNANDO DE. *See* LÁN-CASTER NOROÑA Y SILVA, FERNANDO DE.

ALHÓNDIGA DE GRANADITAS. On September 28, 1810, the city of **Guanajuato**'s outnumbered defenders took refuge in this huge granary to await a relief force to suppress the insurgents led by Miguel **Hidalgo y Costilla**. Before help arrived the insurgents stormed the building, massacring most of those inside. After the insurgents' eventual defeat, the heads of Hidalgo and of his two principal associates, Juan **Aldama** and Ignacio **Allende**, were displayed as a dreadful warning at the corners of the building. Used as a prison until the 1940s, the granary is now a national monument.

ALIJOS ROCKS (*Escollos Alijos*). Group of volanic rocks known to Spanish navigators since at least 1598. Its surface area barely totals 1,000 m^2 in surface area, at 24°57'N, 115°44'W, 300 km west of **Baja California Sur**.

ALL HALLOWS. In Mexico the celebration of the feast of all saints (November 1) tends to merge with the following day, the feast of **All Souls' Day**.

ALL SOULS' DAY. The day following **All Hallows**, the *Día de los Muertos* ("Day of the Dead," November 2), is celebrated rather in the way Americans celebrate the eve of the day before it (Halloween).

Children eat cookies and cakes decorated with skulls and crossbones. Families hold picnics at cemeteries at the graves of relatives. Costume parties feature masks caricaturing celebrities.

ALLENDE. Three **municipios** bear this name. One is 2,052 km^2 in **Chihuahua**, whose county seat is **Valle de Allende**.

A second is 231 km^2 (with 18,486 inhabitants in 1998) in **Coahuila**, 28°20'N, 100°51'W. The county seat was made a **villa** in 1827 as San Juan de Mata and renamed Ignacio Allende in 1832.

The third is 148 km^2 (with 27,773 inhabitants in 2000) located at 25°17'N, 100°01'W in **Nuevo León** and notable for honey, eggs, and oranges.

ALLENDE Y UNZAGA, IGNACIO MARÍA (1779–1811). Born in San Miguel el Grande, a town of **Guanajuato state** since renamed in his honor as San Miguel de Allende, this patriot was a key figure in the **Independence movement** of 1810. He probably should have been in charge of its armed forces, but he initially deferred to Miguel **Hidalgo y Costilla**. He disagreed with Hidalgo's refusal to take **Mexico City** and eventually took command himself, but by then it was too late to reverse the defeats already suffered. Captured at **Acatita de Baján** and sentenced to be shot, his head was displayed on a corner of the **Alhóndiga de Granaditas**.

ALMAZÁN, JUAN ANDREU (1891–1965). Born in **Guerrero**, this **army** officer served with Francisco **Madero** and in 1924 received command of the **Monterrey** army zone. He showed brilliance in suppressing the **Escobar rebellion**. In 1940 he ran as the presidential candidate of the **Partido Revolucionario de Unificación Nacional**, attributing his defeat to fraud—he received only 5.73 percent of the votes.

ALMOJARIFAZGO. A colonial tax on **exports** and **imports** of 7.5 percent, implying a total of 15 percent on anything exported from one part of Spain's domains and imported into another. [L. H.]

ALMONTE, JUAN NEPOMUCENO (1803?–1869). Almonte ruled Mexico, first as president of the conservative faction within the republic from April 18, 1862, until January 12, 1863, then as regent, until October 12, 1863, and next as *lugarteniente del emperador* ("imperial lieutenant") while awaiting **Maximilian**'s arrival, May 20–June 12, 1864.

ALTA CALIFORNIA. Upper California, this pre-1848 name was for what is now the modern state of **California**, in distinction from **Baja California**. The lands north of the Bay of **California** were first explored by Juan Rodríguez de **Cabrillo** in 1542. Englishman Sir Francis **Drake** followed in 1579, and Sebastián **Vizcaíno** in 1602, but Spain did not attempt to occupy or exert authority over Upper California (i.e., north of the Gulf) until 1768. Gaspar de Portolà founded **San Diego** in 1769, and Franciscan missions were established by Junípero **Serra** at **San Francisco** in 1776, **San José** in 1777, and **Los Angeles** in 1781. The area became a constituent state of independent Mexico in 1822 as **Alta California**. American settlers began to arrive in 1841, and were numerous enough to attempt to seize power in the revolt of the "**Bear Flag Republic**" of 1846. The **United States-Mexican War** soon followed and the entire state of Upper California (*Alta*—or *Nueva—California*) was lost in the resulting Treaty of **Guadalupe-Hidalgo**, to become the present-day California in the **United States**. By a supreme irony, the discovery of **gold** that led to the great Californian gold rush was made just one week after Mexico lost sovereignty. *See also* KINO, EUSEBIO FRANCISCO; PICO, ANDRÉS,

ALTAMIRA. Port city of **Tamaulipas** and petrochemical industrial complex with 24,122 inhabitants in 1990, founded in 1749 at 22°50'N, 98°W, as Altamira de N.S. de las Caldas. Excellent surfing conditions attract tourists despite organo-chlorine and heavy metal discharges from some of its factories. The port was privatized in 1994 and is now Mexico's fourth biggest. [L. H.]

ALTAMIRANO. Chiapas municipio of 1,449 km^2 created as San Carlos in 1911 and renamed after the writer in 1935. Located at 16°50'N, 92°05'W, it had 17,026 inhabitants in 1998.

ALTAMIRANO BASILIO, IGNACIO MANUEL (1834–1893). Diplomat, journalist, and writer, this pureblood **Amerindian** from

Guerrero did not learn **Spanish** until he was fourteen. After attending the **Colegio de Letrán** he was caught up in the Wars of the **Reforms** and fought on the liberal side. After the defeat of the French, he helped found *El Correo* (1867) and *El Renacimiento* (1869), took part in forming many cultural societies, and taught literature. His best known works are *Rimas* (a book of poems), *Navidad en las montañas* and *El Zarco* (published posthumously in 1901). He served in diplomatic posts in Spain and France, and died in San Remo, Italy. He was reckoned a disciple of Ignacio **Ramírez**.

ALTIPLANICIE (or ALTIPLANO). High plateau or *meseta* of northern Mexico.

ALTOS HORNOS DE MÉXICO, S.A. (AHMSA). Mexico's largest **iron** and steel complex, established by the government in 1941 at Monclova, **Coahuila**, close to iron ore reserves. It soon surpassed the privately owned **Fundidora de Monterrey** and by 1975 had an annual output three times that of the *Fundidora*. Until 1977 its domestic and foreign sales remained healthy, and it supplied half of all Mexico's iron and steel production. Between 1987 and 1991 sales fell and 2,000 employees were put on "leave without pay" despite protests by the **trade unions**. Carlos **Salinas de Gortari** decided to reverse his predecessor's policy and reduce AHMSA's government-managed administration. In 1991 he allowed Alonso Ancira and Xavier Autrye to buy it from the government in a leveraged buy out and then raised 1.9 billion *pesos* to modernize its mills and expand markets. A period of economic recovery followed, but sales dropped in 1998, creating a two million **peso** deficit The following May, 2.4 billion *pesos* in debt, AHMSA defaulted on its debts and declared bankruptcy. Chief executive Xavier Maza nevertheless predicted that the firm, which then had 19,306 full-time employees (plus a few part-time technical consultants) would retain its position as one of Latin America's leading steel complexes in terms of sales and as a supplier of industrial parts.

ALVARADO. Municipio of **Veracruz state** at 18°46'N, 95°46'W with 49,040 inhabitants in 1998 on 929 km^2. The **cabecera**, on the namesake coastal lagoon, has been since 1867 an important port for coastwise shipping.

ALVARADO CONTRERAS Y MESIA, PEDRO DE (1485?–1541). **Conquistador,** born in Badajoz, Estremadura, second in command to Hernán **Cortés** in the **Conquest** of Mexico. In 1523 he conquered **Guatemala,** El Salvador, and western Honduras, and was appointed by **Charles V** captain general of Guatemala. In 1534, with 2,000 **Indians** and 500 Spaniards he nearly succeeded in conquering Quito. Instead he met Pizarro and Almagro at the Bay of Caráquez and sold his expedition for 100,000 gold *pesos.* He came back to Mexico to consult the **viceroy** about an expedition he was planning into the Pacific, but he arrived just at the outbreak of the **Mixton War.** He joined in and was killed.

ÁLVAREZ ÁLVAREZ, LUIS HÉCTOR (1919?–). Textile manufacturer in **Chihuahua,** and an engineering graduate of M.I.T., with a master's degree from the University of Texas in Austin, he headed the Educational Center for **Ciudad Juárez.** In 1958–1962 he led the **Partido de Acción Nacional** running in that first year as its presidential candidate. He led the party again in 1987–1993 and sat in the **Senate** from 1994–2000.

ÁLVAREZ GUERRERO, ALEJANDRO (1925–). Born in the **Federal District** on December 24, this businessman graduated from **UNAM** in chemical engineering, founded the Association of Electrical Engineers, and in the 1960s became president of the Mexican Institute of Chemical Engineers. A board member of fourteen large corporations, he was director general of Conduit of Mexico from 1970–1972, president of the **Confederación de Cámaras Industriales** from 1972–1973, and creator of the **Trade Ministry**'s Department of Rural Industrialization.

ÁLVAREZ HURTADO, JUAN (1790–1867). President of Mexico from 1855–1856, a soldier and federalist politician from **Atoyac,** he fought for **independence** from 1810, capturing **Acapulco.** Subsequently he fought against **Iturbide,** Anastasio **Bustamante,** and then **Santa Anna,** in the cause of **federalism.** In 1850 he became governor of **Guerrero** and in November 1855 was made president, but he resigned a year later. He later fought against **Maximilian.** He died in La Providencia.

ALZATE Y RAMÍREZ, JOSÉ ANTONIO DE (1737–1799). Priest, historian, cartographer, and scientist from Ozuma, an extremely prolific writer who produced work that is hard to categorize, embracing as it does botany, mathematics, philology, **archaeology**, and **law**. His many foreign honors included membership of the French *Académie des Sciences*. His historical notes have helped clarify Mexico's early colonial period. Expelled with all other **Jesuits** in 1766, he managed to return many years later. His mother's family was kin to *Sor* **Juana Inés de la Cruz**.

AMERICAN-BRITISH COWDRAY HOSPITAL. Private hospital, popularly known as the A.B.C. Hospital, on Avenida Observatorio, **Mexico City**, maintained to American, British, and Canadian standards by the city's Anglophone residents, staffed by both Mexican and American-trained physicians, and reorganized and expanded several times since the 1940s. "Cowdray" honors the family who raised a large endowment from charitable sources to ensure its permanent status. *See also* MEDICAL EDUCATION.

AMERICAN REVOLUTIONARY WAR. In 1779 **Spain** followed her ally **France** in intervening on the colonists' side in the American War of Independence, and an army led by Bernardo de **Gálvez** attacked Florida, capturing **Pensacola**.

AMERICAN SOUTHWEST. *See* FAR NORTH.

AMERICANO ("American"). Originally referring to any inhabitant of the New World, the term came in colonial Mexico to be used as a preferred alternative to **creole**, while the English equivalent began at about the same time to be used to distinguish English settlers on the mainland from those on the Caribbean Islands (the "West Indians"). The Spanish word's normal modern use, to translate "American" (i.e., an inhabitant of the **United States**), is objected to by purists and nationalists alike, who tend to prefer *norteamericano*. This dictionary reserves "American" for any corporation, institution, event, or action not formally pertaining to, nor connected with, the **United States** government, and also for any individual US citizen. [L. H.]

AMERICANS IN MEXICO. *See* AUSTIN, STEPHEN FULLER; BIERCE, AMBROSE; BRANIFF, ALBERT; DANIELS, JOSEPH; FREMONT, JOHN; GUAYMAS; IMMIGRATION; LINDBERG, ANNE MORROW; MCLANE, ROBERT MILLIGAN; MORROW, DWIGHT; O'NEILL, RALPH; PERSHING, JOHN JOSEPH; POINSETT, JOEL ROBERT; SCOTT, WINFIELD; STEPHENS, JOHN LLOYD; TOURISM; TRAVEN, B.; UNITED STATES AMBASSADORS; WALKER, WILLIAM; WILL, BRADLEY RONALD; WILSON, HENRY LANE.

AMERINDIAN (amerindio). This term for Native American is popular in Caribbean English (primarily to avoid confusion with East Indian, i.e., South Asian), and frequent in Mexican Spanish, particularly among anthropologists. This dictionary, deferring to traditional usage, prefers Columbus' misnomer **Indians**. [L. H.]

AMILPA, FERNANDO (1898–1952). Longtime leader of the Union of Bus Drivers, senator from his native **Morelos** from1940–1946 and secretary general of the **Confederación de Trabajadores de Mexico** from 1946–1949. For many years he represented the government on the **Federal Conciliation and Arbitration Board** in management-labor negotiations. Born May 30, he died in **Mexico City**.

AMOROS, ROBERTO (1914–1973). Born June 8, in Coatepec, **Veracruz**, this economist graduated in law from **UNAM** and did graduate study in economics at the University of Rome. In 1946–1951 he was secretary of the office of the presidency, and then from 1952–1958 he was director general of the **Ferrocarriles Nacionales de México**. He formulated many of Mexico's decentralized government agencies. He died in Veracruz on August 14.

AMPARO ("protection"). Writ of relief, on behalf of any citizen, issued by a federal judge to enforce the law. Combining the concept of an injunction with that of a writ of *mandamus* or *habeas corpus*, it can both compel any government official at any level to carry out any constitutional or statutory law and prevent such a one from any action that violates the **law**. These writs are most often sought from the **Supreme Court**, and since 1917 petitioners and petitioning groups have won almost two thirds of these cases. [The *juicio de amparo* was a special interest of the jurist Alfonso **Noriega Cantu Jr.** L. H.]

ANÁHUAC (Nahuátl: "place in the middle of the circle," "place of waters"). **Aztec** name for Mexico's central plateau, the site of **Mexico City.**

ANAYA, PEDRO MARÍA (1795–1854). A soldier who was briefly **president** of Mexico in 1847 and again in 1848, Anaya's fame comes mainly from his heroic defense of **Mexico City** in the **Mexican-American War.** When **United States** General Twigs demanded the surrender of his men, arms, and ammunition, Anaya replied with his famous phrase, *Si hubiera parque, no estaría usted aqui* ("If there had been any ammunition, you would not be here"). After Mexico's defeat he occupied the Presidency briefly, then he resigned.

ANCONA, ELIGIO (1835–1893). Journalist, lawyer, and historian, born in **Mérida**, Ancona, an ardent supporter of Benito Pablo **Juárez.** He founded the pro-Juárez newspaper *La Píldora* and a political newspaper, *Yucatán.* For a time he was governor of **Yucatán** and then a circuit judge, before returning to journalism. His most famous historical work is a history of Yucatán. He also wrote two novels and two plays.

ANDERSON NEVÁREZ, HILDA JOSEFINA (1938–). A feminist politician, born October 10 in **Mazatlán**, she graduated from the **Escuela Normal** of the Federal District. She became a national leader of **women** in politics in the 1960s–1970s, as Secretary for Feminine Action on the **Comité Ejecutivo Nacional** of the **Partido Revolucionario Institucional.** She also served as a federal congresswoman, 1964–1967 and 1970–1973.

ANDRADE DE DEL ROSAL, MARTHA (19??–2000?). Pioneer woman political leader in the **Partido Revolucionario Institucional** who obtained a diploma from the **Escuela Normal** Nacional in **Mexico City** and studied at Claremount College in **California.** In 1951 she organized the *Comisión Nacional de la Mujer* (PRI's National Women's Committee), and in 1952 she joined the PRI's **Comité**

Ejecutivo Nacional. She served as a federal deputy, 1958–1961 and 1964–1967. She organized nursery schools and the Nursery Department of the **Education Ministry** throughout the 1940s and 1950s, becoming Mexico's foremost consultant on preschool education.

ANEXO ("addition"). **Casa del Pueblo**.

ANGELÓPOLIS. Alternative colonial name for **Puebla City**, whence the adjective *anglopolitano*.

ANGOSTURA, BATTLE OF LA. What Americans know as the Battle of **Buena Vista**, Mexicans refer to by this name.

ANGUIANO, RAÚL (1915–2005). Mural painter.

ANIÁN, STRAIT OF. Mythical passage derived from Marco Polo's account of the Island of Anián and believed to separate Alaska from Asia (so providing entry for the Northwest Passage). It was first shown on the Venetian map-maker Bolognini Zalteri's 1566 map of North America. Juan Rodríguez de **Cabrillo** in the 1540s and Sebastián **Vizcaino** in 1596–1602 searched for it in vain (although Martín de **Aguilar**, a member of the latter expedition, thought he had found it). There was an alternative belief locating it much further south, stretching across North America to the Atlantic, or just across Mexico, linking the **Pacific** with the Gulf of **Mexico**.

ANIMALS. *See* CHIHUAHUA; FAUNA; LIVESTOCK.

ANTEQUERA. Villa founded in 1528 has supplied an alternative name for the archdiocese of **Oaxaca**.

ANTHROPOLOGY MUSEUM. *See* MUSEO NACIONAL DE ANTROPOLOGÍA.

ANTI-REELECTION PARTY. *See* PARTIDO ANTIRRELECCIONISTA.

ANTUÑANO, ESTÉBAN DE (1792–1847). Writer, industrialist, and leading economic liberal, British educated, and an adherent of the

Manchester school, he believed the best course for Mexico's **economy** was to increase **manufacturing industry**.

ANZA, JUAN DE (1734–1788). Soldier and explorer, born in Fronteras, **Sonora**, he was one of the officials in charge of expelling the **Jesuits**. In 1775 he marched northward, across southern **California** as far as **San Francisco**, helping to establish missions and forts. In 1777 he was made governor of **New Mexico** and worked to improve its communications with Sonora. He died in Arizpe, Sonora.

APACHE. Already a menace to settlers in Spanish colonial times, these **Indians** of Old Mexico's **"Far North"** made a fierce attack on **Laredo** in 1821. [L. H.]

APARICIO, SEBASTIÁN DE (1502–1600). Probably the first wheelwright and builder of **highways** in **New Spain**, Aparicio's greatest accomplishments include opening up a road between **Mexico City** and **Zacatecas** for transporting **silver**, a venture made possible because he was able to pacify the fierce **Chichimecs** with his love, and not by force of arms. He later became famous as an agriculturalist and navigator. He spent his last years as a Franciscan friar, living a life of great charity and profound humility for which he was beatified by Pius VII in 1789.

APATZINGÁN. Municipio of 2,000 km^2 formed in southern **Michoacán** in 1831, with 100,926 inhabitants in 1998 and 117,949 in 2000. From the late 19th century, dams provided **irrigation** and electric power. Subsequent economic development has owed much to the *Comisión de la Cuenca de Tepalcatepec*, but the area has become notorious as a center of **Narcotics** trafficking. **Apatzingán de la Constitución** is the county seat.

APATZINGÁN CONGRESS. Constituent assembly summoned by José María **Morellos y Pavón** in **Apatzingán** in October 1814. It drew up an abortive republican constitution which called for the **abolition of slavery** and of tribute, the end of the caste system, and equality before the law.

APATZINGÁN DE LA CONSTITUCIÓN. Cabacera of **Apatzingán**, it lies 500 m above sea level at 19°04'N, 102°59'W and was a

Nahuatl settlement refounded by the Franciscans in 1617. In 1998 it had 76,948 inhabitants.

APELLIDO ("surname"). Hispanic custom—formally, legally, and traditionally—is to use two such family names (which themselves may be compound): the paternal, and the maternal or marital. Normally the paternal is given preference, even in the case of a married woman. Exceptions occur when the other name is more distinctive or more prestigious. This is the reason we have entered President Plutarco Elías Calles under **Calles.** The less favored name may be dropped in informal use or indicated just by its initial letter.

The marital *apellido* is usually preceded by *de*. The maternal *apellido* is in very traditional usage preceded by *y* (e.g., Antonio García Cubas in his later works, but Antono García y Cubas in his earlier ones). Spanish language reference sources often ignore these particles in alphabetization.

Anti-colonial feeling at the time of **Independence** led to some substitution of Spanish *apellidos* by Native Indian names, whence (e.g.) Estéban *Moctezuma*. Analogous replacement of the Baptismal name (e.g., *Guadalupe* **Victoria**) also occurs. [L. H.]

APISTA. Supporter of the **Asamblea Popular de los Pueblos de Oaxaca**.

ARBENZ GUZMÁN, JACOBO (1913–1971). Progressive president of **Guatemala**, overthrown in a two-day civil war in 1954 by **United States**-backed rebels invading from Honduras, an act fiercely criticized by Mexican intellectuals and newspaper columnists. Arbenz fled to **Mexico City** where he was granted asylum.

ARBITRATION TRIBUNAL. *See* CENTRO DE ARBITRAJE DE MÉXICO; FEDERAL CONCILIATION AND ARBITRATION BOARD.

ARCHAEOLOGY. The general consensus that man arrived in the New World c.9,500 BC via an ice-covered Bering Sea made it difficult to gain acceptance that logoglyphs in São Paulo state, Brazil, suggested human presence there c.30,000 BC. In September 2003, however, researchers from England's Liverpool John Moores and Bournemouth Universities discovered footprints near **Puebla** in Central Mexico which scholars at Oxford University confirmed on July 4, 2005, as dating from 38,000 BC.

Civilization began in Central Mexico around 1400 BC, and although some sites, like the great pyramid at **Cholula**, were hidden by a failure to grasp their nature, most remained open to the sky and the researcher. Interest in **Mayan archaeology**, however, largely hidden in the rain forest, was only pioneered in the mid-18th century, by King **Charles III**.

Eminent archaeologists of Mexican and Meso-American cultures have included Alfonso **Caso**, Frederick **Catherwood**, Manuel **Orozco y Berra**, and John Lloyd **Stephens**. *See also* BONAMPAK; CHAMPUTEPEC; CHOLULA; COLIMA; CUICUILCO, MILTA; MONTE ALBAN; QUEMADO; TEOTIHUACAN; TULA; VENTA, LA. [L. H.]

ARCHBISHOPS OF MEXICO.

Juan de **Zumárraga**, February 12, 1546–June 3, 1548;

Alfonso de **Montufar**, October 5, 1551–March 7, 1572;

Pedro de **Moya y Contreras**, June 17, 1573–December 7, 1591;

Alonso **Fernández de Bonilla**, May 22, 1592–1600;

García de Santa María Mendoza y Zúñiga, December 6, 1600–October 5, 1606;

Francisco de **García Guerra**, October 29, 1607–February 22, 1612;

Juan **Pérez de la Serna**, January 18, 1613–July 19, 1627;

Francisco de Manso Zúñiga y Sola, August 9, 1627–July 20, 1634;

Francisco Verdugo Cabrera, September 9, 1636–1639?;

Feliciano Vega Padilla, March 22, 1639–December, 1640;

Juan de Mañozca y Zamora, June 14, 1643–December 12, 1650;

Marcelo López de Ancona, April 29, 1652–November 10, 1654;

Mateo de Sagade Bugueiro (a.k.a. Mateo Lazo de Bugueiro), September 19, 1655–January 28, 1664;

Juan Alonso de Cuevas y Davalos, April 24, 1664–September 2, 1665;

Marcos Ramírez de Prado y Ovando, December 15, 1666–May 14, 1667;

Payo **Enríquez Afán de Rivera Manrique**, September 17, 1668–1681;

Francisco de Aguiar y Seijas y Ulloa, June 30, 1681–August 14, 1698;

Juan de **Ortega Cano Montáñez y Patiño**, 1699–December 16, 1708;

Juan Pérez de Lanciego Eguiluz y Mirafuente, March 21, 1714–1728;

Manuel José de Hendaya y Haro, January 25, 1728–October 5, 1729;

Juan Antonio de Vizarrón y Eguiarreta, July 23, 1730–January 25, 1747;

Manuel José Rubio y Salinas, January 29, 1748–July 3, 1765;

Francisco Antonio de Lorenzama y Butrón, April 14, 1766–January 27, 1771;

Ildefonso **Núñez de Haro y Peralta**, March 30, 1772–May 26, 1800;

Francisco Javier de **Lizana y Beaumont**, May 24, 1802–January 1, 1815;

Pedro José de Fonte y Hernández Miravete, September 4, 1815–November 15, 1837;

Manuel Posada y Garduño, December 23, 1839–April 30, 1846;

José Lázaro de la Garza y Ballesteros, September 20, 1850–March 11, 1862;

Pelagio Antonio de Labastida y Dávalos, March 18, 1863–February 4, 1891;

Próspero María Alarcón y Sánchez de la Barquera, December 17, 1891–March 30, 1908;

José Moya y del Río, November 27, 1908–April 22, 1928;

Pascual Díaz y Barreto, June 25, 1928–May 19, 1936;

Luis María Martínez y Rodríguez, February 20, 1937–June 28, 1956;

Miguel Dano Miranda y Gómez, June 28, 1956–July 19, 1977;

Ernesto Corripio y Ahumada, July 19, 1977–September 29, 1994;

Norberto Rivera Carrera, June 13, 1995– [L. H.]

See also EX-ARZOBISPADO.

ARCHITECTURE. Ever since pre-Hispanic times, architecture has been the dominant form of artistic expression in Mexico. Significant practitioners have included Luis **Barragán Morfín**, Adamo **Boari**, José Bento de **Churriguera**, Carlos **Lazo Barreiro**, Pedro **Ramírez Vásquez**, Manuel **Tolsa**, and Francisco **Tres-Guerras**.

AREA. Despite the evacuation of **Nootka** under British pressure in 1795, Mexico inherited at **independence** Spanish claims to virtually the entire western half of North America. The loss, however, of **Texas** in 1836, the **United States** seizure of **Alta California**, **New Mexico**, **Arizona**, and lands to the north in 1848, and the **Gadsden Purchase** of 1854 combined to reduce the territory under the republic's effective control to barely a fourth of that of the United States. Continental Mexico now has a land area of 1,953,128 km^2 (750,000 square miles), and 49,510 km^2 (19,100 sq. miles) of inland water. Mexico's **islands** have a total area of 5,379 km^2 (2,000 sq. miles). This is still enough to make Mexico the second largest of the world's Spanish-speaking countries, surpassed only by the less populous **Argentina**'s 2,800,00 km^2. *See also* CONTINENTAL SHELF; EXTENT; FAR NORTH; GEOGRAPHY; MARITIME SOVEREIGNTY.

ARELLANO, ALONSO DE. Captain in Miguel **López de Legazpi**'s expedition to the **Philippines** discovered in 1564 the regular westerlies in the Pacific in latitudes 40–44°N and led to the establishment of the regular annual **Manila galleon**.

ARELLANO TAPIA, ALICIA (1932–). Born in **Magdalena de Kino, Sonora**, this politician qualified in both dentistry and **law** and married Miguel Pavlovich, a physician and surgeon. A local leader of the **Partido Revolucionario Institucional**, she served as a congresswoman in 1963–1964, then became Mexico's first woman senator from 1964–1970, and in 1973–1976 was mayor of Magdalena. In 1979 she was elected mayor of the state capital, **Hermosillo**, for the 1979–1982 term.

ARGENTINA, RELATIONS WITH. During the Platine war for independence, Argentine privateers were active in the Caribbean against Spanish shipping, leading to Central Americans adopting the horizontally striped blue-white-blue Argentine flag as their own. In 1914 Argentina was one of the "ABC" powers negotiating with the **United**

States over the Mexican situation. It is also to Argentina that Mexico owes the **Estrada** doctrine, while the United States' failure to back up Jean Kirkpatrick's support of Argentina during the 1982 Falkland War demonstrated to all Latin American countries the limitations of the **Inter-American Treaty of Mutual Assistance**.

From 1976, Argentina's **"Dirty War"** led to thousands, mostly artists and intellectuals, seeking political asylum in Mexico. Their influence has been credited for increased Mexican receptivity to Argentine culture and perhaps helps account for the US$ 500,000,000-worth of Argentine cultural imports each year into Mexico, US$ 200,000,000 of them being books.

In 2006 the Argentine team knocked Mexico out of the **World Soccer Cup**. [L. H.]

ARIJIS, HOMERO (1940–). Born in Cutempec, **Michoacán**, this poet studied journalism at the Septién Insitute in **Mexico City**. A writer for various magazines, he became a leading poet after publishing his *La Musa rosa* (1958). His many other works include *La Difícil ceremonia* and *Antes del reino* (both 1963).

ARISTA, MARIANO (1802–1855). Born in **San Luis Potosí**, Arista had a long **army** career before serving as interim president from 1847–1848, and war minister from 1848–1851. He was then proclaimed president by **Congress** from 1851–1853, the first Mexican president to receive a peaceful transfer of power from his predecessor. His administration was admired for its attempt to govern honestly but was frustrated by frequent military uprisings, which led eventually to his resignation and exile in Seville. He died aboard ship when traveling to France. In 1856 he was declared a national hero.

ARIZONA. Until 1848, Arizona was part of Old Mexico's **Far North**. It was made a **United States** territory separate from **New Mexico** in 1863 and a separate U.S. state in 1912.

ARIZONA-SONORA COMMISSION. Binational entity that promotes cultural exchange and trade between the U.S. state of Arizona and its neighbor across the **United States border**, the Mexican state of **Sonora**, in half-yearly meetings since 1959 with its twin, the

Comisión Sonorense-Arizonense. These commissions also advise their respective state governors on problems arising in their common portion of the **United States border** with Mexico.

ARMADA (i.e., marina armada). Fighting **navy**, as opposed to the merchant marine. [L. H.]

ARMADA DE BARLOVENTO. See WINDWARD FLEET.

ARMED FORCES. See AIR FORCE; ARMY; COLEGIO DE DEENSA NACIONAL; ESCUELA SUPERIOR DE GUERRA; NAVY.

ARMENDÁRIZ, PEDRO (1912–1964). One of Mexico's most honored **cinema** actors, he starred in 160 Mexican and thirty foreign films (American, Spanish, and French). He studied aeronautical engineering in California before turning to acting in 1935. His first film, *María Elena*, with Carmen Guerrero, made him a star. In 1937 *Jalisco nunca pierde* established his best remembered role, that of a **charro** (Mexican cowboy), reinforced in 1940 with the self-evidently entitled *El Charro negro*. The image lasted for the rest of his career, despite several non-cowboy roles. In 1941 he realized his personal ambition of starring with the comedian **Cantinflas**, in *Ni sangre ni arena*. In 1942 he had a huge box-office hit, co-starring with Mexico's leading singing actor, Jorge **Negrete** in *Tierra de pasiones*. In that first year of **World War II** he also encouraged patriotism in *Soy puro mexicano* (*I am a real Mexican*). As Mexico's leading box office attraction he could chose his own co-stars, such as Dolores del **Rio** (herself internationally known in the 1930s for her Hollywood films) and María **Félix** (for years the Mexican industry's reigning beauty). In 1946 he costarred with María in ***Enamorada***. His most lauded film, in both Mexico and the **United States**, was *La Perla*, the story of a humble fisherman who finds a pearl and is victimized by a dishonest middleman when he tries to sell it in a big city. On its release with an English soundtrack as *The Pearl*, Orson Wells called it an example of superb acting, showing what the Mexican motion picture industry could produce.

Tall, handsome, with black wavy hair, blue eyes, and a fair complexion, Armendáriz could convincingly play Mexican generals,

French or American executives, and even, in his last film, a Turkish spy (his role in *From Russia with Love*, starring Sean Connery as James Bond). Soon afterward he entered a **Los Angeles** hospital, terminally ill with cancer, and, to avoid longtime suffering, shot himself in the heart with a pistol he had sneaked in with him. The event was front-page news in every major daily newspaper in Latin America and Spain.

ARMY. Spain relied on locally recruited militias for the terrestrial defense of its overseas territories. These provided the officer material for the army of newly independent Mexico, which favored a conservative centralism until its poor performance in the **United States-Mexican War** encouraged a rival popular army to fight and defeat it in the War of the **Reforms.** The new liberal army became eventually the mainstay of the **Porfirato** which was in turn overthrown by what began as a number of regionally-based irregular forces led largely by brilliant, but professionally unqualified, tacticians such as Pancho **Villa** and Emílio **Zapata.** In the aftermath of the **Revolution of 1910** and the internecine quarrels among the rebel generals, it was Plutarco Elías **Calles** who effectively instituted a new army, subordinate to the *sector militar* of what was to become the **Partido Revolucionario Institucional**, and a series of civilian presidents kept the generals in check. This ended the threat of military coups whilst making the army available as the government's last resource against civil unrest, but giving Mexico one of the most ill paid and worst equipped armies in the hemisphere. Modernization and expansion began in the 1970s, with better training and equipment. From the 1980s the army became a principal arm in the war against **narcotics** trafficking. In strength and resources, Mexico's 175,000 strong force (a doubling in 20 years) is currently the fourth largest in the Americas, inferior in numbers only to the armies of the **United States, Cuba,** and **Brazil.** *See also* DEFENSE MINISTRY; HEROICA ESCUELA MILITAR; ESCUELA SUPERIOR DE GUERRA; ZACATECAS MARCH. [L. H.]

ARMY OF THE NORTH. *See* DIVISIÓN DEL NORTE.

ARMY OF THE SOUTH. *See* DIVISIÓN DEL SUR.

ARREOLA, JUAN JOSÉ (1918?–2001). Novelist—*Confabulario* (1952), *La feria* (1963), *Palindroma* (1071), *Inventario* (1977)—and translator.

ARRIAGA. Coastal **municipio** of **Chiapas** with 36,224 inhabitants in 1998 on 653 km², lying between 16°05' and 16°21'N, and between 93°43' and 94°06'W.

ARRIAGA, PONCIANO (1811–1865). Liberal politician who held various posts in his native **San Luis Potosí** and in the federal government. He took part in General Esteban **Moctezuma**'s 1832 campaign against President Anastacio **Bustamante**, served as justice minister in 1852, and was exiled by López de **Santa Anna** to New Orleans where he met Benito Pablo **Juárez**. He has frequently been called the Father of the **Constitution of 1857** because of the extensive work he devoted to it. A strong supporter of Juárez, he died before he could see the Republic's triumph over the Emperor **Maximilian**.

ARRIAGA RIVERA, AGUSTÍN (1925–). Born in **Michoacán**, this administrator graduated in economics from **UNAM** and became professor of economics successively at the **Universidad Michoacana de San Nicolás de Hidalgo**, the University of **Tamaulipas**, and UNAM. As director general of the **Banco Nacional Cinemtaográfica** in 1959–1962 he began the process of increasing the government's role in the **cinema** industry, culminating in Luis **Echeverría**'s expropriation of all film studios and production entities in 1975.

ARROYO MARROQUÍN, ROMARICO DANIEL (1942–). A civil engineering graduate from **UNAM**, with an MSc from Stanford University, this politician was appointed Minister of **Agriculture** and Rural Development by President Ernesto **Zedillo** in January 1998.

ART. Despite the missionaries' zeal to rid **New Spain** of all existing "pagan" artifacts, much pre-Hispanic art remains, chiefly **architecture** but also **sculpture** and **codices**. The essentially baroque styles introduced with the **conquest of Mexico** endured practically until **independence**. The 19th century was dominated by the fashions of contemporary Europe. A genuinely Mexican art comes in with the

Revolution of 1910, particularly evidenced by the **muralists** of the 1930s and 1940s and by the work of a number of outstanding **women** (Leonora Carrington, Olga Costa, Lola Cueto, María Izquierdo, Frida **Kahlo**, Alice Rahon, and Rosa Rolanda). *See also* CONTRABAND; GELMAN COLLECTION; PAINTING. [L. H.]

ART EDUCATION. *See* ACADEMIA DE SAN CARLOS; ESCUELA NACIONAL DE ARTES PLÁSTICAS DE MEXICO; ESMERALDA, LA.

ARTEAGA Y BAZÁN, IGNACIO FERNANDO DE (1731–1783). Spanish naval officer from Huelva, born February 17, the leader of an expedition which left **San Blás** in February 1779 and reached what is now Port Etches on **Hinchinbrook Island**, at 61°N, the northernmost point reached by explorers from Mexico.

ASAIN, RODOLFO (1907–1963). Born in Tula, **Hidalgo**, graduated in **law** from **UNAM**, became a federal district judge. As a justice of the **Supreme Court** from 1936–1940, he wrote in 1938 the opinion under which the government expropriated the **petroleum** industry.

ASAMBLEA POPULAR DE LOS PUEBLOS DE OAXACA (APPO). The "Popular Assembly of the Peoples of Oaxaca," is the umbrella organization of 350 social NGOs in **Oaxaca state**, formed in June 2006 when state **police** attacked a demonstration by striking school teachers. This turned a strike over pay into a demand for the resignation of governor Ulises **Ruiz**. APPO erected barricades and seized radio stations. A local **police** attempt in October to remove a street barrier erupted into a firefight in which American Bradley Ronald **Will** was killed. The federal government held off until October 28, the day after the strike was settled, when 4,500 troops of the **Policia Federal Preventativa** were suddenly airlifted into **Oacaca city** airport. On November 12, Andrés Manuel **López Obrador** announced that the **Partido de la Revolución Democrática** would give APPO its active support, but the new president, Felipe **Calderón Hinojosa**, ordered a clampdown on December 16 that put 150 APPO leaders in a high security prison in **Nayarit**, although 91 were brought back later in the month to prisons in Oaxaca.

The original name, *Asamblea Popular del Pueblo de Oaxaca*, was criticized for the redundancy of *popular* and *del pueblo* ("of the people"), so the change was made to avoid this while preserving the acronym: the ambiguous word *pueblos*, now plural, has been understood as both ethnic ("all the races of Oaxaca") and as emphasizing the rural strength of the association ("all the villages"), or yet to mean a union of localities ("all the population centers"). A "movement," APPO repudiates the idea of its being a political party. [L. H.]

ASOCIACIÓN LATINOAMERICANA DE INTEGRACIÓN (ALADI). Free-trade association of **Argentina**, **Brasil**, Bolivia, **Chile**, **Colombia**, Ecuador, Mexico, Paraguay, **Peru**, Uruguay, and **Venezuela**, headquartered in Montevideo, aimed at reducing tariff barriers and taxes so as to promote member countries' trade and production.

ASOCIACIÓN LATINOAMERICANA DE LIBRE COMERCIO (ALALC). *See* LATIN AMERICAN FREE TRADE ASSOCIATION.

ASOCIACIÓN MEXICANA DE INSTITUCIONES DE SEGUROS (AMIS). Mexican Association of Insurance Institutions, created in 1946, unites all private insurance companies as a lobbying group for negotiations with government, **trade unions**, and the public, and as the organized voice of the insurance industry.

ASOCIACIÓN NACIONAL DE IMPORTADORES Y EXPORTA-DORES DE LA REPÚBLICA MEXICANA (ANIERM). The National Association of Importers and Exporters of Mexico, created in 1940 to promote foreign trade.

ASPE ARMELLA, PEDRO CARLOS (1950–). Born in **Mexico City**, July 7, 1973, this economist became director of economics research at the **Instituto Tecnológico Autónomo de México (ITAM)**, which in 1974 granted him an economics degree with a thesis on Mexican migration and the probability of employment, which was widely quoted in Mexico and the **United States**. In 1978 he received a PhD from M.I.T. with a dissertation on economic transmission mechanisms, and in 1977–1978 was visiting professor of macroeconomics at M.I.T.

In 1978–1982 he was dean of the economics curriculum at ITAM. Having joined the **Partido Revolucionario Institucional** in 1980, he became an advisor in economics to Carlos **Salinas de Gortari**, whom he had met when both were at M.I.T. In 1987–1988 he was minister of programming and budgeting in the cabinet of Miguel De La **Madrid**, and in 1988 finance minister. When Salinas became president, he was very receptive to Aspe's theories favoring the **privatization** of industries that had stagnated under government control and Aspe became the most prominent economist in the land.

ASSASSINATION. *See* HOMICIDE.

ASSEMBLY OF NOTABLES. *See* JUNTA DE NOTABLES.

ASTRONOMY. *See* BÁRCENA, MARIANO; CHAPPE D'AUTE-ROCHE; DIABLO, PINACHO DEL; DÍAZ COVARRUBIAS, FRANCISCO; LEÓN Y GAMA, ANTONIO; OBSERVATORIO NACIONAL ASTRONÓMICO; PALENQUE; VELÁSQUEZ CÁRDENAS Y LEÓN, JOAQUÍN.

ATENEO DE LA JUVENTUD ("Atheneum of youth"). Society concerned with revitalizing the intellectual currents of Mexico, founded in 1909 by Alfonso **Reyes** and other writers.

ATOYAC. A locality on the namesake river, this title was given to the uppermost reaches of the River **Balsas**.

ATTORNEY GENERAL. The Mexican equivalent is **procurador general** at the federal level and **procurador de justicia** at the state level.

AUDIENCIA. The Spanish judges (*oidores*) of the high court with administrative powers heard criminal and civil appeals. Created in medieval Castile as an organ of a centralizing royal government, it acted as a check on royal officials, even the **viceroy**, but came in time to express the views of the local power structure. This was especially significant in that, in the absence or incapacity of a governor or viceroy (e.g., through sudden death), it could, as an *audiencia gob-*

ernadora, exercise an interim executive power. There was originally one *audiencia* for all the **Indies**, that of Santo Domingo, but **Mexico City** was granted the second (and soon, the most important) New World one, with a *regente* and 10 judges, in 1529. Others within the viceroyalty were established at **Guatemala City** in 1542 for all Central America, and at **Guadalajara** in 1549 for **Nueva Galicia** (although remaining subordinate to that at Mexico City until 1572).

The Mexican Audiencia had by the early 1800s come to be **Peninsular** dominated and acted to thwart moves toward **independence** such as the **Junta de México**. *See also* COURTS. [L. H.]

AUDITORIA SUPERIOR DE LA FEDERACIÓN. Agency approved by Congress in December 2000 to replace the **Contadoría Mayor de Hacienda**.

AUGUSTINIANS. Active in propagating the Catholic faith in Mexico, the order also concentrated on building hospitals and succeeded in accumulating great wealth in colonial Mexico.

AUSTIN, STEPHEN FULLER (1793–1836). Texan leader summarily imprisoned by López de **Santa Anna** for journeying to **Mexico City** to plead for more government aid.

AUSTRIAN SUCCESSION, WAR OF. The Eurocentric name for the worldwide conflict that began in the Caribbean as the "War of Jenkins' Ear" in 1739. It is known in North America as "King George's War," was fought in Britain as the "Jacobite Rebellion," and ended with the 1748 Treaty of Aix-la-Chapelle (i.e., Aachen). It involved Mexican **Viceroy** Juan Antonio de **Vizarrón y Eguiarreta** in an expedition to lift the British siege of Cartagena de las Indias (in present-day **Colombia**). [L. H.]

AUSTRIANS. *See* MAXIMILIAN.

AUTOMEX. Mexican maker of Dodge and Chrysler trucks and **automobiles** founded in the 1960s by Octaviano **Campos Sales** and the **Azcárraga** family, with Chrysler as the majority stockholder.

AUTOMOBILES. Automobile manufacturing began in Mexico in 1925 when Ford opened an assembly plant. General Motors followed in 1936 and Chrysler in 1938. In 1952 the government's **Diesel Nacional (DINA)** truck manufacturing corporation began making passenger cars, at first in partnership with Fiat, but later with Renault. In 1964 Toyota and **Volkswagen** were authorized to manufacture in Mexico. In the 1960s and 1970s, Octaviano **Campos Sales** developed the **Automex** Corporation. By 1980 the Mexican production reached 400,000 vehicles a year, and by 2000, over 600,000. The number of vehicles on Mexican **highways** reached 2 million in 1980 and 6 million in 2000.

Although Minister Francisco **Vizcaíno Murray** sought to control automobile emissions in the 1970s, U.S. pollution legislation since then has limited Mexican vehicle **exports**. Not until 1995 did the catalytic converters on Fords made in **Hermosillo** meet U.S. standards.

The need for adequate driver training has caused concern, hence a campaign led by Rafael **Cal y Mayor**.

AVANTE. Organ of the **Partido Popular Socialista** from 1962–1972, when it was replaced by the magazine *Nueva democracia*.

AVIATION, COMMERCIAL. *See* AIR TRANSPORT.

AVIATION PIONEERS. Albert **Braniff**, María Marcos **Cedillo**, and Ralph **O'Neil**.

ÁVILA CAMACHO, MANUEL (1897–1955). "The Gentleman President" of Mexico, 1940–1946, born on April 24 in Teziutlán, **Puebla State**. He studied accounting in **Puebla** and joined the **army** as a lieutenant in 1915, becoming a major in 1918 and a general in 1926. A childhood friend of Vicente **Lombardo Toledano**, in 1919 he became assistant executive officer and close friend of Lázaro **Cardenas**, who made him paymaster of the new Revolutionary **Army** in 1920, and his justice minister during his 1934–1940 presidency. A 1939 interview by *Excelsior* in which he declared that both German and Soviet agents in Mexico had to be watched for reasons of both domestic and external security helped Cárdenas decide to make him his successor, the last of the Revolutionary generals to become Mexico's chief executive. In his inaugural address, following the **election of 1940**, he attempted to end the **Church**-state controversy by proclaiming "Soy creyente" (I am a believer). He took Mexico into **World War II**, began rounding up German and Japanese espionage agents and aided the **United States** war effort with the **Bracero Treaty** and the direct involvement of the Mexican **Air Force**. In 1943 he instituted Mexico's **social security** system, creating the **Instituto Mexicano del Seguro Social**, and his presidency saw 12 million acres of land redistributed. But he reduced the constitutional demand for "socialist education" by appointing a conservative as education minister and changing Article III's requirement in the **Constitution of 1917** regarding **education** from "socialist" to "scientific." He also supported the election of the less radical Fidel **Velásquez Sánchez** to succeed Vicente **Lombardo Toledano** as head of the **Confederación de Trabajadoes de México**.

ÁVILA CAMACHO, MAXIMINO (?–1945). He was "violent, ruthless, arrogant," so unlike his brother, President Manuel **Ávila Camacho**, who made him minister of communications. In 1937–1941 "El Carnicero" (the butcher) had governed **Puebla**, when he made Gustavo **Díaz Ordaz** his protégé. He became wealthy, presumably through **corruption**.

ÁVILA-CORTÉS CONSPIRACY. Rebellion in **New Spain** plotted by the **González de Ávila** brothers and Martín **Cortés y Zúñiga**.

AXAYÁCATL ("visage of water"). Aztec "emperor" (tlatoani), 1470–1481, son of **Montezuma I**, noted for his ferocious repression of revolts by tributary towns. He was succeeded in turn by his two brothers, **Tizoc** and **Ahuitzotl**, and then by his son, **Montezuma II**.

AYALA, PLAN OF. Agrarian reform plan sponsored by Emiliano **Zapata**, that called for the immediate distribution of land to peasants without any compensation to the owners.

AYUNTAMIENTO. Governing body of a **municipio**.

AYUTLA. Municipio in **Jalisco** with 13,480 inhabitants in 1995 on 885 km². The **cabecera**, at 20°09'N, 104°16'W, had 6,625 inhabitants in 1990.

AYUTLA DE LOS LIBRES. City of **Guerrero** at 16°58'N, 99°04'W had 6,214 inhabitants in 1990, **cabecera** of the **municipio** of Ayutla with a 1995 population of 50,500 on 735.4 km².

AYUTLA, PLAN OF. Liberal proclamation of March 1854, issued in **Ayutla de los Libres**, called for a constitutional convention. It led to the downfall of José Antonio **López de Santa Anna** in 1855.

AZANZA, MIGUEL JOSÉ DE (1746–1826). Viceroy of **New Spain** from 1798–1800, a Spaniard, visited the **Indies** as a 17-year-old, accompanying his uncle, Don José Martín de Alegría. After a brief army career, he became a diplomat, with postings in St. Petersburg and Berlin. In 1793 he became war minister before being made viceroy. As such he fortified the port of **San Blas** but fell into the hands of rebels led by Pedro de la **Portilla**. Soon after the rebels defeat Azanza was recalled. He subsequently held high office in Spain, but his support of the puppet regime of Joseph **Bonaparte** led to a death sentence *in absentia* and impoverished exile in Bordeaux, France, where he died.

AZCAPOTZALCO. City in the cultural orbit of **Teotihuacán** to which many refugees fled after the later city was destroyed c.650. In the thirteenth century it became the capital of the **Tepanec Indians** until its destruction by the **Aztecs** and **Chichimec Indians** in 1428. The city is now a **delegación** of the **Federal District**, with 601,524 inhabitants in 1998. It has metal and petrochemical industries.

AZCÁRRAGA JEAN, EMILIO (1968–). Media mogul, the son of Emilio **Azcárraga Milmo**, whom he represented on the board of Grupo Televicentro and its **Televisa** network, and control of which (and board chairmanship) he inherited on his father's death. Wall Street experts proclaimed him a profound media manager with a vision beyond his years.

AZCÁRRAGA MILMO, EMILIO (1930–1997). Media mogul born on September 6 in **Mexico City**, the son of Emilio **Azcárraga Vidaurrota** whose fortune he inherited. *Forbes* magazine reported his gross worth as $2,000,000,000, making him Mexico's wealthiest citizen, if not perhaps its wealthiest resident. He owned Grupo **Televisa, S.A.**, and was a major stockholder in the Automex corporation, maker of **automobiles** and trucks.

AZCÁRRAGA VIDAURROTA, EMILIO (1895–1972). **Radio** and **television** entrepreneur, owner of the Grupo **Televisa**, S.A., and father of Emilio **Azcárraga Milmo**. He had begun his broadcasting empire with station XEW, which first went on the air on September 18, 1930.

AZNAR ZETINA, [ADMIRAL] ANTONIO J. (1904–19??). Born June 12, a graduate of the **Escuela Naval Militar** (Naval College) in **Veracruz**, he rose to be commander of the **Coast Guard**, deputy minister of the **navy** from 1965–1970, and chief of staff of the navy from 1958–1961, modernizing the Naval College's curriculum, adapting it to the technology of seaborne missiles.

AZTEC ("from Aztlán"). Empire of the **Nahuatl**-speaking civilization centered on **Tenochtitlán**, dominated northern and central **Mexico** immediately before the Spanish **conquest of Mexico**. Under their king (**tlatoani**) **Acamapitchli** and his successors, they subjugated most other Indian nations in the previous two centuries (from 1325), achieving by 1519 dominion over nearly 500 small states with 6 million inhabitants spread over 210,000 km^2. As exemplified by their huge temples, they developed an elaborate **architecture** to glorify their "emperor" and their religion of sun worship and human sacrifice. They developed pictograph writing and a literature of poems, philosophy, and mythology. A key to their success was their highly productive, irrigated **agriculture**, which they extended by energetic reclamation of swamps. They have also been known as **Tenochca**, **Mexica**, and **Nahuas**.

The Aztec inheritance has been a powerful element in Mexican nationalism, both in distinguishing the country from its sister

Spanish-speaking republics and as evidence that its nationhood predated the Spanish conquest of Mexico.

AZTEC "EMPERORS" (*tlatoanis*).
Acamapichtli (1375–1395);
Huitzilihuitl (1396–1417);
Chimalpopoca (1418–1426);
Itzcóatl (1427–1440);
Montezuma I (1441–1469);
Axayácatl (1470–1481);
Tizoc (1481–1486);
Ahuitzotl (1486–1502);
Montezuma II (1502–1520);
Cuitláhuac (June–December, 1520);
Cuauhtémoc (1520–1525).

AZTECA T.V. Privatized for US$ 641 million in 1993, when board chairman Ricardo **Salinas Pliego** brought in consultants from America's NBC to strengthen the network's prime time news, long inferior to that of rival **Televisa**. By 1998, Azteca was able to challenge some of the pro-establishment coverage of the dominant **Televisa**. In April 2005 it was at odds with the government over its broadcasting of an attack on Citigroup's 2001 acquisition of Grupo Financiera **Banamex**.

AZTLÁN ("Place of herons"). Lake island (perhaps mythical), far to the northwest of central Mexico, where the **Aztecs** believed their forebears lived as lake fisherfolk until 1111, when their god **Huitzilopochtli** commanded them to migrate south with the promise that they would conquer the world.

AZUELA, ARTURO (1938–). Novelist, whose first work was *El Tamaño del infierno* (1973), won the *Premio Nacional de Novela* in 1980 with his *Manifestación de silencio*.

AZUELA GONZÁLEZ, MARIANO (1873–1952). Novelist from Lagos de Moreno, **Jalisco**, and a doctor by training, his first novel was *María Luisa* of 1907. After the death of **Madero** he joined the army of Pancho **Villa** as a surgeon but then resumed his fiction writing and won worldwide fame with *Los de Abajo* (1915), probably the most famous novel of the **Revolution of 1910**. This first appeared as a serial in *El Paso del Norte* newspaper and has been translated into English five times, notably by E. Munguía as *The Underdogs* (New York: New American Library, 1963) and by Gustavo Pellón in 2006. His other works include *Mala yerba*, translated as *Marcela*.

AZUELA RIVERA, MARIANO (1904–1993). Jurist son of the novelist Mariano **Azuela**, born March 15 in Lagos de Moreno, **Jalisco**. A graduate of **UNAM**, he became professor of **law** at the University of **San Luis Potosí**, and in 1930–1958 at UNAM. He served as senator from Jalisco from 1958–1960, justice of the **Supreme Court** from 1951–1957 and 1960–1972. His legal commentaries have become very important in Mexican legal literature, particularly on the **amparo** and the appellate system.

– B –

B. The sound represented by this letter has been confused in Spain with that of **v** ever since Roman times, whence the frequence alternation in spelling in such words as *Córdoba/Córdova, Carbajal/Carvajal*. It is usual in dictation, etc., to specify it as *b de burro*.

BADILLO GARCÍA, ROMÁN (1895–1963). Lawyer, born February 24, a graduate of **UNAM**, state supreme court justice in **Veracruz** from 1926–1927, leader of the 1934 **Partido Antirreleccionista** (Anti-Reelectionist Party) convention, and a major adviser to President Manuel **Ávila Camacho**, 1940–1946.

BAEZA, FLORENCIO. One of the founders of the **Partido de Acción Nacional (PAN)**.

BAEZA, GUILLERMO (1937–). Politician, born June 20 in **Guadalajara**, a **law** graduate from the **Universidad de Guadalajara**, a **Partido de Acción Nacional** leader in **Jalisco** since 1960, serving as its secretary general in the state, then state chairman, and finally as federal deputy from 1970–1973 and 1976–1979.

BAEZA MELÉNDEZ, FERNANDO (1942–). Lawyer-politician born January 21 in Ciudad Delicias, **Chihuahua**, the son of Florencio **Baeza**, graduated from the *Escuela de Derecho* of **UNAM**, and became active in the **Partido Revolucionario Institucional**, thereby becoming governor of his home state from 1986–1991.

BAJA CALIFORNIA. "Lower California," was so named to distinguish it from "Upper California" (**Alta California**, since 1848 the U.S. state of **California**). Almost all of Baja California is a peninsula separated from the rest of Mexico by the Bay of California. In 1533, some twenty-two Spanish mutineers landed near La **Paz**, and the only two to survive an attack by local **Indians** reported discovering **pearls** there, but when Hernán de Carijalba led an expedition to investigate, he found only a waterless wasteland which the Spanish left to pirates. **Jesuits** established a mission at the future territorial capital La **Paz** in 1720, but this was abandoned in 1750, and only resettled in 1811.

The "Baja's" inhabitants ("*Canchanillas*") numbered 12,000 in 1857, 21,000 in 1869, and 42,000 in 1895. In April 1850 it was divided into the two *partidos* of **Baja California del Norte** and **Baja California del Sur**. These became *distritos* in 1887, *territorios* in December 1930, and states in 1952, although the former is now officially just "Baja California." In 1973, Mexican highway 1 was completed from **Tijuana** to Cabo **San Lucas**. *See also* WALKER, WILLIAM.

BAJA CALIFORNIA DEL NORTE. A territory, and since 1953, a state (officially just "Baja California"—postal abbreviation B.C.), of 70,113 km^2, occupying the northern half of the peninsula of Lower California down to the 28th parallel, 965 km south of the **United States border**. Successive **censuses** have registered populations of 8,000 (1900); 10,000 (1910); 24,000 (1921); 48,000 (1930—when it overtook that of **Baja California del Sur**); 79,000 (1940); 227,000 (1950); 520,000 (1960); 870,000 (1970); 1,178,000 (1980); 1,660,000 (1990); 2,487,367 (2000). This total surpassed 3 million in 2003 and should reach 3.7 million in 2007. The state currently enjoys the largest per capita income in Mexico. The capital is **Mexicali**, and there are five other municipios of which **Tijuana** is the most populous. The island of **Guadalupe** lies within the state's jurisdiction.

BAJA CALIFORNIA DEL SUR (B.C.S.). A territory, and since October 1974 a state, of 73,677 km², occupying the southern half of the peninsula of Lower California, below the 28th parallel, with a population at successive **censuses** of 40,000 (1900); 42,000 (1910); 39,000 (1921); 47,000 (1930); 51,000 (1940); 61,000 (1950); 82,000 (1960); 128,000 (1970); 215,000 (1980); and 317,764 (1990). It was c.382,000 in 1995; 424,041 at the 2000 census; and 490,000 in 2006 (still the least populous Mexican state). The capital is La **Paz**. Industries include **salt production** along the coast.

BAJÍO, El ("alluvial lowland"). The plain of **Guanajuato State** and part of **Michoacán** is drained by the **Lerma** River, a major breadbasket of Mexico, its largest producer of potatoes and sweet potatoes, and also a major producer of **corn**, peanuts, alfalfa, garlic, onions, strawberrites, and **livestock**. [L. H.]

BALBOA, PRAXEDES (1900?–1980). Governor of his native **Tamaulipas** from 1963–1969, born in **Ciudad Victoria**, a UNAM law graduate (1925), a leader in the **Partido Revolucionario Institucional** and key formulator of **labor** and **agrarian reform** laws, and a federal deputy from 1930–1932 and 1935–1937.

BALBUENA, BERNARDO DE (1568–1627). Spanish-born priest who eventually became bishop of Puerto Rico, he is recognized as Mexico's first poet, having migrated with his parents to **Nueva Galicia** at the age of three years and studied at the **University of Mexico** from 1585–1590. His most famous work, *La grandeza mexicana*, describes most eloquently **Mexico City**, for him the most beautiful city of the Americas.

BALDERAS, LUCAS (1797–1847). Army officer, famed for his savage defense of **Mexico City**, killed at the Battle of **Molino del Rey**. A principal street of downtown Mexico City is named in his honor.

BALSAS, RIVER. The longest river on Mexico's Pacific coast. Its 880 km course begins as the **Atoyac**, becomes the Mezquital after its confluence with the **Nayarit**, before taking the name Balsas preferred for its lower reaches. It drains a watershed of 113,200 km².

BAMBA. Folk music originating in **Veracruz State**, featuring a harp, violin, and small guitars.

BANCO DE AVÍO. Government bank founded in 1830 by Lucas **Alemán y Escalada** to make loans to Mexico's nascent **manufacturing industry**. It was effectively abolished in 1842 when López de **Santa Anna** cut off its funding, wanting the money for military purposes.

BANCO DE COMERCIO. Mexico's largest private bank, with branches throughout the Republic, and a widely used *Bancomer* credit card, owned by the multinational Banco Bilboa Vizcaya Argentina (BBVA).

BANCO DE MÉXICO. Mexico's central bank was established in 1925 through the efforts of Alberto **Pani**, to issue currency, operate the national mint, hold government accounts, and act as the reserve bank of last resource for the national banking system. It is the Mexican equivalent of the Bank of England or the United States Federal Reserve system.

BANCO FEDERAL DE FOMENTO ("Federal Development Bank"). *See* CABAL PENICHE, CARLOS.

BANCO NACIONAL CINEMATOGRÁFICA ("National Motion Picture Industry Bank"). Government bank for extending credit to and investing in the **cinema** industry, established in 1941. In the 1960s, and especially during the directorship of Rodolfo **Echeverría Álvarez**, it would implement government policy in denying or limiting credit to studios whose plots were considered unsympathetic, until Manolo **Fábregas** defied it by finding his own finance.

BANCO NACIONAL DE COMERCIO EXTERIOR ("National Bank of Foreign Trade"). Established in 1937 by Luis **Montes de Oca**, this government agency coordinates its activities with the **Nacional Financiera** and the foreign, trade, and industrial development **ministries**.

BANCO NACIONAL DE CRÉDITO AGRÍCOLA ("National Farming Credit Bank"). Established in 1936 to develop **agriculture, fishing, forestry**, and other rural activities, it was absorbed in 1977 by the **Banco Nacional de Crédito Rural**.

BANCO NACIONAL DE CRÉDITO EJIDAL. Established in 1935 to make loans to Native American communal farms (*See* EJIDO), it was absorbed in 1977 by the **Banco Nacional de Crédito Rural**.

BANCO NACIONAL DE CRÉDITO RURAL ("National Bank of Rural Credit"). This bank resulted from a 1977 merger of the **Banco Nacional de Crédito Agrícola** and the **Banco Nacional de Crédito Ejidal**.

BANCO NACIONAL DE DESARROLLO PESQUERO ("National Fisheries Development Bank"). Established June 18, 1979, to provide credit to the **fishing** industry, this bank absorbed the **Banco Nacional de Fomento Cooperativo**.

BANCO NACIONAL DE FOMENTO COOPERATIVO. Established in 1941 to develop **cooperatives**, in 1979 it became an agency within the new **Banco Nacional de Desarrollo Pesquero**.

BANCO NACIONAL DE MÉXICO (B.N.M. or BANAMEX). Despite the title, this is a privately owned nationwide bank and the largest such after the **Banco de Comercio**. It issues the Banamex credit card, and is now part of the Grupo Financiero Banamex. It built up its own art collection, *Acervo Artístico*, whose fate was made uncertain by the mid-2001 acquisition of the Bank by New York's Citibank. In 2005 TV **Azteca** broadcast attacks on the US$ 12.5 million tax-free transaction, and also on a US$ 70 billion transfer of bad loans to the government in the mid-1990s. It also claimed that the government was threatening it with prosecution for stock exchange fraud if it went ahead with the broadcasts.

BANCO NACIONAL DE OBRAS Y SERVICIOS PÚBLICOS. "Banobras" was a 1966 renaming of the Urban Mortgage Bank (*Banco Nacional Hipotecario Urbano*) of 1933, making loans to state and municipal governments for the construction, operation, and expansion of public works.

BANCO NACIONAL DEL EJÉRCITO Y LA ARMADA ("National Army and Navy Bank"). Established by the government in 1946 to grant house purchase mortgages to military personnel and to make loans to businesses operated by them.

BANDITRY. Like most countries that are largely rural and relatively poor, Mexico suffered from chronic banditry in much of the countryside (with highway robbery a constant threat to **postal services**) until this was largely repressed by the draconian methods of the **Porfiriato**—a contributing factor to the consensus among foreign observers that Mexico had been "pacified" and stabilized. Banditry was often connected, at least in the minds of the colonial authorities, with communities of **maroons**. *See also* ACORDADA; MAROONS; RURALES; SANTA HERMANDAD. [L. H.]

BANKERS' ASSOCIATION. *See* ASOCIACIÓN DE BANQUEROS MEXICANOS.

BANKS AND BANKING. Although Mexico had banks earlier in the 19th century than many other countries of the Hemisphere, it had no central bank until the **Banco de México** was established in 1925. Since then Mexican banking has been characterized by a large number of official and semi-official institutions, some of which are detailed in the preceding entries.

The so-called **peso** crisis of 1994–1995 led to an expensive government bailout of the banking system and ultimately, when the opposition **Partido de Acción Nacional** was able to mount an effective protest, to the **Fondo Bancario de Protección al Ahorro** controversy of December 1998 and consequent temporary discouragement of **foreign investment**.

MATT—**Mexicanos y Americanos Todos Trabajando**—now offers a new type of mini-loans to petty entrepreneurs in rural Mexico. [L. H.]

BAÑUELOS, JUAN (1932–). Poet, literary critic and essayist, born in **Tuxtla Gutiérrez, Chiapas**, a **UNAM** humanities graduate, and employed during much of his career as a book publisher's editor while writing for the *Revista Mexicana de Literatura* and other literary journals until he won national recognition with *Ocupación de la palabra* (1965), a book of poems and essays.

BÁRCENA, MANUEL DE LA (1769–1830). Spanish priest who helped secure Mexican **independence** and was a member of the **Regency** headed by Agustín **Iturbide**.

BÁRCENA, MARIANO (1848–1898). Scientist who studied engineering, botany, and the fine arts while working as a harness-maker. His greatest accomplishment was in astronomy and meteorology. In 1877 he inaugurated the Observatory of Astronomy and Meteorology, and in 1880 he was appointed director of what was now the **Observatorio Nacional Astronómico**.

BARRA, FRANCISCO LEÓN DE LA. *See* LEÓN DE LA BARRA, FRANCISCO.

BARRAGÁN, [GENERAL] JUAN (1894–1974). Politician, born on August 30 in **San Luís Potosí** (where he also died on September 28, 80 years later), joined the **Revolution of 1910** in 1913, becoming a general in the 1920s, a senator in 1918–1920, and a federal deputy in 1964–1967 and 1970–1973. In 1954 he helped found the **Partido Auténtico de la Revolución Mexicana**, serving as party president from 1957–1974.

BARRAGÁN, [GENERAL] MIGUEL (1789–1836). President, from 1835–1836, a little over a year until he was fatally stricken with **typhus**. In 1824 he had been made commander general of **Veracruz**. On November 18, 1825, his forces had captured **San Juan de Ulúa**, the last piece of Mexican territory to be liberated from **Spain**.

BARRAGÁN MORFÍN, LUIS (1902–1988). Architect trained initially as an engineer in the Escuela Libre de Ingenieros de **Guadalajara** from 1919–1923.

BARREDA, GABINO (1818–1881). After fighting in the **United States-Mexican War**, this Mexican educator from **Puebla** went to

Paris in 1848–1851 to study medicine. There he got to know Auguste **Comte,** and on his return he did much to spread **positivism** in Mexico. Later he worked closely with Benito **Juárez** as director of the newly created **Escuela Nacional Preparatoria** and in reorganizing the secondary school system to favor science over the humanities. Under his direction, positivism became the official doctrine of Mexico's educational system in the 1870s. It still influences Mexican **education.**

BARRERA, JUAN DE LA (1828–1847). One of the six **Niños Héroes.** Commissioned a lieutenant just before the **United States** attack on **Mexico City,** he died defending the fortifications he had been ordered to build in **Chapultepec Park.**

BARRIOS TERRAZAS, FRANCISCO (1950–). Charismatic **Partido de Acción Nacional** mayor of **Ciudad Juárez,** adopted by his party to run for state governor in 1986, having been endorsed by the media, and, thanks especially to support from a popular priest, Camilo **Daniel.** According to opinion polls, he was favored to win in both Ciudad Juárez and **Chihuahua City,** accounting between them for seventy percent of registered voters. The **Partido Revolucionario Institucional,** however, had just enough "creative" vote tabulations to announce victory. The old worn-out Mexican Communist Party (**Partido Comunista Mexicana**) had become the **Partido Socialista Unificado de México** but was ignored by **Chihuahua** voters. **Inflation** had been brought down, and the PRI took credit for what the federal government and the private sector had accomplished.

BARROS SIERRA, JAVIER (1915–1971). Professor of engineering, born February 25 in the **Federal District** (where he died August 15), he graduated in civil engineering with a master's in mathematics from **UNAM,** where he served as dean of the engineering school from 1955–1958. He was public works minister from 1958–1964 and rector of UNAM from 1966–1970, a period that included the **UNAM student riots of 1968.**

BARTLETT DÍAZ, MANUEL (1936–). A politician, born in **Tabasco** on February 23, a 1959 **UNAM law** graduate, he edited *La **República***

during 1963, studied law in Paris and then began doctoral studies in politics at the University of Manchester (United Kingdom) from 1967–1968, towards a UNAM PhD. In 1981 he became a key adviser to Miguel de la **Madrid**'s presidential campaign, was secretary general of the **Comité Ejecutivo Nacional** of the **Partido Revolucionario Institucional** from 1981–1982, and was governor of **Puebla state** from 1993–1999. In 1999 and early 2000 he campaigned within the PRI for nomination as its presidential candidate. Despite being labeled a "**dinosaurio**" by reformers within the PRI, he showed skill in building up a public demand for his selection, mounted the moment he ended his term as governor. This was an unprecedented action in modern Mexico, where the incumbent has always personally chosen his successor, not independently (as foreign scholars often suggest), but from two or three front-runners endorsed by his inner circle of six or seven advisers, or "**great electors**." However, after the PRI had lost its majority in the lower house (**Cámara de Diputados Federales**) in the **election of 1997**, the preliminary maneuvering among likely candidates widened for the first time since 1929. In March and June 1999 BIMSA (*Buro de Investigaciones de Mercado S,A*, the Mexican public opinion company), released polls showing he had 59 percent and 61 percent respectively of voters in his home state, but **United States** law enforcement authorities had claimed he was linked to the 1985 murder of Enrique **Camarena**. Four former US ambassadors to Mexico expressed their support of Bartlett, saying his good character was well known and that as interior minister he had pushed through the first intelligence-sharing exchange with the US that Mexico had ever had. Unfortunately his foreign **apellido** was also a problem.

BASEBALL (*beisbol*). In 1946, the Mexican baseball leagues were still considered on a par with the lowest minor league American teams, but the quantity and quality of professional baseball players has been gradually improving ever since. Several Mexican baseball players have been successfully recruited by American major league teams. On April 4, 1999, an American National League team opened its season by playing in Mexico, when the San Diego Padres played the Colorado Rockies in **Monterrey**. The Rockies were cheered on to its eight to two victory because Vinny Castilla of Mexico hit a home run for them. *See also* ABANICAR.

BASES ORGÁNICAS DE 1843. The *Bases de Organización Política de la República Mexicana* formed a conservative, centralist constitution, whose main accomplishment was to permit the 1844 election of Antonio López de **Santa Anna**. It was discarded in 1846 and the **Constitution of 1824** readopted.

BASKETBALL (*balconcesto*). Although **soccer** is Mexico's leading **sport**, basketball has, since the 1940s, been slowly narrowing the popularity gap, especially among school teams. Some six million Mexicans play the game, and although the oldest of the three national leagues dates from the 1970s, Mexico won an **Olympics** bronze medal as far back as 1936.

BASSOLS, NARCISO (1898–1959). Statesman, politician, educator, and diplomat who founded the **Escuela Nacional de Economía**. His most important post was as secretary of **education** in the Abelardo **Rodríguez Luján** administration, when he carried out extensive reforms in 1933, extending federal control over state schools and incorporating rural school principles to the urban area. Under **Cárdenas**, he was finance secretary. As a delegate to the **League of Nations** he fiercely defended the causes of Austria, Ethiopia, and the Spanish Republic. He was subsequently minister to the United Kingdom and France, and, in 1945, to the **Soviet Union**. His best known works are *La ley agraria* and *Garantías y amparo*.

BASTÓN. Staff of office (e.g., of the **viceroy**).

BATTLES. *See* ACULCO; ALAMO, EL; ALBARRADA; BUENA VISTA; CALDERÓN, BRIDGE OF; CELAYA, BATTLES OF; CERRO GORDO; CHAPULTEPEC, BATTLE OF; CUATLA; MOLINA DEL REY; MONTE DE LAS CRUCES; NOCHE TRISTE; PUEBLA, BATTLE OF; RELLANO; SALTILLO, SAN JACINTO; SAN MIGUEL CALPULALPAN; TACU-BAYA; TLATELOLCO, BATTLE OF.

BAZAINE, [MARSHAL] FRANÇOIS ACHILLE (1811–1888). Commander of the French expeditionary force in Mexico from 1863–1867 (*See* FRENCH INTERVENTION), having previously fought in the Crimean War and in France's Italian campaign against Austria. During the Franco-Prussian War he was besieged in the fortress of Metz, and, for not having broken through the besiegers' lines, he was sentenced in 1873 to death for cowardice, but he escaped to Madrid, where he died.

BEALS, CARLTON (1893–1979). Liberal American journalist and writer on Latin America, author of *Porfirio Díaz, Dictator of Mexico* (1932). [L. H.]

BEANS. Staple of Mexican traditional diet, includes a great variety, pinto beans being the commonest, followed by black beans, particularly in the South, and kidney beans. The crop totaled 1,364,239 t from 1.9 million hectares in 1994 but only 876,236 t in 2000, whereof **Zacatecas** produced 265,023 t. Almost half the crop is currently dependent on **irrigation**. [L. H.]

BEAR FLAG REPUBLIC. On June 14, 1846, a group of American settlers led by John **Frémont** seized the barracks of **Sonoma**, the capital of the Mexican state of **Alta California**, raised a flag with their bear emblem, and proclaimed the state's independence. Less than a month later, **United States** forces arrived to impose U.S. authority, which was confirmed in the Treaty of **Guadalupe-Hidalgo** two years later.

BECERRA GAYTÁN, ANTONIO (1933–). Marxist politician, he was born in **Chihuahua** on April 19, received an accounting degree from the Colegio Palmore there, and received a master's in psychology from the (unrecognized) Medrano Higher Normal School. He was active in the **Partido Revolucionario Institucional** from 1958 until 1961 when he joined the **Partido Comunista Mexicana** and ran unsuccessfully for the Senate. In 1979 Fidel Castro publicly congratulated him on his appointment to PCM's **Comité Ejecutivo Nacional**. In the 1980s he was active recruiting for the small Revolutionary Teachers' Movement, a Marxist affiliate.

BECKER ARREOLA, JUAN GUILLERMO (1931–). An economist born August 30 in Canatlán, **Durango**, he graduated in law from

UNAM and became a professor of economics there. In 1955 he became director of the Office of **Radio** and **Television** of the **Transport Ministry** (*Secteraría de Comunicaciones y Obras Públicas*). Active in the **Partido Revolucionario Institucional**, he was deputy minister in the **Trade Ministry** in 1974–1976. In 1982–1985 he served as director general of **Diesel Nacional**, the truck manufacturing corporation.

BEEF. Mexico is the world's seventh largest producer of beef. *Carne* ("flesh, meat") is normally assumed to mean *carne de vaca* ("beef").

BÉJAR, FELICIANO (1920–). Painter who sculpts in crystal, plastic, and metal, born in Jiquipán, **Mexico state**. He has had little formal art education, but the artists in his village furthered the development of his talents. *Paisage* and *Caja Tosca* are among his more famous paintings.

BELIZAN BORDER. Mexico's frontier with the former British Honduras lies along the **Hondo** River, stretches for 250 km, and was negotiated by Othón Pompeyo **Blanco Núñez de Caceres**.

BELIZE (Belice). The name since 1971 of the former colony of British Honduras. Regarded by Spain as a part of the captaincy general of **Guatemala**, it was, like most of the Caribbean coast of that government, neglected and unpopulated, so encouraging British interlopers (pirates, smugglers, and cutters of its valuable logwood). The British government's decision in 1862 to regularize the situation by declaring it a crown colony was unpalatable to Spanish speaking countries. Mexico finally recognized the present **Belizan border** in 1893, something Guatemala refused to do until after the area's independence in 1981.

BELLAS ARTES, PALACIO DE ("Palace of Fine Arts"). This art nouveau building with an exterior of Carrara marble is on Juárez Avenue, adjacent to the **Alameda** in downtown **Mexico City**, constructed in 1904–1934 by a team of Italian architects led by Adamo **Boari**, and based on classical European theaters. The Art Deco interior was by Federico Mariscal in 1932. The muraled glass curtain was built by New York's Tiffany jewelry company. It serves as a theater for the **Orquesta Sinfónica Nacional**, the national folklore ballet (*Ballet Folklórico de México*), and for major opera and orchestral concerts.

The building's weight and the soft nature of the city's subsoil have resulted in considerable (and noticeable) subsidence.

BELLATÍN, MARIO (1960–). Novelist, born in **Mexico City** to Peruvian parents. A critic of **machismo**, his first works, *Mujeres de sol* (1986), *Efecto invernadero* (1992) were published in Peru, but his *Flores* (2002) won the Xavier **Villaurrutia** prize. Other novels have included *Salón de beleza* (2000), *El jardín de la Señora Murakami* (2001), and *Shiki Nagaoka: una nariz de ficción* (2002). [L. H.]

BELTRÁN, AMANDO (1905–????). Public administrator, born on February 11. A **law** graduate from **UNAM**, he served as president of the **Federal Conciliation and Arbitration Board** from 1945–1946, secretary of the board of directors of the **Ferrocarriles Nacionales de México** in 1951, and then successively was director of personnel in 1969 and associate administrator from 1969–1973. In 1972 he reported on the number of free rail tickets lavished on federal and state office holders, documenting such situations as the train connecting **Nogales** with **Guadalajara** and **Mexico City** where 80 percent of Pullman passengers held free passes. His attempt to reduce the number of free tickets was overruled by the transport minister and his report was suppressed until 1988, but that specific train was abandoned in the 1990s as uneconomic. In 1998, however, that particular railroad, now with a group of private investors as minority stockholders revived service between **Hermosillo** and Guadalajara with mostly paying passengers.

BELTRÁN BROWN, FRANCISCO (c.1935–). A medical graduate of **UNAM** and professor in the National School of Medicine, this physician was awarded the National Prize of Surgery in 1963 by the Mexican College of Surgeons, appointed Director General of the National Institute of Pediatrics from 1978–1980, and assistant welfare minister from 1980–1982, recognized as an outstanding surgeon in both Mexico and the **United States**.

BENAVENTE, [FRAY] TORIBIO DE (1490?–1568). Franciscan missionary and historian from Benavente (province of Zamora), one of twelve Spanish priests sent to **New Spain** by **Charles V** soon after the Spanish **conquest of Mexico**. He constantly fought to improve the lot of the **Indians** and adopted the name of Motolinía ("the poverty-stricken"), the first indigenous word he heard. He refused to answer violence with violence, preached in many parts of Mexico and Central America, and took part in the founding of **Puebla**. A prolific writer, his most famous work was *Historia de los indios de la Nueva España*. He is buried in the Monastery of San Francisco.

BENEFICIENCIA ESPAÑOLA. A leading hospital of **Puebla**, built with Spanish finance, originally to cater for Spanish immigrants. [L. H.]

BENITO JUÁREZ. (1) **Municipio** of **Quintana Roo** state in which lies **Cancún**. The state's most populous *municipio*, it had 419,815 inhabitants in 2000. In 2005 the **Quintana Roo** state took the unprecedented step of firing its controversial (and politically isolated) mayor Juan Ignacio **García Zalvidea**: either he was corrupt and incompetent (the state's version) or he had been so deliberately starved of state funding that he lacked the resources to run the town properly, or even pay its staff (his version).

(2) **Delegación** of the **Federal District**. [L. H.]

BERENGUER [DE MARQUINA], FÉLIX (1738–1826). Viceroy of **New Spain** from 1800–1803. A naval officer of humble origin, his studies at the Cartagena Naval Academy earned him a mastership in mathematics and astronomy and the post of director of the navy's *Cuerpo de Pilotos*. He then served as governor of the Marianas in 1789–1795. Appointed viceroy in 1799, his arrival was delayed when the British captured him en route and detained him in Jamaica. He reinforced Mexican coastal defenses to keep out American interlopers, while peace with the United Kingdom in 1802 helped Mexico's overseas trade. He resigned the following year over policy differences with the Spanish government.

BERMÚDEZ, ANTONIO J. (1892–????). Born in **Chihuahua**, served as mayor of **Ciudad Juárez** from 1942–1945 and director general of

Pemex from 1946–1958. He directed the government's **Programa Nacional Fronterizo** (National Border Program) of developing new industries along the **United States border** in 1961–1970, encouraging the establishment of **maquiladoras** to create new payrolls for semi-skilled workers.

BERNAL, RAFAEL (1915–1972). Writer of detective fiction: *Un muerte en la tumba* (1946), *Su nombre era muerte* (1947), *El complot mongol* (1969).

BERTRÁN GARCÍA, ALBERTO (1922–2002). One of Mexico's most popular illustrators, engravers, and political cartoonists, he was anti-clerical and against big business. Always loyal to the **Partido Revolucionario Institucional**, he was a leading member of the *Taller de la Gráfica Popular*.

BÉSAME MUCHO. "Kiss me over and over, as if this night were the last time," composed and sung by Consuelo **Velázquez** in 1941 (before, she claimed, she had ever herself been kissed), this became a **World War II** hit, especially for couples separated by the conflict. It has been translated into 20 languages and interpreted by the Beatles, Celine Dion, Plácido Domingo, João Gilberto, and the Russian army chorus. [L. H.]

BETETA, RAMÓN (1901–1965). Newspaper editor and diplomat, born in **Mexico City** on October 7 and dying there on October 15, gained an economics degree from the University of Texas and a PhD from **UNAM**. He served as ambassador to Italy and then to Greece and as finance minister. He edited *Novedades* and the English language *News*, 1958–1964. Mario Ramón **Beteta Monsalve** is his nephew.

BETETA MONSALVE, MARIO RAMÓN (1925–). A nephew of Ramón **Beteta**, he was born July 7 in the **Federal District**, graduated in law from **UNAM** in 1948, gained a master's in economics at the University of Wisconsin in 1950, and became professor of economics at UNAM from 1951–1959. A formulator of structural changes in the **Partido Revolucionario Institucional** in 1972, he has been a long-time key adviser for the **Banco de México**. He was assistant finance minister from 1970–1974 and then minister of finance and public credit from 1975–1976. Under President **López Portillo** he directed the **Sociedad Mexicana de Crédito Industrial** from December 1976. His relatively brief term as governor of **Mexico State** in 1987–1989 boosted his national visibility as a leader. He improved parking facilities and bus services at **Teotihuacán** and brought many new industries into the state.

BIBLIOTECA ("library"). See under following word, except for the *Biblioteca Nacional* (under **National Library**).

BIEBRICH TORRES, CARLOS ARMANDO (1939–). Politician, born in Sahuaripa, **Sonora** on November 19, graduated in law at the Universidad de Sonora and became the state's local **Partido Revolucionario Institucional** chairman. In 1970–1973, he was assistant interior minister. He became governor of Sonora in 1973, a post from which he had to resign in December 1975 after state police killed seven squatters and injured 14 others when forcibly evicting them from land they had occupied for years. The case was widely reported in both the Mexican and American press. A judge ordered him indicted, not for having ordered the **police** action, but for misuse of 36 million pesos in state and federal funds during his governorship. The charge was dropped in 1977 and, after going into a brief seclusion, Biebrich took up activities that kept him away from the public eye.

BIERCE, AMBROSE (1842–1914?). Ohio-born author of *The Devil's Dictionary* (1906) and San Francisco journalist, Bierce disappeared in December 1913 after crossing into Mexico, leading to various tales about his fate. The most likely is that he joined Pancho **Villa**'s army in **Ciudad Juárez**, to die at the battle of **Tierra Blanca** or be captured by the *Federales* and shot as a spy. [L. H.]

BIMBO. Bakery firm founded in Santa María Insurgentes, **Federal District**, in December 1945 as *Panificación Bimbo*. It introduced Mexico to sliced, wrapped loaves of bread, and is now an international conglomerate selling 5,000 products in 16 countries with 44 plants in Mexico, 13 in four American states, 14 in other Latin American and Caribbean countries, and one in Europe. It trades in the **United States** as BBU (Bimbo Bakeries USA). [L. H.]

BIRDS. *See* EAGLE AND SNAKE; FAUNA; QUETZAL.

BIRTHRATE. For centuries Mexico's traditionally high birthrate was offset by the high death rate typical of an undeveloped economy. **Health** improvements during the 20th century changed this situation. By 1973 the annual **population** increase had reached an alarming 3.6 percent. The needed increases in **food** supply, potable water, and **employment**, skilled or unskilled, could not keep up. That year the federal government introduced **Family Planning** Centers (*see* **Centro de Planificación Familiar**), but the birthrate was not seriously reduced until the 1980s. By 1990 the annual population increase had fallen to 2.8 percent, and to 2.2 percent by 1995; by 2001 it was 2.1 percent, and by 2004 only 1.9 percent. Even so, the rate of increase remains beyond the needs of the **labor** market, especially in the rural areas, feeding a steadily increasing migration to the cities and (illegally) across the **United States border**.

BLACK LEGEND (*Leyenda negra*). View spread by **Spain**'s (mostly Protestant) detractors (inspired originally by Bartolomé de las **Casas**' accounts of mistreatment of the **Indians**), that Spanish rule in the **Indies** was inhumane, corrupt, and inefficient.

BLACK MARKET. *See* INFORMAL ECONOMY.

BLACKS (*negros*). Successive colonial censuses reported 18,535 blacks in 1570; 35,089 in 1646; but only 10,000 (compared with 624,461 **mulattoes** and **zambos**) in 1810. As in Argentina, "miscegenation" subsequently reduced their numbers even further. To judge from 2004 articles in the *Houston Chronicle* and the London *Guardian* newspapers, the outside world has only now suddenly awakened to the actual contemporary existence of Afro-Mexicans, a fact that official Mexico has always denied.

From the 1500s onward, **maroons** settled in isolated communities throughout the country, many of which are still inhabited by dark-skinned Spanish speakers who call themselves "blacks" (*negros*). They are largely unaware of either their former status or their African origin, although anthropologists can point to clear African connections in local folklore and folk **dance**. Their numbers can only be estimated, since color is not recorded by the **census**. This is mainly because modern Mexican society has always denied the former existence of **African slavery** anywhere south of **Texas**, even though, at its height in the 17th century, blacks outnumbered whites in many parts of the country. Some 40,000 blacks now live in **Cuajinicuilapa** and a score of smaller places along the **Costa Chica**, a rural stretch of Pacific coastline intersected by the **Oaxaca-Guerrero** state line. A smaller number of blacks lives in **Veracruz**, on the coast of the Gulf of Mexico, where their persistence is related to proximity to the Caribbean. A consequence of the gradual improvement in communications (now even the internet has arrived!) in both areas has led to a new groundswell of consciousness of their identity as Afro-Mexicans, but technology will also as surely erode their existence as pressure and opportunities for interracial marriage increase. [L. H.] *See also* MEXICO NEGRO; PINGUIN, MEMIN.

BLANCO MENDOZA, HERMINIO ALONSO (1950–). Born in **Chihuahua** on July 25, he graduated in economics from the Instituto Tecnológico de Monterrey, did graduate work at the University of Colorado, and took a PhD in economics at the University of Chicago. He has been a professor of economics at the **Colegio de México**, the **Instituto Tecnológico Autónomo de México**, and at Rice University, as well as being a researcher at the Massachusetts Institute of Technology.

In public administration, he has been advisor to the **finance minister** and advisor to the President of the Republic. Until November 1994 he was undersecretary of international commercial negotiations of the department of trade and industrial development, and as such, was Mexico's chief **North American Free Trade Association** negotiator. In 1994–2000 he was secretary of **trade** and industrial development in the cabinet of President **Zedillo**.

BLANCO NÚÑEZ DE CACERES, OTHÓN POMPEYO (1868–1959). Rear admiral from **Ciudad Victoria**, he was appointed in 1897 *Administrador y Comandante del Pontón Chetumal* to negotiate with the **United Kingdom** over the boundary with British Honduras (now **Belize**). On May 22, 1898, he founded at the mouth of the River Hondo what became **Chetumal, cabecera** of the **municipio** now known as **Othón P. Blanco**.

BLANCORNELAS, JESÚS (1936–2006). Journalist who was the founder of *Zeta*.

BLOQUE DE UNIDAD OBRERA. The Workers' Unity Block was a militant coalition of **trade unions** that threatened the **Ruíz Cortines** administration with a national freight strike until **CTM** leader Fidel **Velásquez Sánchez** got the railroad workers' union to withdraw from the Block.

BOARI, ADAMO (1863–1928). Italian architect of the Palacio de **Bellas Artes** and of the *Edificio de Correos* (the headquarters of Mexico's **postal service**).

BOCANEGRA, JOSÉ MARÍA (1787–1862). Interim president of Mexico for six days in December 1829 and holder of several ministerial posts until 1844.

BODEGA Y QUADRA, JUAN FRANCISCO. Ship's captain in Bruno de **Hezeta y Dudagoitia**'s Pacific coast expedition of 1775 who reached 58°N.

BOLSA MEXICANA DE VALORES. Established in its present form in 1933, the **Mexico City** stock exchange is Latin America's largest. In 1976 it absorbed the smaller exchanges in **Monterrey** and **Guadalajara**.

BONAMPAK ("painted walls," in Maya). This archaeological site in **Chiapas**, 121 km south of **Palenque** and its Maya ruins, was discovered in 1946. It displays preserved **Maya** murals dating back to 540, unfortunately deteriorated by the region's severe humidity. In recent years the federal Department of Antiquities and its *Instituto de Antropología* have been able to stop some of the erosion. Striking reproductions of the ruins are displayed at **Mexico City**'s **Museo Nacional de Antropología.**

BONAPARTE, JOSEPH (1768–1844). Elder brother of the French emperor **Napoleon I**, who appointed him leader of his puppet regime in Spain as King Joseph I (*José I*). This attempt to turn Spain into a

French dependency caused a crisis of authority throughout the Spanish empire and was a major stimulus toward the **independence** of the overseas territories. [L. H.]

BONFIL VIVEROS, RAMÓN GUILLERMO (1905–1997). Educator, born in **Hidalgo state**, directed the adult **literacy** campaign for the **education ministry** during the 1960s and was director of teacher education for the ministry from 1970–1976.

BOOKS. *See* CODICES; PRINTING; PUBLISHING AND THE BOOK TRADE.

BORDER PROGRAMS. *See* PROGRAMA INDUSTRIAL FRONTERIZO; PROGRAMA NACIONAL FRONTERIZO.

BORDERS. Mexico has a total periphery of 16,516 km, consisting of 4,583 km of international land frontiers (*See* BELIZAN BORDER; GUATEMALAN BORDER; UNITED STATES BORDER) and 12,273 km of **coastline**, including **islands**, on both the Pacific and the Caribbean. The colonial border of Old Mexico's **Far North** with **Russia**'s American territory is the origin of the southern frontier of the present-day U.S. state of Alaska.

BOTANICAL GARDENS. The 1787 arrival from Spain of the *Real Expedición Botánico* led to the creation in 1791 in the viceregal palace (today's **National Palace**) of the *Real Jardín Botánico de Nueva España* under the care of Vicente **Cervantes**, chair of botany at the University. By 1840, however, it had become badly neglected and **Mexico City**'s principal Botanical Garden is now that of **UNAM**.

BOTANY. *See* FLORA.

BOULBON, RAOUSSET DE (????–1854). French "filibuster" (soldier of fortune) who invaded **Guaymas** in an attempt to occupy the state of **Sonora** and make it an independent country. Defeated by José María **Yáñez**, he was shot by a firing squad on July 13, 1854.

BOURBON REFORMS. Administrative reforms largely inspired by French models, introduced into Spain and its empire under the Bourbon dynasty (1700–1808) but mostly during the reign of **Charles III**. They included a new transatlantic **postal service**, the **intendancy** system, spelling reform, standardization of weights and measures, the first archaeological investigation of **Maya** ruins, the expulsion of the **Jesuits**, and an attempt at a new codification of the **Laws of the Indies**.

The usual Spanish spelling of *Bourbon* is *Borbón*. [L. H.]

BOXING. *See* GARCÍA GONZÁLEZ, ALFONSO.

BRACAMONTES, LUIS ENRIQUE (1923?–). A leading civil engineer, born June 22 in Talpalpa, **Jalisco**, he graduated from **UNAM** in 1946, obtained an M.Sc. and taught engineering at UNAM from 1947–1952. He was director general of the national commission on secondary **highways** from 1952–1964, public works minister from 1970–1976, and has been consultant for the **Ferrocarriles Nacionales de México** and for the construction of several university campuses, public and private housing projects, and leading industrial construction corporations.

BRACERO. Farm field worker or ranch hand. Since the expiry of the **Bracero Treaty**, American farmers have continued to use illegal **emigration** from Mexico to supply much of their labor needs, while the growth of agro-industry and increasing mechanization have steadily decreased the number of jobs for *braceros* within Mexico itself. *See also* AGRICULTURAL LABOR.

BRACERO TREATY. This 1942 arrangement allowed thousands of Mexican farm workers to migrate legally to the **United States** for six-month periods (two harvest seasons a year) to bring in the crops and do other agricultural work while many US farm workers were in the armed forces. The program was renewed in peacetime, lasting until the end of 1964.

BRANIFF, ALBERT (1884–1966). Pioneer American aviator, from Dallas, Texas, who flew Francisco **Madero** over **Mexico City** in 1911, the first passenger **air transport** in Mexican history, commemorated by a plaque at Mexico City's international airport. Until 1977 this plaque spelled Braniff's first name, Spanish style, as

"Alberto," presumably the form he had been registered under at his birth, in Mexico City.

BRAVO, LEONARDO (1764–1812). Creole revolutionary leader, father of Nicolas **Bravo** and a follower of **Morelos**, who distinguished himself as a capable military leader and, as governor of **Tecpán** province, a competent administrator. Captured and executed by the Spanish in 1812, he was declared a national hero in 1823.

BRAVO, NICOLAS DE MÉXICO (1786–1854). Revolutionary who became president in 1823, in 1824 (twice), and in 1840–1841. The son of Leonardo **Bravo**, he fought under **Morelos** and was captured by the Spanish in 1817. He was set free by the **viceroy** in 1820 for himself having freed 500 Spanish prisoners, and he rejoined the insurgents. He spent a period of exile in **Guatemala** and South America, where he fought under Simón Bolívar. **Santa Anna** recalled him from exile in 1839. After his presidency, he was responsible for the defense of **Chapultepec** in the **United States-Mexican War**, was taken prisoner, and retired from public life. He lived for some time in exile in the **United States**, but he died in Chilpaningo in **Guerrero** state.

BRAVO AHUJA, VICTOR (1918–1990). Leading aeronautical engineer and a developer of graduate **education** in engineering throughout Mexico, he was born on February 20, in Tuxtepec, **Oaxaca**. He graduated in engineering from the **Instituto Politécnico Nacional** in 1940, gained a master's from the University of Michigan, became professor of engineering at the IPN, and then moved to the **Instituto Tecnológico y de Etudios Superiores de Monterrey (ITESM)**. There he was successively professor, director of its Summer School (1951–1955), dean of engineering (1955–1958), and president (1959–1960). He also served as governor of **Oaxaca state** from 1968–1970) and education minister from 1970–1976.

BRAVO DEL NORTE, RIO ("wild river of the north"). Mexican name of the border river known in English as the **Rio Grande**.

BRAZIL, RELATIONS WITH. Maximilian's interest in the New World is said to have been first stirred by the visit he paid in 1860 to the court of his cousin, the Brazilian emperor Dom Pedro II.

The imperial Mexican envoy, Escandón, left Brazil on February 8, 1866, and relations were broken off by his secretary, Berruecos, on March 30. Pedro II was indignant at his kinsman's execution the following year, and Brazil did not renew relations with Mexico until after Brazil became a republic following the **army** coup d'état of November 1889.

Brazil was a member of the **Niagara Conference** to negotiate an end to the **Revolution of 1910**.

During the **"Dirty War"** of the later twentieth century, Mexico acted as an intermediary in exchanges of kidnapped diplomats for leftist guerrillas and other detainees in Brazilian government custody. [L. H.]

BRETTON WOODS (NH). Site of the International Monetary Conference in 1944 that fixed world monetary arrangements until the **United States** abandoned the gold standard for the dollar in 1971.

BRIBIESCO SAHAGUÍN, MANUEL. Son of Marta **Sahaguín de Fox** who was accused, along with brothers Jorge and Fernando, by Olga **Warnat**, of influence peddling.

BRIGANDRY. See BANDITRY.

BRITISH IN MEXICO. See CALDERÓN DE LA BARCA, FRANCES ERSKINE INGLÉS; CATHERWOOD, FREDERICK; COOK, JAMES; DRAKE, FRANCIS; GAGE, THOMAS; GREENE, GRAHAM; LAWRENCE, DAVID HERBERT; WARD, H. G.

BROADCASTING. See RADIO; TELEVISION.

BROWNSVILLE. Texan border town on the opposite bank of the **Rio Grande** to **Matamoros**, close to the river's mouth. Its 1998 population was 99,000.

BRUJA. Rural witch or mystic woman, especially in Indian communities, who (for payment) uses "white" magic against evil spirits and to promote amours and uses "black" magic to harm enemies. If she also practices folk medicine, she is a *curandera*. See CURANDERO.

BRUJO. Rural wizard or witch doctor, whose advice, based on Indian myths, often influences peasants in the problems of their daily lives.

BUBONIC PLAGUE. *See* PLAGUE.

BUCARELI CONFERENCE, 1923. In this meeting the **United States** agreed to recognize the government of Álvaro **Obregón** in return for Mexican agreement not to apply the **Constitution of 1917** retroactively against foreign **petroleum** companies and to guarantee the interests of US citizens living in Mexico. The agreement lasted until the nationalization of the companies in 1938.

BUCARELI Y URZÚA, ANTONIO MARÍA DE (1717–1779). **Army** officer from Seville who became **Governor** of **Cuba** on March 19, 1766 until August 14, 1771. He was then **viceroy** of **New Spain** from 1771–1779. Under his administration, the army in Mexico was reduced in size, while the **Indians** in the north were pacified, and (following reports of the Russians pushing south from Alaska) the northern frontier was pushed beyond where **San Francisco** now stands. (*See* PEREZ, JUAN). He also sought to reconcile the Dominicans and Franciscans who were in conflict over their rights in **California**. He gave a new impetus to **mining**, allowing the mine owners to form a more powerful organization. He established free trade with **Spain**, built hospitals, and improved the lot of the mentally ill (*See* HEALTH CARE). He also began building the San Diego fortress to protect **Acapulco**. He died in office of pleurisy and is buried in **Guadalajara**.

His name also occurs as Buccarelli and as Bucarely y Ursua. [L. H.]

BUDGET, FEDERAL. Traditionally, the president of Mexico drew up the budget, the **Cámara de Diputados Federales** debated some details to give opposition members a feeling of importance, and the **Senate** added its formal approval. The budget for the forthcoming calendar year was promulgated before December 15. After the **Partido Revolucionario Institucional** lost its congressional majority in 1997, however, President **Zedillo**'s finance minister José Ángel **Gurría Treviño** was forced into lengthy bargaining with the opposition **political parties**. Approval of the revenue provisions was only secured on December 30 and approval of the expenditure side on December 31.

BUENA VISTA, BATTLE OF (February 1847). One of the most important battles of the **United States-Mexican War**. President Antonio López de **Santa Anna** made a forced march from **San Luis de Potosí** to La Angostura, close to the **Hacienda** of Buena Vista, near **Saltillo**. Despite their long march, his 25,000 troops fought well, and might have won, but Santa Anna, having captured two **United States** flags, broke off the engagement, and rushed to **Mexico City** to proclaim his victory. U.S. commander Winfield **Scott** returned to Washington, where he also proclaimed victory. His artillery fire had in the end proved decisive. The outnumbered American force of 5,000 had inflicted 3,000 casualties, with the loss of just over 700.

BUFA, LA. This mountain peak overlooks **Zacatecas City**. The Los Remedios Chapel, shrine of the local **Huichol Indians**, stands on this peak.

BULLFIGHTING (*fiesta brava*). A spectacle of life and death, rather than a **sport**, bullfighting was brought to Mexico by the Spanish in the 16th century. Each Sunday afternoon during the October-May season finds about 30 of the country's 135 rings in use. The *Plaza de México* in **Mexico City** remains the largest. But bullfighting's popularity has much declined since the 1940s when it was still a major popular entertainment. Now it is as much an attraction for American tourists as for Mexicans, who much prefer other spectator **sports**, such as **soccer** or horse-racing. Far more money is wagered in a week on these sports than on the bulls for an entire season. With fewer ranches specializing in breeding *toros bravos* for the ring, their quality has fallen. The toreadors, cape handlers, mounted picadors who handle the lances, and the others involved are now unionized and have pension funds, but new apprentices are numbered in the hundreds, not in the thousands of the earlier decades of the 20th century. *See also MACARENA, LA*; RODRÍGUEZ, MARIANO.

BULNES, FRANCISCO (1847–1924). Engineer, politician, journalist, and essayist, prominent during the **Porfirato**, articulated the

científico viewpoint and won favor by belittling previous national figures, even Benito **Juárez**. His works include *El verdadero Díaz* ("The Real Porfirio Díaz"), *El verdadero Juárez* ("The Real Juárez"), *La verdad completa sobre México* ("The Full Truth about Mexico"), and, especially, *El porvenir de las naciones hispano-americanos ante las conquistas de Europa y los Estados Unidos* ("The Future of the Hispanic American Nations in the Face of the Recent Achievements of Europe and the United States").

BUÑUEL, LUIS (1900–1983). Catalan film director who lived in Mexico from 1939–1970. *Un Perro andaluz* (1927), his first film, was produced in collaboration with Salvador Dali. The outbreak of the **Spanish Civil War** found him working at New York's Museum of Modern Art. When the war ended, he opted for exile in Mexico, where his output included *Los Olvidados* (1950—about slum life in **Mexico City**), *Robinson Crusoe* (1952), *La Muerte en este jardín* (1956), *Nazarín* (1958), *Diario de una camarera* (1964), *Belle de jour* (1967), and *Via láctea* (1969). He returned to Spain in 1970, where his next film was *Viridiana*.

BUSINESS. *See* CORPORATIONS; TRADE.

BUSTAMANTE. (1) **Municipio** of **Nuevo León** had 2,782 inhabitants in 1998 on 464 km². The **cabecera** lies 100 km north of **Monterrey**.
    (2) Municipio of **Taumalipas** of 1,381 km² had 8,011 inhabitants in 1998. The cabecera was founded in 1749 as San Miguel de los Infantes.

BUSTAMANTE, [GENERAL] ANASTASIO (1780–1853). President of the republic from 1830–1832 and 1837–1841, born in Jiquilpán, **Michoacán**. He fought for **Spain** against **Hidalgo** and **Morelos** and later supported **Iturbide**. He served as vice-president under **Gómez Pedraza** and Vicente **Guerrero**. He was involved in the revolt against Guerrero, becoming President from January 1830 until August 1832 when he was driven into exile in England by revolts led by liberal generals Antonio Méjia in **Texas**, Estéban **Moctezuma** in **Tampico**, and Juan Álvarez in **Acapulco**. The conservatives recalled him in 1836, and he served again from 1837 until overthrown in 1841 by a military coup led by López de **Santa Anna** and **Paredes y Arrillaga**. Generally considered honest and well intentioned, he was often controlled by stronger men.

BUSTAMANTE, CARLOS MARÍA DE (1774–1848). Centrist politician, soldier, historian and newspaper publisher, born in **Oaxaca**. He was an **army** officer in Mexico's first **Independence War**, served as secretary to **Iturbide** in 1821, and edited *El Diario de México*. He is considered an outstanding historian of his period, as in his *Cuadro histórico de la revolución de América* ("Historical Picture of the Revolution in America") and *Apuntes para la historia del gobierno del general Santa Anna* ("Notes on the History of Santa Anna's Government"). In 1847 he became one of the conservative five-man executive power.

– C –

CABAL PENICHE, CARLOS EFRAÍN DE JESÚS (1956–). Chairman in the 1980s and early 1990s of the **Cremi-Unión** banking group, fled to Australia, via Florida, Puerto Rico, and **Spain** when charged with stealing US\$ 700 million from Cremi-Unión through an elaborate self-lending scheme. He was also needed as a key witness in a Swiss bank money laundering case against Raúl **Salinas**, who admitted their association from his prison cell. A witness in the Salinas trial testified that Cabal had received US\$ 200 million from **narcotics** traffickers. He was arrested in Melbourne, Australia, having traveled with hundreds of thousands of dollars, the apparent fruit of his drug trade connections, and a Dominican Republic passport he had bought for US\$ \$50,000. According to Juan Miguel Ponce, head of Interpol in Mexico, he was disguised with a beard and cosmetic changes applied by a Mexican former professional **cinema** makeup artist who committed the error of using his real birth date on his various false passports.

A **Tabasco** native, he became a business executive, courting friends in the government's **Banco Federal de Fomento** with legitimate loans for legal foreign trade activities at first. In 1993 he convinced investors in his bank to join him in buying Del Monte Fresh Produce of Mexico for US\$ 525,000. As its major shareholder, he then controlled 85 percent of Mexican tomato exports. The Mexican government took over Del Monte when Cabral's empire collapsed.

CABALLERO, LUIS G. (1877–1960). Law graduate from the Colegio de San Nicolás, in his native **Morelia, Michoacán,** he served as *Procurador de justicia* (state attorney general) from 1917–1922, and subsequently as high court judge in **Nayarit, Hidalgo, Puebla,** and the **Federal District,** before becoming a **Supreme Court** justice in 1938–1941. There he wrote the majority opinion that German citizens broadcasting anti-US propaganda from Mexican radio stations in English to listeners in the **United States** were violating Mexico's neutrality law. After Mexico entered **World War II,** this opinion was cited as one of the legal justifications of the imprisonment of such "border blaster" broadcasters.

***CABALLITO, El* ("little horse").** Popular name of the statue of **Charles IV** as an imposing military figure (dressed as a Roman general) on a prancing horse, sculptured by Manuel **Tolsa** in 1790. Considered one of the finest works of its kind in the world, it had to be hidden during the wars of **Independence** lest it be destroyed by anti-Spanish mobs. For years it stood at the intersection of the Paseo de la **Reforma** and Avenida **Hidalgo.** After the 1985 **earthquake,** the city planning commission moved the statue to Calzada Tacuba, another west-to-east street, just east of the Avenida Lázaro **Cárdenas,** and across from the north side of the *Edificio de Correos* (**Boari**'s Post Office).

CABAÑAS, LUCIO (1938–1974). Guerrilla fighter, leader of the *Partido de los Pobres* ("Party of the Poor"), who went underground in May 1967 and then from 1971 led an insurrection of roughly 30 rural communities in the Sierra de Atoyac in **Guerrero** whose suppression needed five **army** battalions and 10,000 **police** with air support.

CABECERA. "County seat" or administrative center of a **municipio,** which usually bears the same name.

CABEZA DE VACA, ALVAR. *See* NÚÑEZ CABEZA DE VACA, ALVAR.

CABILDO. In local administration, *cabildo secular* is a colonial term for the governing council of a **municipio**. The institution, imported from medieval Spain, provided many leaders of the **Independence** struggle with a most useful, albeit limited, experience in European-style self-government. After **independence** municipal councils were renamed *consejos municipales,* but the alternative term **ayuntamiento** occurs in both colonial and modern contexts.

The word also denotes the chapter of a cathedral, a *cabildo eclesiástico.*

CABINET. Major departments of state. *See also* MINISTRIES.

CABRERA, LUIS (1876–1954). Lawyer who furnished much of the ideology of the **Revolution of 1910**. He fought not only Porfírio **Diaz**, but was an implacable foe of Victoriano **Huerta**. In 1912 he authored the first modern project for **agrarian reform**. In 1933 he refused an invitation to run as the presidential candidate of the **Partido Antirreeleccionista**. He was also well-known for his translations, including a version of the *Song of Solomon.*

CABRERA, MIGUEL (1695–1785). Religious painter born in **Oaxaca** of Spanish parents. While still a child, his talents attracted the attention of the Archbishop of Mexico, José Manuel Rubio y Salinas, who encouraged and protected him, but he became more noted for the fecundity of his output than for the quality of his works. The more famous of these are *La vida de Santo Domingo, La vida de San Ignacio,* and *Retrato de Sor Juana Inés de la Cruz.* He died in **Mexico City**.

CABRILLO, JUAN RODRÍGUEZ DE (14??–1543). Spanish form of the name of a Portuguese soldier and navigator who went to Mexico with Pánfilo de **Narváez** in 1520 and was with **Cortés** when he conquered **Tenochtitlán**. **Viceroy** Antonio de **Mendoza** sent him to discover the "Strait of **Anián**." He found **San Diego** Bay instead in 1542, making him thus the first European explorer of **Alta California**. He died on San Miguel island in the Santa Barbara Channel on January 3, and his pilot, Bartolomé **Ferrelo**, took over command of the expedition. His discoveries long went unrecognized and unappreciated. **Spain** did not begin to colonize the region until the late 1700s, but the **United States** Postal Service belatedly honored him with a 29-cent stamp in 1992.

CACAO. Native tree of lowland tropical Central America and northern South America which provided a favorite drink of the **Aztecs**, who used its beans as currency. Since it was first drunk by the *conquistadores* at the court of **Montezuma**, it is often claimed to be a distinctively Mexican contribution to world cuisine. Its chief provenance in the colonial period was, however, Venezuela. By the mid-17th century the region around Caracas had obtained a near monopoly of the Mexican market, which was consuming over 80 percent of the Venezuelan crop. By then, unfortunately, the world price of the cacao bean had risen so sharply that most Mexican **Indians** could no longer afford it.

CACIQUE. Arawak term for a native chief, adopted into Spanish soon after the first settlement in Hispaniola, now designates any local or regional boss (a **caudillo** on a local level, so to speak). In Mexico such *caciques* support the dominant federal authority, and in return they are allowed to exercise their own power at the local level as long as this creates no conflict of interest.

CACTI. *See* AGAVE; PRICKLY PEAR CACTUS.

CACTUS MOTH (*cactoblasis cactorum*). Dangerous cactus pest, a native of Argentina, Brazil, and Paraguay. Wingless, it has been widely spread by human beings: to Australia in 1925, South Africa and St. Kitts in 1957 in cactus eradication programs, but since then by accident, being found in Florida in 1989, then in Alabama, and in August 2006 on the Island of **Mujeres**, threatening to reach the mainland and devastate, in particular, Mexico's **prickly pear cactus**. [L. H.]

CÁDIZ CORTES. *See* CORTES OF CÁDIZ.

CAGIGAL DE LA VEGA, [*DON*] FRANCISCO (c.1695–1777). Governor of Santiago de Cuba from 1738–1747 and of all **Cuba** from June 1747–1760 He then served briefly as interim **viceroy** of **New Spain** in 1760, before returning to Cuba as governor of Havana.

The first **apellido** also appears as Cajigal and Caxigal. [L. H.]

CAJERO ("cashier"). State or municipal officer who audits the revenue collected by the tax officials.

CAL Y MAYOR, RAFAEL (1923–). Born in **Chiapas** on September 10, he graduated in engineering from **UNAM**, did graduate study at Yale, and then directed driver training programs throughout Mexico from 1964–1970. A leading consultant on the building of **highways** and their safety, he now heads a large construction corporation and has popularized the need for formal training for all Mexican drivers, whether of private **automobiles** or of trucks.

CALDERÓN, BRIDGE OF. The *Puente de Calderón* on the River **Lerma** was the site of the decisive January 17, 1811, defeat of Miguel **Hidalgo y Costilla** by General **Calleja del Rey** and origin of the title of nobility bestowed upon the victor.

CALDERÓN DE LA BARCA, FRANCES ERSKINE INGLÉS, "Fanny" (1804–1882). Scottish wife of Ángel Calderón de la Barca, marqués Calderón de la Barca, Spain's first ambassador to Mexico in 1829. Her *Life in Mexico* gives her claim to have been one of the best foreign observers ever to have visited Mexico.

CALDERÓN HINOJOSA, FELIPE (1962–). Partido Acción Nacional's successful candidate for president in the **election of 2006**, had been energy minister in the **Fox** administration. A **Morelia**-born, Harvard-educated technocrat, he ran on PAN's claim to have achieved macroeconomic stability and won with a razor-thin majority. His evident need for **Partido Revolucionario Institucional** support in Congress seemed likely to lead him to defend the beleaguered PRI governor of **Oaxaca**. [L. H.]

CALENDAR. Around 200 BC **Zapotec** introduction of writing was accompanied by a system of time reckoning that seems to have been the origin of the elaborate but very accurate **Maya** and **Aztec** calendar of two cycles: a solar year of 365 days and a sacred year of 260 days running in a parallel pattern within a larger cycle of 52 years.

The countries of the Spanish empire replaced the Julian Calendar with the Gregorian in 1583, 170 years before the British empire (including the future **United States**). [L. H.]

CALEXICO. Californian border town of 36,749 (in 2005) opposite **Mexicali**, founded in 1900 as a tent city of the Imperial Land Company. It was named for **California** and Mexico.

CALIFORNIA. (1) Fictional island in the 16th century chivalry romance *Amadis de Gaula*, suggestive of high desert temperatures (*calor* "heat," and *forno* "oven" in Old Spanish), given to the North American coast lands west of the Gulf of **California** and their continuation further north. The Mexican authorities first became fully aware of this coast thanks to the **Manila galleon** that found its best homeward route to be towards California, followed by passage southward close to land. They did not provide the area with a regular administration with its own governor until 1768. Then, in 1804, it was divided into **Baja California** and **Alta California**.

(2) English name for Alta California following its seizure by the **Bear Flag Republic** of 1846 and subsequent **United States** occupation, confirmed by the 1848 Treaty of **Guadalupe Hidalgo**. In 1850 the territory received statehood as the US state of California.

CALIFORNIA, GULF OF. The bay between the peninsula of **Baja California** and the rest of Mexico (also known as the Sea of **Cortés**) is so long (1,100 km–600 miles) and narrow (230 km at its widest) that the peninsula was long thought to be an island. It boasts the best salt water **sport fishing** in the world, and also provides extensive commercial fishing, particularly for **shrimp**.

CALIFORNIA CURRENT. Just as the cold Humbolt current flowing northward from the Antarctic has created the Atacama desert in northern **Chile**, so the Northern Hemisphere's corresponding southerly California current has a similar effect on **Baja California**.

CALIFORNIAN INDIANS. Chemehuevi, Hupa, Maidu, Miwoc, Modoc, Monache, Pomo, Shasta, Yurok, and other tribes of **Alta California** numbered around 300,000 when whites first arrived in 1769.

Largely due to the introduction of European **disease**, they had decreased to about 150,000 by the time of the **United States** annexation in 1848. Exploited, often starved (forbidden to own firearms, they could seldom hunt effectively), and frequently lynched or otherwise murdered, they were reduced by 1860 to barely 30,000.

CALLEJA [DEL REY], FÉLIX MARÍA, CONDE DE CALDERÓN (1753–1828). A most capable general, but one whose cruelty gained him the soubriquet of "the butcher." Born in Medina del Campo, he came to **New Spain** in 1789 as an official of the **Council of the Indies** and was in command of the garrison of **San Luís de Potosí** when his title of nobility was bestowed for his decisive victory over Miguel **Hidalgo y Costilla** at **Calderón** bridge. His 1814 defeat of José María **Morales y Pavón** (who had previously defeated him at **Cuatla**) was the effective end of the initial phase of the **Independence** struggle. As **viceroy** of **New Spain**, 1813–1814, he successfully defended it, reorganizing and strengthening the **army**. Despite his age he was given command in 1819 of an expedition to reconquer Paraguay but was taken prisoner by Rafael **Riego y Núñez** before he could sail.

CALLES, PLUTARCO ELIAS (1877–1945). Born in **Guaymas**, **Sonora**, a teacher before taking part in the **Revolution of 1910**. As early as 1904 he published a newspaper attacking Porfírio **Díaz**, for which he was forced to leave his native city. He later became active in the **Partido de Anti-Reelección** and fought on the side of Álvaro **Obregón** against Victoriano **Huerta** and Pancho **Villa**, rising rapidly to become governor of Sonora in 1917, **interior** minister, 1920–1924, and **president**, 1924–1928. As president he made many reforms in public **education** and **health**, established the forerunner of the **Banco Nacional de Crédito Agrícola**, the **Banco de México**, and the Comisión Agrícola Nacional. However, by enforcing the provisions of the **Constitution of 1917** in regard to the registration of priests, he set off the **Cristero rebellion**. He united all political factions into a single, all powerful **Partido Nacional Revolucionario**, under his leadership. He appointed himself *Jefe Máximo de la Revolución* (Supreme Leader of the Revolution). When Obregón was assassinated immediately after his reelection, he had the Constitution amended to create single six-year presidencies. He then proceeded to secure the appointment of a succession of two-year interim presidents (Emilio **Pontes Gil**, 1928–1930; **Ortiz Rubio**, 1930–1932; Abelardo **Rodríguez**, 1932–1934) whom he controlled as his puppets. He remained the effective, unofficial head of Mexico until Lazaro **Cárdenas** forced him into exile in 1936. He returned in 1941 but stayed out of politics. He died in **California**. *See also* SHEFFIELD, JAMES ROCKWELL.

CAMACHO, SEBASTIÁN (1791–1847). Governor of **Veracruz** in 1837 and 1846. As minister accredited to the **United Kingdom**, **France**, and the **Netherlands**, he was the first Mexican diplomat in Europe.

CÁMARA DE COMERCIO ("Chamber of Commerce"). Under a 1941 federal law, each local chamber must federate with the **Confederación de Cámaras Nacionales de Comercio**.

CÁMARA DE DIPUTADOS FEDERALES (Federal House of Representatives). The lower house was established as the *Cámara de Diputados* on February 24, 1822. The **Constitution of 1917** created 162 congressional districts based on **population**, increased to 178 in 1964, to 194 in 1973, and to 300 in 1979. Until a constitutional amendment in 1964 gave Mexico at least the appearance of being a functioning democracy, with the leader of the **Partido Popular Socialista** becoming the first opposition leader and the **Partido Acción Nacional** gaining twenty seats, all but a handful of seats had been held by the **Partido Republicano Institucional**. The amendment introduced a system whereby additional seats were to be filled by **proportional representation**. When the Chamber was enlarged in 1979, the PRI won 296 of the 300 district seats, whereas six minority parties shared the 100 seats created for them, and the PRI continued to retain the real power. The opposition might engage in lengthy debates but they could only change minor details of legislation. In 1987, the Constitution was amended to allow 200 "party list" seats, it being assumed that the PRI would continue to win almost all the 300 congressional district seats. The landmark **election of 1997** proved that this could no longer be taken for granted, and the PRI found itself deprived of an overall majority in the House for the first time since its founding. As a result the federal budget could only be passed with PAN support.

A deputy's term is for three years, and he may not run for an immediately consecutive term. Currently, each voter casts two ballots, one for the congressional district candidate and one for the party list candidate. *See also* SUPLENTE.

CÁMARA DE DIPUTADOS LOCALES (House of Local Deputies). Unicameral legislature of each Mexican state. Members (whose numbers vary in different states, from 12 to 29) are elected for three-year terms and may not run for immediate reelection. As in the federal government, the executive dominates over the legislature, whose chief power is that of approving or changing the budgets of each **municipio** within the state.

The **election of 1997** reduced but did not overturn the traditional **Partido Republicano Institucional** majorities at state level.

CÂMARA DE SENADORES. *See* SENATE.

CÁMARA INDUSTRIAL. Under a 1941 federal law, every manufacturing or industrial corporation and every wholesaler must join the Industrial Chamber of its industry—cement, footwear, broadcasting, or whatever—which becomes the voice of organized management in negotiations with the government or the **trade unions**. These industry-wide chambers are in turn members of a national federation, the **Confederación de Cámaras Industriales (CONCAMIN)**.

CÁMARA NACIONAL DE LAS INDUSTRIAS DE TRANSFORMACIÓN (CANACINTRA or CNT). The National Chamber of Manufacturing Industries was established by federal law in April 1942 as the organized voice of the newer industrialists who did not have their own chambers in the **Confederación de Cámaras Industriales (CONCAMIN)**. The CANACINTRA has membership in the CONCAMIN, but it also negotiates directly with government and with the **trade unions**. [The decline of the traditional Mexican corporate state since the 1980s has meant a slow decline in the importance of the CANACINTRA, and so has largely left small business with little political influence. L. H.]

CAMARENA, ENRIQUE (1950–1985). "Kiki," a **United States** Drug Enforcement Administration agent, was discovered, tortured, and murdered. At his killers' trial, one witness—a paid informant—claimed Manuel **Bartlett Díaz** had been at the house where Camarena was held. The US Justice Department said that Bartlett had been 650 km away in **Mexico City** at the time, but it refused him a written statement that he was not under investigation unless he would testify before a Los Angeles grand jury. This he refused to do, considering the demand as an insult. *See also* NARCOTICS.

CAMARILLA. Political clique headed by a successful politician who holds a government position. His entourage can be horizontal, among peers who were his classmates in school, or vertical, among rising administrators and their trusted assistants. A *camarilla* is based on close friendships resembling extended family relationships. As its leader rises in government or the **Partido Revolucionario Institucional**, he tries to have his *camarilla* associates promoted into his higher level office. Eventually, such an associate attains a position high enough for him to lead his own *camarilla*. Mexican public life is thus interlaced with political cliques.

Although almost every woman who has reached a state legislature or higher position has been an auxiliary member of some all-male *camarilla*, since the 1980s a few women have formed their own *camarillas*. As more **Partido Acción Nacional** members gain significant posts, so a few more opposition *camarillas* may emerge. Before the rise of Andrés Manuel **López Obrador**, the **Partido de la Revolución Democrática** seemed to have just two major groups: that around the then governor of the **Federal District**, Cuauhtémoc **Cárdenas**, and a rival faction of those who did not closely support him.

CAMINO REAL ("King's highway"). In colonial times, this referred to any highway important enough for its upkeep to be (in theory) the responsibility of the crown, such as any of those linking **Mexico City** with provincial capitals or with important ports.

CAMINOS Y PUENTES ("Highways and bridges"). The *Caminos y Puentes Federales de Ingresos y Servicios Conexos* (formerly the *Departamento de Puentes y Calzadas*) was a federal government agency (serving both the **Transport Ministry** and the **Public Works Ministry**), that built, repaired, and administered directly all federal **highways** and bridges, and, through intergovernmental laws, most state and local roads, including the disbursement of allocated funds and the collection of toll road revenues. It has now been replaced by the *Dirección General de Carreteras*, an agency of the **Transport Ministry**. [L. H.]

CAMPA CIFRIÁN, ROBERTO (1957–). **Mexico City** lawyer and a close associate of teachers' union leader Elba Esther **Gordillo Morales**. He was the presidential candidate of the **Nueva Alianza** in the **Election of 2006**, coming in fifth, with 401,804 votes (0.96 percent).

CAMPECHE CITY. Capital of its namesake state located on the Gulf of **Mexico** coast of the **Yucatán** peninsula, at 19°50'N, 90°30'W, 160 km southwest of **Mérida**. Founded by Francisco de Montejo on a **Maya** site in 1541, its thick walls facing the sea were built against pirate attacks in 1686–1704, but it was not made a city until 1774, nor connected to **Mexico City** by rail until 1951. The population of what is now a 2,922 km^2 **municipio** has grown from 18,000 c.1750 to 71,400 in 1976; 115,000 in 1990; 173,645 in 1998 (of whom 85,150 lived in the city itself); 216,897 in 2000; and 230,910 in 2002. Its retail trade and port activities have been steadily increasing since the 1974 discovery of the state's vast **petroleum** reserves.

CAMPECHE STATE. State of 51,833 km^2, west of **Tabasco**, shares the **Yucatán** peninsula with Yucatán state to the north and **Quintana Roo** to its east, **Guatemala** to the south and the Gulf of **Mexico** to its west. Its area includes 288 offshore **islands**. Its hostility to incorporation into a federal Mexico was always less than that of **Mérida** since its trade passed through **Veracruz** rather than Havana and its local authorities were glad of federal aid to suppress the **Caste War of Yucatán**. The **partido** of Campeche was constituted as a state on May 18, 1858, although it was briefly reincorporated into Yucatán under the **Second Empire**.

The **population** was 86,453 in 1869. At successive **censuses** since then it has been the following: 88,000 (1895); 87,000 (1900); 87,000

(1910); 76,000 (1920); 85,000 (1930); 90,000 (1940); 122,000 (1950); 168,000 (1960); 252,000 (1970); 421,000 (1980); 535,185 (1990); 690,689 (2000); and 754,750 (2005).

It has an arid climate in the north and a humid tropical climate in the south, where rain forests have no road connections to the Gulf coast. Campeche takes its name from the logwood (Mayan *can peche*) that was the first important resource of the region. Its chief products now are **petroleum, shrimp, corn**, and **sugar** cane.

The current municipios are **Campeche** (the capital); Calakmul (23,115 people in 2000 on 13,839 km^2); Calkini (46,899 people on 1,967 km^2); Candelaria (37,681 on 5,519 km^2); Carmen (172,076 on 9,721 km^2); **Champotón**, Escárcega (50,563 on 4,565 km^2); Hecelchakán (24,889 people on 1,332 km^2); Hopelchín (31,214 people on 7,460 km^2); Tenabo (8,400 people on 882 km); and Palizada (8,401 on 2,072 km^2).

CAMPERO, JOSÉ. Army leader from **Colima** in the Constitutionalist forces in 1913 who remained loyal to President Venustiano **Carranza** into 1920. He became briefly governor of **Colima state** during 1935, later serving as a federal deputy and then as executive officer of the federal **senate**. As a newspaper writer in **Chihuahua** and **San Luis Potosí** in the 1930s through the 1960s, he built support for the **Partido Revolucionario Institucional** in northern and central Mexico.

CAMPESINO. Peasant farmer, still one third of the national workforce. The **Revolution of 1910** became, in his name, a fight for social reform: "Land, Bread, and Justice." But that Revolution has done more for the urban worker. Even in the 1970s, after a half century of **agrarian reform**, the *campesino* still used outdated farming methods and implements, and eked out a subsistence with dietary, housing, and clothing standards half as good as those of urban Mexicans. Between 1960 and 1990 the agricultural economy grew two percent a year: one-third the average growth rate of industry. With one *campesino* in four unemployed, the last third of the 20th century saw a steady increase in migration to the cities and to the **United States**. *See also* COFFEE; CONFEDERACION NATIONAL CAMPESINA.

CAMPILLO SÁINZ, JOSÉ (1917–1998). Born October 9, in **Mexico City**, he graduated in **law** from **UNAM**, studied labor law in Italy in the 1930s, and in the 1950s became a leading spokesman for Mexican industrialists and business executives, heading the National Productivity Center and the Committee of International Activities of Private Enterprise. After serving as director of the Mining Industry Chamber, he headed the **Confederación Nacional de Cámaras Industriales**. He was industry and trade minister from 1973–1976 and for several years director of the **Instituto del Fondo Nacional de la Vivienda para los Trabajadores**.

CAMPOS SALAS, OCTAVIANO (1916–1998). Born in **San Luis Potosí** on March 22, he graduated in economics from **UNAM**, did graduate study at the University of Chicago, and became dean of UNAM's School of Economics. After heading the **Sindicato Nacional de Trabajadores de la Educación**, he was an administrator for the Census Bureau, then manager of the **Banco de México**, and, in 1964–1970, industry and trade minister. As an investor in **Automex**, he helped develop automobile manufacturing in Mexico.

CANADA, RELATIONS WITH. New Spain's explorations into its **"Far North"** brought it into conflict with the British trading and settling along the future Pacific coast of **Canada**, notably at **Nootka Island**. Much more recently Canada has become one of Mexico's partners in the **North American Free Trade Association (NAFTA/TLCAN)**.

CANALIZO, VALENTÍN (1794–1850). Born in **Monterrey**, he became a confidant of Antonio López de **Santa Anna**, fighting on his side against **Iturbide** and subsequently, although he changed sides at the end of his life. In 1831 he presided over the courtmartial that sentenced President Vicente **Guerrero** to death. In October 4, 1843, Santa Anna made him interim **president**, until June 1844, and again in September, but a popular uprising provoked by his dictatorial rule ousted him in late November 1844. He died in retirement in **Mexico City**.

CANCHANILLA. Inhabitant of **Baja California**.

CANCÚN ("viper's nest" in Maya). In 1968 a Mayan fishing hamlet of shacks at 21°10'N, 86°50'W in **Benito Juárez municipio** on the northeastern Caribbean coast of **Quintana Roo**, with 117 inhabitants. It was transformed by 1972 into a intentionally-built luxury resort which from the 1980s began attracting celebrities away from **Acapulco**. As poor migrants have flocked here for jobs in the booming tourism business, it has become Mexico's fastest growing city, with 130,000 inhabitants in 2000 and 700,000 in 2006. It suffered severe hurricane damage in October 2005.

CANDELARIA, OUR LADY OF. Among the Indians of **Jalisco** state a special interpretation of the Virgin Mary involved a statue in a church at San Juan de los Lagos in 1541. This *Virgen de la Candelaria* has for centuries been given credit for miracles and remains a part of folk religion among the peasantry. In February various Indian and **mestizo** communities throughout Mexico hold special dances, fiestas, and prayers in her honor.

CANEK, JACINTO (1730–1761). Leader of an unsuccessful **Maya** uprising on November 20, 1761, aiming to wipe out all whites and mestizos. He was captured and executed.

CANNING, GEORGE (1770–1827). United Kingdom foreign secretary and eventually prime minister, responsible for preventing the Holy Alliance of European monarchies from extending its restoration of the absolutist monarchy in **Spain** across the Atlantic. By doing so he effectively secured Hispanic American independence and allowed the **United States** to declare its Monroe Doctrine of no European intervention in the Americas. His motives were primarily commercial: British traders had extremely overly optimistic expectations of a Latin American market freed from Spanish mercantilistic restrictions. [L. H.]

CANTINFLAS (1911–1983). Professional name of Mario Moreno, born August 12, whose movie career began in the 1930s when he wrote and starred in a **Mexico City** stage comedy, *Allí y Allá*. Soon afterwards a major Mexican movie producer had signed him to star in a film version. Dozens of other Mexican films followed, each a box office success throughout Latin America. In 1952 President Miguel

Alemán had quoted a Cantinflas quip about *doubles entendres* in a news conference where Alemán had apparently been misquoted. In 1956 Cantinflas co-starred with David Niven in his only American film, *Around the World in Eighty Days*. The film, adapted from Jules Verne's novel, won an Oscar, and Cantinflas got an award for his role as Passepartout. In 1957 he ranked fourth (after three Argentine stars) in a popularity poll by *La Nación* of Buenos Aires. His death from lung cancer on April 20 drew obituary praise from newspapers throughout the Spanish-speaking world, Europe, and the **United States**. In Hollywood he was compared to Charlie Chaplin for the way his visual talent combined humor and pathos. His will established scholarships for poor, young, aspiring actors.

CANTO, ALBERTO DE. CONQUISTADOR. Founder of **Saltillo**, his attempt to settle **Nuevo León** was later taken up successfully by Luis de **Carvajal y de la Cueva**.

CAPE (*Cabo*). For individual headlands, see under following word.

CAPITAL. Mexico City since the Spanish **conquest**. *See also* CABECERA.

CAPITANÍA GENERAL. *See* CAPTAINCY GENERAL.

CAPTAIN GENERAL (*Capitán general*). Title of Hernán **Cortés** from 1521 until **New Spain** was constituted a **viceroyalty** in 1534, and thereafter the title of a governor of a **captaincy general**.

CAPTAINCY GENERAL. Status of **Guatemala** from 1543 and of **Cuba** from 1581. This meant that, although remaining nominally part of the **viceroyalty** of **New Spain**, they became in most respects a direct dependency of **Spain** itself. [L. H.]

CARABIAS LILLO, JULIA (1954–). Politician and environmentalist, born in **Mexico City**, she obtained a B.Sc. and M.Sc. from **UNAM**. There her research included the ecology of rain forest regeneration and environmental restoration and has resulted in 35 articles and the books *Ecología y autosuficiencia alimentaria*, *La producción* *rural en México: alternativas ecológicas, For Earth's Sake* (a report for the 1992 U.N. Conference on Environment and Development in Brazil), and *Manejo de recursos naturales y pobreza rural.* She was a member of the council of UNAM from 1989–1993 and president of the National Ecology Institute, February-November, 1999, and is currently a member of the Consultative Councils of the National Solidarity Program of the **Procurador General** for Environmental Protection and of the *Fondo Mexicano para la Conservación de la Naturaleza* (National Fund for Conservation). She is on the academic councils of various international environmental organizations, including that of the Program for Advanced Studies in Sustainable Development at the **Colegio de México**.

Although she belongs to no political party, President **Zedillo** appointed her his Environment, Natural Resources, and Fishery Minister. She expressed gratitude at holding such a key post, as the sole woman in previous cabinets had been the Tourism Minister, important to the economy but less fundamental in the long range "health of Mexico's public life and stability." When Rosario **Green** soon thereafter became the second woman in the cabinet as Latin America's first woman foreign minister, she graciously declared Green her senior.

CARACAS CONFERENCE, 1954. The 10th Inter-American Conference was where the resolution attracting most attention was the "Declaration of Solidarity for the Preservation of the Political Integrity of the Americas against International Communist Intervention," to which the Marxist government of Jacobo Arbenz in **Guatemala** replied with a "Declaration of Solidarity for the Preservation of Freedom in Guatemala." The first resolution passed with seventeen votes against one (Guatemala's), with two abstentions: **Argentina** (then ruled by Juan Perón) and Mexico (then under the administration of Adolfo **Ruíz Cortines**). The Mexican far left vigorously supported Arbenz but, knowing Ruiz would never consent to a vote against the Resolution, they were happy at the abstention. President Ruiz was then battling the legacy of **corruption** bequeathed by his predecessor, Miguel **Alemán**, who had tolerated companies securing government contracts through bribery in his eagerness to expand industrialization before his term ended in 1952. In his State of the Union address of September 1, 1954, Ruiz alluded to the condemnation of Arbenz, saying "Mexico supports struggles for freedom in all nations fighting tyranny. But we never support the false leaders claiming to be for freedom while they quietly spread a doctrine that enslaves." Later in his slim *Memoirs* he voiced his resentment of Arbenz having changed the name of the Guatemalan Communist Party to the Guatemalan Labor Party, calling the act "a disservice to genuine organized labor and a trick to deceive others at home and abroad."

CARBAJAL, FRANCISCO S. *See* CARVAJAL Y GRAAL, FRANCISCOS.

CARBAJAL RODRÍGUEZ, JESÚS ANTONIO (1929–). Called *La Tota*, this **soccer** player was a member of the Mexican **world soccer cup** teams of 1950, 1954, 1958, 1962, and 1966. His subsequent career as trainer and manager lasted until 1995.

CARBAJAL SEBASTIÁN, ENRIQUE (1947–). Painter and sculptor from **Chihuaha** known as "Sebastián." Although he did not begin to study art until 1965, he had by 1980 already earned considerable fame in Europe and the Americas.

CARBALLIDO, EMILIO (1925–). Playwright born in **Córdoba, Vera Cruz**, he studied drama at **UNAM**, at universities in the **United States**, and in 1950, as a Rockefeller Institute scholar, he studied and wrote in Europe and Asia. He became famous with *Rosalba* (published 1950) and the staging of *La danza* (1955). His many stage plays stress middle-class psychological problems. His 1958 play *Medusa* brought him international fame and awards.

CARBALLO, EMANUEL (1929–). Noted short story writer, famed for his 1965 collection, *El Cuento mexicano del siglo X*, born in **Guadalajara**. He was a doctoral student at the **Colegio de México** from 1955–1957 and co-founder with Carlos **Fuentes** of the *Revista mexicana de literatura*.

CÁRDENAS DEL RIO, DAMASO (1898–1976). Soldier-politician, elder brother of President Lázaro **Cárdenas**, and named for their father Damaso, owner of a small grocery store in Jiquilpan, **Michoacán**. After fighting in the **Revolution of 1910**, he left active duty with the rank of *General de División* (major general). He was interim governor of his home state in 1930 and one of its federal senators in 1932–1934. As such he helped his brother's presidential campaign in the southwestern states. After the election, he served as an unofficial advisor to the army's Chief of Staff on reserve matters. Although he declined the **Partido Revolucionario Institucional** nomination for governor of Michoacán in 1939, he was elected to the 1950–1956 term and remained active in the party through the 1960s. He died February 4.

CÁRDENAS DEL RIO, LÁZARO (1895–1970). President from 1934–1940, he was born in Jiquilplán, **Michoacán** and fought in the **Revolution of 1910**, rising to the rank of general. He rose steadily in politics, becoming governor of Michoacán, interior minister, and war and navy minister before becoming president. Although he had limited formal education, he was regarded as honest and enjoyed the respect of workers and peasants. Although **Calles** had handpicked him as his successor, he crushed Calles' power and exiled him. He emphasized **agrarian reform**, and his presidency saw some 16 million ha (40 million acres) expropriated and given to peasant **ejidos**. The opposition enjoyed freedom of speech, and Cárdenas' term was the last time Mexico enjoyed true press freedom until 1997. In 1935 he introduced the concept of a legal **minimum wage**. In 1936 he organized the **Confederación de Trabajadores de México** and the **Confederación Nacional de Campesinos**. The former received favored treatment in labor disputes with both foreign and domestic management. In 1937 he nationalized the **railroads**, and in 1938 he expropriated the **petroleum** industry, creating **PEMEX**, giving Mexico the basic fuel and transportation needed for its coming industrialization while laying the basis of the country's economic independence.

In his later years he became more and more an advocate of revolutionary change and was awarded the Stalin Peace Prize. He withdrew from the **Partido Revolucionario Institucional** in 1961 and urged greater social change. During the Bay of Pigs invasion, the Mexican government had to prevent him from going to **Cuba** to give

Fidel Castro his active support. In the 1960s he got the federal government to carry out public works projects in his home state. He stated publicly his belief that the continuing social reform called "The Revolution" depended on public-private mixed enterprise to bolster the economy. He was the driving force behind the **Siderúrgica Lázaro Cárdenas Las Truchas** steel complex.

Although controversial, he is regarded as one of Mexico's greatest post-revolutionary presidents, and is commemorated in the Avenida Lázaro Cardenas, a north-south thoroughfare in downtown **Mexico City**.

CÁRDENAS SOLORZANO, CUAUTÉMOC (1934–). Born May 1, in the **Federal District**, the son of President Lázaro **Cardenas**, he graduated in civil engineering from **UNAM**, 1957 and did graduate research at the French Ministry of Reconstruction in Paris from 1957–1958. With a **Banco de México** fellowship, he worked for the Krupp Corporation in Germany in 1958. Elected a senator from **Michoacán** in 1976, he held various high posts in the **Partido Revolucionario Institucional** from 1977–1979 and served as governor of Michoacán from 1980–1986. He then ran in the 1988 presidential campaign as the candidate of the **Frente Democrático Nacional**—a campaign that caused longtime supporters of his father, and other longtime PRI activitists, to denounce him as a deserter from "the Revolutionary coalition" (i.e., the PRI). He lost the **election of 1988** by only two percent and decided to consolidate his election alliance into a more integrated party, the **Partido de la Revolución Democrática** (without mentioning that one of its components was based largely on the **Partido Comunista Mexicana**): he was PRD president in 1988–1993. Although he said he might run for president again if invited by the PRD, he chose in 1994 to run instead to become the first popularly-elected governor of the **Federal District** (i.e., Mayor of **Mexico City**). His inaugural address promised to reduce crime, but by 1999 the crime in most parts of the city had increased. He ran for president in 2000 as the PRD candidate, but he was thwarted by disunity in the PRD and the death of Heberto **Castillo Martínez**, who might have been able to unify it.

CARGADOR. *See* PORTERS.

CARLOS. For Spanish kings of this name, *see* CHARLES.

CARLOTA, EMPRESS (1840–1927). Spanish name of the Belgian princess Charlotte, an empress consort of **Maximilian**. She returned to Europe in a desperate bid for help to save her husband's regime and his life. She became permanently insane when this failed. [L. H.]

CARNIVAL (*carnaval*). Annual pre-Lenten celebrations, culminating in the dances, parades, and parties of *Mardi Gras* (Shrove Tuesday). In **Mazatlán, Acapulco**, and **Veracruz**—ports catering to tourists— resort activities prevail, but in **Mexico City** and major provincial cities, the celebrations center in private clubs. In small-town and rural Mexico, village carnivals are most intense in Indian communities, where fireworks and folkdancers in bright costumes vie with special theatrical presentations and band concerts.

CARRANZA, VENUSTIANO (1859–1920). Born in **Coahuila**, during the **Revolution of 1910** he supported **Madero**. When Madero's presumed assassin, Victoriano **Huerta**, was taken into **United States** custody, Carranza established a successor administration in **Veracruz**. Meanwhile his rivals Pancho **Villa** and Emilio **Zapata** established a brief period of joint rule in **Mexico City**. In 1915, however, Álvaro **Obregón**'s victory at **Celaya** gave Carranza effective control of the whole country. In his relations with the United States, he steered a middle course, allowing the **Pershing** expedition to enter Mexico, but remaining neutral during **World War I**. A convention summoned by Carranza resulted in the **Constitution of 1917**. As the only revolutionary leader with experience in lawmaking, diplomacy, and administration, he has been called the "legalizer" of the Revolution. From 1917 to 1920 his hold on the presidency was stronger, and he made plans to be reelected, his idea being to govern through the obscure Ignacio Bonillas as his front man for the next presidential term and then to succeed him. When Obregón and Plutarco Elías **Calles** rose up in arms to prevent this, Carranza fled Mexico City, hoping to reach Veracruz and go into exile. He was ambushed on his way and murdered in May 1920. He is commemorated in the central **delegación** of the **Federal District**, "Venustiano Carranza."

CARRERA SABAT, [GENERAL] MARTÍN (1804?–1871). Acting president of Mexico from August–September, 1855.

CARRILLO DE MENDOZA Y PIMENTEL, DIEGO, CONDE DE PRIEGO (1559–1624). **Viceroy** of **New Spain** from 1621–1624, also known as Diego Pimentel y Enríquez de Guzmán. An attempt to reduce what he considered the excessive powers of the archbishop, Juan **Pérez de la Serna**, was countered by excommunication. When he responded by imprisoning the prelate, popular protests were so strong that he had to return to **Spain** in disgrace.

CARRILLO FLORES, ANTONIO (1909–1986). Banker-politician born June 23 in **Mexico City**, the son of Juliàn **Carrillo**. He graduated in **law** from **UNAM**, where he taught from 1936–1952, serving as dean of the law school from 1944–1945. In 1946 he founded the **Comisión Nacional Bancaria y de Valores**. He authored major banking legislation from the 1940s to the 1970s as well as several books on banking law. He was also a top advisor to the **Banco de México** for many years. In 1945–1952, and again in 1977–1979, he was director general of **Nacional Financiera**. As finance minister from 1952–1958 and foreign minister from 1964–1970, he formulated key financial and foreign policies. In 1971–1972 he served as president of the **Instituto Politécnico Nacional**. In 1979 he was elected to the **Cámara de Diputados Federales**. Nabor **Carrillo Flores** is his brother.

CARRILLO FLORES, NABOR (1911–1980). Born February 23 in **México City**, the brother of Antonio **Carrillo Flores**, he graduated from **UNAM** in engineering and in 1942 received a PhD from Harvard. He served as president of UNAM, 1952–1961. Mexico's leading authority on nuclear energy and an active member of the **Consejo Nacional de Ciencia y Tecnología**, he was Mexico's liaison researcher with the U.S. Atomic Energy Commission and its successor, the Nuclear Regulatory Commission. He was a member of the National Commission of **Nuclear Energy** in Mexico from its creation and in 1966 became director of the Mexican Atomic Energy Center.

CARRILLO MARCOR, ALEJANDRO (1908–1988). Born March 15 in **Hermosillo**, he studied at Tulane University and graduated in law from **UNAM**, where he was a professor from 1933–1935. In the 1940s he became dean of the **Colegio Nacional de Guerra** and vice-president of the **Universidad de Trabajadores**. He sat in the **Cámera de Diputados Federales** in 1940–1942 and 1964–1967, in the Federal **Senate** for his native **Sonora** from 1970–1974, and served as ambassador to Saudi Arabia. He directed all publicity for Miguel **Alemán**'s presidential campaign in 1946 and was the publisher of the daily *El Popular* in 1943. A national leader of the **Partido Revolucionario Institucional**, he was the publisher of the government's *El Nacional*, from 1968–1975. He was then governor of **Sonora** from 1975–1979, replacing the discredited Carlos **Biebrich**, untangling the mismanaged state government and returning it to solvency. He was a key formulator of policies that reduced **narcotics** traffic into the **United States**.

CARRILLO OLEA, JORGE (1937–). Army officer born November 19 in Jotula, **Morales**, he was a graduate of the **Heróica Escuela Militar** who got a degree in military administration at the **Escuela Superior de Guerra** from 1962–1965. He then graduated from the armored car course at Fort Knox, Kentucky, from 1967–1968. In 1975–1976 he was undersecretary of tax investigation in the **Finance Ministry**—the only army officer holding such a position outside the Defense Ministry—and Director of National Security at the **Interior Ministry** from 1988–1990. As a colonel in charge of internal security rescue troops, he saved President **Echeverría** when he was attacked at a **UNAM** demonstration in 1975.

CARRILLO PRIETO, IGNACIO (1947–). President Vicente **Fox Quezada** named Carrillo as special prosecutor in January 2002 to fulfill a campaign promise to go after the highest-ranking perpetrators of misdeeds during the 71-year rule of the **Partido Revolucionario Institucional**. [He seems to have been particularly concerned about President Luis **Echeverrá Álvarez**' possible involvement in the **Corpus Christi massacre**. Since the statute of limitations now rules out any murder charge, Carrillo even tried an indictment for genocide of students as a societal group: it failed. L. H.]

CARRILLO TRUJILLO, JULIÁN (1875–1965). Distinguished composer and the father of Antonio and Nabor **Carrillo Flores**, he studied in Mexico City, Leipzig, and Ghent. Later he directed the **Conservatorio Nacional de Música de México**. His compositions include the operas *Matilda*, *Ossian*, and *Zulith*.

CARTOGRAPHY. *See* MAPS AND ATLASES.

CARVAJAL MORENO, GUSTAVO (1948–). **Jalapa**-born politician who studied law at **UNAM** under future President **López Portillo**, the sponsor of his career. A consulting economist for leading industries and government agencies in 1970–1976, he was executive secretary for López during his 1976 presidential campaign. He became assistant labor minister from 1976–1978, head of the **Instituto de Seguridad y Servicios Sociales de los Trabajadores del Estado** in 1978, and secretary general of the **Partido Revolucionario Institucional**. In February 1979 López secured his appointment as president of the PRI to ensure his policies had the party's full support.

CARVAJAL Y DE LA CUEVA, LUIS DE (1539–c.1600). Conquistador and first governor of **Nuevo León** (from 1582), in 1596 he founded **Monterrey**. A **converso**, he was condemned by the **Inquisition** for apostasy and executed.

CARVAJAL Y GRAAL, FRANCISCO S. (1870–1932). Foreign minister, and, as such, acting **president** of Mexico following Victoriano **Huerta**'s resignation, July 15–August 13, 1914.

CASA DE ESPAÑA ("Spain House"). Forerunner of the **Colegio de México**, created to welcome the many Spanish academics and intellectuals exiled by the **Spanish Civil War**. It was a graduate teaching and research center, directed by Alfonso **Reyes**.

CASA DE LA MONEDA ("mint"). *See* MONEDA, LA.

CASA DEL PUEBLO ("house of the people"). This highly effective rural school concept was developed by José **Vasconcelos** as **education** minister. It taught not only the basics (reading, writing, and arithmetic) to all age groups, but also subjects as varied as **music**, the fine arts, and sanitation.

CASA MATA, PLAN DE. Pronunciamiento that led to **Iturbide**'s abdication. Issued in February 1823 by Antonio López de **Santa Anna** and Guadalupe **Victoria**, it called for the end of the **First Empire**, a new **congress**, and a new constitution with a federal form of government. Although it did not specifically call for Iturbide's dismissal, he left office 10 months later.

CASAS, BARTOLOMÉ DE LAS (1474–1566). One of the most famous religious leaders of the New World, he was a wealthy **encomendero** who took up the cause of the **Indians** after observing their extreme suffering, becoming a Dominican priest and their outstanding defender. His *Brevísima relación de la destrucción de las Indias* formed the basis of England's **Black Legend** of Spanish misrule. His relatively short stay in Mexico included the years 1544–1547 as Bishop of **Chiapas**.

CASAS ALEMÁN, FERNANDO (1905–1968). Politician and diplomat, born July 8 in Córdoba, a law graduate from **UNAM** and a leader in the **Partido Revolucionario Institucional**. He was a governor of his native **Veracruz**, then one of its senators, and a key formulator of policy for the **Federal Conciliation and Arbitration Board** in the 1930s. He served as ambassador successively to Greece, Italy, and China. In 1946–1952 he was governor of the **Federal District**. He died in **Mexico City** on October 30.

CASO, ALFONSO (1896–1970). Archaeologist and a **UNAM** graduate, he became a professor of philosophy and anthropology at the University of Chicago, then dean of graduate studies at UNAM. He gained fame as director of the excavations of **Zapotec** culture at **Monte Albán** in **Oaxaca** in 1931–1943. After directing the **Museo Nacional de Antropología**, he became rector of UNAM. In 1946–1949 he was Minister of **Natural Resources** and then headed the **Instituto Indígena Nacional** until his death in November 1970.

CASTAÑEDA, FELIPE (1933–). Sculptor, born in La Palma, **Jalisco state**, who has held one-man exhibits in the United States and Mexico. One of his most famous works is his *Mujer de Manto,* a sculptured figure of polished bronze.

CASTAÑEDA Y ÁLVAREZ DE LA ROSA, JORGE (1921–1997). Diplomat who entered the foreign service with a **law** degree from **UNAM** and at age 30 became ambassador to Saudi Arabia. During the 1960s he represented Mexico at numerous **United Nations, Organization of American States**, and other international meetings, becoming Mexico's chief spokesman on **maritime sovereignty**. After serving as Mexico's chief diplomat at Geneva with the World Health Organization and **International Labour Organisation**, he became assistant foreign minister, and, in May 1977, foreign minister. From 1979 he taught diplomacy at the **Colegio de México** and was also author of some of Mexico's leading textbooks on international relations.

CASTE WAR OF YUCATÁN. This Indian revolt broke out on June 30, 1847, lasting off and on for many years, constituting a serious threat to white control of the peninsula.

CASTELLANOS, ROSARIO (1925–1974). Poet, born in **Mexico City** but brought up in **Chiapas**, died in Israel while serving as Mexican ambassador. She also wrote fiction (*Balún Canán*, 1957) and drama (*El eterno femenino*, 1975).

[Mexico's largest bookstore, opened by President Fox in the *Centro Cultural Bella Época* in the capital's Condesa distict, April 26, 2006, is named after her. L. H.]

CASTELLANOS COUTIÑO, HORACIO (1929 –????). Leading author of constitutional and administrative law, born in **Chiapas**, he was **procurador de justicia** (attorney general) of the **Federal District** before becoming a senator from 1976–1982.

CASTILLIAN (*castellano*). Purist term for the Spanish language, from its origin as the central Iberian dialect of Castile. Its use in much of South America as the nationalists' preferred alternative to *Español* (Spanish) is generally rejected in Mexico as too precious. [L. H.]

CASTILLO LEÓN, AMALIA (1902–1987). Diplomat, born August 18 in **Tamaulipas**, she trained as a teacher, became a professor at teachers' colleges in **Ciudad Victoria** and then in **Mexico City**, and then was a pioneer **woman** leader in the **Partido Revolucionario Institucional** and the first woman on its **comité ejecutivo nacional**. A national leader in child welfare, she became an envoy to the **United Nations**, then ambassador to Sweden and Finland in 1956 and to Austria in 1967. As assistant **education** minister in 1958–1964 she was the first woman in the Mexican cabinet. After being president of the Inter-American Commission of Women, she was ambassador to the International Atomic Energy Organization in 1964–1970.

CASTILLO MARTÍNEZ, HERBERTO (1929–1997). Politician, born in August in **Vera Cruz**, he graduated in civil engineering from **UNAM** and received an honorary doctorate from the Universidad Central de Venezuela. In 1972 he helped found the Mexican Worker's Group of dissidents from the **Partido Comunista Mexicano** and the National Committee for Opinion Polling and Coordination. In September 1974 he helped expand the P.C.M. into the **Partido de los Trabajadores Mexicanos**, later merged into the **Partido de la Revolución Democrática**. An ally of Cuauhtémoc **Cárdenas**, he was expected to be able to unify the PRD around Cárdenas in the election of 2000, but his premature death precluded this.

CASTRO FIGUEROA Y SALAZAR, PEDRO DE. DUQUE DE LA CON-QUISTA, MARQUÉS DE LA GRACIA REAL (168?– 1741). **Viceroy of New Spain** from 1740–1741, born in San Julián de Cela in Corunna province. He left for Mexico in 1739 but was captured by Dutch **pirates** and eventually arrived without proof of his appointment. Only a year later did the **Audiencia** yield to the pleas of the acting viceroy, Archbishop Juan Antonio de **Vizarrón y Eguiarreta**, and let him take up his office. Months later he initiated a strengthening of the defenses of **Veracruz**, but contracted a fatal attack there of dysentery (or of **yellow fever**?) and the Audiencia took over the administration. [L. H.]

CASTRO LEAL, ANTONIO (1896–1976?). Politician and diplomat with a law doctorate from **UNAM**, he served briefly as its president and was then a diplomat in **Chile, Cuba, France, Spain**, and the **United States**, and ambassador to UNESCO before achieving fame as director general of the federal department of fine arts in 1934. In the 1940s he directed movie filming for the government. He helped secure the Palacio de **Bellas Artes** as a national home of symphonies and opera.

CATHEDRAL OF MEXICO CITY. The Western Hemisphere's largest cathedral, built 1573–1791, and measuring 118 m (387 ft.) by 88 m (288 ft.) and standing 55 m (179 ft.) high. In the plateresque style, it is dedicated to Saint **Mary of Guadalupe**.

CATHERWOOD, FREDERICK (1799–1854). English artist who accompanied the explorer John Lloyd **Stephens** to Mayan archaeological sites. His detailed drawings of the ruins, particularly of **Chichén Itzá**, gave many Europeans and North Americans their first acquaintance with the ancient **Maya**.

CATTLE. *See* LIVESTOCK.

CAUDILLO. Spanish term, possibly of Arabic origin (although a diminutive of Latin *caput,* "head," is just as likely), for an autocratic leader, particularly a military usurper, such as Spain's Francisco Franco (*"por la gracia de Dios, caudillo de España"*), usually one ruling over a territory much more extensive than the comparatively humble and puny **cacique**. José Antonio López de **Santa Anna** is the supreme Mexican instance. *See also* PERSONALISM.

CEBALLOS, JUAN BAUTISTA (1811–1857). Acting **president** of Mexico in early 1853, after a distinguished career as a lawyer and a justice of the **Supreme Court**, the increasing opposition to his efforts to bring stability to the country forced him to resign after one month. He was later exiled by López de **Santa Anna** and died in Paris.

CEBRIÁN Y AGUSTÍN, PEDRO, CONDE DE FUENCLARA (1687–1752). Born in Saragossa, he had a diplomatic career before being appointed **viceroy of New Spain** in 1742. He encouraged cultural life and rebuilt part of the **Chapultepec** aqueduct. On leaving office in 1746 he began a *Historia anigua de México*, whose publication was frustrated by his death.

CEDILLO, MARÍA MARCOS (1900–1933). Mexico's first woman aviator. The niece of General Saturnino **Cedillo**, she took off from the family ranch in **San Luis Potosí** in 1920 and flew a **World War I** biplane around the state, and then flew from **San Luis Potosí city** to **Aguascalientes city**. While refueling, she decided to avoid a return trip by night, but the lack of telephones in the rural Mexico of the 1920s meant her family, worried about the delay, had the state police investigate a possible crash. She was eventually killed in a plane crash 13 years later.

CEDILLO, SATURNINO (1890–1939). Last **caudillo** seriously to challenge the authority of the central government. Born on his father's ranch in **San Luis Potosí**, he supported **Madero**, rose to be a wealthy landowner and conservative politician, and was briefly **agriculture** minister in the government of President **Ortiz Rubio**. When his private army was finally defeated by troops of President Lázaro **Cárdenas**, he fled into the mountains but was killed early in 1939.

CÉDULA. (1) Royal decree.
(2) Voting card. Since 1997, this has carried the voter's front-face photograph and signature, inhibiting ringers voting under the names of known non-voters (or voting the cemetery).

CELAYA (Basque *Zalaya*, "flat ground"). This **municipio** of 523 km^2 to the west of Querétaro in **Guanajuato** state had 310,569 inhabitants in 1990 and 382,958 in 2000. Its namesake **cabecera**, "golden gate to the **Bajío**," founded in 1571, at 20°31'N, 100°49'W, was the first city captured by **Hidalgo y Costilla**. Its population was 214,856 in 1990 and 304,400 in 2006.

CELAYA, BATTLES OF. (1) **Hidalgo y Costilla**'s first victory, September 20, 1810.
(2) A pair of decisive battles of the **Revolution of 1910**, fought in April 1915 between the forces of **Obregón**, who supported **Carranza**, and those of Pancho **Villa**. Obregón lost an arm, but Villa was defeated and fled northward leaving Carranza in control of Mexico.

CEMENT INDUSTRY. This industry in Mexico is dominated by CEMEX, a firm founded in 1906 which is now an international conglomerate trading in 32 countries. In Mexico it owns 15 cement manufacturing plants and 22 quarries. Its Construrama building material outlets, founded in 2001, has 2,100 stores (including 750 franchises) in 750 cities.

CENCETTI, ADALBERTO A. (c.1850–c.1910). Italian sculptor, responsible for the huge statute of Benito **Juárez** on the outskirts of **Oaxaca**.

CENSORSHIP. Colonial censorship was threefold: by the local bishop, to guard public morals; by the **Inquisition**, against heresy; and by the Crown, to prevent sedition. In the early nineteenth century, the **Cortes of Cádiz** declared the abolition of political censorship throughout Spain and its empire, but it did not dare challenge the ecclesiastical censorship. Almost immediately after **Independence**, **Iturbide** started suppressing opposition **newspapers**. A few years later President **Bustamante** was doing the same.

The **Constitution of 1857** specifically guaranteed press freedom, but this carried little weight during the **Porfiriato** when recalcitrant newspapers were closed down and their editors imprisoned, exiled (the fate of Ricardo **Flores Magón**), or, if too persistent, killed. A decline in vigilance as the dictator entered his ninth decade clearly signaled the approaching end of the regime. **Madero** permitted a free press, which responded by attacking him viciously. Victoriano **Huerta** introduced a systematic censorship.

The **Constitution of 1917** also guaranteed freedom of the press. Since then governments have generally avoided censorship but (except for the broad toleration of the Lázaro **Cárdenas del Rio** presidency) have pressured the media by providing token import taxes on imported newsprint, bribery, and indirect subsidies. They have similarly kept broadcasting stations loyal by supplying equipment at bargain prices and providing lucrative public service advertising. Mexico really had "bandwagon" journalism, whereby the major **media** were free to make some political criticism, but basically the **Partido Revolucionario Institucional** and the federal government were beneficiaries of gentle treatment.

When its agitation against the Mexico **Olympics** made the Communist *Política* intolerable, it was suppressed not by censorship but by a government embargo on its paper supply.

President **Echeverría's** 1976 takeover of **Excélsior** was a rare example of naked power being used when the usual covert pressure did not suffice. This was uglier than the routine censorship found in many smaller Latin American countries at the time. Mexican **radio** and **television** stations are free to give impartial news coverage to all candidates for public office but at the level of the presidential race, the candidate of the dominant party, the PRI, receives special favorable coverage.

By 1998, press freedom reflected a healthy give-and-take in some editorial pages. Since then top cabinet ministers, and even the president himself, have been targets of blunt and occasionally angry criticism. This has been less evident in **television**, although **Azteca T.V.** has been able to challenge some of the pro-establishment coverage of the dominant **Televisa**. A "Freedom of Information" act was passed in 2002.

[Press freedom in the provinces is still likely to be restricted by violence—Mexico had 10 of the 155 journalists murdered throughout the world in 2006, more than in any other single country except Iraq (*See* GARCIA, ROBERTO MARCOS; GONZALEZ LUGO, HUGO P.; *NOTICIAS*; *ZETA*). As in England, the libel law is still effective in muting criticism of the wealthy or influential, particularly when accused of **corruption** (*See* WORNAT, OLGA). L. H.].

CENSUSES. Early censuses were held in the 1770s, 1831, 1873, and 1895. Since then they have been held in the 10th (the "zero") year of each decade, except when the chaos following the **Revolution of 1910** delayed the next **census** until 1921. For national census totals, see **Population**; for those of individual states, see the state. These are supplemented by estimates for other years, except where they seemed exaggerated (e.g., 5.5 million for **Nuevo León** and 5.4 million for **Oaxaca**, both for 1995).

The census records speakers of indigenous languages but ignores all other ethnic categorization in the supposed interest of not encouraging racism. In actuality it allowed the existence of **blacks** in Mexico and the strong prejudice against them to be officially ignored. [L. H.]

CENTENARY OF INDEPENDENCE. Millions of pesos were spent making Mexico City a showcase for the September 15, 1910, **centenary of Independence** and Porfirio **Diaz**'s 80th birthday, culminating in an elaborate dinner and formal dance held in the great ballroom of **Chapultepec** Castle, with American, French, German, and other foreign diplomats, bankers, and investors almost outnumbering their euphoric Mexican counterparts. As many of the latter took the podium in turn to praise "Mexico's greatest leader since independence," **United States** ambassador Henry Lane **Wilson** cabled President Taft that Mexico had found longlasting stability. Two months later, Mexico exploded in the **Revolution of 1910**.

CENTRAL AMERICA, REPUBLIC OF. Federal state formed from the colonial Captaincy General of **Guatemala**, when it broke away from Mexico in 1822. The Republic was Mexico's southern neighbor until it split into its constituent states 10 years later, the part bordering Mexico becoming the Republic of Guatemala. [L. H.]

CENTRO DE ARBITRAJE DE MÉXICO. Non-governmental tribunal for commercial arbitration. [L. H.]

CENTRO DE ESTUDIOS DE HISTORIA DE MÉXICO. Study center on Mexican history based on the books and documents collected by historian Luis Gutiérrez Cañedo and acquired in 1964 by Condumex, manufacturer of wires and cables for the communication industry. [L. H.]

CENTRO DE ESTUDIOS SUPERIORES NAVALES. The Center for Higher Naval Studies is the **navy**'s equivalent of the **army**'s **Escuela Superior de Guerra**.

CENTRO DE INVESTIGACIÓN Y SEGURIDAD NACIONAL (CISEN). Mexican equivalent of the C.I.A. that replaced since 1989 the *Dirección de Inteligencia y Seguridad Nacional* (DISEN) which had in turn replaced in 1986 the *Dirección Federal de Seguridad Nacional* (DFSN) which had been formed in 1952. All these were subordinate to the **Interior Ministry** until the 2001 creation of the

Public Security Ministry, which involved transferring 800 CISEN staff to the *Policia Federal Preventativa*—PFP. [L. H.]

CENTRO DE PLANIFICACIÓN FAMILIAR. Government-run **Family Planning** Center. The original CPF was open six days a week, and by 1979 6,000 CPFs throughout Mexico were dispensing free contraceptive pills and birth control literature. Until the mid-1980s the centers lacked a budget for evening or Sunday open hours, and at first only 26 percent of women of child-bearing age (and fewer than ten percent of their partners) were using the centers. By the 1990s the ratio improved to one woman in three (and, among the upper and upper-middle classes, slightly more). In 1998 there were over 11,000 CPFs, and the agency was using advertising campaigns, **radio** soap operas and talk shows, **television** programs, comic books, pamphlets, and neighborhood meetings to popularize contraception and "responsible parenthood."

CERDA SANDOVAL SILVA Y MENDOZA, GASPAR DE LA, CONDE DE GALVE (1653–1697). Viceroy of **New Spain** from 1688–1697 who had to expel a French invasion of Venezuela the moment he arrived, securing victory at El Guárico in 1688. He sent expeditions into **Texas** and **New Mexico** and to explore the coast of Florida where he founded **Pensacola** and had success at pacification of **Indians** without punitive methods, but several years of drought and consequent famine produced attacks on retailers and on the viceregal palace. This forced Gaspar de la Cerda to take refuge in the San Francisco convent. With his palace in ruins, he abdicated and returned to **Spain**. [L. H.]

CERDA Y ARAGÓN, TOMÁS ANTONIO MANRIQUE DE LA, MARQUÉS DE LA LAGUNA DE CAMERO VIEJO AND CONDE DE PREDES DE HAVA (1638–1692). Viceroy of New Spain from 1680–1688, the son of the Marquis of Medinaceli. His support of advances into **California**, **Arizona**, and **New Mexico**, the suppression of Indian revolts there, and the formal establishment of **Santa Fé** earned him the title of *el Conquistador*.

CERRO GORDO, BATTLE OF. A decisive US victory in the **United States-Mexican War**. On April 18, 1847, the forces of Winfield

Scott overcame the fortified position of Cerro Gordo, 80 km northwest of **Veracruz**, and could advance unhindered to **Puebla**, 137 km from **Mexico City**. The **United States** Army Corps of Engineers distinguished itself in the battle.

CERVANTES, VICENTE (1755–1829). Spanish botanist who introduced new horticultural methods into **New Spain** and was founder and first director of Mexico's first **Botanical Gardens** until his death.

CERVANTES AGUIRRE, ENRIQUE (1935–). Army officer born in **Puebla**, top of his class at the **Escuela Superior de Guerra**, he graduated from the army's command and staff school, and consistently remained the top-rated among his peers as he advanced from lieutenant to colonel. In 1976, after becoming proficient in English, he served as military attaché in embassy in Washington DC. President **Echeverría** decorated him the same year with the medal of national merit for directing the campaign that uprooted **narcotics** cultivation in **Guerrero**. A brigadier general in 1980, *general de división* in 1983, he then became administrative secretary to the defense minister and then director of the **Heróica Escuela Militar**. In 1983–1984 he was director general of **Defense Ministry** weapons factories.

CERVANTES DEL RÍO, HUGO (1927–1989). Born July 4 in **Mexico City**, this administrator graduated from **UNAM**, where he taught **law** part-time for fifteen years. He became first a youth leader and then legal advisor to the **Partido Revolucionario Institucional**, an administrator in the **navy** ministry from 1952–1956, director general of federal **highways** from 1959–1965, governor of **Baja California del Sur** from 1964–1970, minister of the presidency from 1970–1976, and director general of the **Comisión Federal de Electricidad** from 1976–1980.

CERVANTES HERNÁNDEZ, MARÍA (1925–1989). Engineer born in **Tamualipas**. Her degree from the Institute of Technology in Santiago de Chile made her the first qualified woman civil engineer in Mexico. She also studied at **UNAM**, attended summer sessions of M.I.T., and obtained a certificate in women's studies at the University of Wisconsin in 1983. In 1971 she was a cofounder of *Acción Política*

Feminista and was an engineering consultant on the **Mexico City-Puebla** highway improvement project. She died in Mexico City.

CERVERA PACHECO, VICTOR (1936–). Born April 23, in **Mérida**, this politician never graduated from university, but he became mayor of Mérida in 1971–1973, was active in the **Confederación Nacional Campesina** from 1980–1983, and Minister of **Agrarian Reform** from 1980–1983.

CHALCO. Shantytown 40 km south east of the center of **Mexico City** is regarded as part of Greater Mexico City.

CHAMBER OF DEPUTIES. *See* CÁMARA DE DIPUTADOS FEDERALES.

CHAMIZAL. This 600-acre area between **Ciudad Juárez** and **El Paso**, Texas, was in dispute with the **United States** since a change in the course of the **Rio Grande** in the late-1800s had left it on the US side of the border. The Kennedy administration agreed to return the land to Mexico and compensate El Paso residents for any real estate losses. In September 1964 Presidents Johnson and **López Mateos** met on the spot to finalize the agreement.

CHAMPOTÓN. Campeche river and the **muncipio** at its mouth with 70,554 inhabitants in 2000 on 6,088 km^2. Its capital, at 19°35'N, 90°72'W, was originally founded by the Itza **Maya** while in exile from **Chichen-Itza**, 700–980. When the **Mazapán Confederation** was dissolved in 1194, it became the capital of the **cacicazgo** de *Chakan-Putun* ("region of the savanah"), and in 1517 it was the scene of a Maya victory over Spaniards led by Francisco **Hernández de Córdoba**.

CHAPALA. Mexico's largest freshwater **fishing** lake lies partly in **Jalisco** and partly in **Michoacán**. The largest river flowing into the lake is the **Lerma**, and its principal outlet is the **Grande de Santiago**.

CHAPINGO. Site in Texcoco **municipio, Mexico** state, of the **Universidad Autónoma Chipango**.

CHAPPE D'AUTEROCHE, ABBÉ. Frenchman who came to **Alta California** in the 1770s to observe a transit of Venus.

CHAPULTEPEC. This site in central Mexico was the first capital of the **Aztec** invaders. They were driven from it in 1319.

CHAPULTEPEC, ACT OF. Measure adopted at the **Chapultepec Conference** that declared that all sovereign states in the Western Hemisphere were of equal legal status and that an attack on any one would be considered an attack on all, thereby creating a defensive military alliance of its signatories.

CHAPULTEPEC, BATTLE OF. Last great battle of the **United States-Mexican War**, September 12–13, 1847. The opposing forces were about equal in number, but after an intense artillery barrage and attacks from three directions the US forces managed to take the sixty m high Chapultepec Hill, the last obstacle before **Mexico City**. The strongest resistance came from the far outnumbered San Blas Battalion led by Santiago Felipe **Xicotencatle**, whose martyrs are commemorated as the **Niños Héroes**.

CHAPULTEPEC AQUEDUCT. This colonial **water** supply, stretched over what is now Chapultepec Avenue and ended in a *plaza* known as the *Salto de Agua* ("waterfall"). A few arches were left as a historic monument after its demolition,

CHAPULTEPEC CASTLE. Fortress on a hill in the largest park in **Mexico City**. From 1862–6 and 1876–1934, it was the official residence of Mexico's chief executive, first the Emperor **Maximilian** and then every president beginning with Porfirio **Díaz** until Lázaro **Cárdenas** moved out to the less ostentatious Los **Pinos**. Since November 1940 it has housed the *Museo de Historia*. [L. H.]

CHAPULTEPEC CONFERENCE. The Inter-American Conference on Problems of War and Peace was held in **Chapultepec Castle** in February–March 1945. It was attended by all American republics except **Argentina** to discuss hemispheric security, which led to the Act of **Chapultepec**, the ensuing **United Nations** conference at San Francisco, and an Economic Charter of the Americas.

CHAPULTEPEC PARK. Mexico City's largest public park, containing **Chapultepec Castle** (housing the **Museo Nacional de Historia**), the nearby monument to the **Niños Héroes**, the **Museo Nacional de Antropología**, and adjoining Los **Pinos** (the executive mansion).

CHARLES II (1661–1700). Called "The Bewitched," he was the last Habsburg King of Spain (from 1665, as Carlos II). His death without issue caused the War of the **Spanish Succession**.

CHARLES III (1716–1788). King of Spain (as Carlos III) from 1758–1788. The more important of the **Bourbon reforms** date from his reign. His archaeological interests, first in evidence at Pompeii when he was King Carlo VII of the Two Sicilies, led to his appointing Juan Bautista Muñoz (1745–1799) as historiographer of the Indies and to giving official encouragement to excavations at **Palenque**. [L. H.]

CHARLES IV (1748–1819). King of Spain (as Carlos IV) from 1788–1808. Feeble, physically and intellectually, dominated by his taller wife, Queen María Luisa, cuckolded by his chief minister, Manuel de **Godoy**, and eventually guilty of signing away his throne at **Napoleon**'s demand (March 1808), he is commemorated in **Mexico City** by a most misleading equestrian statue (known as *El Caballito*) of a vigorous military leader. The **viceroy**, who commissioned the statue, suppressed all criticism of the court, threatening with execution anyone who dared gossip about the royal *ménage à trois*. [L. H.]

CHARLES V (1500–1558). Holy Roman **Emperor** and (as Carlos I) King of Spain at the time of the **Conquest of Mexico** (technically as regent for his deranged mother, **Joan** the Mad).

CHARLOTTE, PRINCESS, OF BELGIUM. Future Empress **Carlota**.

CHARRO. Mexican cowboy or rancher, to be distinguished from a *vaquero*, or working rancher. The *charro,* on a silver-adorned saddle, engages in rodeo competitions—from fancy riding to rope tricks. His costume consists of tight riding trousers covering short boots, adorned with silver thread and buttons, a short embroidered jacket similarly decorated, a decorated, wide leather belt and pistol holster, and a silk tie in a flowing bow. The famed *sombrero* (wide brimmed hat) from **Jalisco**, embroidered with gold or silver, has become a folklore symbol for Mexico and is worn by **mariachi** folk musicians.

CHÁVEZ, CARLOS (1899–1978). This outstanding and internationally renowned composer (of operas, ballets, and symphonies) and conductor, succeeded in identifying Mexican **music** with the sociocultural ideas of the **Revolution of 1910**. In 1921 he wrote the ballet *The New Fire* and in 1928 organized the **Orquesta Sinfónica Nacional**. He was a frequent guest conductor in the **United States** and authored *Toward the New Music*.

CHÁVEZ CASTAÑEDA, RICARDO (1961–). Mexican writer of both children's books—*Miedo, el mundo a lado*, 1993; *La niña que tenía el mar adentro*, 2001; *El beso más largo del mundo*, 2004—and adult novels—from *Los ensebados* in 1992 to *El fin de la pornografía* in 2005. His *Generación fría* (1992) is a dictionary of contemporary authors. [L. H.]

CHÁVEZ MORADO, JOSÉ (1909–2002). Painter from **Guanajuato** who worked on Mexican **railroads** before migrating as a laborer to **California** and **Canada**, where he met José Clemente **Orozco** at Pomona College. In 1974 he won the *Premio Nacional de Artes*.

CHÁVEZ OROZCO, LUIS (1901–1966). Born in **Guanajuato** in April, a longtime director of libraries for the **education ministry**, he served as assistant education minister, director of Indian affairs, and head of the *Sindicato Nacional de Trbajadores de la Educación* (the national teachers' union). He was also a prolific writer of essays, articles, and books on Mexican public life, among them the school textbook *Historia de México*

CHAZARO LARA, RICARDO (1920–1993). Born in **Veracruz**, he graduated from the **Escuela Naval Militar**, entered the **navy** in 1942, and rose to vice admiral. In 1976–1982 he was naval minister.

CHETUMAL. The capital since 1915 of **Quintana Roo**, it lies on the mouth of the **Hondo** at 18°30'N, 88°20'W, with a city population of

5,000 in 1950; 48,000 in 1978; and 81,000 in 1995. The **municipio** had 242,423 inhabitants in 1997. Established in 1898 as the port of Payo Obispo, it was renamed in 1936 after Chactemal on the other bank of the river (in what is now **Belize**), capital of the ancient Mayan state of the same name. It was leveled by two hurricanes in the 1940s and by another in 1955. [L. H.]

CHEWING GUM. *See* CHICLE.

CHIAPANECAS. One of Mexico's most popular folk dances spread throughout the country from **Chiapas**. Its rhythmic hand-clapping depends on a two-beat cadence to each measure for three measures, followed by a pause and two loud handclaps. It is played and performed for birthdays, weddings, reunions, or almost any happy celebration or party.

CHIAPAS. The southernmost state of Mexico, borders **Guatemala** (of which it was a province until 1823) and the Pacific Ocean to its east and south and the states of **Tabasco**, **Veracruz**, and **Oaxaca** to its north and west. Its area covers 73,887 km^2 of tropical rainforest, a coastal plain and highlands. Its population was 315,000 in 1895; 361,000 in 1900; 439,000 in 1910; 422,000 in 1920; 530,000 in 1930; 680,000 in 1940; 907,000 in 1950; 1,211,000 in 1960; 1,569,000 in 1970; 1,933,000 in 1976; 2,085,000 in 1980; 3,210,000 in 1990; 3,920,892 in 2000; and 4,293,459 in 2005. One third of the inhabitants are **Indians**.

The chief products of Chiapas are **coffee** and **cacao**. The state has large **Maya** ruins at **Palenque** and Bonampak. Since 1994 it has seen the unrest led by the **Ejército Zapatista de Liberación Nacional**. This prompted the Federal government to investigate rural education in Chiapas and find that most poor rural children were not enrolled in school, although some did attend first and second grade. Interior Ministry observers found that federal welfare programs functioning out of the state capital failed to reach small towns and rural areas, places which continued to suffer severe poverty. Chiapas also houses refugee camps of Mayans seeking asylum from persecution in Guatemala.

Chiapas' capital is **Tuxtla Gutiérrez**, but **Tapachula** is the most populous city.

CHICHÉN ITZÁ ("At the mouth of the Itza people's well"). Archaeological site at 20°40'N, 88°34'W, 120 km (72 miles) southeast of **Mérida** of a **Maya** city built c.600 by **Quetzalcóatl Kukulkán** and more or less abandoned c.900. The remains, first illustrated by Frederick **Catherwood** in 1842, include the 91-step pyramid of Kukulcán, the Temple of the Warriors, the great ball court, and the Caracol, a 12 m high observatory tower, 3.8 m in diameter. In numerous buildings extending over a ten km^2 area, **gold** masks dedicated to the rain god Chac prevail. Inscriptions provide some historical information. An underground water system of deep wells extends over a flat, arid plain.

CHICHIMEC INDIANS. After reaching their zenith in 950–1100, they absorbed the **Toltec Indians**, but by 1247 most of them had been conquered by the **Aztec** empire. In present day Mexico the Chichimecs are concentrated in the state of **Jalisco**.

CHICHIMECS, WAR OF THE (*Guerra Chichimeca*). The 1560–1585 war to bring all the **Chichimec Indians** under Spanish control. *See also* MIXTON WAR.

CHICHUCUATLÁN, SIERRA DE. Range of the Sierra **Madre** Oriental to the immediate northwest of **Mexico City**.

CHICLE. The raw material for chewing gum has been of commercial importance in **Cozumel** and elsewhere in southern Mexico since the early 1900s.

CHIHUAHUA. World's smallest breed of dog, standing no more than 13 cm high at the shoulder and weighing 500 g to three kg. Although named for **Chihuahua state**, this may have been because the state was more familiar to nineteenth century Americans than **Sonora**, where the dog was also bred.

CHIHUAHUA CITY. Capital of **Chihuahua state**, at 28°40'N, 106°09'W, 320 km south of **El Paso,** Texas, founded at 1,415 m in 1708. It was where Miguel **Hidalgo y Costilla** was executed in 1811. It is the headquarters for the cattle and synthetic fiber industries of the state, in a dry, desert region. The city population was 367,000 in 1976; 530,487 in 1990; 671,790 in 2000; and 718,551 in 2005, but the metropolitan area passed 850,000 in mid-2006.

CHIHUAHUA STATE. The largest state in Mexico, created by the July 1823 division of **Nueva Vizcaya** and granted statehood in July 1824. Bordered by **Sinaloa**, **Durango**, **Cohauila**, and **Sonora**, and, beyond the **United States border**, by **Texas** and **New Mexico**, it has an area of 247,000 km². Its population was 267,000 in 1895; 328,000 in 1900; 406,000 in 1910; 402,000 in 1921; 492,000 in 1930; 624,000 in 1940; 846,000 in 1950; 1,227,000 in 1960; 1,613,000 in 1970; 2,000,000 (including 60,000 **Tarahumara** Indians) in 1976; 2,005,000 in 1980; 2,441,873 in 1990; 3,052,907 in 2000; and 3,241,444 in 2005. Mormon and Mennonite settlements contribute to its 35 percent white population, one of the highest proportions in Mexico.

It contains the prehistoric Casas Grandes ruins in its northern desert. In the south, deep gorges and forests include the vast *Barrancas del Cobre* ("Copper Canyon"). It grows **corn**, **cotton**, **wheat**, and alfalfa, but **mining** (of zinc, lead, **gold**, **silver** and **copper**) and cattle ranching (*See* LIVESTOCK) remain its chief economic activities. The home state of Pancho **Villa**, it furnished many troops for the **Revolution of 1910** (*See* GONZALES, Abraham). There are sixty-seven *municipios*, of which Ahumada, Ascención, Camargo, and Jiménez each exceed 10,000 km². Although the capital is **Chihuahua City**, the largest city is **Ciudad Juárez**. Three other municipios, **Cuauhtémoc**, **Delicias**, and **Hidalgo de Porral** have populations over 100,000.

CHILANGO. Somewhat derisive term for an inhabitant of **Mexico City**, said to have come from the slang of **Veracruz** which adopted the **Nahuatl** for "outsider," i.e., outside Veracruz. A politer alternative is *defeño* (from *D.F.* for *Distrito Federal*, the **Federal District**), and there is also *capitolino* ("of the capital city").

CHILDREN'S LITERATURE. Traditionally, writers in Hispanic countries have tended to see writing for children as somehow below the dignity of a serious author. This is fortunately changing, as seen in the work of (e.g.) Ricardo **Chávez Castañeda** and Ignacio **Padilla**.

CHILE, RELATIONS WITH. As one of the "ABC Powers," Chile attended the **Niagara Conference** to negotiate an end to the **Revolution of 1910**. At the end of the **Spanish Civil War**, Mexico and Chile were the only countries in the Americas not supporting the Nationalists. They also were admitting Republican refugees. Immediately after the Chilean armed forces' **coup d'état of** 1973, Mexico admitted thousands of Chileans seeking asylum into its **Santiago** embassy, and, then, immediately after negotiating their safe conduct to Mexico, broke off diplomatic relations (*See* DIRTY WAR). [L. H.]

CHILPANCINGO. Capital since 1853 of **Guerrero** state, at 17°33'N, 99°30'W, officially *Chilpancingo de los Bravo* (honoring **Independence** War hero Nicolas **Bravo** and his family) with a 1990 city population of 97,165 (120,000 in the **municipio**), 284 km south of **Mexico City**, 129 km north of **Acapulco**.

CHILPANCINGO, CONGRESS OF. Convention summonded by **Morelos** in 1813 and presided over by Andrés **Quintana Roo**. It declared Mexico an independent republic.

CHIMALPOPOCA ("steaming shield"). Chief (**tlatoani**) of the **Aztec** state, 1418–1427.

CHINA, RELATIONS WITH. *See* CHINESE IMMIGRATION.

CHINA POBLANA. Peasant woman's costume, originating in **Jalisco** state, having a long green skirt with a red yoke, trimmed with sequins, a white embroidered blouse, a shawl or *rebozo*, and red hair ribbons. It is always worn by performers of the national folk dance, the **Jarabe Tapatío**.

CHINAMPA. Floating garden, pioneered by the Aztecs in the lake on which they built **Mexico City**.

CHINCHINAUTZIN, SIERRA DE. Mountain range to the immediate south of **Mexico City**, reaching 3,951 m in its highest peak, Aguila.

CHINESE IMMIGRATION. Although some Chinese found their way to colonial Mexico via the **Acapulco** galleon, significant numbers only arrived following the commercial treaty of 1899 which permitted the recruitment of Chinese labor for **mining**, railroad building, and **agriculture**. By 1930 Mexico's 12,000 Chinese formed its largest foreign community after the Americans, but hostility, encouraged by the nationalistic aspirations of the **Revolution of 1910** and by the unemployment engendered by the **Depression of the 1930s**, effectively ended further large-scale **immigration**. [L. H.]

CHOCOLATE. *See* CACAO.

CHOLERA. Asian cholera reached Europe in the early 19th century and spread to **Cuba** and Mexico in 1833, with devastating results. [L. H.]

CHOLULA. *Cholula de Rivadavia* is a city 2,135 m above sea level at 19°06'N, 98°31'W and divided into three *municipios*, of which San Pedro Cholula (100,000 inhabitants in 2005) claims to be the longest, continuously inhabited center in the Americas (since c.1500 BC). Until the Spanish **conquest of Mexico** it was the religious center of the **Puebla** basin, but Franciscan missionaries deliberately built Puebla de las Ángeles, just 10 km away as a rival Christian center, which soon displaced it. San Pedro Cholula's prehispanic Great Pyramid remains the largest in the Americas by volume. San Andrés Cholula, on the **camino real** to Puebla, is now home to the private **University of the Americas**.

CHONTAL. Nahatl for "foreigner," designates both a people of **Oaxaca** and the **Maya** *Yokot'an* of **Tabasco**.

CHRISTLIEB IBARROLA, ADOLFO (1919–1969). Leader of the **Partido Acción Nacional**, born March 12 in **Mexico City**, he graduated from **UNAM** in 1941 and taught law there, 1954–1957. As secretary general of PAN, his criticism of the **Partido Revolucionario Institucional** received nationwide attention, and in 1962–1968 he succeeded Luis Héctor **Álvarez** as his party's president. In 1964–1967 he sat in the **Cámara de Diputados Federales**, led the PAN delegation there, and represented it on the **Comisión Federal Electoral**. As secretary of the Mexican bar association, he became a national legal spokesman for conservatives. He died in Mexico City on December 6.

CHURCH, THE. Under colonial rule, the Roman Catholic Church was formally established, with the crown (i.e., the civil administration) exercising legally defined power, the real **Patronato**, over church property and appointments. After **independence**, conservative politicians regarded these powers as having been inherited by the Republican regime, whereas the liberals preferred to regard the Church as inherently hostile to civil authority. Those priests who had supported the **independence** movement had been excommunicated and sometimes even put to death for heresy. During the **Porfiriato** the provisions of the then current **Constitution of 1857** against Church power, and particularly, Church landowning, were largely ignored. The Church acquired extensive estates and charged exorbitant fees for weddings and burials. The reaction against this and the Church hierarchy's generally hostile attitude to social reform became factors in the **Revolution of 1910**. The **Constitution of 1917** provided for detailed enforcement of Church disestablishment in its Article 130. This in turn provoked the **Cristero Rebellion**.

Until these provisions were relaxed by constitutional amendments in 1993–1995, the clergy were forbidden to lead any outdoor religious parade or to wear religious garb, even in private schools. Religious symbols were also banned from classrooms. Catholic, Protestant, and Jewish schools continued to exist, but they identified themselves as French, Italian, American, British, Israeli, etc. "cultural districts." In **Sinaloa**, however, Catholic parochial primary schools openly used nuns as teachers from the 1970s, even publicizing this in school brochures, while the **Procuraduría General de la República** (federal attorney general's office) chose to ignore the occasional protest. A concordat was negotiated in 1992, and diplomatic representatives were exchanged. Pope **John Paul II** made five public visits to Mexico, in 1979, 1993, 1999, 2000, and 2002.

There are 83,000,000 Catholics in present-day Mexico—not including adherents of the heretical **Iglesia Católica Mexicana**—about 87 percent of the population, giving the Republic the world's second largest national Roman Catholic community, after Brazil.

CHURCH ADMINISTRATION. Mexico City was made a bishopric in 1530 and an archbishopric in 1546. The country has currently 14 archdioceses: Acapulco, Chihuahua, Durango, Guadalajara, Hermosillo, Jalapa, Mexico, Monterrey, Morelia, Oaxaca, Puebla, San Luis Potosi, Tlalnepantia, and Yucatán, and 66 dioceses. *See also* ARCHBISHOPS OF MEXICO.

CHURRIGUERA, JOSÉ BENTO DE (1665–1723). Spanish architect, responsible for an extremely ornate style of Baroque architecture, as found in the cathedrals of **Mexico City** and **Zacatecas**.

CHURRIGUERESQUE. Architectural style associated with José Benito de **Churriguera**.

CÍBOLA, SEVEN CITIES OF. Legendary region of great wealth, vainly searched for in 1540–1542 by Francisco **Vázquez de Coronado y Valdés** in Mexico's **Far North** and the modern US Midwest.

CIENTÍFICOS. This group of officials surrounded President Porfirio **Díaz** and composed the "inner circle" of his government. They were so-called from their belief in **Positivism** and the idea that scientific methods of government were the key to progress. They gained prominence in 1892, when their unofficial spokesman, José Yves **Limantour**, became finance minister. Other *científicos* of note were Justo **Sierra**, Manuel **Romero Rubio**, and Rosendo Pineda. They looked to Europe as the model for Mexico, believed in white superiority, denigrated the Indian and the **mestizo** (despite Pineda's being a Zapotec) and equated wealth and power with intelligence. Under their management, Mexico's international credit and monetary stability were very favorably rated, and, outwardly at least, the country appeared to be an ideal model for other underdeveloped countries.

CIFUENTES, RODRIGO DE. 16th-century Spanish painter from Córdoba, the first painter to practice his art in Mexico (and probably in the New World). He painted such notables as La **Malinche**, Hernán **Cortés**, and Antonio de **Mendoza**.

CINCO DE MAYO. *See* FIFTH OF MAY.

CINEMA. Outstanding Mexican motion pictures have ranged from *Mecánica nacional* of 1971, directed by Luis Alcoriza, to *Enamorada* of 1946 and *María Candelaria* of 1943, both directed by Emilio **Fernández Romo**. *Like Water for Chocolate* has been a recent success internationally.

As early as 1900, feature-length silent films were occasionally produced in Mexico. Contemporary documentaries recorded the fighting and other events of the **Revolution of 1910**. The México-Lex company, established in 1915, was active in producing silent films from 1918 to 1923. Mexico's first talking picture was Miguel Conteras' *El Águila y la serpiente* of 1929. *Santa* of 1932 was Mexico's first talkie where the sound had been recorded directly onto the film.

In the 1930s, the dubbing of Hollywood and other foreign films with Spanish soundtrack limited Mexican film production. However, *Vámonos con Pancho Villa* of 1935 was an early success, and in 1936 *Allá en el Rancho Grande* starring Tito Guízar launched the genre of ranch or rural life comedies which flourished into the 1960s, reaching its heights in the 1940s and 1950s with films staring **Cantiflas** and Tin Tan and such singing stars as Jorge **Negrete**, Pedro Infante, and Pedro **Arméndariz**. The golden age of the Mexican cinema ran from the 1950s to the 1970s, attracting large audiences not only in Mexico, but throughout Latin America and Spain, and among Spanish speakers in the **United States**. From the 1940s through the 1970s, the industry was developed by directors such as Emilio **Fernández Romo**, and stars such as Cantiflas and Dolores Del **Río**. The opening of the modern studios of Churubusco, Azteca, Clasa, Tepeyac, Cuauhtémoc, and Mexico City, in 1946, gave Mexico the largest film industry in Latin America. Its output of feature length films increased steadily to achieve an annual total of 122 in 1950. Daily **television** broadcasting began that year, and, as elsewhere, film output began falling in the face of rising production costs and video competition. In 1972 Mexico produced only 64 films. In 1975 all production studios were expropriated by the government and became part of **CONACINE**.

Although the rock-and-roll era of the late 1970s was notable for Mexican musicals which included the singing of translated songs from the Beatles, by 1979, with the rapid growth of T.V. and the closure of thirty percent of Mexico's movie theaters, annual output had fallen to less than half that of 1972. Serious dramas such as *El*

Elegido of 1982, starring Katy Jurado (who has gained minor fame in Hollywood), recaptured some of the movie-goers. In the 1990s, many Mexican movie studios concentrated on films made for television and cable release, while Spanish-language television stations in the United States affiliated with either the Univisón or the Telemundo networks of Mexico provided reruns of Mexican films of the 1950s–1970s in their late-night programming. *See also* ARMENDÁRIZ, PEDRO; ARRIAGA RIVERA, AGUSTÍN.

CITIES. *See* TOWNS AND CITIES.

CITLATLTÉPETL. Alternate name for **Orizaba** volcano.

CITY. *See* CIUDAD.

CIUDAD ("city"). Historically, a town with a higher status than a **villa**, usually the **cabecera** ("seat") of a **municipio** (county). It is a purely administrative concept, not depending on physical size or population.

CIUDAD ACUÑA. Small border city of **Coahuila State** at 29°20'N, 100°58'W, across the **Rio Grande** from Del Rio, Texas, **cabecera** of the **municipio** of Acuña with a population in 2000 of 110,388, making it the state's fifth most populous city. Nevertheless, only gravel roads connect the city to major **highways** running southward.

CIUDAD JUÁREZ. Founded in 1581 at 31°42'N, 106°59'W as a convenient crossing point of the **Rio Grande**, originally known as El Paso del Norte—a name kept by its twin community of El Paso in **Texas**. It was renamed in 1888 to honor Benito **Juárez** who had made it his capital in 1861–1867. The most populous city of **Chihuahua state**, its population was 550,000 in 1976, 1,218,817 in 2000, and growing at an annual rate of three percent. As with other major ports of entry, **tourism** and cross-border trade place additional burdens on the municipal facilities, from road repair to street lighting, park facilities, and supplemental sewage disposal. A Federal Betterment Board has therefore been created to supplement local funding. Board members are selected for three-year terms from among civic, business, labor, and industrial leaders and activists in public life.

[Unfortunately the city has in recent years gained notoriety for unsolved crimes against **women**, particularly poor single women working in **maquilladoras**. Over 450 have been kidnapped, raped, and murdered since 1993. L. H.]

CIUDAD NEZAHUALCÓYOTI. Capital of the **município** of **Nezahualcóyoti**.

CIUDAD OBREGÓN. Most of the public and private buildings of this city at 27°28'N, 109°59'W, on the **Yaqui River**, date from after 1925, when this city was founded in the **município** of Cajeme in southern **Sonora**. It was named in honor of Álvaro **Obregón**. Its population was 193,000 in 1976 and 321,000 in 1995. It has the Technological Institute of Sonora, some of the state's major grain elevators, flour mills, **cotton** gins, fertilizer plants, and agricultural implement factories. It is also a processing center for the **livestock** industry.

CIUDAD UNIVERSITARIA. Main campus of the **University of Mexico** on the Avenida Insurgentes Sur, at the far southern end of **Metro** line 3. UNAM was transferred here from downtown in 1952.

CIUDAD VICTORIA. Capital city of **Tamaulipas** since 1825, founded October 6, 1750, as the Villa de Santa María de Aguayo.

CIVIL CODE (*Código Civil*). Federalism implies, and the **Constitution of 1917** specifies, that each **state** have its own **law** codes, while the national **congress** legislates civil law only for the **Federal District** and the former territories. In fact, however, the code for the Federal District has been copied by each individual state almost verbatim.

The turbulence of the years following **independence** precluded any early replacement of Spanish law. Although **Oaxaca** enacted its own civil code in 1827–1828, little else had been done when Benito **Juárez** introduced a draft code in 1861. In 1866 the **second empire** promulgated a code based on the French Napoleonic code of 1804. This influenced the definitive code of 1870, which drew also on the draft of 1861, the draft Spanish code of 1851, and the codes of Portugal, Sweden, Switzerland, and Prussia. It was supported by a code of civil procedure promulgated in 1872. A new code in 1884 was almost a literal restatement of that of 1870. The social and political changes introduced by the **Revolution of 1910** led President **Calles** to impose a new federal code with such novel features as gender equality that went into effect September 1, 1932. [L. H.]

CIVIL WARS. *See* CASTE WAR OF YUCATÁN; DIRTY WAR; FRENCH INTERVENTION; INSURRECTIONS; REFORMS, WAR OF THE; REVOLUTION OF 1910; YAQUI.

CLAVEL, ANA (1961–). Novelist from **Mexico City**, winner in 1999 of Spain's Alfaguara prize. Clavel's "fantastic realism" is exemplified in *Cuerpo náufrago* about a woman who magically changes her sex. Other works are *Fuera de escena* (1984), *Los deseos y su sombra* (1999), and the short story collection *Cuando María miré al mar* (1991). [L. H.]

CLAVIJERO, FRANCISCO JAVIER (1731–1787). Jesuit priest and one of the most famous historians of his era, best remembered for such works as the *Storia antica del Messico*. He mastered many natural sciences, was an expert in classical literature, and knew many languages, including more than twenty languages and dialects of **New Spain**. After the banishment of the **Jesuits**, he settled in Italy, where his *Historia de la Antigua o Baja California* was published in 1789. He died in Bologna.

CLIMATE. Although Mexico lies wholly in the tropics and subtropics (*See* EXTENT), its climate is shaped by its **topography** and by uneven **rainfall** distribution. The hottest areas, with average temperatures of 25°C–30°C, are found below 1,000 m above sea level in the north, and below 1,800 m in the south. Temperate climates with averages of 18°C–20°C are found in the 1,000–2,000 m altitudes in the north, 1,800–2,400 m in the south. The snow line begins at 4,000 m elevation in the north, 4,500 m in the south, but winter snow occurs in much of the **altoplanicie** of northern Mexico.

The country suffers from autumnal **hurricanes** from both the Caribbean and the Pacific. [L. H.]

CLOTHES AND CLOTHING. *See* COSTUME.

CLOUTHIER, MANUEL (1934–1989). Manuel de Jesús Clouthier del Rincón, known as "Maquió," was a **Sinaloa** businessman who founded the *Movimiento Familiar Cristiano.* He became president of the **Partido del Acción Nacional**, running unsuccessfully as their candidate for governor of his state in 1986 and for President of the Republic in 1988. He died in a car crash on October 1, in which foul play was alleged. [L. H.]

COAHUILA. Officially *Coahuila de Zaragoza*, and originally part of **Nueva Extremadura**, Coahuila's 151,571 km^2 make it the third largest state in Mexico. In the final decades of **New Spain**, Coahuila was part of the **intendancy** of **San Luis Potosí.** The **Constitution of 1824** created the *Estado Libre de Coahuila y Tejas*, dissolved by the 1836 independence of **Texas.** Coahuila was united with **Nuevo León** from mid-1857 until 1864 when it supported **Maximilian**, specifically in order to regain its autonomy. The first leaders of the **Revolution of 1910**, Francisco **Madero** and Venustiano **Carranza**, both came from Coahuila.

The present-day state borders **Nuevo León** to its east, **Chihuahua** to its west, **Durango** to its south, and shares a 512 km border with **Texas** in the United States to the north. Its population at successive **censuses** was 236,000 (1895); 297,000 (1900); 362,000 (1910); 394,000 (1921); 436,000 (1930); 551,000 (1940); 721,000 (1950); 908,000 (1960); and 1,115,00 (1970). It was estimated as 1,335,000 in 1976 and recorded as 1,557,000 in 1980; 1,972,000 in 1990; 2,296,070 in 2000; and 2,495,200 in 2005.

The Sierra **Madre** Oriental divides Coahuila into western and eastern plateaus. The state's constituent *municipios* are **Saltillo** (the current state capital), Ramos Arizpe, Arteaga, Parras de la Fuente, General Cepeda to the southeast, **Torreón** (the most populous city until the recent expansion of **Ciudad Juárez**), San Pedro de las Colonias, Francisco I. Madero, **Matamoros**, and Viesca in the Laguna region; **Monclova** (the former state capital from 1687 when Coahuila was separated from Durnago), Ciudad Frontera, Castaños, Candela, Abasolo, Nadadores, San Buenaventura, Escobedo, Lamadrid, and Sacramento in the center; Sierra Mojada, Ocampo, and Cuatro Ciénegas in the desert zone; **Ciudad Acuña**, Guerrero, Hidalgo, Jiménez, **Piedras Negras**, Allende, Morelos, Nava, Villa Unión, and Zaragoza in the north; and (Ciudad) Juárez, Melchor Múzquiz, Progreso, Sabinas, and San Juan de Sabinas in the coal **mining** area—Coahuila is also Mexico's chief producer of **coal**, hence the location here of the **Altos Hornos** steel complex. Since the 1950s, **irrigation** has brought **cotton**, **corn**, **wheat**, and grape cultivation to the Laguna region of this desert state. It is Mexico's major **wine** producer.

COAL. Although Mexico has some coal mines, chiefly in **Coahuila**, but also in **Sonora**, output is inadequate for the needs of the modern **economy**, and particularly for the **iron and steel** industry. [L. H.]

COAST GUARD (*Guardacostas*). Currently a branch of the **navy**; in the 18th century, it was a system of privateers employed to defend Spanish sovereignty in the Americas by attacking foreign shipping in the surrounding seas (*See* LANCASTER NORONA Y SILVA, FERNANDO DE).

COASTLINE. Modern Mexico has a total coastline of 11,933 km, one of the longest of all the American republics. The mainland has 8,475 km on the Pacific and 3,118 km on the Gulf of **Mexico** and the Caribbean Sea. Mexico's **islands** give it an additional 340 km.

COATZACOALCOS. This **Petroleum** exporting port of **Veracruz-Llave** on the namesake river, at 18°09'N, 94°26'W, had 267,212 inhabitants in 2000. An Olmec settlement refounded in 1522 as Espíritu Santo, it became a port as Coatzacoalco in 1825, was renamed Puerto México in 1900, and became Coatzacoalcos in 1936.

COATZACOALCOS, RIVER. Eastward flowing river of **Oaxaca** state and **Veracruz-Llave**, navigable in its lower reaches.

COCOA. Powder from the **cacao** bean, so called from European confusion with the coconut.

CODICES. The **Aztec** and the **Maya** cultures each possessed a writing system and a literature. Although most examples of the codices on which they wrote were systematically destroyed in the **Church**'s campaign against paganism, one example sent to **Charles V** was captured en route by a French privateer and (after he had found himself an English buyer) ended up in Oxford University's Bodleian Library. There its beauty so impressed Edward **King**, Viscount Kingsborough, that he made it his life's work to track down, collect, and reprint all surviving such codices. [L. H.]

CODINA, GENARO (1851–1901). Musical composer from **Zacatecas** who showed promising ability, using the harp to compose. His best-known work, the *Zacatecas March,* is still widely played. His fame was such that he toured the United States with his own orchestra, the Típica Zacateca.

COFETEL. Federal agency charged with regulating the Telephone Industry (*See* TELEPHONES).

COFFEE. Coffee, native to highland Ethiopia, reached Mexico in the late eighteenth century, and by the mid-19th century it had become a key part of its **economy**. It is grown inland from the Caribbean coast, from central Mexico southwards, with the best quality coming from **Oaxaca** and **Chiapas**. Mexico is also one of the world's largest producers of certified organic coffee, mainly for the American market. Although cultivation remains in Mexican hands, it is marketed by international agri-business, notably Bristol Myers Squibb de Mexico, Nestlé México, Sabormex, and Unilever de México. Starbucks opened its first coffee shops in **Mexico City** in 2002.

Historically, the labor demands of coffee cultivation at harvest time stimulated much **internal migration** (20,000 in the 1920s) and, from the mid-twentieth century, an even higher rate of seasonal immigration from **Guatemala** (up to 200,000). The industry's contribution to the national economy reached $700 million a year. Mexico was the world's fourth largest coffee producer, but the ending of the **International Coffee Organization**'s national quota system in 1989 effectively halved the world price, besides making it inherently unstable. This has so impoverished small coffee growers in Mexico as to make them signficant contributors to the **emigration** flow into the **United States**. [L. H.]

COINAGE. The first Mexican coins were badly minted items, dubbed **macuquino**, of **silver** and copper. The first **gold** coins were issued in

1679. Improved technique produced the beautiful **columnario** issue of 1732.

Decimalization was introduced by the **Second Empire** and continued with after the restoration of the Republic.

Early twenty-first century Mexico coins exist in the denominations of 10 centavos, 20 centavos, 50 centavos, and one, two, five, and 10 pesos. The obverse bears the **eagle and serpent**; the reverse shows the value. *See also* MINT; PESO; REAL. [L. H.]

COLEGIO DE DEFENSA NACIONAL. Top academic military institution, established in 1981. A selection of senior **armed forces** officers (colonels and above) are trained there in national security policy, resource management, foreign relations, and economics.

COLEGIO DE INGENIEROS CIVILES DE MÉXICO. The Institute of **engineering education** formed in 1946, but its antecedents went back to the *Real Seminario de Minería* of 1792.

COLEGIO DE LETRÁN. Prestigious 19th-century high school in **Mexico City**.

COLEGIO DE MÉXICO. Important gesture of the Mexican government at the outset of **immigration** of loyalist refugees from the **Spanish Civil War** was the 1938 creation of the **Casa de España**. In 1940 this was reorganized as "Mexico College," and is now an independent, élite institution funded by the Ford, Rockefeller, and other foundations, by UNESCO, and by the Mexican government. Its alumni hold top positions in Mexican government and universities. It has 200 full-time and 100 part-time students following three-year masters' and five-year doctoral courses in the social sciences and humanities. It has an Oriental Studies Center and offers Asian and African linguistics. **Cosío Villegas** was director until 1966, when his successor was the economist Víctor **Urquidi**. Its numerous publications include the quarterly *Foro internacional*.

COLEGIO DE SAN NICOLÁS OBISPO. Colonial precursor of the **Universidad de San Nicolás de Michoacán**, founded by Vasco de

Quiroga in 1540, thus anteceding the **University of Mexico** although only having the status at the time of a college. Its 18th century rectors included Miguel Hidalgo and his more famous son Miguel **Hidalgo y Costilla**. José **Morelos** studied there under the younger Hidalgo, and during the early years of the **independence** struggle, both helped to keep the college open.

COLEGIO DE SANTA CRUZ DE TLATELOLCO. School for Indian noblemen, founded by Archbishop Juan de **Zumárraga**.

COLEGIO NACIONAL DE AGRICULTURA. The 1853–1916 forerunner of the *Escuela Nacional de Agricultura* since 1978 has been part of the **Universidad Autónoma Chipango**.

COLIMA CITY. Capital of the namesake state, at 19°14'N, 103°41W, and an altitude of 4,100 m (13,500 ft.), 450 km west of **Mexico City**, and 320 km south of **Guadalaja** along a winding highway, and 50 km from the Pacific Ocean, founded by a **conquistador** in 1523. It has agricultural industries and **salt production**. It had 91,000 inhabitants in 1976 and 127,000 in 1995. Many buildings were destroyed and 28 people killed when a 7.6 (Richter) magnitude earthquake hit the town on the evening of January 21, 2003.

COLIMA STATE ("Col."). Small state (5,455 km^2) in southwestern Mexico of ten *municipios*, with a 112 km coastline on the Pacific, is bordered by **Jalisco** on the north and east, and **Michoacán** on the southeast. Its population was 56,000 in 1895; 65,000 in 1900; 78,000 in 1910; 92,000 in 1921; 62,000 in 1930; 79,000 in 1940; 112,000 in 1950; 164,000 in 1960; 241,000 in 1970; 317,000 in 1976; 346,000 in 1980; 429,000 in 1990; 542,647 in 2000, and 567,996 in 2005. The state's two volcanoes draw many geologists. Volcán Nevada is dormant, but Volcán de Fuego is Mexico's most dangerously active volcano, having erupted in the late 1980s and again in 1991, when it produced a new dome rising 30 m above the crater rim. The **Revillagigedo Islands** lie within the state's jurisdiction.

Tropical **agriculture** and livestock dominate the state's economy. The town of Comala, eleven km NNW of Colima City, has an artisan community that has being crafting elaborate wood furniture, sold all over Mexico, for 200 years. Las **Hadas** is a recently developed coastal resort.

The federal government, in partnership with private enterprise, now operates a toll highway between **Colima City** and its port of **Manzanillo**.

COLINA, RAFAEL DE LA (1898–1984). Diplomat, born in Tulancingo, **Hidalgo**, he earned an M.Sc. from **UNAM**. He served as Mexican consul in Missouri, **Texas**, Pennsylvania, **Louisiana**, Massachusetts, and **California**, as director of the Consular Corps, ambassador to the **United States** from 1949–1952, to Japan from 1962–1964, and then to the **Organization of American States** from 1965–1976. He was a key advisor on foreign policy to Mexican presidents during the 1960s and 1970s.

COLOMBIA, RELATIONS WITH. New Spain sent a naval expedition in 1740 to lift the British siege of Cartagena. Mexico took part in the abortive 1826 **Congress of Panama** on Latin American cooperation.

COLÓN DE PORTUGAL, PEDRO NUÑO. Duque de Veragua y de Vega Real, marqués de La Jamaica y de Villamizar, Conde de Gelves, knight of the Golden Fleece (????–1673). A descendant of Christopher **Columbus**, he had a career in public administration culminating in his appointment as **viceroy** of **New Spain** in 1672. When he reached **Mexico City**, November 20, 1673, he was elderly and physically worn out and died five days later. [L. H.]

COLONIA ("colony"). In the administration of the **Federal District**, this was a division of a **delegación**.

COLOSIO, LUIS DONALDO (1950–1994). Assassinated presidential candidate. Born in Magdalena, **Sonora**, February 10, he made frequent visits as a teenager to nearby **Nogales** and Tucson in Arizona. After preparatory school in Sonora, he took an economics degree at the **Instituto Tecnológico de Monterrey**, a master's in urban economics and development from the University of Pennsylvania in 1974–1975, followed by a doctorate. He came through his studies to understand that, as Mexico continued to modernize, the private sector would become more importent than the public. Subsequently he taught at **UNA**, at the **Collage de Mexico** (in 1979) and then at the private Anáhuac University.

Active in the **Partido Revolucionario Institucional**, he sat in the **Cámara de Diputados Federales** in 1985–1988, and then in the **Senate** from 1988–1991. In 1987–1992, he was president of the **Comité Ejecutivo Nacional** of the PRI. Supported by **Salinas de Gortari** and the PRI's inner circle, he was their favorite candidate to become the next President and received the official nomination to run on November 28, 1993. A gentle man in private life, he was deeply troubled by the unrest in **Chiapas** led by the **Ejército Zapatista de Liberación Nacional**, and went into deep depression for a week, locked in his home library, searching for a way peace might be negotiated. On March 6, 1994, he made a brave speech distancing himself from Salinas, openly contradicting the assertion that Mexico was becoming a developed nation. He said flatly in a national broadcast that it was still in the Third World. He also suggested a possible connection between leaders of **narcotics** cartels and highly placed persons close to the president. He promised vigorously that when elected he would separate the government from the party apparatus. Two weeks later, on March 23, while campaigning in the midst of a large political rally at **Tijuana**, he was shot at close range, apparently by Mario **Aburto**. The mystery of who had hired the gunman continues. Speculation alternated between blaming "dinosaurs" fighting his threat to the PRI's influence, and those fearful of his public call for a crusade against narcotic "kings" in his native Sonora.

Not since the 1928 murder of Alvaro **Obregón** when seeking a second term, had a Mexican presidential candidate been assassinated, but after Colosio's funeral, when national outrage began to subside a little, the PRI officially nominated Ernesto **Zedillo** in his stead. When he had been elected and inaugurated on December 1, 1994, the media allowed the assassination to drop out of the news. After Raúl **Salinas de Gortari**'s conviction, however, unofficial investigations erupted, looking into Colosio's anti-**corruption** stance and Raúl's involvement with criminals. Speculation continues into the new century. *See also* CENSORSHIP.

COLUMBUS, CHRISTOPHER (1451–1506). Genoese sailor, Cristoforo Colombo, known in Spanish as Cristóbal Colón, planted the flag of Castile in the New World on October 12, 1492.

COLUMBUS DAY (*Día de la Raza*). Anniversary of Christopher **Columbus**'s landfall on October 12, 1492, now celebrated internationally to honor the worldwide community of speakers of Spanish.

COLUMBUS RAID. In 1916, Pancho **Villa**, wishing to prejudice Mexico's relations with the **United States** and so embarrass his rival, Venustiano **Carranza**, led a raid into New Mexico, briefly occupying the town of Columbus where some U.S. citizens were killed. As expected, the United States retaliated by sending a punitive expedition into Mexico, led by General J. J. **Pershing**. While Villa was never captured by Pershing's forces, indications are that he was badly wounded. An unexpected result was that the people of Columbus erected a statue to Villa in their town square.

COLUMNARIO ("having columns"). Colonial coins minted from 1732 bore on the reverse a representation of the twin columns of Hercules, linked by a ribbon bearing the motto *"plus ultra"* the origin of the **dollar sign**. Such coins were the first in Mexico with milled edges (to prevent the clipping that compromised the value of the earlier **macuquino** coins.

COMADRE. A godmother in **compadrazgo**, i.e., in relation to the child's real parents (or the mother in relation to her children's godparents)—the original meaning of the English word "gossip"—as opposed to a *padrina* (the godmother in relation to the child). [L. H.]

COMANDANCÍA GENERAL DE LAS PROVINCIAS INTERNAS. *See* PROVINCIAS INTERNAS, COMANDANCÍA GENERAL DE LAS.

COMERCIO, MINISTER DE. *See* TRADE MINISTRY.

COMISIÓN FEDERAL DE ELECTRICIDAD (C.F.E.). The federally owned Electricity Commission was created in 1941 to compete with privately owned power companies. In 1960–1962, President **López Mateos** expropriated all such companies, putting them under the C.F.E. For the first time, uniform rates prevailed throughout Mexico, a great help for industrial growth. The C.F.E.'s director general is a member of the president's cabinet and enjoys high-level autonomy.

COMISIÓN FEDERAL ELECTORAL (C.F.E.). The Federal Electoral Commission comes under the **interior ministry**. It supervises voter registration, elections, and vote tabulation at all levels of government. It certifies political parties as meeting legal minimum requirements for recognition, candidates require its certification to be included on the ballot, and it supervises the conduct of campaigns and elections. Its endorsement of the **Partido Acción Nacional** presidential candidate as victor in the **election of 2006** was rejected on the left and the C.F.E. headquarters were bombed November 6, 2006.

COMISIÓN NACIONAL BANCARIA Y DE VALORES (C.N.B.V.). The National Banking and Securities Commission was founded in 1946 by Antonio **Carrillo Flores**.

COMISIÓN NACIONAL DE ÁGUA (C.N.A.). Mexico's National Water Commission was created in 1989, a successor to the *Comisión Nacional de Irrigaciones* of 1926, with the National Weather Service (*Servicio Meteorológico Nacional*), becoming one of new body's dependent agencies. [L. H.]

COMISIÓN NACIONAL PARA EL REPARTO DE UTILIDADES (CNRU). The National Committee for Profit Sharing, was created in 1962 to ensure that, after deductions for taxes, profits on invested capital, and funds for expansion, repairs, and modernization, a percentage of remaining profits are distributed through a local committee to all full-time employees. Each worker's share is based on his or her lowest and highest wages for the year and the number of days worked.

COMISIÓN SONORENSE-ARIZONENSE. Mexican partner of the **Arizona-Sonora Commission** in joint promotion of trans-border cooperation.

COMITÉ EJECUTIVO NACIONAL (CEN). The National Executive Committee of the **Partido Revolucionario Institucional** consists of the party president, a secretary general, and secretaries for agrarian, labor, popular, financial, and political affairs and for press and public relations, recruitment, and social action. It controls the geographical hierarchy of the party as well as the three vocational sectors (popular, labor, and agrarian). Within each state the PRI has a *comité ejecutivo estatal.*

COMITÉ NACIONAL DE PRODUCTIVIDAD E INNOVACIÓN TECNOLÓGICA, A.C. (COMPITE). The National Productivity Council, a not-for-profit organization, founded in 1997.

COMITÉ NACIONAL DE REPARTO DE UTILIDADES. *See* COMISIÓN NACIONAL PARA EL REPARTO DE UTILIDADES (CNRU).

COMO AGUA PARA CHOCOLATE. *See LIKE WATER FOR CHOCOLATE.*

COMMERCE. *See* TRADE.

COMMUNICATIONS MINISTRY. *See* TRANSPORT MINISTRY.

COMMUNISM. *See* PARTIDO COMUNISTA MEXICANA.

COMONFORT, IGNACIO (1812–1863). President from 1855–1857, born in **Puebla**, he helped Antonio **López de Santa Anna** to overthrow President Anastacio **Bustamante** in 1833. In 1855 he was regarded as the prime candidate for the presidency, but deferred to Juan **Álvarez Hurtado**, who then made Comonfort his war minister. Despite his reputation as a conciliator, Comonfort enraged soldiers and churchmen by abolishing their **fueros**, a recipe for civil war. When Álvarez was forced out, Comonfort became provisional president, serving from December 1855 to November 1857. During these years he faced several uprisings that he suppressed. When the liberal **Constitution of 1857** went into effect, he accepted it without enthusiasm as the Plan of **Tacubaya** would have overturned it. He was elected president in 1857, but Félix **Zuloaga**

forced him to resign in January 1858. He fled to the **United States** and then to **France**. When European intervention was threatened by the **London Convention**, he returned to support Benito **Juárez**, his constitutional successor, and was killed in an ambush on November 14.

COMPADRAZGO. Relationship of ritual kinship (among all social classes, both rural and urban) formed when someone acts as the sponsor of another's child at christening, confirmation, or marriage, creating lifelong mutual obligation and (usually) friendship. Besides forming strong social and political ties between families of equal rank, *compadrazgo* can also create a patron-client relationship when the godparent outranks the parents socially. [L. H.]

COMPADRE. Relationship of a godfather (**compadrazgo**) to the godchild's actual parents, or the father in relation to his child's godparents (as opposed to a **patrino**). The feminine is a **comadre**. [L. H.]

COMPAÑÍA EXPORTADORA IMPORTADORA MEXICANA S.A. (CEIMSA). The government's export-import company of 1949–1961, the predecessor of the **Compañía Nacional de Subsistencias Populares (CONASUPO)**.

COMPAÑÍA MEXICANA DE AVIACIÓN (C.M.A.). Mexico's principal privately-owned airline was founded in **Tampico** as the *Compañía Mexicana de Transportes* (C.M.T.), flying weekly payrolls and passengers to the oilfields in **Veracruz**. On August 20, 1924, CMA was incorporated by Gustavo and Alberto Salinas, former military pilots, to provide commercial air links between **Mexico City**, **Saltillo**, Tampico, and **San Luis Potosí**. By 1941 CMA served all major provincial cities, plus several major cities in the **United States**. By 1960 it had replaced all its propeller aircraft with jets. Throughout the 1970s its annual profits contrasted with the annual deficits of its government-owned competitor, **Aeroméxico**. In 1980 Mexicana flew thirty percent more domestic and twenty percent more international passengers than its rival. *See also* AIR TRANSPORT.

COMPAÑÍA NACIONAL DE SUBSISTENCIAS POPULARES (CONASUPO). The government's National Company of Popular

Subsistence, or more accurately, Basic Commodities Corporation, had its origin as a successor to CEIMSA, the government's export-import company, which functioned from 1949–1961. It buys **corn**, **beans**, **wheat**, **rice**, **coffee**, sorghum, and other major crops at subsidized prices and stores them in a government chain of warehouses. Thousands of CONASUPO retail stores throughout Mexico sell food (including bakery goods, condensed milk, and other canned goods), working clothes, and a few toys and basic appliances almost at cost, to provide the poor with necessities and encourage commercial groceries and supermarkets to hold down prices. *See also* DÍAZ BALLESTEROS, ENRIQUE; HANK GONZÁLEZ, CARLOS; JÍMENEZ CANTU, JORGE; MÚGICA MONTOYA, EMILIO.

COMPTROLLERSHIP GENERAL, MINISTRY OF THE (*Secretaría de la Contraloría y Desarrollo Administrativo*, **SECODAM**). This federal government ministry was created in 1994 to replace the *Secretaría de la Contraloría de la Federación*—SECOGEF—of 1982. Its purpose was to manage and modernize administrative processes in government and public administration, and in particular to fight **corruption** and make procedures more transparent. On April 11, 2003 SECODAM became the **Public Administration Ministry**.

COMTE, AUGUSTE (1798–1857). French rationalist philosopher, the founder of **Positivism**.

CONACINE. National Motion Picture Company (*Corporación Nacional Cinematográfica*), a government **cinema** monopoly.

CONCHELLO, JOSÉ ÁNGEL (1923–1998). Leader of the **Partido Acción Nacional**, born September 1st in **Monterrey**, he graduated in law from **UNA** and studied industrial development in Canadian universities. He has been on the PAN national executive since 1969, and was party president in 1972–1975. In 1953 he represented Mexican employers at the International Labor Organization. He was advisor for the **Confederación de Camaras Industriales** and the **Confederación de Cámaras Nacionales de Comercio** and was a columnist for *El Universal*, the magazine *La Nación*, and many other periodicals. He sat in the **Cámara de Diputados Federales** in 1967–1970 and 1973–1976 and ran as PAN candidate for governor of **Nuevo León** in 1979. He was also professor of sociology at the **Universidad Iberoamericana**.

CONFEDERACIÓN CAMPESINA INDEPENDIENTE (CCI). Independent Peasant Farmer Federation, formed in 1963 by Ramón Danzos Palomino, Vicente **Lombardo Toledano**, Braulio **Maldonado Sánchez,** Genaro **Vázquez Rojas**, and others, to challenge the official **Confederación Nacional Campesina**. However, the CCI was co-opted in 1970.

CONFEDERACIÓN DE CÁMARAS INDUSTRIALES (CONCAMIN). Federation of Industrial Chambers to which each individual **cámara industrial** must belong. The amount of dues each pays determines the number of its votes within a CONCAMIN assembly.

CONFEDERACIÓN DE CÁMARAS NACIONALES DE COMERCIO (CONCANACO). All local chambers of commerce are legally required to belong to this National Confederation of Chambers of Commerce, the organized voice of retail management in negotiating with the government or **trade unions**.

CONFEDERACIÓN DE TRABAJADORES DE MEXICO (C.T.M.). The Mexican Federation of Labor was a confederation of Mexican **trade unions** organized in 1936 by Vicente **Lombardo Toledano** along the lines of the American C.I.O. to fill the void left by the discredited and decadent **Confederación Regional Obrera Mexicana**. In its early years it boasted a membership of 250,000 factory workers, 90,000 miners, 17,000 petroleum workers, and 80,000 transport workers. It was President Lázaro **Cárdenas'** most powerful source of support and, as a result, it received his backing to strike on numerous occasions. When he reorganized the official party into the **Partido de la Revolución Mexicana**, the C.T.M. became the official spokesman for the labor sector, enjoying official status in the government. It was the dispute between the C.T.M. and the foreign-owned petroleum companies which led to their nationalization in 1938. It enjoyed its most militant period during Cárdenas' term of office, but it has grown more conservative during succeeding administrations, concentrating more on economic and social issues, rather than on political ones. The C.T.M. has long since been purged of radical leftists and communists. It is made up of 20 national unions, 31 state federations, and more than 100 local and regional federations. Estimates of current strength range from 500,000 to well over 1,000,000. It continues to be the official spokesman for labor within the **Partido Revolucionario Institucional**.

CONFEDERACIÓN GENERAL DE TRABAJORES (C.G.T.). The General Federation of Labor was an attempt in 1920 by the newly formed **Partido Comunista Mexicana** to build a trade union base. During 1921 C.G.T. leaders were trained in Moscow, but fewer than 80,000 workers joined before it began to dissolve in 1928.

CONFEDERACIÓN NACIONAL CAMPESINA (CNC). The National Peasants' Federation was established in 1936 by President Lázaro **Cardenas** at the urging of León **García Pujou** and others to give the **campesino** an organized voice for negotiating benefits and aid from the government. The CNC also became the core unit of the agrarian sector of the **Partido Revolucionario Institucional**, lobbying for such needs as **agrarian reform**, bank loans and credits, and government subsidies for fertilizers. *See also* LEYVA VELÁSQUEZ, GABRIEL; ROJO GÓMEZ, JAVIER; SOTO Y GAMA, ANTONIO DIAZ.

CONFEDERACIÓN NACIONAL DE ORGANIZACIONES POPULARES (CNOP). This sector of the **Partido Revolucionario Institucional** was for professionals and all those not affiliated with the party's peasant or trade union sectors. It was founded by Carlos A. **Madrazo**, Antonio **Nava Castillo**, and others on February 7, 1943.

CONFEDERACIÓN PATRONAL DE LA REPÚBLICA DE MÉXICO (COPARMEX). The Employers' Federation of Mexico, founded in 1929, was a voluntary association of employers from the retail trade, manufacturing industries, wholesalers, and other private-sector management. It lobbies and negotiates with government and **trade unions**.

CONFEDERACIÓN REGIONAL OBRERA MEXICANA (CROM). The Regional Federation of Mexican Workers was founded March 22, 1918, by labor leader Luis **Morones**. By 1916 it claimed a two million membership and during the 1920s was Mexico's most powerful **trade union** federation. After the **Confederación de Trabajadores Mexicanos** was established in 1936, it eclipsed the CROM, and by the 1970s CROM was just a token federation with very little influence in politics or government.

CONFEDERACIÓN REVOLUCIONARIO DE OBREROS Y CAMPESINOS (CROC). The Revolutionary Federation of Workers and Peasant-Farmers was developed in 1952 and 1953 by President **Ruiz Cortines** to give the **Partido Revolucionario Institucional** some competition, particularly in government and management negotiations, so strengthening the government's position through labor pluralism. By 1954, CROC had a membership of 435,000 before it began to level off. Through the 1970s it remained a medium-sized federation supportive of both the government and the PRI.

CONGREGA (or _congregación_). This name was given by the Spaniards to any Indian town. They segregated the **Indians** by forcing them to live in these settlements to protect them from being taken advantage of, to assure a readily-available labor supply, and to facilitate their conversion to Christianity. The greater part of such resettlement occurred in the late 1500s and early 1600s.

CONGRESO DE TRABAJO. Annual meeting of **trade unions**, established under official auspices at the February 1966 _Asamblea Nacional Revolucionaria del Proletariado_ in **Mexico City**. [L. H.]

CONGRESS (_Congreso_). Mexico's federal congress consists of two houses: the **Senate** and the **Cámara de Diputados Federales**. The legislature has, however, always been dominated by the power of the executive branch, i.e., the **president**.

CONGRESS OF PANAMÁ (_Congreso de Panamá_). In pursuit of his dream of a Latin American confederation, Colombian president Simón Bolívar summoned a Pan-American Conference of all Latin

American nations at Panama City, then part of Colombia from June 22–July 15, 1826. Only a few nations attended, and their pride and jealousy prevented any useful outcome of the conference. A plan for a second congress at **Tacubaya** proved abortive.

CONQUEST OF MEXICO, SPANISH. Hernán **Cortés** sailed from **Cuba** in 1519 with 500 soldiers, sixteen horses, fourteen cannons, and forty-seven muskets. On the coast of **Veracruz** he was greeted by an envoy of the emperor **Moctezuma** who gave the invaders **gold** and **silver** ornaments. This prompted them to march to the **Aztec** capital **Tenochtitlán** in search of more wealth, with the aid of La **Malinche** as interpreter. In 1521 the Spaniards easily subdued Moctezuma and his warriors, who had never seen horses or gunfire. The bearded Spaniards also fit the Aztec legend of the god **Quetzalcóatl** who was supposed, some day, to send representatives from the sea to the east. After Moctezuma was killed in a riot between Spaniards and Aztecs and his successor **Cuauhtémoc**'s resistance was overcome, the conquest of *central* Mexico was complete.

Expeditions southward followed almost immediately but took two decades to extend Spanish authority firmly into Central America.

To the immediate north lived **Indians** who had never submitted to the Aztecs. Their conquest required another seventy years, which included the **Mixton War** and the War of the **Chichimecs**. Beyond that, in what became the "**Near North**," progress was even slower. **Monterrey**, for instance, was not founded until 1598. And in the "**Far North**" no serious attempt at conquest was made, except for **New Mexico**, before the late 17th century. Thanks to the nature of the country and the fierceness of Indian resistance, this vast area had hardly been settled in any density when it was annexed by the **United States** in 1835–1848.

[The impact of the conquest went far beyond the political, introducing European **disease**, ideology (the Catholic **Church**), technology (especially in **agriculture** and **livestock** raising), and the **Spanish language**. L. H.]

CONQUISTADOR ("conqueror"). Any explorer or soldier of fortune who took part in the original Spanish conquest and settlement of the New World, notably, in Mexico's case, Hernán de **Cortes**, but also Pedro de **Alvarado y Mesia**, Juan de **Grijalva**, Nuño Beltrán de

Guzmán, Francisco de **Ibarra**. The term applied originally to those fighting to liberate Spain from the Moors. [L. H.]

CONSEJO NACIONAL DE CIENCIA Y TECNOLOGÍA (CONA-CYT). The federal government's National Science and Technology Council.

CONSEJO NACIONAL DE SALUD. Council reestablished in its present form in the mid-1980s to decide the broad lines of health policy, meeting quarterly and formed by the 32 state secretaries of health, with the federal minister of health as chairperson.

CONSEJO POLÍTICO NACIONAL (C.P.N.). The **Partido Revolucionario Institucional**'s national council is a permanent collegiate policy-making body, subordinate to the party's *Asamblea Nacional*, and consisting of the party president, secretary general, and former presidents of the **Comité Ejecutivo Nacional**, 32 state committee chairmen, and 15 representatives from the agrarian, labor, and popular sectors. [L. H.]

CONSERVADORES. Political conservatives, originally within the **Cortes of Cádiz**, but soon anywhere in Latin America.

CONSERVATION. *See* ECOLOGY.

CONSERVATIVE PARTY. *See* PARTIDO CONSERVADOR.

CONSERVATORIO NACIONAL DE MÚSICA DE MÉXICO. The National Conservatory of Music was founded July 1, 1866, as the *Conservatorio de Música de la Sociedad Filarmónica de México*, the result of an initiative of the Second **Empire**, to succeed the *Academia Filarmónica Mexicana* of 1825, claimed to have been Latin America's first formal music conservatory. Although it adopted its present name in 1868, this was changed again in 1908, 1913, and 1921, and only changed back, this time definitively, in 1930. [L. H.]

CONSOLIDATION, LAW OF (*Ley de consolidación*). A **cédula** of the Spanish crown required lands held by religious orders to be sold for the benefit of the treasury, tantamount to the nationalization of such land. During the years it was in effect, 1805–1809, the Spanish treasury received over 10 million *pesos*.

CONSORTIUM FOR RESEARCH ON MEXICO ("Profmex"). This NGO, chartered in California since 1982 and registered in Mexico as an *asociación civil*, has a worldwide membership of 105 universities, organizations, and think tanks, and over 700 individuals (academics and specialists from government, private corporations and multilateral agencies, to conduct independent analysis of Mexico's public policies and development model and its role in world affairs. Its internet journal, *Mexico and the World Webjournal*, began in 1996.

CONSTANZO, ADOLFO DE JESÚS (1962–1989). Palo Mayombe (Puerto Rican voodoo) cult leader and **narcotics** dealer of **Matamorros** was born to a Cuban in Miami. He had himself shot to avoid arrest for the murder of an American student, Mark Kilroy.

CONSTITUENT ASSEMBLY OF 1856 (*Congreso Constituyente de 1856*). Assembly responsible for the **Constitution of 1857**. It met in Mexico City, February 17, 1856–February 5, 1857.

CONSTITUENT ASSEMBLY OF 1916–1917. The **Querétaro** Convention, an assembly gathered at Querétaro by President Venustiano **Carranza** between October 1916 and February 1917, expedited the final draft of the **Constitution of 1917**.

CONSTITUTION OF 1812. *See* SPANISH CONSTITUTION OF 1812.

CONSTITUTION OF 1814. *See* APATZINGÁN CONGRESS.

CONSTITUTION OF 1824. Constitution reflecting the Liberals' commitment to decentralization, largely drafted by Valentín **Gómez Farías** and Miguel **Ramos Arizpe**. It was modeled on that of the **United States** of America and on the **Spanish Constitution of 1812** (from which it took several sections verbatim). It created a federal republic of 19 states, 4 territories, and a **Federal District**. As originally provided in the US Constitution, the candidate coming in second in the presidential election was made the vice president.

CONSTITUTION OF 1836. *See* SIETE LEYES.

CONSTITUTION OF 1843. *See* BASES ORGÁNICAS DE 1843.

CONSTITUTION OF 1846. Another liberal attempt to secure a federal constitution.

CONSTITUTION OF 1857. Constitution of reformer Benito **Juarez**, proclaimed in February, 1857, could not be put into effect until the fall of the **empire** in 1867. It disestablished the **Church** and nationalized its property, but this provision and others on **agrarian reform** were ignored during the long years of the **Porfirato**, 1876–1911. It provided for a single-house legislature and no **vice president**. Any president dying in office would be succeeded by the chief justice of the **Supreme Court**. A 1904 amendment increased the presidential term to six years and restored the vice presidency.

CONSTITUTION OF 1865. The *Estatuto Provisional del Imperio Mexicano* was a tribute to the modern and very liberal outlook of the Emperor **Maximilian**, while its total failure to achieve any practical application gave ample evidence of his inability to exercise any real independence of his very conservative supporters. [L. H.]

CONSTITUTION OF 1917. Drafted by the **Constituent Assembly of 1916–1917**, besides defining political rights (freedom of speech and the press, and the suffrage), it broke with the past with article 27 on the land. This article divorced subsoil mineral rights from surface property ownership, declaring them the property of the nation. Only with a government concession could any entity develop **mining** resources. The article also provided for the return of communal farms (**ejidos**) to the villages from which the **Porfirato** had taken them. Article 123 became the magna charta of organized **labor**, guaranteeing the right to organize, the right to strike, and the right to an eight-hour day with extra pay for overtime. It also obliged large employers to provide schools for the children of workers in communities lacking them. Article 130 secularized elementary **education**, ended the **Church**'s existence as a legal corporation, and nationalized the Church's property. Its clergy were forbidden to hold any public office or lead any political party. It was the enforcement of this article that provoked the **Cristero Rebellion**.

In 1995, however, federal court decisions affirmed by the **Supreme Court** allowed President **Zedillo** to change administrative regulations to lift the ban on clerical garb. Almost no priests or nuns, however, have so far resumed wearing cassocks or habits.

The Constitution abolished once again the office of vice president, providing instead for the Congress to elect an interim president for two years and then hold a special election. It refused **female suffrage** for fear of the Church's influence on **women**.

It interpreted the call for "**no reelection**" to mean single, four-year term presidencies, but Plutarco **Calles** had this amended to allow reelection after an interval. This enabled Alvador **Obregón** to be elected for a second term in 1928. When, however, Obregón was assassinated, the constitution was amended to restore the original prohibition, but changing the term from four years back to the earlier six, the famous "sexennium."

CONSTITUTIONALISTS. Supporters of Venustiano **Carranza** against Victoriano **Huerta** from 1913.

CONSULADO. A guild of merchants. Its prime function was to administer commercial law, but it was also important in promoting and controlling economic development. Election of its officers was usurped by the crown as Spanish administration underwent centralization in the late 1400s. With the creation of Spain's American empire and the decision to make Seville the only port from which ships might legally sail to the Indies, that city's *Consulado* came effectively to govern all transatlantic trade. Mexico City was unique in being permitted its own *Consulado* as early as 1592. It would be another two hundred years before this privilege was extended to other New World cities such as Buenos Aires, Caracas, and Havana.

CONTADORÍA MAYOR DE HACIENDA (C.M.H.). Agency of the executive, created in 1824 to take over the functions of the Mexican colonial version of the Spanish *Tribunal Mayor de Cuentas*. There are also individual *contadorías* at state level. In 1918 the C.M.H. became the *Departamento de la Contraloría de la Federación*, but the hostility of all federal **ministries** to any external audit secured its abolition in 1932. In December 1936 the C.M.H. was then reconstituted as a commission of the **Cámara de Diputados Federales**, (and reformed in December 1978), but in 1946 some of its functions were entrusted to the new *Secretaría de Bienes Nacionales y Inspección Administrativa,* renamed the *Secretaría del Patrimonio Nacional* and then *Secretaría de Patrimonio y Fomento Industrial* until such audit functions passed to the *Secretaría de Programación y Presupuesto* and eventually, via the *Secretaría de la Contraloría de la Federación*—SECOGEF (from 1982), to the *Secretaría de la Contraloría y Desarrollo Administrativo*—SECODAM (**Comptrollership General** from 1994). In 2000 Congress voted to replace the C.M.H. with a new **Auditoria Superior de La Federación**. [L. H.]

CONTEMPORÁNEOS. Literary journal of 1928–1932, edited by Salvador **Novo**.

CONTINENTAL SHELF. Mexico's continental shelf has an estimated **area** of 500,000 km^2. *See also* ISLANDS; MARITIME SOVEREIGNTY.

CONTRABAND. The wealth of the New World, particularly in precious metals, and Spain's inability to provide enough consumer goods or even shipping space to satisfy demand encouraged smuggling. This smuggling, particularly by the French, Dutch, and English, from early in the colonial era led to military measures such as the **Windward Fleet** to frustrate it. In modern times Mexico's principal illegal trading is in **narcotics** and in "people smuggling" of undocumented migrants across the **United States border**.

There is also much export of stolen art. An estimated 1,000 pieces have been smuggled abroad since 1999. Although all export of colonial art has been outlawed since 1972, there have been virtually no prosecutions for breaching this prohibition. [L. H.]

CONTRALORÍA GENERAL. *See* COMPTROLLERSHIP GENERAL.

CONTRERAS, JESUS F. (1866–1902). Artist who at an early age demonstrated extraordinary ability in the fine arts, specializing in sculpture under the renowned master Manuel **Noreña**. He assisted the master in the construction of the statue of **Cuauhétemoc** on the Paseo de la **Reforma**. The bronze statues in relief forming part of the *Monumento a la Raza* are perhaps his best-known work. His most impressive work is the marble statue in **Mexico City**'s **Alameda** Park, *Malgré Tout* ("despite everything").

CONVENCIÓN DE AGUASCALIENTES. *See* AGUASCALIENTES, CONVENTION OF.

CONVENCIÓN DE SOLEDAD. *See* SOLEDAD, CONVENCIÓN DE.

CONVENTION OF LONDON. *See* LONDON CONVENTION.

CONVERSO. A Sephardi and his descendants (*See* JEWS) who accepted baptism as a condition of residing in Spanish domains after 1492. Many continued to practice Judaism in secret and all were liable to be suspected of so doing. Technically, this was apostasy, a capital offense.

COOK, [CAPTAIN] JAMES, R. N. (1728–1779). Yorkshireman whose explorations of the Pacific included the coast of what is now British Colombia. His March 31, 1778, visit to **Nootka** Island led to conflicting British and Spanish claims to the island and an international incident.

COOPERATIVES. *See* BANCO NACIONAL DE FOMENTO COOPERATIVO; FIDEICOMISO.

COORDINACIÓN DE FUERZAS DE REACCIÓN Y APOYO INMEDIATO (C.F.R.A.I.). Coordination of Rapid Response and Assistance Forces, a branch of the **Public Security Ministry**, formed in 2001, mainly from former military policemen. Subordinate to it is the specialized counter-terrorist unit, *Fuerzas Especiales*.

COPPER. Mexico has the world's 10th largest output of copper.

COQUET, BENITO (1915–1994). Social security pioneer, an attorney, born in Jalapa, **Veracruz.** He sat in the **Cámara de Diputados Federales,** served as director of the **Instituto Nacional de Bellas Artes,** ambassador to Cuba, Minister of the Presidency (1956–1958), and then Director General of the **Instituto Mexicano de Seguridad Social** (1958–1964). As director, he extended social security coverage. After his retirement he drafted a measure for further extensions which was put into effect in 1984.

CORA. Indian group (also known as *Nyari*) in southern **Durango** and in **Nayarit.** It numbered about 10,200 in the mid-1990s.

CORDERO, JUAN (1824–1884). Painter from **Puebla,** one of Mexico's greatest, he studied in Rome at an early age and gained wide popularity in Mexico. Two of his most famous works are *Moses and the Annunciation* and *The Adulterous Woman.*

CÓRDOBA. This Spanish city has given its name to Mexican cities in **Durango** and **Veracruz-Llave.** The more important is the latter, founded November 29, 1617, at 18°53'N, 96°56'W and 860 m above sea level, to defend the **camino real** between **Mexico City** and **Veracruz** from attacks by **maroons.** It was where in 1821 the Treaty of Córdoba was signed to ratify the Plan of **Iguala.** It suffered a severe earthquake in 1973. The 2000 population of the city was 150,821, and the population of the **municipio** was 177,288. [L. H.]

CORN (*maíz*). The staple cereal of Meso-America began as a domestication of the native teosinte grass, in the valleys of **Tehuacán** and **Oaxaca** from about 8,000 BC. Before 2,000 BC, however, the seed cases were not soft enough nor the seeds big enough for corn to become the region's staple food. Corn reached something like its present form around 1,000 BC. Currently Mexico is the world's fourth largest corn producer (after the **United States,** China, and **Brazil**), growing in 2003 about 20 million *tonnes* on 7.8 million ha, with the greatest contribution coming from **Jalisco.**

CORONA DEL ROSAL, ALFONSO (1906–). Important **Partido Revolucionario Institucional** leader, an **UNAM** law graduate, and a reserve officer who rose to be *general de división* (major general), he sat in the **Cámara de diputados federales** from 1940–1943 and in the **Senate** from 1946–1952. He later served as governor of his native **Hidalgo**, head of the **Banco Nacional del Ejército y la Armada**, minister of the national patrimony, i.e., **natural resources** (1964–1966), and governor of the **Federal District** (1966–1970). He headed the PRI Youth (*Juventud del PRI*), held various positions on the **Comité Ejecutivo Nacional**, and was party president from 1958 to 1964.

CORONADO, FRANCISCO. *See* VÁZQUEZ DE CORONADO Y VALDÉS, FRANCISCO.

CORPUS CHRISTI MASSACRE. On June 10, 1971, at the height of the "**dirty war**," about 10,000 protestors or rioters (according to your political viewpoint) marched on the **Instituto Político Nacional**, demanding that the federal government spend more on **education**. There was a confrontation with "truckloads" of **Halcones**, involving truncheons and firearms and causing 80 admitted deaths. The **police** were involved only at the end, but the 200 they then arrested have never, it is claimed, been seen again. A resulting inquiry was closed down by Luis **Echeverría Álvarez**, president at the time, as it did not seem to be getting anywhere. In 2002, however, President Vicente **Fox Quezada** decided to reopen the matter and appointed Ignacio **Carrillo Prieto** as special prosecutor. [L. H.]

CORRAL, RAMÓN (1854–1912). Politician from Álamos, **Sonora**, held various posts, the most important of which were Governor of Sonora, interior minister (from 1879), and Porfirio **Díaz'** **vice president** (from 1904). His close association with Díaz and his reputation for selling the **Yaqui** Indians into what amounted to economic slavery made him one of the most hated men in Mexico. His resignation on May 25, 1911, was simultaneous with that of Diaz. He died in exile in Paris.

CORREA, VICTOR MANUEL (1917–1996). The first member of a conservative opposition party to govern a state since the **Revolution of 1910** was born on October 18, in **Mérida**, of which he was mayor in 1967–1970, He helped elect two **Partido Acción Nacional** members to the municipal council and two to the state legislature. He ran for governor of **Yucatán** in 1969 and 1975, founded the trust department for the **Banco del Sudeste**, and popularized the trust concept throughout Yucatán.

CORREGIDOR. Colonial administrator of a *corregimiento* (a territory reserved for **Indians**).

CORRIDO. Originally an Andalucian romantic narrative in octosyllabic verse, the word in a Mexican context generally denotes a chapbook of popular poetry, similar to the Luso-Brazilian *literatura de cordel*.

CORRO, JOSÉ JUSTO (1794–1864). President of Mexico from 1836–1837, succeeding on the death of Miguel **Barragán**, he governed during the difficult time when **Texas** became independent. As a rather undistinguished chief executive, he accomplished little except the abandonment of the federalist **Constitution of 1824** in favor of the centralist **Siete Leyes**.

CORRUPTION. The Spanish Crown was well aware of the need to guard against dishonest officials. Each administrator could be the subject of the **visita** (or outside review) at any time and on his departure was subject to the juicio de **residencia** reviewing his tenure, often conducted by his successor to be. No such restraints limited the opportunities of post-**Independence** rulers. The depredations of López de **Santa Anna** are merely an extreme case of self-enrichment by those in power. The **Revolution of 1910** promised reform but all too often placed in power the humble who were simply overcome by the novel opportunities presented by high office. The successful prosecution of transport minister Eugenio **Méndez Docurro** was unprecedented, but it encouraged action against others. In 1998–1999 the federal attorney general for the first time undertook an extensive examination of the **sestenio** of Carlos **Salinas de Gortari**, so far reaching that Gortari preferred exile to facing his accusers.

In mid-2001, Transparency International ranked Mexico 51st among the nations in descending order of rectitude, scoring 3.7 on its 10 point scale (where 10 = perfection), behind **Chile** (18th), Uruguay

(36th), Costa Rica (40th), **Brazil** (46th), and Colombia (50th), but ahead of **Argentina** (57th), and Venezuela (69th). *See also* MORDIDA; WORMAT, OLGA. [L. H.]

CORTÉS, HERNÁN, 1° MARQUÉS DEL VALLE DE OAXACA (1485–1547). Spanish conqueror of Mexico, born in Medellín in the border province of Extremadura. He studied at Salamanca without graduating, fought in Italy under the *Gran Capitán*, and was invited out to Hispaniola by his kinsman Nicolás de Ovando. He later became the secretary and confidant of Diego Velázquez, the conqueror of **Cuba**, who made him mayor of Santiago de Cuba. Velázquez commissioned him to follow up Juan de **Grijalva**'s exploration of the Mexican coast. The governor later cancelled the mission as a result of intrigue (and Cortés' amorous involvement with a niece of Velásquez), but too late to stop him sailing, in 1518, with 500 men in 10 ships. He landed in **Yucatán**, sailed up the coast and on July 9, 1519, he founded Villa Rica de la Vera Cruz, today's **Veracruz**. Having horses, firearms, and the help of **Indians** hostile to the Aztecs, also benefiting from various **Aztec** superstitions and predictions, he entered their capital, **Tenochtitlán**. Although driven out on the **Noche Triste**, he returned to defeat the Aztecs decisively at **Tlateloclo** on August 13, 1521.

After this victory he was showered with honors, including his marquisate and huge tracts of land in Mexico. Besides administering the new colony, he led an expedition into **Central America**. Once again he fell victim to intrigue and returned to Spain in 1540 in the forlorn hope of defending himself. He fought in a Spanish expedition to Algeria. Then he retired, forgotten, to his native village where he died. His body, however, was brought back for burial in Mexico.

CORTÉS, MARTIN (1522–1595?). Illegitimate son of Hernán **Cortes** and La **Malinche**, and supposedly the first **mestizo**, born to an Indian woman and a Spanish **hidalgo**. Involved like his half-brother Martín **Cortés y Zúñiga** in the **Ávila-Cortés conspiracy**, he too was arrested and exiled to Spain for life.

CORTÉS, SEA OF. *See* CALIFORNIA, GULF OF.

CORTES OF CÁDIZ. Legislature of the Spanish resistance movement against the puppet regime of Joseph **Bonaparte**, summoned by the

Junta Central. It met on the Isla de León off Cádiz, from 1810–1814. With representatives from the entire Spanish empire (among them Miguel **Ramos Arizpe** from **New Spain**), it introduced extensive administrative reforms in the Spanish territories it controlled worldwide and drafted the liberal **Spanish Constitution of 1812**. [L. H.]

CORTÉS Y ZÚÑIGA, MARTÍN, 2° MARQUÉS DEL VALLE DE OAXACA (1532–1589). Son and heir of Hernán **Cortés** by his second wife, Juana de Zúñiga, he accompanied his father back to Spain in 1540 and fought at the Battle of St. Quintin in Flanders. He returned in 1563 to a great welcome in Mexico. There the abortive uprising led by the **González de Ávila** brothers attempted to install him as captain general of **New Mexico** in virtual independence of Spain. Sentenced to death, he was reprieved, but exiled in Spain and forbidden ever to return to Mexico.

COSALÁ. Small **Sinaloa** town with 5,300 inhabitants in 1990, located at 24°21'N, 106°41'W, 155 km from **Culiacán**. Its altitude is 200 m, Founded in 1550 as Reales Minas de las 11,000 Vírgenes, notable for having been capital of the former Estado de **Occidente** from 1826–1827, it was one of the major **mining** centers of northwestern Mexico in the late 19th century. It is the **cabecera** of its namesake **municipio** of 2,429 km^2, with a population of 17,000 in 1990.

COSÍO VILLEGAS, DANIEL (1898–1976). One of Mexico's leading writers and historians, he was born July 23 in **Mexico City**. He studied law at **UNAM**, and then economics and history at Harvard, Cornell, Wisconsin, and London universities. He founded the **Fondo de Cultura Econòmica** in 1935 and helped establish the **Colegio de México** in 1940. There he set national standards for doctoral studies. He also was advisor to several finance and foreign ministers and directors of the **Banco de México**, Mexican representative at the **Bretton Woods** conference, ambassador to UNESCO (1957–1959) and then its secretary general in 1959. His many publications include the 5-volume *Historia moderna de México* (1963), *La sucesión presidencial* (1975), and *La sucesión: desenlace y perspectivas* (1975). He died on March 11 in his native city.

COSTA CHICA. This 325 km (200 mile) stretch along the Pacific coast of **Guerrero** and **Oaxaca** from southeast of **Acapulco** to Puerto Ángel is a zone of poor subsistence farming inhabited by **blacks** and **Indians**. It was only recently made accessible by road with the construction in the 1960s of a rough rural road from Acapulco, some 250 km (160 miles) to the northwest. This road cut the journey time from a week's donkey ride to a three-hour bus ride. Electricity and **television** have followed. [L. H.]

COSTUME. *See* CHARRO; CHINA POBLANA; GUAYABERA; JAROCHO; OTONÍ; REBOZO; SARAPE; WRESTLING.

COTTON. Mexico has been growing cotton since 5000 BC. Despite problems with pink bollworm, mid-20th century Mexico was the second largest producer of cotton and one of the world's five largest exporters, selling half its crop abroad. Then internal consumption began to rise, while reduced profitability discouraged production. Exports fell from 800,000 bales (of 500 lbs) in 1975 to 300,000 in 1985. Since joining **NAFTA**, Mexico has become a major importer of American cotton (200,000 bales in 1992). Genetically modified cotton was introduced in 1996. By 2000 this genetically modified cotton was planted on 26,300 ha, a third of Mexico's crop acreage. [L. H.]

COUNCIL OF NOTABLES. *See* JUNTA DE NOTABLES.

COUNCIL OF THE INDIES. The usual English name for Spain's executive council and supreme court for her American empire, successively the *Junta de Indias* (1504), *Consejo de Indias* (1519), and *Real y Supremo Consejo de las Indias* (1524). The members were prominent Spaniards appointed by the Crown, consisting after 1571 of a president, four to five councilors, a *fiscal*, a *relator* and several minor officials. It became subordinate to the new **navy** ministry (*Secretaría de Marina y de las Indias*) in 1714, was reduced to advisory status in 1790, and abolished in 1812. **Ferdinand VII** revived it in 1814, but it was definitively abolished after his death in 1834. [L. H.]

COUPS D'ÉTAT (*golpes de estado*). Mexico suffered several abrupt changes of government by force in the first half of the 19th century, but it has been free of them since that time. The **Revolution of 1910** saw many attempted *golpes*, such as the murder of President **Madero** and the challenges to President **Carranza** in 1915–1920. None of these attempts had the essential quality of sudden success, and generally sustained fighting followed even the more successful ones.

COURTS. The modern system consists of a **Supreme Court**, 91 circuit courts, 49 courts of appeal, and 185 district courts. *See also* ACORDADA; AUDIENCIA.

COZUMEL (Mayan "isle of swallows"). Mexico's largest inhabited island, a flat, limestone, oval island, 47 x 15 km, totaling 647 km², at 20°30'N, 86°57'W, 19 km off the shore of northeast **Quintana Roo** (of which it is a **municipio**). It was already important as a trading center in the 1300s. Thirty-two island sites have **Maya** ruins, but the most impressive was bulldozed to build a **World War II** airstrip. The Spanish, under Juan de **Grijalva**, arrived from **Cuba** in May, 1518, seeking **Indians** to enslave. By 1570 **smallpox** had reduced the pre-conquest population of 40,000 to just 30. In the 1700s, Henry Morgan and others used the island as a pirate hideout. Abraham Lincoln is said to have planned its purchase as a place to which to deport freed slaves, but his plan was frustrated by the **Caste War of Yucatán.** A small **chicle** industry developed there in the early 1900s. Its modern development for **tourism** (now its only economic resource) began when Jacques Cousteau revealed the coral reefs of Palencar and their underwater attractions for scuba divers in 1959. Unfortunately the reefs have been damaged by the building of a pier for cruise liners in the 1990s. The island's dense vegetation was devastated by Hurricane **Wilma** in 2005.

San Miguel de Cozumel is the only town. It had 60,091 inhabitants in 2000 and 90,000 in 2003.

Singer Kirsty MacColl was killed there when she was struck by a speedboat belonging to millionaire Guillermo González Novás on December 18, 2000. The case still needs to be settled.

CRACK, MANIFIESTO DEL. Literary program of 1996 adhered to by the so-called *Grupo Crack* of Ricardo Chávez Castañeda, Igancio **Padilla**, Pedro Ángel **Palou**, Eloy **Urroz**, and Jorge **Volpi**, who co-authored *Crack, instrucciones de uso* in 2005. [L. H.]

CREELMAN, JAMES (1859–1915). This Canadian-born journalist on February 17, 1908, secured an interview with Porfirio **Diaz** in which the president said he believed Mexico was ready for an opposition party, and that, if he lost in 1910, he would peacefully turn over power to it. The president's failure to keep this promise fueled the opposition to his rule that eventually erupted into the **Revolution of 1910**.

CREMI-UNIÓN, GRUPO FINANCIERO. Banking group of the 1980s, headed by Carlos **Cabal Peniche**.

CREOLE (*criollo*). Originally the Portuguese *crioulo*, a term for a "tame" slave (i.e., one born in captivity) the word came to denote anything (**coffee**, longhorn cattle, cuisine, life style, culture) developed in the New World from European or African sources. It was used as an insult by *Peninsulares* for the descendants of Spanish settlers in the Americas, who turned it instead into a proud self-designation, completely free of the suggestion of racial mixing that the word often bears in English or French. Although frequently very wealthy, these "white Creoles" came to resent the discrimination they increasingly suffered as Spain tended more and more to reserve positions of political and ecclesiastical power for expatriate Spaniards (seen in Madrid as more objective, more loyal, and less corrupt). A significant factor in unifying creole discontent was the formation of the Army of **New Spain** in 1761, a move prompted by fear of a British invasion: When creole recruits met at **Jalapa**, they came for the first time to realize what a powerful class they constituted. On the eve of the fight for **independence** in 1810 it is estimated that they made up one million of Mexico's population of just over six million.

The word itself was less popular in Mexico than elsewhere in the New World. *Americano* was the preferred alternative.

CRIME. *See* BANDITRY; CONTRABAND; CORRUPTION; HOMICIDE; LAW; MACHISMO; NARCOTICS; PISTOLERO; POLICE; PRISONS.

CRIMINAL CODE. *See* PENAL CODE.

CRISTERO REBELLION. Provoked by Plutarco Elias **Calles'** attempt to enforce the registration of priests required by the **Consti-**

tution of 1917, it led to violence and bloodshed. Most churches were without priests for the three years it lasted (1927–1930), and only clandestine services were being held. The name came from "¡Viva Cristo Rey!" the battle cry of the fanatically fervent *cristeros*, who were particularly strong in **Jalisco** and **Michoacán**. In 1928 one of them, José de **León Toral**, assassinated Álvaro **Obregón**, but documented accounts of the barbarism practiced by both sides was not available until an Interior Ministry report of 1934 was made public in 1984. Government supporters, particularly rural schoolteachers, had their earlobes cut off and a cross carved on each arm. Captured rebels were beaten up and sometimes castrated. Although the total number of victims (on both sides) has never been released, thousands were eventually forced to flee for safety to the **United States**.

When it became clear than neither side would prevail, U.S. ambassador Dwight **Morrow** negotiated a settlement, in effect from June 26, 1929. The key government compromise was to tolerate religious instruction in school. Although some violence continued through the 1930s, particularly in **Veracruz-Llave**, the settlement marks the end of the last major **Church** and State controversy in Mexico. Both sides had realized that a truce was needed for the good of the country and themselves. *See also* GOYTORTUA, JESÚS.

CROCKETT, DAVY (1786–1836). This American frontiersman and patriot was long believed to have died in the **Alamo**. In 1999 a Texan family auctioned off for several thousand dollars the diary of a lieutenant colonel in José Antonio López de **Santa Anna**'s army. According to the diary, Crockett did not die in the Alamo but tried to flee and was killed by a Mexican marksman. Researchers found, however, that the diary had been written in far off **Mexico City**, and not until 1840, in an attempt to win favor from Santa Anna, who was then trying to rebuild his image among the Mexicans after his defeat at **San Jacinto**. [L. H.]

CROIX, CARLOS FRANCISCO DE, MARQUÉS DE CROIX (1699–1786). Born in France, of Flemish descent, Croix was taken to Spain as a child and entered royal service as a youth. Appointed **viceroy** of **New Spain** and intendant of the Royal Treasury in 1766, he was ordered to expel the **Jesuits**. This provoked a rebellion that received support particularly in **Guana-juato**, **Pátzcuaro**, and **Valladolid**. He sent expeditions of inspection into **Sonora** and Upper and Lower **California**. He promoted the use of Spanish among the **Indians** and introduced a national lottery to improve viceregal finances. He built the fortress of San Carlos (named for **Charles III**) in **Veracruz**. He returned to Spain in 1771 and was appointed Captain General of Valencia, where he died. [L. H.]

CROIX, TEODORO DE (1730–1791). *Comandante General* of the **Provincias Internas** from 1776–1786.

CRUICKSHANK GARCÍA, JORGE (1915–1989). First minority-party senator since the **Revolution of 1910**, born on July 29 in Tehuantepec, **Oaxaca**. He graduated from the *Escuela de Ingeniería Mécanica y Eléctrica* (School of Mechanical and Electrical Engineering). In 1938 he became secretary of the National Socialist Youth of Mexico, and in 1940 a professor at the **Instituto Politécnico Nacional**. In 1943 he was elected to the governing council of the **Universidad de los Trabajadores**. He helped draft the constitution of the **Sandwiched National de Trabajadores de la Educación** whose national committee he joined in 1947. In 1948–1951 he represented civil servant **trade unions** on the **Instituto de Seguridad y Servicios Sociales de los Trabajadores del Estado**. In 1948 he helped Vicente **Lombardo Toledano** found the **Partido Popular Socialista**, and in January 1969 he became its secretary general. The first PPS deputy in the Oaxaca state legislature in 1968, he sat in the **Cámara de Diputados Federales** in 1964–1967 and 1970–1973 and was elected to the **Senate** for 1976–1982.

CRUZ, JUANA INÉS DA LA. *See* JUANA INÉS DE LA CRUZ, SOR.

CUADERNOS AMERICANOS. A leading academic journal, each issue of which is a monograph, published in Mexico City since 1943.

CUAJINICUILAPA. Village of the **Costa Chica** with 8,000 residents who make it the largest Mexican town with a black majority. It boasts a modest *Museo de las Culturas Afromestizas*, perhaps the only official place in Mexico to recognize the country's heritage of **African**

slavery. **Blacks** elsewhere in Mexico are seldom aware of their origins, let alone proud of them. [L. H.]

CUARTÓN. Administrative subdivision of a **partido**.

CUATEQUIL. Indian name for the colonial **repartimiento**.

CUATLA, BATTLE OF. Outstanding victory of the patriots led by José María **Morelos y Pavón** over royalists led by General **Calleja del Rey**. *See also* MENDOZA, NARCISO.

CUAUHTÉMOC. (1) City of **Chihuahua state** with 124,378 inhabitants in 2000.

(2) **Delegación** of the **Federal District** at 19°30'N, 99°10'W, occupying much of central **Mexico City**.

CUAUHTÉMOC, TLATOANI (1495/1502?–1525). Last **Aztec** emperor, son of Anuízotl, and nephew and son-in-law of **Moctezuma II**, regarded as a national hero in modern Mexico. During the reign of his cousin **Cuitláhuac** he led the **Aztec** armies, successfully containing the forces of Hernán **Cortes** for several months. He succeeded to the crown on March 1, 1521, but by August most of **Tenochtitlán** was in Spanish hands and the Aztecs were finally defeated on the 13th. He and his chief officials tried to flee by canoe, but they were captured. His subsequent tortures and the stoicism with which he bore them are legendary. Although his feet were put in boiling oil, he never revealed the location of the treasures lost by the Spaniards during the **Noche Triste**. He was then taken on Cortés' expedition to Honduras and hanged en route, at Izancánac, in **Tabasco**, for treason on March 5, 1525.

The name means "falling eagle," a metaphor for the setting sun. It sometimes appears in the form *Cuahtémoctzin* (or *Guatemótzin*), incorporating a title indicative of nobility.

Golden objects found during the 1969 building of the **Metro** are thought to have been part of "Cuauhtémoc's treasure."

CUAUHTÉMOC S.A. Monterrey brewers who produce *Carta Blanca* and other brands in Latin America's largest brewery, founded in 1890 by the German-Mexican José Schneider.

CUBA, RELATIONS WITH. Cuba's Governor **Velásquez de Cuéllar** sent a small reconnoitering expedition to the coast of **Yucatán**, from which came Cortés' 1519 expedition. It remained easier for settlers in Yucatán to trade with Cuba than with other locations in Mexico until **railroads** provided an overland link after **World War II**. From 1535–1821 **Mexico City** was the seat of the **viceroyalty** of **New Spain**, which nominally included the **Captaincy General** of Cuba, a practically autonomous jurisdiction extending to Florida and **Louisiana**.

Mexico achieved its **independence** in 1821 and was sympathetic to Cubans wishing to end Spanish rule. The *Águila Negra* conspiracy was formed by Cubans exiled in Mexico. On April 6, 1869, Mexico recognized the rebels' **República en Armas** as a belligerent.

The chaos of the Mexican revolution of 1910–1917 led to some **emigration** of Mexicans to Cuba. Afterwards Mexico was used as a refuge for Cubans at odds with their government, notably Fidel Castro who outfitted his *Granma* expedition there.

Thanks to foreign minister Manuel **Tello**, and in accord with the **Estrada doctrine**, Mexico refused to break with Cuba in 1962, although its government condemned the **Soviet Union**'s introduction of nuclear missiles into Cuba and supported the **United States** naval blockade. For the ten years from 1962–1972, Mexico and Canada were the only Western Hemisphere countries that retained diplomatic relations with Cuba. In 1968 the riots of the Plaza de **Tlatelolco** owed much to the efforts of 26 Cuban agents, who were later arrested. Photographs of their confiscated passports appeared on the front page of *Excelsior*.

In 1976 Mexico negotiated an agreement with Cuba for shared **fishing** for **grouper** off **Yucatán**.

President **López Portillo** paid an official visit to Cuba in 1981, and in the 1980s Mexico cultivated friendly relations with Sandinista **Nicaragua** in a forlorn hope of counteracting Cuban influence there. In the mid-1990s when the **Chiapas** uprising occurred, there was evidence that some of the rebels had been trained in Cuba. Mexico maintains a friendly posture toward Cuba, while criticizing the United States trade embargo and strongly opposing the Helms-Burton Act. Mexican investment in Cuba by way of **joint ventures** has increased significantly since the 1980s. Mexican exports to Cuba in January–October 1995 were up 77 percent over 1994, when they totaled

$269,000,000—0.4 percent of all her exports. Cuba sold $12,000,000 worth of goods to Mexico in 1994.

Relations with Cuba began to cool after the 2000 election of President **Vicente Fox Quesada**. The new President publicly questioned the policies of the Cuban regime. Mexico withdrew its ambassador after allegations of Cuban meddling in a Mexican political scandal. Mexico was also unhappy with a speech by Fidel Castro accusing Mexico of blindly following U.S. directives in supporting a **United Nations** resolution criticizing human rights protection in his country.

[In February 2005, the U.S. government ordered an American-owned hotel to expel Cuban guests who had come to conduct "secret" negotiations with American business interests. The **Mexico City** authorities saw this act as infringing on Mexican sovereignty, a reaction that proved so popular among ordinary Mexicans in an election year that the federal government felt obliged to support it. L. H.]

CUE DE DUARTE, IRMA (1938–). First woman secretary general of the **Partido Revolutionario Institucional**'s **Comité Ejecutivo Nacional** (August–December 1984), born on May 7 in Tierra Blanca, **Veracruz**. She earned her law degree in 1959 from **UNAM** with a thesis on the writ of **amparo**. Since then she has been a professor there of public administration. In 1982–1985, she sat in the **Cámara de diputados federales** and was a member of the PRI's advisory council on political and economic policies.

CUERNAVACA. Capital of **Morelos** at 18°57'N, 99°15'W, now only 82 km south of **México City** via a toll expressway which cuts through mountain passes. Its population was 314,000 in 1976 and 501,000 in 1995. The city contains the Palace of Hernán **Cortés**, used as his head-quarters during his **conquest of México**. Its corridors have world-famous murals of Mexican history by Diego **Rivera**, commissioned in 1928 as a goodwill gesture by **United States** ambassador Dwight **Morrow**. With a year-round spring climate, Cuernavaca is a tourist resort that also has the vacation homes of high-level government officials, entertainment celebrities, and other wealthy Mexicans.

CUETO RAMÍREZ, LUIS (1901–1977). Career **army** officer, made a brigadier general in 1956, a student of **police** administration, released by the army so he could serve as police chief of the **Federal District** from 1961–1969. As such, he directed police operations during the violent student riots of the period.

CUEVAS, JOSÉ LUIS (1934–). The works of this modern painter and sculptor became known internationally in the 1980s. His pictures and ceramics are exhibited in the *Museo José Luis Cuevas* on Academia Street in **Mexico City**'s historic district.

CUEVAS, MARIANO (1879–1949). Jesuit historian and university professor best remembered for such important works as his **church** history, *Historia de la iglesia en México* (1928), and his general national history, *Historia de la nación mexicana* (1940).

CUEVAS CANCINO, FRANCISCO (1921–). Diplomat, born May 7 in **Mexico City**. He obtained a law degree from the **Escuela Libre de Derecho** in 1943, and a master's in civil law from McGill University in Montreal in 1946. After further studies in London, England, he became a professor at the **Colegio de Mexico**. He served as legal advisor to the Mexican delegation to the **United Nations** in 1960–1961, was ambassador successively to the U.N. in 1965–1970, to Belgium in 1980–1982, to the **United Kingdom** in 1982–1086, and to Austria in 1986–1988. In retirement he wrote several works on foreign relations.

CUICUILCO. This site now is in the **Federal District** at the intersection of Avenida Insurgentes Sul and the Anillo Periférico. It was one of the oldest cities in the Valley of **Mexico**, dating back perhaps to 1200 BC. Part of it was buried in volcanic ash c.300 AD, but the site seems to have been abandoned after an eruption on April 24, 76 AD, or possibly after one in 30 AD. [L. H.]

In the south of the city stands the round pyramid complex that forms the oldest surviving ceremonial center in the Valley of **Mexico**, dating from c.600 BC.

CUITLÁHUAC (1476–1520). Penultimate **Aztec** "emperor" (**tlatoani**), he succeeded on the death of **Moctezuma I** in June 1520. Free from the latter's many superstitions, he was able to drive the

Spaniards from **Tenochtitlán**, killing many during the famous **Noche triste.** Within six months, in December 1520, he himself was dead of **smallpox.** His successor was **Cuauhtémoc.**

CULIACÁN. (1) Westward flowing river of **Sinaloa state.**

(2) Name of the capital city of **Sinaloa** state, officially Culiacán Rosales, 50 km from the Pacific, founded by Nuño Beltrán de **Guzmán** in 1531. It had 264,000 inhabitants in 1976; 601,700 in 1990; and 745,532 in 2001.

(3) **Municipio** of the same name extends over 4,759 km^2, from 25°10' to 24°S and from 106°56' to 107°43'W. Since 1970 its local authorities have favored the **Church,** allowing it to flout the restrictions imposed by the **Constitution of 1917** two decades before these were legally relaxed.

CULTURE. *See* ART; DRAMA; MUSIC; NOVELS; POETRY; SPORT.

CURANDERO. Practitioner of folk medicine, whose training was in a rural school or apprenticeship rather than in a recognized medical school. *Curanderos* use herb and other traditional remedies and tend to practice in relatively isolated towns and regions. Even in the cities of the **United States** border region, however, one can find herb shops selling home remedies with no prescription required. *See also* BRUJA.

CURRENCY. *See* CACAO; COINAGE; DOLLAR; EXCHANGE RATE; PESO; REAL.

– D –

DANCE. *See* BLACKS; CHIAPANECAS; JARABE TAPATÍO; JAROCHO; MACARENA; MARIMBA; QUETZAL DANCE; TEENEK INDIANS; TOTOMEC INDIANS; YAQUI.

DANIEL, CAMILO. This priest in July 1986 suddenly found himself an important endorser of Francisco **Barrio** as **Partido de Acción Nacional** candidate for governor of **Chihuahua**. At a time when the

Church still understood it was to remain silent in political campaigns, Father Daniel suddenly began to function as he might have after the 1995 easing of restrictions on the clergy expressing political opinions. He had been preaching a very mild form of Liberation Theology (but not the clumsy mixture of Christian and Marxist ideas being spread by radicals in Central America), and he merely campaigned at non-political meetings for more efficient welfare programs at state and national level. Barrio lost, and Father Daniel's hunger-strike protest at the rigged vote count was quickly forgotten.

DANIELS, JOSEPHUS (1862–1948). This former **United States** Secretary of the Navy and North Carolina newspaper publisher was appointed ambassador to Mexico in 1934. Although the Mexican people received him at first with hostility, his genuine friendliness toward them reversed this initial feeling. He was sympathetic to **Cárdenas**' ideas and helped to calm US-Mexican relations when the **petroleum** industry was nationalized in 1938.

DANZOS PALOMINO, RAMÓN (1918–). This teacher from **Sonora**, a member of the **Partido Comunista Mexicano**'s central committee from 1936–1981, was a leader of socialist youth groups since the 1950s. In 1963 he helped found the **Confederación Campesina Independiente**. In 1964 he established the People's Electoral Front to encourage votes for the **Partido Popular Socialista (PPS)** instead of the dominant **Partido Revolucionario Institucional**. From 1935 until the mid-1970s, he organized various groups of squatters who temporarily seized farmlands in the northern states.

DÁVILA AGUIRRE, VICENTE (1893–1960). Born in **Cohuila**, he graduated in engineering in the **United States**. As a military commander in 1915–1920 he supported **Carranza**. As governor of **San Luis Potosí**, he enforced the reforms of the **Revolution of 1910**. He was discredited politically for supporting Adolfo de la **Huerta**'s abortive rebellion of 1923.

DÁVILA Y PADILLA, AGUSTÍN (1562–1604). A Mexican-born historian and Dominican religious, he was named "Preacher of the

King" and "Chronicler of the Indies" by Phillip III, who commissioned him to write his most famous work, *Historia de la provincia de Santiago de la Nueva España del Orden de Santo Domingo*, published in 1596. From 1598 he was archbishop of Santo Domingo, the city where he later died.

DAY OF THE DEAD. *See* ALL SOULS' DAY.

DE ("of," "from"). For names beginning with this prefix, see under following word (e.g., LANDA, Diego de).

DEATH RATE. Better **public health** measures have been drastically reducing the death rate almost every year since 1905, when it was 33.2 per thousand. It was down to 22 per thousand by 1930, 23.4 per thousand by 1940, 10.1 per thousand by 1970, and to 5.4 per thousand by the late 1990s, despite widespread infectious and parasitical **disease** among the poor. By 2006 it was down to 4.74 per thousand. *See also* INFANT MORTALITY.

DEBT MORATORIUM. *See* FOREIGN DEBT MORATORIUM.

DECENA TRÁGICA, LA ("Tragic Ten Days"). This refers to the 10 days from February 9–18, 1913, when **Madero**'s government was subjected to open anarchy and cannon fire, leading to the **Embassy Pact** and the takeover of power by General Victoriano **Huerta**.

DECIMALIZATION. *See* COINAGE.

DECLARATION OF INDEPENDENCE. *See* INDEPENDENCE.

DEDAZO ("finger pointing"). In this tradition of **presidential succession** under the **Partido Revolucionario Institucional** the outgoing president chose his successor from among three or four leading contenders. [The failure of President **Zedillo** to endorse his choice in this way may well have contributed to the PRI's losing the **election of 2000**. In contrast, the first **Partido de Acción Nacional** president, **Fox Quezada**, successfully handpicked his successor in more or less the traditional manner. *See also* GREAT ELECTORS. L. H.]

DEFEÑO. *See* CHILANGO.

DEFENSE MINISTRY (*Secretaría de la Defensa Nacional,* **SEDENA**). The constitution of the **Apatzingán Congress** decreed a *Secretaría de Guerra.* The brief **First Empire** instituted a *Secretaría de Estado de Guerra y Marina* in November 1821. This was revived in 1843 as the *Ministerio de Guerra y Marina,* but redesignated a *"secretaría"* in 1861. A decree of November 1937 adopted the new international fashion of "national defense" (*defensa nacional*), but only two years later a separate naval department (*Departamento de Marina Nacional*) was created. The **Air Force** remains part of the Defense Ministry. [L. H.]

DEFORESTATION. Mexico's rate of deforestation is second only to that of Indonesia, totaling three million acres a year in 1993–2000. Not only is much of it economically misguided, but it is often driven by the **narcotics** industry, either directly for drug cultivation or as a means of money laundering. It is aided by both violence and Mexico's endemic **corruption** and inadequate **law** enforcement. Actual lumber production has been falling, unable to compete with imports of soft woods from the **United States**, the 1994 output of 5.9 million m^2 being the lowest for two decades. [L. H.]

DEGOLLADO, SANTOS (1811–1861). Guananjuato-born reformer, politician, and soldier, Egollada sought to limit the power of the **Church**, fought **corruption** in government, and led a strong effort to improve **agriculture** by scientific means. In 1847 he was rector of the newly reopened **Colegio de San Nicolás**, and later war minister under **Juárez**, a position from which he was later dismissed for recommending foreign mediation in a dispute with British landowners. Known as the "Hero of Defeats" for losing more battles than he won, he was ambushed and killed by the conservative General Leonardo Márquez.

DEL ("of the"). For words and names so beginning, see under following word (e.g., RÍO, Andrés del).

DELEGACIÓN. Since December 1928, this was an administrative subdivision of the **Federal District**, replacing the **municipio**. There were originally 12, plus a *Departamento Central*. In 1941 the latter was merged with General Anaya (only created as a *municipio* in 1924) as the *Ciudad de México*. In 1970 this was split into four (Benito Juárez, **Cuauhtémoc**, Miguel Hidalgo, and Venustiano Carranza), making a current total of 16 (the others being Álvaro Obregón, Azcapotzalco, Coyoacán, Cuajimalpa, Gustavo A. Madero, Iztacalco, Iztapalapa, Magdalena Contreras, Milpa Alta, Tláhuac, Tlalpan, and Xochimilco). Each is divided into wards called *colonias* (e.g., 74, including the downtown *Zona Central*, in the case of the central delegation of Venustiano Carranza). [L. H.]

DELICIAS. The municipio of **Chihuahua state** had 116,426 inhabitants in 2000, was established in 1932, and was named for the railroad station serving the *Hacienda Delicias*. Its namesake **cabecera** at 28°10'N, 105°30'W claims to be Mexico's youngest city. [L. H.]

DEPARTAMENTO. This refers to a division of a **state** under the **Siete Leyes** from 1837–1841.

DEPRESSION OF THE 1930S. The economic effects of the **Escobar Rebellion** left Mexico in a poor state to cope with the problems created by the world's worst economic depression. The depression's effects included the country being forced off the **gold standard** in July 1931. It shared with Russia, China, Turkey, and Italy, however, the distinction of not suffering a traumatic change of government (having, like them, already had its own violent revolution a decade before). [L. H.]

DEVELOPMENT MINISTRY (*Secretaría de Fomento*). This was a forerunner of the **Trade Ministry**.

DÍA, El. This **Mexico City** newspaper gives its editorial support to the **Partido Popular Socialista**.

DIA DE LA NACIÓN. The National Day is September 1st.

DIA DE LA RAZA. *See* COLUMBUS DAY.

DIA DE LA REVOLUCIÓN. This is celebrated on November 20, the anniversary of the outbreak of the Mexican **Revolution** when **Madero** declared himself **president**. It is one of Mexico's national **holidays**.

DIA DE LOS MUERTOS. *See* ALL SOULS' DAY.

DIA DE LOS REYES. *See* TWELFTH NIGHT.

DIABLO, PICHACO DEL. This 2830 m peak in **Baja California del Norte** is the site of the **Observatorio Nacional Astronómico.**

DIARIO OFICIAL. This official daily gazette of Mexico promulgates all federal laws.

DÍAZ, FÉLIX (1868–1945). This nephew of Porfirio **Diaz** in early October 1912 led an unsuccessful revolt in **Veracruz** against his uncle's successor, **Madero**, and was imprisoned in **Mexico City**. He was released by Manuel **Mondragón** and led an attack on the presidential palace, beginning the **Decena Trágica**, which was ended by the "**Embassy Pact**" and the accession of Victoriano **Huerta** as provisional president. Díaz was to have succeeded **Huerta** as president, but the latter sent him instead to a diplomatic post in **Japan**. After his return he led another abortive revolt, this time against **Carranza**, for which he was exiled in 1919 and not allowed to return until 1937. He died in the city of **Veracruz.**

DÍAZ, PORFÍRIO (1830–1915). José de la Cruz Porfirio Díaz, was president of Mexico seven times and exercised presidential power in his own right, or behind a nominee (Manuel **González** from 1880–1884), from 1876 until the **Revolution of 1910**. He was "reelected" in 1884, 1888, 1892, 1896, 1900, 1906, and 1910. Born in **Oaxaca** on September 16 , he studied at the Institute of Oaxaca under **Benito Juárez**, worked as a librarian, and studied law. He began his military career when he joined the 1855 fight for the Plan de **Ayutla**. In the Wars of the **Reform** and the fight against **Maximilian** he was one of Mexico's most distinguished generals, capturing **Mexico City** in 1867. After campaigning several times for the presidency, he finally overthrew Lerdo de **Tejada** and was named provisional president in 1876 and definitive president on November 29, 1876.

His controversial rule gave Mexico a stability it had not known since **Independence**. The countryside was pacified by his brutal **Guardia Rural**. He disregarded the masses, considering that **Indians** were good for little more than hard physical labor, and that Mexico's future lay with the whites.

His inner group of advisers, the **científicos**, led by José Yves **Limantour** achieved a balanced budget for the first time in 1894, encouraged **foreign investment** and the building of **railroads**, particularly those lines connecting with the **United States**. Diaz made their policies possible by his *Pan o palo* ("bread or the club"), rewarding cooperation and chastizing any opposition. He was a master at manipulating his supporters, such as the **Church** (whose power he allowed to increase), the **army**, politicians, great landowners (he allowed the expropriation of huge tracts of Indian lands), and foreign business interests.

It was easy to mistake oppression for tranquillity. Foreign observers regarded him as a truly progressive figure. U.S. secretary of state Elihu Root called him "one of the greatest men to be held up for the hero worship of mankind." The brilliant **Centenary of Independence** celebrations impressed outside observers. But in the rural areas, the natives were already restless, circulating rifles bought by selling their livestock, leaving their farms devoid of the cows and goats they had depended on for milk, meat, and hides. On November 20, their pent up fury burst into scattered warfare against army posts. The **Revolution of 1910** would force Diaz into exile in Paris and continue for a decade until the last of the Porfiriato administrators had been cleared out of office.

Perhaps his best known quotation, reflecting a widespread feeling among Latin Americans was *¡Pobre México, tan lejos de Dios y tan cerca de los Estados Unidos!* ("Poor Mexico, so far from God and so close to the United States").

DÍAZ BALLESTEROS, ENRIQUE (1916–). Morelos-born law graduate and administrator with the **Ferrocarriles Nacionales de México**, he joined the **Compañía Nacional de Subsistencias Populares** in 1961, becoming its director in 1979.

DÍAZ CERECEDO, CANDIDO (1927–). Born February 2 in **Veracruz**, he graduated from **UNAM** in law in 1960, joined the **Partido Socialista de los Trabajadores** in 1979, and ran as its candidate for governor of Veracruz in 1980, and for president of Mexico in 1982. A teacher in the Federal District, he had worked as a milkman, blacksmith, and charcoal maker. As mayor of Chicontepect, Veracruz, he helped found several union locals for workers who had not been organized before.

DÍAZ COVARRUBIAS, FRANCISCO (1833–1889). Teacher, geographer, and astronomer from **Veracruz**, he taught at the *Colegio de Minería*, forerunner of the **Colegio de Ingenieros Civiles de México**. He made original contributions in astrophysics and correctly predicted the 1857 solar eclipse. He worked in the **Juárez** government and headed a Mexican commission to Japan in 1874 to study the planet Venus.

DÍAZ DE ARMENDÁRIZ, LOPE, MARQUÉS DE CADEREITA (1574–16??). **Viceroy** of **New Spain** from 1635–1640, his administration was noted for public works and action against piracy.

DÍAZ DE LA VEGA, [GENERAL] RÓMULO (1804?–1877). Supporter of **Iturbide**, he fought at various times against Texans, French, and Americans. In 1855 he was **president** of Mexico for just two days in August, and then again from September 12–October 4. Forced into exile, he returned when the conservatives gained power and fought against **Juárez**. Captured, he was freed in view of his long history of fighting Mexico's foreign enemies. He was allowed to live a secluded life in **Puebla** where he died.

DÍAZ DEL CASTILLO, BERNAL (c.1495–1581). This companion of Hernán **Cortés** accompanied him to **Tenochtitlán** and then south to Honduras where he witnessed the death of **Cuauhtémoc** at the hands of the Spanish. His *Verdadera historia de la conquista de la Nueva España*, compiled over 40 years later in response to apocryphal accounts of the Spanish **Conquest of Mexico**, is the best contemporary work on the subject, thanks to its detailed description of events, even though it was not written in a scholarly manner. The original version appeared in Madrid in 1632, but the 1904–1905 edition in two volumes by Mexican historian Genaro **García**, based on the original manuscript in Guatemala City, probably gives a more faithful rendition.

DÍAZ DÍAZ, DANIEL (1934–). Transportation minister in 1984–1988, he was born March 17 in Huandacareo, **Michoacán**. He graduated in 1954 from **UNAM** in civil engineering, joined the **Partido Revolucionario Institucional** in 1956, and then earned a master's in economic programming at the Center for Economic Programming in France in 1964, and was professor of planning at UNAM from 1965–1982. He apprenticed in public administration at the **United Nations** Center for Industrial Development and during 1975 was professor of architecture at UNAM. In 1972–1976 he was director general of programming for the **Public Works Ministry**.

DÍAZ INFANTE, LUIS (1896–1962). An attorney from **León, Guanajuato**, he served as a federal deputy, as acting governor of Guanajuato, a federal judge, and ultimately as a justice of the **Supreme Court** from 1950–1958. Although a member of the **Partido Revolucionario Institucional**, he caused a furor by joining the far-right **Unión Sinarquista Nacional** which supported opposition conservatives against the PRI.

DÍAZ INFANTE ARANDA, ERNESTO (1930–). Born January 6 in the Federal District, he graduated in law from the **Universidad de San Luis Potosí** in 1954. In 1967–1968 he was a judge at the district court in **Chihuahua**, then a judge of the First Collegiate Court in Civil Matters at the federal level in 1968–1979. He published studies on the history of the **Supreme Court**, where he became a justice himself in 1979–1988. Luis **Diaz Infante** is a kinsman.

DÍAZ ORDAZ, GUSTAVO (1911–1979). President of Mexico from 1964–1970, he was "the most conservative since 1910." A committed Catholic, born March 11, in San Andrés, **Puebla**, he graduated in law from the **Universidad de Puebla**, where he became a law professor and then vice president. He served in the federal **congress** as a deputy from 1943–1946 and as senator from 1946–1952, was prosecuting attorney in Puebla, and a justice of the state supreme court. As interior minister from 1958–1964 his vigor against opponents of the **Partido Revolucionario Institucional** led him to imprison David Alfaro **Siqueiros**. As president, he faced the most serious challenge to public order since the **Revolution of 1910**, when student riots in July–October 1968 culminated in a massacre in the Plaza of **Tlatelolco**. His administration stressed the construction of public housing and expansion of the petrochemical industry through government investment. He also held the **peso exchange rate** steady while reducing **foreign debts** from US$ 6 billion to US$ 4 billion.

In December 1976 he became ambassador to Spain, but he resigned in August 1977 over disagreement with President **López Portillo**'s policy toward Spain. He returned to law practice in Mexico City, dying there on July 15.

DÍAZ SERRANO, JORGE (1921–). Director general of **Pemex**, he served four years' imprisonment for embezzlement of US$ 34 million. Born in Nogales, **Sonora**, on February 6, he graduated in mechanical engineering from the **Instituto Politécnico Nacional** in 1941 and did graduate study at the University of Maryland. In 1946–1958 he was a key executive with Fairbanks Morse machinery corporation in Mexico and in private electrical, marine transportation, and petroleum equipment companies. He became director of Pemex in December 1976, putting into the field the largest team of full-time geological surveyors ever assembled in Latin America. These surveyors found Mexico had 40 billion barrels of proven oil reserves (against the 11 billion found in previous incomplete surveys in 1938), and a probable total of over 60 billion. Devising a daily production schedule of 2.5 million barrels for the 1980s, he made Mexico one of the world's major **petroleum** producers and exporters. Such success received worldwide praise and seemed to put him above criticism. When in 1981 some of Mexico's biggest customers were offered cheaper oil from other countries, he boldly lowered his prices by four dollars a barrel. For this, President **López Portillo** had him fired. Knowing he was still enormously popular, the president saved face by appointing him ambassador to the Soviet Union, a major oil exporter. Both Diaz Serrano and López Portillo enjoyed American media praise for keeping Mexico out of **OPEC**.

In 1983 President De La **Madrid** told Congress to expose any **corruption** in Pemex and Díaz Serrano, by then a federal senator, was suddenly charged with fraud in his former position. On July 30, the lower house voted unanimously to remove him from the Senate, so ending his immunity from prosecution. The federal attorney general released details of the charges, and Federal Judge Jorge Reyes Tariaba of the Ninth Penal Court refused him bail. When the President said he would try to recover some of the stolen funds, Díaz Serrano suddenly filed for divorce from Elvia Moreno de Díaz Serrano. Though they were personally compatible he admitted doing this to prevent some of his wealth from being impounded. When his lawyer warned him of the impending seizure of his enormous private yacht (larger than Queen Elizabeth II's own *Britannia*), its captain was able to sail out of **Acapulco** and hand it over to his former wife in the French Riviera before the federal police arrived—an international media sensation.

After four years, Díaz Serrano was released without having to report to any parole or probation officer. It was estimated that his total embezzlement was nearly one billion dollars, a world record that earned him a brief entry in the *Guinness Book of Records*.

DIAZ SOTO Y GAMA, ANTONIO. *See* SOTO Y GAMA, ANTONIO DIAZ.

DIDAPP, JUAN PEDRO. Durango-born diplomat and journalist, his early 20th century articles condemned one-man rule and advocated political parties. These had no immediate effect but did help stir greater interest in politics. He was executed by **Huerta**'s agents for allegedly spying for **Carranza**.

DIEMECKE, ENRIQUE ARTURO (1952–). Musician, born in Mexico of German parents, he became in the 1990s the principal conductor of the **Orquesta Sinfónica Nacional de México**. He has been a guest conductor of major symphonic orchestras around the world, from New Zealand to France.

DIESEL NACIONAL (DINA). This is the government's national truck and automobile manufacturing enterprise.

DIET. *See* CUISINE; FOOD SUPPLY.

DIEZMOS. *See* TITHES.

DINOSAURIO ("dinosaur"). This was a pejorative term of the late 20th century for an old style political boss who helped keep the ruling clique of the **Partido Republicano Institucional** in power by replenishing their allies. They secured government positions as soon as they retired or left for other jobs.

DIRTY WAR (*Guerra Sucia*). The limited success of many Latin American governments against the **guerrilla** war tactics of the far left led, during the later 1960s, the 1970s, and early 1980s, to a "no holds barred" response by the **police**, secret police and **armed forces**. Without traditional legal oversight of their actions, doubtless many of their victims were innocent, or guilty only of holding subversive opinions. This has made it fashionable to condemn those involved on the government side. There does however seem to be little philosophical difference between the attitude of the authorities in Mexico, or in **Brazil**, **Chile**, Paraguay, **Argentina**, Uruguay, or **Guatemala** (to cite them in the order of increasing repressive vigor), and the extra-legal methods being practiced since 9/11 by the governments of the **United States** and the **United Kingdom** against the comparable threat of terrorist attacks by Muslim *jihadis*.

But the **Partido Revolucionario Institucional** was concerned to preserve its leftist reputation, at least internationally. This is why, officially, Mexico had not only condemned human rights abuses elsewhere in Latin America but had actively facilitated, for example, the escape of Brazilian guerrillas ransomed for U.S. ambassador Elbrick in 1969 and Japanese consul Okuchi in 1970. Mexico had also granted asylum to those many Chileans who had evaded arrest in 1973 by entering the Mexican embassy and to Guatemalans fleeing oppression in their country, while simultaneously refusing to acknowledge any such activities by its own security forces until March 2006 when accusations by the National Security Archive (an American NGO) received wide news agency coverage. In particular, 74 named Mexican officials were specifically accused of responsibility for 275 disappearances. The **Fox** government's response was a promise to release details of all Mexican counterinsurgency activities for the period 1964–1982, evidently in order to help it discredit the PRI in the coming 2006 elections.

The November 6, 2006, bombing of three buildings in **Mexico City** has shown that political violence is still being resorted to. *See also* ABUJAMAL, MUMIA; CABAÑAS, LUCIO; UNAM STUDENT RIOTS OF 1968.

DISEASE. European diseases introduced with the 16th century Spanish **conquest of Mexico** decimated the aboriginal population, who did not develop a natural immunity until the late seventeenth century. *See also* CHOLERA; HOOF AND MOUTH DISEASE; INFLUENZA; LEPROSY; MEASLES; MUMPS; PLAGUE; SMALLPOX; TTPHUS; YELLOW FEVER.

DISTRITO FEDERAL. *See* FEDERAL DISTRICT.

DIVISIÓN DEL NORTE. This was the name given to the forces of Pancho **Villa**, at one time numbering 50,000, although the División's strength ebbed rapidly after his fortunes began to wane from c.1915 and his defeat at **Agua Prieta**.

DIVISIÓN DEL SUR. The army led in the **Revolution of 1910** by Emiliano **Zapata**.

DIVORCE. This was introduced by Venustiano **Carranza** in 1914 for a number of grounds, including desertion.

DOLLAR. This name derived from *Johachimsthaler*, an inhabitant or product of Johachimsthal, the Bohemian (Czech) valley that was the principal source of **silver** for Austria's 18th century mint. The word then came to be applied in English to Spanish America's silver **peso** (minted from Mexican silver) and adopted by the newly independent United States as its own currency unit. [L. H.]

DOLLAR SIGN. From 1732 the **columnario** version of the Spanish and Spanish-American **peso** symbolized its national origin by bearing a representation of the twin columns of Hercules at the entrance to the Mediterranean, linked by a length of twisted ribbon. This became the $ sign (originally with two vertical lines) used for both **United States** and Latin American currencies. Mexico and the other Latin American countries still using the sign often add "M.N." (*moneda nacional*) to make it clear when "$" refers to "national" and not U.S. money. [L. H.]

DOLORES HIDALGO. This village near **Querétaro** but in **Guanajuato state**, originally Dolores, was renamed in honor of its parish priest Miguel **Hidalgo y Costilla**, whose **Grito de Dolores** marked the beginning of Mexico's modern **independence** struggle.

DOLPHIN, USS. This is the name of a US naval vessel stationed off **Tampico**, from which a small landing party seeking gasoline wandered into a restricted area and were arrested. Demands for an apology were not, in **United States** eyes, sufficiently complied with, and a naval occupation of **Veracruz** followed. **Huerta**'s diversion of troops in response weakened his military position elsewhere, while the occupation itself deprived his government of the city's customs revenues.

DOMESTIC TRADE. *See* INTERNAL TRADE.

DOMÍNGUEZ, BELISARIO (1863–1913). This physician supported Francisco **Madero** and became a senator; but when he publicly denounced General Victoriano **Huerta** for killing Madero, he was murdered himself. This so enraged Congress that Huerta dissolved it and appointed a new, docile Congress in 1914.

DOMÍNGUEZ, [JOSÉ] MIGUEL (1756–1830). This lawyer actively worked for Independence from 1808, when **Napoleon** forced **Charles III** and his son the future **Ferdinand VII** to abdicate and made his brother Joseph **Bonaparte** king of Spain. Domínguez was arrested and dismissed from his position as mayor of **Querétaro**. After independence he served in 1823–1824 on the provisional *junto de gobierno* and later as president of the **Supreme Court**. He died in **Mexico City**.

DON ("sir"). This title used before a person's given name (cf. the British *Sir*) originally marked a member of the gentry. By the early

19th century it had come into indiscriminate use for any respectable citizen (cf. the British "esquire"), although some Mexican patriots repudiated it as too much associated with the former colonial power. In modern Mexico its use denotes affectionate respect. The feminine form is Doña. [L. H.]

DON JUAN TENORIO. This traditional Spanish play about the noble philanderer is performed at fiestas on various religious **holidays**, particularly in villages on the day of the local patron saint. In the Mexican version, Don Juan repents his sins and goes to heaven.

DONIS, ROBERTO (1934–). This painter, born in **San Luis Potosí**, studied at La **Esmeralda** in **Mexico City**. He has taken part in over 50 group exhibitions in the Americas and Europe. *Corte transversal de un pensamiento* is a representative work.

DOUGLAS, ARIZONA. This **Arizona** border town of 14,312 (2000 census) was named for copper mining pioneer James Douglas. It is located at 31°20'N, 109°32'W, opposite **Agua Prieta**. [L. H.]

DOVALI JAIME, ANTONIO (1905–1981). The director of **Pemex** from 1970–1976 increased oil production enough to make Mexico a **petroleum** exporting country. Born October 3 in **Zacatecas**, he graduated from **UNAM** in engineering and later served as the dean of its engineering school from 1959–1966. He became director of construction for the **Ferrocarriles Nacionales de México**, building the railroad linking **Chihuahua** state and its Copper Canyon with the Pacific coast of **Sinaloa**, 1952–1961.

DRAKE, [SIR] FRANCIS (1546–1596). This English privateer was regarded by Spain as an outright pirate. His 1577–1580 circumnavigation included many attacks on Spanish shipping and ports on the western coasts of the Americas and a landing in **San Francisco** Bay where he posted a claim to the surrounding territory as "New Albion."

DRAMA. Mexican dramatists include Juan Ruiz de **Alarcón y Mendoza**, Enrique **Carballido**, Carlos **Fuentes**, Federico **Gamboa**, Elena **Garro**, Luis Josefina **Hernández**, Vicente **Leñero**, Salvador **Novo**,

Elena **Poniatowska**, José **Rosas Moreno**, and Rodolfo **Usigli**. Its actors include Manolo **Fábregas** and María **Félix**.

DRESS. *See* COSTUME.

DRUG TRADE. *See* NARCOTICS.

DUCOING GAMBA, LUIS HUMBERTO (1937–). Born May 15, he graduated in **law** from the University of his native **Guanajuato**. In 1964 he became a national leader of the **Confederación Nacional Campesina**. As a federal deputy he pushed agrarian legislation. He was governor of Guanajuato from 1973–1979.

DUPRE CENICEROS, ENRIQUE (1914–1988). Leader of the **Confederación Nacional Campesina**, he was born in **Durango** and educated at **UNAM**. As a federal deputy and later, a senator, he was a key formulator of legislation on **irrigation** and water usage from 1952–1962. He was governor of his home state, 1962–1966 and a long-time policy advisor for the Department of Agrarian Affairs and its successor, the **Agrarian Reform Ministry**.

DURAN, DIEGO (1538–1588). This **mestizo** priest and historian translated **Aztec** literature and culture for Spanish colonial officials.

DURANGO CITY (*Victoria de Durango*). The capital of **Durango State** and its largest city, at 24°01'N, 104°40'W, 800 km northwest of **Mexico City** and 1,920 m above sea level, was founded in 1563 and named for the birthplace in Biscay of Francisco de **Ibarra**. The population was 210,000 in 1976; 581,000 in 1995; and 491,436 in 2000. Its economy stresses lumber and mineral processing, foundries, textiles, and **tobacco**. It is an important railroad and highway link between El Paso, Texas, and **Mexico City**.

DURANGO STATE. Mexico's fourth largest state with an area of 119,648 km² is bordered by **Chihuahua**, **Sinaloa**, **Zacatecas**, **Coahuila** and **Nayarit**. It had a **population** of 144,331 in 1857; of 173,942 in 1869; and at successive **censuses** of thereafter of 294,000 (1895); 370,000 (1900); 483,000 (1910); 337,000 (1921); 404,000

(1930); 484,000 (1940); 630,000 (1950); 761,000 (1960); 934,000 (1970); 1,182,000 (1980); 1,349,378 (1990); 1,448,661 (2000); and 1,509,117 (2005). It has 38 *municipios*, of which the most important are **Durango City**, Gómez Palacio, and Lerdo.

[Constituted an **intendancy** in 1786 and a state at Mexican **Independence** in 1824, it had previously been part of **Nueva Vizcaya**. Its western region is dominated by the Sierra **Madre** Occidental, with pine and oak forests. The northern region is desert, except for the irrigated farmlands in the Laguna district, formed by hydroelectric projects on the **Nazas** River. Other rivers are the **Humaya, Presidio, Piaxtla,** and **Mezquital.** The capital is **Durango City.**

The economy is based on mining (**silver, gold,** lead, **copper,** and iron ore), ranching, **corn,** and **cotton.** L. H.]

DZIB CARDOZO, JOSÉ (1921–). This attorney and oceanographer was born January 12 in **Campeche**. As professor of oceanography at the **Universidad Autónoma de Campeche**, he has had a national influence on legislation on **fishing** in Mexican waters and on all major research on the oceans. In 1961 he encouraged state universities facing the Gulf of **Mexico** or the Pacific Ocean to organize or expand degree programs involving the fishing industry. He also promoted practical fishing schools for skilled tradesmen.

– E –

EAGLE AND THE SERPENT, THE. The *Águila y la serpiente* national symbol of an eagle perched on a **prickly pear cactus**, holding a snake in its talons, displayed on the national **flag** and elsewhere (e.g., on some of the **coinage**) derives from an **Aztec** legend. Such an apparition was how the sun god **Huitzilopochtli** indicated where the new **capital** should be built. The symbol has also provided the titles of a book by Martín Luis Guzmán and of a pioneer motion picture, Mexico's first "talkie," *El Águila y la serpiente* of 1929, directed by Miguel Conteras. [L. H.]

EAGLE PASS. This **Texas** border town is opposite **Piedras Negras** and 140 miles southwest of **San Antonio**. Eagle Pass was founded in

1850 on the site of an old smugglers' crossing, El Paso de Águila de Escondido. It is on the **Rio Grande** facing the mouth of the Escondido river, a place which became a Texas Militia camp in the 1840s. It became in 1871 the seat of Maverick County. Population has grown from 2,729 in 1900 to 7,247 in 1950; 21,307 in 1980; and 22,413 in 2000. Since the completion of Highway 57 it has been a major gateway into Mexico. [L. H.]

EARTHQUAKE OF 1985. The worst earthquake since **Independence** (8.1 on the Richter scale) struck **Michoacan** on September 19 and severely damaged **Mexico City**. Within hours, the Del Prado Hotel had disappeared from the capital's Juárez Avenue facing **Alameda Park**, along with several smaller hotels nearby, the Steele Corporation building, and buildings housing some 20 large industrial corporations. The death toll may have been as high as 30,000.

EARTHQUAKE OF 2005. On August 11, 2006, a 5.9 earthquake had its epicenter in **Michoacán** and was felt in **Mexico City**, 125 miles to the northwest.

EARTHQUAKES. The entire **Pacific Rim**, i.e., the shoreline countries on both sides of the Pacific Ocean, constitutes a region of great seismic activity, the so-called *Rim of Fire*.

ECHAVE IBIA, BALTASAR (c.1580–1660). Mexican-born painter son of **Echave Orio**. His works represent the transition from Renaissance to Baroque style. The few works that remain are housed in the **Escuela Nacional de Artes Plásticas de México**.

ECHAVE ORIO, BALTASAR, EL VIEJO (1548–1630). The elder Baltasar Echave was born in Guipúzcoa, Spain, arrived in Mexico c.1580, and was married there. An excellent painter of this period, his *La Visitación* and *La Anunciación* can be seen at the **Escuela Nacional de Artes Plásticas**. Other works are in the National Cathedral in **Mexico City**.

ECHEVERRÍA, [FRANCISCO] JAVIER (1797–1852). President of Mexico for five days in September 1841. Born in Jalapa, **Veracruz**, he occupied various political and cultural posts both before and after his presidency. He died in **Mexico City.**

ECHEVERRÍA ALVÁREZ, LUIS (1922–). President of Mexico, 1970–1976. Born January 17, in **Mexico City,** he graduated in law from **UNAM** in 1945, did graduate work in Santiago de Chile, then served as law professor at UNAM, 1947–1949. He subsequently became director of publicity for the **Partido Revolucionario Institucional,** a member of the party's national executive committee, and then executive officer. He began in government as director of accounts for the **navy** ministry, then executive officer for the **education ministry.** As interior minister in 1964–1970, he was blamed by student leader Eduardo **Valle** for having ordered paratroopers to back up the **police** once wild shooting had caused many student and police deaths in the Plaza de **Tlatelolco** riots of October 1968. Media commentators said that Valle's statement neither excused **Díaz Ordaz**'s handling of the 1968 power challenge nor fully indicted Echeverría. The latter, however, would receive post-factum blame after a few years by UNAM historians and political scientists. As president he became involved in more direct violence with young voters than any other modern chief executive. An attempt at rapprochement with young radicals, including the bringing into his cabinet and circle of advisers of leftist UNAM professors, notably Pablo **González Casanova,** ended in 1975 when, ignoring a warning from González Casanova, he confronted a howling group of Marxist students defacing murals at the UNAM library. He asserted that he "understood" their frustrations and would explain the government's stand on problems. A stone thrown by one of their leaders hit him on the forehead, an act of disrespect unheard of since the **Revolution of 1910** had stabilized in 1920 the situation into relative civility. On television he called the student a fascist, an act of political expediency to avoid further antagonizing the far-left groups involved. His pointing out on campus that his cabinet then included the highest ever proportion of UNAM graduates (78 percent) brought him no sympathy. He organized his own group of club-bearing students to keep the far-left rioters in check. *Excélsior*'s comment was that it was a tale of two groups of rowdies, and that Echeverría's behavior was "beneath the dignity of the office of the presidency." His response was to obtain control of the rival newspaper *El Universal* and secure the hiring of his own stooges onto the staff of *Excélsior*.

Within the PRI, Echeverría was consistently on the political left. The courtesy visit paid by the president and his wife on the Communist painter David Álfaro **Siqueiros** shortly before the latter's death was perhaps as much a proclamation of Echeverría's political sympathies as of the regard in which he held one of Mexico's greatest artists.

In foreign affairs, he adopted a Third World position, vigorously supporting the Communist, Socialist, and Arab blocks in the **United Nations** in an abortive bid to become UN Secretary General. He expropriated the tobacco production industry in 1972 and movie production (*See* CINEMA) in 1975. In 1976 he pushed extensive expropriations of medium-sized farms in **Sonora**, **Sinaloa**, and other northern states, engendering a controversy over the constitutionality of his actions.

His **sexennium** saw a severe contraction of the lucrative tourist industry, including a boycott by **United States** Jews in response to his pro-Arab foreign policy. A severe increase in **inflation**, a US$ 3.5 million trade deficit in 1975, a decline in industrial production, and massive capital flight (not unconnected with foreign investors' alarm at his **tercermundismo**) forced him to devalue the **peso** in September 1976, from 12.50 to the dollar, to 30, ending 22 years of currency stability.

In 1977 he became ambassador to UNESCO and in 1978 ambassador to Australia. [In July 2006 he was briefly under house arrest for alleged responsibility for student deaths in the Plaza de Tlatelolco riots. He was released under the statute of limitations. L. H.]

ECHEVERRÍA ÁLVAREZ, RODOLFO (1917–). Brother of President Luis **Echeverría Álvarez**, and for some years a film and theater actor under the name "Rodolfo de Anda." A federal deputy, 1951–1955 and 1961–1964, and a senator, 1964–1970. A key formulator of government policy for the **cinema** industry since 1964, especially during the periods when he headed the Mexican Actors' Union (*Asociación Nacional de Actores,* ANDA). In 1970–1976 he was director general of the **Banco Nacional Cinematográfica**.

ECHEVERRÍA RUIZ, RODOLFO (1946–). Son of Rodolfo **Echeverría Álvarez**, he was Director of Youth for the **Partido Revolucionario Institucional**, then PRI Executive Officer from 1970–1976, before becoming assistant labor minister in the **López Portillo** cabinet.

ECOLOGY. Like all developing countries, Mexico has a mixed environmental protection record. **Deforestation** is a long-standing problem. The conflict over **salt production** and the protection of whale breeding areas on the coast of **Baja California del Sur** is a recent example.

Although a law to protect soil and water was passed in the 1940s, the government's main concern was to develop the internal **economy** by import substitution with intensive exploitation of **natural resources** and to direct state intervention to encourage industrialization. Even the 1972 creation within the *Secretaría de Salubridad y Asistencia* of the Under-secretariat for Improving the Environment was mainly concerned with immediate matters of public health. Change began with the 1982 creation of the *Secretaría de Desarrollo Urbano y Ecología*, SEDUE, which in 1992 became the *Secretaría de Desarrollo Social*, SEDESOL. A separate **environment ministry** was finally achieved in 1994. *See also* CARABIAS LILLO, JULIA; PARTIDO VERDE ECOLÓGICO DE MÉXICO. [L. H.]

ECONOMIC COMMISSION FOR LATIN AMERICA (ECLA). A regional commission of the **United Nations**—in Spanish, *Comisión Económica para América Latina* (CEPAL)—established in 1948 in **Santiago**, Chile, to help Latin American governments promote the economic development of their countries and improve the standards of living of their people. In recent years ECLA/CEPAL has undertaken research on problems of multilateral trade and economic agreements and has concerned itself with specific areas such as **population**, **manufacturing industry**, **agriculture**, **energy**, science and technology, the **environment**, and the participation of **women** in development. It meets biennially, with inter-session work entrusted to a Committee of the Whole.

ECONOMIC EXPLOITATION ZONE (E.E.Z.). *See* MARITIME SOVEREIGNTY.

ECONOMICS MINISTRY (*Secretaría de Economía*, **SE**). Ministry whose aim is to promote the growth of Mexican business enterprises in size and competitiveness. Trade and industry were administered under the **First Empire** by the *secretaría* of internal and external affairs, then from 1853 by that of development, settlement, industry, and trade. The **Constitution of 1917** created a separate trade and industry ministry. A reorganization of 1977 created a *Secretaría de Patrimonio y Fomento Industrial*, whose division in 1982 established a *Secretaria de Comercio y Fomento Industrial*, immediate forerunner of the present SE. [L. H.]

ECONOMY, THE. Before the **Revolution of 1910**, the Mexican economy depended on **agriculture** and **mining**. Diversification began in the 1920s, and since the 1940s industrialization has been a government budget and policy priority. Government investment created a mixed economy, with the government controlling 88 percent of the 30 largest industries in 1982 but less than 40 percent by the 1990s. During 1985–1987, President Miguel de la **Madrid** had privatized almost 1,000 government-owned enterprises that had been inefficient, often providing unpopular products or poor service, and usually running deficits. **Telephones** and **air transport** were sold to private investors.

Mexico's assets include its **petroleum** reserves, its expanding **manufacturing industry**, and **tourism**, offset by a **population** growing faster than the job market. But despite **inflation** and unemployment, Mexico has progressed during this century into a nation with an urban majority increasingly using consumer goods and credit. *See also* INFORMAL ECONOMY; MAQUILLADORAS; SOCIAL CLASSES.

EDUCATION. Education was a **Church** matter in colonial times. The 19th century liberals, particularly Valentín **Gómez Farias**, sought to secularize it, but provision was very limited until the **Revolution of 1910**, whose **Constitution of 1917** declared it to be free, secular, and compulsory between grades 1 and 6. By the mid-20th century, the federal government was maintaining a national university, **UNAM**, and 39 state and technical universities and institutes of higher learning. Federal and state governments shared responsibility for secondary schools, and local government was also involved in primary level provision. The **population** explosion of the 1970s meant in practice, however, that one child in three was denied admission, and the 1978 dropout rate at sixth grade reached 70 percent. The average education level was the fourth grade in 1970, but was fifth grade by 1990.

With the removal of restrictions on teaching by religious orders, **Church** primary and secondary schools expanded modestly in the late 1990s. *See also* HIGHER EDUCATION; PRIMARY EDUCATION; SECONDARY EDUCATION.

EDUCATION MINISTRY. The **Constitution of 1917** abolished the *Secretaria de Instrucción Pública y Bellas Artes* of 1905 as an intrusion on municipal independence, although the federal government retained control of **education** in the **Federal District** and federal territories. Within two years the number of public schools had fallen from 344 to 148, and it was clear that most *municipios* were unable to fulfil their new responsibilities. José **Vasconcelos**, rector of what became **UNAM**, was given an *ad hoc* role to reform Mexican education, pending a constitutional amendment to permit the creation of a *Secretará de Educación Pública* (SEP) in September, 1921. *See also* PEDRO RAMIREZ VAZQUEZ.

"EFFECTIVE SUFFRAGE: NO REELECTION" (*¡Sufragio efectivo: no reelección!*). A slogan of strict adherence to the principles of the **Constitution of 1857** used successfully by Porfirio **Diaz** in 1876 to prevent Sebastián **Lerdo de Tejada** from perpetuating himself in office. After Diaz had himself famously failed to follow his own doctrine, the Plan of **San Luis Potosi** revived the slogan as the rallying cry of the **Revolution of 1910**. It has been reproduced on every Mexican official document since then. *See also* REELECTION.

EHRENBERG, FELIPE (1943–). A native of **Mexico City**, best known as a pioneer of experimental and conceptual art. He began his artistic career as a painter and draftsman, and his early mentors included muralist José **Chávez Morado** and avant-garde artist Mathias Goeritz. After a brief exile in England from 1968, he returned in the mid-1970s, joining the Mexican group movement, when a number of Mexican artists began working collectively staging performances reflecting their response to current socio-political issues. In the 1980s he led self-publishing workshops for artists, students, and teachers in Mexico. These gave them the tools to publish works reflecting the needs of their local regions and organized a similar project for Nicaraguans after the fall of Somoza. In addition, with the establishment of a program called H2O Talleres de Comunicación, Ehrenberg helped to establish 800 new community presses and over 1,000 community murals throughout Mexico. In the 1990s Ehrenberg published elaborate books with strong sculptural elements. He also created a series of installations and performance pieces focusing on border politics between the **United States** and Mexico in the age of the **North American Free Trade Agreement (NAFTA)**, California's Proposition 187, and the **Zapatista** liberation uprising. His work in the late 1990s reflected the theme of violence, and his more recent work includes the creation of dynamic exhibitions on the Internet. He currently lives in São Paulo as Mexico's cultural attaché to **Brazil**. [L. H.]

EISENSTEIN, SERGEI MIKHAILOVICH (1898–1948). Russian film director, responsible for the classic film of the Mexican **Revolution of 1910**, *Viva México*.

EJÉRCITO DEL NORTE. *See* DIVISIÓN DEL NORTE.

EJÉRCITO ZAPATISTA DE LIBERACIÓN NACIONAL (EZLN). On the morning of January 1, 1994, a clandestine **guerrilla** organization of 8,000 men took over two small **Chiapas** towns, Ocosingo and Villa Margarita, at gun point. Meanwhile José Pérez Méndez, an Indian self-proclaimed leader of a faction of this "Zapatist Army of National Liberation," had gathered **Mexico City** journalists in San Cristóbal de la Casas to proclaim its message of democracy, equality and dignity. Later in the day, units of the Mexican **army** arrived and at least 145 died in the ensuing battle. A few days later the "*Zapatistas*" withdrew into the dense Chiapas rainforest, returning to make repeated confrontations in the towns. During 1995–1999, various federal negotiators made temporary agreements with the EZLN, and the media lost interest. In 2001 it led a 16-day motorcade from Chiapas to Mexico City to demand an "indigenous rights" law, but by December 2006 the media was boasting of the EZLN being a "spent force," of no significance beyond its rhetoric.

EJIDITARIO. A member of an **ejido**; anyone over 18 in the community (based on permanent residence and kinship), whether he or she actually engages in farming or not.

EJIDO. A form of communally-owned farm, existing before the **Spanish conquest** and still found in **Indian** and **mestizo** villages. During the **Porfiriato**, such farms were expropriated and given to favored government administrators or sold to large landowners. Their restitution to their communities was a goal of the **Revolution of 1910**, secured in the **Constitution of 1917**. Each ejido assembly elects its own commission president, secretary, and treasurer to run the farm and a grievance committee to check on their administration. They have, however, been plagued by inefficient farming methods and low yields. In 1991 **Congress** amended the Constitution, effective January 6, 1992, to allow ejidos (under **Agrarian Reform Ministry** supervision) to sell or rent small parcels off to individual **ejiditarios** and to lease or share the farming of such parcels as long as the community's crop yields were not negatively effected. Constitutional changes since 1995 have ended the collective ownership of ejidos. Peasant owners may continue traditional farming as part of the village cooperative, or they may lease individual plots and farm each of them independently.

EL ("the"). With the now traditional exception of the republic of El Salvador, and the thoroughly anglicized **El Paso** and **Los Angeles**, all words and names beginning with the definite article are alphabetized under the following element.

EL PASO. Texas border town, originally El **Paso del Norte**, founded at 31°47'N, 106°24'W as a Jesuit mission in 1659, the twin of **Ciudad Juárez** on the Mexican side. With 598,590 inhabitants in 2005, it is, after **San Diego**, the second largest city in the **United States border** region.

ELECTION OF 1920. Won by Álvaro **Obregón Salido** with 95.70 percent of the votes against 4.21 percent recorded for his opponents.

ELECTION OF 1924. Won by Plutarco Elias **Calles** with 84.15 percent of the vote against 15.85 percent for Ángel **Flores**.

ELECTION OF 1928. Won by Álvaro **Obregón Salido**, running unopposed.

ELECTION OF 1929. Won by Pascual **Ortiz Rubio** (PNR) with 93.55 percent of the vote against 5.33 percent for José **Vasconcelos**.

ELECTION OF 1934. Won by Lázaro **Cárdenas del Rio (PNR)** with 98.19 percent of the vote against Antonio J. **Villareal**, with 1.08 percent

ELECTION OF 1940. In a foregone conclusion, Manuel **Ávila Camacho** (93.9 percent of the vote) defeated both General Juan Andreu **Almazán** on the right—he claimed his mere 5.73 percent the result of fraud—and Francisco **Múgica** on the left. The new **Partido de Acción Nacional** (PAN) had no candidate, but many of its members supported Almazán. The quasi-fascist movement, **Sinarquismo**, failed to play any significant role.

ELECTION OF 1946. Miguel **Alemán Valdés'** victory with 77.91 percent of the vote was marred by electoral fraud by the **Partido Revolucionario Institucional**, leading to serious riots in **Guanajuato state** in which dozens died. Opposition candidate Ezequiel **Padilla** of the **Partido Democrático Mexicano** was backed by the **Partido de Acción Nacional** and ran a vigorous campaign (winning 19.33 percent), but the outcome was never in doubt, particularly as Padilla was identified too strongly as pro-American.

ELECTION OF 1952. Won by Adolfo **Rúiz Cortines (Partido Revolucionario Institucional)** with 2,700,000 votes (74.32 percent), defeating FPP's Miguel **Henríquez Guzmán** who received 580,000 votes (15.88 percent), Efraín **Gonexiles Luna (Partido de Acción Nacional)** who received 286,000 votes (7.82 percent), and Vicente **Lombard Tolerant (PPS)** who received 73,000 votes (1.99 percent).

ELECTION OF 1958. Won by Adolfo **Lopez Mateo** with 90.43 percent of the vote against 9.42 percent for **Partido de Acción Nacional** candidate Luis Hector **Alvarez**.

ELECTION OF 1964. Won by Gustav **Diaz Aertex** with 88.82 percent of the votes, defeating José **Gonzales Torres (Partido de Acción Nacional)** with 10.98 percent of the votes.

ELECTION OF 1970. Partido Revolucionario Institucional candidate Luis **Echeverria Alvarez** won with 11,900,000 votes (86.02 percent) to **Partido de Acción Nacional** candidate Efraín **Gonzales Morin**'s 2,000,000 (13.98 percent), more than any previous PAN candidate.

ELECTION OF 1972. The congressional election in July was the first with **Partido Communist Mexicana** candidates on the ballot. They won 10 percent of the total vote for the **Proportional Representation** of minority parties.

ELECTION OF 1976. José **Lopez Portillo (Partido Revolucionario Institucional)** was elected unopposed.

ELECTION OF 1982. Won by the **Partido Revolucionario Institucional**'s Miguel de la **Madrid Hardwood** with 70.99 percent of the votes over Pablo Emilio Madder **(Partido de Acción Nacional)** with 15.68 percent and Arnold Martín Vertigo with 3.48 percent. The election was notable for the candidacy of Ignacio **Gonzales Gailes**, director general of the **Union Sinarquista Nacional**, but running on the **Partido Democrático Mexicano** ticket and coming in fourth, with 1.85 percent. Other candidates totalled 3.53 percent.

ELECTION OF 1988. During the final vote tabulation it was alleged that both presidential candidates (Carlos **Salinas de Gortari** and Cuauhtemoc **Cárdenas**) had each secured 49 percent of the votes, the rest having been lost, marked incorrectly, or given to minor candidates. Following widespread rumors of actual vote-rigging, investigations by government, the parties, and the media eventually concluded that Salinas had won with 50.47 percent, that Cárdenas had only 30.9 percent, and a third candidate, Manuel J. **Clouthier**, from the **Partido de Acción Nacional** had 17.07 percent. Such a tiny overall triumph shook the **Partido Revolucionario Institucional**, from its **Comité Ejecutivo Nacional** down to local committees.

In the congressional elections, the PRI won 233 seats, the PAN 38, and leftist parties 29. With **proportional representation** seats added, the PRI had 260, the PAN 101, the **Partido de la Revolución Democrática** 34, the **Partido Popular Socialista** 32, the **Partido Auténtico de la Revolución Mexicana** 31, the **Frente Democrático Nacional** 22, and the **Partido Mexicano Socialista** 19.

ELECTION OF 1994. Ernesto **Zedillo Ponce de León** (**Partido Revolucionario Institucional**) won with 50.2 percent, defeating Diego **Fernández de Cevallos Ramos** (**Partido de Acción Nacional**) with 26.7 percent, Cuauhtémoc **Cárdenas** with 17.1 percent, and Cecilia Soto (PT) with 2.8 percent. Other candidates received a total of 3.2 percent.

ELECTION OF 1997. In the July 6 elections for the **Cámara de Diputados Federales**, the **Partido Revolucionario Institucional** lost its overall majority, winning only 239 seats. The **PRD** won 125, the **Partido de Acción Nacional**, 122, with two minor parties sharing the other 14. In the **Senate**, the PRI, won all 64 geographically-assigned seats, but only 32 of those under **proportional representation**. Of the remaining 32, the PAN secured 23 and the PRD nine. The **Instituto Federal Electoral** reported that the PRI received 41 percent of **television** news coverage during the four month campaign period, PRD got 26.3 percent, PAN got 20 percent, and five smaller parties received the remaining 12.7 percent (measuring only of quantity of air time, irrespective of whether the content was objective or partisan). Although all state legislatures retained their PRI majorities, several found these had so declined as to barely exceed the combined PAN and PRI opposition.

ELECTION OF 2000. Held in July, it was won by **Partido de Acción Nacional** candidate, Vicente **Fox**. PAN also won 51 **senate** seats (against 60 for the **Partido Revolucionario Institucional** and 17 for the **Partido de la Revolución Democrática**), and 221 congressional seats (against 211 for the PRI and 68 for the PRD).

ELECTION OF 2003. This local election involved the governorships of 10 states, with PRI taking **Chihahua** and **Durango** from the **Par-**

tido de Acción Nacional, and the PRD winning **Zacatecas**. Some 40 percent of local legislator's posts and those of 1,600 mayors were also in dispute. Much of the **Partido Revolucionario Institucional** recovery was attributed to a widespread fear of government plans for privatizing the **Sistema Pública de Salud de México**. The elections for the lower house of **Congress** gave PRI 224 seats, PAN 149 seats, the **Partido de la Revolución Democrática** 97, and others 30. The net result was that the PRI remained the largest and best-organized of Mexico's parties, holding most state governorships and a plurality in the national **senate**. [L. H.]

ELECTION OF 2006. Held on Sunday July 2 for the president, for the mayoralty of **Mexico City**, and for 628 seats in the two houses of **Congress**.

(1) PRESIDENTIAL. Although Felipe **Calderón Hinojosa** ran on the provision of more employment through "trickle down" economics while Andrés Manuel **Lopez Obrador** ("AMLO") promised greater social welfare provision, both ran largely negative campaigns. Calderón's labelling of AMLO as "a danger to Mexico" (comparing him with Venezuela's Chávez) was eventually ruled unconstitutional and ultimately had to be withdrawn. As the one clear opponent of legalized **abortion**, Calderón alone received the active endorsement of the **Church**.

In the end, Calderón received 15,000,284 votes; AMLO came a very close second with 14,756,350; and Robert **Madrazo Pintado** a poor third with only 9,301,441. Patricia **Mercado Castro** received 1,127,963 and Roberto **Campa Cifrian** only 401,504. As expected, Calderón did best in the prosperous north, while AMLO had his strongest support in **Mexico City** and in the impoverished south.

Lopez Obrador has, with much leftist support including that of James Kenneth Galbraith, complained of a faulty result. Not only had the government tried to have him declared judicially ineligible to run, but the electoral roles had been "scrubbed" of felons and other persons deemed ineligible to vote. The percentage claimed for Calderón apparently exceeded the cumulative overnight tally by (it was alleged) the addition of invalid ballots. AMLO's reported total was considerably less than the total of his party's congressional votes. The first 10,000 boxes counted were abnormally in favor of Calderón, and the results from 223 boxes disappeared in mid-count. There were also the usual cries from the loser of employer intimidation and vote buying in rural areas.

The **Comisión Federal Electoral** carried out a partial recount (11,839 ballot boxes). According to the American *Center for Economic and Policy Research,* which investigated a random 1,706 of these, this recount had disallowed 1,302 votes for Calderón (0.54 percent, just below his national majority of 0.55 percent!) while increasing corresponding votes for Lopez Obrador, not in any credible relationship, but by a mere 77.

AMLO organized massive protest rallies in the capital but didn't give his supporters any guidance on how they might effectively intervene. It was expected that he would (like Al Gore) eventually bow to the inevitable and accept the official result, which was judicially confirmed September 5. Although 55% of Mexicans agreed, according to an opinion poll, that there had been some fraud, two thirds of these accepted the C.F.E.'s verdict that such fraud had not been sufficient to make it necessary to reverse the result.

(2) CONGRESSIONAL. The PAN became the largest party in the House with 206 seats; PRD had 160; PRI fell to 121; the **Nueva Alianza** won 9; and the *Partido Alternativo Socialdemócrata y Campesino* (PASC) won 4. In the Senate PAN slightly improved its position, winning 52; PRD more than doubled its seats winning 36; PRI fell to 38; and the Nueva Alianza and PASC achieved one each.

(3) GUBERNATORIAL. The PAN's candidates won in Aguascalientes, Baja California, Jalisco, Guanajuato, Morelos, Querétaro, San Luis Potosi, Tlaxcalá, and Yucatán. [L. H.]

ELECTIONS. *See* SUFFRAGE.

ELECTRICITY. *See* CHYMOSIN FEDERAL DE ELECTRICIAN.

ELIAS CALLS, PLUTARCH. *See* CALLS, PLUTARCH ELIAS.

ELIZONDO ALCALDE, SALVADOR (1932–2006). UNAM professor, critic, translator, and novelist: *Farabeuf; o, crónica de un instante* (1965).

EMBASSY PACT. Negotiation, sponsored by **United States** ambassador Henry **Wilson**, whereby Félix **Diaz** agreed to support Victoriano **Huerta** in a coup to overthrow President **Madero**.

EMERITENSE. Pertaining to or inhabiting **Mérida**.

EMIGRATION. [There was some emigration to **California** in the **gold** rush of 1849, but this was soon discouraged by a special tax on non-English-speaking miners. The chaos of the **Revolution of 1910** provoked much short-term migration, particularly to California and **Cuba**. In the late 1920s, the defeat of the **Cristero Rebellion** forced "thousands" to seek refuge in the **United States**. During **World War II** the **Bracero** program facilitated the supply of **agricultural labor** to American farmers, L. H.]

Since then, illegal migration from Mexico to the southwest of the **United States** (which already had a history going back decades) has increased enormously, propelled by Mexico's high **birthrate**, the difference in living standards, and the greater demand for labor north of the Rio Grande. In 1999 the U.S. Immigration Service estimated that 7 million to 12 million Mexicans were working illegally in the United States or receiving welfare benefits there. It also claimed that the number of their agents on or near the border was inadequate to apprehend more than a small proportion of undocumented Mexicans crossing it. In 1998 Francisco Solís, director general of Mexico's immigration and emigration service, caused a political uproar when, in an interview with CNN, he declared he would do nothing to hamper illegal border crossings. Mexicans needed jobs and the annual **population** growth required the escape valve of the **United States border**. Direct protests from the White House to Los **Pinos** followed firm protests from the U.S. secretary of state to Mexico's foreign minister. The Mexican government officially denounced Solís' views and insisted that its **family planning** program and expansion of the **economy** were alleviating the problem.

The migration rate was estimated in 2006 as being an annual net loss of 0.432 percent of the Mexican **population**.

EMILY, HURRICANE. The second major hurricane of the 2005 season, it made landfall on **Cozumel** as a category 4 storm in mid-July, hit the mainland just north of Tulum in **Quitana Roo**, and then crossed the Bay of Campeche to hit **Tamaulipas**.

EMPEROR (*emperador*). Title borne by **Charles V**, Spanish head of state at the time of the **Conquest of Mexico**, as Holy Roman Emperor, 1520–1554; by Agustín **Iturbide**, 1821–1823, as Agustín I, *emperador constitucional del império mexicano*; and by the Austrian archduke Ferdinand Maximilian von Habsburg as the Emperor **Maximilian**, 1863–1967. The Aztec ruler's title, **Tlatoani**, is also traditionally and usually translated as "emperor." [L. H.]

EMPIRE. Mexico began its independent existence with the status of an empire (*imperio*). This **First Empire** lasted from September 1821 to February 1823. The **Second Empire**, May 1864 to May 1866, never extended to the entire country. [L. H.]

EMPLOYERS' FEDERATION. *See* CONFEDERACIÓN PATRONAL DE LA REPÚBLICA DE MÉXICO.

EMPLOYMENT. The economies of the New World were historically short of labor, hence the imposition of forced labor on the **Indians** and the use of **African slavery**. Improved techniques and productivity and failure to compete with cheaper (often subsidized) imports led in the later 20th century to a decline in agricultural employment. This caused **internal migration** to the cities and **emigration** to the **United States**, plus a growth of the **informal economy**. A palliative to a serious unemployment problem was the encouragement of **maquilladoras** in cities along the **United States border**. [L. H.]

ENAMORADA. A 1946 film set in **Cholula** during the **Revolution of 1910**, directed by Emilio **Fernández Romo**, and starring Pedro **Armendáriz** as a general and María **Félix** as the love interest. Distributed with subtitles as *The General and the Señorita*, this was widely seen in North America and earned the award for the best foreign film of its year in Canada.

ENCINAS JOHNSON, LUIS (1912–1982). A **UNAM** law graduate, born in **Hermosillo**, who became known nationally for leading a vigorous public life despite seriously impaired vision and the effects of the

leprosy he had suffered in his youth. He was attorney general of **Sonora**, state supreme court justice, rector of the **Universidad de Sonora** from 1956–1961, state governor from 1961–1967, and director general of the **Banco Nacional de Crédito Agrícola** from 1970–1973.

ENCOMENDERO. Conquistador or other Spanish settler "entrusted" with an **encomienda**.

ENCOMIENDA ("trust"). A system introduced from medieval Spain whereby a settler in the New World was given responsibility by the Crown for converting and acculturating a group of **Indians**. The Indians were obligated to offer their free **labor** in return. Such "wards" remained technically "free," and there was (in theory) no associated land grant. The system was so abused that legal restrictions were introduced in the very first Laws of the Indies in the 1540s, but it was not effectively suppressed until the last century of colonial rule. *See also* REDUCCION; REPARTIMIENTO. [L. H.]

ENERGY MINISTRY (*Secretaría de Energía*, SENER). Created in 1994 by a reformation of the *Secretaria de Energía, Minas y Industria Paraestatal*, SEMIP, itself formed in 1982 when the earlier *Secretaría de Patrimonio y Fomento Industrial* was renamed on losing responsibility for **trade** and industry. *See also* MINISTRIES. [L. H.]

ENGINEERING EDUCATION. The importance of the **mining** industry led the colonial regime to establish the *Real Seminario de Minería* in 1792, which became almost immediately the *Real Colegio de Minería*, dropping the honorific *real* at **independence**. This became the *Escuela de Minas*, then under the **Second Empire** *Escuela Politécnica*. It was reformed by Benito **Juárez** in 1867 as the *Escuela Especial de Ingenieros*. Renamed in 1883 the *Escuela de Ingenieros*, a title later qualified as *Nacional,* it grew from 203 students in 1904 to 1000 by 1945. The present **Colegio de Ingenieros Civiles de México** was inaugurated March 7, 1946.

The *Escuela de Artes y Oficios para Hombres* of 1856 evolved into the *Escuela de Ingeniería Mécanica y Eléctrica* (EIME) in 1921, renamed in 1932 *Escuela Superior de Ingeniería Mécanica y Eléctrica* (ESIME). [L. H.]

ENGLAND. The pre-1707 predecessor of the **United Kingdom** was chronically at war with Spain and its empire from the 1580s, with the Pacific coast attacks by Francis **Drake** an early manifestation.

ENRÍQUEZ AFÁN DE RIVERA MANRIQUE, [FRAY] PAYO, DUQUE DE ALCALÁ (1610–1684). Augustian friar from Seville who became bishop of **Guatemala** in 1657, archbishop of Mexico in 1667, and acting **viceroy** of **New Spain** in 1673. As viceroy he finished the fortifications of the castle of **San Juan de Ulúa** and subsidized missionary expeditions. He resigned in 1681 to retire to the Convent of Nuestra Señora del Risco in Ávila, Spain, where he died. [L. H.]

ENRÍQUEZ COYRO, ERNESTO (1901–). Educationalist. Born in **Mexico City**, he graduated from the University of Barcelona, and then took a law degree at **UNAM**. In 1951 he reorganized the Ministry of **Natural Resources** (*Patrimonio Nacional*) and was the founder and first dean of UNAM's School of Political and Social Sciences. In 1958–1964 he served as assistant **education** minister.

ENRÍQUEZ DE ALMANZA, MARTÍN (15??–1583). Fourth **viceroy** of **New Spain**, 1568–1580. He drove English privateers out of Mexican waters (*See* ENGLAND), undertook various public works including the Cathedral, the San Hipólito hospital, the Santa Clara convent, and the Colegio de Santa María de Todos los Santos, established the Holy **Inquisition** and admitted the **Jesuits**. His concern for the welfare of the **Indians** included paying them for work on government projects and promulgating the **Tanda Law**. In 1581 he succeeded Francisco de Toledo as viceroy of Peru and died in office. [L. H.]

ENRÍQUEZ DE GUZMÁN, LUIS, CONDE DE ALBA, DE LISTE Y DE VILLAFLOR (1600–1663). Named **viceroy** of **New Spain** in 1649, he assumed office the following year and concerned himself with combating administrative **corruption**. In 1653 he left to become viceroy of **Peru**. [L. H.]

ENSENADA. Port and tourist center of **Baja California**, at 31°51'N, 116°38'W, 120 km (70 miles) south of the **United States border**.

ENVIRONMENT MINISTRY. Francisco **Vizcaíno Murray** became Director of Environmental Protections in 1972. An *Instituto Nacional de Ecología*, INE, was created in 1992 and followed in December 1994 by the establishment of a *Secretaría de Medio Ambiente, Recursos Naturales y Pesca*, SEMARNAP, which was reformed in November 2000 as the *Secretaría de Medio Ambiente y Recursos Naturales*, SEMARNAT, when fisheries were transfered to the **Agriculture Ministry**. [L. H.]

ENVIRONMENTAL ISSUES. *See* ECOLOGY.

EPIDEMICS. *See* DISEASE.

ESCANDÓN, JOSÉ DE, CONDE DE SANTA GORDA (1700–17??). Soldier from Santander in northern Spain who led expeditions to settle the further regions of the "**Near North**" and neighboring regions of the "**Far North**" in 1746–1755, creating the new jurisdiction of **Nuevo Santander** and establishing its first 20 settlements.

ESCOBAR REBELLION, 1929. "The Railroad and Banking Revolt" led by General José Gonzalo Escobar with 30,000 troops, opposed to the succession of Emilio **Pontes Gil** and the anti-clerical laws. In March the rebels captured **Ciudad Juárez** and then attacked **Monterrey** while systematically destroying **railroads** and robbing banks. There were 2,000 deaths but by late May the rebellion had been suppressed by Juan Andrés **Almazán**, aided by arms and aircraft from the **United States**. [L. H.]

ESCOBEDO, MARIANO (1826–1902). The *juarista* general to whom Emperor **Maximilian** surrendered his sword at **Querétaro** on May 15, 1867.

ESCOCESES ("Scotsmen"). In a Mexican context, members of the Scottish Rite of **Freemasonry**, favored by the conservatives. *See also* WARD, H. G.

ESCUELA DE AVIACIÓN MILITAR. The **Air Force** college was established in November 1915 and directed in 1921–1925 by Ralph **O'Neil**. It is now located in **Guadalajara**. [L. H.]

ESCUELA LIBRE DE DERECHO ("independent law school"). Formed in 1912 when a group of professors and students broke away from the *Escuela Nacional de Derecho* (which survives as the *Escuela de Derecho* of **UNAM**). Its first rector was Agustín **Rodríguez** and until the arrival of private universities in the 1950s it was the only law school not under a public university or other government agency. It owes its high reputation in large part from the fact that its faculty grades students exclusively on their performance in oral examinations.

ESCUELA MILITAR. *See* HERÓICA ESCUELA MILITAR.

ESCUELA NACIONAL DE AGRICULTURA. The National School of Agriculture, forerunner of the **Universidad Autónoma Chipango**.

ESCUELA NACIONAL DE ARTES PLÁSTICAS DE MEXICO. Originally the **Academia de San Carlos**, renamed in 1867 the *Escuela Nacional de Bellas Artes*.

ESCUELA NACIONAL DE ECONOMÍA. Founded in the 1930s by Narciso **Bassols**.

ESCUELA NACIONAL PREPARATORIA (E.N.P.). National Preparatory School. Its first director in the 1870s was Gabino **Barreda**.

ESCUELA NAVAL MILITAR. Naval academy at **Veracruz**.

ESCUELA SUPERIOR DE GUERRA. The Superior War School, equivalent to the **United States** Army Command and General Staff, offers selected captains a 3-year course in administration, strategy, and tactics. The **navy** has a similar **Centro de Estudios Superiores Navales**. [L. H.]

ESCUTIA, JUAN (1827–1847). Officer cadet from **Nayarit**, newly enrolled in the **Escuela Militar** when he became one of the "**Niños Héroes**" of the Battle of **Chapultepec**. He is popularly believed to have jumped over a cliff to his death, wrapped in the Mexican flag so it would not fall into the hands of the Americans.

ESMERALDA, LA. Famous school of painting and sculpture in **Mexico City**.

ESPINOSA, PATRICIA (1958–). Ambassador successively to the **United Nations**, Germany, and Austria. He was appointed foreign minister by President Felipe **Calderón Hinojosa**. [L. H.]

ESPINOSA DE LOS MONTEROS, ANTONIO (1903–1959). Economist with a master's from Harvard, a founder of **UNAM**'s School of Economics, director general of **Nacional Financiera**, 1935–1949, and ambassador in Washington, 1945–1948.

ESPINOSA VILLARREAL, OSCAR (1953–). A **Mexico City**-born graduate in business administration from **UNAM** who directed **Nacional Financiera** from 1987–1988, was president of the **Bolsa Mexicana de Valores** (Mexico City stock exchange) from 1988–1991, and governor of the **Federal District**, December 1, 1994–December 5, 1997.

ESQUIVEL, LAURA (1951–). Novelist and former kindergarten teacher, author of one of Mexico's most famous novels of recent years, *Como agua para chocolate* (1989), a tale of early 20th century northern Mexico whose heroine, forced to remain single to care for her elders, channels her frustrated passion into her cooking. Translated into 29 languages, it became a 123-minute film directed by Alfonso Arau, *Like Water for Chocolate* (1992), then the highest grossing foreign film released in the **United States**.

In February 2006 she published a fictionalized biography of La **Malinche**. [L. H.]

ESTADO. Spanish for "state" (all senses). *See also* SECRETARIO DE ESTADO; SIEGE, STATE OF; STATES.

ESTADOS UNIDOS MEXICANOS ("United Mexican States"). Since 1824, the official title of the federal Republic of Mexico, but not used on the **coinage** until 1905.

ESTANCO. A colonial method of taxing morally questionable luxuries such as playing cards and **tobacco** products by making their manufacture and distribution a state monopoly with artificially high retail prices. Introduced as one of the French-inspired **Bourbon Reforms**, it persisted into early independent **Mexico**. *See also* TAXATION. [L. H.]

ESTRADA DOCTRINE. A principle of foreign policy named for Argentine jurist José Manuel Estrada (1842–1894) and adopted by Mexico in 1930. Diplomatic relations with foreign governments would be determined by factual rather than legal considerations. The choice of government being the internal interest of the nation concerned, Mexico would only deny recognition to any new regime only if such recognition would violate Mexico's own national interest. The doctrine has not, however, been applied consistently. While it was used to justify Mexico's refusal to conform to the **Organization of American States'** decision to break off relations with Castro's **Cuba**, it did not prevent diplomatic ruptures with **Spain** under Franco nor with **Chile** under Pinochet. [L. H.]

ESTRADA REYNOSO, ENRIQUE (1889–1942). Opposition politician, younger brother of Roque **Estrada Reynoso**, he studied engineering in **Guadalajara** and joined the **Revolution of 1910** under General Rafael **Tapia**. He became a career officer, serving as governor of his native **Zacatecas**, 1920–1923; war minister, 1920–1923; and making major general in 1923. His support of Adolfo de la **Huerta**'s 1923 rebellion led to six years' exile in the **United States**. On his return he immediately supported another rebellion (the **Escobar Rebellion of 1929**). Later he accepted membership in what would become the **Partido Revolucionario Institucional**, and became federal deputy from 1937–1940, senator from 1940–1942, and director general of the **Ferrocarriles Nacionales de México** from 1941 until his death on November 11, 1942. He has been cited as an example of an opposition leader who was co-opted by the PRI back into the governmental system.

ESTRADA REYNOSO, ROQUE (1883–1966). Opposition politician, elder brother of Enrique **Estrada Reynoso**, a 1906 law graduate of the **Universidad de Guadalajara**, and a brigadier general in the 1913–1915 battles of the **Revolution of 1910**. Secretary to Francisco

Madero, he became executive secretary to Venustiano **Carranza** from 1914–1915 and was the major opposition candidate for president against Álvaro **Obregón** in 1920. After supporting Adolfo de la **Huerta**'s 1923 rebellion, he was exiled in the **United States**. After his return he was co-opted into the **Partido Revolucionario Institucional** and became a federal **Supreme Court** justice from 1941–1952.

ETHNICITY. *See* BLACKS; CREOLE; IMMIGRATION; INDIANS; JEWS; MESTIZO; RAZA.

EX-ARZOBISPADO. The former Archbishop's Palace in **Tacubaya**.

EXCÉLSIOR. **Mexico City** daily newspaper, founded on March 10, 1917, by Félix **Palavicini** as Mexico's first modern news-oriented paper, with news reports instead of editorial views on the front page. It became the country's leading paper, and, from 1932, it was cooperatively owned by key employees, although, like other papers of the time, supporting the official party (the future **Partido Revolucionario Institucional**. In the 1950s–1960s, under the direction of the distinguished journalist Julio **Scherer García**, it became the first Mexican newspaper of the time to voice criticism of the government if not of the president himself.

By the 1970s its readership of 250,000 (and 300,000 on Sundays) included important government officials and business and civic leaders throughout Mexico, but its independence led in 1972 to a boycott by the private sector.

An **UNAM** riot in 1975 led the paper to stray from the unofficial stance of never directly attacking the Mexican president, no matter who held the post. In June 1976 dozens of slum dwellers, led by Humberto Serrano, a spokesman for President **Echeverria** within the PRI, invaded an 88 ha property owned by *Excelsior*, threatening not to leave until the paper's executive director, Julio Scherer García was fired. They promised squatters they could stay in the meanwhile. At its July 8 stockholders' annual meeting, only Echeverria supporters were allowed to speak, and private armed door guards intimidated their opponents. Scherer was dismissed without a word of criticism of his competence or excellent managerial record. Leading newspapers the world over, the *New York Times*, France's *Le Monde*, and Brazil's

Estado de São Paulo among them, condemned the firing. Scherer founded the center-left *Proceso*, to which the now semi-official *Excelsior* reacted by including an occasional editorial page columnist to challenge the magazine by giving an anti-establishment view, but one with a different emphasis to that found in *Proceso*. The paper gradually recovered its ability to run other occasional stories critical of government administrators, particularly when ousted staffers regained control after the end of Echeverría's presidency. In the 1980s and 1990s the paper slowly recovered a little of its former prestige. After the PRI lost control of the **Cámara de Diputados Federales** (the lower house of the federal congress) in 1997, *Excélsior* displayed even more independence than before 1976, but its criticisms of the ruling party, presidency, and senate were usually balanced by accompanying presentations of the government's side. In 1998 with circulation still falling, it offered its support to PRI candidate Francisco **Labastide Ochoa**. A year later co-op members fired their leader, but the paper's financial problems continued. By 2000, when Labastide lost, its circulation stood at 350,000 (and 400,000 on Sundays). It owed $70 million in taxes and other debts, but a proposal to sell out to Miguel **Aldana Ibarra** fell through. In January 2006, however, it was reported that the paper was being sold to radio station owner Grupo Imagen for US$ 55.5 million. *See also* CENSORSHIP; *UNO MAS UNO*.

EXCHANGE RATE. The **peso** stayed roughly even with the **United States dollar** until the **Porfiriato** (it had originally been the same coin): 0.97 to the dollar in 1821; 0.96 in 1850; 1.09 in 1877. By 1894 it had fallen to half this (1.98 to the dollar), a value it kept, with small fluctuations through the **Revolution of 1910** and until the 1920s (2.06 to the dollar in 1900; 2.01 in 1910; 1.91 in 1917; 2.03 in 1925). The **Depression of the 1930s** reduced it to 2.65 in 1931; 3.50 in 1933; 3.60 in 1935; and, with nationalization of the **petroleum**, briefly even further, to 5.19. After a slight recovery stabilized it during **World War II** at 4.85 in 1940–1949, it was devalued to 8.65 in 1949–1954, and then again to 12.50 for the 22 years from 1954–1976, a period when the **International Monetary Fund** used the *peso* as one of the world's stable currencies.

In September 1976 it was allowed to float, inducing constant **inflation** ever since, with a decline to 26.50 to the dollar in 1977. Significant falls since then have been largely the result of capital flight, notably during the **Moratorium crisis** of August 1982 (reaching 150.00 on the free market in 1983 and 195.00 in 1984), and during the so-called "peso crisis" of December 1994 into early 1995. In 1995 the "new peso" (**nuevo peso**) was introduced, at a rate of 5.84 to the **dollar**, falling to 6.12 by July.

Subsequent six monthly rates:

January 1996—7.52	July 1996—7.57
January 1997—7.83	July 1997—7.87
January 1998—8.23	July 1998—8.92
January 1999—10.20	July 1999—9.52
January 2000—9.50	July 2000—9.83
January 2001—9.77	July 2001—9.17
January 2002—9.16	July 2002—10.20
January 2003—10.62	July 2003—10.46
January 2004—10.92	July 2004—11.47
January 2005—11.26	July 2005—10.67
January 2006—10.62	July 2006—10.98
January 2007—10.83	

Interpretation should take into account the 21st-century fall in the international value of the U.S. dollar. [L. H.]

EXECUTIVE. *See* PRESIDENT.

EXILES. Important groups of exiles in Mexico have included German and Austrian communists, Spanish Republicans, and leftist refugees from the Southern Cone (Argentina, Brazil, Chile, Paraguay, and Uruguay) during the **Dirty War**. There is also the problem of asylum seekers fleeing ethnic and political persecution in Central America (particularly in **Guatemala**), many of the exiles being housed in refugee camps in **Chiapas**. [L. H.]

EXPORTS. *See* CACAO; COFFEE; NARCOTICS; PETROLEUM; SILVER; SISAL; TOBACCO.

EXTENT. Modern (post–1848) Mexico stretches in a funnel shape from the **United States border** at 32°43'05"N down to the Isthmus of

Tehuantec, south of which it broadens out toward the border with **Guatemala** at 14°30'45"N. Continental Mexico extends east-west from 86°44'W to 107°08'W. Mexican sovereignty also extends to a number of **islands**. *See also* AREA; CONTINENTAL SHELF; FAR NORTH; MARITIME SOVEREIGNTY.

EXTERNAL DEBT. *See* FOREIGN DEBTS.

EZETA. *See* HEZETA.

– F –

FÁBREGAS, MANOLO (1921–1995). Cinema, radio, and **television** actor, director, and producer. Born July 15 in **Mexico City** as Manuel Sánchez Navarro Jr., the son of theater actor Manuel **Sánchez Navarro** and film actress Fanny Schiller. He graduated from the Texas Military Institute in 1938 and took his stage name in honor of his famous grandmother, Virigina Fábregas. As a theater actor manager in the late 1940s, he adapted such Broadway hits as *Life with Father*. In 1959 his Spanish version of *My Fair Lady* (in which he played Professor Higgins) had made him Mexico's leading producer-director. His 1970 production of *Fiddler on the Roof* broke Mexican theater box office records. His film *Mécanica nacional* (1971), about crazed automobile racing fans, avoided government censorship (e.g., of a man slapping his daughter, dressed in the then novel miniskirt) by raising finance from private loans. The film had a successful three-month opening run in 1971, followed by a further six months at another **Mexico City** cinema, and was still playing in 1973. He also hosted a *Tonight* and a *Weekend* talk show on television until the late 1970s. He operated his own Teatro San Rafael and Teatro Manolo Fábregas, Mexico's leading live-drama theaters. He produced, directed, or starred in Broadway hits from *Barefoot in the Park* to *Man of La Mancha*, plus Mexican plays from *Tenorio* to *Muerte de Juárez* and *Juan Derecho*.

After his death, which captured media attention throughout the Spanish-speaking world, his widow, Rafaela Fábregas, became executive director of his theaters and his project of continuing development of legitimate theater production in Mexico.

FÁBULA, ISIDRO (1882–1964). An attorney, born in **Mexico State**, June 28, who served as foreign minister under President **Huerta**, 1913–1915, and in 1915–1920 as ambassador successively to Italy and **Spain**, to **Brazil**, **Chile**, and Uruguay, and to **Argentina**. In 1937–1940 he was Mexican envoy to the **International Labour Organisation**, and in 1946–1952 a judge of the International Court at the Hague. He died in Mexico City on August 12.

FAESLER, JULIO (1930–). An attorney who became an economics and finance professor at the **Instituto Politécnico Nacional**, and then director of its doctoral program in foreign trade. In 1970–1976 he directed the government's **Instituto Mexicano de Comercio Exterior** and has been a longtime advisor on Mexico's import and export policies.

FALCON DAM (*Represa Falcon*). A popular flood control and **irrigation** project based on the furthest downstream international dam on the **Rio Grande**, at 26°33'N, 99°09'N, completed under the **Ruiz Cortines** and Eisenhower administrations in October 1953, and behind which a 27,520 ha (98,960 acre), 100 km (60 mile) long reservoir, *Falcon Lake*, has formed. [L. H.]

FALCONS. Sometimes used to translate **Halcones.**

FAMILIES. The extended family has a social and political significance shaping both public and private life and includes the ritual kinships of **compadrazgo**. These relationships are basic units in political parties, lobbying groups, and in the political cliques essential in obtaining appointments to non-routine governmental positions. **Divorce** has been permitted since 1914. *See also* KINSHIP; MACHISMO; WOMEN. [L. H.]

FAMILY PLANNING. Not until April 1972 (when Jorge **Jiménez Cantu** was health minister) did any Mexican government publicly advocate family limitation. Decades of **Church**-State political conflict had nullified the impact of Papal encyclicals against birth control, but

machismo fostered a pride in irresponsible fatherhood. In 1973 the burgeoning **birthrate** led the federal government to introduce the **Centro de Planificación Familiar**. Although the annual population increase had been brought down to the planned three percent by 1990, with half of all Mexicans still under 25 years of age, the nation still faced a birthrate too large for the availability of employment, potable water, food, and education.

In the 1990s Mexico's equal rights for **women** group ran newspaper advertisements telling women that limiting pregnancies was their only hope of achieving equal rights.

Induced **abortion** remains illegal.

FAR NORTH (*El Norte Grande*). Those territories which passed to **United States** sovereignty in 1848 and are now known to Americans as the *South West* (of the United States).

Although, right from the beginning of Spanish colonization individual *conquisadores* and missionary priests explored deep into the heartland of North America, the fierceness of Indian resistance, the low density of Spanish settlement, and the great distances involved meant that **Mexico City**'s hold over these vast spaces was precarious in the extreme and, despite the expeditions of José de **Escandón**, became more so with the 1767 expulsion of the **Jesuits**. That problem was (at least nominally) solved by having the Dominicans take over Jesuit missions in **Arizona**, **New Mexico**, and **Baja California**, while the Franciscans, led by Junípero **Serra**, continued the attempts to "christianize" (i.e., Hispanize) **Alta California**. In 1776 Spain's colonial secretary, José de Gálvez, formed a new administration, the *Comandancia general de las **Provincias Internas*** to strengthen royal control and respond to constant Indian raids.

The furthest Spanish exploration along the coast was to **Hinchinbrook Island** at 61°N, beyond even the 58°N reached by the 1775 voyage of Juan Francisco **Bodega y Quadra**. But soon a retreat from the more extreme Spanish pretensions was begun by withdrawal from Vancouver Island in the face of British pressure after the second **Nootka Convention** of 1794, followed by the acceptance, by a much weakened **Spain**, of the Treaty of **Limits of 1820**. Although the rest of this huge area was eventually lost through conquest by the United States, an important predisposing factor was the way economic ties to the latter were allowed to develop. Politicians in Mexico City were not only physically distant but also ignorant and uninterested, believing, for instance, that the territories were a fiscal drain when in fact they paid considerably more in **taxation** to the center than they cost (a fact concealed by bad record keeping!). *See also* TEXAS. [L. H.]

FARELL CUBILLAS, ARSENIO (1921–). Born June 30 in **Mexico City**, he graduated from **UNAM**, where he was a law professor for 25 years and served as legal consultant from the Aviation Pilots' Union, the Cinema Production Workers' Union, and for the Society of Authors and Composers. He was president of the National Chamber of Alcohol and Sugar Industries, director general of the **Comisión Federal de Electricidad**, 1973–1976, and of the **Instituto Mexicano de Seguridad Social**, 1976–1982. He was **labor** minister, 1982–1994, under both De La **Madrid** and **Salinas Gortari**, and minister of the **Contraloria General** under **Zedillo**, 1994–2000. In 1998 he received media praise for his unprecedented publishing of guidelines for judicious spending that a federal budget should follow. Such ideas had previously come only from presidents, and then rarely.

FARIAS, LUIS M. (1920–1999). Born in **Monterrey** on June 6, he became a professor of philosophy at **UNAM** (where he had graduated in **law**) and president of the National Federation of University Students. In 1946–1958, he was **television** and **radio** commentator of the XEW and XEW-TV networks and head of the XEW Union of Artists from 1946–1964. In 1951 he became founder-director of the National Association of Broadcast Announcers. In June 1962 he used his broadcasting experience to arrange all press and broadcasting coverage for the **Mexico City** meeting between presidents Kennedy and **López Mateos**. He served as executive officer for the **Tourism Ministry**, 1964–1967; director of information for the **Interior** Ministry, 1958–1964; governor of **Nuevo León**, 1970–1973; and director of *El Nacional*, 1975–1979.

FARMING. *See* AGRICULTURE.

FASCISM. *See* SINARQUISMO.

FAUNA. Characteristic wildlife of the drier parts of northern and central Mexico includes coyotes, vultures, reptiles, and scorpions. The mountains harbor mountain lions (*pumas*), bears, wolves, and eagles. Coastal swamplands such as those of **Ahome** are home to crocodiles. The rainforests of **Southern Mexico** have **jaguar**s, tapirs, monkeys, **iguana**, and parrots.

A breeding program for some threatened species is in progress on the island of **Tiburón**. *See also* CACTUS MOTH; FISHING; OCTOPUS; QUETZAL; TUNA; WHALES.

FEDERACIÓN DE PARTIDOS DEL PUEBLO DE MÉXICO (F.P.P.M.). Federation of Parties of the Mexican People, an opposition group formed in 1950 by dissidents from the **Partido Revolucionario Institucional**. Although it only registered 100,000 voters in two-thirds of Mexican states, its 1952 presidential candidate, **Henríquez Guzmá,** drew 580,000 votes. **García Barragán**, as party president and campaign director stressed its anti-crony platform. In 1954, however, the **Comisión Federal Electoral** cancelled the FPPM's status as a registered party over technicalities in registering voters.

FEDERACIÓN DE SINDICATOS DE LOS TRABAJADORES EN SERVICIO DEL ESTADO (F.S.T.S.E.). The Federation of Civil Service Unions, formed in 1938, unites all **trade unions** of federal employees. In disputes with government, it appeals to a special arbitration tribunal. It maintains its own separate **social security** system, the **Instituto de Seguridad y Servicios Sociales de los Trabajadores del Estado**. There is a similar federation of state and municipal civil service unions.

FEDERAL CONCILIATION AND ARBITRATION BOARD (*Junta Federal de Conciliación y Arbitraje—*JFCA). Sometimes translated as "Federal Labor Board," it was established on September 22, 1927, to resolve conflicts between labor and management. An agency of the **Labor Ministry**, it includes government, employer, and trade union representation and has subordinate local boards (JLCAs) and sectoral panels. Their powers include that of declaring a strike unlawful. Often established unions represented on these boards will urge the withholding of legal recognition from new, rival unions. [L. H.]

FEDERAL DEVELOPMENT BANK. *See* BANCO FEDERAL DE FOMENTO.

FEDERAL DISTRICT (*Distrito Federal*). The republican **constitution of 1824** confirmed **Mexico City** as the national capital, and (in imitation of the special status of the District of Columbia in the **United States**) detached its administrative area from **Mexico state** and made it directly dependent on the federal government, except during the suspension of federalism in 1837–46. The district's original 222 km^2 was enlarged to 1,700 km^2 in 1854, downsized to 1,479 km^2 in 1900, and is now 1,485 km^2 (573 sq. miles), bordering Mexico state to its north and **Morelos state** to the south. It contains Mexico City itself and many surrounding suburbs, with a population of 269,534 in 1857, 225,000 in 1869, and at subsequent **censuses** of 485,000 (1895); 541,000 (1900); 721,000 (1910); 906,000 (1921); 1,230,000 (1930); 1,757,000 (1940); 3,050,000 (1950); 4,871,000 (1960); 6,874,000 (1970); 8,831,000 (1980); 8,236,960 (1990) and 8,605,239 (2000). The actual administration was carried out by locally elected *municipios* (7 in 1824, 22 in 1854, 13 in 1903, 14 in 1924) until these were replaced in December 1928 by the *Departamento Central* and 12 *delegaciones* (*See* DELEGACION). These were mere agencies of the Department of the Federal District, which would be headed by a federally appointed **governor**, usually referred to in English as the mayor. The heads of his department parallel the key administrators in a state and in a **municipio**. The department had its own system of federal courts and is represented in the federal Congress by two senators and the number of deputies appropriate to its population.

Limited powers of local government were conferred in 1987 with each of the now 16 *delegaciones* electing its own council and the district as a whole having a popularly elected *Asamblea de Representantes*.

On October 20, 1993, a constitutional amendment restyled this *Asamblea Legislativa de Representantes*, with the increased power established in clause IV of Article 73 of the Constitution, to sit until November 1994. From March 15, 1995, the ordinary periods of this assembly's sessions would be held according to the dates in the *Diario Oficial* decree implementing the amendment. Cuauhtémoc **Cárdenas** became the first elected mayor in the election of July 6, 1997, serving for three years from December 2, 1997.

In the second half of the 20th century the city began to outgrow the bounds of the Federal District to become one of the world's megalopolises. *See also* MEXICO CITY CONURBATION.

FEDERAL ELECTORAL COMMISSION. *See* COMISIÓN FEDERAL ELECTORAL.

FEDERAL ELECTRICITY COMMISSION. *See* COMISIÓN FEDERAL DE ELECTRICIDAD.

FEDERALISM. The Liberal **Constitution of 1824** made Mexico, on paper, a federation. Although the centralizing Conservatives reestablished a unitary state through the **Constitution of 1836**, this was in effect for only a decade. Since then, except during the brief Conservative **Empire** of the 1860s, Mexico has been officially *Los Estados Unidos Mexicanos*. But in reality, federalism has never been a powerful force in Mexico, which has always been ruled by a strong central government. Its states have never enjoyed any degree of real autonomy.

FELIPE DE JESÚS, SAINT (1575–1597). Mexico's first saint, a Franciscan priest who abandoned his studies for the priesthood and was then sent by his wealthy parents to the **Philippines**. There, after leading a life of luxury and debauchery, he eventually mended his ways and was ordained. On his return voyage to Mexico City to celebrate his first mass, however, his ship was intercepted off the coast of **Japan**, and he and four other priests were tortured and killed.

FÉLIX, MARÍA (María de los Ángeles Félix Guereña, 1915?–). Actress, dubbed La Doña. Born in Alamos, **Sonora**, she debuted in *El Peñón de las ánimas* (1942) and soon achieved stardom and box office success. Otavio **Paz** calls her, in the prologue to his collection of photographs of her, *Una Raya en la agua* (1997) "the world's most beautiful woman." In 1946 she became an international star, playing opposite Pedro **Armendáriz**'s general in *Enamorada*. *Juana Gallo* (1960) was the first of several films in which she temporarily gave up roles in evening gowns or skimpy costumes to don male attire, defeating a male villain while wearing **charro** riding breeches and a pistol belt. When she wore such attire in her 1969 **television** series *Constitución*, she was credited with successfully encouraging Mexican women to wear pants in public for the first time. During her career she won two *Arieles de Oro* (equivalent to the Hollywood *Oscar*) and two *Arieles de Plata* as the runner-up actress of the year. Three of her five husbands were Augustín **Lara**, Jorge **Negrete**, and Diego **Rivera**. Her only child was an artist, Enrique.

FÉLIX SERNA, FAUSTINO (1913–1986). Businessman-politician, born May 3 in Pitiquito, **Sonora**. He obtained a diploma from Sonora teacher training college, organized the Caborca Cotton Company, a Sonora trucking service, and founded the Sonora Truckers' Union. He was elected successively councilman and then mayor in **Ciudad Obregón**, deputy in the federal **Congress**, and governor of Sonora state, 1967–1973.

FEMALE SUFFRAGE. Despite the exclusion of female suffrage from the **Constitution of 1917**, seven states came to allow **women** to vote in municipal or state elections, beginning with **Yucatán** in 1922 and **San Luis Potosí** in 1923. Efforts by Lázaro **Cárdenas Del Rio** at the federal level, however, were stalled by Congress and then doomed by the simple fact of being embraced by opposition candidate Juan Andreu **Almazán** in 1940. Eventually, in 1953, a constitutional amendment sponsored by **Ruiz Cortines** extended the right to vote to women in all elections—federal, state, and local.

FERDINAND VII (1784–1833). King of **Spain** in patriot eyes from 1808, but only effectively so when **Napoleon**'s troops were driven out of Spain at the end of the Peninsular War in 1814 and he was released from French captivity. When the news of his ouster by Napoleon in favor of the latter's brother Joseph **Bonaparte** on May 2, 1808, had arrived in the Americas, a rift opened there, as in Spain itself, between those who accepted the new regime and those who continued to regard Ferdinand as Spain's legitimate king. The **viceroy**, José de **Iturrigaray** tried to exploit the situation to his own advantage, but he was deposed by Spaniards loyal to King Joseph and replaced by the elderly Pedro **Garibay**. By then fear of Indian and mestizo support for the insurgency led by Miguel **Hidalgo y**

Costilla and José María **Morelos** with its implied threat of social revolution had united the upper classes. Once the outcome of the Peninsular War had reunited Spain under a restored and absolutist Ferdinand VII, Spain's continued rule in Mexico seemed assured.

The situation was reversed when in early 1820 rebel army officers in Spain led by Rafael **Riego y Núñez** forced Ferdinand into pursuing liberal policies. The threat of Mexico's being subject to such a government united the conservatives. Within a year even the newly appointed viceroy was ready to accede to the Plan of **Iguala** for an independent New Spain under conservative rule. **Canning** in the **United Kingdom** and Monroe in the **United States** each seized the opportunity to issue a formal undertaking to oppose any move by another European power to support Spain in the Americas.

By the end of his reign, Ferdinand had lost all Spain's mainland American empire.

FERNÁNDEZ DE BONILLA, ALONSO (????–1600). Fourth archbishop of Mexico, appointed 1592.

FERNÁNDEZ DE CEVALLOS RAMOS, DIEGO (1941–). UNAM trained lawyer, senator, and unsuccessful **Partido de Acción Nacional** candidate in the **election of 1994**.

FERNÁNDEZ DE CÓRDOBA, DIEGO, MARQUÉS DE GUADALCÁZAR (1578–1630). Spanish official, born in Seville, who accompanied Margaret of Austria on her 1599 journey to marry Phillip III, and who became **viceroy of New Spain** in 1612. As such, his achievements included the aqueduct from Santa Fe to La Mariscala, the draining of the Valley of **Mexico**, founding the cities of Córdoba and Lerma, and suppressing the revolt of the **Tepejuan** Indians. He left in 1621 to become viceroy of **Peru**. [L. H.]

FERNÁNDEZ DE LA CUEVA [ENRÍQUEZ], FRANCISCO, DUQUE DE ALBURQUERQUE, MARQUÉS DE CUELLAR, CONDE DE LEDESMA Y DE HUELMA (1617–1676). Barcelonaborn Spanish soldier-administrator who fought in Flanders. Made **viceroy** of **New Spain** in 1653, he was the first such to suffer an assassination attempt. He finished the cathedral and founded **Albuquerque**

but lost Jamaica to the English. Returning to Spain in 1660, he became viceroy of Naples. [L. H.]

FERNÁNDEZ DE LA CUEVA ENRÍQUEZ, FRANCISCO (16??–1733). **Viceroy** of **New Spain**, 1702–1711, who lived extravagantly while civil servants went unpaid and poverty and **banditry** spread. [L. H.]

FERNÁNDEZ DE LIZARDI, JOSÉ JOAQUÍN (1776–1827). A journalist and precursor of **independence** who used the 1812 period of freedom from **censorship** in **Mexico City** to propagandize for liberation from Spain. His *Periquillo sarniento* of 1816, published by Mariano **Galván Rivera**, has been called Mexico's first important novel.

FERNÁNDEZ MACGREGOR, GENARO (1883–1959). Lawyer who founded and (until the 1950s) published the *Mexican Journal of International Law* and was assistant foreign minister from 1911–1914. Then, as a key legal adviser for the **foreign ministry**, 1917–1924, he helped revolutionary Mexico secure a renewal of diplomatic recognition by the **United States**. In the 1940s he served as a judge of the International Court of Justice at the Hague.

FERNÁNDEZ MANERO, VÍCTOR (1898–). Physician, born in **Villahermosa**, who served as a deputy in the federal **Congress** and in 1936–1939 as governor of his native **Tabasco**. In 1940 he joined the cabinet, and by 1943 he had created the **Health Ministry** from the former department of health. He later served as ambassador, first to **France**, then to Yugoslavia.

FERNÁNDEZ ROMO, EMILIO (1904–1986). Film director. Born March 26, in Sabinas, **Coahuila**, he supported Adolfo de la **Huerta** and was exiled with him to **Los Angeles**. There he trained as an actor and film technician at various Hollywood studios, observing the editing of Sergei **Eisenstein**'s *Viva México*. Returning to Mexico he was billed as *El Indio,* for Indian features inherited from his **Kikapú** mother. His *María Candelareria* (1943) which established him as a leading director was followed in the same year by *Flor silvestre* with

Dolores del **Rio**, both photographed by Gabriel Figueroa. *Enamorada* in 1946 brought international stardom to Pedro **Armendáriz** and María **Félix**. His *Islas Marías* about the harsh penal colony led to prison reform, and *Un Día de vida* (1950) became one of Latin America's most acclaimed and successful films. Among other artistic and financial successes were *Salón México*, 1949; *La Red*, 1953; *La Choca*, 1974; *Soy puro mexicano*, *La Bien amada*, and, codirected with John Ford, *The Fugitive* (1947).

FERRELO, BARTOLOMÉ. Pilot on Juan Rodríguez **Cabrillo's** expedition of 1542 who took over command on the latter's death. He reached 44°N, the latitude of Eugene, Oregon, before turning back. The expedition returned in April 1543.

FERRIES. *See* GUAYMAS; PROGRESO; SERVICIOS MARÍTIMOS DE TURISMO.

FERROCARRIL MEXICANO. Railroad corporation registered in London during the **Second Empire** as *The Imperial Mexican Railway Company*. Faced with bankruptcy, it ceased construction in 1866 but was encouraged to resume work by Benito **Juárez** who, desperate to develop the country's transportation infrastructure, offered a generous subsidy. The line from **Veracruz**, with a branch to **Puebla**, reached **Mexico City** on December 20, 1872. Since the **privatization** of the 1990s, *Ferrocarril Mexicano S.A.* has become the largest of Mexico's **railroads**.

FERROCARRILES NACIONALES DE MÉXICO. National Railways of Mexico, formed in 1937, when President Lázaro **Cárdenas del Rio** expropriated the privately owned **railroads**. The exception was the Ferrocarril del Pácifico, running between **Nogales** and **Guadalajara**, which operated semi-autonomously during a long period of transition. In the post-**World War II** period, service on the National Railways deteriorated as the bureaucracy sought to satisfy the railroad workers' trade union (*Sindicato de Trabajadores Ferrocarrileros de la República Mexicana*—STFRM), and the railroad sank increasingly into debt. Much of this was due to keeping cargo rates below cost as a subsidy to farmers. In 1958 the Communist leaders of the railwaymen's union ordered slow working and in 1959 began one-hour stoppages of passenger trains in furtherance of their wage demands. When the government refused to give way, the union began two-hour stoppages of freight trains every four hours, with an immediate impact on the delivery of perishable foods. These stoppages only ended when President **López Mateos** threatened prosecutions for treason of union head Demetrio **Vallejo** and party secretary David Álvaro **Siqueiros**. There was also the issue of the free passes given to top officials of the presidential cabinet, to members of the federal **congress**, to leaders of state legislatures, and to various civil servants, federal, state, and municipal, and their families. According to the annual report for 1982, as many as 80 percent of sleeping car passengers between the **United States border** and **Mexico City** were riding free. The 1980s saw many less-used lines closed. From 1995 onwards, a series of privatizations took place, not only to make the railroads solvent but also to improve service. FCNM's ferry services were hived off as the privatized **Servicios Marítimos de Turismo**.

FICTION. *See* NOVELS.

FIDEICOMISO. A government development lending agency for **cooperatives**, such as the *Fideicomiso Pesquero* for fishing cooperatives. Others provide for small businessmen, for skilled workers in **tobacco**, **sugar**, and related industries, and for small-scale artisans such as **silver**smiths.

FIFTH OF MAY (*Cinco de Mayo*). Anniversary of the 1862 Battle of **Puebla** which set back the progress of the **French Intervention** and establishment of the **Second Empire** by two years. For this it is regularly celebrated as a national holiday throughout Mexico, and it is such an assertion of their allegiance by those of Mexican birth or descent in the United States that Americans confuse it with the anniversary of Mexico's Declaration of **Independence** (September 15–16, 1810).

FILIBUSTER. A cognate, and originally a homonym, of "freebooter," i.e., pirate, it came in the mid-19th century to mean any (but particularly an American) soldier of fortune in the Caribbean or Mexico. The most notorious was William **Walker**. Others were John **Frémont** and Raousset de **Boulbon**.

FILMS. *See* CINEMA.

FINANCE MINISTRY. Established in 1821 as the *Secretaría del Tesoro*, it became the *Secretaría de Hacienda* in 1824, the *Ministerio de Hacienda* in 1843, and in 1854 *Secretaría de Hacienda* once again. Since 1917 it has been the *Secretaría de Hacienda y Crédito Público* (Ministry of Finance and Public Credit, SHCP). It has authority over treasury reserves and deposits, the federal reserve banking system, the currency (including the mint), and interest rates. It collects federal taxes and other revenue, disburses federal expenditures, and administers credit and investments extended by government through decentralized government agencies and banks. *See also* BUDGET, FEDERAL.

FINANCIAL CRISIS OF 1982. In August capital flight provoked by a large current account deficit led Mexico into declaring a **moratorium** on its **foreign debts**. This provoked general loss of investor confidence in all Latin American countries and a region-wide economic depression lasting the rest of the decade.

FINANCIAL CRISIS OF 1994. An overvalued **peso**, a chronic balance of payments deficit covered by short term borrowing, and the political shocks of events in **Chiapas** and the murders of reputed reformers Luis Donaldo **Colosio** and José Francisco **Ruiz Massieu** led to severe capital flight which obliged the **Banco de México** to allow the currency to "float," i.e., suddenly depreciate.

FINANCIERA NACIONAL AZUCARERA (FINA). The government's **sugar** industry development bank, created in 1943 as the *Financiera Industrial Azucarera*, changed its name in 1963 and liquidated in April, 2006.

FINANCIERO, EL. Daily business newspaper, founded 1980.

FINE ARTS NATIONAL INSTITUTE. *See* INSTITUTO NACIONAL DE BELLAS ARTES.

FINE ARTS PALACE. *See* BELLAS ARTES, PALACIO DE LAS.

FIRST EMPIRE. The constitutional form, the *Imperio Mexicano*, adopted soon after Mexico achieved independence in February 1821, with Agustín **Iturbide** as **emperor**. It was extended in January 1822 to include the former captaincy general of **Guatemala** but ended with the exile of Iturbide in March 1823, followed by the separation of the Central American states (except **Chiapas**) from Mexico in July 1823.

FISHING. An autonomous federal agency under the ministry of trade and the **navy**, the *Departamento de Pesca* was created in December 1976, under the direction of Fernando Rafful, a career public administrator, to deal with all commercial fishing and with the fish conservation and exploitation in lakes, rivers, and territorial waters (*See* HYDROGRAPHY). In 1982 fisheries became a separate ministry, but in 1994 it was downgraded to an undersecretariat within the **Environment Ministry**. Whereas this was seen as a shift of emphasis to conservation and sustainability, the undersecretariat's November 2000 transfer to the **agriculture ministry** (*Secretaria de Agricultura, Ganadería, Desarrollo Rural, Pesca y Alimentación*) would seem to suggest a further policy change to one of *fomento* (i.e., encouraging output). The legislation continues to pay at least lip service to the "rational use of marine resources."

Catches of **octopus, grouper**, and abalone are regulated by quota; in other sectors, reliance is placed on closed seasons, restrictions on vessel size, permitted gear, etc.

The economically most important products of the industry are **shrimp**, followed by **tuna**, octopus, grouper, **squid, sardine**, and **shark**.

Sport fishing is an important tourist attraction. *See also* PEARL FISHING; SARDINE. [L. H.]

FLAG. Tricolors have been associated with a repudiation of the old order ever since the United Provinces of the Netherlands adopted one of horizontal bands of orange, white, and blue in their revolt against 16th-century Spain, inspiration of the red, white, and blue vertical tricolor of revolutionary France.

Mexico's national flag, a red, white, and green vertical tricolor, dates from October 1821: red for the union of *americanos* and Spaniards, white for the **Church**, and green for **independence**, the ideas of the Plan de **Iguala**. Benito **Juárez** reinterpreted these colors as representing the blood of heroes, hope, and unity.

The central emblem, omitted until 1968 from the merchant ensign, began as a crowned eagle with wings spread. The first republican flag, of February 1823, substituted the uncrowned Aztec **eagle and serpent** design, its lower half surrounded by a semicircle of laurel and olives. The flag of the **Second Empire** imitated that of the second French empire in having a small crowned eagle in each corner. The spread eagle became one viewed from the side in 1917, but only in 1984 was it decided to reverse its position on the back of the flag so that both sides would match.

The proportions of the flag were originally two to three, except under the Second Empire, which changed them to 4.7 to 1.2. The present four to seven proportion was decreed in 1968.

Confusion with Italy's similar tricolor (introduced in 1797 with the red and white for Milan and the green for Lombardy) were finally resolved in time for the **Olympic Games** of 1968. The eagle and serpent symbol (with a diameter three quarters of the width of the central panel) would henceforth be carried on the merchant ensign as well as on the national flag. The current flag regulations date from December 8, 2005.

The flag of **Hidalgo y Costilla**'s revolt was a blue square having centered within it a white square in which a crowned eagle perched on a cactus over a three-arched bridge circling in turn the letters V, V, and M, for *Viva Virgen María*. *See also* NAVAL JACK. [L. H.]

FLAG DAY (*Dia de la bandeja*). The national flag day, February 24, was first celebrated in 1937. [L. H.]

FLEET. *See* NAVY; TREASURE FLEET.

FLORA. The traditional "**Near North**" is largely **matorral** characterized by spiny shrub and cactus, but much of the higher land bears temperate oak or pine forest. Central Mexico is divided between the forested highland (over 800 m), natural prairie in the drier east, and subtropical plants along the wetter Pacific coast. Southern Mexico bears perennial tropical rainforest, except in the drier areas along the Caribbean which have deciduous tropical forest. Some **islands** still conserve a few of their unique aboriginal species. *See also* AGAVE; BOTANICAL GARDENS; FORESTS; LEUCAENA; MOCIÑO, JOSÉ; POINSETT, JOEL ROBERTS; PRICKLY PEAR CACTUS; TREES. [L. H.]

FLORES, ÁNGEL (1883–1926). Revolutionary general, governor of **Sinaloa**, 1920–1924, who was the defeated conservative presidential candidate in the **Election of 1924**.

FLORES, MANUEL ANTONIO. *See* FLOREZ MARTÍNEZ DE ÁNGULO, MANUEL ANTONIO.

FLORES FERNÁNDEZ, EDMUNDO (1918–2004). Economist and public administrator whose writings influenced Mexican trade policies. He was a visiting professor at the Woodrow Wilson School of International Affairs, 1972–1974, ambassador to **Cuba**, 1974–1975, director of the **Partido Revolucionario Institucional**'s **Instituto de Estudios Políticos, Economicos e Sociales**, 1975–1976, and director of the **Consejo Nacional de Ciencia y Tecnología**, from 1976.

FLORES MAGÓN, ENRIQUE (1887–1954). Regarded as a precursor of the **Revolution of 1910**, although playing a much less active role than his elder brothers. He died in **Mexico City**.

FLORES MAGÓN, JESÚS (1871?–1930). Born in **Oaxaca**, he helped his brother Ricardo **Flores Magón** found *La Regeneracion*. When it was banned, he gave up all pretence of being a revolutionary and withdrew from politics.

FLORES MAGÓN, RICARDO (1873–1922). Lawyer and revolutionary leader, the most active of the three brothers, and generally regarded as the intellectual precursor of the **Revolution of 1910**, publishing an opposition newspaper, *El Demócrata* in 1893 which Porfirio **Díaz** had promptly closed. Along with his elder brother Jesús **Flores Magón**, he then, in 1900, started *La Regeneración*. After fleeing his consequent incarceration, he resumed its publication in San Antonio, Texas, and founded the underground **Partido Liberal**. In 1911 he led a rebellion in **Baja California**, but never joined forces with what he termed **Madero**'s "bourgeois revolution." For writing seditious literature, he was sentenced in 1918 to 20 years in the **United States** federal penitentiary at Fort Leavenworth, dying a very embittered man.

FLORES SÁNCHEZ, OSCAR (1907–1986). Lawyer who served as federal senator from his native **Chihuahua** from 1952–1958, as its governor from 1968–1974, and then as **López Portillo**'s **procurador general** (attorney general) from 1976–1982, noted for his vigorous campaign against the **smuggling** of **narcotics** into the **United States**.

FLORES TAPIA, ÓSCAR (1917?–1998). Born in **Saltillo**, trained as a teacher, he served as senator from his native **Coahuila** from 1970–1976. Within the **Partido Revolucionario Institucional**, he has been director of publishing, a member of its **Comité Ejecutivo Nacional**, secretary for popular action, and head of the **Confederación Nacional de Organizaciones Populares**.

FLOREZ MARTÍNEZ DE ÁNGULO, MANUEL ANTONIO, CONDE DE CASA FLÓREZ (1723–1799). Native of Seville who served as **viceroy** of New Granada from 1776–1781, and of **New Spain** from 1787–1789. In the former post he built **highways**, reformed hospitals, encouraged industry and **agriculture**, developed free trade, established the first public printing press in **Bogotá**, improved the defenses of Cartagena de las Indias, and fought British incursions on the Mosquito Shore. In the latter, he recovered taxing powers that had been delegated to a *superintendente* and formed three new regiments. [L. H.]

FOLK DANCE. *See* DANCE.

FOLK MEDICINE. *See* BRUJA; CURANDERO.

FOLK MUSIC. *See* BAMBA; CHIAPANECAS; *GOLONDRINAS, LAS*; HUAPANGO; JARABE; JAROCHO; *LLORONA, LA*; *MACARENA, LA*; *MAÑANITAS, LAS*; MARIACHI; MARIMBA; *RANA*; TAPATÍO.

FOLKLORE. *See* MYTH.

FOMENTO. Economic development (often with a hint of governmental stimulation); modern usage prefers the politically neutral *desarrollo*. [L. H.]

FONDO BANCARIO DE PROTECCIÓN AL AHORRO (FOBAPROA). Approval of the 1999 federal budget was delayed when the **Partido de Acción Nacional (PAN)** protested at the US\$ 65 billion in liabilities amassed by FOBAPROA in the federal government bailout of the banking system during the **peso** crisis of 1994–1995. After negotiation between Congress, the presidency, and banking officials, the PAN and **Partido Revolucionario Institucional** leaders in the **Cámara de Diputados Federales** reached a compromise on December 11, 1998, allowing **Banco de México** governor Guillermo **Ortiz** to remain at his post. *See also* BANKS AND BANKING.

FONDO DE CULTURA ECONÓMICA (F.C.E.). Founded in 1935 (to remedy the lack of modern works in Spanish on economics) by Daniel **Cosío Villegas**, who directed it for many years, finally permitting the government to buy a partnership after its success as Spanish America's publisher of quality books. It opened a Brazilian subsidiary in the early 1990s.

FONDO DE PROMOCIÓN DE INFRAESTRUCUTRA TURÍSTICA (INFRATUR). Federal agency for investment in the infrastructure of the tourist industry, builds various facilities needed to encourage **tourism**.

FONDO NACIONAL DEL CONSUMO DE LOS TRABAJADORES (FONACOT). Federal agency to help upgrade workers' consumption, chiefly by subsidies on a few essentials.

FONDO NACIONAL DE LA VIVIENDA PARA LOS TRABAJADORES. *See* INSTITUTO DEL FONDO NACIONAL DE LA VIVIENDA PARA LOS TRABAJADORES.

FONDOS ("funds"). Twelve development agencies created by President **Díaz Ordaz** in 1965 as major government lending outlets for each of several economic sectors, including **tourism**, **fishing**, housing, and **sugar** production.

FONTE, BARTOLOMÉ DE. Legendary Spanish admiral who supposedly discovered the Strait of **Anián** (leading to the Atlantic) in his 1640 exploration of the Pacific coast of North America.

FOOD AND FOOD SUPPLY. Long self-sufficient in basic foodstuffs, globalization has in recent years reduced Mexican production in face of cheaper (and sometimes subsidized) food exported from the **United States** and elsewhere. *See also* AGRICULTURE; BAJIO, El; BEANS; COFFEE; COMPANIA NACIONAL DE SUBSISTENCIAS POPULARES; CORN; FONDO NACIONAL DEL CONSUMO DE LOS TRABAJADORES; HIDALGO STATE; WHEAT. [L. H.]

FOOT AND MOUTH DISEASE. *See* HOOF AND MOUTH DISEASE.

FOOTBALL, ASSOCIATION. *See* SOCCER.

FOREIGN CLUB. A very profitable casino controlled by Plutarco Elías **Calles**, catering to middle and lower income Mexicans. **Cárdenas** closed it down (although permitting some other forms of gambling to continue), thereby incurring the wrath of the man who had done so much to put him in power.

FOREIGN DEBT MORATORIUM. (1) In 1861, Benito **Juárez**, faced with a depressed state of its **economy** and depleted treasury, declared a two-year moratorium on interest payments on Mexico's foreign public debts. This led to the **London Convention** and provided the excuse for the subsequent **French Intervention**.

(2) In the **Financial Crisis of 1982** Mexico again suspended interest payments on its foreign debts, undermining foreign investor confidence, with serious consequences throughout Latin America. [L. H.]

FOREIGN DEBTS. During **Díaz Ordaz**'s presidency, the external debt fell from US$ 6 billion to US$ 4 billion. At the end of 1999, however, Mexico owed the **International Monetary Fund** US$ 7.42 billion, much of it accrued during the **financial crisis of 1994** that had followed the December 1994 devaluation of the **peso.**

Nevertheless, in April 1999, finance minister Ángel **Gurría Treviño** rejected a preventative credit line offered by the IMF for 2000–2006, stating that Mexico's new policies of fiscal caution and firm debt management made this unnecessary.

FOREIGN EXCHANGE. *See* EXCHANGE RATE.

FOREIGN INVESTMENT. The **United Kingdom** was Mexico's chief source of foreign investment during the early 19th century but was gradually replaced by the **United States.** [L. H.]

FOREIGN MINISTRY (*Secretaría de Relaciones Exteriores*, **SRE**). The **First Empire** established in November 1821 a *Secretaría de Negocios y Relaciones Interiores y Exteriores*, with José Manuel de **Herrera** as Mexico's first foreign minister. Early in 1822 this became the *Ministerio de Relaciones Exteriores e Interiores*. The **Siete Leyes of 1836** dropped the inclusion of "interior relations," and while the **Constitution of 1857** redesignated all ministries as "secretariats," there was a temporary return in 1861–1891 to the style *Ministerio de Relaciones Exteriores y de Gobierno*. [L. H.]

FOREIGN RELATIONS. *See* INTERNATIONAL RELATIONS.

FOREIGN TRADE. *See* EXPORTS; IMPORTS.

FORESTS. Despite rapid **deforestation** in recent decades, a quarter of Mexico's land area is still wooded. Even the largely desert north has some impressive forests, especially **Chihuahua.** The woodlands of central Mexico have the world's highest number of species of oak and pine. The unique ability of cloud forest to obtain moisture from the surrounding atmosphere provides a significant contribution to the water supply to **Mexico City.** Tropical southern Mexico has lowland rainforest, broadleaf forest, and montane forest, parts of **Chiapas** being the wettest areas in Mexico and home to almost a third of the native **flora.** [L. H.]

FOX QUEZADA, VICENTE (1942–). Born in **Mexico City**, July 2, he was brought up in rural **Guanajuato**, studied business administration at the **Universidad Iberoamericana** and at Harvard, worked for Coca Cola de México, and managed corporations in the **livestock** breeding and agro-industry fields. He joined the **Partido de Acción Nacional** in 1987, was elected governor of Guanajuato on its ticket in a landslide in 1995, and became its candidate for the 2000 presidential election. He won, ending the dominance that the **Partido Revolucionario Institucional** had enjoyed since 1929. His wife is Marta **Sahaguín de Fox**.

[His presidency, however, ended on a sour note. His handling of the unrest in **Oaxaca** was criticized as heavy-handed, his lawyers were suing him for not paying them for defending him against a charge of rigging the **election of 2006**, and Congress forbade him to leave the country after he left office—he had intended to join his daughter in Australia. L. H.]

FRAGA MAGAÑA, GABINO (1899–1982). A **Morelia**-born lawyer who headed the *Comisión Nacional Bancaria y de Valores*, CNBV (National Banking and Securities Commission), and served as assistant foreign minister and as a **supreme court** justice. He is best known as a founder of the *Instituto de Administración Pública* (Institute of Public Administration) in the 1950s, promoting the concept of **higher education** for federal civil servants.

FRAIRE, ISABEL (1934–). A writer for literary magazines, she became nationally known in the 1970s for translating and publishing the poetry of Ezra Pound and T. S. Eliot. Her own volume of poems, *Solo esta luz* (1969), brought her international recognition.

FRANCE, RELATIONS WITH. Valois, France's traditional rivalry with Habsburg, Spain, manifested itself in the 16th century in expeditions to the New World by its privateers. This enmity continued under the Bourbons until the War of the **Spanish succession** gave the Spanish throne to a junior branch of the Bourbons, creating the informal alliance between Spain and France known as the "Family Compact." This lasted until the French Revolution and **Napoleon I**'s intervention in Spain in 1808. Although French territorial ambitions in North

America had already been effectively ended by the **Louisiana** Purchase, a desire for influence in the New World continued, as evinced by the coinage of the term "Latin America" in the 1830s to suggest a commonality of interests among its "Latin" countries in opposition to the Anglo-Saxon, Protestant, and Common Law North. This found its most aggressive expression in the **French Intervention** of 1863–1866.

An early French visitor was the abbé **Chappe d'Auteroche** who came to California in the 1770s to observe a transit of Venus. *See also* CAMACHO, SEBASTIÁN; FRENCH IMMIGRATION; PASTRY WAR. [L. H.]

FRANCHISE. *See* SUFFRAGE.

FRANCO SODI, CARLOS (1904–1961). An **Oaxaca** lawyer who served as director of the **Mexico City** federal penitentiary, as **procurador general** (attorney general) of the **Federal District** from 1946–1952, and then of the federal government from 1952–1958, after which he served as a **supreme court** justice from 1956–1961. His many articles and commentaries on criminal **law** helped modernize the penal code in the 1940s, 1950s, and 1960s.

FREEMASONRY. At the end of the 18th century, in the wake of the French Revolution, the Freemasons became important vehicles in the spread of political and economic liberalism. This was an ideology to which the **Church** was fiercely opposed, although it made its objection ostensibly on the theological ground that Freemasons had sworn not to reveal their secrets, even in the confessional. Masonic deism was also seen a repudiation of papal authority in faith and morals. In the 1820s, Mexico shared with Brazil the distinction of being the first Catholic countries whose national leaders had embraced Freemasonry, with priests actually serving as masters of lodges. The York and Scottish Rites both became active in Mexico in 1822. The conservatives tended to be Scottish Rite Masons—**Escoceses**—and the liberals to be York Rite Masons—**Yorkinos**—of whom Vicente **Guerrero** became grand master in 1824. Benito **Juárez**, responsible for the **Constitution of 1857** which disestablished the Church, was a leading mason. Most presidents since the **Revolution of 1910** have been 32-degree masons. Since 1924 it has been traditional for the incumbent president to wear a masonic ring to symbolize his support of the separation of **Church** and state and of the curtailment of religiously-based partisan politics. *See also* RINCON, VALENTIN. [L. H.]

FRÉMONT, JOHN. American explorer and soldier of fortune whose June 1846 occupation of **Alta California** (the "**Bear Flag Republic**") caused a revolt in **Mexico City** and the overthrow of President Mariano **Paredes y Argillaga**.

FRENCH IMMIGRATION. In 1828, Mexico permitted former members of Napoleon's Imperial Guard to settle in **Los Angeles** to reward their service to Mexican **independence**. About 800 settled in what was then a town of under 5,000 and came to dominate it socially until the 1870s. In French Town, around the present-day city hall, stood the house of Jean-Louis Vignes, a native of Bordeaux who began both **California**'s orange and **wine** industries. He planted *El Aliso* (named for its ancient sycamore), one of California's first vineyards on 42 ha (104 acres) outside the town, between present-day Cesar E. Chavez Avenue and the 110 Freeway. This became one of the world's largest vineyards, producing 150,000 bottles a year, including the first Californian "champagne." [L. H.]

FRENCH INTERVENTION. The 1861 **foreign debt moratorium** led to the **London Convention** which involved direct intervention by the country's principal creditors, the **United Kingdom**, Spain, and **France**. But the first two countries withdrew when it became clear that France intended to install a puppet regime favoring its own interests. In 1863 Dubois **Saligny**, French minister in **Mexico City,** conspired with Mexican conservatives hostile to Benito **Juárez** to form a **Junta de Notables** to consider a new constitution. The Junta would eventually offer allegiance to Archduke **Maximilian** as **emperor** of Mexico, who in turn would sign the Convention of **Miramar** to guarantee French military support. The *Expédition du Méxique*, 35,000 strong, was commanded by General François Achille **Bazaine**. It took **Puebla** in early 1863 and **Mexico City** in June 1963. After the Union's victory in the American Civil War, **United States** pressure eventually secured a French withdrawal, fatally reducing Maximilian's troop strength to his 25,000 Mexicans. *See also* BOULBON, RAOUSSET DE; LONDON CONVENTION. [L. H.]

FRENTE CARDENISTA. *See* PARTIDO DEL FRENTE CARDENISTA DE RECONSTRUCCIÓN NACIONAL.

FRENTE DEMOCRÁTICO NACIONAL (FDN). The National Democratic Front, an alliance of the **Partido Mexicano Socialista**, the **Partido Popular Socialista**, and the **Partido Auténtico de la Revolución Mexitana**, formed to support the presidential candidacy of Cuauhtémoc **Cárdenas** in the **election of 1988**.

FRENTE ELECTORAL POPULAR. The Popular Electoral Front, a far-left organization led by Braulio **Maldonado Sánchez** in the **election of 1964**.

FRENTE URBANO ZAPATISTA. Marxist guerrilla group responsible for the 1971 kidnapping of Julio **Hirschfeld Alamada**.

FUCA, JUAN DE. Greek pilot living in **New Spain** in 1588–1594 who is supposed to have discovered the strait named after him at 47°–48°N, between Vancouver Island and the northwestern part of the state of Washington. [L. H.]

FUENTE, JUAN RAMÓN DE LA (1951–). Physician born in **Mexico City** on September 5. Graduating in medicine from **UNAM**, he specialized in psychiatry at the Mayo Clinic in Rochester, Minnesota, earned an MSc, served as an associate professor at the University of Minnesota, and returned to do research at the *Instituto Nacional de Nutrición* and the *Instituto Mexicano de Psiquiatría*. He became director of UNAM's Department of Medicine, then director of UNAM's program of health research. In 1994–1995 he served as minister of health and was later charged by President **Zedillo** with suppressing the 10-month-old UNAM **student strike of 1999**.

A member of the *Sistema Nacional de Investigadores* at the highest level, he is on the board of governors of the "Salvador Zubirán" National Nutrition Institute and of the technical council of the *Fundación Mexicana para la Salud*.

The author of over 100 works on health **education** and other aspects of medicine, his distinctions include the Washington Award to Merit in Psychiatry (1979), the Miguel Alemán Valdés award in health (1987), the National Science Award of the Academy of Scientific Research (1989), and the Eduardo Liceaga award from the National Academy of Medicine (1992).

FUENTES, CARLOS (1928–). Novelist and playwright, educated at **UNAM** in law and at universities in Europe and the **United States**. He has been Mexico's most influential writer ever since his 1954 short story collection *Los Días enmascarados*. He edited the magazine *El Espectador* and in 1955 helped revive the ***Revista mexicana de literatura***. His 1958 novel *La Región más transparente*, translated as *Where the Air Is Clear* (1960), "the best novel of modern Mexico," examines the social structure of his native Mexico City by focusing on the financial ruin of a former leader of the **Revolution of 1910**. Subsequent novels include *Las Buenas conciencias* (1958) portraying provincial life, *Aura* (1962) about Mexican belief in ghosts, *La Muerte de Artemio Cruz* (1962), translated as *The Death of Artemio Cruz* (1966), whose dying protagonist symbolizes Mexican history since 1910, and *Cambio de piel* (1967), a story narrated by an aging nihilist who has to spend a night with other travelers in the Aztec city of **Cholula** and probes through flashbacks the decline of modern society. This brought him international fame and was translated into English as *A Change of Skin* (1968), as well as French, Russian, Czech, Portuguese, German, Japanese, and other languages.

Fuentes' plays include *Todos los gatos* (1970), and he has written six film scripts, notably *Tiempo de morir* (1966). His countless socialist-influenced political and economic essays and articles have appeared in *The Saturday Review*, *The New York Times*, *The London Times*, several European magazines, and, particularly in *Siempre*.

FUENTES, MARIO (1934–). A Cruillas-born artist, trained at **UNAM**, famous for his sculpture *Cristo* (at San Nicolás de las Garzas) and the paintings *Familia* and *Mujer*.

FUERO. Legal term derived from the Latin *forum*, name of the central square in Roman cities, often used as an open-air court. As the source of legal decisions, it became during medieval and colonial times the name for a charter bestowing special rights and obligations on a town, corporation, or social group, such as the *fuero eclesiástico* (possessed by the **Church**, particularly controversial for conserving the clergy's right to be tried only in ecclesiastical courts), the *fuero militar* (by the **army**, giving soldiers a similar right to be tried only in military courts), and the *fuero académico* (by the university). [L. H.]

FUERTE, El ("the fort"). Town on the left bank of its namesake river, founded in 1568 as San Juan Bautista de Carapoa, but after its destruction by **Indians**, rebuilt as a fort in 1610. On September 12, 1824, it became the first capital of the Estado de **Occidente**, a dignity transferred to **Cosala** on August 28, 1826. Since 1830 it has been in **Sinaloa**. Made a **ciudad** in 1906, its 1990 population was 10,300. It is the **cabecera** of the namesake **municipio** whose 1990 population was 86,100 on 4,034 km².

FUERTE, RIVER. River of **Sinaloa state** that empties into the Pacific at Los **Mochis**.

FUERZA AERONAVAL. The **navy**'s air arm was formed in 1918. It used mainly American equipment but also a few aircraft manufactured in Mexico until the 1990s when it began buying Russian aircraft. Its main role is air-sea search-and-rescue and coastal patrol. In 2001 it had 68 fixed-wing airplanes and 50 helicopters.

FUERZAS DE LIBERACIÓN NACIONAL. Guerrilla group formed in **Monterrey** in August 1969, apparently the origin of the **Ejército Zapatista de Liberación Nacional**.

FUGA, LEY DE. *See* LEY DE FUGA.

FUNCIÓN PÚBLICA, SECRETARÍA DE. *See* PUBLIC ADMINISTRATION MINISTRY.

FUNDIDORA DE MONTERREY. Founded in 1900 as a privately-owned corporation by investors from Mexico, **France**, the **United States**, and Italy. Its blast furnace came into operation in 1903, thirty years before **Argentina** had its own steel plant, and forty years ahead of **Brazil**. Other facilities were added within a month and the plant became Latin America's first integrated **iron and steel** plant.

– G –

GACETA DE MÉXICO. Mexico's first newspaper, begun in 1665.

GACHUPIN ("wearer of spurs"). Derogatory term, particularly in colonial times, for a **Peninsular** (a Spaniard) as a wielder of political power. It is probably **Nahuatl** in origin.

GADSDEN, JAMES (1788–1858). United States minister to Mexico and railroad tycoon who negotiated the 1854 **Gadsden Purchase** on behalf of President Franklin Pierce, after his initial offer to buy **Baja California**, **Sonora**, **Sinaloa**, **Durango**, and **Chihuahua** for $50,000,000 had been rejected.

GADSDEN PURCHASE. An 1854 treaty, known in Mexico as the Treaty of **Mesilla**, negotiated by President Antonio López de **Santa Ana** and James **Gadsden** whereby the United States purchased 76,845 km^2 (29,270 sq. miles) of border territory in the **Mesilla Valley** for US$ 10 million in gold. This was done so that the Southern Pacific Railroad from **Texas** to **California** might avoid the higher elevations farther north. Santa Ana appropriated the money, a theft that was partly responsible for his overthrow in 1855.

GAGE, THOMAS (1597–1655). An English Catholic who came to Mexico as a Dominican but later travelled overland to Panama where he took a ship to Europe. Back in England he converted to Anglicanism and published a best-selling account of his travels. [L. H.]

GALÁN, JULIO (1959–2006). Iconoclastic painter from Múzquiz, a **Coahulia mining** town, who achieved fame when he moved to New York in 1984 and was given attention by Andy Warhol. His narcissistic blend of folk imagery and pop art derived from his painful early years as a closet homosexual in the provincial Mexico of the mid-20th century. His international reputation began with the Paris showing of his *China Poblana* in 1989. He subsequently returned to live in **Monterrey**. [L. H.]

GALEANA. (1) A town of 1,200 in 1990 of **Chihuahua** state at 30°08'N, 107°38'W, founded in 1767 as the Presidio de Buenaventura, renamed in 1778 as the *Villa de San Juan Nepomuceno*, made the **cabecera** of a namesake **municipio** in 1820, and renamed for Hermenegildo **Galeana** in 1829.

(2) A city of **Nuevo León** at 24°50'N, 100°04'W, founded 1678 as San Pablo de los Labradores, made a **villa** and renamed for the **Independence** hero in 1829. It became a **ciudad** in 1877. Although its 7,155 km² make its *municipio* the largest in the state, it had only 39,519 inhabitants in 2000.

GALEANA, HERMENEGILDO (1762–1814). Born in **Guerrero** to an English father and Mexican mother, brother to José and Juan Pablo **Galeana**, he became an officer in the army of **Morelos**, whose life he saved in the Battle of **Cuatla**. Galeana's actions during the 1813 siege of **Acapulco** were decisive in the port's fall to the patriots. His great leadership won him the nickname *Tata* ("uncle") Gildo from his followers. Killed in an ambush, he was declared a national hero when Mexico had gained **independence**.

GALEANA, JUAN PABLO (1760–1814). Patriot soldier, brother to Hermenegildo and José. He played a key role in the sieges of **Cuatla** and **Acapulco**. He probably died in the same ambush as his brother, but his body was never found.

GALINDO, SERGIO (1926–1993). Novelist, born in **Jalapa** and for ten years director of publications at the **Universidad de Veracruz**. His *La Justicia de enero* (1959) led to changes in the **immigration** service. His *El Bordo* (1960) popularized the psychological probing of the reforms of the **Revolution of 1910**.

GALLEON (*galeón*). The large ocean-going warship of c.1550–1700, superseding the smaller caravels of the earliest explorations. [L. H.]

GALVÁN LÓPEZ, FÉLIX (1910–1988). Army officer. Born in **Guanajuato**, he graduated from the **Colegio Militar** in 1930, rising to be a **general de división**. As inspector general of the army in the 1960s, he modernized technical training of all enlisted personnel and brought computers into the **armed forces'** general operations. In 1976 he became defense minister.

GALVÁN RIVERA, MARIANO (1782–1876). Mexico's first modern book publisher. His successes included **Fernández de Lizardi's** *El Periquillo sarniento*. His conservative views led him to accept membership of the **Junta de Notables**, which resulted in his imprisonment after the fall of **Maximilian**. Eventually released, he died in **Mexico City**.

GÁLVEZ, [DON] BERNARDO DE, CONDE DE GÁLVEZ (1746–1794). Soldier and administrator. Born in Málaga, Spain, he fought in Portugal and Algeria and taught in the Military Academy at Ávila before being sent to the **Indies** in 1779 as military governor of **Louisiana**. As such he commanded the brilliant 1781 campaign that drove the British out of western **Florida** and captured **Pensacola**. This made a significant contribution to the patriots' victory in the **American Revolutionary War**, because his mixed force of regulars, militia, and some American volunteers kept the enemy out of the strategic Mississippi River Valley. The city of Galveston, Texas, was so named to remember these contributions to American independence and a 15-cent US stamp was issued for the same reason in 1980.

In 1782 he was made Captain General of Florida and Louisiana, then Governor of **Cuba** from February 4–April 7, 1785, and succeeded his father, Matias de **Gálvez**, as **viceroy** of **New Spain** in 1785. There he sought to increase food production, particularly of **corn** and **beans**, and began a public works program to relieve unemployment, rebuilding **Chapultepec Castle** and giving **Mexico City** its first public lighting. He was disliked, however, by the **Audiencia** whose false reports led Madrid to suspect his great popularity and he was recalled the following year. Already in poor health, he died eight years later. [L. H.]

GÁLVEZ, JOSÉ DE (1729–1787). In 1765–1772 he served as Spain's last and greatest visitor-general in **New Spain**, where his chief mission was to set up the **intendancy** system. During his first year he secured the recall of the **viceroy**, Joaquín de **Monserrat**, after which he injected an unprecedented efficiency into the colonial administration. He oversaw the expulsion of the **Jesuits** in 1767 and countered expansion by **Russia** south from Alaska by sending Junípero **Serra** into **California** and establishing garrisons and missions at **San Diego** and **Monterrey**. He recommended numerous reforms, particularly relating to **mining** and **taxation**. [L. H.]

GÁLVEZ, MATÍAS DE (1717–1784). **Viceroy** of New Spain, 1783–1784. Brother of Don José de **Gálvez**, his military career led to his being made captain general of **Guatemala** and **president** of its **audiencia**. As such he fought the British on its Caribbean coast and was rewarded with the viceroyalty. During his administration he divided **Mexico City** into four quarters, improved its **police** service, helped establish the **Academia de San Carlos**, collected documents for an intended general history of the Indies, and revived the *Gaceta de México*. He fell ill on his last day in office and died shortly thereafter. [L. H.]

GAMBLING. The **Lotería Nacional** began in the 1760s. Gambling on **jai alai** and horse racing has been legal since the 19th century. Gambling on **bullfighting** has a long tradition. Casino gambling (e.g., the **Foreign Club**), however, has been illegal since 1934. [L. H.]

GAMBOA, FEDERICO (1864–1939). **Modernista** novelist, playwright, and diplomat, born in **Mexico City**. A foreign service career culminated in his becoming foreign minister in 1913. After **Huerta**'s downfall, he went into exile, returning in 1923 to make his living by teaching and writing. His best known work is the novel *Santa*, the basis of several motion picture versions. His most famous play is *La Venganza de la gleba*.

GAMIO, MANUEL (1883–1960). Anthropologist and archaeologist born in **Mexico City**, considered one of the world's experts on the Indian civilizations of Mexico. He became under-secretary of **education** in 1925, and directed the **Instituto Interamericano de Estudios Indígenas** from 1942 until his death.

He made a detailed study of **Teotihuacán**, discovering its Temple of **Quetzalcóatl**, and doing research on the population of the surrounding valley.

His many works include *Investigaciondes arqueológicas en México*, *El Templo de Quetzalcóatl*, and *La Población del Valle de México*.

GÁNDARA LABORÍN, CÉSAR. Businessman-politician. Born in **Sonora** into a family tracing its descent from 16th century conquistadors, he has since the 1950s owned the largest hotels and motels in the state and has been president of the national hotels association. He was mayor of **Hermosillo**, 1958–1961, secretary of state for Sonora, 1967–1973, and was active in the **Arizona-Sonora Commission** in the 1960s–1980s.

GANTE, PEDRO DE. *See* PEDRO DE GANTE.

GARCÍA, GENARO (1867–1920). Historian. His is the most faithful and complete edition of Bernal **Díaz del Castillo**'s *Verdadera historia de la conquista de la Nueva España*.

GARCÍA, JESÚS (1881–1907). "The hero of Nacozari," a locomotive fireman who saved the town by driving a burning train loaded with dynamite out of town. He took it a safe distance away but was killed, still on the footplate, when it exploded.

GARCÍA, ROBERTO MARCOS (19??–2006). Assistant director of the regional weekly *Testimonio* assassinated in **Veracruz**, November 21.

GARCÍA BARRAGÁN, MARCELINO (1895–1979). An **army** general who became a political reformer. A director of the **Heróica Escuela Militar**, he was made **governor** of his native **Jalisco**. In 1950 he helped General **Henríquez Guzmán** organize the **Federación de Partidos del Pueblo de México**. After this was outlawed in 1954, he rejoined the **Partido Revolucionario Institucional**, and in 1964–1970 served as defense minister.

GARCÍA CANTÚ, GASTÓN (1917–2004). Historian, author of *El socialismo en México en el siglo XIX*; *El Pensamiento de la reacción mexicana*; *La Intervencion francesa en México*; and *Las invasiones norteamericanas en México*.

GARCÍA CONDE, PEDRO (1806–1851). Politician, cartographer, and **army** officer. Attracted to soldiering at a very early age, he was already a general at age 34. He was at the same time active politically in his native **Sonora**. Because of his mapping skills, he was chosen to fix the new northern boundary after the **United States-Mexican War** of 1846–1848.

GARCÍA CRUZ, MIGUEL (1909–1969). An **Oaxaca** engineer who became a leading demographer and pioneer in **population** studies at Mexican universities in the 1950s. He served as secretary general (the second highest administrator) of the **Instituto Mexicano de Seguridad Social**, 1943–1958, and headed the Social Welfare Commission.

GARCÍA CUBAS, ANTONIO (1832–1912). Engineer and geographer. He graduated with honors in geography from the Colegio de Ingenieros and managed to stay free of politics, being well regarded by both **Maximilian** (who made him a member of the Order of **Guadalupe**) and **Juárez** (who appointed him to a high position in the **Development Ministry**). He published his memoirs, *El Libro de mis recuerdos* and a *Curso de geografía*.

GARCÍA GONZÁLEZ, ALFONSO (1909–1961). Lawyer who served as **governor** of **Baja California del Norte**, 1947–1952, ambassador to Colombia, 1952–1958, and director general of **tourism**, 1959–1961. He was also head of the Mexican Sports Federation. As an undergraduate he had been heavyweight boxing champion of Mexico. In the 1950s he promoted Mexican boxing teams at the Central American and Pan American Games and at the **Olympics** and helped develop Mexican professional boxing.

GARCÍA GRANADOS, FRANCISCO (1786–1841). Soldier and politician. He helped write the **Constitution of 1824**, served as Guadalupe **Victoria's** finance minister and held numerous other offices, among them that of **governor** of **Zacatecas**, where he was responsible for so many improvements that he was called affectionately *Tata* ["father"] *Pachito*. He fought López de **Santa Ana** but was defeated and retired from public life, dying in **Zacatecas City**.

GARCÍA GUERRA, [FRAY] FRANCISCO (15??–1612). Viceroy of **New Spain,** 1611–1612. Born in Frómista, Palencia, he became a Dominican prior in Valencia and, chosen by Phillip III as Archbishop of Mexico in 1607, he was already an old man when made acting viceroy in 1611. A dutiful administrator, he died of a fall when getting into his carriage. [L. H.]

GARCÍA ICAZBALCETA, JOAQUÍN (1825–1894). Historian, one of the most capable of his era, praised for his erudition by the Spanish scholar Ramón Menéndez y Pelayo. His *Historia de la conquista del Perú* is a translation of **Prescott**, but his greatest work is probably the *Bibliografía mexicana del siglo xvi.* He died in **Mexico City**.

GARCÍA PONCE, JUAN (1932–2003). Author of 14 novels (including *Figura de paja*, 1964), essays, and a play.

GARCÍA PUJOU, LEÓN (1898–1972). An agrarian leader from **San Luís Potosí**, a founder of the **Confederación Nacional Campesina**, a deputy in the federal **Congress**, 1928–1930 and 1937–1940, and a federal senator, 1940–1946.

GARCÍA RAMÍREZ, SERGIO (1938–). Lawyer from **Guadalajara** who as a federal judge in the 1960s pioneered the modern rehabilitation of delinquent children. He served as assistant minister of **natural resources** and as assistant interior minister, 1972–1976. He founded Mexico's first prison without bars and is a leading authority on the **penal code**.

GARCÍA SAÍNZ LAVISTA, RICARDO (1930–). An attorney, born June 8 in **Mexico City,** who became head of the **Finance Ministry**'s **income tax** department, 1956–1958; assistant director of **social security**, 1966–1976; minister of programming and the budget, November 1977–May 1979. He is best known for his vigorous leadership of the **Asociación Nacional de Importadores y Exportadores de la República Mexicana**—ANIERM—(National Association of Importers and Exporters) in the 1960s.

GARCÍA ZALVIDEA, JUAN IGNACIO. Populist politican elected mayor of **Benito Juárez** on the **Partido Verde Ecológico de Méx-**

ico ticket but controversially fired in July 2004 by **Quintana Roo** state. A month later the Federal **Supreme Court** ordered his reinstatement. After a year the state had its way, immediately thereafter announcing a special grant of US$ 30 million for unpaid city workers and suppliers, appointing a "citizens' council" to form an interim administration and beginning an audit to account for the city's US$ 90 million debt. Accused of overspending on social services and padding the city's pay-rolls, García maintained that he had to attend to the needs of the poor majority, living without running water next door to **Cancún**'s lavish hotels. Meanwhile the city's phenomenal growth, both in population and tourist infrastructure, imposed a need for more services and the city workers to provide them. The immediate cause of the state intervention had been a march on city hall by 1,400 unpaid (unionized) city workers, joined (García maintained) by **Partido Revolucionario Institucional** thugs sent in to provoke a riot. The business community backed the state action wholeheartedly, as did a majority of the city council. Inefficient or not, a leftist mayor was clearly inappropriate for Mexico's most important tourist town, although the manner of his ousting reportedly shocked many **Mexico City** liberals. Although he eventually regained his office and finished his term, he was jailed in November 2005 on **corruption** charges, supposedly to prevent him running for state governor. [L. H.]

GARIBAY, PEDRO (1729–1815). An elderly general when he was appointed acting **viceroy** of **New Spain**, 1808–1809, following the imprisonment of José de **Iturrigaray**. An upright and hardworking administrator, his chief care was to send money and arms to those fighting the French occupation of Spain. [L. H.]

GARRIDO CANABAL, TOMÁS (1890–1943). A **Calles** supporter who was agriculture minister in the 1934–1940 **Cárdenas del Río** administration.

GARRIDO DÍAZ, LUIS (1898–1973). Law professor at the **Universidad de Michoacán**, then rector there, 1924–1928. Rector of **UNAM**, 1948–1953. He co-founded ANUIES, the Mexican association of universities and institutes of higher education, served on the federal bench, was an assistant manager of *El Nacional*, and in the

1950s–1960s was executive secretary of the government's national savings bonds program.

GARRO, ELENA (1916?–1998). Born in **Puebla** (different sources cite birth dates of 1916, 1917, and 1920) but brought up in **Mexico City**, she became one of the few Mexican women to win fame as a playwright and film scriptwriter. She is best known for her plays *La señor en su balcón* (1959) and *La dama boba* (1964) and the novel *Los recuerdos del porvenir* (1963). A very political writer, she was married to Octavio **Paz**, 1936–1962, with whom she had her daughter, Helena. In 1937 they visited Spain to give propaganda support to the Republicans, but in July 2006 documents released by the **United States** Central Intelligence Agency revealed that during the "**Dirty War**" she had infiltrated the student movement of 1968 as a Mexican government spy. [L. H.]

GASCÓN MERCADO, ALEJANDRO (1932–). **Partido Popular Socialista** politician, president of its youth division, 1953–1956, member of its national committee, press and publicity secretary, director of economic studies, and then PPS executive officer, serving as deputy in the Federal **Congress**, 1970–1973. He was also president of the National Federation of Boarding Schools for Workers' Children. A native of **Nayarit**, he was brother to Julián **Gascón Mercado**.

GASCÓN MERCADO, JULIÁN (1925–). Physician and surgeon, born January 28 at Tepic, **Nayarit**, and trained at **UNAM**. **Partido Revolucionario Institucional** candidate for the governorship of his native state, he also received the **Partido Popular Socialista** nomination, thanks to his brother, Alejandro **Gastón Mercado**, and served 1964–1970.

GAXIOLA, FRANCISO JAVIER (1896–1978). **Toluca**-born lawyer who founded the Mexican Bar Association in 1923; was **governor** of **Baja California del Norte**, 1929–1932; industry and trade minister, 1940–1944; and president of the National Council of Lawyers, 1957–1972.

GELMAN COLLECTION. A major collection of 20th century Mexican art formed by Jacques and Natasha Gelman and housed in Phoenix Art Museum, Phoenix, Arizona. [L. H.]

GENERAL AGREEMENT ON TARIFFS AND TRADE (GATT).
The forerunner of the **World Trade Organization**. Mexico was
admitted in June 1986 after nine months of negotiations.

GENERAL DE DIVISIÓN. Mexican **army** rank equivalent to that of
major general.

GEOGRAPHY. Most of modern Mexico's territory resembles a funnel,
with the wide end winding along the 3,000 km (1,900 mile) **United
States border**. South of the narrow end of that funnel, the **Tehuantepec** Isthmus, tropical forest lands unfurl as the **Chiapas** highlands,
running to the **Guatemalan border**. The western **Baja California**
peninsula encloses the Gulf of **California**, and a dry southeastern corner becomes the flat **Yucatán** peninsula. More than half of Mexico's
2,007,711 km² rises over 975 m (3,200 feet) above sea level, with the
terrain ranging from deserts to swamps. Both **rainfall** and **population**
are unevenly distributed. *See also* AREA; EXTENT; FLORA;
FAUNA; HYDROGRAPHY; TOPOGRAPHY. [L. H.]

GERMANS IN MEXICO. Charles V's position as Holy Roman
Emperor led to some Germans settling in the New World during his
reign, but the first really significant German to visit **New Spain** was
probably Alexander **Humboldt** in 1803–1804. The accession of
Adolf Hitler led to several German Communists seeking a Mexican
refuge in the 1930s–1940s. *See also* SCHREITER, HELMUT
OSCAR; TRAVEN, B.

GERMANY, RELATIONS WITH. *See* GUERRA OLIVARES,
ALONSO; U-BOATS; WORLD WAR I; WORLD WAR II.

GERZSO, GUNTHER (1915–). He occupies a singular place as an
abstract painter in a land that reveres recognizable imagery.

GIL PRECIADO, JUAN (1909–1999). Professor of mathematics;
dean of the *Escuela Politécnica* of the **Universidad de Guadalajara**;
mayor of **Guadalajara**, 1956–1958; **governor** of his native **Jalisco**,
1959–1964; and agriculture minister, 1964–1970, in which capacity
he made the **United States**-Mexican Hoof-and-Mouth Disease Commission effective.

GINER DURÁN, PRAXEDES (1893–1978). Soldier-politician from Camargo, **Chihuahua**, he served under Pancho **Villa**, 1911–1918, and later became a **general de división**. Elected to the **Cámara de Diputados Federales** and then to the **Senate**, 1928–1934, he helped former president Plutarco **Calles** to form the **Partido Nacional Revolucionario**, forerunner of the **Partido Revolucionario Institucional**.

GIULIANI, RUDOLPH (1944–). Sometime mayor of New York City whose "zero tolerance" policy is credited with cutting New York's **crime** by 60 percent. As a result his consultancy group was paid $4.3 million in 2004 to find a solution to the Mexican capital's crime problem. [L. H.]

GOBERNACIÓN, SECRETARÍA DE. See INTERIOR MINISTRY.

GODFATHER SYSTEM. See COMPADRAZCO.

GODOY, MANUEL DE, PRÍNCIPE DE LA PAZ (1767–1854). Manuel Godoy Álvarez de Faría, chief minister of King **Charles IV** of Spain, responsible for the alliance with **France** which led to the loss of the Spanish **navy** at Trafalgar and eventually to **Napoleon**'s attempt to make his brother Joseph **Bonaparte** puppet King of Spain in 1808. [L. H.]

GOLD. Although the Spanish began **mining** gold very soon after the Spanish **conquest**, especially in **Guanajuato**, **Zacatecas**, and **San Luis Potosi**, it has never been as important for the Mexican economy as the more widespread **silver**. The gold in **Alta California** that led to the great gold rush was discovered just after Mexico lost the province to the **United States**.

GOLD STANDARD. New Spain with its abundant **silver** had set the monetary standard of the later Spanish empire (and even the infant **United States**) with the quality of its silver **dollar** (or **peso**). Following the United Kingdom's 1815 adoption of the gold standard, however, the silver standard became increasingly difficult to maintain, particularly toward the end of the 19th century when silver was suffering a chronic depreciation against gold. Thanks to finance minister José **Limantour**, Mexico joined almost all the rest of the world community in adopting the gold standard in the 1890s, only (like most of the world) to be forced off it during the **Depression of the 1930s**. *See also* COINAGE. [L. H.]

GOLONDRINAS, LAS **("the swallows").** A traditional Mexican folksong, played at engagement parties, retirement banquets, and other special festivities.

GOLPE DE ESTADO. *See* COUPS D'ÉTAT.

GÓMEZ ARIAS, ALEJANDRO (1906–1990). Lawyer from **Oaxaca** who helped form the **Partido Popular Socialista** and was its vice president in 1948.

GÓMEZ FARIAS, VALENTÍN (1781–1858). Guadalajara-born physician who became an outstanding liberal leader, fighting for a free press and a reduction of the power of the **Church**. He helped draft the **Constitution of 1824** and served for many years as López de **Santa Ana**'s vice president. As early as 1833 he held the presidency for two brief periods while Santa Ana was away on military missions. He urged **Congress** to pass many liberal measures, including the abolition of **tithes** and a reduction in the size of the **army**, whereupon Santa Ana forced him into exile. After a brief, unsuccessful liberal uprising in 1840, he again had to go into exile, a fate he suffered a third time for trying to reduce the power of the clergy. He succeeded Santa Ana as president in 1846–1847, and opposed the Treaty of **Guadalupe-Hidalgo**. Once more his running battle with the Church drove him into exile. In 1850 he was nominated unsuccessfully for president, but he saw his anti-clericalism triumph in the **Constitution of 1857**. His other achievements included the establishment of the **National Library** and the creation of a national agency to foster secular **education**.

GÓMEZ GÓMEZ, RODRIGO (1897–1970). An accountant and banker, director general of the **Banco de México**, 1952–1970, who in 1960 led the movement for Mexico to join the **Asociación Latinoamericana de Libre Comercio (ALALC)**.

GÓMEZ MORÍN, MANUEL (1897–1972). Founder of the **Partido de Acción Nacional (PAN)**. Born in **Chihuaha**, February 27, he graduated in **law** from **UNAM**, 1918; served as a law professor there, 1919–1972; as dean of the law school, 1922–1924; and rector, 1933–1934; and also as assistant finance minister, 1919–1921. He presided over the PAN's first assembly and was elected party president, 1939–1949. Every three years beginning in 1940, he had PAN field increasing numbers of congressional candidates, winning the first seats in 1946. In 1946, 1952, 1958, 1964, and 1970, he helped the PAN national assembly choose a presidential candidate.

GÓMEZ MORÍN TORRES, JUAN (1924–). Lawyer son of Manuel **Gómez Morín**, he was the **Partido de Acción Nacional**'s secretary general, 1969–1972, has long been on its national executive committee, and has served in the **Cámara de Diputados Federales**.

GÓMEZ PEDRAZA, MANUEL (1790–1851). President of Mexico for 11 months in 1828 and for 4 months in 1833, he was born in **Querétaro**, fought for **Spain** against the insurgents, but after **Independence** became a supporter of **Iturbide**. Declared president in 1828, he was deposed by López de **Santa Ana** and went into exile in **France**. His brief 1833 presidency was noted for the expulsion of all **peninsular** Spaniards from Mexico. He was forced to resign, but subsequently held various high offices, and died in **Mexico City**.

GÓMEZ SEGURA, MARTE (1896–1973). An agricultural engineer who served as federal deputy and senator, **governor** of his native **Tamaulipas**, and as agriculture minister, 1928–1930 and 1940–1946. As the modernizing rector of the **Escuela Nacional de Agricultura** in 1923–1924, he moved it to a new site at **Texcoco** where it eventually developed into the **Universidad Autónoma Chilango**.

GÓMEZ VELASCO, ANTONIO (1897–1987). Soldier-politician, born September 3, in Sayla, **Jalisco**. An **army** captain in 1913, he rose to be a **general de división**, served as assistant defense minister, introduced modern physical education into the army, and received **France**'s Legion of Honor for his **World War II** service. In 1954 he helped found the **Partido Auténtico de la Revolución**

Mexicana, of which he was a long-time leader, becoming its president in 1977.

GÓMEZ ZEPEDA, LUIS (1905–1994). Born in **Aguascalientes**, an administrator of the **Ferrocarriles Nacionales de México (FCNM)** from 1937, he was secretary general of the Railroad Workers' Union (*Sindicato de Trabajadores Ferrocarrileros de la República Mexicana*—STFRM), 1962–1968, and director general of the FCNM, 1972–1982. He was also a member of the **Comité Ejecutivo Nacional** of the **Partido Revolucionario Institucional** and a senator, 1964–1970.

GONZALES, ABRAHAM (1865–1913). José Abraham Pablo Ladislao González Casavantes, an ally of **Madero** who became governor of **Chihuahua** but was killed when he was about to leave for **Mexico City** to rescue the president.

GONZÁLEZ, EPIGMENO (1778–1858). A merchant who took an active role in the 1810 uprising, and was with **Hidalgo y Costilla** when the decision was made to begin the **Independence** struggle. When the Spanish discovered his house was the patriot's arsenal, he was imprisoned and then exiled to the **Philippines**. He eventually returned to **Guadalajara**, where he died.

GONZÁLEZ, MANUEL (1833–1893). Politician from **Matamoros** who originally fought against the liberals, but supported **Juárez** following the **French intervention** and became a close confidant of Porfirio **Díaz** who had him appointed president, 1880–1884, during which time Diaz served as minister of development (*Fomento*). Despite charges of **corruption**, González's administration made notable economic progress, implementing **metrification**, opening the **Mexico City** to El **Paso** railroad, and laying the submarine cable connecting **Veracruz** and **Tampico** with **Brownsville**, Texas. Although the press attacked him vigorously he never made use of **censorship** laws against it. He died while serving a third term as governor of **Guanajuato**.

GONZÁLEZ APARICIO, LUIS (1907–1969). Architect from **Veracruz** who was in charge of the reconstruction of the state government building in **Hermosillo**. He then directed government **housing** projects in **Morelos state**. In 1950–1952 he headed the **Papaloapan** River Commission, and in the 1950s–1960s he instituted the federal modern market construction program.

GONZÁLEZ AZCOAGA, PEDRO (1945–). Partido Auténtico de la Revolución Mexicana administrator, national executive committee member, and party president (January 1973–1975). He was born in **Campeche** on November 11.

GONZÁLEZ BLANCO, SALOMÓN (1900–1992). Born April 22 in Playa, **Chiapas**, he graduated in **law** from **UNAM**, where he was a part-time law professor for 15 years. He served successively as a judge of the state supreme court, a judge of the federal district court in **Villahermosa**, the assistant director of accounting in the **Finance Ministry**, director of conciliation, and then executive officer in the **Labor Ministry**, minister of labor, 1958–1964, and **governor** of **Chiapas**, 1978. His numerous writings helped shape modern labor law in Mexico.

GONZÁLEZ BOCANEGRA, FRANCISCO (1824–1861). Author of the lyrics of the **national anthem**. Although expelled from Mexico because of his Spanish parentage, he returned years later to his native **San Luís Potosí**, and in 1853 won a contest for the words of the anthem. He died of typhus in **Mexico City**.

GONZÁLEZ CASANOVA, PABLO (1922–). Born February 11 in **Toluca**, left-wing professor of political science, with a PhD in political sociology from the Sorbonne, his *Democracia en México* (1965) is the most widely read textbook on Mexican government. He became dean of **UNAM**'s School of Social and Political Sciences, and in 1964–1970, head of its Instituto de Investigaciones Sociales. Appointed rector of UNAM by President **Echeverría** in 1970, he was forced to resign in 1972 for having failed to end numerous student strikes. In media interviews in 1975 he denounced student violence, particularly the attack on the president, thereby getting himself denounced by the Young Communist League.

GONZÁLEZ COSIO, MANUEL (1915–). Engineer who served as a federal deputy, senator, and **governor** of his native **Querétaro** from 1961–1967. During the 1950s he developed and directed federal water and conservation policies for areas of desert and forest.

GONZÁLEZ DE ÁVILA, ALONSO (15??–1566). An early advocate of **independence**. He was executed when his plot to place a son of Hernán **Cortés** on a separate Mexican throne was discovered.

GONZÁLEZ DE ÁVILA, GIL (15??–1566). Executed with his brother Alonso **González de Ávila** for participating in their **independence** plot.

GONZÁLEZ DE LA VEGA, FRANCISCO (1901–1976). Born in **Durango**, he graduated from **UNAM**, where he taught **law**, numbering among his students future Presidents **Alemán**, **López Mateos**, **Díaz Ordaz**, and **Echeverría**, through whom he shaped penal law from the 1940s through the 1970s. In 1946–1952 he was **procurador general** (attorney general of Mexico), in 1957 he founded the **Universidad de Durango** in 1957, and he was also president of the Mexican Academy of Penal Sciences.

GONZÁLEZ FERNÁNDEZ, JOSÉ ANTONIO (1952–). Politician, born March 8 in **Mexico City**, earned a law degree from the **Escuela Libre de Derecho** and a master's in public administration from the University of Warwick, England. He was an administrator in, successively, the **Interior Ministry** (1974–1975), the **Finance Ministry** (1977–1978), and the **Education Ministry** (1978–1981). In 1981 he became a state deputy in **Guerrero**, in 1982 the administrative secretary of the **Universidad Pedagógica Nacional**, and then joined the **Health Ministry** (as director of legal affairs, 1982–1983; chief officer, 1983–1984; and undersecretary for sanitary regulations, 1985). He was legal attaché in the Washington embassy, 1987–1988; assistant director of the **Comité Ejecutivo Nacional** of the **Partido Revolucionario Institucional**, 1993–1994; majority representative from the **Cámara de Diputados Federales** to the **Instituto Federal Electoral** in 1994; and minister of **labor**

and social planning, May 13, 1998–November 30, 2000; and president of the PRI in 1999.

GONZÁLEZ GARZA, ROQUE (1885–1962). Briefly president of Mexico, January 16–June 10, 1915, with the support of the Zapatistas.

GONZÁLEZ GOLLAZ, IGNACIO (1929–). Director general of the **Unión Sinarquista Nacional**, 1959–1994, and its presidential candidate in 1982. Born in October in **Jalisco**, he had dropped out of the **Universidad Autónoma de Guadalajara** before graduation to become a full-time activist in the movement.

GONZÁLEZ HINOJOSA, MANUEL (1912–). Lawyer from **San Luis Potosí**, law professor at the **Universidad Iberoamericana**, a founding member of the **Partido de Acción Nacional**, and its president in 1969–1972 and 1975–1978, he sat in the **Cámara de Diputados Federale** from 1967–1970 and 1973–1976.

GONZÁLEZ LUGO, HUGO PEDRO (1909–). Lawyer-politician from **Nuevo Laredo**, he sat in the **Cámara de Diputados Federales**. Then in 1945 he became **governor** of **Tamaulipas**, until removed by President **Alemán** for freeing the **police** chief of **Ciudad Victoria**, who had murdered the editor of *El Mundo,* the local daily, for criticizing his administration in 1951. González went on to become manager of the federal National Bonded Warehouses, 1949–1952, and, in 1970, ambassador to Bolivia.

GONZÁLEZ LUNA, EFRAÍN (1898–1964). One of the founders of the **Partido de Acción Nacional**, and its 1952 presidential candidate. Born in Autlán, **Jalisco** on October 18. A law graduate of the **Universidad Autónoma de Guadalajara**, he became in 1921 the leader of the Catholic Association for Mexican Youth and helped increase **Church** influence in Mexican public life. He died September 10 in **Mexico City**. Efraín **González Morfin** is his son.

GONZÁLEZ MARTÍNEZ, ENRIQUE (1871–1952). Guadalajara-born poet, physician, and diplomat: *Poeias* (1938–1940). His work is post-modernist, although strongly influenced by **modernismo**.

GONZÁLEZ MORFIN, EFRAÍN (1929–). Son of Efraín **González Luna** and also a **Partido de Acción Nacional** presidential candidate in the **election of 1970**. Born June 5 in **Guadalajara**, he had studied philosophy and economics at the University of Innsbruck and the Sorbonne. He also had led the PAN's youth group, becoming a member of its national executive committee in 1960, and a member of the **Cámara de Diputados Federales**, 1967–1970.

GONZÁLEZ ORTEGA, [GENERAL] JESÚS (1824–1881). Soldier-politician. A strong supporter of the liberals and Benito **Juárez**, he was made **governor** of **Zacatecas** in 1858, defeating the conservative forces in the state in 1859. By then, as chief justice of the **Supreme Court**, he was ex officio vice president of Mexico. His continued successes against the conservatives (culminating in victory at the Battle of **San Miguel Calpulalpan**) so increased his prestige that his supporters asked Juárez to step down in his favor. Juárez refused and González later fell into disfavor through his inability to defeat General **Mejía**. Shortly after the Battle of **Puebla** he succeeded **Zaragoza** but was defeated and taken prisoner. He escaped into exile in New York City. Later he tried unsuccessfully to claim the presidency of Mexico. He died in **Saltillo**.

GONZÁLEZ TORRES, JOSÉ (1919–1998). Born September 16 in **Michoacán**, a lawyer who became secretary general of the **Partido de Acción Nacional**, 1959–1962, and its unsuccessful candidate for president in the **election of 1964**.

GOOD NEIGHBOR POLICY. Although associated with **United States** President Franklin Roosevelt (who took it over from his predecessor, Herbert Hoover), the expression originates in Fanny C. Gooch's *Face to Face with the Mexicans*.

GORDILLO MORALES, ELBA ESTHER (1945–). The powerful leader since 1989 of the **Sindicato Nacional de Trabajadores de la Educación**. A history teacher from Comitán, **Chiapas**, she joined the SNTE and the **Partido Revolucionario Institucional** in 1970, becoming secretary general of the PRI before resigning in 2005 and being expelled in 2006 for her close association with **Nueva Alianza**

presidential candidate Roberto **Campa Cifrián**. A Christmas Day 2006 article in the Paris newspaper *Le Monde* accused her of **corruption** and of breaking way on any progressive reform of Mexican **education**. [L. H.]

GOROSTIZA, JOSÉ (1901–1973). A diplomat **from Tabasco** who served in the **United Kingdom**, Italy, **Cuba**, Norway, and **Guatemala**, and at the **United Nations**. He was director general of the Mexican diplomatic service, 1946–1949, ambassador at the 1947 Pan American Conferences of 1947 in **Petrópolis** (where the **Inter-American Treaty of Mutual Assistance** was negotiated) and of 1948 at Bogotá (where the **Organization of American States** was formed). He was subsequently ambassador to Greece, foreign minister in 1964, and, as head of the National Commission on Nuclear Energy, 1965–1970, developed Mexico's basic **nuclear energy** policies.

GOVERNMENT FINANCE. *See* BUDGET; FINANCE MINISTRY; TAXATION.

GOVERNOR (*Gobernador*). The executive officer administering a colonial *gobierno* or a modern Mexican **state** (or the **Federal District**). *See also* SECRETARIO DE ESTADO.

GOYTORTÚA [SANTOS], JESÚS (1910–1979). The **San Luis Potosí**-born author of *Pensativa* (1945), a best-selling novel of the **Cristero Rebellion**, of *Lluvia roja* (1946), of *Sucedió en Jalisco* (1972), and of the short story collection *El jardín de lo imposible* (1938). [L. H.]

GRANADERO. A member of the black-uniformed riot **police**.

GRANDE DE SANTIAGO, RIO. River of 412 km that flows into the Pacific from Lake **Chapala** which is fed by the River **Lerma**.

"GREAT ELECTORS." A theory, first put forward without attribution by *Proceso*, that half a dozen top advisors, including the top labor leader, the spokesman for **manufacturing industry**, the spokesman for the retail trade, two key **Partido Revolucionario Institucional**

administrators, and up to two others conferred with the outgoing president of the republic to choose his successor. Octavio **Paz**, with top-level sources of information, contended that the theory was true only in 1994, the year when the PRI was reeling after its original candidate, Luis **Colosio**, had been murdered by an unknown assailant. *See also* DEDAZO; PRESIDENTIAL SUCCESSION.

"GREAT HURRICANE." A storm of October 1780 which killed 2,000 along the eastern shore of the Gulf of **Mexico**.

GREATER MEXICO CITY. *See* MEXICO CITY CONURBATION.

GREEN MACIAS, ROSARIO (1941–). Zedillo's foreign minister, January 7, 1998–2000, the first woman to hold such a post anywhere in Latin America. A graduate in international relations at **UNAM**, she obtained a master's in economics at the **Colegio de México**, specialized in international economics and Latin American fiscal problems at Columbia University, and then took a course specializing in Latin American economic integration at the Institute for Latin American Integration (INTAL) in Buenos Aires. In 1968–1983 she was a professor and researcher at the Colegio de México. She was also Mexico's senior diplomat at the **United Nations** agencies in Geneva, 1972–1974, and an advisor to the Center for Third World Economic Studies in 1979–1989. She has also been ambassador to the German Democratic Republic. In 1984 she became director general of the **Foreign Ministry**'s Martías Romero Institute of Diplomatic Studies, guiding newly appointed ambassadors in the Mexican foreign service. From time to time she teaches a course on international economic problems at UNAM. In 1990 President Zedillo elevated her to senior adviser on relations with other Latin American republics.

Professor Green has authored over 50 articles in academic journals, in Spanish, English, and French, analytical columns for such major **newspapers** as *El Universal* and *El Día*, and nine books, of which four have been translated into English: *Mexican Foreign Political Indebtedness, 1940–1973* (1976); *State and Transnational Banking in Mexico, 1981* (1984); *The Economy: Module for Teaching Middle Education* (1976); and *Foreign Debt in Mexico* (1988). She was associate editor of *Foro internacional*, 1968–1972 and 1979–1980. She is publisher of the *Mexican Journal of Foreign Policy* and has been a consultant to the **Consejo Nacional de Ciencia y Tecnología (CONACYT)**.

GREEN PARTY. *See* PARTIDO VERDE ECOLOGISTA DE MÉXICO.

GREENE, GRAHAM (1904–1991). The English novelist recounted his travels in Mexico in *The Lawless Road*. (American title was *Another Mexico*). His *The Power and the Glory* (1940) is a novel set during the persecution of the **Church** in the 1920s. A movie version was made in 1962. [L. H.]

GRIJALVA, JUAN DE (1490–1527). Navigator from Segovia sent by his uncle Diego **Velázquez de Cuéllar** in 1518 to explore the coast to the west of **Cuba**, i.e., the **Yucatán** Peninsula. He reached **Cozumel** and then sailed along the coast northward, as far as the River **Tabasco** where he heard of a powerful ruler called **Moctezuma**. He named the new country **New Spain** (from a supposed resemblance to his home country) and returned to Cuba. He was killed by **Indians** on a subsequent voyage to Olancho in Honduras, but his explorations led to Hernán **Cortés**' 1519 expedition and to Spain's eventual conquest of Mexico and Central America.

GRIJALVA, RIVER. River of 700 m that rises near Huehuetenongo in **Guatemala** as the Mezcalapa and empties into the Pacific. It receives an arm of the **Usumocinta** 16 km before its mouth.

GRIMM GONZÁLEZ, GUILLERMO (1938–). Politician, born July 19 in **Mexico City**. He earned a business administration degree from the **Universidad Iberoamericana**, and was professor of marketing there, 1965–1967. In 1982–1988 he served as undersecretary of **tourism**, one of the first non-graduates of **UNAM** to reach cabinet rank. His subordinate appointees for recreation and for hotel development were also Universidad Iberoamericana graduates, and in 1983 he was to hire yet another fellow alumnus to direct the **Fondo de Promoción de Infraestrucutra Turística**.

GRITO DE DOLORES ("Cry from Dolores"). The revolutionary speech made by Miguel **Hidalgo y Costilla** outside his parish church in the village now renamed **Dolores Hidalgo**, on the morning of September 16, 1810. He condemned those Spaniards who supported the French imposed rule of Joseph **Bonaparte**, professing his allegiance to **Ferdinand VII** and his Catholic faith. He did not preach a break with **Spain**, but such a desire was the eventual result. This was also the case in similar refusals elsewhere in Spanish America to back the new puppet regime in Spain.

GROUPER. This fish is hunted on the **Yucatán** continental shelf by Mexican fishermen and by industrial fleets from Mexico and **Cuba**, under a bilateral agreement of 1976, reviewed every other year. The total catch has fallen from 15,000 t in the early 1990s to 10,000 t in the early 21st century. [L. H.]

GRÚA Y TALAMANCA, MIGUEL DE LA, MARQUÉS DE BRANCIFORTE (1750–????). Viceroy of **New Spain**, 1794–1798. Born in Sicily, he married the sister of Manuel de **Godoy**, prime minister of Spain, and used his viceregal office chiefly for self-enrichment, seizing the properties of French residents in New Spain and **Louisiana**, and selling offices and **army** ranks. He was eventually accused of **corruption** and relieved of his office. [L. H.]

GRUPO FINANCIERO CREMI-UNIÓN. *See* CREMI-UNIÓN.

GUADALAJARA. "The City of Roses," capital of the 1786 **intendancy** of the same name, previously the province of **Nueva Galicia**, which became **Jalisco** state after independence. It is located at 20°40'N, 103°21'W, 500 km (300 miles) west-northwest of **Mexico City** at 1,567m (5,200 ft) above mean sea level, founded by Nuño Beltrán de **Guzmán** who named it for his birthplace in Spain. With a 20,000 population in 1800 and 60,000 at mid-century, it was Mexico's third largest city. A quarter century later it had 75,000 residents, reaching parity with **Puebla**. It has now been Mexico's second city for well over a century, and in 2005 had 1,600,940 inhabitants. Its greater metropolitan area (which includes neighboring Tlaquepaque, Tonalá, and Zapopan) reached 2 million by 1970 and was estimated as 4,425,950 in 1998.

Possessing a year-round temperate climate, many parks, fountains, and broad avenues, it is called the "Pearl of the West." Clustered downtown are several buildings from the 1860s or earlier. The Byzantine-looking cathedral dates from 1618. The Degollado Theatre was built, to resemble Milan's *La Scala* in 1856. Many public buildings bear murals by José Clemente **Orozco**. It has two universities (**Universidad Autónoma de Guadalajara** and **Universidad de Guadalajara**) and a medical school with more foreign students—including 2,000 Americans—than any other in the Western world. The city is the agricultural and wholesale distributing center of western Mexico, and second only to **Mexico City** as a retail center. Industries range from chemicals and cement to textiles and lumber, although it is outranked by **Monterrey** in industrial output. The suburb of Tlaquepaque is famous for ceramics.

GUADALUPE, ISLA DE. An oceanic island of volcanic origin at 28°53'N, 118°18'W, 241 km (145 miles) west of **Baja California del Norte**, 35 km by 10 km, reaching an altitude of 1,300 m. Important for its marine **fauna**, it is the last refuge of the Northern elephant seal (*mirounga angustiostris*) and is the only breeding ground of the native fur seal (*arctocephalus townsend*), but its ecosystem has been disastrously affected by erosion caused by goats (imported by whalers) which have destroyed its ridge top cloud forest. It was declared a nature reserve in 1925. Local fishermen exploit its lobsters and abalone. Surrounding rocks include *Isla Adentro* and *Isla Afuera*, 3 km off the island's southern tip. [L. H.]

GUADALUPE, ORDER OF. Order of honor instituted by Agustín de **Iturbide** which went out of existence on his overthrow, but enjoyed a brief revival by López de **Santa Anna** in 1853–1855 and another during the reign of **Maximilian**.

GUADALUPE, VIRGIN OF. *See* MARY OF GUADALUPE, SAINT.

GUADALUPE HIDALGO. Suburb of **Mexico City**, the former Tepeyac Hill, site of the shrine of Saint **Mary of Guadalupe**, and where the Treaty of **Guadalupe Hidalgo** was signed.

GUADALUPE-HIDALGO, TREATY OF. Signed February 2, 1848, at the conclusion of the **United States-Mexican War**, the Treaty cost

Mexico half its national territory (what are now the states of **California**, Nevada, **Arizona**, **New Mexico**, and Utah, plus an extension of Texas to the **Rio Grande**) in return for an indemnization of US$ 15,000,000 and the U.S. assumption of its citizens' claims against Mexico, amounting to a further US$ 3,000,000.

GUAJE. Spanish for **Leucaena** and the word origin of **Oaxaca State**.

GUANAJUATO CITY. Capital of **Guanajuato State**, founded as a **mining** center in 1554 (at 21°02'N, 101°28'W, and 1,996 m above sea level, 370 km northwest of **Mexico City**), it was until the 1840s Mexico's major **silver** producing area. Its pottery and toy factories and historic buildings of the 1810s attract **tourism**. The municipal population was 61,000 in 1976; 130,000 in 1995; and 141,196 in 2000, of whom 78,000 were living in the city.

GUANAJUATO STATE. A state of 30,567 km² in central Mexico, including the **Bajío** plain, created as an **intendancy** in 1786. Its **population** was 729,103 in 1857; 874,000 in 1869; and at successive **censuses** thereafter it has been 1,047,000 (in 1895); 1,062,000 (1900); 1,082,000 (1910); 860,000 (1921); 988,000 (1930); 1,046,000 (1940); 1,329,000 (1950); 1,736,000 (1960); 2,270,370 (1970); 3,006,110 (1980); 3,982,513 (1990), 4,406,568 (1995); 4,663,032 (2000); and 4,893,812 (2005). It has 46 *municipios* of which the most populous are León (1,134,842 inhabitants in 2000); Irapuato (440,134 inhabitants in 2000); Celaya (382,958); Salamanca (226,654); Pénjamo (144,426); **Guanajuato City**, Allende (134,880); Silao (134,337); Valle de Santiago (130,821); **Dolores Hidalgo** (123,834); and San Francisco del Rincón (100,239). Fraud in the **election of 1946** led to riots and the dismissal of governor Ernesto **Hidalgo**. *See also* DOLORES HIDALGO; GUANAJUATO CITY.

GUANOS Y FERTILIZANTES. The government agency for fertilizers.

GUARDIA RURAL. *See* RURALES.

GUATEMALA, CAPTAINCY GENERAL OF. Colonial administration theoretically subordinate to the **viceroyalty** of **New Spain**

embracing all Central America (but not Panamá). It achieved **Independence** as part of **Iturbide**'s Mexican **Empire** but broke away as the Republic of **Central America** in 1822 (except for **Chiapas**, which opted to remain part of Mexico), only to break up in 1840 into the five present-day successor states. [L. H.]

GUATEMALA, RELATIONS WITH. Guatemala, the dominant member of the República Federal de Centro-América, became an independent polity with the breakup of the federation in 1840. In 1871 Juárez's government played a key role in the successful revolt against Vicente Cerna, the last conservative president of Guatemala. In 1906 Mexico supported **United States** intervention in Guatemala to end that country's war with El Salvador and Honduras, and the consequent **San José Conference**. The United States sponsored overthrow of the radical **Arbenz** government in 1954, thereby installing a fiercely anti-Communist regime in Guatemala whose "**Dirty War**" repression of the **Maya** has created a chronic refugee problem for southern Mexico. *See also* BELIZE; CARACAS CONFERENCE.

GUATEMALAN BORDER. Mexico's border with Guatemala stretches 962 km, and is frequently crossed by undocumented immigrants. [L. H.]

GUATEMÓTZIN. Alternative name of the **Aztec** ruler **Cuauhtémoc**. It also occurs as *Guatemoc*.

GUAYABERA. A man's combination hip-length shirt-jacket worn in tropical regions, particularly Mexico and **Cuba**, outside the trousers, over an undershirt in place of a coat. Made of **cotton**, it has lapels and four large pockets. [L. H.]

GUAYMAS. A leading port of northwestern Mexico on the Gulf of **California** in **Sonora** state, at 27°54'N, 110°52'W, 130 km (80 miles) south of **Hermosillo**. Its economy rests on commercial **fishing** (particularly of **shrimp**), the processing of marine products, the export of **cotton**, and as a resort for sport fishing. A daily ferry connects it with La **Paz**; and it is a major highway, rail, and air link to **Mexico City**. Named for the Guaymas, pre-Hispanic ancestors of today's **Seris**, the town became a military base and port in 1767. The railroad connection with **Nogales** on the **United States border** was completed in 1882. The **census** population was 103,138 in 2000; 101,507 in 2005; but the general area including the adjacent tourist resort of San Carlos (popular with American and Canadian retirees) totals some 150,000.

GÜERMES PACHECO Y PADILLA, JUAN VICENTE DE, 2ND CONDE DE REVILLA-GIGEDO (1740–1799). Viceroy of **New Spain**, 1789–94 (and among the most effective holders of that office). Born in Havana while his father Juan Francisco de **Güermes y Horcasitas** was captain general of Cuba, he entered the Spanish army in 1755, captained the Palace Guard in **Mexico City** and fought at Ceuta and Panama and before Gibraltar and was then made viceroy of the Plate (*Rio de la Plata*) but was sent to Mexico instead before he could take up the appointment. As a notable reforming viceroy he improved the administration, provided Mexico City with a new fresh water supply and its first service of coaches for hire, promoted its cultural life, founded the first **Botanical Gardens**, and established street lighting there and in other cities. [L. H.]

GÜERMES Y HORCASITAS [ARGUAYO], JUAN FRANCISCO DE, CONDE DE REVILLA-GIGEDO (1682–1768). Captain General of **Cuba**, March 18, 1734–April 1746, and subsequently **viceroy** of **New Spain**, 1746–1755. As such he carried out many reforms, including more effective tax collection, corrected many abuses and prevented the French in **Louisiana** from expanding westward. His title of count was bestowed in 1749. His residence, the House of Tiles, is now a restaurant. [L. H.]

GÜERMEZ. Tamaulipas city founded by José de **Escandón** on January 1, 1749, as San Fernando de Güermes (named for **Viceroy** Juan Francisco de **Güermes y Horcacitas**).

GUERRA OLIVARES, ALONSO (1897–1967). A diplomat from **Nayarit** who served as a senator and as assistant foreign minister. As ambassador to the Federal Republic of Germany, 1953–1964, he helped expand Mexican trade with the European Common Market (the present European Union).

GUERRA SUCIA. *See* DIRTY WAR.

GUERRERO. State (abbreviation "GRO") of 63,794 km², formed in 1847 from parts of **Puebla** and **Mexico State**, bordering the Pacific and named for Vicente **Guerrero**, but essentially recreating the former province of **Tecpan**. Its **population** was about 270,000 at around 1860. At successive **censuses** since then it has totalled 418,000 (1895); 479,000 (1900); 594,000 (1910); 567,000 (1921); 642,000 (1930); 733,000 (1940); 919,000 (1950); 1,187,000 (1960); 1,597,000 (1970); 2,110,000 (1980); 2,620,000 (1990); 3,079,649 (2000), and 3,115,202 (2005). Its 76 *municipios* include **Acapulco**, **Iguala**, and **Taxco**. The capital is **Chilpancingo**. *See also* ABARCA ALARCON; RAIMUNDO.

GUERRERO, PRAXEDES (1882–1910). Supporter of Francisco **Madero** who launched raids into Mexico from his exile in the **United States** even before the start of the **Revolution of 1910**. He was killed in late December, 1910, leading his men into combat near Janos in **Chihuahua**.

GUERRERO, VICENTE [RAMÓN] (1782–1831). Liberal president of Mexico, 1829. He fought alongside **Morelos**. When the latter was executed, Guerrero's band of guerrillas was one of the main sources of resistance to the Spanish, however weak and sporadic this resistance was. He later joined **Iturbide** and his Plan of **Iguala**, playing a major role in Mexico's final bid for **independence**. In December 1828, having lost the election to Manuel **Gómez Pedraza**, he used the military assistance of López de **Santa Anna** to secure the presidency. A year later Santa Anna replaced him with Vice president Anastasio **Bustamente**. Guerrero then tried to flee into exile but was betrayed by the captain of the Italian ship on which he had embarked, who sold him to Bustamente's minister, José Antonio Facio, for $50,000. He was then shot for treason on January 14. When the Liberals returned to power, Guerrero was exonerated so completely that the new state of **Guerrero** was named in his honor, and he has ever since been regarded as a national hero.

GUERRILLA ("little war"). Spanish term, from the Peninsular War against **Napoleon**, for a campaign by irregular forces using hit-and-run tactics in a war of attrition against the occupation forces of a foreign regular **army**, and usually meaning in English a participant in such a war (*guerrillero* in Spanish). *See also* DIRTY WAR; EJÉRCITO ZAPATISTA DE LIBERACIÓN NACIONAL; FRENTE URBANO ZAPATISTA; LOZADA, MANUEL.

GUILLÉN VICENTE, RAFAEL SEBASTIÁN (1957–). Real name of *Subcomandate* Marcos, leader of the **Ejército Zapatista de Liberación Nacional**. A former Marxist philosophy student, he presented himself as a Robin Hood figure, adapting Clausewitz to say he was waging guerrilla warfare "as politics by other means." Claiming to be an Indian and wearing a full black mask over face and neck, he was by April 1994 holding twice-weekly press conferences. He was only exposed as the son of a wealthy furniture retailer in **Tampico** on February 9, 1995. His public relations campaign, complete with t-shirts, buttons, key-rings and even condoms with his name on the box, had been a publicist's dream. Media liberals in the **United States** rushed to glamorize him, and Octavio **Paz** commented that "the media spectacle so well perfected by the United States" had "finally come to Mexico." At his campaign's height in mid-1994, 70 percent of urban Mexicans recognized him as head of the "**Zapatista**" movement.

When the **North American Free Trade Association** became operative in 1994, Marcos alarmed peasants in **Chiapas** by convincing them that the lower tariffs this would introduce would make them unable to compete with farmers in the **United States**.

GUITARRÓN ("large guitar"). An oversized Mexican guitar that uses the strings of a bass viol and serves as a string bass in an orchestra.

GULF. *See* CALIFORNIA, GULF OF.

GURRÍA TREVIÑO, [JOSÉ] ÁNGEL (1950–). Finance minister, 1998–2000. Born May 8 in **Tampico**, he graduated in economics from **UNAM**, obtained a master's in public finance from the University of Leeds, England, and then studied financial administration at Harvard, and international relations at the University of Southern

California. In 1968 he became an analyst in the international department of the **Comisión Federal de Electricidad**. He also became an active member of the **Partido Revolucionario Institucional** where he has been a member of the commissions on international affairs, modernization, and ideology. He has also been private secretary to the director of **Nacional Financiera** and its assistant manager of international affairs, permanent Mexican delegate to the **International Coffee Organisation**, general director of Public Credit, and member of the team renegotiating Mexico's **foreign debts**, deputy minister (*subsecretario*) of finance, one of the negotiators of the financial chapter of **NAFTA**, and general director of NAFIN. **Zedillo** made him his foreign minister on December 2, 1994, transferring him to finance on January 5, 1998.

In late 1998 he was the administration's negotiator with the leaders of the **Partido de Acción Nacional** and **Partido de la Revolución Democrática** to secure passage of the **budget** through the **Cámara de Diputados Federales**, achieved December 31. In April 1999 he made financial history by rejecting a credit offer from the **International Monetary Fund** as unnecessary. In February 2006 he became secretary general of the Organization for Economic Cooperation and Development.

Gurría has authored several works on foreign debt, including *La Política de la deuda externa*, and "La Reestructuración de la deuda: el caso de México," his contribution to *Administración pública contempránea de México*. He is also an *officier* of France's Legion of Honor.

GUTIÉRREZ, EULALIO (1881–1939). Eulalio Martín Gutiérrez Ortiz, chosen provisional president of Mexico in succession to Victoriano **Huerta**, October 1914, by the Convention of **Aguascalientes**. Driven out of **Mexico City** by the approach of **Obregón**, he attempted briefly, but futilely, to govern from **Nuevo León**.

GUTIÉRREZ BARRIOS, FERNANDO (1927–). Respected elder statesman, called upon on May 20, 1999, to plan a primary election to allow popular choice of the **Partido Revolucionario Institucional** presidential candidate for the **election of 2000**.

GUTIÉRREZ NAJERA, MANUEL (1859–1895). Poet, born in **Mexico City**. Although considered a Romantic, he was the forerunner of

modernismo in Mexico. His mastery is shown in his *Odas breves* and in the poems "Tristissima nox" and "Serenata de Schubert." He also wrote much prose, where description of reality is prominent, contributing to about 40 **newspapers** and to literary magazines under more than 20 pen names.

GUTIÉRREZ RINCÓN, EFRAÍN (1897–19??). Soldier-politician who graduated from **UNAM** in engineering, fought under Emiliano **Zapata**, 1915–1916 as a captain and key staff officer. **Governor** of his native **Chiapas**, 1937–1940, then director general of the **Banco Nacional de Crédito Agrícola**.

GUTIÉRREZ ROLDÁN, PASCUAL (1903–19??). Economist from **Mazatlán** with a degree in agronomy and doctorate in economics. He directed all government steel plants, 1952–1958, then headed **Pemex**, 1958–1964.

GUTIÉRREZ RUIZ, DAVID GUSTAVO (1940–). Economist from **Tabasco** with graduate studies at the Sorbonne. He represented Mexico before the European Common Market in 1963, governed **Quintana Roo** from 1971–1975, and in 1976 was appointed director of **Guanos y Fertilizantes**.

GUZMÁN, MARTÍN LUIS (1887–1976). Novelist and journalist from **Chihuahua** who fought under Pancho **Villa** and **Carranza**. His experiences in the **Revolution of 1910** led him to concentrate on native themes in his fiction, creating a genuinely Latin American novel. His best known work, *El Águila y el serpiente, la sombra del caudillo* (1928) was translated into English by Harriet de Onís in 1965 as *The Eagle and the Serpent*. In 1942 he founded the magazine *Tiempo*, remaining its publisher until 1974.

GUZMÁN, NUÑO BELTRÁN DE (????–c.1545). Conquistador from Guadalajara, Spain, who personified the "**black legend**" of Spanish misrule. While governor of **Pánuco**, 1526–1528, he confiscated many *encomiendas* and gave them to his friends, sold many **Indians** into slavery (often after deliberately encouraging them to rebel), and forced the *caciques* to pay him heavy tribute. "Bloody Guzmán" and his **audiencia** were excommunicated in 1529. Fearing further punishment, he fled north, exploring as far as **Sinaloa** (where he founded **Culiacán**) and eventually settling in **Jalisco** (where he founded **Guadalajara**). When the authorities became aware of his many further excesses, he was recalled to **Mexico City**, tried there, imprisoned for two years there, and then imprisoned for the rest of his life back in Spain. He had pompously named his area of exploration "España Mayor," but after his arrest it became "**Nueva Galicia**."

GUZMÁN NEYRA, ALFONSO (1906–1994). Lawyer from **Veracruz** who was a leader in the **Partido Revolucionario Institucional** and a key campaign adviser for **Ávila Camacho** in 1940 and **Alemán** in 1946. Appointed a judge in the federal **Supreme Court**, 1952–1976, he served as chief justice, 1959–1964.

GUZMÁN WILLIS, MANUEL (1900–1973). A ranch owner who headed and developed the Association of Cebu Cattle Ranchers, served as mayor of **Tampico**, and in 1952–1958 was senator from **Tamaulipas**.

– H –

HACENDADO. Owner of a **hacienda**. Such people, as symbols of the old order, were a prime target of the insurgents of the **Revolution of 1910**.

HACIENDA ("property, wealth"). The word has two distinct meanings:
    (1) The royal or governmental treasury; the **finance ministry**.
    (2) A large landed estate. Most of those in Mexico before the **Revolution of 1910** had come into existence after the Spanish **conquest of Mexico**, evolving in almost every case (illegally) from an **encomienda**, and cursing Mexico with the problem of **latifundia**. It has been estimated that, at the close of Spanish rule, all the country's best land was divided among a mere 5,000 *haciendas*.

HADAS, LAS. Resort on the coast of **Colima state**, near **Manzanillo**, developed in 1974 by a Bolivian multimillionaire tin magnate living in **Colima City**. His opulent hotel attracted Hollywood and Mexican **cinema** and **television** stars and famous athletes. The 1979 film *Ten*, filmed entirely at Las Hadas, made actress Bo Derek an international star overnight. By the 1990s, Las Hadas had become popular with deep-sea anglers.

HALCONES ("hawks"). Pro-government protesters and street demonstrators, organized as groups by the federal authorities in 1968, and used to counterbalance anti-government rioters, particularly in 1971, 1974, and 1975, helping the **police** (unofficially) to contain left-wing, often Communist, violence, especially at schools and universities. Both *halcones* (sometimes translated "falcons") and their adversaries were mostly students or former students ranging in age from the teen years to their early twenties, although they have been alleged to be simply an elite squad of the police.

HANK GONZÁLEZ, CARLOS (1927–2001). Billionaire businessman-politician and **Partido Revolucionario Institucional** power broker, born August 28 in **Galeana**, son of a German-born teacher at the **Colegio Militar**. He was a school teacher, 1941–1951; mayor of **Toluca**, 1955–1957; member of the **Comité Ejecutivo Nacional** of the PRI and of the **Cámara de Diputados Federales**; director general of the **Compañía Nacional de Subsistencias Populares**; governor of **Mexico state**, 1970–1976; governor of the **Federal District**, 1976–1982 (creating 34 new, broad thoroughfares after extensive slum clearance); and minister of **tourism** and agriculture, and credited with the slogan "any politician who is poor is a poor politician."

Around 1976 he became an adviser on public policies to successive presidents ("the Cardinal Richelieu of his generation"), from **López Portillo** to **Salinas de Gortari**, and was considered for president himself until he pointed out that his father's nationality at birth made him ineligible. With interests in transportation, manufacturing, and construction in every Mexican state, and also in some American corporations, his wealth was given in *Forbes* magazine as US$ 1.1 billion. Generous to his friends and supporters, he is known to have made interest-free loans to politicians in financial need. Suggestions in the late 1990s that some of his enterprises might have had money laundering links with the **narcotics** trade proved inconclusive.

HANK RHON, CARLOS (1948–). Financier son of Carlos **Hank González** and Julia Rhon. He helped found **Taesa** and directs the family's banking and communications holdings. President Clinton's 1999 announcement that he was recertifying Mexico as a reliable ally in the binational war on the **narcotics** trade was made soon after a visit from Carlos Hank Rhon.

HANK RHON, JORGE (1953–). Unlike his circumspect father, Carlos **Hank González**, and elder brother, Carlos **Hank Rhon**, Jorge has tended to be seen in public with various entertainment celebrities and with government officials in social settings. One news photograph of him posing with **United States** customs officers at the border crossing south of **San Diego** ran in Southern California newspapers, but also in **Mexico City** dailies. He monitors the family-owned Agua Caliente racetrack in **Tijuana**, as well as off-track gaming interests on both sides of the **United States border**. The **election of 2004** saw him elected Tijuana's mayor as the **Partido Revolucionario Institucional** candidate. This eccentric multimillionaire owns a private zoo of 20,000 animals.

HAT DANCE. *See* JARABE TAPATÍO.

HAY, EDUARDO (1877–1941). Soldier-politician, a graduate in engineering from the University of Notre Dame, who was chief of staff for President **Madero** in 1911, then a top adviser to Presidents **Carranza**, 1915–1920, and **Obregón**, 1920–1924. In 1935–1940 he served as foreign minister.

HEADS OF GOVERNMENT. In **New Spain** the head of government (under successive **kings of Spain**) was, first, Hernán **Cortés** until 1534, and thereafter the **viceroy**. During the **Second Empire** the head of government was the **prime minister**. Otherwise successive **heads of state** (the emperor Agustín **Iturbide** and successor **presidents**) have been their own heads of government.

HEADS OF STATE. *See* AZTEC "EMPERORS"; ITURBIDE, AGUSTÍN; KINGS OF SPAIN; MAXIMILIAN; PRESIDENTS.

HEALTH CARE. *See* AMERICAN-BRITISH COWDRAY HOSPITAL; BENEFICIENCIA ESPAÑOLA; BIRTH RATE; DEATH RATE; DISEASE; INFANT MORTALITY; MEDICAL EDUCATION; SISTEMA PÚBLICA DE SALUD.

HEALTH MINISTRY. Created in 1943 as the *Secretaría de Salubridad y Asistencia* (Health and Welfare Ministry) from the then *Department of Salubridad*. In 1982 it became the *Secretaría de Salud* (SSA), which oversees the **Sistema Pública de Salud**.

HENEQUÉN. The normal word for **sisal** in the **Spanish** of Mexico and Central America, often used in English language works on the region. [L. H.]

HENESTROSA, ANDRÉS (1906–). A widely syndicated newspaper columnist from **Oaxaca** who was also Mexico's leading historian of the press, publishing, and the media, and a film producer. He was director of literature for the **Instituto Nacional de Bellas Artes**, 1952–1958, and sat in the **Cámara de diputados federales**, 1958–1961 and 1964–1967. He retold local folktales in *Los hombres que dispersó la danza* (1929), authored hundreds of short stories and essays from the 1940s through the 1970s, and published the magazines *El Libro y el pueblo* and *Letras patrias*.

HENRÍQUEZ GUZMÁN, [GENERAL] MIGUEL (1896–1972). A soldier-politician, born August 4 in Piedras Negras, **Coahuila** who joined the **Revolution of 1910** in 1912 as a cadet guarding President **Madero**. In 1950 he challenged the inner-circle selection of presidential candidates (*See* PRESIDENTIAL SUCCESSION) and was expelled from the **Partido Revolucionario Institucional**, whereupon he formed the **Federación de Partidos del Pueblo de México**, becoming its (unsuccessful) presidential candidate in the **election of 1952**.

HERMOSILLO. Capital of **Sonora** state at 29°05'N, 110°57'W, 290 km (180 miles) south of the **Arizona** border. Its population was 410,000 in 1995 and 689,902 in 2004. It has textile mills and **cotton** gins, the **Universidad de Sonora** with a modern state library nearby, and is the trade and financial center for a large part of northwestern Mexico. In 1953 it was among the first Mexican cities to create Civic Betterment Boards to help the municipal government finance parks, street lighting, and other local services.

Although four presidents—**Calles, Obregón**, De la **Huerta**, and Abelardo **Rodríguez**—who had been governors of Sonora were closely associated with the leadership that spawned the dominant **Partido Revolucionario Institucional**, Hermosillo became the first state capital to elect an opposition (**Partido de Acción Nacional**) mayor, Jorge Valdez Múñoz for 1967–1970.

HERNÁNDEZ, JOAQUÍN. "La Quina," all-powerful head of the **petroleum** workers' trade union (*Sindicato de Trabajadores Petroleros de la Republica Mexicana*—STPRM), who had, in an informal way, more to say about the operation of **Pemex** than the director general. He extorted payment from anyone wishing to be hired and from any contractor or supplier wishing to do business. His reign ended in 1988 when President **Salinas de Gortari** ordered his arrest.

HERNÁNDEZ, LUISA JOSEFINA (1928–). The first woman professor of drama at **UNAM**, where she had received her first degree before doing graduate work as a Rockefeller scholar at Columbia University. Her 1951 play *Aguardiente* won many prizes. Her other plays, from 1957 to 1964, stress social satire. She has also published five novels.

HERNÁNDEZ CORZO, RODOLFO (1909–????). Mexico's leading educator and research scientist in biochemistry. Born in **Chiapas**, with a chemistry degree from the **Instituto Politécnico Nacional** and a PhD from Stanford, he was dean of the IPN school of biological sciences and, until 1958, IPN president. During the 1960s and 1970s he directed the government's wildlife conservation programs.

HERNÁNDEZ DE CÓRDOBA, FRANCISCO (1475–1518). Conquistador who arrived in **Cuba** in 1511 and was ordered by governor Diego **Velázquez de Cuéllar** to outfit an expedition to explore **Yucatán**. He set sail on February 9, 1517, but suffered fierce attacks by local **Indians** and shortly after his defeat at **Champotón** returned to Cuba with his surviving companions. He died there of the wounds he had received.

HERNÁNDEZ DELGADO, JOSÉ (1904–1990). Lawyer from **Guanajuato** who directed the **Nacional Financiera** from 1952 through 1970.

HERNÁNDEZ HERNÁNDEZ, FRANCISCO (1913–1997). A former deputy and senator, born in Capulalpan, **Tlaxcalá**, who from the 1940s through the 1960s served alternately as director of the congressional library and as editor of the *Diario official*.

HERÓICA ESCUELA MILITAR. The military academy (*Escuela Militar*) at **Chapultepec** Castle (founded in 1823) was the scene of the last conflict of the **United States-Mexican War** of 1848, and famed for the sacrifice of the **Niños Héroes**, hence its current name as the "Heroic Military School." Located now in a **Mexico City** suburb, it offers annually a four-year course for 245 **army** cadets who graduate as second lieutenants. The **navy** has a comparable school in **Veracruz** and the **air force** one in **Guadalajara**.

HERRERA, ENRIQUE (1938–). A social science professor, born in **Mexico City**, he served as assistant minister of communications, 1970–1976, and founded **Noticias Mexicanas**.

HERRERA, JOSÉ JOAQUÍN (1792–1854). President of Mexico, 1848–1851. This mild-mannered and honest soldier politician from **Jalapa** initially supported **Spain** against the Patriot insurgents, but in the final struggle for **Independence** joined forces with **Iturbide**, attaining the rank of brigadier general. While acting-president in 1844–1845 he wanted to negotiate with President **Polk**, but he was overthrown by more militant forces led by Mariano **Paredes y Arrillaga**. He opposed the war, but he served as the next-man-in-line to **Santa Anna** and was elected president at the war's end.

HERRERA Y RIVERO, VICENTE DE. Viceroy of **New Spain**, 1784–1785.

HEZETA Y DUDAGOITIA, BRUNO DE. Second in command to Juan **Pérez**'s expedition along the Pacific coast in 1774, and given command in 1775 after Pérez had failed to sail as far north as he had been instructed. One of his ships, commanded by Juan Francisco **Bodega y Quadra**, reached 58°N. The expedition, suffering badly from scurvy, got back to **San Blás**, November 20, 1775. A subsequent expedition was led in 1779 by Ignacio de **Arteaga**. [L. H.]

HIDALGO (*hijo de algo*, "son of something"). (1) A inheritor of landed property, and hence, a minor Spanish nobleman.

(2) **Municipio** of **Michoacán** state, with 106,421 inhabitants at the census of 2000, named for Miguel **Hidalgo y Costilla**.

(3) One of Mexico's most popular names for a street.

HIDALGO, AVENIDA. In **Mexico City**, a west-to-east thoroughfare along the northern side of the **Alameda**.

HIDALGO, ERNESTO (1896–1955). *Excelsior* journalist who was **governor** of his native **Guanajuato state** from September 1943 until January 1946. Then President **Ávila Camacho** removed him from office after law and order broke down with dozens dead in riots prompted by **Partido Revolucionario Institucional** electoral fraud. The **Comisión Federal Electoral** subsequently made some reforms.

HIDALGO DE PARRAL. *See* PARRAL.

HIDALGO STATE. State (postal abbreviation "Hgo") named for Miguel **Hidalgo y Costilla**. It borders **San Luis Potosí**, **Puebla**, **Verazruz**, **Tlaxcala**, **Mexico State**, and **Querétaro**. Created by separation from Mexico State, January 15, 1869, and enlarged from 13,040 km^2 to 20,987 km^2 in the late 20th century, it now has 84 *municipios*. The **population** at successive counts has been 404,207 (in 1869); 548,000 (1895); 605,000 (1900); 646,000 (1910); 622,000 (1921); 678,000 (1930); 772,000 (1940); 850,000 (1950); 995,000 (1960); 1,194,700 (1970); 1,547,000 (1980); 1,888,000 (1990); 2,235,591 (2000); and 2,354,514 (2005).

Besides providing **Mexico City** with meat and dairy produce, the **economy** depends on alfalfa, **corn**, beans, barley, maguey, wheat, alfalfa, **sugar** cane, and (particularly in the past) on the mining of iron, copper, **silver**, gold, lead, mercury, and zinc. Cities include **Pachuca** de Soto (the capital), **Tulancingo**, and the site of the **Toltec** capital of **Tula**.

HIDALGO Y COSTILLA, MIGUEL (1753–1811). Priest revered as the "Father of his Country" because he initiated, in 1810, the insurrection that culminated in Mexican **independence**. A **creole**, he was born on a **hacienda** at San Diego Corralejo in **Guanajuato state** where his father was the administrator, and studied at what is now the **Universidad de San Nicolás** in **Morelia**, and, subsequent to his 1778 ordination, became its rector. Aware of the new ideas of the age, he narrowly escaped imprisonment by the **Inquisition** in 1800 for translating works by French revolutionary writers into Spanish. Instead, he was banished to the village now known as **Dolores Hidalgo**. As its parish priest, he associated himself closely with the **Indians**. His interest in the welfare of his flock led him into such forbidden economic activities as grape growing and silk worm culture. He was originally lukewarm to the idea of independence, and his **Grito de Dolores** was primarily a call for allegiance to **Ferdinand VIII**, whom Napoleon I had recently ousted as king of Spain in favor of his brother Joseph **Bonaparte**.

That Hidalgo's feelings had become much stronger was evident in September 1810, when word reached him that the authorities were about to arrest him. So, in the early morning of September 16, he gathered his parishioners together, distributed arms, and told them that this was the start of a new era which would mean independence from Spain. He then set forth to capture **Guanajuato City**. Passing through Atotonico, he came across an image of St. **Mary of Guadalupe** which he adopted as his rallying standard. After taking **Celaya**, he reached Guanajuato with his force swollen, by workers from the nearby **silver** mines, to about 100,000 followers. The 500 or so Spanish defenders were massacred when the insurgents stormed the **Alhóndiga de Guanajuato**. In the subsequent sacking of the city, Hidalgo was forced to fire on his own supporters as the only way to control them. By late October, he was at the gates of **Mexico City**, occupying what is today the Colonia del Valle neighborhood. But he hesitated there, fearful of what his mob would do to the City. When, after defeats at **Aculco** and **Monte de las Cruces**, he moved instead northward toward **Querétaro**, he lost at least half of his disappointed army through desertion. He then turned back to **Morelia**. In **Guadalajara** he received one of his warmest welcomes, and the title of Serene Highness. Basking in false glory, he took the title of Captain General of America, showing an extreme pride much in contrast with the humility of his successor, José María **Morelos y Pavón**. Nevertheless, he was a true patriot who cared for those who had no power to fight injustice. He established an insurgent newspaper, *El Despertador Americano*, and on December 10 proclaimed the **abolition of slavery**. His fortunes now turned dramatically for the worse. In January 1811, royalist forces under General **Calleja del Rey** routed the insurgents (now commanded by Ignacio **Allende**) at **Calderón Bridge**. In their subsequent flight, Hidalgo and Allende were ambushed and captured in March at **Acatita del Baján**. After trial by the **Inquisition** for heresy, he was defrocked and handed over to the secular authorities. They had him shot at **Chihuahua** on July 31. His head was displayed high above the Alhóndiga until 1821. In 1824 his body was buried with full honors in Mexico City.

Although a failure as a revolutionary, he made a sincere effort to help the poor, raise their standard of living, and create a united and prosperous Mexico. To the Mexican people he symbolizes the union of **Creole** and **Indian**, of the ruling classes and the poor, something that would not occur for another century, if then.

His name is remembered in a **municipio** of **Michoacán**, in **Hidalgo state**, and elsewhere: as a street name it recurs throughout the Republic. *See also* FLAG, NATIONAL.

HIGHER EDUCATION. Each state has a public university, but these institutions are more dependent on federal funding than on state funding. The federal government is directly responsible for **UNAM**, the **Universidad Autónoma Metropolitana**, the **Instituto Politécnico Nacional**, the **Universidad Autónoma Chipango** (the former National Agricultural College) and several technological institutes and centers. During the 1960s and 1970s, industrialists and philanthropists began to help fund private universities, as did **Church** groups. In 1999 there were 18 private universities and several other degree-granting technical institutes, among them the **Universidad Iberoamericana**, the **University of the Americas** in **Mexico City** and its namesake in **Puebla**, and the distinguished **Instituto Tecnológico de Monterrey**. In mid-1999 the Internet Language School of Mexico began its first operations, teaching English to students in **Mexico City**. *See also* ENGINEERING EDUCATION; LEGAL EDUCATION; MEDICAL EDUCATION.

HIGHEST POINT. This is the **Orizaba Volcano**, 5,700 m.

HIGHWAYS. Highways were first developed for the **postal service** of the ancient **Maya** and **Aztec** civilizations. The Spanish empire had a system of roads maintained by the crown (*See* CAMINO REAL). Independent Mexico established a highway department, *Puentes y Calzados* (later **Caminos y Puentes**).

By 1996 Mexico had 94,248 km of paved highways and 157,752 km of unpaved highways. They were carrying 80 percent of Mexico's freight and 95 percent of passengers. A system of modern toll roads have been built to parallel major intercity routes. *See also* APARICIO, SEBASTIÁN DE; AUTOMOBILES; PAN AMERICAN HIGHWAY. [L. H.]

HIJO PRODIGO, EL. Literary magazine founded by Octavio G. Barreda, April 15, 1943, lasting until 1946, and associated with Octavio **Paz** and Spanish loyalist **refugees**. Its title was inspired by John Donne's "We are all prodigal sons." [L. H.]

HINCHINBROOK ISLAND. The most northerly point (61°N) reached by 18th century explorers from **New Spain**.

HINOJOSA, COSME R. (1879–1965). Director general of **postal services** in the 1920s–1930s. He was also a long-time head of the national pawnshop (**Monte de Piedad** Nacional) and formulated the law that pawned national relics might not be resold if museums had claims on them for their historical value to the nation.

HIRSCHFIELD ALMADA, JULIO (1917–). An engineer-businessman from **Mexico City** who rose to vice president of the H. Steel Company, manufacturer and retailer of office furniture and watches throughout Mexico, and then served as director general of **airports**, 1970–1973 and minister of **tourism**, 1973–1976. In September 1971 his kidnapping by the Marxist guerrillas of the **Frente Urbana Zapatista** brought into the open the far-left **guerrilla** violence of 1970–1976 that President **Echeverría** had tried to keep out of the news (*See* DIRTY WAR). Hirschfield was released for a 3,000,000 **peso** ransom.

HOJALATA Y LÁMINA (HYLSA). Iron and steel producer, founded by private investors at **Monterrey** in 1946. It later added a steel plant in **Puebla**.

HOLIDAYS. Mexico's official national holidays are January 1 (New Year), February 5 (Constitution), March 21 (Benito **Juárez**), May 1 (**May Day**), September 1 (**Día de la Nación**), September 16 (**Independence Day**), October 12 (**Columbus Day**), November 20 (**Revolution Day**), and December 25 (Christmas). Religious holidays that are normally observed but without official endorsement are **Twelfth Night**, Maundy Thursday, Good Friday, **All Hallows, All Souls' Day**, and December 12 (honoring Mexico's **patron saint**, Saint **Mary of Guadalupe**). *See also* FIFTH OF MAY.

HOLY OFFICE. *See* INQUISITION.

HOMELAND SECURITY. *See* PUBLIC SECURITY MINISTRY.

HOMICIDE. Mexico is notorious for its high murder rate. Although this has been declining in recent years (down from 17.58 per 100,000 in 1994 to 13 per 100,000 in 2003), it is still among the world's highest, after Papua New Guinea, Pakistan, **Colombia** (63 per 100,000 in 2003), South Africa (51 per 100,000 in 2003, down from 75.3 per 100,000 in 1994), Jamaica and **Venezuela** (both 32 per 100,000 in 2003), **Brazil** (23 per 100,000), Croatia (22.8 per 100,000), and Russia (19 per 100,000), but with no figures available from China, India, or Iraq. These figures compare with 5.7 per 100,000 in the **United States** overall (but 46 per 100,000 in the District of Columbia, 20 per 100,000 in Puerto Rico, and 13 per 100,000 in **Louisiana**), 1.41 per 100,000 in England and Wales, and 0.95 per 100,000 in **Spain**.

A particular problem is the high rate of rape-murders along the **United States border** and especially in **Ciudad Juárez** and **Chihuahua City**. **Narcotics** traffic-related murders accounted for 2,221 deaths in 2006, being highest in **Michoacán** (567), **Sinaloa** (562), **Guerrero** (350), **Tamaulipas** (306), and **Nuevo León** (170), and up from 1,080 in 2001.

Mexico also has currently the second worst record in the world for murders of journalists (*See* CENSORSHIP).

Important judicial executions and political assassinations in Mexican history include those of Carranza, Colosio, Comonfort, Hidalgo y Costilla, Iturbide, Jaramillo, Madero, Maximilian, Montezuma II, Morelos y Pavón, Obregón, Trotsky, Victoria, Vila, and Zapata. *See also* DIRTY WAR; TLATELOLCO, PLAZA DE. [L. H.]

HONDO RIVER. River marking the **Belizan border** and the southern boundary of **Quintana Roo**.

HOOF AND MOUTH DISEASE. *See* GIL PRECIADO, JUAN.

HORA DE VERANO ("summer time"). Daylight saving time, an advance of one hour over normal ("winter") time, was first introduced in **Baja California** in 1942, then tried for one experimental summer in 1988 in the **Yucatán Peninsula**, before being applied nationally from 1996. A federal law of May 1, 2001, decreed it should last from the first Sunday in April until the last Sunday in October in all **time zones**. [L. H.]

HOUSE OF REPRESENTATIVES. *See* CÁMARA DE DIPUTADOS.

HOUSING. *See* HUMAN SETTLEMENTS MINISTRY; INSTITUTO DEL FONDO NACIONAL DE LA VIVIENDA PARA LOS TRABAJADORES; SHANTY TOWNS.

HOUSTON, SAM (1793–1863). The architect of Texan independence from Mexico, effectively secured by his victory at the Battle of **San Jacinto**.

HOY. Magazine of the 1970s, now defunct.

HUAPANGO. Folk **music** that shifts back and forth from a rapid beat to slower rhythms, similar to that of the Spanish flamenco. It originated in **Veracruz state.**

HUARACHE. An **Indian** sandal, still very popular in Mexico.

HUASTEC. *See* TEENEK INDIANS.

HUERTA, ADOLFO DE LA. (1881–1954). Revolutionary figure and provisional president, May–November, 1920. Born in **Guaymas**, he had served as provisional governor of **Sonora** and minister of the interior. In 1920, no longer considering himself a follower of **Carranza**, he approved the Plan of **Agua Prieta**. After turning over the presidency to Álvaro **Obregón**, he became finance minister. At the end of 1923 he broke with Obregón, and General Guadalupe **Sánchez** proclaimed him provisional president again. This rebellion failed, and he lived in exile in **Los Angeles** until 1936 when he became inspector general of Mexican consulates. Later he served as director general of civil pensions. He died in **Mexico City**.

HUERTA, RAMÓN MARTÍN. *See* MARTÍN HUERTA, RAMÓN.

HUERTA, [GENERAL] VICTORIANO (1845–1916). President, February 1913–July 8, 1914. As a **Jalisco**-born officer under Porfirio **Diaz**, he became a brigadier general in 1902. After **Madero** came to power, Huerta was given command against the forces of Pascual **Orozco**, whom he defeated and made off with millions of pesos doing so. For this Madero relieved him of his command, only to employ him again against the forces of Félix **Díaz**. This time, however, he allied himself with Díaz and worked closely with **United States** ambassador Henry Lane **Wilson** in order to assume the presidency himself. In the process he was (at least indirectly) responsible for the deaths of Madero and of Vice president **Pino Suárez**, which made his regime unacceptable to U.S. President Woodrow **Wilson**. He also alienated the United States when he obtained loans from the British-owned El Águila Petroleum. Huerta, a heavy drinker, proved to be not only extremely cruel, but also inept. Repression and **censorship** were exacerbated by a wide use of political assassination.

Rebellions in **Coahuila** led by Venustiano **Carranza**, in **Chihuahua** led by Pancho **Villa**, in **Sonora** led by Álvaro **Obregón**, and in the south by **Zapata**, marked the beginning of his downfall. Serious military reverses, allied to United States intervention (the *Dolphin* affair) led him to resign July 8, 1914, and flee the country, publicly blaming President Woodrow **Wilson**'s intervention, He eventually ended up in Newman, New Mexico, where he was arrested on conspiracy charges and died from cirrhosis of the liver while in custody.

HUICHOL. An Indian group, numbering in the mid-1990s about 49,800, concentrated in **Jalisco**, but also living in southeast **Durango**, **Nayarit**, and **Zacatecas state**, among the last to come under Spanish rule. Only nominally Catholic, they consider the deer a sacred animal and use the hallucinogenic plant peyote to communicate with spirits and pagan gods.

HUIPIL. A straight, shapeless, sleeveless blouse worn by Indian and mestizo peasant women.

HUITZILÍHUITL ("hummingbird's feather") (13??–1417). Chief (**tlatoani**) of the **Aztec** state, from 1396, between **Acamapitchli** and **Chimalpopoca**. He married a daughter of **Tezozómoc**.

HUITZILOPOCHTLI. The principal **Aztec** deity, god of war, often identified with the Sun, known as the "Hummingbird God" and as the "Lord of the Universe."

To make his perilous daily journey across the sky, he needed the sustenance of human blood, hence the importance to the Aztecs of human sacrifice. His temple was the largest in **Tenochtitlán** and occupied the site where **Mexico City**'s cathedral now stands.

He is said to have told his followers to begin a pilgrimage southward under his protection and guidance until they saw an eagle perched on a cactus with a snake in its mouth. That would be where Tenochtitlán was to be built and the origin of Mexico's national **snake and serpent** emblem.

HUIZAR GARCÍA DE LA CADENA, CANDELARIO (1883–1970). Mexican composer of *Pueblerinas* (1931).

HUMAN SETTLEMENTS MINISTRY. (*Secretaría de Asentimientos Humanos y Obras Públicas—SAHOP*). This was the combination in December 1976 of the **Public Works ministry** and the Department of Human Settlements. The latter agency had been created in 1971 to help cope with the staggering problem of slum clearance and the high rate of **internal migration** from the countryside into the cities. SAHOP's first minister was Pedro **Ramírez Vázquez**. It has since become the **Social Development Ministry**.

HUMAYA. River of **Durango state**.

HUMBOLDT, ALEXANDER (Friedrich Alexander, baron [Freiherr] von Humboldt, 1769–1859). Prussian scientist, traveler, and prolific writer (younger brother of the linguist Wilhelm), probably the best known scientist of his era, who visited the Americas—**New Spain**, **Cuba**, **Central America**, New Grenada (modern Colombia), Ecuador, and **Peru**—from 1799–1804, accompanied by the French botanist Aimé Bonpland, studying climatology, geology, oceanography, and biogeography. He was in Mexico March 22, 1803–March 7, 1804, taking copious notes of his observations later incorporated in his 30-volume *Voyage aux régions équinoxiales du Nouveau Continent* (1807–1834). Places he visited included **Cuernavaca**, **Guanajuato**, **Pachucha de Soto**, and **Querétaro**. He made phenomenal use of his time in the country, exploring **silver** mines, mountain peaks, and canals. He even carried out astronomical observations on the great Aztec pyramid at **Cholula** on his way to **Veracruz** to take ship for Havana.

HURRICANES. Mexico suffers a major hurricane every five to seven years. Notable hurricanes have included the **"Great Hurricane"** of October 1780; **Racer's hurricane,** which struck **Matamoros** in 1837; the three hurricanes in the single year of 1898, all of which hit the **Yucatán** Peninsula; the hurricane of August 1909, in which 1,500 died in Yucatán and **Tamaulipas**; that of 1933 in **Matamorros**; the hurricane of August 1951, when 115 lives were lost in **Tampico**; Hurricane Hilda I in September, 1955 (166 killed in Tampico); Hurricane Gert of September 21, 1993 (76 killed, again in Tampico), Hurricane Gilbert of September 1988 (which hit the Yucatán Peninsula as a category 5 storm, and then came ashore again in Tamaulipas, just south of Brownsville, Texas). Hurricanes of 2005 were **Emily** and **Wilma**. On September 1, 2006, Hurricane John hit land northeast of Los Cabos, **Baja California**, with 160 kph winds; and on September 16, category 3 Hurricane Lane hit the Pacific coast between **Mazatlán** and **Culiacán**. *See also* TREASURE FLEET.

HUXLEY, ALDOUS [LEONARD] (1894–1963). The English novelist visited Mexico in the mid-1930s, describing his visit in *Beyond the Mexique Bay*.

HYDROGRAPHY. Most Mexican rivers, including the longest, the **Rio Grande**, flow into the Gulf of **Mexico**. The others include, from north to south, the **Coatzacoalcos**, the **Tamesí**, the **Pánuco**, the Grijala, the **Papaloapan**, and the **Usumacinta**, while the **Hondo** empties into the Caribbean south of the Gulf. Several underground rivers have formed in the limestone of **Yucatán**.

West coast rivers (again, north to south) are the Colorado, whose long course through the American South West terminates by its emptying into the head of the Gulf of **California**, the **Yaqui**, the **Fuerte**, the Huavapan, the San Pedro, the **Grande de Santiago**, and the **Balsas**.

The **Salinas**, **Salvador**, and **San Juan** are tributaries of the Rio Grande.

Minor rivers include the **Cullacán**, **Humaya**, **Mezquital**, **Nazas**, **Orizaba**, **Plaxtla**, **Presidio**, **Sinaloa**, and **Tehuantepec**.

All but the Rio Grande are more obstacles to be forded or bridged than navigable aids to inland penetration.

There are also several inland lakes. **Mexico City** began as an island in one of them. The others include Lake **Chalapa** and **Pátzcuaro Lake**, as well as artificial creations such as the large reservoir behind **Falcon Dam**.

– I –

IBARGÜENGOITIA, JORGE (1928–1983). Sardonic novelist (*Los relámpagos de agosto*, 1964; *Las muertas*, 1977), short story writer (*La ley de Herodes*, 1967), and playwright from **Guanajuato**, killed in an aircrash in Madrid. [L. H.]

IBARRA, FRANCISCO DE (1539–1575). Conquistador who became **governor** and **captain general** of **Nueva Vizcaya**, founded **Durango City**, and opened many **silver** mines in **Zacatecas**.

IBARRA IBARRA, GUILLERMO (1911–1980). A lawyer from Alamos, **Sonora**, who became president of the **UNAM** student federation in 1933, a judge of the Federal Tax Court (*Tribunal Fiscal de la Federación*), then head of the **Federal Conciliation and Arbitration Board**, and director of *El Nacional,* 1948–1956. As a senator in 1958–1964 he helped introduce **proportional representation** in congressional elections, despite himself being a leader of the **Partido Revolucionario Institucional**.

IBARRA MÚÑOZ, DAVID (1930–). Economist and a certified public accountant from **Mexico City** who served as director of planning for the **Public Works** Ministry; as the **United Nations' Economic Commission for Latin America**'s director for Mexico, 1967–9; assistant director general (1970–1976) and then director general (1976–1977) of **Nacional Financiera**. In 1977–1982 he was finance minister. He is known throughout Latin America for his many articles and books on economic development.

IGLESIA CATÓLICA MEXICANA. The "Mexican Catholic Church," with 370,000 communicants, has no ties to the Vatican, but is affiliated to the New Mexico diocese of the Protestant Episcopal Church and allows the ordination of **women** (having currently one woman priest).

IGUALA. A **municipio** of **Guerrero state** of 567 km^2 with 39,732 inhabitants in 1960; 83,328 in 1980; and 123,960 in 2000. The **cabecera** is **Iguala de la Independencia**.

IGUALA, PLAN OF. Drawn up at **Iguala** by Agustín **Iturbide** on February 24, 1821, as a conservative basis for **independence** from **Spain** and agreed on with the **viceroy** in the Treaty of **Córdoba**. Its three main points were equality under the law for **Creoles** and Spaniards, Roman Catholicism as the only acceptable religion, and the establishment of an independent **empire**, under **Ferdinand VII**, or another

European royal acceptable to Mexico. Eventually, Iturbide himself became **emperor**. Mexico's red-white-green national **flag** was meant to symbolize the three principles of Iguala.

IGUALA DE LA INDEPENDENCIA. A city in **Guerrero state** at 18°20'N, 99°35'W, 128 km (80 miles) south of **Mexico City**, with a 1976 population of 88,000. Founded by the **Chontal** Indians in 1347, conquered by **Itzcóatl** in 1440, it became the **cabecera** of an **encomienda** in 1560, and is now *cabecera* of the 567 km² **municipio** of Iguala, with 39,732 inhabitants in 1960; 83,328 in 1980; and 123,960 in 2000. *See also* ABARCA ALARCON, RAIMUNDO.

IGUANA. A large lizard native to the subtropical and tropical zones of Mexico, considered edible by **Indians**, up to 1.5 m (5 ft.) from head to tailend when fully grown.

ILLITERACY. *See* LITERACY.

IMMIGRATION. Although contemporary Mexico is economically attractive to **Guatemalans** and Hondurans, many of these and other Central Americans enter Mexico en route to (mostly illegal) onward migration into the **United States**. Mexico's relatively low living costs also attract American and Canadian retirees. *See also* AFRICAN SLAVERY; AMERICANS IN MEXICO; AUSTRIANS; BLACKS; BRITISH IN MEXICO; CHINESE IMMIGRATION; EXILES; FRENCH IMMIGRATION; GERMANS IN MEXICO; JEWS; RUSSIANS IN MEXICO; SPANISH CIVIL WAR. [L. H.]

IMPORTERS' AND EXPORTERS' ASSOCIATION. *See* ASOCIACIÓN NACIONAL DE IMPORTADORES Y EXPORTADORES DE LA REPÚBLICA MEXICANA.

IMPORTS. The **mercantilism** of **Spain** in the colonial period, by forbidding most foreign imports, encouraged a widespread **contraband** trade. During the early **independence** period, free trade was introduced but made subject to tariffs seen purely as a source of revenue. In the mid-20th century, Mexico, like other larger Latin American countries, pursued an economic policy based on import substitution through the development of **manufacturing industry** behind tariff barriers, which were steadily increased so as also to help solve balance of payment crises. The **financial crisis of 1982** led to a strict licensing of all imports, but this very soon came to be regarded as no longer a viable option. In June 1986 Mexico joined the **General Agreement on Tariffs and Trade**, limited licensing to 28 percent of imports by value, reduced the average import tariff to 13 percent and the maximum tariff to 50 percent. Mexico's entry into the **North American Free Trade Association** accelerated this trade liberalization by imposing the obligation to abolish most restrictions on trade with Canada and the **United States** (77 percent of all imports in 1997) by 2004. NAFTA membership was followed by negotiations to liberalize trade with **Chile**, Bolivia, Venezuela, Colombia, Ecuador, and the countries of Central America and the Mercosur (a regional trade agreement between four countries—Brazil, Argentina, Uraguay, and Paraguay. [L. H.]

IMPUESTO AL VALOR AGREGADO. *See* VALUE-ADDED TAX.

IMPUESTO ESPECIAL SOBRE PRODUCCIÓN Y SERVICIOS (IEPS). "Special tax on goods and services," levied *inter alia* on drinks and tobacco. [L. H.]

INCOME DISTRIBUTION. In 1920, 2 percent of Mexican families received half the **gross domestic product**. Thanks to government policies, there has been considerable improvement since. In 1965, 1.8 percent of families received 15 percent of the GDP. One initiative was a profit-sharing law enacted in 1962 which created the **Comité Nacional de Reparto de Utilidades** to enforce profit sharing. During the early 1970s the buying power of wages was increasing by 6.4 percent a year.

From the 1990s onward, however, globalization, **privatization**, and the modernization of the **economy** in general have together reduced the average salary (by 28 percent by 1993), at the same time doubling the number of Mexicans living below the **poverty** line to about 30 percent of the nation, with the **campesino** particularly disadvantaged. *See also* MINIMUM WAGE. [L. H.]

INDEPENDENCE. September 15, 1810, the date of the **Grito de Dolores**, is regarded as the date of Mexico's first declaration of independence (*Acta de Independencia*), originally made on the night of September 15–16, 1810. Effective independence, however, only came with the last **viceroy**'s acceptance of independence as a *fait accompli* in the 1821 Treaty of **Córdoba**, **San Juan de Ulúa** remained Spanish until November 18, 1825. *See also* CENTENARY OF INDEPENDENCE.

INDEPENDENCE, WAR OF. Conflict begun with Miguel **Hidalgo y Costilla**'s revolt of 1810–1811, continued under José María **Morelos y Pavón** until 1815, and then by Guadalupe **Victoria** as a **guerrilla** campaign until separation from **Spain** was secured by Agustín **Iturbide** in 1821. The struggle was only ended by the fall of **San Juan de Ulúa** in 1825. [L. H.]

INDEPENDENCE DAY. *Día de la Independencia.* Celebrated on September 16th, but often confused by Americans with the *Cinco de Mayo* (**May the Fifth**).

INDIAN AFFAIRS. The official *Instituto Nacional Indigenista* of 1949 was reconstituted July 5, 2003, as the *Comisión Nacional para el Desarrollo de los Pueblos Indígenas*, whose website is www.cid.gob.mx.

INDIAN LANGUAGES. There are 53 native languages (of which **Nahuatl** remains the most widespread) still spoken in Mexico, although use of the **Spanish language** continues to expand at their expense, for social and economic reasons. The situation where Spanish speaking grandchildren can only converse with their monoglot Indian grandparents through the intermediary of a bilingual parent has parallels wherever the dominant language has sufficient kudos: e.g in Brittany in France. [L. H.]

INDIAN WARS. *See* APACHE; CASTE WAR OF YUCATÁN; CERDA Y ARAGÓN, TOMÁS ANTONIO MANRIQUE DE LA; CHICHIMECS, WAR OF; CONQUEST OF MEXICO, SPANISH;

FAR NORTH; MIXTON WAR; UGARTE Y LOYOLA, JACOBO DE; INSURRECTIONS.

INDIANS (*indios*). Despite the increasing substitution of "Native American" or "**Amerindian**," Columbus' misnomer (from **Indies**) remains the most widely used term in both English and Spanish, for the aboriginal populations of the Americas—in Mexico, for pre-Hispanic groups ranging from **Aztecs** to **Zapotecs**. For the date of their first arrival, *See* ARCHAEOLOGY.

In the colonial period Indian labor was exploited by the **encomienda** and **reducción** systems until their separate legal status was abolished by the **Spanish Constitution of 1812**. *See also* OBRAJE.

Estimation of how many Indians there are in Mexico's present population is complicated by problems of definition. Used (as it often is) as a social term rather a cultural or linguistic one, would give a total of 10 million or so, but probably as much as 30 percent of the population are of predominately Indian descent, and many more Mexicans have enough Indian blood to affect their physical appearance. The number officially regarded as Indian, about 8 million, is the largest indigenous total in any country of the Americas. The most numerous groups in present-day Mexico are, in descending order, the **Nahua, Maya**, Zapotec, **Mixtec, Otomí, Tzeltal, Totonac, Maazahua, Tzotzil**, and **Huastec**. *See also* CALIFORNIAN INDIANS; CHONTAL; CORA; HUICHOL; LACANDÓN; MAYO; MESTIZO; MIXE; PAPAGO; PIMA; SERI; TARASCAN; TEPEJUAN; TOJOLABAL; TRIQUE INDIANS; YAQUI; ZACATEC INDIANS. [L. H.]

INDIES (*Indias*). Official title of the Americas during the Spanish colonial period, whence **Council of the Indies, Laws of the Indies**, etc.

INDUSTRY. *See* MANUFACTURING INDUSTRY.

INDUSTRY, MINISTRY OF. *See* TRADE MINISTRY.

INFANT MORTALITY. Deaths during the first year of life were at the rate of 375 per 1000 live births in the 1890s. This has since fallen to 225 per 1,000 in 1922; 125 per 1,000 in 1930; 60 per 1,000 in 1970; 40.4

per 1,000 in 1980; 31.1 per 1,000 in 1990; 21.7 per 1,000 (98th among the nations of the world, after **Argentina** and **Chile**) in 2002; to 20.91 per 1,000 in 2005. [For comparison, the rate in **Brazil** was then 25.8 per 1,000; and in the **United States**, 6 per 1,000. Deaths per 1,000 during the first five years of life fell from 46 in 1990 to 27 in 2005. [L. H.]

INFLATION. Although the **peso** was originally the same **silver** coin as the 18th century **United States dollar**, it slowly lost relative value and by the 1960s was worth about 30 U.S. cents. Inflation increased markedly following the **foreign debt moratorium** of August 1982, reaching in some years of the following decade over 40 percent and in late 1987 the equivalent of 225 percent. In December 1994 the Mexican government devalued the peso 14 percent. To deal with the consequences, President **Zedillo** instituted an austerity program that included a 5 percent increase in the **value-added tax** and higher electricity rates. The U.S. government, acting through the **International Monetary Fund**, the Inter-American Development Bank, and commercial banks underwritten by U.S. government funds, made Mexico a US$ 20 billion loan to help Mexico stabilize its currency. As a result, the annual inflation rate fell to 10 percent in 1995 through 1997. *See also* EXCHANGE RATE.

INFLUENZA. The mid-16th century epidemic spread from Europe to Mexico in 1558–1559. Mexico also suffered in the worldwide "**Spanish flu**" of 1918–1919.

INFORMAL ECONOMY. As in most Third World countries, lax law enforcement and a large number of workers excluded by lack of formal qualifications from legal employment has created a large "black," unregulated **economy** on the fringes of officially sanctioned activities. [L. H.]

INQUISITION, HOLY. The royal *Tribunal del Santo Oficio* was established in Spain in 1478, independent of the Papal Inquisition, to enforce religious orthodoxy, hunt out apostasy among *conversos* (**Jews** who had accepted baptism to avoid expulsion from Spain's domains in 1492 and their descendants), and root out "dangerous" literature. It was formally established in the **viceroyalty** in 1569 by

Pedro **Moya y Contreras** (who located it, initially, in Santo Domingo). Its control of political expression lasted until the **Cortes of Cádiz** abolished it in 1813, and religious censorship persisted even longer.

It is ironic that, although the Holy Office did not prosecute **Indians** in **New Spain** after 1575, the first person to be tried by it there was an Indian, Marcos of Acolhuacán. Of the 600 cases tried during the 16th century, only 13 were sentenced to death in the sixteenth century and it is doubtful if more than 60 people were put to death through the actions of the Holy Office in Mexico during the entire three-hundred year colonial period.

Among those who have suffered at its hands have been Manuel **Abad y Queipo**, Luis de **Carvajal**, Miguel **Hidalgo y Costilla**, and [Fray] José Servando Teresa de **Mier**.

INSTITUTO DE ESTUDIOS POLÍTICOS, ECONOMICOS Y SOCIALES (IEPES). The **Partido Revolucionario Institucional**'s Institute of Political, Economic, and Social Studies, whose function is to orient and train rising political appointees in positions in public life.

INSTITUTO DE SEGURIDAD Y SERVICIOS SOCIALES DE LOS TRABAJADORES DEL ESTADO (ISSSTE). The Institute of Social Security for Government Workers (organized in the **Federación de Sindicatos de los Trabajadores en Servicio del Estado**).

INSTITUTO DEL FONDO NACIONAL DE LA VIVIENDA PARA LOS TRABAJADORES (INFONAVIT). The Institute of the National Fund for Workers' Housing has since 1971 been financing low-cost home mortgages, low-rent public apartments, and slum clearance. This federal program funds and builds housing which the private sector cannot underwrite.

INSTITUTO FEDERAL ELECTORAL. The Federal Electoral Institute, an autonomous agency of the **Interior Ministry** whose responsibilities extend to approving (or censoring) campaign advertising. [L. H.]

INSTITUTO INDÍGENA NACIONAL. National research institution on Mexico's aboriginal peoples, i.e., the **Indians**.

INSTITUTO INTERAMERICANO DE ESTUDIOS INDÍGENAS. Pan American Institute for the Study of Native Americans, founded in 1942.

INSTITUTO MEXICANO DE COMERCIO EXTERIOR (IMCE). The government's Foreign Trade Institute.

INSTITUTO MEXICANO DEL PETROLEO (I.M.P.). The Mexican **Petroleum** Institute is a research entity for **Pemex**.

INSTITUTO MEXICANO DEL SEGURO SOCIAL (IMSS). The Mexican Social Security Institute was created in 1943 to provide retirement pensions and medical care for workers in the private sector. Each worker contributes 8 percent of his salary and his employer another 8 percent into the worker's IMSS fund. *See also* MARTÍNEZ DOMÍNGUEZ, GUILLERMO.

INSTITUTO NACIONAL DE BELLAS ARTES (INBA). The Federal Government's National Institute of Fine Arts, created by a law of December 1946, is a semi-autonomous agency of the **Education Ministry**. Its director administers a symphony orchestra, a classical ballet company, a folklore ballet company, a music conservatory, art museums and galleries, the **Museo Nacional de Antropología**, libraries, and various artistic activities throughout Mexico.

INSTITUTO NACIONAL DE ESTADÍSTICA, GEOGRAFIA E INFORMÁTICA (INEGI). The Government's national statistical office, formerly the *Dirección General de Estadística*, which Gilberto **Loyo** had reorganized in the 1950s.

INSTITUTO NACIONAL DE LA VIVIENDA. *See* INSTITUTO DEL FONDO NACIONAL DE LA VIVIENDA PARA LOS TRABAJADORES.

INSTITUTO NACIONAL DEL CAFÉ. The National Coffee Institute is the government agency controlling **coffee** prices, exports, and domestic distribution by private producers, and investing in production.

INSTITUTO PANAMERICANO DE GEOGRAFÍA E HISTORIA (I.P.G.H.). Spanish name of the **Pan American Institute of Geography and History**.

INSTITUTO POLITÉCNICO NACIONAL (IPN). The National Polytechnic Institute in **México City** was a 1937 conversion by Wilfrido **Massieu** of the College of Railroad Workers, which he had helped found in 1920. The IPN is a federal institute of higher learning second only to **UNAM**. It stresses engineering, medicine, dentistry, the physical sciences, and most major technological specialities. Like other Mexican universities, it maintains its own preparatory schools (grades 10–12) which combine high school and community college level courses, preparatory to entrance into IPN.

INSTITUTO TECNOLÓGICO AUTÓNOMO DE MÉXICO. The Autonomous Technological Institute of Mexico.

INSTITUTO TECNOLÓGICO Y DE ESTUDIOS SUPERIORES DE MONTERREY (ITESM). The **Monterrey** Institute of Technology, a private university, Mexico's leading higher institution for engineering education.

INSURANCE ASSOCIATION. *See* ASOCIACIÓN MEXICANA DE INSTITUCIONES DE SEGUROS.

INSURRECTIONS. *See* ACORDADA REVOLT; ARISTA, MARIANO; ASAMBLEA POPULAR DE LOS PUEBLOS DE OAXACA; ÁVILA-CORTÉS CONSPIRACY; BEAR FLAG REPUBLIC; BOULBON, RAOUSSET DE; BUSTAMANTE, ANASTASIO; CABAÑAS, LUCIO; CANEK, JACINTO; CEDILLO, SATURNINO; CIVIL WARS; EJÉRCITO ZAPATISTA DE LIBERACIÓN NACIONAL; ESCOBAR REBELLION; GUERRILLA; HUERTA, ADOLFO DE LA; INDEPENDENCE, WAR OF; INDIAN WARS; IZÚCAR; LOZADA, MANUEL; PORTILLO, PEDRO DE

LA; RIO GRANDE, REPUBLIC OF; RIOTS; URAGA, JOSÉ L.; YAQUI.

INTENDANCY (*intendencia*). A new administrative unit based on a French model (whence the traditional English spelling) introduced by Spain in the late 1700s as part of the **Bourbon reforms** to increase efficiency and limit **corruption**. The **intendant** (*intendente*) was concerned with finance (particularly revenue collection), industry (enforcement of the trade laws, but also the encouragement of any economic activities likely to increase revenue), defense, and justice. The system was planned in 1767 but intense opposition prevented its introduction into **New Spain** until 1786, the **viceroyalty** being then divided into 12 intendancies: **Durango, Guadalajara, Guanajato, México, Michoacán, Oaxaca, Puebla, San Luis Potosí, Sonora, Veracruz, Yucatán**, and **Zacatecas**. The **viceroys** rightly feared it would erode their powers, which became increasingly symbolic. Their suspicion and obstruction and the eruption of the **independence** movement denied the new system any fair opportunity to prove itself.

The administrative division of an intendancy was a **partido**. [L. H.]

INTERAMERICAN CONFERENCE ON PROBLEMS OF WAR AND PEACE. *See* CHAPULTEPEC CONFERENCE.

INTER-AMERICAN TREATY OF MUTUAL ASSISTANCE. Known by its Spanish initials as TIAR, the treaty, negotiated at the August 1947 Inter-American Conference in **Petrópolis**, was signed in **Rio de Janeiro** and revised in 1975. It provided that an armed attack on any **Organization of American States** member would be treated as an attack on all. The **United States** decision that the 1982 Falkland War between **Argentina** and the **United Kingdom** did not qualify as such showed the Treaty to be fatally flawed. [L. H.]

INTERIOR MINISTRY (*Secretaría de Gobernación*—SEGOB). Government department corresponding to the **United Kingdom** Home Office or the **United States** Department of Justice and whose usual translation is taken from European practice: "Internal Affairs" might be more appropriate. The **Constitution of 1917** established the ministry as the liaison between the federal executive and the governments of the states and *municipios*. It directs the **Comisión Federal Electoral** and is the final executive authority over **immigration, emigration**, prisons, **radio, television**, the **cinema, crime** prevention, the federal **police**, criminal **justice**, and other sensitive aspects of public life which may also be the concern of other ministries and semi-autonomous agencies.

Its incumbent holds the most senior cabinet post below that of the president (and one frequently held just before its holder becomes himself president of the republic). He is the president's chief agent in dealing with all other entities of the executive branch and with the legislative and judicial branches.

During the 1958–1976 period some of the ministry's powers were transferred to the ministry of the **presidency**, and in 2001 it lost its homeland security responsibilities to the new **Public Security Ministry**. [L. H.]

INTERNAL MIGRATION. Mexico shares with most other Third World countries a chronic problem of flight from the impoverished rural areas to the big cities, particularly to the huge **Mexico City Conurbation**. The causes closely resemble those fostering **emigration** to the **United States**. *See also* URBANIZATION. [L. H.]

INTERNAL TRADE. By the 21st century conglomerates such as **Bimbo, Cemex**, the Walgreens-owned **Sanborns**, and **Wal-Mart** were already dominating much of Mexican retailing. *See also* COMPAÑÍA NACIONAL DE SUBSISTENCIAS POPULARES; HIRSCHFIELD ALMADA, JULIO. [L. H.]

INTERNATIONAL COFFEE AGREEMENT. Mexico was one of the seven Latin American countries signing the first International **Coffee** Agreement of 1957. It played a leading role in the revised agreement of 1968. Seen as a restraint on free trade, its system of national quotas ceased to be effective in 1989. [L. H.]

INTERNATIONAL COFFEE ORGANISATION. Headquartered on London's Oxford Street, with Spanish as one of its three working languages, its primary purpose was implementing the **International Coffee Agreement**. [L. H.]

INTERNATIONAL LABOR DAY. *See* MAY DAY.

INTERNATIONAL LABOUR ORGANISATION (I.L.O.). Originally the **League of Nation**'s International Labour Office, it became, under the **United Nations**, the International Labour Organisation, usually referred to in American sources as the International Labor Organization. It is headquartered in Geneva, Switzerland.

INTERNATIONAL MONETARY FUND (IMF). By the end of 1999, Mexico's **foreign debts** included US$ 7.42 billion owed to the Fund (headquartered in Washington, DC, and underwritten by the **United States** government) but was sufficiently confident in its financial policies to reject an offer of a preventative credit line for the 2000–2006 period.

INTERNATIONAL RELATIONS. *See* FOREIGN MINISTRY.

IRAPUATO. Most populous *municipio* of **Guanajuato** state with 440,134 inhabitants in 2000.

IRISH. *See* KING, EDWARD; SAINT PATRICK BATTALION.

IRON AND STEEL. Mexico has the world's 13th largest output of iron ore.

The country's steel industry began in 1900 when Mexican, American, and French investors created the **Fundidora de Monterrey**, the first integrated iron and steel mill in Latin America. When **World War II** brought a shortage of steel, President Manuel **Ávila Camacho** set up **Altos Hornos de Mexico S.A.** as a government corporation. Mexico's next large steel corporation, **Hojalata y Lámina (HYLSA)**, was started by private investors in 1946. **Tubos de Acero de Mexico (TAMSA)**, also privately funded, followed in 1955. By the 1960s, 53 plants were producing iron and steel, insuring Mexico's status as an industrialized nation. In 1976 the government created **Siderúrgica Lázaro Cárdenas Las Truchas (SICARTSA)**.

The industry is still mainly located in the north, particularly in **Monterrey** and **Monclova**, and although Mexico has about enough iron ore for its needs, the industry suffers from the country's lack of adequate **coal** deposits. Production in 1971 was 3,780,000 tons more than any Latin American country except Brazil, but insufficient for Mexico's own needs.

In 1986 the federal government publicly admitted that it had put billions of dollars not only into SICARTSA but into other plants that it had bought from private corporations, only to see most of them consistently lose money.

In 1992, President Carlos **Salinas de Gortari** privatized the steel mills with the public endorsement of his entire cabinet and all top officers of the **Partido Revolucionario Institucional**. More significantly, the automobile producers welcomed the move. In 1995, steel and iron exports to other developing countries constituted an economic boom in the now privatized industry. In May 1999, the private Grupo Imsa formed a joint venture with steelmaker Ispat International to produce and distribute flat-rolled steel products throughout Latin America.

IRRIGATION. Artificial irrigation was used by the **Olmecs**. Today only 7 percent of Mexico's total land **area** is under natural **rainfall** cultivation. On January 9, 1926, a federal law of irrigation created the *Comisión nacional de Irrigaciones* (National Irrigation Commission) to introduce a modern administration of water resources. Soon after his December 1946 inauguration, President Miguel **Alemán** got Congress to create a Ministry of Hydraulic Resources, which was merged in December 1976 with the Ministry of **Agriculture**. The federal government is thus concerned with all hydroelectric projects, as well as the administration of rivers and lakes (*See* HYDROGRAPHY). Within each **municipio** there are federally controlled Boards of Water and Drainage, coordinating with state and local officials on matters of sanitation and the household and personal use of water. The result has been that, since 1980, 14 percent of Mexico's total area is now under cultivation or grazing.

In 1989 the *Comisión Nacional de Irrigations* was restyled into the **Comisión Nacional del Agua**—National Water Commission.

ISABEL. Spanish for "Elizabeth," although Spain's two queens of this name are traditionally referred to in English as "Isabella." The earlier was the queen regnant of Castile and León whose marriage to Ferdinand of Aragon created a unified Kingdom "of the Sain" by taking Grenada, the last Muslim-ruled territory in the Peninsula. She sought racial and ideological unity by expelling the **Jews**, and despatched **Columbus** on his fateful voyage, all in the same year of 1492. For this, she and her husband were awarded the soubriquet of their "Catholic majesties," just as the kings of France were the "Most Christian" rulers, those of Portugal the "Most Faithful," the Austrian Habsburgs were their "Apostolic" majesties, and English monarchs have been, since the young (and still Catholic) Henry VIII's attack on Lutheranism, "Defenders of the Faith." [L. H.]

ISIDORE, HURRICANE. A category 3 storm of September 14–26, 2002, which formed southeast of Jamaica and hit the **Yucatán** Peninsula at Telchac Puerta, September 22 with winds of 250 km/h, weakened over land, and two days later headed back over the Gulf to Louisiana.

ISLANDS. The main ones on the **continental shelf** are **Cozumel**, **Mujeres**, **Tiburón**, and **Tres Marias**, but there are over 200 smaller ones in **Campeche state** alone. The chief oceanic islands are the *isla de* **Guadalupe**, the **Revillagigedo islands**, and the **Alijos** rocks. The islands in the Pacific have a total **area** of 4,600 km^2; those in the Gulf of **Mexico** and the Caribbean total 779 km^2. *See also* COASTLINE; MEXCALTITÁN; SAN JUAN DE ULÚA.

ISLAS BRAVO, ANTONIO (1885–1949). Lawyer who fought under Pancho **Villa**, was a federal deputy, 1924–1926, and **supreme court** justice.

ISTHMUS OF TEHUANTEPEC. *See* TEHUANTEPEC ISTHMUS.

ITALY, RELATIONS WITH. Early Italian settlers in **New Spain** included priests and printers. Italy also supplied many of the books imported into the early colony. The great wave of Italian emigration in the later 19th and earlier 20th centuries went, however, far more to the **United States**, **Argentina**, **Brazil**, and Venezuela than to Mexico.

Despite the near contemporaneity of their adoption, the similarity of the national **flag** of Italy to that of Mexico would seem to be pure coincidence.

ITURBE, [GENERAL] RAMÓN F. (1889–1970). Soldier from **Sinaloa**, second in command to Álvaro **Obregón** during the 1912–4 battles in the north, at the beginning of the **Revolution of 1910**. In 1940 he was expelled from the **Partido Revolucionario Institucional**'s forerunner, the **Partido Revolucionario Mexicano** for supporting the presidential candidacy of Juan Andreu **Almazán**.

ITURBIDE, AGUSTÍN (1783–1824). Emperor of Mexico, as Agustín I, 1822–1823. Born in what is now **Morelia**, he fought for the Spanish against the **independence** movement until the liberals seized power in Spain in the **Spanish Revolution of 1820**. At that time he proclaimed the Plan of **Iguala**, to use independence to continue conservative rule in Mexico, symbolized by his adoption of the imperial title soon afterwards. Overthrown and forced into exile in Europe, he was provided with a pension on condition that he never return. However, hearing rumors that **Ferdinand VII** was about to mount an invasion of Mexico, he offered his services to the new Mexican republic and set sail without waiting for the reply. He landed at Soto la Marina, near **Tampico**, was arrested, and shot for treason, July 19.

ITURRIGARAY, JOSÉ DE (1742–1815). José de Iturrigaray y Aróstegui, **viceroy** of **New Spain**, 1803–1808. Born in Cadiz of Navarrese descent, he entered the army as a cadet in 1759, was an infantry lieutenant by 1762, and captain in the *Carineros Reales* by 1777. He fought against the **United Kingdom** and Portugal in 1762 and against France in 1793. His friendship with Manuel de **Godoy** gave him an entry into politics and his appointment as viceroy. When he heard of the 1808 abdications in Bayonne of both **Charles IV** and his son **Ferdinand VII**, he refused to recognize either the puppet regime of Joseph **Bonaparte** or the authority of the **Junta Central** in Cadiz. Instead he set up a **Junta de México**, which split between a **Creole** majority wanting independence and a minority wanting Spanish rule to continue. When it seemed the former would prevail, the minority faction of Spanish merchants, with the support of the **Audiencia**, assaulted his palace and imprisoned him. Eventually, back in **Spain**, he was tried by the regime of the restored Ferdinand VII. He died before the trial had ended.

ITZÁ. The **Maya** group who founded **Chichén Itzá**.

ITZCÓATL ("Obsidian Snake"). Leader (**tlatoani**) of the Aztecs, 1427–1440 and real founder of the **Aztec** empire, responsible for bringing 24 settlements under Aztec rule and making **Tenochtitlán** the most important center in the Valley of **Mexico**. He was succeeded by **Montezuma I**.

IXTAPA. *See* ZIHUATANEJO.

IXTAPAN DE LA SAL. A famous spa near **Cuernavaca**.

IXTLACCÍHUATL ("white woman" in Nahuatl). Mexico's most famous volcano, on the eastern rim of the central Valley of Mexico surrounding **Mexico City**, rising to 5286 m (17,342 ft.) above sea level. It is associated with nearby **Popocatépetl** in the legend of the Aztec Princess Ixtla, betrothed to the warrior Popo if he could defeat her father's enemies. This he did, but rivals sent back false news of his death, whereupon Ixtla fell ill and died. The conquest by the white-skinned Spaniards reinforced the legend, and the twin volcanoes became symbols of the conquest as well as of fertility.

IZAMAL. Maya ruins in **Yucatán state**.

IZÚCAR. Town in **Puebla state** at 18°38'N, 98°30'W, now officially Izúcar de Matamoros, 80 km (50 miles) south of **Puebla City**. Locale of an Indian revolt in 1780, it fell to José María **Morelos y Pavón** in late 1810, resisting a royalist counterattack on March 2, 1811, before the rebel army decided to abandon it.

– J –

J. This letter was originally an *i* with a descender used as a flourish at the end of words, but it came in 16th century Spanish to denote the same sound as **x**, and in the spelling reform of 1723 replaced it, except as an archaism, and as a matter of national pride in many Mexican **toponyms**, especially, of course, *México* (for which the Spanish Academy prescribes *Méjico*). Its use also alternates with *g* in some proper names, e.g., *Jeronimo* versus *Gerónimo*. [L. H.]

JACOBIN SOCIETY. The deprecatory name the conservative **Escoceses** (Scottish rite masons) gave to the rival, liberal **Yorkinos** (York rite masons). [The reference is not to the Stuart pretenders (*Jacobites*) but to the French revolutionaries. L. H.]

JAGUAR. The New World leopard, the largest feline of the Americas (up to 1.8 m long and weighing up to 120 kg), formerly widespread in forested areas of **Meso-America**, and a major symbol in the religion, **literature**, and **art** of the pre-Hispanic **Olmec**, **Maya**, and **Aztec** civilizations. **Deforestation** is both reducing the animal's prey base and fragmenting its population into ever smaller and more isolated pockets. The Mexican subspecies is the *panthera onca arizonensis*. [L. H.]

JAI ALAI. The Basque ball game known in Spain as *pelota*.

JALAPA. Xalapa de Henríquez (from Nahatl *xallapam* "spring in the sand"), capital of **Veracruz state** and location of the state **Universidad de Veracruz**, at 1,375 m (4,500 ft.) above sea level on the slopes of the Sierra **Madre** Oriental, at 19°35'N, 96°50'W, 65 km (40 miles) from the Gulf of **Mexico**. It is the third biggest city in the state (population 185,000 in 1976; 279,451 in 1990; 395,590 in 2000). A traditional link on the highway and railroad between **Veracruz** and **México City**, it has preserved a section of colonial era buildings with cobbled streets. Despite the retention of the initial *x* in the official spelling, the airport code is JAL.

JALAPEÑO. Pertaining to or inhabiting **Jalapa**. The feminine *jalapeña* is also the name of a very spicy local cheese, now found throughout Mexico.

JALISCO. A coastal state of 124 *municipios* on 80,157 km^2 of southwestern Mexico, bordered on its north by **Nayarit** and on its east and south by **Michoacán** and Lake **Chalapa**, officially spelled *Xalisco*. Its northern sector is part of the central Mexican plateau. The rest is the mountainous basin of the **Lerma River** and a narrow coastal lowland. It is a leading producer of cattle, milk, horses, and corn. It had 804,058 inhabitants in 1857 and 924,580 in 1869. Successive **cen-**

suses since then have recorded populations of 1,108,000 (1895); 1,154,000 (1900); 1,209,000 (1910); 1,192,000 (1921); 1,255,000 (1930); 1,418,000 (1940); 1,747,000 (1950); 2,443,000 (1960); 3,297,000 (1970); 4,372,000 (1980); 5,303,000 (1990); 6,322,002 (2000); and 6,752,113 (2005). Mexico's most populous state in the 1910s and 1920s, it was overtaken by **Veracruz** and the **Federal District** in the 1930s, and by **Mexico state** in the 1960s. The capital is **Guadalajara**, under which name the future state had been made an **intendancy** in 1786. An inhabitant is a *Jaliscense*.

Local folk customs typify what is popularly thought of as "Mexican": **mariachi** music, fancy **charro** costumes (including the broad brimmed *sombrero*, and the brightly colored striped **sarape**), and **tequila**.

JAPAN, RELATIONS WITH. Mexico sent an **air force** squadron to fight in the Japanese occupied **Philippines** during **World War II**. *See also* DÍAZ COVARRUBIAS, FRANCISCO; FELIPE DE JESÚS, SAINT.

JARA RODRÍGUEZ, [GENERAL] HERIBERTO (1884–1968). He fought in many battles of the **Revolution of 1910**, often in his native **Veracruz state**. In 1914 he commanded naval cadets against US forces landed from USS *Dolphin*. He was a leader of the radicals in the **Constituent Assembly of 1916–1917**, responsible for most of the basic land, **labor**, and other social reforms written into the **Constitution of 1917**. He later served as a federal senator, then **governor** of Veracruz state, 1926–1930, and, in 1940–1946, **navy** minister, such an appointment of an **army** general causing widespread criticism in the press and the navy.

JARABE TAPATÍO. The Mexican hat dance, from **Jalisco**, the national folk dance of Mexico. A man in a **charro** suit and a woman in a **china poblana** dress dance with vigorous stomping, circling a large *sombrero*.

JARAMILLO, JUAN DE (14??–154??). Spanish captain who, on the urging of Hernán **Cortés**, married La **Malinche** in 1524, and returned to live with her in Spain. He came back to Mexico in 1526.

JARAMILLO, RUBÉN (1900–1962). Peasant organizer who had fought under Emiliano **Zapata** in 1913–1918. He began his organizing in the 1930s. From 1940 he led numerous groups of squatters, protesting the slowness of the distribution of nationalized farmlands. His headquarters were in Tlaquiltenango in his native **Morelos**, but his efforts ranged from **Baja California** to **Chiapas**. In 1958 he became loosely allied with Jacinto **López**, organizing temporary land seizures in northern states. He also received help from the **Movimiento de Liberación Nacional**. By then he had become the best-known symbol of peasant alienation in Mexico and the most effective rural critic of the **agrarian reform** program. Early in 1962 his squatters began occupying farms throughout central Morelos, including some belonging to State Governor Norberto López Avelar. Federal troops were called in when state forces proved inadequate. In a gunfight on May 23, an **army** captain kidnapped Jaramillo and his wife and later killed them as rebels, although neither was armed nor leading any guerrillas. In subsequent land seizures through the 1970s, no other squatters had the public impact of those led by Jaramillo in 1958–1962.

JARDÍN BOTÁNICO. *See* BOTANICAL GARDENS.

JAROCHO. A nickname for a resident of **Veracruz state**, often applied specifically to folk dancers and musical groups of men in white cotton trousers and jackets and peaked straw hats playing **bamba** music. The women dancers wear lace and embroidered white dresses and use white fans.

JECKER, JUAN B. (1810–1871). A Swiss who in 1859 negotiated a loan equivalent to US$ 15,000,000 to conservative elements in Mexico at a usurious rate. When Benito **Juárez** declared a moratorium on **foreign debts**, Jecker, now a French citizen, sought his government's help in securing repayment. This was the official reason for the subsequent **French intervention**.

JEFE MÁXIMO DE LA REVOLUCIÓN. "Supreme leader of the Revolution," a title given to Plutarco Elías **Calles**.

JEFE POLÍTICO. Term for an administrator at any level, introduced by the liberal **Spanish Constitution of 1812**, which was briefly restored in the **Spanish Revolution of 1820**, changing thereby the title of the **viceroy** to that of *Jefe Político Superior.*

JENKINS' EAR, WAR OF. *See* AUSTRIAN SUCCESSION, WAR OF.

JESUITS. The order was expelled from all Spain's domains in 1767 with some 2,600 brothers driven out from the whole of Spanish America, not without provoking popular rebellions in their support, as in **Guanajuato**. Soon afterwards the order was dissolved by the Vatican but survived in Russian-occupied Poland, protected by Catherine the Great. After the Napoleonic Wars Rome allowed it to be reconstituted and members were permitted to return to Mexico in the mid-19th century. They now run the **Universidad Iberoamericana**. *See also* ALEGRE, FRANCISCO JAVIER; CLAVIJERO, FRANCISCO JAVIER.

JEWS. Many Sephardic Jews who accepted baptism to avoid expulsion in the 1490s (*See* CONVERSO) settled in the New World in the (rather misplaced) hope of escaping the attentions of an ever-suspicious **Inquisition**. Other Jews (also mostly Sephardim) settled in a more tolerant Mexico after **Independence**, although the disruptions and civil disorder of the **Revolution of 1910** encouraged many of these to emigrate to **Cuba**. [L. H.]

JICOTÉNCAL. *See* XICOTÉNCATL.

JIMÉNEZ. City of **Tamaulipas** founded February 17, 1749, as the Villa de Santander de los Cinco Señores by José de **Escandón** and made the capital of **Nuevo Santander**.

JIMÉNEZ, JOSÉ MARIANO (1781–1811). An **independence** leader who fought with Miguel **Hidalgo y Costilla**. A mining engineer, born in **San Luís Potosí** city. Supervising canon manufacture was one of his main contributions to the cause. After Hidalgo was driven from

Guanajuato, Ignacio **Allende** ordered the now Lieutenant General Jiménez to begin **insurrections** in the north. He took **Saltillo** and **San Antonio**, Texas, but was captured at **Acatita de Baján** in March 1811 and executed by firing squad on July 26.

JIMÉNEZ, MIGUEL BERNAL (1910–1956). Composer of the symphonic suite *Michoacán* (1940), of *Noche en Morelia* (1941), and of the opera *Tata Vasco* (1941), based on the life of Vasco de **Quiroga**.

JIMÉNEZ CANTU, JORGE (1914–). Politician. A physician graduate of **UNAM**, he headed the National Commission for School Construction in the 1950s, was general manager of the **Compañía Nacional de Subsistencias Populares** from 1964–1969 (directing numerous programs for improvements in rural crop marketing), served as health and welfare minister from 1970–1976 (promoting **family planning** in provincial cities and towns), and **governor** of **Mexico state** from 1975–1981.

JIQUILPÁN. A tiny village in western **Michoacán**, birthplace of President Lázaro **Cárdenas del Río**.

JOAN. English form of **Juana**, as in Queen Joan the Mad (*Juana la Loca*, 1479–1555), elder sister to English Queen Catherine of Aragon and mother of the Emperor **Charles V** who began his reign as regent in her name, she having been considered incapacitated since 1505.

JOHN PAUL II, POPE (1920–2005). Only months after his accession (and on his first foreign trip), His Holiness (Karol Wojtyla) became the first Pope to visit Mexico, January 26–31, 1979, when he opened the third Latin American Conference of Bishops in **Puebla** and visited the shrine of St. **Mary of Guadalupe**, **México City**, **Monterrey**, **Guadalajara**, and **Oaxaca City**. He came again in August 1993 and made another five-day visit in 1999, conducting mass for 100,000 in Mexico City's Aztec Stadium on January 25, deploring the spread of **Protestantism** and the shortage of priests, while reiterating his opposition to the ordination of **women**. He made his fifth and last visit in July 2002.

JONGUITUD BARRIOS, CARLOS (1922–). Politician, prominent in the **Partido Revolucionario Institucional** since the 1960s, he served as senator from **Mexico state**, and in 1976 entered the cabinet as director of the **Instituto de Seguridad y Servicios Sociales de los Trabajadores del Estado**.

JORNADA, LA. Left-wing daily newspaper founded by Elena **Poniatowska**.

JOSEPH I (José I). Title adopted in Spain by Joseph **Bonaparte**.

JOURNALISM. Until the 1950s, journalists were mostly trained for newspaper or magazine work through trade schools entered after the tenth grade of public school. **UNAM** then created a journalism school, but few students graduated and even fewer found employment with major publications. The Carlos Septién García School of Journalism has been more successful. Founded in 1949, it is recognized by the **Education Ministry** as a degree-granting institution. It awards a licenciature (with the title *licenciado en periodismo*) after a university-level course and maintains an advisory board of editors from major **Mexico City** dailies. Broadcasting journalists mostly train at trade schools. *See also* CENSORSHIP; MEDIA; NEWSPAPERS; PRINTING; PUBLISHING AND THE BOOK TRADE; RADIO; TELEVISION.

JUAN CARLOS I, KING OF SPAIN (1938–). The king paid a state visit to Mexico in 1978.

JUAN RULFO PRIZE. Juan **Rulfo**'s memory has been honored in the **Guadalajara** International Book Fair's $100,000 literary prize given annually since 1991, open to all Latin American and Caribbean writers. In 2006, however, the novelist's heirs took legal action against the use of his name without their permission. The prize goes on, but its name may have to be changed.

JUANA INÉS DE LA CRUZ, SOR. (1651–1695). "The Tenth Muse," the most brilliant woman of colonial Latin America. Famed for her poetry (especially *Liras* and *Sueño*), she also possessed considerable knowledge of foreign languages, **astronomy**, **painting**, and mathematics. She entered the Convent of St. Jerome at age 18 and for the next 25 years concentrated on study and writing. She died of an epidemic disease caught while nursing other nuns. Her face appears on the current 200 **peso** bill.

JUÁREZ GARCÍA, BENITO PABLO (1806–1872). President of Mexico, 1858–1872. A full-blooded **Zapotec Indian**, born March 21 in the mountain village of San Pablo Guelatao, **Oaxaca**, he is held in the highest esteem in his country, which has bestowed on him the prestigious title *Benemérito de las Américas* ("Hero of the Americas"). He is regarded by many as its greatest statesman and politician. He lost both his parents at age three and was fostered by an uncle. At 12, still illiterate and knowing no Spanish, he was helped to study by a Franciscan who detected his outstanding scholastic aptitude. He originally planned to enter the priesthood but eventually decided to become a lawyer and enter public life. In 1831 he was elected to Oaxaca city council, became a state legislator, and in 1848 state governor. Exiled to New Orleans by López de **Santa Anna**, he returned to support the Plan de **Ayutla**, helped pass the **Reform Laws** (notably the **Ley Juárez**) and draft the **Constitution of 1857**, and was elected chief justice of the **Supreme Court**. He was arrested, however, by Félix **Zuloaga**. He managed to escape and became, in liberal eyes, president as the constitutional successor of the deposed Ignacio **Comonfort**, but he only took effective power with the Battle of **San Miguel Calpulalpan**. Forced to leave **Mexico City** by the **French intervention**, he established his government successively at San Luis **Potosí**, **Chihuahua**, and El **Paso del Norte** (now **Ciudad Juárez**) and continued to enjoy **United States** recognition and support. When France withdrew its military support of **Maximilian**, Juárez's forces were able to capture and execute him. Having already served a nominal two terms, Juárez campaigned successfully for reelection in October 1867 and for a fourth term in 1871, dying in office of a heart attack on July 19 the following year.

His fondest ideal was that people should be governed by laws, not the whims of the powerful: *El respecto al derecho ajeno es la paz y la democracia es primero* ("Respect for the rights of others is the basis of peace, and democracy is foremost"). He practiced honesty in government and always insisted on it in others, but his respect for the democratic process sometimes took on an exaggerated form, considering its evolutionary state in Mexico at the time, and he would allow the legislature long periods of debate over issues which he should have insisted be resolved in much less time.

Ironically, the socialist father of the Italian fascist leader Mussolini was to christen his son Benito in admiration at Juárez' judicial murder of the former ruler of Austrian-occupied northern Italy.

JUICIO DE AMPARO. *See* AMPARO.

JUNTA CENTRAL (*Junta Suprema Cental Gubernativa*). The council, based eventually in Cádiz, that sought to coordinate the fight against the puppet regime of Joseph **Bonaparte** in Spain, until January 1810 when it transferred its authority to a Regency Council. It summoned a parliament for the entire Spanish empire, the **Cortes of Cádiz.**

JUNTA DE GOBIERNO. A committee, usually of three, who provide an interim government in times of emergency, as in the period following the end of the **First Empire** and that led by Pedro **Vélez** in the last week of December, 1829.

JUNTA DE MÉXICO. Throughout the Spanish empire, the immediate reaction to the enforced abdication of **Ferdinand VII** was to set up *ad hoc* committees to govern in his name. That in **Mexico City** was among those suspected of really seeking **independence** from **Spain** and, despite support from the **Viceroy** José de **Iturrigaray** (who miscalcuated the balance of forces), was soon overthrown by the **Peninsular** interest.

JUNTA DE NOTABLES ("Council of Worthies"). The group of Mexican conservatives that offered the imperial crown to the Austrian Archduke **Maximilian** in French-occupied **Mexico City** in 1863. It included high **Church** dignitaries unhappy at the anti-clerical **Constitution of 1857**. *See also* FRENCH INTERVENTION; SALIGNY, DUBOIS.

JUNTA FEDERAL DE CONCILIACIÓN Y ARBITRAJE. *See* FEDERAL CONCILIATION AND ARBITRATION BOARD.

JUNTA MEXICANA. *See* JUNTA DE MÉXICO.

JUNTA NACIONAL AMERICANA. Rebel government established August 19, 1811, at Zitácuaro in eastern **Michoacán** by Ignacio **López Rayón** who became its *"Ministro universal de la nación."*

JUNTA SUPERIOR DE GOBIERNO Y REGENCIA DEL IMPERIO. The Imperial Regency Council governed Mexico from June 18, 1863, until May 20, 1864, when power devolved on the Emperor **Maximilian**'s Lieutenant Juan Nepomuceno **Almonte**.

JUSTICE. Mexico has no separate ministry of justice; its role is performed by the *Subsecretaría de Asuntos Jurídicos y Derechos Humanos* of the **Interior Ministry**. *See also* COURTS; LAW. [L. H.]

JUZGADO GENERAL DE INDIOS. A special court established in 1573 to help the **Indians**, who could appear before it to denounce abuses committed against them by Spaniards and others in authority. It was a good example of the Spanish crown's sincere efforts to eliminate exploitation of its Indian subjects.

– K –

K. This letter is superfluous in normal Spanish, where it is usually replaced by *c* or *qu*, except for such international abbreviations as "kg" (*quilograma*), "km" (*quilometro*), and "kph" (kilometers per hour), in foreign names, and in transcribing, or transliterating, from **Maya**, **Nahuatl**, and other **Indian** languages. [L. H.]

KAHLO, FRIDA (originally Frieda) (1907–1954). Mexico's most famous woman artist, and an icon of feminism. Born in **Coyoacán** to a Hungarian Jewish photographer and his **mestizo** wife, she was severely crippled by polio in 1910 and was almost killed in a bus crash in 1925 which left her unable to bear children and affected her health for the rest of her life. She is best known for her striking self portraits. Triumph and pain, and the harshness of life, her own and that of **women** in general, form a constant theme of her brightly colored paintings, many of which are self portraits. Although the French communist surrealist painter André Breton claimed the credit for "discovering" her internationally, she rejected the label "surrealist" for her own work. Greatly influenced by pre-Columbian and folk art, her paintings embody *Mexicanidad*: the national pride that pulsed through Mexico in the post-Revolution era and has greatly influenced *Chicana* artists since. She met her husband, Diego **Rivera** (whom she accused of borrowing her ideas without ever giving her the credit), when she joined the **Partido Comunista Mexicana** in 1928. She became his model, and they married in 1929. Her house in Coyoacán is now a museum of her life and work. Since the mid-1970s, she has been a rolemodel for women in the Mexican-American and feminist communities. Frida Kahlo is honored on a 34-cent US postage stamp of 2001, and her life has inspired two novels in English. [L. H.]

KENNA, HURRICANE. A category 5 Pacific hurricane, the strongest for decades, passed offshore of **Puerto Vallarta**, hit the coast at **San Blas**, and dissipated over land in northeast Mexico, October 15, 2002.

KIKAPÚ (or KICKAPOO). Indian group numbering some 200 in 1995, living in **Coahuila** state.

KING, EDWARD, VISCOUNT KINGSBOROUGH (1795–1837). An Irish nobleman whose enthusiasm for Mexican antiquities led to his death in a Dublin debtors' prison, unable to pay for the completion of his lavishly produced collection of **codices**, *Antiquities of Mexico*, 1830–1848.

KINGS OF SPAIN. During Mexico's colonial period, these were House of Habsburg (*Casa de Austria*):

> Charles V (*Carlos I*), 1520–1556, but reigning in Spain from 1516, although as regent for his mother, **Joan** the Mad;
> Philip II (*Felipe II*), 1556–1598;
> Philip III (*Felipe III*), 1598–1621;

Philip IV (*Felipe IV*), 1621–1665;
Charles II (*Carlos II*), 1665–1700, "the Bewitched."

House of Bourbon (*Casa de Borbón*):
Philip V (*Felipe V*), 1700–1746;
Ferdinand VI (*Fernando VI*), 1746–1759;
Charles III (*Carlos III*), 1759–1788;
Charles IV (*Carlos IV*), 1788–1808;
Ferdinand VII (*Fernando VII*), March–May, 1808.

House of Bonaparte:
Joseph **Bonaparte** (*José I*), 1808–1814.

House of Bourbon, restored:
Ferdinand VII (*Fernando VII*), 1814–1821, but reigning in Spain
until 1833.

KINO, [PADRE] EUSEBIO FRANCISCO (1645–1711). Early
explorer of **California**. A Spanish Jesuit, he founded settlements,
missions, and churches in **Sonora**, 1687–1700, including the mission
of **San Xavier del Bac**. He is buried in the principal church of the
city of **Magdalena de Kino**, in northern Sonora.

KINSHIP. Among **Indian** groups and rural and small-town **mestizo**
societies, kinship plays a vital social and political role. Elaborate distinctions are made for first, second, and more remote cousins, and for
paternal and maternal in-laws. Biological and marital relationships
are supplemented by the ritual kinship of **compadrazgo**. *See also*
FAMILIES.

KUKULCÁN. Maya name for the god known to the Aztecs as **Quetzalcóatl**.

– **L** –

LA ("the"). For Hispanic words and names beginning with the definite
article, see under the following element (e.g., MADRID, MIGUEL
DE LA).

LABASTIDA, JAIME (1939–). Writer from Los Mochis, **Sinaloa**,
and a **UNAM** philosophy graduate. He has contributed essays and

short stories to the *Revista mexicana de literatura* and most other leading Mexican magazines. In 1960 he published the anthology *La Espiga amontinada*.

LABASTIDA OCHOA, FRANCISCO (1942–). Partido Revolucionario Institucional candidate for the July 2, 2000, presidential election. He lost, ending the PRI's 71-year-long hold on the presidency. Born in Los Mochis, **Sinaloa**, August 14, he graduated in economics in 1964 from **UNAM**, where he taught. He did graduate work at the **Economic Commission for Latin America** and served in the **Finance Ministry** as an analyst, 1962–1963, becoming active in the PRI in 1964. He headed the automobile transportation office in the **Transport Ministry** in 1966–1967 and returned to the Finance Ministry as fiscal director in 1976–1979. He was minister of energy and mines in 1982–1986, ambassador to Portugal in 1993–1994, **agriculture** minister from January 23, 1995–January 3, 1998, and then interior minister, resigning in May 1999 to run for president. He is married to María Uriarte de Labastida, who holds a PhD in art history from UNAM, and he has co-authored *Planeación para el desarrollo*.

LABNÁ. Maya ruins in **Yucatán state**.

LABOR. *See* AFRICAN SLAVERY; AGRICULTURAL LABOR; EMPLOYMENT; ENCOMIENDA; INCOME DISTRIBUTION; INFORMAL ECONOMY; LABOR MINISTRY; MAY DAY; MINIMUM WAGE; REDUCCIÓN; TRADE UNIONS.

LABOR MINISTRY (*Secretaría de Trabajo y Previsión Social—* STPS). Originating in 1911, as the Department of Labor within the Ministry of Development and Industry (*See* TRADE MINISTRY), it did not become a separate ministry until 1932 and only added "social insurance" to its title in 1940. It enforces the labor code, all federal, state, and local labor laws, and oversees labor-management relations. It administers federal conciliation and arbitration boards, the National **Minimum Wage** Commission, (*Comisión Nacional de Salarios Mínimos*), and the **Comité Nacional de Reparto de Utilidades**.

LABOR UNIONS. *See* TRADE UNIONS.

LABRA GARCÍA, WENCESLAO (1896–1974). Politician from Zumpango, **México State**, who served three terms in the **Cámara de Diputados Federales**, and was a senator, 1934–1971, and governor of his home state, 1937–1941. He was a longtime member of the **Comité Ejecutivo Nacional** of the **Partido Revolucionario Institucional**, and its secretary for organization and statistics. In 1936 he was a founder of the **Confederación Nacional Campesina**.

LACANDÓN. A Mayan **Indian** group in the **Usumacinta** River Valley of **Chiapas** state, which has remained relatively isolated from Mexican culture and preserves its **Maya** dialect. Short in stature, Lacandlons wear their hair long and loose, and they supplement some basic **agriculture** with hunting. They numbered about 500 in 1978 and only 300 in 1995. A private museum in **San Cristóbal de las Casas** preserves their history from pre-Hispanic times.

LAGOS CHÁZARO, FRANCISCO (1879–1932). Briefly the (nominal) president of Mexico, June 6–October 10, 1915.

LAJOUS, ADRIAN. Director general of **Pemex**, appointed December 1994. An economist trained at Cambridge University, England, he cut operational duplications, and ended extortion in **Tabasco state**. When thousands of wells had been drilled there in the 1970s and 1980s, local politicians, with the connivance of Pemex officials, had persuaded the peasants whose land had been ruined to block access. These same politicians then collected bribes from Pemex for getting the peasants to end the blockade. Lajous ended these payments suddenly and completely. He shrank the workforce from 230,000 in 1988 (the result of **corruption** under Joaquín **Hernández**'s domination of the oil workers' union) to 130,000 in 1998.

LAKES. *See* HYDROGRAPHY.

LÁNCASTER NOROÑA Y SILVA, FERNANDO DE, DUQUE DE LINARES, MARQUÉS DE VALDEFUENTES (1640–1717). **Viceroy** of **New Spain**, 1711–1716. Also referred to as "Alencastre," he strove to suppress **corruption** and **contraband** (he built a frigate for **coast guard** purposes), and rebuilt the palace of the **Mexico City**

ayuntamiento, leaving with a high record of achievement despite his age. [L. H.]

LAND LAW OF 1883. The law, designed to encourage foreign settlement of rural Mexico, allowed the chartering of surveying companies who were empowered to survey public land (understood as including all land for which no written title could be produced) for subdivision and settlement, with the right to a third of all land surveyed. In 1894, after thus acquiring one fifth of the total land mass of Mexico (and selling most of it in large blocks to **hacienda** owners), the companies secured changes in the law that were even more favorable to them.

LAND REFORM. *See* AGRARIAN REFORM.

LANDA, DIEGO DE (1514–1579). Spanish bishop, responsible for converting the **Maya**. His *Relación de las cosas de Yucatán*, the earliest description of **Maya** civilization, remains a classic to this day. Unfortunately his burning of Mayan **codices** (manuscripts) destroyed almost all primary sources on the subject.

LANZ DURET, FERNANDO (1916–). An attorney from **Campeche** who became a writer for *El Universal* and Mexico's leading war correspondent in 1942–1945, chronicling Mexico's participation in **World War II**. He sat in the **Cámara de Diputados Federales** in the 1950s and in the Senate in 1958–1964.

LARA, AUGUSTÍN (1900?–1970). Composer of the hit song *Granada* and first husband of María **Félix**.

LAREDO, TEXAS. United States border town across the **Rio Grande** from **Nuevo Laredo**, founded in May 15, 1755, as a post on the highway to **San Antonio**, *San Agustín de Laredo* (named by José de **Escandón** for Laredo, a town near his native Santander in Spain). Laredo suffered a serious attack by Comanches and Apaches in 1821. The population was 800 in 1789; 3.512 in 1880; 11,319 in 1890; 122,899 in 1990.

LAS ("the"). For words and names beginning with the definite article, see under following element (e.g., CASAS, Bartolomé de las).

LASCURÁIN PAREDES, PEDRO (1858–1952). Foreign minister to President Francisco **Madero**, whom he succeeded at 22:24 hrs, February 18, 1913, only to resign in favor of Victoriano **Huerta** at 23:20 hrs.

LATIFUNDIA. Spanish rule in Mexico, as in most other parts of the Americas, created a pattern of very large estates, *haciendas*, monopolizing the ownership of all good land, but often administered by the agents of an absentee landlord (**hacendado**) living in **Mexico City** or Europe. **Agrarian reform** (i.e., the distribution of such **hacienda** land to the peasants) was a major program of the **Revolution of 1910**.

LATIN AMERICAN FREE TRADE ASSOCIATION (LAFTA). In Spanish, the *Asociación Latinoamericana de Libre Comercio* (ALALC). Set up in April 1961 following the 1960 Treaty of Montevideo, of which Mexico was a signatory, it was replaced in 1980 by the **Asociación Latinoamericana de Integración**. *See also* GÓMEZ GÓMEZ, RODRIGO; MARTÍNEZ BÁEZ, ANTONIO.

LATIN AMERICAN TOWER. *See* TORRE LATINOAMERICANO.

LAVALLE URBINA, MANUELA (1908–1996). An attorney from **Campeche** who became the first woman to be made a federal judge. She presided over the high court (*Tribunal Superior*) of the **Federal District**, 1947–1952, directed social welfare for the **Interior Ministry**, 1952–1963, and was a senator, 1964–1970.

LAW, THE. When the Spanish came to Mexico in 1521, they brought with them a legal system (the *Sete Paribas* of 1250) based on Roman law, modified by medieval conceptions of Christian morality and equity, which affected particularly the law of matrimony, seen as a holy sacrament, and that of money-lending, castigated as usury. Roman law tried to prescribe for every conceivable human action that might be subject to legal sanction, leaving little room for judicial initiative. The task of the judge was merely to find the correct legal prescription to fit the particular case being heard. Some trials were assigned a jury, especially when the case involved a serious crime, and the burden of proof was on the prosecution. All accused were entitled to legal representation, even if the state had to provide it, but no release on bail was permitted for serious charges if apprehended "red handed," a powerful incentive for errant drivers to flee the scene of any road accident.

To cope with the special situation of the Americas, Spain made piecemeal adaptations that were eventually codified as the **Laws of the Indies** in 1680, but further modifications due to the great economic and political changes of the 18th century left the law badly in need of codification again. The **supreme court** throughout the colonial period was the **Audience**.

Despite new codifications since **independence**, customary law still has currency in some Indian communities. *See also* ADMINISTRATIVE LAW; AMPERE; CIVIL CODE; FUEGO; LEGAL EDUCATION; PENAL CODE. [L. H.]

LAW COURTS. *See* AUDIENCIA; SUPREME COURT.

LAWRENCE, DAVID HERBERT (1885–1930). The English novelist's visit in the 1920s resulted in his *Mornings in Mexico*, a collection of descriptive essays, and *The Plumed Serpent*. [L. H.]

LAWS OF THE INDIES. The legislation resulting from the Spanish conquest of the New World was codified in 1512–1513, in 1542, and again in 1680, with a 3-volume supplement in 1791. A complete revision in 12 volumes, the *Nova recopilación* was begun in 1805, but it was still unfinished when Mexico became independent. [L. H.]

LAWS OF THE REFORM. *See* REFORM LAWS.

LÁZARO CÁRDENAS. Locality of **Michoacán** currently being developed as a major container port.

LAZO BARREIRO, CARLOS (1914–1955). The architect of **UNAM**'s new campus, built in 1949–1952, 18 km (11 miles) from downtown **Mexico City**. He was a professor of architecture at UNAM, 1943–1955.

LEAD. Mexico is the world's fifth largest producer of lead.

LEAGUE OF NATIONS. Mexico was a member of this post-**World War I** predecessor of the **United Nations**.

LEGAL EDUCATION. The longest established law school is that of **UNAM** (formerly the *Escuela Nacional de Derecho*). The most prestigious is probably the independent **Escuela Libre de Derecho**.

LEIVA, JUAN DE (1604–c.1678). Juan de Leyva y de la Cuerda, marqués de Leyva and conde de Baños, **Viceroy** of **New Spain**, 1660–1664. His viceroyalty has been characterized by woeful economic policies and a mistreatment of his subordinates. On returning to Spain, he entered a Carmelite convent in Pastrana, where he died. [L. H.]

LEÑERO, VICENTE (1933–). Novelist (*Los albañiles*, 1963), and playwright (*Martirio de Morales*, 1981).

LEÓN ("lion"). (1) A northern Spanish city and a medieval kingdom, constituent of the union of Castile and Leon (*"A Castilla y a León, Nuevo Mundo dió Colón"*), joined in 1516 with Aragon as the united kingdom "of the Spains." It inspired the name of **New Spain**'s "kingdom" of **Nuevo León**, and of several cities throughout the Americas.

(2) An industrial city of central Mexico in the state of **Guanajuato**, 400 km (250 miles) northwest of **Mexico City**, at 1770 m (5,800 ft.) above sea level, officially *León de los Aldama*. Founded in 1576, it is a center for marketing cattle and hides and manufacturing leather goods, having the largest output of shoes in Latin America. In 1978 its over 600 tanneries and shoe factories produced 200,000 pairs a day: its 1995 production was 1,100,000 pairs. It also makes electronic goods, plastics, and textiles. The population was 413,799 at the 2000 census.

(3) A city and former capital of Nicaragua, whence the name of the *comandancia general* of León (Nicaragua, Costa Rica, and El Salvador) within Mexico's short-lived **First Empire**.

LEÓN, LUIS L. (1891–1991). Agriculture minister under President Elías Plutarco **Calles**.

LEÓN, NICOLAS (1859–1929). Physician, teacher, and historian from **Michoacán**. He practiced medicine only briefly, later working as a museum curator, ethnologist, and anthropologist, and in many other professions. His hundreds of works include *Hombres ilustres y escritores michoacanos* and *Tradiciones y leyends piadosas de México*.

LEÓN DE LA BARRA, FRANCISCO (1863–1939). Catholic leader and politician, Porfirio **Díaz**'s last foreign minister who became interim president of Mexico between the resignations of Diaz and his Vice president Ramón **Corral** on May 25, 1911, and the accession of Francisco I. **Madero** on November 6.

LEÓN MURILLO, MAXIMILIANO (1925–). A secondary and preparatory school teacher from **Michoacán** who became a leader of the **Partido Popular Socialista**. As a PPS deputy in Congress in 1970–1973, he helped the **Partido Revolucionario Institucional** draft key **petroleum**, **labor**, and **television** legislation.

LEÓN TORAL, JOSÉ DE (????–1928). Participant in the **Cristero Rebellion**, he murdered Álvaro **Obregón**, while he was having breakfast in a **Mexico City** restaurant on July 17, 1928.

LEÓN Y GAMA, ANTONIO (1735–1802). A self-educated mathematician, physicist, and astronomer who was born and died in **Mexico City**. The subjects of his scholarly papers ranged from medicine to a study of the moons of Jupiter.

LEPERO. A slang term applied to someone who is uncouth and vulgar (or, in the many jokes of which a *lepero* is the butt, merely stupid).

LEPROSY. Hanson's disease, this disfiguring and chronic affliction was introduced in its diffuse form by the Spanish **conquest of Mexico**. Hernán **Cortes** himself founded the Hospital of St. Lazarus (1528–1927). Later, the **Manila Galleon** would bring the nodular form from the **Philippines**. The first statistics, for 1927, indicate 1,450 cases, **Guanajuato** being the most affected state. Although the total was still 1,470 in 2001 (in a much larger national **population**), this was less than that of any country of the Americas except for Canada, the **United States**, **Guatemala**, **Belize**, and Chile. There is little reason to fear the disease is being spread into the US through Mexican **immigration**. [L. H.]

LERDO DE TEJADA, MIGUEL (1812–1861). Liberal politician, finance minister, 1855–1859, a justice of the **Supreme Court**, and author of the **Ley Lerdo**.

LERDO DE TEJADA [Y CORRAL], SEBASTIÁN (1825–1889). President of Mexico, 1872–1876. A liberal who was foreign minister under Benito **Juárez**. He became chief justice of the **Supreme Court** and therefore Juárez's constitutional successor. His administration restored diplomatic relations with **France**, undertook tariff and **taxation** reform and significant school and railroad construction, and amended the **Constitution of 1857**, restoring the Senate. Lerdo was successful in the presidential election of October 1872; but when he sought reelection in 1876, Porfirio **Díaz** issued his Plan de **Tuxtepec** and rose in revolt. Lerdo fled into exile in New York City where he died.

LERMA, RIVER. Flows through **Jalisco** to Lake **Chalapa**.

LETRÁN, COLEGIO DE. *See* COLEGIO DE LETRÁN.

LETRAS LIBRES. Monthly literary magazine, inspired by *Plural*, and *Vuelta*, published in Mexico City and Madrid editions since January 1999. [L. H.]

LEUCAENA (Spanish *guaje*). A native of Mexican and Central American lowlands now widely grown abroad, one of the few woody tropical legumes that is very digestible and of low toxicity. The plant can be a shade tree, windbreak, stabilizing hedge, or source of green manure. Its trunk provides timber, poles, postwood, fuel, cellulose pulp, and charcoal. Its foliage and seed provide fodder, human food, and tea. Its gum can substitute for gum arabic. The toxins that make it unsuitable for non-ruminant livestock can be extracted and used to make fungicides and insecticides. [L. H.]

LEVA. Recruitment, largely of the poor and uneducated (but excluding unacculturated rural **Indians**), for military service, as arbitrary and brutal as the 18th century press gang system of the British royal navy. [L. H.]

LEY DE FUGA ("law against flight"). The right of the **police** or other authority to shoot dead someone trying to escape from arrest or imprisonment, notoriously used by the **rurales** to give legal cover to the murder of detainees. Often a cell door would be left open in the hope that the detainee would try to walk out.

LEY IGLESIAS. One of the **Reform Laws** of 1857, it removed cemeteries from the control of the **Church**.

LEY JUÁREZ. The first and most significant of the **Reform Laws**, authored by Benito Pablo **Juárez García**, severely limiting the power of the military and **Church** courts (*See* FUEGO), a major cause of the **War of the Reforms**.

LEY LERDO. Law of 1856, drafted by Miguel **Lerdo de Tejada**, which limited **Church** land ownership to that needed for its day-to-day operations.

LEYVA VELÁSQUEZ, GABRIEL (1896–1985). Politician from Humayes, **Sinaloa**. As a young officer under General Álvaro **Obregón**, he fought in the battles of 1911–1920. His father was a close friend of Francisco Ibdalecio **Madero**, and most of his relatives were precursors of the **Revolution of 1910**. He was acting governor of Sinaloa, 1935–1937; a member of the **Cámara de Diputados Federales**, 1937–1940; and a senator, 1940–1946 and 1970–1976. When elected governor of Sinaloa in 1957, he was a dominant member of the **Comité Ejecutivo Nacional** of the **Partido Revolucionario Institucional**. During his term (through 1962) he ended long-term attempts of squatters to take over unfarmed lands, even though he had been secretary general of the **Confederación Nacional Campesina**.

LIBERAL PARTY. *See* PARTIDO LIBERAL.

LIFE EXPECTANCY. A falling **birthrate** and public health improvements have increased life expectancy at birth from 45 years in 1940 to 65 years in 1980, 71 years in 2000, and 75.4 in 2006 (78.3 for females, 72.6 for males).

LIKE WATER FOR CHOCOLATE. English title of the best-selling novel *Como agua para chocolate* by Laura **Esquivel** and of the motion picture based upon it.

LIMANTOUR, JOSÉ YVES (1854–1935). French-born politician who was undersecretary of finance and then finance minister (1892–1910), during the later **Porfiriato**. A leader of the **científicos**, he instituted many reforms, such as nationalizing the **railroads**, abolishing the **alcabala**, and lowering many import duties. He took Mexico onto the **gold standard**, paid off in 1890 the last of Mexico's debt to the **United States**, and so improved the country's international financial standing that he was able to negotiate foreign loans at interest rates of only 4 percent. Unlike many of his fellow politicians of the period, he was an honest and able administrator. The **Revolution of 1910**, however, forced him into exile in Paris, where he died.

LIMAR ASPEREZAS ("smooth over differences"). A phrase used by cliques within Mexican political parties when they negotiate a compromise without losing face in public controversy.

LIMITS, TREATY OF, 1820. Agreement between **Spain** and the **United States** confirming the 1819 sale of Florida and the acceptance of the River Platte as Mexico's northern border.

LIMÓN ROJAS, MIGUEL (1943–). Education minister, 1994–2000. Born in **Mexico City** on December 17, he graduated in law from **UNAM** with highest honors, did graduate work at the Université d'Aix in Marseilles, France, and then taught law, first at UNAM and then at the **Universidad Autónoma Metropolitana**, where he became director of Social Sciences and Humanities. In 1983–1988 he was director general of the **Instituto Nacional Indígena** where he modernized some federal programs to help **Indians** gain access to **secondary education**. In 1988–1994 he was undersecretary for population and migratory services in the **Interior Ministry** and became education minister in December 1994. In

1999 he developed a plan to orient teachers in the use of computers in teaching.

Within the **Partido Revolucionario Institucional** he has served as subdirector of social studies in the **Instituto de Estudios Políticos, Economicos y Sociales** and as president of the National Forum of Professional and Technical Specialists.

He represents Mexico from time to time on the **United Nations'** Commission for the Prevention of Discrimination against Ethnic Minorities. In 1998 he became president of the Mexican branch of the International Development Society.

LINARES. Early name of the diocese of Nueva León, now the archdiocese of **Monterrey**.

LINDBERGH, ANNE MORROW (1906–2001). Writer, daughter of financier-ambassador Dwight **Morrow**, wife of aviator Charles Lindbergh (whom she met at a diplomatic reception in **Mexico City**), and herself a pilot.

LITERACY. The literacy rate among Mexicans grew from 17.9 percent of the total **population** in 1895 to 22.3 percent of those over 12 years of age in 1900 and to 33.9 percent of those over 10 in 1921. Figures since then are of percentages of those over 15 years of age: 38.5 in 1930, 46.0 in 1940, 56.8 in 1950, 66.5 in 1960, 74.2 in 1970, 83.0 in 1980, 87.4 in 1990, 89.3 in 1995, 90.5 in 2000, and 92.2 in 2003 (94 percent of males, 90.5 percent of females).

LITERARY MAGAZINES. *See CONTEMPORÁNEOS; HIJO PRODIGO; LETRAS LIBRES; NEXOS; PLURAL; REVISTA MEXICANA DE LITERATURA; TALLER; VUELTA.*

LITERATURE. *See* CODICES; DRAMA; NOVELS; POETRY.

LIVAS VILLARREAL, EDUARDO (1911–1991). Politician born January 21 in **Monterrey**, where he graduated from the city law school in 1933. He was a member of the organization founding the **Universidad de Nuevo León** in 1933 and was a long-time member of its board of regents. As a senator in 1958–1961 he led the congressional campaign to expropriate the electric power companies. As governor of **Nuevo León** from 1961–1967 he ended the recurrent strikes and unrest at the University.

LIVESTOCK. Just as *carne* ("meat") normally means beef, so *ganadería* ("livestock rearing") normally refers to that of bovine cattle, the technique of raising of which was a major Spanish contribution to the economy of the New World, and not least to that of those parts of Mexico that were annexed by the **United States** in 1835–1848. **Sheep farming**, swine, and poultry were also introduced by the Spaniards, but they have never achieved an equivalent cultural (or economic) significance. [L. H.]

LIZANA Y BEAUMONT, FRANCISCO JAVIER DE (1750–1811). Viceroy of **New Spain**, 1809–1810. Professor in the universities of Alcalá and Zamora and bishop of Zamora and Teruel, he was appointed archbishop of **Mexico** in 1803, where he arrived in January 1804. The **Junta Central** of Cadiz appointed him viceroy to replace Pedro **Garibay**. He handed over his archiepiscopal duties to Chief Inquisitor Juan Alfaro and took up his new office in September 1808, promptly arousing the hostility of the *peninsulares* by his readiness to fill offices with *americanos* and his refusal to proceed against those who were openly seeking **independence**. This led the **audiencia** to demand his resignation, secured on May 9, 1809. He resumed his duties as archbishop and died in **Mexico City**.

LLORONA, LA ("weeping woman"). Nationally popular folksong from the **Tehuantepec Isthmus**, often played at wedding receptions and engagement parties.

LOBO MORALES, HUMBERTO (1945–). Director of the employers' association of his native **Nuevo León**, assistant manager of Sada enterprises and managing director of Protexa Industries, both in **Monterrey**, local representative of Herreria Vulcano, and board member of the Banco Mercantil de Monterrey and of the Banco General de Monterrey.

LOCAL GOVERNMENT. *See* AYUNTAMIENTO; CABILDO; CUARTÓN; DELEGACIÓN; DEPARTAMENTO; FEDERAL DISTRICT; INTENDANCY; MUNICIPIO; PARTIDO; STATES.

LOMBARDINI, [GENERAL] MANUEL MARÍA (1802–1853). President of Mexico, February to April 1853, when he handed over his office to Antonio López de **Santa Anna**, whom he had always strongly supported. He died the following December.

LOMBARDO TOLEDANO, VICENTE (1894–1968). Mexico's best known socialist and most successful Marxist. Born in Teziutlán, **Puebla**, in 1919, he graduated in law from the **UNAM**, where he taught until 1933. He was a member of the Mexican Labor Party, 1921–1932; was acting governor of **Puebla**, 1923; a councilman in the **Federal District**, 1924–5; member of the **Cámara de Diputados Federales**, 1926–1928 (for the Labor Party) and again, 1964–1967 (for the **Partido Popular Socialista**); organizer and secretary general of the **Confederación de Trabajadores Mexicanos**, 1936–1940; president of the Moscow-oriented Latin American Federation of Workers (*Confederación de Trabajadores de América Latina*), 1938–1963; secretary general of the Mexican Socialist League (*Liga Socialista Mexicana*), 1944–1945. He joined the **Partido Revolucionario Mexicano** and worked within it and its successor, the **Partido Revolucionario Institucional** until he founded the **Partido Popular** (the future **Partido Popular Socialista**) in 1948. He was PPS presidential candidate in the **election of 1952**, and although unsuccessful, helped establish PPS strength in a few states, such as **Nayarit**, in some congressional districts, and in scattered local governments. In 1963 he founded the **Confederación Campesina Independiente**, which challenged the pro-government **Confederación Nacional Campesina** until coopted in 1970.

LONA REYES, ARTURO (1925–). Prelate. Born November 1, in **Aguascalientes**, he was ordained in 1952, headed the Catholic seminary in Aguascalientes, and was made Bishop of **Tehuantepec** in 1971. His is noted for his active campaign to help the poor and to work with peasant organizations to better their communities.

LONDON CONVENTION. Agreement reached by **France**, **Spain**, and the **United Kingdom**, October 31, 1861, for a joint occupation of the **Veracruz** custom house to collect import duties to pay the amounts that the **foreign debt moratorium** was withholding. Faced with **Napoleon III**'s plans for a wider, politically motivated **French intervention**, the other powers withdrew in the early spring of 1862 and negotiated with Mexico a separate Convención de **Soledad**.

LONG BEACH, CA. At 35°48'N, 118°09'W, this southern **California** community was first settled from Mexico in 1784. It is now a major port with 490,166 inhabitants in 2006, but it has become virtually a suburb of **Los Angeles**, 30 km (20 miles) to the north. [L. H.]

LONGORÍA KOWALSKY, EDUARDO. Nephew of Octaviano **Longoría Theriot**, a senior member of the board of the Banco de Londres y México, and a major stockholder in many Longoría enterprises, helping make his family one of the wealthiest in Mexico.

LONGORÍA PENN, OCTAVIANO. Son of Octaviano **Longoría Theriot**, he is the manager of the Banco Longoría chain. His wife, Josefina, is daughter to Antonio L. Rodríguez.

LONGORÍA THERIOT, OCTAVIANO (1905–1986). "Chito" Longoría, businessman from **Nuevo Laredo**, claimed kinship by marriage to Francisco I. **Madero**. Born March 23, he graduated from Peacock Military Academy in **San Antonio**, **Texas**, and attended the junior college of Pearce School, Philadelphia. He became president of the Banco Longoría in 1932; then president of Empresas Longoría; president of Banco Continental; a board member of the **Banco de Comercio** (Bancomer) national chain of banks; with interests in a variety of enterprises from pharmaceuticas to transportation. In 1974 he became a founding member of the Mexican Council of Businessmen. His first wife was the late Alice Penn; his second is Jeanette Hermann of San Antonio. His daughter Sara Alicia married Eduardo Brittingham.

LÓPEZ, JACINTO (1906–1971). Leader of the **Unión General de Obreros y Campesinos de México**, and associate of Rubén **Jaramillo**.

LÓPEZ DE LEGAZPI, MIGUEL. Adelantado, leader of the expedition from **New Spain** that captured Manila, future capital of the **Philippines**, in 1571.

LÓPEZ DE SANTA ANNA, ANTONIO. *See* SANTA ANNA, ANTONIO LÓPEZ DE.

LÓPEZ MATEOS, ADOLFO (1910–1969). President of Mexico from 1958–1964. Ideologically a centrist, he was generally popular and succeeded in guiding Mexico through the shock waves of the Cuban Revolution of 1959 (*See* CUBA, RELATIONS WITH). He accomplished more in **agrarian reform** than any president since **Cárdenas del Río**. It was through his efforts that Mexico opened important new trade links with the Far East and became a member of the **Asociación Latinoamericana de Libre Comercio (LAFTA)**. His administration made **education** the largest item in the budget. Thousands of schools were built, teachers received pay incentives for working in rural areas, an adult literacy campaign was begun, and government-approved textbooks were distributed gratis to public school children. Public health campaigns in rural areas significantly reduced tuberculosis, polio, and malaria. One of his government's most popular, but relatively minor, accomplishments was the recovery of the **Chamizal** area of disputed sovereignty.

LÓPEZ NOGALES, ARMANDO (1950–). Elected **Partido Revolucionario Institucional** governor of **Sonora** in 1997.

LÓPEZ OBRADOR, ANDRÉS MANUEL (1953–). Politician known as AMLO and as *El Peje*, he was active in the **Partido Revolucionario Institucional** in his native **Tabasco** before joining the **Partido de la Revolución Democrática** in 1994. His being beaten bloody by the **police** while protesting for Indian rights probably helped his rise within the party, which he led in 1996–1999, serving as mayor of **Mexico City** from 2000–2005, and, despite running unsuccessfully for president in the **election of 2006**, formally proclaimed himself "president" at a mass meeting in the **Zócalo** on November 20th, the anniversary of the **Revolution of 1910**. His supporters' efforts, however, to physically prevent **Calderón**'s inauguration on December 1 were a dramatic failure. [L. H.]

LÓPEZ PACHECO [CABRERA Y BOBADILLA], DIEGO, DUKE OF ESCALONA, MARQUIS OF VILLENA AND MOYA, COUNT OF XIQUENA AND SAN ESTEBAN DE GORMAZ (1599–1645). Viceroy of New Spain from 1640–1642 and the first grandee of Spain to be receive such an appointment. This ended when the Bishop of **Puebla** had him imprisoned for supposed collaboration with the Portuguese who were then fighting a war of independence to end their 60 year "union of crowns" with Spain. He was cleared but when King Philip IV offered him reinstatement, he pleaded ill health and was made viceroy of Navarre instead. [L. H.]

LÓPEZ PORTILLO Y PACHECO, JOSÉ (1920–2004). President of Mexico, 1976–1982. Born June 16 in **Mexico City**, he graduated in law in 1945 from the **Universidad de Chile** in Santiago de Chile and in 1946 from **UNAM**. There he taught law from 1947–1958 and founded the UNAM doctoral program in public administration. In 1958–1972 he was a member of the **Comité Ejecutivo Nacional** of the **Partido Revolucionario Institucional**; in 1959–1960 technical director in the Ministry of **Natural Resources**; in 1960–1965 director general of the federal boards of material improvement in all seaports and cities along national borders. In 1965–1968 he was legal affairs director in the Ministry of the **Presidency**. In 1970–1972 he was assistant minister of Natural Resources. In 1972–1973 he was director general of the **Comisión Federal de Electricidad**, and in 1973–1976 he served as finance minister.

Taking over the presidency at a time of grave economic crisis, he moved to reassure the business community and foreign investors, implementing the **International Monetary Fund**'s program of reducing imports and public expenditure, stimulating exports, and keeping down wages. His national development plan for 1979–1990 divided Mexico into eleven zones to decentralize the **manufacturing industry**, giving tax credits to new investors and to investment in areas with high employment levels. Industrializing ports reduced electricity, natural gas, and fuel oil rates. Profits from non-renewable **petroleum** resources were used to invest in industries with products from renewable resources, with the goal of creating 600,000 jobs a year, to reduce unemployment and **emigration** to the **United States**. Despite his 1977 visit to President Carter, and Carter's 1979 return visit to Mexico, their negotiations produced few positive results. The United States refused to improve access for either Mexican goods or Mexican immigrants and delayed selling Mexico F-5 supersonic fighters until 1981. López Portillo gave verbal support to Third World causes and the reintegration of **Cuba** into the hemispheric community, while providing Sandinista Nicaragua with economic aid, and making a three-day visit to Havana during the Mariel boat lift of 1980.

The end of his presidency saw the **financial crisis of 1982** to which he responded by nationalizing the banks, instituting rigid foreign exchange controls, and accusing the United States of continuing to impose its will on Central America and the Caribbean.

López Portillo wrote two novels, both published in 1976 in both Spanish and as an English translation. *Quetzalcoatl* has the Aztec god promising Mexicans security, but they demand freedom instead. *Don Q* has lawyers questioning the efficiency of government bureaucracy.

He died of pneumonia on February 18.

LÓPEZ PORTILLO Y PACHECO, MARGARITA (1918–). Elder sister of President **López Portillo y Pacheco**, born in **Guadalajara**, she is an established writer of **television** scripts, **radio** scripts, film scripts, and magazine articles. In December 1976 she became director of the bureau of radio, television, and **cinema** of the **Interior Ministry**, supervising all non-commercial broadcasting and the government's own daily news and information programs.

LÓPEZ RAYÓN, IGNACIO (1773–1832). Patriot. A lawyer by profession, he dedicated himself to administering the family mines. Soon after the war for **independence** began, he became Miguel **Hidalgo y Costilla**'s secretary and confidant. Later he commanded troops in the north and in central Mexico, where he took **Zacatecas**, and where, after Hidalgo's death, he attempted to set up a government, the **Junta Nacional Americana**, but could only fight a **guerrilla** campaign. He attended the Congress of **Chilpancingo**. The Spaniards finally captured him in 1817, but they did not execute him. After **independence** in 1820 he became mayor of **San Luis Potosí** and, for a while, chief administrator of **Jalisco**. He died in **Guadalajara**.

LÓPEZ Y FUENTES, GREGORIO (1897–1966). Writer whose novel *El indio* won the *Premio Nacional de Literatura* for 1935.

LORENZO FRANCO, JOSÉ RAMÓN (1935–). Navy minister, 1994–2000. Born January 2 in Apizaco, **Tlaxcala,** he graduated as a marine engineer from the **Escuela Naval** and took command courses at the **United States** Naval War College. He became chief of staff for naval security at the **Centro de Estudios Superiores Navales,** then inspector and comptroller general at the **Naval Ministry,** served as naval attaché at Mexico's embassies in Washington, DC, and Paris, and received Brazil's Tamandaré medal of merit for coordinating naval studies with Brazil.

LORET DE MOLA MEDIZ, CARLOS (1921–1986). Politician and political writer. He has been editor of the *Diario de Yucatán,* a member of the **Cámara de Diputados Federales** from 1961–1963, a senator from 1964–1970, and **governor** of **Yucatán** from 1970–1976. He is nationally known as one of the few leaders within the **Partido Revolucionario Institucional** to have written specific criticism of the pressures exerted on government officials by the establishment leadership. His *Confesiones de un gobernador* (1978) detailed inner-circle agreements. He was the most effective critic among government officials of the **Echeverría** presidency.

LOS ("the"). With the now traditional exception of the Americanized city of *Los Angeles,* for words and names beginning with this definite article, see under following word.

LOS ANGELES, CALIFORNIA. Although Juan Rodríguez de **Cabrillo** had visited the Indian village of Yangana at 36°03'N, 118°24'W in 1542, it was only in 1771 that an expedition from **San Diego** led by priest Junípero **Serra** and soldier Garpar de Portolá established a mission there, *Nossa Senhora la Reina de los Ángeles de Porciúncula,* which became a settlement in 1781. In 1800 the population was still a mere 315 Mexicans. After 1828 there was significant **French Immigration.** Despite stiff resistance, the city fell to the Americans in January 1847. During the Mexican **Revolution of 1910**

it played the role of refuge for *émigrés* that Miami would play during the Cuban Revolution of 1959. [L. H.]

LOTERÍA NACIONAL. As in many other Hispanic countries, the colonial national lottery (introduced by **Viceroy** Carlos Francisco de **Croix** in the 1760s) has continued since **Independence**. It is held twice weekly, its proceeds going toward hospital care for the poor. Agents selling tickets have to have a government license. *See also* GAMBLING.

LOUISIANA. Named for King Louis XIV by late 17th century French explorers whose claims covered 13 of the present day US states. In 1763 the huge territory was passed to Spain, whose late 18th century governor, Bernardo de **Gálvez**, played an important role in the **American Revolutionary War**. Early in the 19th century, **Napoleon** forced the Spanish government to hand it back, but when he failed to reconquer Saint Domingue (modern Haiti) he decided to abandon his dream of a new French empire in North America and negotiated with President Jefferson a sale of the entire territory to the **United States**. [L. H.]

LOYO, GILBERTO (1901–1973). Mexico's leading statistician in the 1940s–1970s. An economist from **Veracruz**, he became dean of the school of economics of **UNAM** in 1944–1952 and originated courses in demography there and at other Mexican universities. He was director general of the **censuses** of 1940 and 1950. As trade minister (*secretario de industria y comercio*), 1952–1958, he modernized the *Dirección Nacional de Estadística*, forerunner of the **Instituto Nacional de Estadística, Geografía e Informática**. He chaired the National Commission on the **Minimum Wage** from 1963–1972.

LOZADA, MANUEL (1828–1873). Guerrilla leader who resisted federal government attempts to regain control of his native state of **Nayarit** after **Maximilian**'s fall in 1867. His cruelty earned him the title "Tiger of Nayarit." He was finally caught and executed by federal troops.

LUCHA LIBRE. *See* WRESTLING.

LUGO LAGUNAS, JOSÉ (1871–1963). A lawyer from **Guerrero** who in 1909 became a leader of the **Partido Antirreeleccionista** against the **Porfiriato**. As **governor** of Guerrero in 1910–1913 he opposed the growing power of Victoriano **Huerta**. In the **Constituent Assembly of 1916–1917**, he wrote much of what became Article 123 (on **labor** rights) of the **Constitution of 1917**.

LUJÁN RODRÍGUEZ, ABELARDO. *See* RODRÍGUEZ, ABELARDO LUJÁN.

LUNA KAN, FRANCISCO (1926–). A physician from **Mérida** who became an active developer of the **sisal**, fiber, rope, and cord industries of his native **Yucatán**. A senator who became a leader in Congress in 1970–1976, he was then elected **governor** of his state, 1976–1982.

LUQUE, EDUARDO (1910–19??). A lawyer from **Querétaro** who became a leader in Congress as a deputy (1943–1946, and 1961–1964) and senator (1946–1952 and 1964–1970). He dominated congressional committees on credit, **agriculture**, and constitutional matters, and became speaker of the Senate. He headed the **Federal Conciliation and Arbitration Board** and in 1958–1961 organized the custom offices for **Quintana Roo**.

– M –

MACARENA, LA. A two-step dance tune imported from Spain in colonial times and now played by the band at **bullfighting** contests, before the action begins, between each fight, and at the conclusion of the afternoon's six fights.

MACHETE. The long (60 cm–1 m: two to three feet) cutlass, used in the Caribbean region as the peasant's all purpose tool for cutting cane, brush, branches, and coconuts, and for repairing fences and houses. *Machetes* with engraved steel blades and decorated handles are displayed at *fiestas* and other special events.

MACHISMO. The quality of being **macho** includes virility, strength, and courage. It is the cult of an assertive masculinity, which for centuries prompted the fathering of large families, and encouraged men to take pride in begetting further children outside marriage. The opposite of compromise (seen as weakness) in personal or public life, its political meaning is that of defeating opponents—domestic or foreign—or winning them over, having one's own views and policies predominate.

[A downside has been a degree of tolerance of violence against **women**, particularly in the privacy of the home. L. H.]

MACUQUINO. Term for the poor quality **coinage**, misshapen and of irregular thickness, typical of the products of Spanish colonial mints through the mid-18th century and whose lack of milled edges tempted clipping (shaving bits from the edges, so debasing their value).

MADELEINE, HURRICANE. Pacific hurricane of 1976 whose 144 mph winds crossed the coast near **Zihuatanejo**.

MADERO GONZÁLEZ, FRANCISCO IBDALECIO (1873–1913). President of Mexico from 1911–1913. Born into a landowning family in **Coahuila** and educated in Europe and the **United States**, he led the opposition against Porfirio **Díaz**, setting off the **Revolution of 1910**, the first major social upheaval of the 20th century. After making a very moderate proposal in his *La Succesión presidencial de 1910*, he was elected in October 1911 and served until forced to resign on February 18, 1913, by Victoriano **Huerta**. A week later he was murdered while in the custody of Major Francisco Cárdenas of the **Rurales**, generally assumed to have been acting on Huerta's orders.

An idealist without previous governmental or political experience, he was unable to control the forces that he had unleashed by forcing Díaz to resign. His supporters were united only in hatred of Diaz, and few wanted the liberal and legalistic democracy he was offering. Although he proved to be generally inept (perhaps too naïvely trusting), he is regarded as a hero in Mexico today, although his defects are recognized.

MADERO GONZÁLEZ, GUSTAVO A. (1875–1913). Congressman brother of President Francisco **Madero González**, murdered, like his brother, at the end of the "**Decena trágica**."

MADRAZO, CARLOS A. (1915–1969). A **Tabasco** lawyer, a major reformer within the **Partido Revolucionario Institucional** and a founder of the Party's **Confederación Nacional de Organizaciones Populares.** He sat in the **Cámara de Diputados Federales** and was **governor** of Tabasco from 1959–1964. As president of the PRI in 1964–1965, he initiated party primaries in **Baja California del Norte** and **Chihuahua state,** but he could not end the inner-circle self-replenishment system based on personal relationships (*See* PRESIDENTIAL SUCCESSION). His death in a plane crash on June 4 ended his life-long efforts to make PRI nominations for public offices more accessible to rank-and-file members through primaries or open conventions, instead of the rubber-stamping of candidates already chosen by the leadership.

MADRAZO CUÉLLAR, JORGE (1953–). **Procurador general** (attorney general) involved in the July 1999 dismissal of charges against bankers accused of laundering profits from **narcotics** exported to the **United States.**

MADRAZO PINTADO, ROBERTO (1952–). Former governor of **Tabasco state**—and a **Partido Revolucionario Institucional** *dinosauro* ("dinosaur")—who in 1999 became a candidate for president of Mexico after the PRI announced a primary in 2000 for the party nomination. The long-time practice of the nominee being chosen by the incumbent's **"dedazo,"** or by a few **"Great Electors,"** had ended. Madrazo became the PRI candidate thanks largely to the party's successes under his leadership in the **election of 2004**, but he placed a poor third in the **election of 2006**.

MADRE, SIERRA. The name of two high parallel mountain ranges, one third of the way inland from the western divide and one fourth of the way inland from the Gulf of **Mexico**. They made the construction of east-west **highways** and **railroads** difficult and expensive. Although Mexico is still better served by its north-south routes, many new highways and regional **railroads** have been built since the 1950s, often by tunnelling through these mountains. The *Sierra Madre Occidental*, which rises to 4,000 m, is continued north of the

United States border by the Sierra Nevada and the Cascade Range and southward by the *Sierra Madre del Sur*. The more easterly range is the *Sierra Madre Oriental*, the southward continuation of the Canadian and American Rocky Mountains. Between these two ranges lies Mexico's high Central Plateau, the **Altiplanicie**.

MADRID, TREATY OF, 1670. In return for relief from privateers and **pirates**, Spain conceded English sovereignty over Jamaica, Barbados, a few other Caribbean islands, and most of the territories adjoining the Atlantic seaboard of North America between Florida and Maine. [L. H.]

MADRID HURTADO, MIGUEL DE LA (1934–). President of Mexico from 1982–1988. Born December 12 in **Colima**, he graduated in law from **UNAM**, obtained a master's in public administration from Harvard, became a professor of law at UNAM, assistant director of finance for **PEMEX**, and director of public credit in the finance ministry, 1972–1976. He represented Mexico at various international economic conferences, held administrative posts with the **Banco de México** and with the **Banco Nacional de Comercio Exterior** (from May 16, 1979), and was planning minister under **López Portillo**, under whom he had been a student at UNAM. In succeeding his former teacher, he hoped to bring about an era of more liberal political discourse and make use of his banking and public finance experience. His presidency began with guarded optimism, but the nation was still nursing grievances between the traditional right and the far left, particularly over the **Tlatelolco** plaza deaths. He publicly promised no programs or policies he could not complete within his **sexennium**. He ignored the attempts of leftists within and without the **Church** to push Liberation Theology, replying when questioned, "the devout can figure out the truth themselves." His administration was notable for a doubling of presidential appointments to high positions of non-UNAM graduates. He particularly favoured those from the **Universidad Iberoamericana**.

He responded to the **earthquake of 1985** with personal courage, visiting sites where walls could have fallen at any moment. Broadcasting to the nation, he said Mexicans would rebuild without begging for foreign help. This electrified even his political opponents and brought him a popularity not seen in Mexico for a politician for many years. He used the occasion to decry the previous failed efforts to decentralize. If industries would relocate to **Monterrey, Guadalajara, Puebla,** or cities near the **United States border,** and elsewhere, the jobs they provided would lure employees to relocate also.

His last year in office saw him still popular, with **inflation** brought under control, slowly decreasing each quarter. He had now begun **privatization,** selling off government-owned industries that had been running deficits.

MADRINA. A godmother, in relation to her godchild (as opposed to a **comadre**). Like that of the child to its godfather (**padrino**), the relationship is lifelong. *See also* COMPADRAZGO.

MAGAÑA, GILDARDO (1891–1939). An accountant from **Michoacán** who was a general under Pancho **Villa,** then became chief of the **División del Sur** upon the death of Emiliano **Zapata** in 1919. He was the leading intellectual of the Zapatist reform movement. He was **governor** of **Baja California del Norte,** then of Michoacán, 1936–1939. He was also a major advisor to his lifelong friend Lázaro **Cárdenas del Río** during the latter's presidency.

MAGAÑA NEGRETE, GUMERSINDO (1939–). Business executive from Irapuato, **Guanajuato,** and one of the founders there of the **Partido Demócráta Mexicano** in 1971. He helped get the PDM on the ballot for the 1979 congressional elections. Since the idea for the party was first mooted in the 1960s, he has worked to get **Sinarquista** members to join the PDM, of which he has been president since 1978.

MAGDALENA DE KINO. The farming village of Buqubavic of 300 people discovered in 1541 by Francisco **Vázquez de Coronado y Valdés** became Eusebio Francisco **Kino**'s mission station of *Santa María de Buquivaba* in June 1688. It is now in **Sonora** state, became a **ciudad** in 1917, and suffered a serious fire at its local **Pemex,** July 22, 1959.

MAGDALENA RIVER. River of 322 km rising near **Nogales** and flowing through **Magdalena de Kino** (whence its name) to empty in the Gulf of **California.**

MAGUEY. *See* AGAVE.

MAIL. *See* POSTAL SERVICE.

MAIZE. *See* CORN.

MALDONADO SÁNCHEZ, BRAULIO (1903–1992?). A lawyer from San José, **Baja California del Norte**, who became the new state's first elected **governor** in 1953–1959. Founder and secretary general of the Leftist **Partido Socialista**, 1931–1932, he joined the **Partido Nacional Revolucionario** (now the **Partido Revolucionario Institucional**) in 1934. In 1958–1963 he worked to create the non-official **Confederación Campesina Independiente** in an unsuccessful campaign for more socialism in agrarian affairs. He led the far-left **Frente Electoral Popular** against **Díaz Ordaz** in the **election of 1964**.

MALINCHE, LA (1495–1528?). (1) Spanish form of Malintzín, name of Hernán **Cortés'** mistress and Indian interpreter, who had learned Spanish from an explorer who had been shipwrecked earlier. Martín **Cortes** was their son. Born in **Veracruz**, the daughter of an Aztec governor, this beautiful and highly intelligent woman was also known as Doña Marina. She was, through her knowledge of **Nahuatl** and **Maya** and hence of the dissension and intrigues among the various Indian nations, a key factor in the Spanish **Conquest of Mexico**. Later, Cortés arranged for her marriage to Juan **Jaramillo**, who took her for the rest of her life to Spain, where she gained the respect of influential families.

(2) Laura **Esquivel's** sympathetic fictionalized biography *La Malinche* portrayed her as a champion of the Maya against **Aztec** oppression. It appeared in February 2006 and in an English translation by Ernesto Mestre-Reed in July.

(3) A dormant volcano in **Tlaxcalá state**.

MALINCHISMO. The exaltation of anything foreign and the undervaluing of anything native to Mexico. The term, derived from La **Malinche**, may even denote an outright betrayal of national interests so gross as to amount to high treason.

MAÑANITAS, LAS ("the dawns"). A popular folksong, sung in the early morning of someone's birthday, but also during the subsequent celebrations.

MANCERA, ANTONIO SEBASTIÁN DE TOLEDO, MARQUÉS DE. *See* TOLEDO, ANTONIO SEBASTIAN DE.

MANERO, ANTONIO (1896–1964). A banker who directed the Regulatory Commission of the banking system in the 1920s–1930s, founded the National Labor Bank in 1929 and the Industrial Bank of the State of Mexico in 1943.

MANGA DE CLAVO. The ancestral ranch in **Veracruz state** of General López de **Santa Anna**.

MANILA GALLEON. An annual voyage from the Philippines to **Acapulco** leaving in February or April, taking **silver** to exchange for spices and for beeswax for lighting (that from South East Asia was better quality and longer lasting than that from North America). The voyages began in the late 1560s, after Alonso de **Arellano** had pioneered the route although Manila only became their destination after the city fell to the Spanish in 1571. They continued until 1815, when the cargo was offloaded at **Zihuatanejo** as Spain had lost control of Acapulco in 1813. *See also* GALLEON. [L. H.]

MANJARREZ, HÉCTOR (1945–). Novelist who wrote *No todos los hombres son románticos* (1983), *Pasaban en silencio nuestros dioses* (1987), and *El otro amor de su vida* (1999). He also was a short story writer, poet, and essayist. [L. H.]

MANRIQUE ARIAS, DANIEL (1939–). Distinguished painter, trained at La **Esmeralda**, who originated the *Arte Acá* movement in the Tepito region of **Mexico City**, an effort to bring the art of mural painting to the masses. His works include *La Puerta* and *La Tapia*.

MANRIQUE DE LA CERDA Y ARAGÓN, TOMÁS ANTONIO. *See* CERDA Y ARAGÓN, TOMÁS ANTONIO MANRIQUE DE LA.

MANRIQUE DE ZÚÑIGA, ÁLVARO (1545?–1590). Viceroy of **New Spain** from 1585–1590. A younger son of the 4th duke of Bejar, he was himself rewarded for his good service to the crown with the marquisate of Villamanrique. Appointed February 26, he reached Mexico with his wife on November 18, For his first task he was charged to regularize the capital's **wine** trade. He soon found himself arbitrating between the regular clergy (whom he favored) and the friars (Dominican, Franciscan, and Augustinian) who had the support of the general population. To combat **contraband** and **piracy**, he created a corps of Militia to fight on land and consti-tuted a **coastguard** of two ships to fight at sea. An unhappy juris-dictional conflict arose with the almost independent **audiencia** of **Guatemala** which assailed Madrid with so many false accusations against the viceroy that the **Council of the Indies** appointed as **vis-itador** Pedro Romanos, bishop of **Tlaxcalá** and a personal enemy of Manrique. He had him dismissed and his property seized. The ex-viceroy was only allowed to return to **Spain**, penniless, six years later. [L. H.]

MANUFACTURING INDUSTRY. In the colonial period, Spanish mercantilism discouraged local industries. Some industrialization took place during the **Porfiriato**, but the most significant develop-ments occurred during the mid-20th century period of deliberate import substitution.

Currently industry employs 23 percent of the workforce, while producing 28 percent of the gross domestic product and 33 percent of the country's exports. *See also* ALAMAN Y ESCALADA, LUCAS; ANTUÑANO, ESTÉBAN; AUTOMOBILES; OBRAJE. [L. H.]

MANZANILLA SCHAFFER, VICTOR (1924–). Politician from **Mexico City**, a law graduate from **UNAM**, where he taught law, sociology, and then economics. A long-time adviser to the **Partido Revolucionario Institucional** on economics and politics, he was a member of the **Comité Ejecutivo Nacional** of the PRI, of the **Cámara de Diputados Federales** (1967–1969) and a senator from **Yucatán** (1970–1976). He headed the National Revolutionary Coali-tion in the 1960s.

MANZANILLO. Port town of **Colima City**, at 19°03'N, 104°20'W, with one of the few natural harbors on Mexico's Pacific coast, developed for **tourism** by Bolivian millionaire Antenor **Patiño**.

MAPS AND ATLASES. Not only does the **Museo Nacional de Historia** have an important map collection, but the **Museo Nacional de Antropología** has one of pre-Hispanic maps. Important cartographers include José Antonio de **Alzate y Ramírez** and Pedro **García Conde.** [L. H.]

MAQUILLADORAS ("makeup assistants in a theater"). Assembly plants built by multinational corporations in Mexico or other developing countries specifically to assemble parts imported from the **United States** (or some other developed country), using low cost local **labor**, and returning the resultant finished products to the country of origin. Such plants are naturally located close to international borders or to suitable ports.

The lower labor rates derive from the lower living costs, relatively high levels of unemployment in developing countries, and the employers' preference for young female (and non-unionized) workers. This has impact on both traditional family structures and the relative status of **women**. Nevertheless, wage rates of US$ 4.00 per day in 2001 were sufficient to attract migrants from rural areas all over Mexico. [Unfortunately even these rates are proving uncompetitive with those paid in China, and recent years have seen significant contraction in the *Maquilladora* industry, although this has been partly offset by a growing interest by the Chinese electronic industry in opening its own assembly plants in **Tijuana** as a backdoor into the American market. L. H.]

The American term "twin plants" is a misnomer, since the corresponding plants on the U.S. side of the border are mere receiving sites for transshipment of the finished products to their U.S. consumers. For several years the U.S. federal tax code has in effect subsidized such plants by limiting import duties on their products to the value added by their assembly, complementing the encouragement given to such plants by Mexico's **Programa Industrial Fronterizo**. U.S.-owned *maquilladoras* near the **United States border** with Mexico began with electronic appliances and musical instruments. Subsequent additions included automobile brake assembly units for Ford and General Motors.

In 1986, polls in **Arizona** and **California** found the *maquilladoras* helped allay a public opinion that was apprehensive of the increasing number of Mexican illegal immigrants entering the US in search of jobs they could not find inside Mexico.

By 1993 there were 2,143 American-owned *maquilladoras* in Mexico; by 1999 there were 3,012, from **Tijuana** to **Ciudad Juárez** to **Matamoros**, employing 1,021,724 Mexicans (removed from the welfare rolls and added to the number of Mexican income tax payers).

Since 1998 the *maquilladora* concept has been extended to data processing. By 2000 Mexico had some 500 American-owned data processing plants, earning the Mexican **economy** US$ 300 million a year. For obvious technical reasons, such data processing does not have to be performed near the border (although much of it is, since telephone links are cheaper there), and large cities are often preferred as offering a sufficiently large labor market with computer skills and adequate English. This is why Current Technologies, Inc. has a branch in **Puebla**, and Newport Beach Data of California has a branch at **Monterrey**.

MARCHA DE ZACATECAS. *See* ZACATECAS MARCH.

MARCOS, *SUBCOMANDANTE.* The alias of Rafael Sebastián **Guillén Vicente**.

MARGAIN, HUGO B. (1913–1997). Lawyer, born February 13 in **Mexico City**, who became Mexico's most influential diplomat. He directed the Retail Tax Bureau, then the Federal Income Tax Bureau (1951–1959), and then in the **Trade Ministry** he was executive officer and subsequently deputy minister (1961–1964). In 1962–1963 he directed the **Comité Nacional de Reparto de Utilidades**. He was ambassador in Washington, 1965–1970, in London, 1973–1976, and then again in Washington, 1976–1982. He was President **López Portilla**'s senior diplomat, ranking immediately after the foreign minister.

MARGIL DE JESÚS, [FRAY] ANTONIO (1657–1726). Franciscan missionary from Spain who spent over 50 years in many regions of **New Spain**, from **Texas** to **Yucatán**, traveling everywhere on foot.

Among the many schools he founded was the *Colegio de la Cruz* in **Querétaro**. He died in the monastery of San Francisco de México and has been beatified for his great religious work among the **Indians**.

MARIACHI. Mexico's prototype folk music. A mariachi orchestra consists of two violinists, two trumpeters, three guitarists, and a bass guitarist who plays the **guitarrón**. Wearing **charro** costume, they take turns singing solos, duets, trios, and other combinations. The songs cover all facets of Mexican culture, but especially ranching and farm life.

MARIMBA. A wooden xylophone, the native musical instrument of **Chiapas**, but played throughout **Guatemala** and rural Mexico.

MARINA, DONA. *See* MALINCHE, LA.

MARITIME SOVEREIGNTY. Mexico's territorial waters were extended in the mid-20th century a further 9 nautical miles, from 3 nautical miles (5.58 km) out to sea from the shore to 12 nautical miles (22.3 km), making the total **area** of seas under Mexican sovereignty 231,831 km^2 (less than half the **continental shelf**). The concept of a 200 nautical mile (371 km) wide zone of exclusive economic dominion (for **fishing** and mineral exploitation) was subsequently also adopted. This Economic Exploitation Zone (E.E.Z.) increases the total sea **area** under Mexican jurisdiction to almost 3,000,000 km^2. [L. H.]

MAROONS (*CIMARONES*). Runaway black slaves who formed their own self-governing communities, under a leader frequently known as *Yunga*, in isolated places often high in the mountains, whence the name (from *cima*, a high peak). They were the bane of colonial civil governments throughout "Plantation America," from Mexico to Brazil. [L. H.]

MÁRQUEZ, [GENERAL] LEONARDO (1820–1913). Conservative fighter during the **War of the Reforms**, nicknamed *El Tigre* ("tiger") *de Tacubaya* for his wholesale shooting of prisoners.

MARTÍN HUERTA, RAMÓN (1957–2005). Ramón Martín Huerta, politician. He was born in San Juan de los Lagos, Mexico, on January 24, 1957, and married María Esther Montes Hernández. They had two sons and one daughter.

As a young man, he headed the Catholic Association of Mexican Youth but then moved to the city of **León** in the state of **Guanajuato** at the age of 22. There he got a degree in Business Administration and within five years (1984–1987) headed the state's Association of Industrialists (*Asociación de Industriales del Estado de Guanajuato*). He turned to politics in the late 1980s, first winning a local seat in León, later in the federal parliament in **Mexico City**. It was in 1987 that he introduced the **Partido de Acción Nacional** leader Manuel Clouthier—then heading the opposition—to businessman Vicente **Fox Quesada**. Together they persuaded him that he could help overthrow the long stranglehold on power by the **Partido Revolucionario Institucional**. Martín Huerta was Fox's campaign director when the latter failed to win the governorship of Guanajuato in 1991, and again in 1995, when Fox did win. In 1999 he stepped down to run for the presidency of Mexico, naming Huerta as interim governor. On winning, he made Huerta deputy minister of the **Interior**.

Growing insecurity, particularly along the **United States border**, led to public disillusionment, expressed in street protests. Dozens of people were being killed every month, mostly the victims of "turf wars" among rival Mexican drug lords, fighting for the lucrative cocaine and marihuana routes into the United States. In August 2000 Fox turned to his old friend to lead Mexico's fight against **narcotics** trafficking and related violence, naming him head of the **Public Security Ministry**, which oversees the uniformed federal **police** and some special army units. Martín Huerta, considered to be on the far right of his **Partido de Acción Nacional**, immediately sent hundreds of police and soldiers to border towns such as **Tijuana**, **Reynosa**, **Nuevo Laredo**, and **Matamoros** in an operation he called **Mexico Seguro** ("A Secure Mexico"). However, it was like plugging a flooded dyke with his finger, as the trafficking, killings, and kidnappings not only continued but intensified. Soon he had to face the fact that two of the country's biggest rival drug lords, Osiel Cárdenas and Benjamín Arellano Félix, both in jail near **Mexico City**, had joined forces and were running the narcotics trade from behind bars by computer and cellular phone. Aware that this was possible only through the collusion of prison guards, Martin Huerta made the guards undergo drug tests and lie-detection, but there was no sign that the drug lords were scaling back their activities. His efforts made him one of the country's most marked men. The fact that he was on his way to the maximum security La Palma prison, September 21, 2005, when his helicopter crashed near Huixquilucan caused obvious speculation that the Bell-412 had been shot down. Rescue workers reported, however, that the aircraft had slammed into a 3,300 m (11,000 ft.) mountaintop in thick cloud and fog. [L. H.]

MARTÍNEZ, JUAN JOSÉ (1782–1863). Patriot nicknamed *El Pípila* (a slang term for a domesticated turkey). He was a miner who joined Miguel **Hidalgo y Costilla**'s **independence** movement and led the attack on the **Alhóndiga de Granaditas**, pushing a huge stone statue slowly forward to its thick wooden door which was then set on fire, allowing the revolutionaries to gain entry. **Guanajuato** has a huge statue of Martínez overlooking the city. He died in **San Miguel de Allende**, probably of tuberculosis.

MARTÍNEZ BÁEZ, ANTONIO (1901–2001?). Jurist and historian from **Morelia** who was legal head of the *Banco Nacional Hipotecario Urbano* (predecessor of the **Banco Nacional de Obras y Servicios Públicas**) and director of indemnifications for the **agriculture ministry** in the 1930s. He headed the National Banking Commission in 1941–1943, the **Financiera Azucarera** in 1943–1946, was trade minister from 1948–1952, and head of the National Securities Commission from 1953–9, reorganizing Mexico's stock markets. In 1959–1960 he was president of the *Colegio de Abogados* (the Mexican bar association), and in 1968 he represented Mexico in the **Asociación Latinoamericana de Libre Comercio (LAFTA)**, securing lower tariffs on Mexican exports.

MARTÍNEZ CORBALA, GONZALO (1928–). A civil engineer from **San Luis de Potosí** who was president of the Mexican Society of Engineers, publisher of the professional magazine *Ingenería civil* in the 1960s, and head of the Mexican Planning Association. As a federal deputy in 1964–1967, he led the movement in Congress that forced Ernesto **Uruchurtu** to resign as **governor** of the **Federal District**. In 1972–1974 he was ambassador to **Chile**.

MARTÍNEZ DE LA VEGA, FRANCISCO (1909–1985). A well-known leftist writer from **San Luis Potosí** who co-founded *Siempre* in 1951 and was secretary general of the **Partido Popular Socialista,** 1951–1955. After representing the PPS in the **Cámara de Diputados Federales**, 1958–1959, he became interim **governor** of **San Luis Potosí state**, 1959–1961 by representing both the PPS and the dominant **Partido Revolucionario Institucional** as a coalition appointee to fill an unexpired term.

MARTÍNEZ DE NAVARRETE ROMERO, IFIGENIA (1930–). A leading economist and economics adviser to the **Partido Revolucionario Institucional**, professor at **UNAM**, where (uniquely for a woman) she was dean of the school of economics from 1970–1972, and a member of President **Díaz Ordaz**'s council of economic advisers from 1964–70. She is married to Alfredo **Navarrete Romero**.

MARTÍNEZ DOMÍNGUEZ, ALFONSO (1922–). Politician from **Monterrey** who built his power base as secretary general from 1949–1952, of the **Federación de Sindicatos de los Trabajadores en Servicio del Estado**. He sat in the **Cámara de Diputados Federales**, 1952–1955, and 1964–1967, becoming leader of the House. He was head of the **Confederación Nacional de Organizaciones Populares**, 1961–1965, and president of the **Partido Revolucionario Institucional**, 1968–1970. He became **governor** of the **Federal District** in 1970, but had to resign after the 1971 student riots. He served as governor of **Nuevo León state**, 1979–1985.

MARTÍNEZ DOMÍNGUEZ, GUILLERMO (1924–). Economist and journalist from **Monterrey**, and brother of Alfonso **Martínez Domínguez**. He has been a columnist for *Hoy*, *Excelsior*, and *La Prensa*. In 1953 he won the National Prize for Journalists for exposing fraud in the **Instituto Mexicano del Seguro Social**. He was director of prices for the **Trade Ministry** before heading the Small

Business Bank. He was then director general successively of the **Comisión Federal de Electricidad** (1964–1970) and the **Nacional Financiera** (1970–1976).

MARTÍNEZ TORNEL, PEDRO (1889–1957). An engineer from **Veracruz** who built the shipping port of **Salina Cruz, Oaxaca**, in 1923, and modernized it in 1957. He was a top administrator of the **Ferrocarriles Nacionales de México**, 1935–1943, then assistant minister (1943–1945) and minister of public works (1945–1946). In 1940, however, he had directed Juan **Almazán**'s unsuccessful run for president, thereby cutting himself off for high office after 1946.

MARTÍNEZ VERDUGO, ARNOLDO (1925–). Communist politician. In the 1940s–1950s he was a state government clerk in his native **Sinaloa**. In 1945–1949 he was national head of Communist youth (*Juventud Comunista de México*), and has been active in the **Partido Comunista Mexicano** since 1949, a member of its Central Committee since 1955 and secretary general since 1964. After years of lobbying he got PCM candidates certified on the ballot for the **election of 1979**.

MARY OF GUADALUPE, SAINT. Patron Saint of Mexico since 1754. In 1531 Juan Diego, a poor Indian laborer, saw a vision of Our Lady with an Indian physiognomy on Tepeyac Hill, now the northern suburb of **Mexico City**, Villa de Guadalupe Hidalgo. After Bishop Juan de **Zumárraga** demanded proof of the vision, Diego presented him with fresh roses and a painting of the Virgin inside his coat, which sufficed to convince the prelate of the Indian's sincerity. The shrine, built there in 1709, was where the Treaty of **Guadalupe-Hidalgo** was signed. It became a basilica in 1908. The cult of the saint, which venerates motherhood, is especially strong among Mexican women. Her feast is on December 12. She is also the patron of the **Cathedral of Mexico City**.

MASONS. *See* FREEMASONRY.

MASS MEDIA. *See* MEDIA.

MASSIEU, WILFRIDO (1878–1944). An engineer who directed the Military Industry College and then the College of Railroad Workers (1920–1937), which he helped convert into the **Instituto Politécnico Nacional**, of which he became first president, 1937–1944.

MASTRETTA, ANGELES (1949–). Novelist from **Puebla** currently living in **Mexico City**, married to fellow writer Héctor Aguilar Camin. She was the author of *Arráncame la vida* (1985), *Mal de amores* (1996), and the short story collection *Mujeres con ojos grandes* (1990), reissued in a bilingual edition as *Women with Big Eyes* (2004). [L. H.]

MATAMOROS, MARIANO (1770–1814). Patriot priest and warrior for whom **Matamoros** city was renamed.

MATAMOROS, TAMAULIPAS. A border city, at 25°52'N, 97°30'W, opposite **Brownsville** Texas. It boasts Mexico's oldest US consulate, established in 1850. The site was discovered by Alonso Álvarez de Piñeda in 1519, named *Paraje de los esteros hermosos* ("place of the beautiful marshes") in 1706, settled by 12 families in 1774 as *San Juan de los esteros hermosos*, renamed by missionaries in 1793 *Nuestra Señora del refugio de los esteros hermosos*, made a port in 1820 with 2,320 inhabitants, renamed in 1826 to honor Mariano **Matamoros**, and in 1834 granted **ciudad** status. It boomed on **cotton** exports during the **United States** Civil War. In 1876 it was the base for Porfirio **Díaz**'s revolt following the Plan of **Tutepec**, which took him to the presidency. The great hurricane of September 3, 1933, caused huge floods.

The **municipio** had 418,141 inhabitants in 2000 on 4046 km². It witnessed a **cotton** boom in 1948–1962, until synthetics decreased world demand. Its **agriculture** now depends on sorghum, but since 1970 **maquiladoras** have also been important to its economy. [L. H.]

MATLAZÁHUATL. A colonial-era **disease**, probably **typhus**. [L. H.]

MATORRAL. The semi-desert characteristic of the lower lands of northern Mexico.

MAXIMATO. The years 1924–1936 when Mexico was effectively controlled by Plutarco Elias **Calles**, the self-styled *Jefe Máximo* of the Revolution.

MAXIMILIAN, EMPEROR OF MEXICO (1832–1867). Born Archduke Ferdinand Maximilian von Habsburg, younger brother of Austrian Emperor Francis Joseph, he had been governor of the Austrian province of Lombardy until this was ceded to the newly united Kingdom of Italy in 1859. At that time his interest in maritime affairs led to his being made head of the Austrian navy. Maximilian's interest in the New World is said to having been awakened when he made a short visit to **Brazil** in 1860. Following the **French Intervention** in Mexico, a delegation of prominent Mexican conservatives to **Miramar** in October 1863 offered him the throne of Mexico on behalf of the **Junta de Notables**. A spurious plebiscite was held to reassure him that the offer had general popular support, and he accepted the crown, April 10, 1864. His rule over what was essentially a French puppet government created by the Convention of **Miramar** began with his arrival in **Veracruz** in May 1864, but government was in the hands of Lieutenant Juan Nepomuceno **Almonte** until he reached Mexico City on June 12. Early in his reign he alienated his supporters by proclaiming such liberal ideas as freedom of the press and the separation of **Church** and State and naming a liberal, José Fernando Ramírez, to be his foreign minister. Although his regime was always hovering on the brink of bankruptcy, it managed some Hausmann-style improvements to **Mexico City** that are perhaps (along with the decimalization of the **coinage**) its only permanent legacy.

Benito **Juárez** fought the emperor uncompromisingly, even though Maximilian once offered him a high position in his government. In October 1865, believing Juárez had given up and fled the country, and hoping firmness would end an apparently now futile civil war, Maximilian decreed the death penalty for all rebels captured in arms. In the end, this was to supply the chief justification for his own execution, June 19, 1867, following the downfall of his regime on May 15, an execution that caused consternation among monarchists abroad and precluded the renewal of Brazilian diplomatic relations with Mexico until the abdication of his cousin Pedro II in 1889.

Mexicans today tend to look upon Maximilian as a well-meaning foreigner who was woefully naïve about the political realities of Mexico.

MAY DAY. The first of May is celebrated in Mexico as in many other countries as (International) **Labor Day**, a date originally chosen to protest President Grover Cleveland's suppression of the black Pullman car attendants' strike in Chicago on that day in 1894. [L. H.]

MAY THE FIFTH. *See* FIFTH OF MAY.

MAYA. The lands of the Maya include all of the **Yucatán** peninsula, much of **Chiapas** and **Tabasco**, all of **Belize** and **Guatemala**, and the western-most parts of Honduras and El Salvador, a total of some 325,000 km². The Maya-speaking **Teenek Indians** have been isolated from the rest of the Maya nation since very early times.

The original hunter-gatherer Maya developed village communities based on agriculture in the highlands around 1,800 BC. This "Pre-Classic" culture spread into the lowland forests and swamps around 1,000 BC. The first stone pyramids were erected around 500 BC and cities with monumental architecture characterize the "Late Pre-Classic" period of 400 BC–250 AD.

The cities of the "old empire" Mayan period (300–900 AD) gave evidence of an advanced knowledge of astronomy with a calendar actually more accurate than our present-day Gregorian system. Their chief center within the present boundaries of Mexico was at **Palenque** in Chiapas. At the 8th century height of this "Classic" period, there were around 40 major cities with up to 100,000 people each. Estimates of total population range beyond 10 million; and over-population, along with chronic intercity warfare, have been suggested as causes of the civilization's eventual decline and collapse. A new theory links Mayan decline with that of China's Tang dynasty, seeing both as victims of a 7th to 9th century worldwide change in wind flow in tropical areas, producing a prolonged period of drought and famine.

The post-900 "new empire" period is noted for its pyramids and temples at **Chichén Itzá** and **Uxmal** in Yucatán, and politically for the **Mazapán confederation**.

The Spanish conquest of the Maya, attempted by Francisco de **Montejo** in 1527–1535, was largely accomplished by his son, Francisco de **Montejo** the younger, in 1540–1546.

Survivors of the ancient Maya are still the predominant **Indian** nation in **Meso-America**. Those living in southern Mexico (the states of Yucatán, **Campeche**, **Quintana Roo**, and Chiapas) numbered about 600,000 in the mid-1990s, making them the largest Indian group in Mexico after the **Nahua**. The **Lacandón** are a Mayan subgroup. Only about half, however, of the Mexican Maya (350,000 in 1975) still speak Mayan, and although neighboring **Guatemala** still has three million Mayan speakers, virtually all the Honduran Maya are now Spanish speakers.

MAYAN ARCHAEOLOGY. *See* CATHERWOOD, FREDERICK; CHARLES III; COZUMEL; IZAMAL; LABNÁ; MAYA; PALENQUE; STEPHENS, JOHN LLOYD; UXMAL.

MAYAN LANGUAGES. The proto-Mayan of 2,000 BC had developed into at least two languages by the Classic period, although the Choltí dialect seems to have served as the norm in diplomatic communication between the rival cities and in monumental inscriptions. The present-day Maya speak over 30 different, though related, languages. [L. H.]

MAYO. **Sonora Indian** group of 56,600 (1995 estimate).

MAYORGA, MARTÍN DE (172?–1783). **Viceroy** of **New Spain**, 1779–1783. Appointed while serving as captain general of **Guatemala** and president of its **audiencia** and just as Spain had decided to join her French ally in intervention in the **American Revolutionary War**. He organized an expedition to Florida, led by Bernardo de **Gálvez** to aid the rebels there. Meanwhile a terrible outbreak of **smallpox** produced such high and widespread mortality that he offered his resignation (which was declined). In 1780 oppression led to a revolt of **Indians**, put down by his Captains José Antonio de Urízar and Tomás Pontón. He died just as he reached Cãdiz on his return to Spain. [L. H.]

MAZA, MARGARITA (1826–1871). Wife of Benito Pablo **Juárez**, and a member of a family occupying a high social position. She bore him eight daughters and four sons.

MAZAHUA. **Indian** nation of 180,000 (1995 estimate) living in the states of **Mexico** and **Michoacán**.

MAZAPÁN CONFEDERATION. A league of the principal late **Maya** cities, dissolved in 1194.

MAZATLÁN. A city of **Sinaloa** state (of which it was state capital, 1859–1873), and Mexico's largest commercial port on the Pacific, at 23°12'N, 106°25'W, with a population of 315,180 in 1990 and 343,000 in 1995. It is a headquarters for commercial **fishing**, merchant shipping, and industries related to marine products. It is also a tourist resort for bathing, yachting, and sport **fishing**.

MCALLEN. Texas border town opposite **Reynosa**.

MCLANE, ROBERT MILLIGAN (1815–1898). American soldier, politician, and diplomat sent to Mexico in 1859 to discover which of the contending regimes the **United States** should recognize. He opted for the Liberals when Benito **Juárez**'s foreign minister Melchor **Ocampo** accepted the humiliating Transit and Trade Treaty of 1858 which would have given the US a permanent sovereign right of passage across the **Tehuantepec Isthmus**, tariff reductions, and the right to military intervention, for a single payment of US$ 4 million. Fortunately for Mexico, the US Senate, bitterly divided between North and South, failed to ratify the treaty.

McLane resigned as envoy in 1860 and went on to become governor of Maryland and then US minister in Paris. [L. H.]

MEASLES. The second (after **smallpox**) of the killer diseases introduced by European contact. It ravaged **Cuba** in 1529, spread to Florida and Central Mexico in 1531, and reached the highland **Maya** in 1532. Further outbreaks accompanied the **smallpox** epidemics of 1563–1564 and 1615–1617. [L. H.]

MEDIA. By the 1970s, **radio** and **television** stations, government and privately owned, already blanketed Mexico. Whereas less than one-fifth of adult Mexicans buy or read daily **newspapers**, over 95 percent obtain their news from broadcasting. *See also* CENSORSHIP; PUBLISHING AND THE BOOK TRADE.

MEDICAL EDUCATION. Although most medical schools are in **Mexico City**, there are also medical schools in the major provincial cities. That in **Guadalajara** has, since the 1970s, enrolled dozens of **United States** citizens who have mastered sufficient Spanish, most of them white males denied entry into American schools because of affirmative action preferences for **women** and non-whites.

MEJÍA, IGNACIO (1814–1906). Soldier, politician, and confidant of Benito Pablo **Juárez**. He was noted for his honesty; and when Porfirio **Díaz** could not bribe him into collaboration, he had to force him into exile by levying false charges.

MEJÍA, TOMÁS (1823–1867). After Miguel **Miramón**, the best known conservative general in the **War of the Reforms**. He became genuinely devoted to the Emperor **Maximilian** and was executed with him on the Hill of the Bells.

MELGAR, AGUSTÍN (1829–1847). One of the **Niños Héroes**. Having lost both parents when very young, he was allowed to enroll in the **Escuela Militar** in **Chapultepece Park**, ultimately dying in its defense. He killed at least one American and was wounded twice before being killed himself.

MELO, JUAN VICENTE (1932–1996). A physician and dermatologist from **Veracruz**, he became a fine **art** critic, and then a full-time writer, editing *Universidad de México* and writing for *Siempre*, the *Revista mexicana de literatura*, and other periodicals. His short story volume, *La Noche alucinada* (1956), and his novel, *La Obediencia noctura* (1969), made him known nationally for his characterizations of lonely Mexicans.

MÉNDEZ, JUAN N. (1820–1894). Briefly interim president in 1876–1877.

MÉNDEZ DOCURRO, EUGENIO (1923–). Politician from **Veracruz** dismissed for **corruption**. An engineering graduate from the **Instituto Politécnico Nacional** with a master's from Harvard, he directed the IPN, 1959–1962; was assistant minister of communications, 1964–1970; then minister, 1970–1976. In 1977 the **López Portilla** administration charged him with stealing 80 million pesos while minister under **Echeverría**. He was forced to resign his 1977 position as undersecretary of **education** and to repay a fourth of the alleged fraud. For the first time in modern Mexican history, a **procurador general** (federal attorney general) documented misappropriation of funds by a high-ranking administrator, producing false invoices and cancelled checks. The case against Méndez triggered a general probe of many bureaucrats in the most extensive anti-corruption investigations and trials of public officials ever held in Mexico since **Independence**.

MENDIETA, [FRAY] GERÓNIMO DE (c.1525–1604). Franciscan missionary, famed for his *Historia eclesiástica indiana*, an account of the conversion of the Mexican **Indians** in the 16th century. Born in Victoria, Spain, the youngest of a large family, he learned to speak **Náhuatl** so well that he became a better orator in that language than in Spanish. He died in the Monastery of St. Francis in Mexico after a long illness.

MENDIETA Y NÚÑEZ, LUCIO (1895–1988). A sociologist from **Mexico City** who co-founded the schools of social sciences and of economics at **UNAM** and published the *Revista sociológica mexicana* in 1939–1946.

MENDOZA, ANTONIO DE (1493–1552). First **viceroy** of **New Spain** and one of the most outstanding, appointed 1534, serving 1535–1550. Born in Granada of wealthy parents, he began service at the Spanish court at a young age and, after a varied career which included diplomatic service in Hungary, he was named viceroy for an indefinite period—a unique privilege as all his successors would be limited to six-year terms. Charged with curtailing the power of the **audiencia** and of Hernán **Cortés**, he adopted a more humane policy toward the **Indians** and many were converted. His accomplishments included a population **census**, the foundation of the **University of Mexico**, the introduction of **printing**, the establishment of a **mint**, and the founding of the Colegio de Santa Cruz de Tlatelolco for the education of Indian noblemen. He despatched expeditions into **Arizona**, **New Mexico**, and the coasts of **California**. He founded the cities of **Guadalajara** and of Valladolid, now **Morelia**. Mendoza was so successful that in 1549 he was appointed viceroy of **Peru**, an office he took up in 1551. He lies buried in Lima.

MENDOZA, NARCISO (1800–after 1864). Revolutionary hero. As a boy he helped defend his native city of **Cuatla** against Spanish troops led by General **Calleja del Rey**. When they were about to burst into the city, he fired a cannon at them point-blank, giving **Morelos** the chance to regroup. There is a statue to Mendoza on the outskirts of **Cuernavaca**.

MENDOZA Y LUNA, JUAN MANUEL, MARQUIS OF MONTESCLAROS (1571–1628). **Viceroy** of **New Spain**, 1603–1607, in which post he undertook the draining of **Mexico City**'s lakes to obviate flooding and built a reservoir of drinking water. In 1607 he was made viceroy of **Peru**, returning to Spain in 1615. [L. H.]

MERCADO CASTRO, PATRICIA (1957–). Daughter of small farmers from **Ciudad Obregón**, **Sonora**. She became leader of the new **Partido Alianza Social-demócrata y Campesina** and its presidential candidate in the **Election of 2005**, in which she championed equal opportunity and **women**'s right to abortion.

MERCANTILISM. The 17th–18th century economic doctrine adopted by all Europe's colonial powers which saw the colonies as existing solely to enrich the mother country. Foreign trade was discouraged and usually outlawed, fostering a huge **contraband** trade, while settlers were stopped from producing anything that might cut into the profits of metropolitan growers, manufacturers, or middlemen: e.g., in the case of Mexico, olive and grape cultivation and **wine** production. [L. H.]

MÉRIDA. Capital of **Yucatán**, lying on a low, flat plain, surrounded by **sisal** plantations, at 20°59'N, 89°39'W. The city's water is pumped from wells by windmills. Mérida was founded in 1542 by Francisco **Montejo** the younger on the site of Tho, an ancient city of the **Maya**. The Spanish built on top of Mayan temples and other structures. The Montejo home of 1549 has been preserved in the main plaza near the Cathedral. For centuries the city was isolated from the rest of Mexico, and even its port of Progreso traded more with Havana than with **Veracruz**. Air transport began to lessen this isolation in the 1940s, but the city had no rail link with the federal capital until 1950 and none by road until 1961.

Mérida is a center of **sisal** products: rope, cordage, sackcloth, sacks, and fabric hats. It is also a tourist center for the Mayan sites of **Chichén Itzá** and **Uxmal**. It has a state museum and is the location of the **Universidad de Yucatán**.

The **municipio** had 705,055 inhabitants in 2000.

MERINO RABAGO, FRANCISCO (1919?–1994). Banker from **Irapuato**. He was director of credit for the **Banco Nacional de Crédito Ejidal**, 1956–1958, then its assistant general manager, 1959–1960 and 1971–1975, becoming in 1975 director general of the **Banco Nacional de Crédito Rural**. During the **López Portillo** administration of 1976–1982 he was **agriculture** minister.

MESILLA, TREATY OF. Name by which the **Gadsden Purchase** is known in Mexico.

MESILLA VALLEY. Territory in the far north of **Sonora** and **Chihuahua** which the **Gadsden Purchase** transferred to **Arizona** and **New Mexico**.

MESO-AMERICA. A term, most often used in archaeology, for Central America, but frequently including the southern half of Mexico. [L. H.]

MESTIZO (feminine *mestiza*). Someone of mixed Indian and European descent: an estimated 55 percent of the Mexican population in the 1990s. Someone of mixed Indian and African descent was a **zambo**. *See also* INDIANS.

METATE. A carved stone for grinding **corn**, a major household tool in **Indian** villages. Also used throughout rural Mexico and in the town houses of the poor.

METRIFICATION. The total implementation of the Metric system of **weights and measures** was made during the presidency of Manuel

González. Its use throughout this *Dictionary* includes *t* to mean the metric ton(ne) of 1,000 kg. [L. H.]

METRO. Mexico's first underground rapid transit railway opened in **Mexico City** in 1969. French-designed, like that of Montreal, it serves 95 stations on nine routes totalling 120 kms (75 miles). [L. H.]

METZLIAPÁN ("moon lake"). Mystical name for Lake **Texcoco**.

MEXCALTITÁN, ISLA. Small island (about 1 km across) settlement (1,300 inhabitants) and tourist resort, constructed artificially c.4,000 BC in the *Marisma Nacional* (coastal swampland) of **Nayarit** state. [L. H.]

MEXICA. A term for the **Aztec** people, perhaps from **Metzliapán**.

MEXICALI. Capital of **Baja California del Norte**. Located opposite **Calexico**, California, it is the only Mexican state capital on the **United States border**. An agricultural center, it had a population of 640,000 in 1995 and of 764,602 in 2000.

MEXICAN. Spanish distinguishes between *mexicano* (inhabiting or pertaining to the whole Republic) and *mexiquense* (inhabiting or pertaining to **Mexico State**). An inhabitant of **Mexico City** is a *defeño* or a **chilango**. An inhabitant of the colonial **viceroyalty** of **New Spain** was a **novohispano**. **Mexica** is a synonym of **Aztec**. [L. H.]

MEXICAN-AMERICAN WAR. *See* UNITED STATES-MEXICAN WAR.

MEXICAN BORDER. *See* UNITED STATES BORDER.

MEXICAN INSTITUTE OF SOCIAL SECURITY. *See* INSTITUTO MEXICANO DE SEGURIDAD SOCIAL.

MEXICAN REVOLUTION. *See* REVOLUTION OF 1910.

MEXICANA. *See* COMPAÑÍA MEXICANA DE AVIACIÓN.

MEXICANO-NORTEAMERICANA, GUERRA. *See* UNITED STATES-MEXICAN WAR.

MEXICANOS Y AMERICANOS TODOS TRABAJANDO (M.A.T.T.). A not-for-profit bank formed in **Monterrey** in 1980 and now associated with the **San Francisco**-based Kiva website, modelled after Mohammed Yunus' Grameen Bank. It provides short-term loans of under $100 to microenterprises in rural areas, 90 percent of them run by **women**.

MEXICO. Derived from **Mexica**, a name for the Aztecs, it came to designate their capital, i.e., **Mexico City**, and only replaced **New Spain** as the official name of the whole country following **independence**. [L. H.]

MEXICO, GULF OF (*GOLFO DE MÉXICO*). The northwestern extension of the **Caribbean Sea** to which it is connected by the 210 km-wide (131 mile-wide) **Yucatán Channel** and the 180 km-wide (112 mile-wide) **Florida Strait**. It is ringed by the **United States** coastline from Key West to the mouth of the **Rio Grande**, the Mexican coast thence from **Matamoros** to **Yucatán**, and some 500 km of the northern coast of **Cuba** between 84°57'W (Cape San Antonio) and the Hicacos Peninsula at 23°12'N. [L. H.]

MEXICO, VALLEY OF (*VALLE DE MEXICO*). Populated from the retreat of the last ice age around 12,000 BC. Although it accounts for only 14 percent of the territory of post-1854 Mexico, it is home to over half of its present-day **population**. *See also* VALLE DE MÉXICO, ESTADO DEL.

MEXICO CITY (*CIUDAD DE MEXICO*). The national capital was built in 1520 on the site of the Aztec **Tenochtitlán**, at 2,240 m (7,349 ft.) above sea level, on the dried-up bed of Lake **Texcoco**, in the area known to the Aztecs as **Anáhuac**, 320 km (200 miles) west of **Veracruz City** on the Gulf of **Mexico**, and 306 km (190 miles) northeast of **Acapulco** on the Pacific. Much of the original **Aztec** street layout can still be traced. The **population** plunged after the Spanish **conquest of Mexico** to a nadir of 90,000, before beginning to recover in the early 18th century. Then in the 1730s, a terrible outbreak of **typhus** (or perhaps **plague**) set it back from 110,000 to 70,000. By the **census** of 1772 it had climbed back to 112,463. It was about 137,000 in 1800; 150,000 at **Independence**; 180,000 under the **Second Empire**; 331,781 at the census of 1895; and 470,659 in 1910 (compared to 721,000 for the entire **Federal District**). By 1970, the Federal District had 7,005,855 inhabitants within a Greater **Mexico City Conurbation** of 8,541,070. Thirty-five years later, these figures have increased to 15,000,000 within the Federal District but 20,000,000 within the conurbation, which is now one of the world's most populous cities and expected to double by 2020.

Three bombs damaged central city buildings (the offices of the **Comisión Electoral Federal** and the **Partido Revolucionario Institucional** and a branch of a foreign bank) in an apparent leftist political protest on November 6, 2006.

The city's principal avenue, running southwest from downtown to **Chapultepec Park** is called the Paseo de la **Reforma**, and the next in importance is called *Insurgentes*, although both were laid out under the **Empire**. The chief 18th century contribution to the city's layout is the **Alameda**. The central downtown square, the **Zócalo**, dates back to the Aztecs.

MEXICO CITY AUDIENCIA. *See* AUDIENCIA.

MEXICO CITY CONURBATION. Greater Mexico City (the *Area Metropolitana*, or *Zona Metropolitana del Valle de México*) vies with Tokyo-Yokohama for the title of the world's most populous city, depending partly on one's definition. In the 1970–1990 period, the extent of the built-up area grew from 650 km^2 to 1,600 km^2 while the population doubled, from ten to twenty million. It now stretches some 60 km north-south and 45 km east-west. Expansion has been most rapid toward the south and east. Districts include V. Carranza, Cuauhtemoc, Ixtacalco, Benito Juárez, Ixtapalapa, Coyoacán, Tlahuac, Xochimilco, Milpa Alta, Tapan, Magdalena Contreras, Álvaro Obregón, Cuajimalpa de Morelos, Miguel Hidalgo, Az Capotzalco, and Gustavo A. Madero. Places in **Mexico State** currently regarded as within Greater Mexico City include Amecameca, **Chalco**, and **Netzahualcóyoti**. The poor tend to live to the north, east, and southeast of the central city, the middle classes within the center, and the wealthier prefer localities to the west and south of the center.

The yearly rainfall ranges from 600 mm in the northwest to 1,100 mm in the cooler (15°C average) southeast.

The conurbation's altitude is too high for mosquito-borne **malaria**, and it reduces humidity to 30 percent less than that at sea level. But there is a serious problem of thermic inversion, whose frequency increases with altitude, creating a high degree of air pollution. Since January 1986 it has frequently reached danger levels, much of it due to the high density of its automobile traffic, which the **Metro** is unable to alleviate to anything close to the required degree. The pollution is hemmed in by the city's surrounding hills: the Sierra de **Pachuca** to the north, outcrops of the Sierra **Madre** Oriental to the northeast, the Sierra de **Chichinautzin** to the south, the Sierra de las Cruzes to the southwest, and the Monte Alto and Monte Bajo ranges to the west. Ironically, the magnificence of their snow-capped peaks has not been visible at ground level since the 1960s. There are also serious problems with the water supply, due to the city's location on a former lake with no outlet to the sea, problems which have never been solved since Aztec times.

The magapolis lies in an earthquake zone. The **earthquake of 1985** was the most serious in recent years.

Social problems include a high **crime** rate which led to the 2004 recruitment of former New York mayor Rudolph **Giugliani** to advise on measures to combat it.

A denizen of this megalopolis is (impolitely) called a **chilango**. [L. H.]

"MÉXICO SEGURO." An anti-drug smuggling operation along the **United States border** initiated in 2005 by Ramón **Martín Huerta**.

MEXICO STATE (*ESTADO DE MEXICO*). State (postal abbreviation "Mex") lying north and west of the **Federal District**, on a plateau 2,500 m (8,000 ft.) above sea level. A mountain range running northwest to southeast separates the Valley of **Mexico** from the state capital of **Toluca**. The state's economy rests on cereals, **sugar**, **maguey** cactus, fruit, dairy produce, cattle, copper and **silver**

mining, and **manufacturing** (automobiles, metal products, fibers, woolen goods, cement, and bricks). Although much of the state now lies within Greater **Mexico City**—and has been connected with the downtown area by the **Metro** since the 1980s—some 90,158 ha were reforested in the late 1990s.

Created in 1786 as an **intendancy**, it lost Mexico City when this was constituted as the **Federal District** by the **Constitution of 1824**, regaining it briefly while Mexico ceased to have a federal structure in 1836–1847. It subsequently lost territory to **Guerrero** in 1849, and to **Hidalgo** and **Morelos** in 1869, decreasing its **population** from 1,029,629 in 1857 to only 599,810 in 1869. Since then its inhabitants have numbered, at successive **censuses**: 837,000 (1895); 934,000 (1900); 989,000 (1910); 885,000 (1921); 990,000 (1930); 1,146,000 (1940); 1,393,000 (1950); 1,898,000 (1960); 3,833,000 (1970); 7,564,000 (1980), 9,816,000 (1990); 13,096,686 (2000); and 14,007,495 (2005). In 2006 they were estimated to number 14,400,000, making it the Republic's most populous state. [L. H.]

MÉXICO-TENOCHTITLÁN. A "porte-manteaux" word to refer to **Mexico City** throughout its existence, from the time of the **Aztec** city of **Tenochtitlan** through to today's modern megapolis.

MEZCAL. An alcoholic drink made from fermented **agave** (maguey cactus). It originated in **Oaxaca** but is now a standard drink throughout Mexico.

MEZQUITAL. A river of **Durango state**.

MICHELENA, JOSÉ MARIANO DE (1772–1852). Revolutionary leader who pursued a military career despite having a law degree. He was a key organizer in a failed **independence** plot of 1808, which led to his imprisonment, but he was promptly released by the sympathetic **viceroy**, Francisco Javier de **Lizana y Beaumont**. He then left for Spain and took part in the Peninsular War. After Spain's liberation from Napoleon he remained there until Mexican independence. When he returned he occupied an important post in the government of Nicolás **Bravo** besides being himself acting **president** five times

(May, July, October 1823, January and May, 1824). Later he occupied important diplomatic posts in Europe. He died in his native **Morelia**.

MICHOACÁN. (**Nahuatl** *michamacuan*, "place of the fishermen"). Created as the **intendancy** of **Valladolid de Michoacán** in 1787, it is now a state officially known as Michoacán de Ocampo, of 59,928 km² with 112 *municipios*, of which the most populous are **Morelia** (the capital), **Uruapan** (265,699 inhabitants in 2000), Lázaro Cárdenas (171,100), Zamora (161,918), Zitácuaro (138,050), **Apatzingán** (117,949), and **Hidalgo** (106,421). The state's total **population** was 554,585 in 1857 and 618,072 in 1869. Since then it has been the following at successive **censuses**: 890,000 (1895); 936,000 (1900); 992,000 (1910); 940,000 (1921); 1,048,000 (1930); 1,182,000 (1940); 1,423,000 (1950); 1,852,000 (1960); 2,324,000 (1970); 2,869,000 (1980); 3,548,200 (1990), 3,985,667 (2000); and 3,966,073 in 2005 (making it Mexico's 7th biggest state). It has Lakes **Chalapa** (shared with **Jalisco**) and **Pátzcuaro**. On its Pacific coast is the **SICARTSA** steel complex and Mexico's second largest iron ore reserves. It was the home state of both Lázaro **Cárdenas del Río** and Felipe **Calderón Hinojosa**.

As the most important state for the import of cocaine, it has a very serious organized **crime** problem, with 523 murders (35 of them **police** officers) in 2006 alone. *See also* ABAD Y QUEIPO, MANUEL; AGUILAR TALAMANTES, RAFAEL. [L. H.]

MIER, [FRAY] JOSÉ SERVANDO TERESA DE (1765–1827). A liberal religious from **Monterrey** who first gained fame by giving his interpretation of how Saint **Mary of Guadalupe** arrived in Mexico, for which he was promptly jailed by the **Inquisition**. Although an opponent of **Iturbide**, he spoke out against the liberal **Constitution of 1824** as a disaster for Mexico.

MIGRATION. *See* EMIGRATION; IMMIGRATION; INTERNAL MIGRATION.

MILPA. In most of Mexico's major **Indian** languages, a clearing for **corn** cultivation, a cornfield.

MINA, FRANCISCO JAVIER (1789–1817). Spanish soldier and revolutionary who fought for Mexican **independence**. After fighting in the Peninsular War, he was persuaded by Fray José Servando Teresa de **Mier** and other Mexican liberals to lead the *Ejército Auxiliador de la República Mexicana* in the cause of Mexican **independence**. Although victorious in several battles, he was captured with Pedro **Moreno** after attacking **Guanajuato** in October 1817 and shot.

MINIMUM WAGE. The first legal minimum wage (of 1.50 pesos a day) was decreed for the **Federal District** on January 5, 1934. Vicente **Lombardo Toledano** succeeded in getting a minimum hourly wage of 3.50 pesos during the presidency of Lázaro **Cárdenas del Río**. It is now enforced by the C.N.S.M. (*Comisión Nacional de Salarios Mínimos*—National Minimum Wage Commission), but varies geographically. In 2007 a daily rate of 50.57 pesos is payable in all of **Baja California**, the **Federal District**, and the more prosperous parts of **Chihuahua**, **Guerrero**, **Mexico State**, **Sonora**, **Tamaulipas**, and **Vera Cruz**. A daily rate of 49 pesos applies in **Jalisco**, **Nuevo León** and most of the rest of the states just named. All the rest of Mexico constitutes *Area Geográfica C* and has a daily rate of 47.60 pesos.

MINING. Mineral extraction has been important since pre-Hispanic times. The most abundant metals are **gold**, **silver**, mercury, graphite, **lead**, antimony, manganese, **copper**, molybdenum, and wolfram. Other important minerals are iron, sulfur, fluor spar (calcium fluoride), **coal** (in **Coahuila**), and marble. Expansion of the industry through foreign investment was greatly encouraged when traditional Spanish law of subsoil ownership was abrogated by the new mining code of 1884. This and the introduction of the new cyanide process increased gold production from 1.5 million **pesos**' worth in 1877 to 40 million peso's worth in 1908, and silver output from 25 million peso's worth to 80 million peso's worth in the same period.

MINISTER. (1) In this dictionary, used for a cabinet member in charge of a large department of state: *secretario* in modern Mexican usage (but sometimes *ministro* in the 1800s), *secretary* in the **United States**. His immediate assistant, *subsecretario*, is translated as "deputy minister."

(2) International usage for the head of a legation (diplomatic mission), prior to the wholesale upgrading of legations into embassies, and their heads into ambassadors, in the 20th century (1898 in the case of the U.S.-Mexico relationship). Unawareness of this change has allowed many anachronistic references to "ambassadors," who were in fact but ministers, to creep into scholarly literature. [L. H.]

MINISTRIES. The **First Empire** was administered through four *secretarías*: those of **justice** and **church** affairs, war and **navy**, finances, and of internal and external affairs. A reorganization in 1853 added a secretariat of development, settlement, industry, and **trade**. The **Constitution of 1917** created a separate trade and industry ministry. A law of 1946 created a *Secretaría de Bienes Nacionales y de Inspección Administrativa* which in 1958 became SEPANAL, the *Secretaría de Patrimonio Nacional*, responsible for **natural resources**. A ministerial reorganization of 1977 which created a *Secretaría de Patrimonio y Fomento Industrial* was followed by another in 1982, creating a *Secretaria de Comercio y Fomento Industrial* and a *Secretaria de Energía, Minas y Industria Paraestatal*, SEMIP, and yet another in 1994, creating a *Secretaría de Energía*.

Currently there are 18 major departments of state (*secretarías*) whose heads (*secretarios*) are members of the president's cabinet: the **agrarian reform ministry**, the **agriculture ministry**, the **defense ministry**, the **economics ministry**, the **education ministry**, the **energy ministry**, the **environment ministry**, the **finance ministry**, the **foreign ministry**, the **health ministry**, the **interior ministry**, the **labor ministry**, the **national security ministry**, the **naval ministry**, the **public administration ministry**, the **social development ministry**, the **tourism ministry**, and the **transport ministry**. [L. H.]

MINT (*La Casa de Moneda de México*). Mexico's national mint, the oldest in the New World, began in 1519 as a private concession to Hernán **Cortes** and was only established as a formal branch of government when Antonio de **Mendoza** became the first **viceroy** in 1535, and located it in the building that currently houses the National **Monte de Piedad**. In 1562 it was moved to the **National Palace**. Enlargement and improvement of its accommodation there in the late 17th century and during the course of the 1700s led Alexander von

Humbolt to describe it as the "largest and richest" mint in the whole world.

The widespread collapse of law and order ushered in by the **independence** struggle made it unsafe to ship new coins out of **Mexico City**, so stimulating the creation of provincial mints, some of which were not closed down until 1905, only to reappear briefly during the anarchy following the **Revolution of 1910**.

Although the mint remains headquartered in Mexico City, most of its production (which includes **coinage** for foreign customers) was moved in 1983 to a new mint in **San Luis Potosí**. [L. H.]

MIRAMAR. Palace on the Adriatic near Trieste, residence of **Maximilian** at the time he was offered the throne of Mexico. There he signed the Convention of Miramar whereby he was to receive military assistance from the French emperor, **Napoleon III**, in return for Mexico's assuming responsibility, not only for all outstanding **foreign debts**, but also for the cost of the 20,000-strong French expeditionary force, effectively tripling the burden on the Mexican treasury. [L. H.]

MIRAMÓN, [GENERAL] MIGUEL (1832–1867). Provisional president of the conservative faction in Mexico, 1859–1860, during the **War of the Reforms,** and their best general. Faithful to the Emperor **Maximilian** to the end, he was captured with him at **Querétaro** and shortly afterwards shot, along with the Emperor and General Tomás **Mejía**, June 19.

MITLA. A city lasting from 600 to 1521, built by the **Zapotec** but in the 14th century occupied by the **Mixtec**, whose highly developed civilization left huge buildings and temples including a Hall of Columns with mosaic designs and hieroglyphs. The site lies 32 km (20 miles) southeast of **Oaxaca City**.

MIXE. Indian nation of 69,000 (1995 estimate) living in **Oaxaca** state.

MIXTEC. The fourth largest **Indian** nation in Mexico today, of some 280,000 people (1995 estimate) living in **Oaxaca** (where they are the second largest Indian group, after the **Zapotec**), **Guerrero**, and **Puebla** states. The Mixtecs are related ethnically and linguistically to the Zapotec, whose pre-Hispanic cities of **Mitla** and **Monte Albán** they came to occupy.

MIXTON WAR. A fiercely fought campaign in **Jalisco** in 1541–1542 to overcome the nomadic **Chichimeca** tribes (who were preventing the Spaniards from pushing northwards, just as they had previously stopped the **Aztec** advance). It was in this war that Pedro de **Alvarado** lost his life.

MOCHIS, LOS. Pacific coast city on the **Fuerte** river, 30 m above mean sea level at 25°55'N, 109°10'W, 200 km from **Culiacán**, **cabecera** of the **Sinaloa municipio** of **Ahome**, It first became important as a railroad terminus. [L. H.]

MOCIÑO, JOSÉ (c.1770–c.1820). An outstanding scientist who was most famous for his work in botany. He was a student and colleague of the French botanist Sessé whom he accompanied on scientific expeditions throughout **New Spain**, where both men discovered and categorized many **flora**. He went back with Sessé to **Spain**, and after the latter's death, settled for a while in France He later died in Spain. The most famous of his many works is his *Flora mexicana.*

MOCTEZUMA (NAHUATI *MOTECUHZOMA*). Normal form in Spanish of the Aztec personal name **Montezuma**, given to a river of **Hidalgo state**.

MOCTEZUMA, ESTÉBAN. General who led a revolt from **Tampico** which overthrew President Anastacio **Bustamante** in 1832.

MOCTEZUMA CID, JULIO RODOLFO (1927–). A **Mexico City** lawyer who was assistant director of planning for the ministry of the **presidency** in 1964, and then its director of investments, 1965–1970. During 1971–1973 he was legal consultant for the ministers of finance and the presidency and for the head of the **Compañía Nacional de Subsistencias Populares (CONASUPO)**, thereby influencing major policies of the **Echeverría** administration. From December 1976 to November 1977 he was himself finance minister, and then he became coordinator for the **finance ministry** and the ministry for planning and the budget, as President **López Portillo**'s chief financial and economic adviser.

MODERADOS. The "middle-of-the-roader"s of the early **independence** era, principally upper class **Creoles** opposed to both a monarchy and the privileged status of the **Church** and clergy.

MODERNISMO. Late 19th century literary (and predominantly poetic) movement, the Hispanic equivalent of French and English symbolism, and corresponding to Art Nouveau in other contemporary art forms. Originally developed by the Nicaraguan Rubén Darío, its first important Mexican practitioners were Amado **Nerva** and (arguably) Enrique **González Martínez**. It shares nothing but the name with the Brazilian *modernismo* of the 1920s. [L. H.]

MODERNISTA. Adhering or pertaining to **Modernismo**.

MOLINA DEL REY, BATTLE OF, 1847. Lucas **Balderas** was killed here.

MOLINA ENRÍGUEZ, ANDRÉS (1866–1940). Lawyer who became a general in the **Revolution of 1910**. His work *Los Grandes problemas nacionales* (1910) on the social ills of the time had a great effect on the developing ideology of the Revolution. He is regarded as the chief architect of **agrarian reform** and had great influence on drafting Article 27 of the **Constitution of 1917**.

MONCAYO, JOSÉ PABLO (1912–1958). A composer of **Huapango** music.

MONCLOVA. Town of **Coahuila** (and its original capital) which has a steel mill. The **municipio** had a population of 193,657 in 2000. It was founded during the brief **viceroyalty** of Melchor **Portocarrero Laso de la Vega**.

MONEDA, LA. *See* COINAGE; MINT.

MONEY. *See* COINAGE; DOLLAR; EXCHANGE RATE; PESO; REAL.

MONSERRAT Y CIURANA, JOAQUÍN DE, MARQUÉS DE CRUÏLLES, SEÑOR DE BENALFAQUÉ, DE CATAMAR-RÚA Y DE LLOMBO (1700?–1771). Viceroy of New Spain, 1760–1766. Born in Valencia, he received a commission for the Spanish foot guards when very young and became governor of Badajoz. Within a year of his appointment as viceroy he was accused of embezzling government funds, and a six-year investigation by the Visitor General José de **Gálvez** led to his recall. During this time he put down a rebellion in **Yucatán** and led a naval attack on Havana which recovered Cuba from its British occupiers. His trial took place in Spain where he was granted the titles of Baron of Patraix and of Planes and allowed to return to **New Spain** to hand over his staff of office formally to his successor, Carlos Francisco de **Croix.** [L. H.]

MONSIVÁIS, CARLOS (1938–). Essayist (*Aires de familia: cultura y sociedad en América latina,* 2000), winner of the 2006 Juan **Rulfo** prize. [L. H.]

MONTE ALBÁN. Zapotec, and later, **Mixtec,** mountaintop site 10 km (six miles) west of **Oaxaca City,** excavated in 1931 by Alfonso **Caso.** The delicate gold, **silver,** and jade jewelry, masks, and implements he found are now in the state museum in Oaxaca City.

MONTE DE LAS CRUCES, BATTLE OF. Royalist victory over insurgents in central Mexico, October 30, 1810.

MONTE DE PIEDAD. An officially sponsored pawnshop, found throughout the former Spanish empire. That in **Mexico City** is *"nacional." See also* HINOJOSA, COSME R.

MONTEJO, FRANCISCO DE (1448–1550). Conquistador, one of Hernán **Cortés'** principal allies, who was sent to Spain to defend the latter's interests. In 1527 **Charles V** authorized him to explore and colonize **Yucatán.** He got control of Yucatán and **Cozumel,** and also of Honduras, until Pedro de Alvarado drove him out. In old age he lost his lands and returned to Spain, where he died.

MONTEJO, FRANCISCO DE, THE YOUNGER. In 1540–1546 he completed the conquest of the **Maya**, first attempted by his father, and in 1542 he founded the city of **Mérida**.

MONTEMAYOR, CARLOS (1947–). A writer from **Parral**, **Chihuahua**. Novels: *Minas del retorno* (1982), *Guerra en el paraíso* (1991); poetry: *Abril y otras estaciones* (1997); short stories: *Las llaves de Urgell* (1971). [L. H.]

MONTENEGRO Y NERVO, ROBERTO (1885–1968). Mexican painter from **Guadalajara** who specialized in surrealist murals. In 1934 he became the first director of the *Museo de Arte Popular* (Museum of Mexican Popular Art in Mexico City).

MONTERREY. Capital of **Nuevo León**, Mexico's third largest city, and its second largest industrial center, at 25°40'N, 100°15'W, 537 m above sea level, 240 km (150 miles) south of the **United States border**, with a population within the **municipio** of 11,000 in 1803; 15,000 in 1862; 47,000 in 1878; 88,000 in 1920; 333,000 in 1950; 1,110,997 in 2000; and 1,139,417 in 2005; but 3,593,274 in the whole metropolitan area. Founded in 1596 by Luis de **Carvajal**, the city was the **viceroyalty**'s control point for trade routes through the Sierra **Madre** Oriental. Modernization began in 1888 when the **railroads** from **Texas** and **Mexico City** reached Monterrey. In 1903 the **Fundidora de Monterrey** went into production. Large supplies of natural gas from **Tamulipas state** and iron ore from Nuevo León state itself and from **Coahila state** have aided industrialization. The city has the largest cement and glass factories in Mexico, and the **Cuauhtémoc S.A.** brewery. Other factories produce paper, plastics, automobile equipment, and electronic and electrical appliances ranging from **television** receivers to refrigerators. The *Centro de Productividad de Monterrey*, second only to the National Productivity Center in Mexico City, trains skilled workers. The city has the **Universidad de Nuevo León** and the private **Instituto Tecnológico de Monterrey**.

MONTES DE OCA, FERNANDO (1829–1847). One of the **Niños Héroes**. Born in Atzcapozalco, he died in defense of **Chapultepec Castle**, fighting on when the battle was lost, despite orders to retreat.

MONTES DE OCA, LUIS (1894–1958). An accountant who became President **Carranza**'s financial envoy to the United States in 1915. As comptroller general, 1924–1927, he was Mexico's monetary reformer. He became director general of the **Banco de México** and in 1937 founded the government's **Banco Nacional de Comercio Exterior**. He was a long-time spokesman for Mexican presidents to the National Banking Council and began the widespread practice of appointing public accountants to high federal offices.

MONTEZUMA. Traditional English form of the **Aztec** name that appears as *Motecuhczoma* in **Nahuatl** and as *Moctezuma* in Spanish.

MONTEZUMA I. Moctezuma Ilhuicamina ("heaven's bowman"), **Aztec** "emperor" (**tlatoani**), 1441–1469, nephew of **Itzcóatl**. His military conquests extended the Aztec empire to the northeast and south, until checked toward the end of his reign by a catastrophic famine, whose eventual ending was attributed to the practice of human sacrifice.

MONTEZUMA II (1475–1520). Moctezuma Xocoyótzin ("valiant lord"), **Aztec** "emperor" (**tlatoani**), 1502–1520. It was during his reign that the first hotels were established in **Tenochtitlán** and a botanical garden built in Oaxtepec, **Morelos**. He lived in extraordinary luxury, attended by 300 servants, his daily meals consisting of hundreds of different courses, from which he chose a sampling. His plates were of **gold** and **silver**, and he enjoyed ocean fish brought to his court the day they were caught by a relay of runners. He was killed by a stone thrown by one of his own subjects while trying to persuade them to surrender to the Spaniards.

MONTUFAR, ALFONSO (????–1572). Second archbishop of Mexico, appointed October 5, 1551.

MORA, JOSÉ MARÍA LUIS (1794–1850). Liberal politician who worked closely with Valentín **Gomes Farías** and is recognized as the principal theoretician of Mexican liberalism. López de **Santa Anna** banished him, but he returned when Santa Anna himself had to go into exile. He died in Paris, and his remains were not brought back to Mexico until 1963.

[In 1981 his name was chosen for **Consejo Nacional de Ciencia y Tecnología**'s new postgraduate research institute in history and the social sciences in **Mexico City**, the *Instituto de Investigaciones Dr. José Maris Luis Mora*. L. H.]

MORALES BLUMENKRON, GUILLERMO (1908?–). A broadcaster, born in **Puebla**, who directed government programs 1934–1936, then originated the government's "National Hour," sent out from all radio stations each Sunday night (and still running in 1979). He was president of the Association of Advertising Agencies, 1957–1959; head of the National Chamber of Broadcasters, 1968; interim **governor** of **Puebla state**, 1973–1974; and owner of 20 leading radio stations and a leading network official.

MORATORIUM. *See* FOREIGN DEBT MORATORIUM.

MORDIDA ("bite"). In Mexico, a bribe paid to **police** and other civil servants, particularly in finalizing negotiations of public contracts with private companies and services, and hence, any bribe, large or small—probably the most pervasive form of **corruption** in Mexican life.

MORELIA. Capital city of **Michoacán** founded in 1541 as **Vallodolid** and renamed for the **Independence** hero José **Morelos**. Located in a fertile valley at 1,890 m (6,200 ft.) above sea level, at 19°45'N, 101°10'W, 200 km (125 miles) west of **Mexico City**, it has preserved many colonial buildings, including the Spanish governor's palace. Home to the venerable **Universidad de San Nicolás**, the city had a 1995 population of 315,000 and 568,700 in 2003. At the 2000 census, the whole **municipio** had 620,532 inhabitants.

MORELOS STATE ("Mor"). Lying just south of the **Federal District** and bounded on the southwest by **Guerrero** and on the southeast by **Puebla state**, it is the Republic's second smallest state (4,941 km²), formed from **Mexico State** as a *Departamento* in 1862, only becoming a state in April, 1869, and not acquiring its present boundaries until 1923. Named for Jesús María **Morelos y Pavón**, it is divided into 33 *municipios*. The capital is **Cuernavaca**, which like other mountain cities of Morelos enjoys a spring-like mild climate. Morelos, a major producer of **sugar** cane and **rice**, has been credited at successive **censuses** with 121,409 inhabitants (1869); 160,000 (1895 and 1900); 180,000 (1910); 103,000 (1921); 132,000 (1930); 183,000 (1940); 273,000 (1950); 386,000 (1960); 616,000 (1970); 947,000 (1980); 1,195,000 (1990); 1,555,296 (2000); and 1,612,899 (2005). Emiliano **Zapata** was a native.

MORELOS Y PAVÓN, JOSÉ MARÍA (1765–1815). Patriot from **Valladolid**, now renamed **Morelia** in his honor. Although regarded as a **creole**, he was probably a **mestizo** with some African ancestry. He began as a mule driver, and his knowledge of the terrain of southern Mexico enabled him to become an outstanding military and **guerrilla** leader during the initial struggle for **independence**. He studied under Miguel **Hidalgo y Costilla** at the **Colegio de San Nicolás** and became a priest. When Hidalgo began his insurrection, Morelos volunteered to be a chaplain, but he was ordered to lead the revolutionary movement in the south. He took over the leadership of the movement on Hidalgo's death, his outstanding feat being the defeat of **Calleja del Rey** at **Cuatla**. After capturing **Acapulco**, he convened the Congress of **Chilpancingo** to declare independence, using, in contrast to Hidalgo, the humble title "Servant of the Nation." Despite a series of defeats he convened the **Apatzingán Congress**, but before the constitution it drew up could be put into effect he was captured on his way to **Tehuacán**, tried, and shot by firing squad, December 22.

The death of this capable leader signalled the end of the Independence movement begun by Miguel **Hidalgo y Costilla**. Mexico regards him second only to Hidalgo as a hero, but he had far more military ability. His face appears on the 50 peso bill.

MORENO, PEDRO (1775–1817). Patriot, active in the revolutionary movement from 1814, working closely with Francisco Javier **Mina**, with whom he was captured and shot, October 1817. Lagos de Moreno in the state of **Jalisco** is named after him.

MORONES, LUIS N. (1890–1964). Labor leader who founded the **Confederación Regional Obrera Mexicana (CROM)**. A short and extremely overweight individual, Morones was known for his **corruption**, but continued to wield decisive labor influence because he maintained good relations between labor and President Plutarco **Calles**, who made him minister of industry, trade, and labor, further enhancing his power. Although the CROM lost power and influence under President Emilio **Portes Gil**, Morones continued to be wealthy. When **Cárdenas del Rio** rose to power, Morones was exiled to the United States in 1936, but he returned later to head the now powerless CROM. He died in **Mexico City**.

MORROW, DWIGHT (1873–1931). **United States** ambassador to Mexico from 1927. His appointment marks the beginning of the best era of cooperation between the United States and Mexico and is an excellent example of how one man can influence relations between two countries. He had a genuine love and respect for the Mexican people and was greatly instrumental in negotiating an end to the **Cristero** Rebellion. He personally paid for the murals painted by Diego **Rivera** at the Palace of **Cortés** in **Cuernavaca**.

His daughter was the writer Anne Morrow **Lindbergh**.

MOTION PICTURE INDUSTRY. *See* CINEMA.

MOTOLINÍA. Native name adopted by Fray Toribio de **Benavente**.

MOVIES. *See* CINEMA.

MOVIMIENTO DE LIBERACIÓN NACIONAL (M.L.N.). Far left movement founded in 1961, which gave some assistance in the land seizures carried out by Rubén **Jaramillo**. *See also* VAZQUEZ ROJAS, GENARO.

MOYA, LUIS (18??–1911). Hero of the **Revolution of 1911**, born in **Zacatecas state**, who won numerous battles, liberated the city of **Zacatecas** and Ciudad Lerdo, but fell to a stray bullet in Sombrerete as he dismounted to visit kinsfolk in the town, which he had just liberated.

MOYA PALENCIA, MARIO (1933–). Lawyer who was public relations administrator for the **Ferrocarriles Nacionales de México**, 1955–1958; assistant director of real estate for the Ministry of **Natural Resources** (*Patrimonio Nacional*), 1959–1961; director general of the **Cinema** Bureau of the **Interior Ministry**, 1964–1968; assistant interior minister, 1969–1970; and then interior minister, 1970–1976. He was President **Echeverría**'s choice as his successor, but the **Partido Revolucionario Institucional** inner circle preferred José **López Portillo**.

MOYA Y CONTRERAS, PEDRO DE (1535?–1591). Sixth **viceroy** of **New Spain**, 1583–1585, first inquisitor and third archbishop of Mexico. Born in Pedroches (province of Córdova), he became a child page of Juan de Ovando (president of the **Council of the Indies**), who made him his private secretary and paid for his studies at Salamanca University where he became a doctor of civil and canon law. He went on to become a schoolmaster at the cathedral of the Canary Islands and, around 1568, inquisitor of Murcia. Within the year he was sent to establish the Holy **Inquisition** in the **viceroyalty**, choosing to locate it initially in Santo Domingo. He strove to learn the main **Indian languages** and to improve the education of his clergy. An outbreak of plague in 1576 demonstrated his humanitarian concern for the Indians who were the most affected. His fame and the favorable reports on him that the viceroy sent back to Spain led to his appointment as visitor to tackle official **corruption**, which had increased greatly on the viceroy's death. His efforts were remarkable in reaching further up the hierarchy than ever before. He became viceroy himself on November 25, 1584, and in 1585 he summoned the Third Provincial Mexican Council which declared there was no justification for Indian slavery. Phillip II recalled him in mid-1586 to become president of the Council of the Indies and got the Pope to make him patriarch of the Indies.

His name also appears as Pedro Moya de Contreras. [L. H.]

MÚGICA, [GENERAL] FRANCISCO JOSÉ (1884–1954). Soldier-politician of radical socialist views. As delegate to the **Constituent Assembly of 1916–1917**, his was a key influence on the anti-clerical, **agrarian reform**, and **labor** rights provisions of the **Constitution of**

1917. He governed his native state of **Michoacán** in 1920–1922, then directed federal prisons, served as trade and industry minister, 1934–1935, public works minister, 1935–1939, and governor of **Baja California del Sur**, 1940–1946. As a close friend of President Lázaro **Cárdenas del Rio**, he might have become president in 1940, but many in the **Partido Revolucionario Institucional** found his radicalism too extreme, especially since he had helped secure political asylum in Mexico for Leon **Trotsky**.

MÚGICA, HUGO. Eldest son of General Francisco **Múgica**, who enrolled him at the Texas Military Institute in **San Antonio** to insure he would be bilingual. The elder Múgica encouraged his colleagues to send their sons to the **United States** for **secondary education** or college to insure their familiarity with American industrial and military culture and the English language. Hugo returned to Mexico for his **higher education**, entered the Mexican **air force**, and, as a colonel, became the Mexican president's personal pilot.

MÚGICA MONTOYA, EMILIO (1926–). Economist, born May 1926 in **Mexico City**, graduated from **UNAM**, where he taught economics, 1951–1973. He was an economist for the ministries of communications, **national patrimony** (1948–1952), and the **Nacional Financiera**. He then became an administrator successively for the **Compañía Nacional de Subsistencias Populares (CONASUPO)**, the **Ferrocarriles Nacionales de México**, and the Finance Ministry (1959–1975). He was coordinator for all publicly owned industries in 1975–1976, and then became minister of communications and transport.

MUJERES, ISLAND OF (*ISLA MUJERES*). A 3 km-long island and **municipio** of **Quintana Roo** at 21°11'N, 86°42'W, 8 km across the Bahía de Mujeres from **Cancún**. The island has a **fishing** village and is a tourist resort. Its population in 2000 was 11,313.

MULATTO. Person of mixed African and European descent. *See also* BLACKS, ZAMBO.

MUMPS. One of the killer diseases that came with the Spanish **Conquest of Mexico**, it is first recorded in **Mesoamerica** in 1550.

MUNICIPIO. The basic (and lowest) Hispanic unit of local government, roughly corresponding to an Anglo-American county (often with several towns and a surrounding rural area), although often misleadingly translated "municipality." It is normally named for the **cabecera** (county seat) but there is a long Hispanic tradition of its governing body (the **cabildo**, now known as the **ayuntamiento**) neglecting the rural area. Mexico in 1979 was divided into 2,359 *municipios*. [L. H.]

MÚÑOZ LEDO, PORFIRIO (1933–). Leader of the **Partido de la Revolución Democrática** in the lower house, and current president of the party. Born July 23, in **Mexico City**, he graduated in law at **UNAM**, did graduate studies in economics and political science at the Sorbonne, 1956–1959; served as a political adviser and analyst for the **Partido Revolucionario Institucional**, 1960–1972; Mexican envoy to **UNESCO**; assistant director for graduate education at the **Education Ministry**, 1961–1965; secretary general of social security, 1966–1970; adviser on federal housing throughout the 1970s; assistant minister of the **presidency**, 1970–1972; labor minister, 1972–1975; president of the PRI, 1975–1976. In 1976 he became education minister and pushed expansion of vocational training and institutions of higher education, but resigned in December 1977 over policy disagreements. He ultimately left the PRI to join the PRD, which he headed in 1993–1996. After the **election of 1997** he became PRD leader in the **Cámara de Diputados Federales**, helping it to forge a loose coalition with the **Partido de Acción Nacional** to control a majority of votes in the 1997–1999 sessions. In 1999 he indicated his wish to be the PRD's presidential candidate but lost out to Cuauhtémoc **Cárdenas Solorzano** and gave his support to Vicente **Fox Quesada** who appointed him ambassador to the European Union. On his return in February 2004 he announced his intention to avoid any party allegiance and to promote consensus politics, but in early 2006 he was supporting the PRD presidential candidate Andrés Manuel **López**.

MURALISTS. Mural **painting** has been called the supreme form of Mexican artistic expression. It most famous practitioner is probably Diego **Rivera**. Others include Raúl **Anguiano**, Daniel **Manrique**

Arias, José **Chávez Morado**, Roberto **Montenegro y Nervo**, José Clemente **Orozco**, David Alfaro **Siqueiros**, and Rufino **Tamayo**. *See also* BONAMPAK.

MURDER. *See* HOMICIDE.

MURILLO VIDAL, RAFAEL (1904–). Lawyer who served as a judge in the state courts of Veracruz and **Nayarit**, a member of the **Cámara de Diputados Federales**, postmaster general, senator (1964–1968), **governor** of his native **Veracruz** (1968–1974). Since 1946 he has been a leader of the **Confederación Nacional de Organizaciones Populares**, helping federal bureaucrats control the **Partido Republicano Institucional**.

MUSEO NACIONAL DE ANTROPOLOGÍA. The National Anthropology Museum opened at its present site in **Chapultepec Park** in 1962 in one of the world's best designed museum complexes, after decades of being housed in several colonial era buildings in downtown **Mexico City**. Its exhibits, maps, artifacts, and dioramas depict both ancient and modern Indian cultures from throughout Mexico. Simulations of the pyramids of **Teotihuacán** and of **Maya**, **Zapotec**, and **Aztec** temples combine scaled-down structures and murals. The museum has the original Aztec sacrificial stone, an Aztec **"Sun Stone,"** and Aztec, Maya, and Zapotec **codices**. Taped music, mannequins in typical clothing, and household and work scenes from present-day cultures include every Indian group in the country. The architect was Pedro **Ramírez Vásquez**.

MUSEO NACIONAL DE HISTORIA. The National History Museum has occupied **Chapultepec Castle** and adjacent modern buildings since its founding in 1940. With paintings, maps, dioramas, flags, weapons, uniforms, documents, furniture, and many other artifacts, it traces Mexican history since the **Conquest**.

MUSIC. Among prominent musicians and composers are Julián **Carrillo Trujillo**, Carlos **Chávez**, Genaro **Codina**, Enrique Arturo **Diemecke**, José Pablo **Moncayo**, Jaime **Nunó**, Juan **Osorio Palacios**, Manuel María **Ponce**, Silvestre **Revueltas**, José **Rocabruna**,

Juventino **Rosas**, and Riog **Tovar**. *See also* FOLK MUSIC; SYM-PHONY ORCHESTRAS.

MUTUAL ASSISTANCE PACT. *See* CHAPULTEPEC, ACT OF.

MÚZQUIZ, Melchor (1790–1844). Interim president of Mexico in 1832.

MYTH. *See* FOLKLORE.

– N –

NACIONAL, BIBLIOTECA. *See* NATIONAL LIBRARY.

NACIONAL, EL. Government-controlled daily newspaper, published from 1929 in **Mexico City**, directed, August 20, 1975–September 4, 1979, by Luis M. **Farias**. It became the handy reference for all official policy changes and federal and state appointments (reported in detail), and was widely subscribed to for this reason. Its headquarters were owned by the **Interior Ministry**.

After the **Partido Revolucionario Institucional**'s close-won victory in 1988, and the opposition gains in the state and local elections of 1991 and 1994, a movement gradually grew within **Congress** to phase out the paper's subsidies. It was felt that the party was being harmed by the emphasis given to its views in this government mouthpiece. In 1998 Congress voted to defuse criticism of the PRI by ending these subsidies. Although its editors considered **privatization**, the paper was clearly not viable without government advertising and official subscriptions. Its last edition appeared on September 30, 1998, with historical sketches of its 69 years covering Mexican public life. A few thousand extra copies were printed as souvenirs for PRI activists.

NACIONAL FINANCIERA (NAFIN). Government bank created in 1934 as a government agency to buy real estate. It subsequently expanded its activities into such diverse fields as transportation, electric power, and **irrigation**, to become the prime official financial agency for promoting economic development, making low interest loans for approved projects. In 1933 it created the **Bolsa Mexicana de Valores**, the Mexican stock market. Since 1947 NAFIN has been the only government entity authorized—subject to **foreign ministry** approval, and (if a formal treaty is involved) to Senate ratification—to negotiate foreign loans. In this it has been highly successful.

NACO. A slang term with a connotation similar to that of **lepero**.

NACOZARI. Sonora town remembered for the heroism of Jesús **García**, whence its official name of Nacozari de García. At the 2000 census the **municipio** had 14,365 inhabitants.

NAHUA. Any speaker of **Nahuatl** but the term is prefered in modern Mexican usage for the dominant **Aztec**. The present day Nahuas number 1,200,000 and inhabit chiefly the states of **Puebla**, **Veracruz**, **Hidalgo**, **Guerrero**, **San Luis Potosí**, **Tlaxcalá**, **Morelos**, and **México**, although there are some Nahuatl speakers further south, in Central America.

NAHUATL. Language of the **Nahua** peoples, the first of whom, the **Toltec**, reached central Mexico from upper California in the 6th century. *See also* CODICES.

NAO DE CHINA. Alternate name for the **Manilla Galleon**.

NAPOLEON I (1769–1821). Napoleon Bonaparte, Corsican-born "Emperor of the French" whose 1804 sale of **Louisiana** gave the **United States** a common border with Mexico, compromising Spanish (and then Mexican) rule over what became the American Southwest. His 1808 intervention in **Spain** caused the Peninsular War and a crisis of authority throughout the Spanish empire that eventually resulted in successful seizure of power by local American **creole** elites, except in **Cuba**, Hispaniola, and Puerto Rico.

It was his adoption of the title of **emperor** (hitherto reserved in the western world to the titular head of Germany's "Holy Roman Empire") that inspired imitation by **Iturbide** in Mexico and Pedro I in Brazil. [L. H.]

NAPOLEON III, EMPEROR OF THE FRENCH (1808–1873). Nephew and step-grandson of **Napoleon I** whose desire to increase and extend French influence in the Americas led him to persuade **Maximilian** of Habsburg to head a French-dominated **Second Empire** in Mexico. [L. H.]

NARCOTICS. Mexico has been a major exporter of marihuana into the United States. In 1972 it replaced Turkey as the major supplier of heroin (both home grown and imported from Central America). A vigorous Mexican-United States control program, however, reduced Mexico's share of the U.S. heroin market from 90 to 50 percent by 1979. Since then the most important narcotic trade across the **United States border** with Mexico has been of cocaine, accounting for three quarters of all the Colombian cocaine reaching the United States. In the 1990s, Mexico found itself with nationwide criminal organizations ("cartels") shipping the drug overland, by sea, and even by air, using small private aircraft and remote airfields—the pilots, Americans among them, were being paid US$ 25,000 per trip. In 1997 the U.S. Drug Enforcement Administration launched an extensive investigation into both the smuggling and the resulting money laundering of the profits of over US$ 10 million a month. In March 1999 the DEA publicly linked the leaders of the two main cartels, that of the Arellano Félix brothers of **Tijuana** and the Vicente Carillo Fuentes cartel of **Ciudad Juárez** to "a few highly placed Mexican government officials." Although no charges were levelled at billionaire businessman Carlos **Hank González**, Mexican attorney general Jorge Madrazo admitted that his office had in 1997 investigated lower level administrators in Hank's many enterprises and that although no indictments were made, the large sums they handled might have included laundered funds, **Partido de Acción Nacional** congressman Adolfo Aguilar Zinzer also headed an inconclusive probe into Hank's activities. On May 10, 1997, 24 Mexican drug traffickers and bankers were trapped in Mesquite, Nevada, and jailed, but all charges were dropped as prejudicial to ongoing trade negotiations. In July the Mexican foreign ministry secured the release of four of the 24 who had been facing prosecution on related charges by Madrazo, although the others were fined and put on probation.

Amphetamine-based drugs manufactured primarily for export to the United States are a recent addition to the trade.

In February 2005 it was reported that a drug cartel had acquired a Russian ground-to-air missile originally supplied to the Communists in Nicaragua and that Nahum Acosta, responsible for the President's travel arrangements, had been selling the cartel information, implying that the narcotics industry was intending to murder President **Fox** by shooting his airplane down. *See also* CAMARENA, ENRIQUE. [L. H.]

NARD. River (tributary of the **Balsas**), and namesake state of 26,979 km^2, named for the *Nyari* or **Cora** Indians, on the southcentral Pacific coast, including the **Tres Marías** islands and **Mexcaltitán**. Its capital is **Tepic**, and until 1917 the area was the Territory of Tepic. The Sierra **Madre** Occidental traverses the state northwest to southeast, making the eastern part of the state a mountainous, lumber-producing region of forests and valleys. The western part produces such tropical crops as **cotton, sugar, coffee**, and palm oil. **San Blas** is the major port. There are 19 *municipios*: Acaponeta, Ahuacatlán, Amatlán de Ceñas, Bahia de Banderas, Compostela, Del Nayar, Huajicari, Ixtlán del Rio, Jala, **Jalisco**, Rosamorada, Ruz, San Blas, Santa María Laguinillas, Santiago Laguinillas, Santiago Ixcuintla, Tecuala, Tepic, Tuxpan, and La Yesca. Its bordering states are **Sinaloa**, **Zacatecas**, and **Durango** to the north; **Jalisco** to its east and south, The state's **population** in successive **censuses** has totaled: 149,000 (1895); 150,000 (1900); 171,000 (1910); 163,000 (1921); 168,000 (1930); 217,000 (1940); 290,000 (1950); 390,000 (1960); 544,000 (1970); 726,000 (1980); 825,000 (1990); 920,185 (2000); and 949,684 (2005). *See also* LOZADA, MANUEL. [L. H.]

NARVÁEZ, PÁNFILO DE (1470–1528). Conquistador from Valladolid, Spain, who helped Diego **Velázquez de Cuéllar** conquer Cuba, adopting far harsher measures toward the Indians than Velázquez approved of. After his 1527 return to Spain, he led a 300-man expedition to **Florida**, accompanied by Alvar **Núñez Cabeza de Vaca** as his treasurer. The expedition failed to find gold and was decimated by Indian attacks. On September 22, 1528, Velázquez sent him to Mexico to apprehend Hernán **Cortés**, but he was outmaneuvered when Cortés persuaded his men to abandon him. He died when his ship was wrecked in a storm.

NATERA, PÁNFILO (1882–1951). Second in command to Pancho **Villa**, 1913–1920, and **governor** of his native state of **Zacatecas**, 1940–1944.

NATIONAL ACTION PARTY. *See* PARTIDO DE ACCIÓN NACIONAL.

NATIONAL AGRICULTURAL CREDIT BANK. *See* BANCO NACIONAL DE CRÉDITO AGRÍCOLA.

NATIONAL ANTHEM (*Hino Nacional Mexicano*). Lyric by Francisco **González Bocanegra** (1853), music by Jaime **Nuno** (1854). The first verse is as follows:

Ciña ¡oh Patria! tus sienes de oliva / de la paz el arcángel divino / que en el cielo tu eterno destino / por el dedo de Dios se escribió.

Mas si osare un extraño enemigo / profanar con su planta tu suelo / piensa ¡oh Patria querida! que el cielo / un soldado en cada hijo te do.

And the chorus:

Mexicanos, al grito de guerra / el acero aprestad y e bridón / y retiemble en sus centros la tierra / al sonoro rugir del cañón.

NATIONAL ANTHROPOLOGY MUSEUM. *See* MUSEO NACIONAL DE ANTROPOLOGÍA.

NATIONAL BASIC COMMODITIES CORPORATION. *See* COMPAÑÍA NACIONAL DE SUBSISTENCIAS POPULARES.

NATIONAL BORDER PROGRAM. *See* PROGRAMA NACIONAL FRONTERIZO.

NATIONAL COMMITTEE FOR PROFIT SHARING. *See* COMITÉ NACIONAL DE REPARTO DE UTILIDADES.

NATIONAL CONFEDERATION OF CHAMBERS OF COMMERCE. *See* CONFEDERACIÓN DE CÁMARAS NACIONALES DE COMERCIO.

NATIONAL FEDERATION OF GOVERNMENT WORKERS. *See* FEDERACIÓN DE SINDICATOS DE LOS TRABAJADORES EN SERVICIO DEL ESTADO.

NATIONAL FEDERATION OF POPULAR ORGANIZATIONS. *See* CONFEDERACIÓN NACIONAL DE ORGANIZACIONES POPULARES.

NATIONAL FLAG. *See* FLAG.

NATIONAL FUND FOR TOURISM DEVELOPMENT. *See* FONDO DE PROMOCIÓN DE INFRAESTRUCUTRA TURÍSTICA.

NATIONAL FUND FOR WORKERS' CONSUMPTION. *See* FONDO NACIONAL DEL CONSUMO DE LOS TRABAJADORES.

NATIONAL FUND FOR WORKERS' HOUSING. *See* INSTITUTO DEL FONDO NACIONAL DE LA VIVIENDA PARA LOS TRABAJADORES.

NATIONAL HEALTH COUNCIL. *See* CONSEJO NACIONAL DE SALUD.

NATIONAL HEALTH SERVICE. *See* SISTEMA PÚBLICA DE SALUD DE MÉXICO.

NATIONAL HOLIDAYS. *See* HOLIDAYS.

NATIONAL LIBRARY (*Biblioteca Nacional*). Proposed in **Congress** in 1828, formally decreed by a law passed in 1833 at the instigation of Vice president Valentín **Gómez Farías**, it was not definitively established until November 1867—with 91,000 volumes confiscated from religious foundations including the old University and so, heavily weighted with theology and scholasticism. A collection of 4,500 volumes on Mexico and its history, purchased as the basis of a national library by the Emperor **Maximilian**, had been auctioned off at the fall of the **empire**. Nevertheless, the content of the National Library has since been enlarged, by legal deposit, purchases, and donations, and considerably broadened in scope. By 1910 it had doubled to 200,000 volumes. It reached its first million holdings in 1981, and now houses 3 million.

Control, administration, and physical location have varied over the years and, apart from José María Vigil (director, 1880–1909), its directors have been changed frequently, particularly during the **Revolution of 1910**. Since 1929 it has been administered by **UNAM**. The former Church of St. Augustine was acquired to house the library in 1867, but its adaptation took until 1883. Transfer to the UNAM campus was proposed in the 1950s but only effected in 1979. By then the new building was too small, and the collections could only be united on the new site when additional accommodation was built in 1993. [L. H.]

NATIONAL PALACE (*Palacio Nacional*). This stands on the east side of **Mexico City**'s **Zócalo** on the site of **Montezuma**'s own palace, which Hernán **Cortes** knocked down in 1521 to replace it with a residence for himself. This was acquired by the crown in 1562 and largely rebuilt in 1693. An extra floor was added in 1926. During the colonial period, as the *Palacio Real* ("Royal Palace"), it was the **viceroy**'s official residence but also housed other government offices, notably the royal **mint**, and even the **Botanical Gardens**. After **independence** it became the official residence of the president of the republic until 1876, when Porfirio **Diaz** moved into **Chapultepec Castle**. The modern building is notable for **mural painting** of Mexican history by Diego **Rivera**. [L. H.]

NATIONAL PATRIMONY. *See* NATURAL RESOURCES.

NATIONAL PAWN SHOP. *See* MONTE DE PIEDAD.

NATIONAL PEASANTS' FEDERATION. *See* CONFEDERACIÓN NACIONAL CAMPESINA.

NATIONAL PROLETARIAN DEFENSE COMMITTEE OF MEXICO. A committee set up in 1935 at the suggestion of President

Lázaro **Cárdenas del Río**, to organize Mexican labor into a general confederation. It was a forerunner, so to speak, of the **Confederación de Trabajadores Mexicanos**.

NATIONAL PUBLIC WORKS BANK. *See* BANCO NACIONAL DE OBRAS Y SERVICIOS PÚBLICAS.

NATIONAL SCHOOL OF ECONOMICS. *See* ESCUELA NACIONAL DE ECONOMÍA.

NATIONAL SECURITY MINISTRY. *See* PUBLIC SECURITY MINISTRY.

NATIONAL SYMPHONY ORCHESTRA. *See* ORQUESTA SINFÓNICA NACIONAL DE MEXICO.

NATURAL GAS. Mexico is the world's 13th largest producer of natural gas (*See* PEMEX).

NATURAL RESOURCES. Although a county's natural resources of mineral wealth, forests and other natural vegetation, and marine life may be described in Spanish as its *recursos naturales*, a more emotive phrase is *patrimonio national* (i.e., the nation's birthright or inheritance). A law of 1946 created a *Secretaría de Bienes Nacionales y de Inspección Administrativa* which in 1958 became the *Secretaría de Patrimonio Nacional*, SEPANAL. A ministerial reorganization of 1977 which replaced this with a *Secretaría de Patrimonio y Fomento Industrial* was followed by another in 1982, dividing its responsibilities between a *Secretaria de Comercio y Fomento Industrial* and a *Secretaria de Energía, Minas y Industria Paraestatal*, SEMIP. Further reorganization in 1994 divided the latter into an **Energy Ministry** and an **Environment Ministry**. *See also* AGRICULTURE; FISHING; FORESTS; MINING. [L. H.]

NAVA CASTILLO, ANTONIO (1906–). Politician from **Puebla**, a co-founder of the **Confederación Nacional de Organizaciones Populares** and its secretary general, 1944–1946; director of the federal penitentiary in **Mexico City**, 1955–1956; a member of the **Cámara**

de **Diputados Federales**; and elected **governor** of his home state in 1963, but forced to resign in 1964 for failing to end disruptive strikes by university students which had led to federal troops being sent in.

NAVAL AIR ARM. *See* FUERZA AERONAVAL.

NAVAL JACK (*Pabellon de Proa*). This is a diagonal white, green, red tricolor flag, rising left to right, bearing an anchor on the central panel.

NAVAL MINISTRY (*Secretaria de la Marina*). This ministry covers both the merchant and the fighting navies and is also responsible for cooperation with the Departamento de **Pesca**. Although imperial Spain had established a *Secretaría de Marina y de las Indias* in the 18th century, Mexico's naval affairs were originally part of the **Defense Ministry** (in its various guises), only becoming an independent ministry, the *Secretaría de Marina Nacional*, in 1939. [L. H.]

NAVARRETE LÓPEZ, JORGE EDUARDO (1940–). Diplomat from **México City**. An economics graduate from **UNAM** (1963); he became ambassador to Yugoslavia, 1977–1978; a delegate to the **United Nations**, 1978–1979; undersecretary at the **Foreign Ministry**, 1979–1985; ambassador to the **United Kingdom**, 1986–1989; ambassador to China, 1989–1994 (when he negotiated a trade agreement to sell Mexican **cotton** to the People's Republic); and, thanks to his continued contacts in Belgrade, a key adviser to the Foreign Ministry during the Kosovo conflict.

NAVARRETE ROMERO, ALFREDO (1923–1999). Economist, born July 24 in **Mexico City**, an economics graduate of **UNAM** with a PhD in economics from Harvard. He directed **Nacional Financiera**, 1953–1970; the **Financiera Azucarera**, 1970–1972; was subdirector of finances for **Pemex**, 1972–1976; and has been an economic adviser for the **United Nations**, the **Organization of American States**, the World Bank, and the Mexican **finance ministry**.

He is married to Ifigenia **Martínez de Navarrete Romero**.

NAVARRO, HÉCTOR (1937–). Painter and educator, teaching at the **Universidad de Guadalajara**. He has had many exhibitions in both

Mexico and the **United States**, and his works can be seen at many museums in both countries. Of note are his paintings *Personaje Mitomano* and *Situación de Ubicuidad.*

NAVY (*MARINA ARMADA*). Spain had created the **Windward Fleet** in the 17th century to patrol the Caribbean and the Gulf of **Mexico**, and in the 18th century commissioned a **coast guard** of privateers. Despite its long **coastline** on two oceans, independent Mexico has never emphasized naval strength. Its few warships remained in port during the **United States-Mexican War** as the only way to avoid their destruction. Some build-up occurred during the **Porfirato** including a **Escuela Naval Militar** at the main navy base at **Veracruz**, but the force was still too small to play much of a role in the **Revolution of 1911**. Some small warships were bought from the **United States** and Canada in the 1920s and the 1940s. There has been further expansion since, mainly for coastal surveillance and fishery protection. By 1996 it had a volunteer force of 37,000, but lacked submarines, fast-attack craft, and air defense missiles. Ten years later its personnel had increased to 46,972, but its strength was still concentrated in coastal patrol vessels: the only larger ships were two destroyers and six frigates. Officers train at the *Escuela Naval Militar* and those selected for senior command at the **Centro de Estudios Superiores Navales.** *See also* FUERZA AERONAVAL; NAVAL MINISTRY; SAINZ DE BARANDA, PEDRO. [L. H.]

NAZAS. River of **Durango state**.

NEAR NORTH (*EL NORTE CHICO*). That part of northern **New Spain** that became the northern states of Mexico after the 1848 loss of the "**Far North**," i.e., **Baja California**, **Sonora**, **Sinaloa**, **Chihuahua**, **Coahuila**, **Nuevo León**, and **Tamaulipas**. These states contribute 62 percent of modern Mexico's land **area**, but only 25 percent of its **population**. [L. H.]

NEGRETE, JORGE (1911–1953). Mexico's leading singing actor from his 1936 debut. His 38 films included *El Fanfarrón* (1938) and *Historia de un amor* (1941). Among the mostly patriotic songs he popularized were *Jalisco* and *Allá en el rancho grande*. The good-looking Negrete became María **Félix**'s second husband but was unable to prevent her from divorcing him to marry the far less handsome Diego **Rivera**. A native of **Chihuahua**, he died in Los Angeles.

NEGRETE, PEDRO CELESTINO (1777–1846). Provisional **president** of Mexico, March 31–April 30, 1823.

NERVA, AMADO [RUIZ DE] (1870–1919). Poet and diplomat, he began as a journalist, but first became famous as a novelist with *El Bachiller* (1896). Early in the 20th century he entered the foreign service, at the same time acquiring fame as a poet. Like his friend Rubén Darío, a **modernista**, he followed in the path of **Gutiérrez Nájera**. His most famous and most popular poem is *La Amada inmóvil* (1912), inspired by the death of his beloved Ana Cecilia Luisa Daíllez, his companion of 10 years.

NETHERLANDS, RELATIONS WITH. The Dutch fight for independence from Spain, 1580–1609, 1621–1648, soon spilled over into the Americas in the form of seaborne attacks on Spanish shipping, coastal towns, and islands. *See also* CAMACHO, SEBASTIÁN; WINDWARD FLEET.

NETZAHUALCÓYOTL. *See* NEZAHUALCÓYOTL.

NEVADA, SIERRA DE ("snowed upon"). As a name for a high mountain range, almost as common in the Hispanic world as that of *"Grande"* for a river. One such is the range to the immediate east and southeast of **Mexico City**, which includes the peaks of **Popocatepetl**, **Tláloc**, Telapon, and **Pelayo**. The lands of the modern US state of Nevada were nominally Mexican before 1848. [L. H.]

NEW MEXICO (*NUEVO MEXICO*). A part of Mexico's old **Far North** with its own governor from 1696 until **independence**, but acquired by the **United States** in 1848. After losing what became the territory of **Arizona** in 1863, the remaining 315,113 km^2 received statehood in 1912. [L. H.]

NEW SPAIN (*NUEVA ESPANA*). The official name of Spain's first New World **viceroyalty** (1521–1821), embracing all territories north of Panamá. **Cuba** (then including Florida and **Louisiana**) and **Guatemala** (then including all Central America) were, however, captaincies general, and for most purposes directly dependent on Spain, so that the viceroy's effective authority was limited to Mexico (albeit then a far larger Mexico including all the "**Far North**" lost to the United States in the 1830s–1840s). Judicially, however, his authority controlled not only the **audiencia** of **Mexico City**, but also those of **Guadalajara**, Guatemala, **Santo Domingo**, and Manila. [L. H.]

NEWS, THE. English-language daily, owned by *Novedades* and published from the third floor of the *Novedades* building. When Ramón **Beteta** became manager in 1958, he cautiously encouraged *The News* to be as objective as conditions permitted in reporting on Mexican government activities, which resident American, Canadian, and British businessmen and their families expected, having such coverage in their hometown papers.

NEWSPAPERS. Newspaper publishing began in 1665 with the *Gaceta de México*. The first daily, *El Diario de México*, was started in 1805 by Carlos de Bustamante. Soon afterwards weekly newspapers became important in igniting the fight for **independence**.

By the 1930s the most prominent dailies (and President **Cárdenas'** regular reading) were *Excélsior* and *El Universal*. In the mid-20th century, fewer than half of all Mexican voters read daily newspapers. As a source of political news, **radio** was more important for most Mexicans. By 1946 the greater metropolitan areas of **Mexico City, Guadalajara,** and **Monterrey** shared almost 60 percent of the country's total daily newspaper readership. To control content, government used the patronage of state agencies' advertising rather than **censorship**.

Development of the provincial press has been slow because Mexico City dailies circulate nationally among government and civic leaders. These national papers, plus those of **Guadalajara** and **Monterrey**, provide 60 percent of total daily newspaper circulation. The rest of Mexico, with 80 percent of the population, has 40 percent of the newspaper circulation. *See also JORNADA; NEWS, THE; NOVEDADES; PRENSA; REFORMA; UNO MAS UNO.*

NEXOS. Left-wing literary journal, edited 1983–1995 by Héctor Aguilar Camín (husband of frequent contributor Àngeles **Mastretta**).

NEZAHUALCÓYOTL (1402–1472). Poet king of the **Acolhuas**. His father was deposed by **Tezozómoc** of **Azcapotzalco**, and both father and son had to flee for their lives, eventually finding refuge in **Tenochtitlán**. For over 10 years Nezahualcoyotl lived in exile, but he regained his father's throne in 1431 and ruled Texcoco until his death. When young he had been a brave warrior, but he had soon showed outstanding ability as a poet and scientist also. As king he had many public works carried out, including palaces, aqueducts, public baths, and the most famous hanging gardens in the Americas. His face appears on the current 100 peso bill.

NEZAHUALCÓYOTL. "Netza," a **município** of **Mexico State**, named after the **Texcoco** king, formed in 1964 by the merger of Chimalhuacán, La **Paz**, and Ectepec. By 1995 it was Mexico's sixth most populous municipio with a population of 1,256,115, but more recent estimates, suggesting almost three times this number, would put it in second place. The administrative seat is **Ciudad Nezahualcóyotl**. Situated northeast of **Mexico City** but within the Greater Mexico City area, the *município* houses some of the conurbation's poorest inhabitants, many of them in virtual shantytowns.

NEZAHUALPILLI. Son of **Nezahualcóyotl**, whom he succeeded as king of **Texoco** in 1472.

NIAGARA CONFERENCE. A meeting at Niagara Falls, Ontario, Canada, in 1914, called for by **Argentina, Brazil, Chile**, and the **United States** to end the **Revolution of 1910** through peace negotiations between Victoriano **Huerta** and Venustiano **Carranza**. It failed, primarily because Carranza demanded Huerta's unconditional surrender.

NIERMAN, LEONARDO (1932–). One of Mexico's most outstanding 20th century painters, he prepared for his career by studying physics and the psychology of color at **UNAM**. He has had exhibitions all over the world, and his works (e.g., *Pájaro de fuego* and

Influencia Solar) are characterized by brilliant colors which at times seem to emit fire.

NIÑOS HÉROES ("Child heroes"). The cadets of the **San Blas Battalion**, killed at the Battle of **Chapultepec**, and commemorated by a huge monument in Chapultepec Park: Juan de la **Barrera**, Juan **Escutia**, Fernando **Montes de Oca**, Francisco Márquea, Vicente **Suárez**, and Agustín **Melgar**. The **Heróica Escuela Militar** was so renamed in their honor.

NISHIZAWA, LOUIS (1920–). Painter and sculptor from **Mexico state**, trained at the **Escuela Nacional de Artes Plásticas de Mexico** and at the Center of Japanese Artists in Tokyo. He has had art exhibitions in many parts of the world. One of his most famous works is *Naturaleza muerta*.

¡NO REELECTION! *See* "EFFECTIVE SUFFRAGE: NO REELECTION"; REELECTION.

NOBAL. Spanish for **prickly pear cactus**.

NOCHE TRISTE. The "sad night" or "night of sorrows" of June 30–July 1, 1520, when **Cuitlahuac** drove the Spaniards out of **Tenochtitlán** with heavy losses.

NOGALES. Sonora town on the **United States border**, opposite Nogales, Arizona. The two communities are very unequal (in 2000 the Mexican town had 159,787 inhabitants in the **municipio**—and over 320,000 if the surrounding area be included—its U.S. twin only 12,000) but they cooperate in fire fighting, traffic control, and other daily tasks, despite the international boundary. They form a natural pass in the mountains for north-south highways connections, and (especially in the 1960s–1970s) for **narcotics** smuggling.

NOOTKA. Location on the Pacific coast of the north of Vancouver Island, at 50°N, 170 km (45 miles) north of Tofino, from the name given to the local **Indians**. Although Juan José **Pérez Hernánez** had traded there from his ship in 1774, the first European to step ashore was

British Captain James **Cook** in 1778, followed in 1785 by fur trading vessels of the East India Company, which built a shipyard. News of this led in June 1789 to an occupation by forces from **New Spain** under Estéban José Martínez, who erected a 16-gun Fuerte San Lorenzo. This became an international incident when British ships were seized. The resulting Anglo-Spanish conventions of 1790 and 1794 required the return of the seized ships and the eventual abandonment of the Mexican settlement (Santa Cruz de Nootka) in 1795. [L. H.]

NOPAL. Spanish for **prickly pear cactus**.

NOREÑA, MIGUEL (1843–1894). One of Mexico's most famous sculptors of his era. His works include the statues of Benito **Juárez** in **Oaxaca** and in the **National Palace** in **Mexico City**. His most famous statue is that of **Cuauhtémoc** on the Paseo de la **Reforma** in Mexico City.

NORIEGA CANTU JR., ALFONSO (1909–1988). A law professor at **UNAM**, 1939–1971, and at the **Universidad Iberoamericana**, 1971–1979, where his course and research on legal guarantees and appeals did much to raise the prestige of the UIA among Mexican jurists. He was a recognized authority on the *juicio de amparo*.

NORTE CHICO, EL. *See* NEAR NORTH.

NORTE GRANDE, EL. *See* FAR NORTH.

NORTEAMERICANO. In Latin American and especially Mexican Spanish, seldom having the wider sense of "North American," the term is used rather to refer specifically to the **United States** (often called in older usage, the *Estados Unidos del Norte*). A less frequent alternative, *Estad(o)unidense*, occurs, as does the ambiguous **Americano**. [L. H.]

NORTH AMERICAN FREE TRADE ASSOCIATION (NAFTA/ TLCAN). A treaty among the **United States**, Mexico, and Canada, lowering various tariffs on goods and services traded between them. The U.S. Congress approved the treaty on November 17, 1993, to take effect in January 1994, despite opposition from American labor leaders, fearful of the competition from cheaper Mexican workers. Mexican President Carlos **Salinas de Gortari**, whose Congress had already given its approval, urged U.S. passage on the grounds that the consequent increase in international trade would lessen illegal **migration** to the United States from Mexico. In fact it did not. On the other hand, the claim by "Subcomandante Marcos" (Rafael Sebastián **Guillén Vicente**) that poor Mexican farmers would find themselves unable to compete with American agribusiness was not borne out either. Increased American trade into Mexico led to increased demand for Mexican farm products, and hence more rural employment, while banks became readier to lend to farm owners to modernize their equipment and get fertilizer on credit. There was also a modest increase in Mexican trade with Canada.

NOTABLES, JUNTA DE. *See* JUNTA DE NOTABLES.

NOTICIAS. **Oaxaca** newspaper whose offices were invaded by state **police** in 1995 after it had published criticism of the state government.

NOTICIAS MEXICANAS (NOTIMEX). The Mexican news and information agency, founded by Enrique **Herrera** in 1968.

NOVEDADES. **Mexico City** daily newspaper, whose coverage of national news was improved by manager Ramón **Beteta** in the early 1960s. He adopted some of the reportorial norms he had introduced to the associated *News*, but with much more caution, and continued much of its traditional bandwagon journalism. That is, the paper tended to support most federal government policies.

NOVELLA, PEDRO FRANCISCO. Acting **viceroy** of **New Spain**, 1821. An artillery general and governor of **Mexico City**, he was the last effective holder of the office, which he spent having to fight insurgents to the exclusion of meeting the normal needs of the viceroyalty. His replacement, Don Juan **O'Donojú y O'Riana** arrived at Veracruz on July 30, 1821, but never took office.

NOVELS. The story of the Mexican novel really begins with José Joaquín **Fernández de Lizardi**'s "costumbrista" *El periquillo sarniento*. In the later 19th century the most important novelists were probably Amado **Nerva** and Federico **Gamboa**. Mariano **Azuela González** was Mexico's first novelist to win an international reputation, with *The Underdogs*. Also inspired by the **Revolution of 1910** was Marín Luis **Guzmán**'s *The Eagle and the Serpent*. The 1940s saw Rodolfo **Usigli**'s *Ensayo de un crimen*, José **Revueltas'** *Los muros del agua*, Jesús **Goytortúas'** *Pensativa*, and Agustín **Yáñez**'s *Al filo de agua*. The post-**World War II** "boom" in the publishing of Latin American literature, a phenomenon due chiefly to Spanish publishers turning to transatlantic authors when works by their fellow Spaniards were increasingly threatened by the rigid censorship of the Franco regime, included (in chronological order) important novels by Josefina **Vicens**, Juan **Rulfo**, Rosario **Castellanos**, Sergio **Galindo**, Elena **Garro**, Juan José **Arreola**, Vicente **Leñero**, Jorge **Ibargüengoitia**, Gustavo **Sainz**, Salvador **Elizondo**, José Emilio **Pacheco**. Rafael **Bernal**, José **Revueltas**, Elena **Poniatowska**, Juan Vicente **Melo**, Paco Ignacio **Taibo** II, and Luis **Zapata**.

Among novel writers coming into prominence in the last quarter-century: Gerardo de la **Torre**, Jaime del **Palacio**, Juan García **Ponce**, María Luisa **Puga**, Sergio **Pitol**, Angeles **Mastretta**, Héctor **Manjarrez**, Fernando del **Paso**, Laura **Esquivel**, Enrique **Serna**, Carlos **Montemayor**, Juan **Villoro**, Luis Humberto **Crosthwaite**. Even more recent are Mario **Bellatín**, Ana **Clavel**, David **Toscana,** and the "Crack group" of Ricardo **Chávez Castañeda**, Igancio **Padilla**, Pedro Ángel **Palou**, Eloy **Urroz**, and Jorge **Volpi**. *See also* NOVO, SALVADOR; REBOLLEDO, EFRÉN; SALAZAR MALLÉN, RUBÉN. [L. H.]

NOVEMBER 20. *See* REVOLUTION DAY.

NOVO, SALVADOR (1904–1974). A prolific writer of essays, plays, poems, novels, and popular histories. After a master's in literature from **UNAM**, he became editor of (and contributor to) *Contemporáneos*, 1928–1933; professor of drama at the **Conservatorio Nacional**, 1930–1933; director of public relations for the **Foreign**

Ministry, 1930–1934; head of theatrical productions and direction of the drama school of the new **Instituto Nacional de Bellas Artes**, 1946–1956; and official historian of **Mexico City**, 1965–1974. His novel *El Joven* (1928) portrays Mexico City as seen by a young man. His *Nueva grandeza mexicana* (1948) is a popular history of Mexico.

NOVOHISPANO. Inhabiting, or pertaining to, **New Spain**.

NUCLEAR ENERGY. Construction of the first stage of Mexico's sole nuclear plant for generating electricity, at Laguna Verde in **Veracruz state**, 60 km northeast of **Jalapa**, was authorized in July 1990 and by 2005 was contributing 3 percent of the nation's electric power, It failed, however, to reach international safety standards, and in March 2005 the Comisión Federal de Electricidad decided it should be closed and dismantled. *See also* CARRILLO FLORES, NABOR; GOROSTIZA, JOSÉ.

NUCLEAR NONPROLIFERATION TREATY. *See* TLATELOLCO, TREATY OF.

NUECES RIVER. The western boundary of **Texas** until the victory of **San Jacinto** allowed the insurgent Texans to push the territory of their new republic onward to the **Rio Grande**.

NUEVA ALIANZA (PANAL). The New Alliance, a political party "con la fuerza de la educación," formed July 14, 2005, led by Miguel Ángel Jiménez Godinez, who was succeeded in 2006 by Tomás Ruiz González. In the **election of 2006** it won a **Senate** seat, nine seats in the House, and one governorship. Its presidential candidate was Roberto **Campa Cifrián**. The party's economically liberal ideology has led it to give general support to the Felipe **Calderón Hinojosa** presidency. [L. H.]

NUEVA ANDALUCÍA. Early name for **Baja California**.

NUEVA DEMOCRACIA. Since 1972, the magazine of the **Partido Popular Socialista**.

NUEVA ESPAÑA. *See* NEW SPAIN.

NUEVA EXTREMADURA. A colonial jurisdiction that included present-day **Coahuila, Texas,** and **New Mexico.** There was also a colonial "Nueva Extremadura" in **Chile.** Spain's impoverished southwestern province of Extremadura produced many of the early explorers of the New World.

NUEVA GALICIA ("New Galicia"). A colonial "kingdom" centered on **Guadalajara** (declared its capital in 1560), including modern-day **Aguascalientes, Jalisco,** and **Zacatecas,** and lasting until the establishment of Intendencias in 1787.

NUEVA VIZCAYA ("New Biscay"). A colonial "kingdom" of 610,000 km^2 (372,200 sq. miles) originally established in 1575 by the Basque **conquistador** Francisco de **Ibarra,** embracing **Coahuila** and **Texas** until 1726. From 1777 until 1786 it consisted of what are now **Sinaloa, Durango,** and **Chihuahua.** It then became, until **independence,** the **Intendancy** of Durango.

NUEVO LAREDO. City of **Tamaulipas,** the cross-border twin of **Laredo,** Texas, with a 2000 population of 310,915, on the direct route between **Monterrey** and **San Antonio,** Texas. It is a processing center for agricultural **exports** into the **United States** and has several **maquilladoras** (cross-border assembly plants). The **municipio** in recent decades has shown independence from the **Partido Revolucionario Institucional,** giving support in the 1960s for the **Partido de Acción Nacional,** and in 1973 electing its mayor and council members from the **Partido Auténtico de la Revolución Mexicana.**

NUEVO LEÓN. A northern state of 64,555 km^2 and 51 *municipios* whose **population** was 145,779 in 1857; 171,000 in 1869; and at successive **censuses** thereafter: 309,000 (1895); 328,000 (1900); 365,000 (1910); 336,000 (1921); 418,000 (1930); 541,000 (1940); 740,000 (1950); 1,079,000 (1960); 1,695,000 (1970); 2,513,000 (1980); 3,049,000 (1990); 3,834,141 (2000); and 4,199,282 (2005). It borders **Tamaulipas** to the east, **San Luis Potosí** to the south, and

Coahuila to the west and north, where it also has a 15 km border with **Texas**. Its western and southern regions are crossed by the Sierra **Madre** Oriental. The northern part is desert, with a hot, dry climate. Its Salinas, Salvador, and San Juan rivers are tributaries of the **Río Grande** on the **United States border**. **Silver** and lead are mined. **Irrigation** allows the growing of **cotton**, citrus fruit, **wheat**, and **corn**. The capital is the large industrial city of **Monterrey**, which benefits from the **natural gas** and **petroleum** pipelines running to it across the state from **Tampico** on the coast.

[After an initial attempt to settle the area by Alberto del **Canto** had been frustrated by the **Chichimec Indians**, an expedition led by Luis de **Carvajal y de la Cueva** had more success and a "New Kingdom of León" was established in 1582. Real development had to await early 19th century **immigration** of Germans, French, Italians, East Europeans and Americans, attracted by cheap land. L. H.]

NUEVO MÉXICO. Spanish for **New Mexico**.

NUEVO REINO DE LEÓN. Original colonial name of **Nuevo León**.

NUEVO SANTANDER. A colonial jurisdiction in Northern Mexico, established in 1746 to end Indian raids, by José de **Escandón**, embracing present-day **Tamaulipas** and southern **Texas** up to the **Nueces River**. Its capital is now known as **Jiménez**.

NÚÑEZ CABEZA DE VACA, ÁLVAR (1490–1560). Conquistador whose travels took him from Florida to Paraguay. Born in Jerez de la Frontera in Andalusia of a noble family, he was in 1527 made the treasurer of Panfilo de **Narváez**'s expedition to **Florida**. After shipwreck and capture by **Indians**, Núñez Cabeza de Vaca escaped and journeyed through what is now the southern **United States** and northern Mexico to reach **Sonora** and then **Mexico City** in 1536, his wanderings giving him an atypical sympathy for the Native Americans. He was then sent to Paraguay to become its new **adelantado**, arriving in March 1542 after a crosscountry journey across what is now southern **Brazil**. He was too sympathetic to the Indians for the settlers' liking. They rebelled and sent him back to Spain in 1545. Exiled by the **Council of the Indies**, he was later exonerated and granted a pension.

NÚÑEZ DE HARO Y PERALTA, ILDEFONSO (1729–1800).
Viceroy of **New Spain**, 1787. This Spanish prelate had been installed
as archbishop of Mexico in 1772 and was made acting viceroy for a
few months pending the installation of Manuel Antonio **Florez**
Martínez de Ángulo. [L. H.]

NÚÑEZ KEITH, GUILLERMO (1921–). Radio announcer from
Guaymas, he was by the 1940s–1950s the leading network
announcer in **Mexico City** on radio, and later on **television**. In 1952
he was head of the Inter-American Congress of Announcers and
came to own several leading radio stations throughout Mexico and
the Publimex public relations agency. In 1967–70 he sat in the
Cámara de Diputados Federales. Into the 1980s he was often the
official announcer when a president of the republic was broadcasting.

NUNÓ, JAIME (1824–1908). Jaime Nunó Roca, composer of the
music of the **National Anthem**. Born in a small town in Catalonia,
Spain, he was admired and respected for his musical ability. He held
important musical posts in Spain, Mexico, and the **United States**. He
died in New York City.

NUTRITION. *See* FOOD SUPPLY.

NYARI INDIANS. *See* CORA.

– O –

OAXACA CITY (*OAXACO DE JUAREZ*). Capital city of **Oaxaca**
state, 17°05'N, 96°45'W in the Oaxaca Valley of the Sierra **Madre**,
founded in 1521 at 1525 m (5,000 ft.) above sea level, on sites of
Zapoteca and **Mixtec** centers that had been founded in 1486. The
Spanish called it *Segura de la Frontera* until it was granted "royal
city" status as *Nueva Antera de Oaxaca* in 1532. Most public buildings are constructed with the gray-green local stone, and all buildings

tend to have extra thick walls as protection against **earthquakes**, such as those of 1931 and 1957. On a hilltop on the edge of the city is A. A. **Cencetti**'s huge statue of Benito **Juárez**, erected in 1891. The population was estimated in 2003 at 526,000.

[In November 2006 the city was occupied by 4,500 **Policia Federal Preventativa** to take over control from opponents of the governor. The disturbances cost a dozen dead, 100 missing, and 200 arrests. More than 700 colonial-era buildings had been destroyed or damaged, many of them by the methods used to obliterate antigovernment slogans. The P.F.P. were also reported to have begun investigating the local state **police**. L. H.]

OAXACA STATE (*NAHUATL HUAXYACAC***—"place where leucaena trees grow").** The native state of Benito **Juárez** (postal abbreviation "Oax"), occupying 95,363 km^2 on the southern Pacific coast and originally created as an **intendancy** in 1787. Parallel southern ranges of the Sierra **Madre** running through the state northwest to southeast create two watersheds. The **Papaloapan** and **Coatzacoalcos** rivers flow through the state of **Veracruz** into the Gulf of **Mexico**. The **Tehuantepec** River flows into the Pacific. The economy stresses cereals, fruit, **sugar**, **coffee**, and tobacco. The population, which includes many **Zapotec** and **Mixtec Indians**, grew from 525,938 in 1857; to 601,850 in 1869; 883,000 in 1895; 949,000 in 1900; and 1,040,000 in 1910; falling to 976,000 in 1921, but it then reached 1,085,000 in 1930; 1,193,000 in 1940; 1,421,000 in 1950; 1,727,000 in 1960; 2,015,000 in 1970; 2,400,000 in 1976; 2,369,000 in 1980; 3,020,000 in 1990; 3,438,765 in 2000; and 3,506,821 in 2005.

Mexico's poorest state, with **Indians** forming the mass of its population, it was involved in a virtual insurrection during 2006, led by the **Asamblea Popular de los Pueblos de Oaxaca**. [L. H.]

OBRAJE. Any post-**conquest** manufacturing venture exploiting Indian **labor**. Particularly, in Mexico, a textile mill. [L. H.]

OBREGÓN SALIDO, ÁLVARO (1880–1928). President of Mexico, 1920–1924. A native of **Sonora**, he entered politics as mayor of Hutabampo, and in 1912 he became an active participant in the **Revolution of 1910**. He allied himself with the forces of Venustiano **Car-**

ranza and defeated Pancho **Villa** at the battle of **Celaya**, where he lost an arm. Elected president with 95.79 percent of the votes, he began putting together a working coalition which would ultimately evolve into the **Partido Revolucionario Institucional**. He signed the unpopular agreements with the **United States** arising out of the **Bucareli Conference, 1923**, even though this was inconsistent with the aims of the Revolution, and he showed a heavy hand against the **Cristeros**. He had just been elected for a second presidential term in the **election of 1928** when he was assassinated by José de **León Toral**.

Ciudad Obregón was founded in his honor in 1925.

OBSERVATORIO NACIONAL ASTRONÓMICO. Mexico's National Observatory was inaugurated by President Porfirio **Díaz** on March 6, 1877. The following year it was moved from the **National Palace** to **Chapultepec Castle**, in 1883 to the **Ex-Arzobispado**, **Tacubaya**, and in 1942 to Tonanzintla. Building the present observatory, Mexico's highest, on the 2,850 m high Picacho del **Diablo**, was begun by **UNAM** rector Guillermo Sobrón in 1971 and inaugurated in 1979. Mexico also has an important 50 m diameter astronomical telescope at **Puebla**, inaugurated in November 2006.

OCAMPO, MELCHOR (1814–1861). Liberal politician from **Michoacán**. He studied law and science before entering politics in 1840. He opposed the 1848 peace treaty of **Guadalupe Hidalgo** and was subsequently exiled by López de **Santa Anna** to New Orleans. There he met Benito **Juárez** and Ponciano **Arriaga**, became a dedicated liberal, and later became Juárez's interior minister and acting trade and foreign minister. As a prominent liberal he worked closely with Juárez in drafting the **Reform Laws**, but he was criticized for signing the 1858 Transit Treaty with **United States** envoy Robert **McLane**. He retired from government work in 1861 but was captured by the forces of Leonardo **Márquez** and shot that June.

OCAÑA GARCÍA, SAMUEL (1931–). Physician from Arivechi, **Sonora**. Born September 7, he trained in the **Instituto Politécnico Nacional**, did graduate studies in respiratory diseases, and in 1964 became director of the regional hospital in Navojoa, Sonora. He was mayor of Navojoa, 1973–1976; director for Sonora of the **Partido**

Revolucionario Institucional's economic and social studies; assistant secretary of the state government, 1977–1978; and state secretary general and Sonora head of the PRI, 1978–1979. In 1979–1985 he was **governor** of Sonora.

OCARANZA, FERNANDO (1876–1965). A physician who was dean of **UNAM**'s medical school, 1925–1934, then rector, 1934–1939. A long-time leader of the Mexican Red Cross and the **Consejo Nacional de Salud**, he pioneered comparative physiology in Mexico.

OCCIDENTE, ESTADO DE. State existing from 1824 until 1830, when it was divided into the present-day states of **Sonora** and **Sinaloa**. Its first capital was El **Fuerte**.

OCTOPUS. In 1997, with a catch of 25,000 t and high world prices, octopus became Mexico's third most valuable **fishing** harvest, but there has since been a fall to around 16,000 t, due to lower prices. Most of this fishing occurs around **Yucatán** and **Campeche**, by small artesanal inshore boats, and by industrial, medium-sized, vessels further out. [L. H.]

O'DONOJÚ Y O'RIANA, JUAN (1762–1821). Appointed **viceroy** of **New Spain**, 1821, but never assumed office. An **army** general who had been captain general of Andalucia, he was sent by Spain's new liberal regime as *jefe político superior* to replace Viceroy **Apodaca**. Instead he proved well disposed to those seeking **independence** and signed with **Iturbide** the Treaties of Córdoba of August 24, 1821, accepting the new status quo, ordering the withdrawal of Spanish troops and, following the September 14 **declaration of independence**, sat briefly, until his death, as a member of the five-man regency council, under Iturbide's presidency.

OFICIAL MAYOR. The executive officer or chief administrator of any government agency or office.

OIDOR ("hearer"). A justice of the **Audiencia**.

OIL. *See* PETROLEUM.

OJEDA PAULLADA, PEDRO (1934–). Official of the **Partido Revolucionario Institucional**; procurator general of the Republic, 1971–1976; minister of labor and social security, 1976–1981; and president of the **Federal Conciliation and Arbitration Board**, 1995.

OLACHEA AVILES, AGUSTÍN (1893–1974). A former **army** general, he was governor of **Baja California del Sur**, 1929–1931, 1946–1951, and 1952–1956, and of **Baja California del Norte**, 1931–1935, In 1944–1958 he was an inner-circle adviser of presidents and cabinet ministers, influencing **tourism, mining,** and public works policies. In 1956–1958 he was president of the **Partido Revolucionario Institucional**.

OLID, FRANCISCO DE (1488?–1524). Spanish **conquistador** who arrived in the New World in 1518 and played an important role in Hernán **Cortés'** conquest of Mexico. In 1524 he was sent south to conquer Honduras, but after founding Triunfo de la Cruz he renounced his allegiance to Cortés, and captured Cortés' emissaries, Francisco de las Casas and Gil González de Ávila. Rather foolishly he invited his captives to a meal, whereupon they attacked him with their table knives. He fled, wounded; but they followed, caught him, tried him, and had him beheaded.

OLIVARES SANTANA, ENRIQUE (1920–). Politician from San Luis, **Aguascalientes,** with a teaching diploma who became a member of the Aguascalientes state legislature. He then became a member of the **Cámara de Diputados Federales**, 1958–1961; state governor of Aguascalientes, 1962–1968; secretary general of the **Partido Revolucionario Institucional**, 1968–1970; senator, 1970–1976; head of the **Banco Nacional de Obras y Servicios Públicas**, 1976–1979; and on May 16, 1979, he became interior minister. Since 1970 he has also been a key official of the **Comité Ejecutivo Nacional** of the PRI, formulating PRI policies, including the party's structural reforms of 1972 and 1979, which broadened the base of popular participation.

OLLOQUI LABASTIDA, JUAN JOSÉ DE (1931–). Economist and diplomat, born November 5 in **Mexico City**. He graduated in **law** from **UNAM**, obtained a master's in economics at George Washington

University, and became successively professor of economics at UNAM and the **Universidad Iberoamericana**; director of currency for the **finance ministry**; head of the National Securities Commission (the *Comisión Nacional Bancaria y de Valores*); executive director of the Inter-American Development Bank, 1966–1970; and ambassador in Washington, where he helped reduce the tension caused by some of President **Echeverría**'s policies. In 1976 he became a deputy foreign minister.

OLMEC. The Olmec **Indians** (from the Aztec *Olman* "land of rubber") built the first pre-Hispanic high civilization in Mexico from 1200 BC to 100 BC, on the La **Venta** coastal plain of **Veracruz** as far as **Tabasco**, with a hieroglyphic script, pyramids, spacious temples, jaguar mosaics, and colossal carved heads 3 m (10 ft.) or more in height. Their mathematics included the concept of zero. Their culture penetrated as far south as **Chiapas**, but by 300 AD it had been absorbed by the **Maya**.

OLYMPICS. [Mexico first participated in the Paris summer Olympics of 1900, coming third in polo. It did not take part again until 1924 and never in the winter games before 1928. It won two silver medals at Los Angeles in 1932, three bronze at Berlin in 1936, a silver at Helsinki in 1952, a gold and a bronze at Melbourne in 1956, and a bronze at Rome in 1960, and again at Tokyo in 1964. L. H.]

Despite some countries' misgivings about the altitude, the games were held in **Mexico City** in 1968, Pedro **Ramírez Vázquez** being chosen chairman of Mexico's organizing committee. The **Partido Comunista Mexicano** was bitterly opposed to the games being held in Mexico. During 1967 every issue of the party organ *Política* urged the public to protest until the games were cancelled, to save wasting on a prestige project what the government should have been spending on welfare and **education**. This opposition culminated in the riots in the Plaza de **Tlatelolco**, six days before the games opened. They were held nevertheless, resulting in Mexico's best ever outcome: three gold, three silver, and three bronze.

[A silver medal in boxing was won at the 1972 Munich games, a gold and a silver at Montreal in 1976, a silver and three bronze at Moscow in 1980. In 1984 at Seoul, Mexico won both gold and silver in the 20 km walk, another gold in the 50 km walk, two more silvers in boxing and in wrestling, and a bronze in cycling. The two bronze won in 1988 (Seoul) were in boxing and diving. A silver was won in 1992 (Barcelona) and a bronze in 1996 (Atlanta). In 2000 at Sydney Mexican athletes won a gold, two silver, and a bronze. At the 2004 Athens games, Mexican women won three silver medals and a male entrant won a bronze. *See also* REVUELTAS, JOSÉ. L. H.]

OÑATE, JUAN DE (1549–1624). Explorer born in **Guadalajara** who colonized large sections of **New Mexico**, and travelled as far north as Kansas, founding many settlements along the way.

O'NEIL, RALPH (1896–1980). Aviation pioneer, born in **Durango** to an Irish American father and Mexican mother, he served with the **United States** army air corps from 1917–1919, shooting down 11 enemy aircraft. In July 1920 he was given command of the Mexican **air force**. He helped defeat the 1923 rebellion of Adolfo de la **Huerta**. On February 11, 1921, he was made head of the **Escuela de Aviación Militar**, but he left Mexico, December 1, 1925, to develop a flying boat service from Miami to Buenos Aires. [L. H.]

OPERADORA DE TEATROS. A nationwide chain of motion picture theatres in which the government is a major stockholder. It competes with *Películas Nacionales* and *Oro* **cinema** chains, in which the government also holds large blocks of stock.

ORDAZ, DIEGO DE (1480–c.1532). Conquistador who became one of Hernán **Cortés'** most trusted officers, although Cortés had at one time arrested him for his loyalty to Diego **Velázquez de Cuéllar**. After giving valuable service to Cortés, he took on the conquest of New Granada (modern **Colombia**) and Venezuela, but he was not successful, and died on his way back to Spain.

ORGANIZACIÓN CAMPESINA DE LA SIERRA DEL SUR. *See* AGUAS BLANCAS.

ORGANIZATION OF AMERICAN STATES (O.A.S.). Transformation at Bogotá, **Colombia**, in 1948 of the **Pan-American Union** of

American Republics, already responsible for the **Pan American Highway** and the **Pan American Institute of Geography and History**. In 1959 the O.A.S. created the Inter-American Development Bank (*B.I.D.: Banco Interamericano de Desarrollo*).

O.A.S. membership has since been extended to western hemisphere countries of the Commonwealth (Trinidad and Tobago joined in 1967, **Canada** in 1972), but at its January 1962 meeting in Punta del Este, Uruguay, the O.A.S. voted 14–1 (**Cuba**) with six abstentions (**Argentina, Bolivia, Brazil, Chile, Ecuador**, and **Mexico**) to suspend Cuban participation. While most Latin American delegates realized the threat Cuba posed, because of the Marxist-Leninist ideology of its government, its support of **guerrilla** movements, and its involvement with the **Soviet Union**, there was no precedent or legal basis for expulsion, nor even, according to the arguments of some of the largest and most influential member states, for suspension. Mexico offered a compromise resolution claiming that Marxism-Leninism ran against the principles and objectives of the O.A.S. Others argued that similar measures should be taken regarding other dictators in the hemisphere. The **United States** delegates used significant leverage to gain the necessary majority. In 1964 the O.A.S. voted 15–4 (Bolivia, **Chile**, Mexico, and Uruguay) to impose comprehensive political and economic sanctions on Castro's Cuba. These were only lifted in 1975. [L. H.]

ORGANIZED LABOR. *See* TRADE UNIONS.

ORIVE ALBA, ADOLFO (1907–). An engineer from **Mexico City** who built the hydroelectric dams in **Sonora**, 1935–1938; directed the National Irrigation Commissions, 1940–1946; and was then minister of hydraulic resources, 1947–1952. In 1970 he became director of the **Siderúrgica Lázaro Cárdenas Las Truchas (SICARTSA)**.

ORIZABA. A river and namesake city, of **Veracruz state**, at 18°51'N, 97°06'W, 130 km (81 miles) west of the Gulf of **Mexico** and 293km (182 miles) southeast of **Mexico City**, at 1228 m (4,030 ft.) above sea level, visited by **Cortés** but not made a **villa** until 1774 and a **ciudad** only in 1830. Its 28 km^2 **municipio** had 118,593 inhabitants in 2000 and was a center of the **coffee** industry, with **sugar** and jute mills, cigar factories, and marble quarries.

ORIZABA VOLCANO (*Volcán Pico de Orizaba*). Mexico's highest peak (5,747 m: 18,855 ft.), hence called *Citlaltépetl* ("mountain of stars") by the Aztecs. Standing 95 km (60 miles) west of **Veracruz City**, on the line between **Veracruz State** and **Puebla State**, it had a pre-Hispanic temple dedicated to the "sacred fire." Although it had eruptions between 1545 and 1566 and in 1687, it is presently inactive.

ORLANDO, FELIPE (1911–). Mexican-born painter who grew up in **Cuba**, and studied art under Cuban masters in his formative years. Besides being an accomplished painter, he has studied music and archaeology, and is considered an authority on African transculturation in the Americas. The Museum of Modern Art in New York is one of the many museums with his work on permanent exhibition.

OROZCO, JOSÉ CLEMENTE (1883–1949). Painter of the **Revolution of 1910**, famous for his murals of Mexican history and Mexico's struggle for social justice.

OROZCO, [GENERAL] PASCUAL (1882–1915). A supporter of **Madero** who won several key opening battles in the **Revolution of 1910**, capturing **Ciudad Juárez** in 1911. He then broke with Madero, accusing him of nepotism and **corruption** and called for radical social and political reform in the *Plan Orozquista* of March 25, 1912. Victoriano **Huerta** defeated his forces at **Rellano**, driving Orozco into exile in **Texas**, where he died.

OROZCO Y BERRA, MANUEL (1816–1881). Lawyer, engineer, historian, and archaeologist who was chief justice of the **Supreme Court** just before **Maximilian** became **emperor**. After his execution, Orozco served a brief prison term, but he was soon back in official favor. He is also noted for his 4-volume *Historia antigua y de la conquista de Mexico* (1880–1881) and his *Materiales para una cartografía mexicana* (1871).

ORQUESTA SINFÓNICA NACIONAL DE MEXICO (OSNM). The national symphony orchestra was founded in 1928 by Carlos **Chávez** in the Palacio de **Bellas Artes**. Besides its government funding, it receives grants from the Flintridge Foundation, the California

Arts Council, the San Francisco Arts Commission, the Hewlett Foundation, and the **United States** National Endowment for the Arts. Every year it gives concerts in major cities in the provinces, the United States, and Europe. Its size—101 musicians, with five flutes, five oboes, and two concertmasters; instead of the usual 72–82 musicians, two flutes, two oboes, and a single principal violinist—gives it enormous sound. Its guest conductors have included Stravinsky, Klemperer, and Bernstein. Mexican conductors have included Chávez himself, Silvestre **Refueltas**, Manuel **Ponce**, Julio **Carillo**, and Enrique Arturo **Diemecke**.

ORTEGA CANO MONTÁÑEZ Y PATIÑO, JUAN DE (1627–1708). Viceroy of **New Spain**, 1696 and 1701. Cleric who served in Mexico as *fiscal* of the **Inquisition** before being consecrated in 1673 as bishop of Guadiana in **Durango**, then in 1684 as bishop of **Michoacán**, and in 1699 as archbishop of **Mexico**. He served twice as acting viceroy—in 1696 (when he had to confront the first student strike in the Americas) and in 1701.

ORTIZ, GUILLERMO. Finance minister at the time of the **peso** crisis of 1994–1995 and blamed by **Partido de Acción Nacional** for the consequent liabilities acquired by the **Fondo Bancario de Protección al Ahorro**. In late 1998, the consequent scandal briefly threatened his subsequent position as governor of the **Banco de México**.

ORTIZ DE DOMÍNGUEZ, JOSEFA (1768–1829). Patriot heroine and wife of Miguel **Domínguez**, mayor of **Querétaro**, whom she convinced of her belief in **independence**, which derived from her concern for the oppressed and downtrodden. Their house was used to plot rebellion, and when the conspiracy was discovered, it was she who warned the others, causing them to advance the date of their insurgency to September 16, 1810. She was eventually captured and held in a convent. She was freed on her promise to cease her revolutionary activities. Greatly disappointed by the rise of Agustín **Iturbide** and the conservatives, she died in **Mexico City**.

ORTIZ MENA, ANTONIO (1908–). A lawyer from **Parral, Chihuahua**, who directed nationalization, 1940–1945; ran the *Banco*

Nacional Hipotecario Urbano, 1946–1952; and was director general of the **Instituto Mexicano del Seguro Social**, 1952–1958; and finance minister, 1958–1970. From 1971–1987 he was president of the Inter-American Development Bank.

ORTIZ RUBIO, PASCUAL (1877–1963). President of Mexico, 1930–1932. An engineer from **Michoacán**, he entered politics as a supporter of Francisco **Madero**. A mild ineffectual man, he was known as *Don Nopalitos* ("Mr. Clubless") from the cliché that Mexico's rulers used *pan o palo*. As one of the figurehead presidents who served as frontmen for Plutarco **Calles** after the end of his 1924–1928 term, Ortiz held office from February 1930 to September 1932, when Calles forced him to resign and go into a brief exile in the **United States**. Despite being generally controlled by Calles at the end of a telephone line and enduring such insulting graffiti as *Señor Singonados* ("No Gonads"), he was allowed some initiatives by his master, including the promulgation of the **Estrada doctrine** and the federal labor code. He died in **Mexico City**.

OSORIO DE ESCOBAR Y LLAMAS, DIEGO (????–1673?). **Viceroy** of **New Spain**, 1664. Bishop of **Puebla** who served as acting viceroy for just three and a half months, during which short time he replenished an empty treasury (and even sent money back to Spain), and improved the fortifications of **Campeche city**. [L. H.]

OSORIO PALACIOS, JUAN (1920–1997). A leading concert violinist in the 1960s–1970s, born in **Mexico City**. He was concertmaster with the **Orquesta Sinfónica Nacional de México**, 1939–1948; member of the National University Symphony; secretary general of the music workers' trade union, 1946; and a member of the **Cámara de Diputados Federales**, 1951–1955 and 1958–1961, promoting the national development of the arts.

OTEYZA FERNÁNDEZ, JOSÉ ANDRÉS (1942–). Economist, born November 21, in **Mexico City**. He graduated in economics from **UNAM**, 1965; obtained a master's in economics at Cambridge University, England; taught at UNAM, 1968–1970; worked as an economist for the Ministry of **Natural Resources**, 1965–1968; and for the

Banco de México, 1968–1970. He was chief analyst for government-owned enterprises, 1970–1971; director general of research for the Natural Resources ministry, 1974–1975; and then minister of Natural Resources itself (and the chief policy formulator for government-owned enterprises), from December 1976 through 1982.

Since 1969 he has also been an editor and contributor for the leading Mexican economics journals *Investigación económica*, *El Trimestre económico*, and *El Economista mexicano*. In 1972 he became advisory editor for the *Carta de México*, published by the Mexican president's office.

OTHÓN P. BLANCO. Municipio of **Quintana Roo** containing the state capital of **Chetumal** and named for Admiral Othón Pompeyo **Blanco Núñez de Caceres**. Its population was 150,000 in 1990 and 208,164 in 2000.

OTOMÍ. Indian nation of **Mexico** and **Hidalgo** states, numbering in the mid-1990s about 280,000 (roughly equal to the **Mixtec**), and famed for their weaving, particularly of red woolen garments, and of fancy baskets made from cactus fiber. Men and women wear red wool sashes with white work clothes or fancy party costumes. **Querétaro** was originally an Otomí town.

OUR LADY OF GUADALUPE. *See* MARY OF GUADALUPE, SAINT.

OZUMACINTA. Former spelling for the River **Usumacinta**.

– P –

PACHECO, JOSÉ EMILIO (1939–). Writer, editor, and literary critic from **Mexico City**, nationally known since the 1960s. His novel *Morirás lejos* (1967) condemned persecution of religious minorities. In 1969 he won the national prize for **poetry**. In 1972 his short story collection, *El Princípio del placer*, evoked national nostalgia for simpler times. *Las batallas en el desierto* appeared in 1981.

PACHECO Y OSORIO, RODRIGO, MARQUIS OF CERRALBO (1570–1640). Viceroy of **New Spain**, 1624–1635, during which period he had to improve its naval strength against constant Dutch, French, and English attacks. He had also to improve **Mexico City**'s flood defenses following a serious inundation. [L. H.]

PACHUCA. Located 2,500 m above sea level at the foot of the Sierra **Madre** Occidental at 20°07'N, 98°44'W. The **Aztec** Pachoacan and colonial Real de Minas de Pachuca, became in 1869 the capital of **Hidalgo state**, renamed Pachuca de Soto to honor Manuel Fernando Soto, who had been chiefly responsible for the creation of the new state. The city stagnated with the decline of **silver** mining in the early 20th century, but growth resumed in the 1960s (when it became in effect an outlying suburb of **Mexico City**) with the arrival of other industries including cement and manganese production and manufacturing. It had 175,000 inhabitants in 1995. Its namesake **municipio** occupies 14,563 ha and its mountainous countryside is of great natural beauty. The woods of Mineral del Chico National park, 21 km from Pachuca, are ideal for mountaineering, rock climbing, **sport fishing**, and hiking. [L. H.]

PACHUCA, SIERRA DE. Mountain range to the north of **Mexico City**, reaching 3,000 m. in Huasca de Ocampo.

PACTO DE SOLIDARIDAD ECONÓMICA (P.S.E.). An economic restructuring program introduced in 1986 involving an incomes policy, extensive **privatization** of state-run enterprises, price controls, an increase of government revenue through both higher taxes and more efficient tax collection, and a decrease in government expenditure.

PADILLA. Tamaulipas city founded by José de **Escandón**, January 6, 1749, as the Villa de San Antonio de Padilla, named in honor of María Padilla, wife of **viceroy** Juan Francisco de **Güermes y Horcasitas**. [L. H.]

PADILLA, EZEQUIEL (1890?–1971). Diplomat and politician who served under Emiliano **Zapata** and Pancho **Villa** and ran unsuccessfully for president in the **election of 1946**. His many diplomatic posts included ambassador to the **United States**, delegate to the **United Nations**, and foreign minister.

PADILLA, IGNACIO (1969–). Short story writer from **Querétaro**, born in **Mexico City**. He grew up in South Africa, edited the Mexican edition of *Playboy* in the 1990s, and has been Mexico's cultural attaché in London. His acknowledged influences include García Márquez, Borges, Cortázar, and such non-Hispanics as Julian Barnes and Kazuo Ishiguro. His works include the short story collection *Subterráneos* (1989), the novels *El año de los gatos amurallados* (1994) and *La catedral de los ahogados* (1995), and the children's story *Los papeles del dragón típico* (1991). [L. H.]

PADILLA NERVO, LUIS (1898–1985). Diplomat from **Michoacán**, and a graduate of **UNAM** who did graduate studies at the University of London, England, and at George Washington University. A veteran diplomat since 1918, he served as ambassador to Uruguay, El Salvador, Panama, Costa Rica, Denmark, **Spain**, and Austria. He headed the Mexican delegation to the **United Nations**, 1945–1952 and 1958–1964, and was president of the UN General Assembly, 1951–1952. He was foreign minister, 1952–1958, and a justice of the International Court at the Hague, 1964–1972.

PADILLA SEGURA, JOSÉ ANTONIO (1922–). An electrical engineer from **San Luis Potosí** who was vice president of the **Instituto Politécnico Nacional** in the 1950s, and then its rector until 1964, when he expanded doctoral level **engineering education**. In 1964–1970 he was minister of communications and transport, and from 1971, director of government owned steel mills.

PADRINO. A godfather, in relation to his godchild (as opposed to a **compadre**). The feminine is a **madrina**. *See also* COMPADRAZGO. [L. H.]

PAINTING. This *Dictionary* includes entries for Raúl **Anguiano**, Feliciano **Bejar**, Miguel **Cabrera**, Enrique **Carbajal Sebastián**, Rodrigo de **Cifuentes**, Juan **Cordero**, José Luis **Cuevas**, Roberto **Donis**, Baltasar **Echave Ibia**, Baltasar **Ehave Orio**, Felipe **Ehrenberg**, Mario **Fuentes**, Julio **Galán**, Gunther **Gerzso**, Frida **Kahlo**, Daniel **Manrique Arias**, Roberto **Montenegro y Nervo**, Héctor **Navarro**, Leonardo **Nierman**, Louis **Nishizawa**, Felipe **Orlando**, José Clemente **Orozco**, Diego **Rivera**, José Luis **Rodríguez Alconcedo**, David Alfaro **Siqueiros**, Juan **Soriano**, Rufin **Tamayo**, Leticia **Tarrago**, Eduardo **Terrazas**, José María **Velasco**, Cristóbal de **Villalpando**, Moises **Zabludowsky**, Armando **Zúñiga**, and Francisco **Zúñiga**. *See also* ESMERALDA, LA; MURALISTS. Information on individual painters is available from the website http://mexico.udg.mx/arte/pintores.

PALACIO ("palace"). The term is used for any government building, from a town hall up to the **National Palace**. For other individual *palacios*, see under previous word (e.g., BELLAS ARTES, PALACIO DE LAS).

PALACIO, JAIME DEL. Short story writer: *Parejas: tres narraciones enlazadas* (1981), *Seis mujeres: relatos* (2003).

PALAFOX Y MENDOZA, JUAN DE (1600–1659). Viceroy of New Spain, 1642–1649. Born in Navarre, a doctor of Sigüenza university, appointed a fiscal of both the War Council and the **Council of the Indies** in 1626 and elected bishop of **Puebla** in 1639. He arrived in Mexico in 1640 and was made viceroy two years later. As bishop and viceroy he was notable for his energetic church building and his efficient tax gathering which enabled him to come to the financial aid of Cuba and assist in improving its defenses.

He is responsible for the magnificent **Palafoxian Library** which he built up in Puebla. He wrote much criticism of the **Jesuits** and was ordered to return to Spain in 1649. [L. H.]

PALAFOXIAN LIBRARY (*Biblioteca Palafoxiana*). An outstanding collection, open to the general public, of 42,556 books (in a score of languages)—including 9 incunabula—and 5,346 manuscripts, established in **Puebla** in 1646 by Bishop and **Viceroy** Juan de **Palafox Y Mendoza** and still in its original building. On June 17, 2005, UNESCO declared it one of the "Memoirs of Humanity," particularly for its coverage of the history of the New World.

PALAVICINI, FÉLIX F. (1881–1952). Founder of **Excélsior**, and author of a 4-volume history of Mexico.

PALENQUE. Ruined **Maya** city in the tropical rainforest of **Chiapas**. Its temples and other large buildings (among them, notably, an observatory) were erected in 514–784. By 800 the site had been abandoned and its inhabitants had migrated to the **Yucatán** peninsula. European knowledge of ancient Mayan civilization really dates from the discovery of its ruins by a local priest, Antonio de Solís, in 1746, although those of Copán in Honduras had been reported in 1576.

PALOU, PEDRO ÁNGEL (1966–). Puebla-born civil servant, soccer referee, and rector of the **University of the Américas**, turned novelist: *Amores enormes* (1991); *En la alcoba de un mundo, una vida de Xavier Villaurrutia* (1992); *Con la muerte de los puños* (2003); *Malheridos* (2004); and *El diván del diablo* (2005). [L. H.]

PAN AMERICAN HIGHWAY (*Carretera Panamericana*). An international strategic project for an Alaska to Tierra del Fuego automobile highway, proposed in 1923, formally agreed at Buenos Aires in 1936, and largely completed by 1970, thanks in no small part to the **United States** having provided two thirds of the construction costs during **World War II**. Three branches of this highway cross the **United States border** to unite at **Mexico City**. There they form a single trunk route south to the **Guatemalan border** and on to Darien in southern Panama, where the 90 km "Darien gap" still breaks the connection with the highway's continuation across the length of South America. There is also a fourth branch that runs from Havana across western **Cuba** to provide, in theory, a link across the **Yucatán** Peninsula to the main highway.

PAN AMERICAN INSTITUTE OF GEOGRAPHY AND HISTORY (PAIGH). The oldest specialized agency of the **Organization of American States**, founded at the VIth (Havana) Pan American Conference of the Amercian Republics and located in **Tacubaya**.

PAN AMERICAN UNION. The Third Pan American Conference of Latin American nations meeting with the United States in Rio de Janeiro in 1906 established the Union of American Republics and created the Pan American Union, based in Washington, DC, to act as its central coordinating agency. The first Pan American conference on Mexican soil was the **Chapultepec Conference** in early 1945. At the Bogotá conference of 1948, the organization became the **Organization of American States**, although the Pan American Union has continued as its central secretariat.

PAN O PALO ("bread or club"). A reference to the two traditional ways of exercising authority in Mexico, "stick" or "carrot," both to categorize different styles of leadership, and a twofold approach by the same leader—Porfirio **Díaz**, for instance, always ready to reward collaborators and repress the uncooperative.

PANAMA, CONGRESS OF. *See* CONGRESS OF PANAMA.

PANI, ALBERTO J. (1878–1955). Politician and diplomat who served in various posts from the time of the **Revolution of 1910**, distinguishing himself as finance minister in the government of Alvaro **Obregón**, replacing Adolfo de la **Huerta** who led an unsuccessful coup. Pani strengthened the power of his ministry and, through his efforts, a strong central bank, the **Banco de México**, was founded.

PÁNUCO. Colonial jurisdiction named for a river of 510 km with a watershed of 107,200 km^2. Known in its upper reaches as, successively, the Tula, San Juan, and Montezuma, it becomes the Pánuco at its union with the Temporal and empties into the Gulf of **Mexico** at **Tampico** in **San Luis Potosi state**. [L. H.]

PAPAGO. One of Mexico's smallest **Indian** groups. Together with the **Pima**, they numbered in the mid-1990s 490 individuals, in **Sonora** and **Sinaloa**.

PAPALOAPAN, RIVER. Eastward flowing river of **Oaxaca state** and **Veracruz-Llave**.

PARACAIDISTA ("parachutist"). A squatter, one who invades unguarded or disputed land and begins to farm it as his own, having arrived unannounced, as if suddenly "fallen from the sky."

PAREDES Y ARRILLAGA, [GENERAL] MARIANO (1797–1849). President of Mexico, January 4–July 28, 1846. Having supported López de **Santa Anna** in 1841, he deposed him in 1844. He then seized power from Acting President José Joaquín **Herrera**, to prevent him from negotiating with **United States** President **Polk**, and was accused of weakening Mexico in the face of the enemy (who invaded in April 1846) in the hope of establishing a monarchy in Mexico. Subsequently exiled, he lived for a while in the United States, but died in **Mexico City**.

PARRAL. Municipio of **Chihuahua state** at 26°N, 105°W, 222 km by road from the state capital, with a population of 88,197 in 1990; 100,821 in 2000. Founded in 1631 as Real de Minas de San José de Parral, it was the capital of **Nueva Vizcaya**, 1640–1731, and became Hidalgo de Parral in 1833. Pancho **Villa** died here in 1923. From 1567 until the early 1930s the area was important for **silver** mining.

PARTIDO. (1) A *partido pedáneo*, a subdivision of an **intendancy** under the 1785 *Ordenanza de Intendentes*. "*Pedáneo*" refers to the fact that the official in charge of such an administration did so as a delegate of the intendant. The subdivision of a *partido* was a **cuartón**.

(2) A *partido político*, i.e., a political party. *See* POLITICAL PARTIES.

PARTIDO ALIANZA SOCIALDEMÓCRATA Y CAMPESINA. The Social Democratic and Farmers' Party, formed in 2005, made Patricia **Mercado Castro** its presidential candidate in the **Election of 2006**.

PARTIDO ANTIRRELECCIONISTA. A party of the early 20th century dedicated to the principle of "No **Reelection**." *See also* CABRERA, LUIS; CALLES, PLUTARCO ELIAS; LUGO LAGUNAS, JOSÉ.

PARTIDO AUTÉNTICO DE LA REVOLUCIÓN MEXICANA (PARM). The Authentic Party of the Mexican Revolution, a moderately conservative opposition party, founded in 1954 by Generals Juan **Barragán**, Antonio **Gómez Velasco**, and Juan B. **Treviño**.

Since 1958 it has won a handful of congressional district seats, and since 1964 a few minority-party seats in the **Cámera de Diputados Federales**, and six mayoral races. Its current president is Rosa Maria Denegri.

PARTIDO COMUNISTA MEXICANA (P.C.M.). Founded in 1919, the Mexican Communist Party attempted in 1920–1928 to build a **labor** base with the **Confederación General de Trabajo**. Between 1921 and 2001 the P.C.M. has held 18 party congresses, but it remained unregistered for electoral purposes (although legal) because for decades its membership did not rise above 5,000. In 1978, however, it claimed 80,000 members and fielded minority **proportional representation** candidates for the **Cámera de Diputados Federales** and Valentín Campa ran as a write-in candidate for president. In 1958 Demetrio Vallejo, a leader of the *Sindicato de Trabajadores Ferrocarrileros de la República Mexicana* (Railroad Workers' Union) caused millions of dollars of damage to the economy through slowdowns and unauthorized stoppages of trains until he was jailed under the federal penal code for social dissolution. For the PCM's part in the 1959 railroad strikes, the then secretary general, David Alfaro **Siqueiros** was also convicted of social dissolution and jailed 1960–1962.

The party journal was the weekly *Oposición*. Its youth movement, the Juventud Comunista de Mexico, was active within student federations, and helped enlarge the bloody riots of 1968.

The party line was consistently pro-Moscow, denying any connection with the Communist September 23rd League of **guerrillas**. In 1981 it became the **Partido Socialista Unificado de Mexico** and in 1989 it was absorbed (as a tiny faction) into the **Partido de la Revolución Democrática**. *See also* MARTÍNEZ VERDUGO, ARNOLDO.

PARTIDO CONSERVADOR. Conventional name for the loose grouping of conservative politicians (**conservadores**) in early independent Mexico.

PARTIDO DE ACCIÓN NACIONAL (PAN). "National Action Party," the main conservative opposition party since its founding by

Manuel **Gómez Morín**, Efraín **González Luna**, Manuel **González Hinojosa**, and Antonio L. **Rodríguez**, in September 1939. It backed Juan Andreu **Almazán** for president in 1940, obtained legal recognition in 1946, and secured its first congressional seats in 1948. Its representation was increased following the introduction of **Proportional Representation** in 1964, and again in 1979. It was then very small in comparison with the **Partido Revolucionario Institucional** but was showing strength **in Yucatán** and **Baja California del Norte**. Although it supports private enterprise and opposes government action as a tool to effect social change, it began in the 1960s, under the leadership of Adolfo **Christlieb Ibarrola**, to move away from its former close identification with the conservative elements in society towards a more centrist position. In 1997, the PAN in alliance with the **Partido de la Revolución Democrático**, obtained an overall majority in the **Cámara de Diputados Federales**. The party's current president is Carlos Castillo Peraza.

PAN's electoral appeal remains greatest in the north, where it achieved its first successes. It competes strongly with the PRI in the central states, but remains comparatively weak in most of the south. *See also* VICENCIO TOVAR, ABEL.

PARTIDO DE ANTI-REELECCIÓN. *See* PARTIDO ANTIRRE-ELECCIONISTA.

PARTIDO DE LA REVOLUCIÓN DEMOCRÁTICA (P.R.D). Party of the Democratic Revolution, founded by Cuauhtémoc **Cárdenas Solórzano** in October 1988, replacing the Partido del Frente Cardenista (although some members of the latter have continued it as the **Partido del Frente Cardenista de Reconstrucción Nacional**). In 1989 the P.R.D. absorbed the **Partido Socialista Unificado de Mexico**. As the party on the left of the **Partido Revolucionario Institucional**, it was able to get the support of many **trade unions** following the death of long-term **Confederación de Trabajadores de México** leader Fidel **Velázquez Sánchez** in 1999. Yet it has never got quite the intense degree of support that the CTM had given the PRI during the 35 years of Velázquez's dominance. Successive party presidents have been Cuauhtémoc Cárdenas (1988–1993), Roberto **Robles Carnica** (1993), Porfirio **Múñoz Ledo** (1993–1996), Andrés

Manuel **López Obrados** (1996–1999), Pablo Gómez Álvarez (1999), Amalia García Medina (1999–2002), Rosario Robles (2002–2004), Leonel Godoy Rangel (2004–2005), and Leonel Cota Montaño (from 2005). In the **election of 2006** its candidate, Andrés Manuel **López Obrador**, came within 0.5 percent of winning the presidency.

PARTIDO DE LOS TRABAJADORES MEXICANOS (P.T.M.). The Mexican Workers' Party, founded by Heberto **Castillo Martínez** in 1974, later merged into the **Partido de la Revolución Democrática**.

PARTIDO DEL FRENTE CARDENISTA DE RECONSTRUC-CIÓN NACIONAL (P.F.C.R.N.). Party formed, as the *Partido del Frente Cardenista*, to support the presidential candidacy of Cuauhté-moc **Cárdenas** in the **election of 1988**. The bulk of the party became the **Partido de la Revolución Democrática**, but a rump survived, adding "de reconstrucción nacional" to the original title, running Rafael **Aguilar Talamantes** as its candidate in the 1994 presidential race and wining 0.77 percent of the national vote.

PARTIDO DEL TRABAJO (P.T.). Labor Party, currently headed by a *Comisión coordinadora* ("coordinating commission"), composed of José Narro Céspedes, Alberto Anaya, and Marcos Cruz.

PARTIDO DEMÓCRATA CRISTIANO. "Christian Democrat Party," present title of the former **Partido Demócrata Mexicano**.

PARTIDO DEMÓCRATA MEXICANO (P.D.M.). The "Mexican Democrat Party," a right-wing party favoring private enterprise, a reduced bureaucracy, and traditional Catholic values in government policies and programs. It was formed, with the same initials as the earlier and somewhat similar **Partido Democrático Mexicano**, when, in Irapuato, **Guanajuato**, on May 23, 1971, Juan Aguilera Azpeitia convened a national meeting of former **Unión Sinarquista Nacional** members and convinced them that discredited right-wingers could gain status and political influence through the pro-posed P.D.M. The conference adopted a party charter and elected Baltasar Ignacio Valádez as president. By 1975 the new party had

100,000 registered members and ran candidates for seats in the **Cámera de Diputados Federales** in all states and the **Federal District**. In 1978 the party elected Gumersindo **Magaña Negrete** to lead it in fighting for congressional seats in the **election of 1979**. It adopted Ignacio **González Gollaz** as its presidential candidate in the **election of 1982**. It is now the **Partido Demócrata Cristiano** but is still known as the P.D.M.

PARTIDO DEMOCRÁTICO MEXICANO (P.D.M.). The "Mexican Democratic Party," a right-wing party, formed in 1946 by Ezequiel **Padilla** who became its presidential candidate in the **election of 1946**. The party soon faded and was effectively replaced by the **Partido Demócrata Mexicano**, which usurped its initials.

PARTIDO LIBERAL. (1) Name of several political parties in Latin America claiming principles derived from those of the liberal wing of the **Cortes of Cádiz**, and a way of referring to the loose grouping of similarly minded politicians in early independent Mexico, whence the **Unión Liberal** of the **Porfiriato**.

(2) The "Liberal Party," a clandestine anti-Porfirio **Díaz** party founded in 1906 by Ricardo **Flores Magón**. [L. H.]

PARTIDO MEXICANO DE LOS TRABAJADORES. See PARTIDO DE LOS TRABAJADORES MEXICANOS.

PARTIDO MEXICANO SOCIALISTA. The Mexican Socialist Party was founded in March 1987 but merged with the **Partido de la Revolución Democrática** in May 1989.

PARTIDO NACIONAL REVOLUCIONARIO (PNR). The "National Revolutionary Party" was formed by President Plutarco **Calles** in March 1929 to draw agrarian activists, **trade union** leaders, military groups, and government bureaucrats into one unified, all powerful party and make the social Revolution permanent. It was chartered in a convention convened in **Querétaro**. Its name was changed in 1938 to **Partido Revolucionario Mexicano (PRM)**.

PARTIDO NUEVA ALIANZA (PANAL). See NUEVA ALIANZA.

PARTIDO POPULAR. The "People's Party," founded June 20, 1948, by Vicente **Lombardo Toledano,** Jorge **Cruickshank García,** and Alejandro **Gómez Arias.** It later became the **Partido Popular Socialista.**

PARTIDO POPULAR SOCIALISTA (PPS). A renaming of the **Partido Popular** to show its Marxist orientation. The PPS was responsible for creating the **Unión General de Obreros y Campesinos de México.** Lombardo was the PPS presidential candidate in the **election of 1952.** In subsequent elections it fielded candidates for the Congress, state legislatures, and municipal governments, but supported the **PRI** candidates for president. Since 1964 it has won a few seats in each election for the **Cámara de diputados federales.** Jorge **Cruickshank García** became PPS secretary general in 1968 on the death of Vicente **Lombardo Toledano** and in 1976 became the first PPS senator. The party's greatest strength has been in the states of **Nayarit, Oaxaca,** and selected areas of **Morelos, Mexico state,** and the **Federal District.**

The PPS is supported editorially by *El Día,* and (jointly with the **Partido Revolucionario Institucional**) by *Siempre.* The party organ, *Avante,* was replaced in 1972 by *Nueva democracia.* Indalecio Sáyago Herrera is the party's current secretary general. *See also* GASCÓN MERCADO, ALEJANDRO; MARTÍNEZ DE LA VEGA, FRANCISCO.

PARTIDO RADICAL. The Radical Party, a political grouping that came together in 1824 to oppose any amnesty for Spaniards accused of crimes during the War of **Independence,** 1810–1821. In 1828 the party supported President **Santa Anna.** In 1846 it championed the plan to nationalize **Church** property. In 1857 it supported the Plan of **Tacubaya** and President Ignacio **Comonfort.** When Comonfort left Mexico in 1858 and Benito **Juárez** came to power, the Radicals were discredited and their party began to fall apart.

PARTIDO REVOLUCIONARIO DE LOS TRABJADORES (P.R.T.). The Workers' Revolutionary Party is currently headed by Pedro Peñalosa as coordinador.

PARTIDO REVOLUCIONARIO DE UNIFICACIÓN NACIONAL (PRUN). The Revolutionary Party of National Unification was formed in 1940 by General Juan **Almazán** for his unsuccessful presidential candidacy of that year and dissolved after the election.

PARTIDO REVOLUCIONARIO DEMOCRÁTICO. *See* PARTIDO DE LA REVOLUCIÓN DEMOCRÁTICO.

PARTIDO REVOLUCIONARIO INSTITUCIONAL (PRI). The Institutional Revolutionary Party was a 1946 renaming of the **Partido Revolucionario Mexicano (PRM)** to emphasize the institutionalization of the **Revolution of 1910**, and organizationally continues the structure of the PRM. It has a national executive committee, the **Comité Ejecutivo Nacional (CEN)**, 31 state committees, a **Federal District** committee, and a committee in each **municipio**. Every three years, a general assembly (*Asamblea Nacional*) of 3,000 delegates and alternates representing the general membership endorses the programs and principles which the CEN has proclaimed. The **Consejo Político Nacional** is a permanent council subordinate to the *Asamblea Nacional*.

To improve the party's image and that of **Congress, proportional representation** was introduced in 1964. That image, however, dropped dramatically after the dubious result of the **election of 1988**, and dropped further after the 1994 political murder of Luis **Colosio**. It began to improve rapidly when President **Zedillo** appointed a non-PRI attorney general, whose vigorous probing ended with the conviction of Raul **Salinas de Gortari**. A brief recovery in PRI's electoral fortunes followed the choice of Roberto **Madrazo Pintado** to be party boss in 2002.

PRI's electoral decline is most noticeable in the north of the country. It remains competitive in the center states and is still dominant in most of the south. In 2006, dissatisfaction with the PRI governor of **Oaxaca** caused not only violent opposition within the state but probably explains the bombing of PRI offices in **Mexico City**, November 6th.

PARTIDO REVOLUCIONARIO MEXICANO (PRM). The Mexican Revolutionary Party, founded in 1938, the successor of the **Partido Nacional Revolucionario (PNR** of 1929) and destined to become in 1946 the **Partido Revolucionario Institucional (PRI).**

The old military sector of the PNR was phased out and replaced by a popular sector, whose functions from 1943 were exercised by the **Confederación Nacional de Organizaciones Populares**, which also came to dominate the **labor** and agrarian sectors, in as much as the CNOP includes government bureaucrats and the professional class.

PARTIDO SOCIALISTA DE LOS TRABAJADORES (P.S.T.). The Socialist Workers' Party, founded in 1973 by Rafael **Aguilar Talamantes** who became its secretary general and got it registered for the **election of 1979** when it fielded candidates for deputy in all 31 states and the **Federal District**. The party's seven cofounders and its central committee members came from Heberto **Castillo Martínez's** National Committee for Opinion Surveys and Coordination. After Castillo's death, the PST could barely achieve enough votes to remain a recognized party and outside the Federal District had trouble finding a member willing to run for office. Most of its active members left to join the **Partido de la Revolución Democrática Mexicana**. Aguilar Talamantes is currently president of the **Partido del Frente Cardenista de Reconstrucción Nacional**.

PARTIDO SOCIALISTA UNIFICADO DE MÉXICO (PSUM). The Unified Socialist Party of Mexico was formed in November 1981 by a merger of the **Partido Comunista Mexicana**, the Movimiento de Acción y Unidad Socialista, the Partido del Pueblo Mexicano, and the Partido Socialista Revolucionario. In 1989 it was absorbed by the **Partido Revolucionario Democrático de Mexico**.

PARTIDO VERDE ECOLOGISTA DE MÉXICO (P.V.E.M.). Mexico's Green Party, founded May 14, 1993, one of whose members served briefly as mayor of **Benito Juárez (Cancún)**. Its predecessor, the *Partido Verde Ecologista Mexicano*, formed in 1986, had been denied legitimacy in 1990 because "ecological concerns" were not appropriate to a *political* party. It contested the congressional **election of 2006** in alliance with the **Partido Revolucionario Institucional**, winning 18 of the alliance's 121 House seats. [L. H.]

PASO, FERNANDO DEL. Novelist: *Noticias del imperio*. 1987.

PASO DEL NORTE, EL. Pre-1836 name of **El Paso, Texas,** and pre-1888 name of its border twin, **Ciudad Juárez.**

PASTRY WAR (*Guerra de los Pasteles*). Popular name of the Franco-Mexican war of 1838. French citizens with claims totalling 600,000 pesos for depredations suffered during civil conflicts included a French pastry maker in **Tacubaya** whose business had been shot up by a group of Mexican officers. French warships occupied **San Juan de Ulúa,** and, with the help of **United Kingdom** mediation, received a guarantee of the entire claim, whereupon their ships returned home. *See also* YÁÑEZ, JOSÉ MARÍA.

PATERNALISM. The style of government, closely related to **personalism,** where the leader's interest in his followers encourages him to implement his policies without regard to institutional approval, such as acts of the legislative or judicial branches of government. An interesting example occurred some years ago in **Mexico state,** whose governor, feeling that excessive consumption of **pulque** was economically harmful to the drinkers' dependents, unilaterally forbade its sale in public places (but not its delivery to private homes), making inspection flights by helicopter to ensure compliance with his decree.

PATIÑO, ANTENOR (1896–1982). Bolivia's wealthiest tin mine owner who moved to Mexico when his mines were nationalized in 1952. In Mexico he developed the port of **Manzanillo** into a resort for rich tourists by building the Las Hadas hotel complex. In 1960–1962 he developed the luxury María Isabel Hotel in **Mexico City,** then sold its majority stock to the Sheraton Hotel chain and the Mexican government.

PATRIA CHICA ("little fatherland"). The tendency, very prevalent in Mexico, to fix one's primary loyalty at the level of the state or other immediate environment, rather than at that of the nation: the example of Robert E. Lee's allegiance to Virginia rather than the union at the onset of the American Civil War is analogous. Such sentiments steadily diminished as the **United States** evolved from a mainly agrarian and rural to an industrial and urbanized society, and one can anticipate a similar evolution in Mexico.

PATRIMONIO NACIONAL. *See* NATURAL RESOURCES.

PATRON SAINT. Since 1754, Saint **Mary of Guadalupe**.

PATRONATO. State control of **Church** income and secular aspects of its administration, in return for official enforcement of its religious dogma, secured by the Spanish crown in the middle ages. This was accepted as part of their political inheritance upon **independence** by most Latin American republics but came increasingly into conflict with the liberal secularization of modern politics. The resulting political battles to retain or end this formal establishment of religion raged particularly fiercely in the Mexico of the 1830s and 1850s. Only as a result of the **Revolution of 1910** were Church and state definitively separated.

PÁTZCUARO. A town, **municipio**, and tourist resort in **Michoacán**, located on the namesake lake, with 35,000 inhabitants in the 1970s; 77,872 in 2000.

PÁTZCUARO LAKE. One of the most beautiful lakes in Mexico, occupying some 422 km^2 of **Michoacán**, 20 km long and 14 km wide at its greatest extension. It is rather shallow, averaging 7.6 m depth, and is famous for its white fish. These are caught by local **Indians**, using very distinctive and traditional large fishing nets shaped like butterflies.

PAVÓN, JOSÉ IGNACIO (1791–1866). Briefly president of the conservative faction in 1860 during the War of the **Reforms**, in succession to Miguel **Miramón**.

PAZ, LA. (1) Capital of **Baja California del Sur** (and formerly of **Baja California** territory), **fishing** port and resort, with a 2000 population of 196,907. **Jesuits** established a mission there in 1720, only to abandon it after an outbreak of **smallpox** in 1750. It was resettled in 1811 and became the territorial capital in 1829.

(2) Former **município** of **Mexico state**, now part of **Nezahualcóyoti**.

PAZ, OCTAVIO (1914–1998). Internationally known man of letters, winner of the Nobel Prize for Literature. Born in **Mexico City**, he studied law, literature, social sciences, and humanities at **UNAM**, and wrote essays, **poetry**, popular history, political commentary, **novels**, and non-fiction works about Mexican and international public life. In 1943 he obtained a Guggenheim Fellowship to study literature in the **United States** and in Europe. His *El laberinto de la soledad* (1950), translated into English as *The Labyrinth of Solitude*, on daily life and widespread attitudes in Mexico, influenced mass demand for reform and government responses. It was followed by *El arco y la lira*, a 1956 book of poetry. In 1943–46 he was associated with the journal *Hijo Prodigo*. By the 1960s he had become Mexico's most distinguished living writer and one of its most influential ones of the century. His *Posdata,* 1970 (translated as *The Other Mexico*), stirred national consciousness about technological development. Having served as Mexican ambassador in several major European countries, he resigned as ambassador to India to protest the handling of the **UNAM student riots of 1968**. His views had appeared in *Hoy* and *Siempre* for some years when in 1970 he became editor of a new magazine, *Plural*. In 1971 he editorialized against **Echeverría's** refusal to have the **procurador general** investigate the beating up by unidentified street fighters of students protesting government handling of protests at the **Instituto Politécnico Nacional**. His death on April 4 produced appreciative obituaries throughout the world's press.

PEARL FISHING. First mentioned in regard to 16th-century **Baja California**.

PEASANT ASSOCIATIONS. *See* ORGANIZACIÓN CAMPESINA DE LA SIERRA DEL SUR.

PEDRO DE GANTE (1486–1572). "Peter of Ghent," so called from the Flemish city where he was born (connected to Spain with the marriage of Queen **Joan** the Mad of Castile to Philip the Handsome, Duke of Burgundy). Thanks to Bartolomé de las **Casas**, he became an outstanding missionary in **New Spain**, establishing many schools and churches. He is still loved in Mexico today. He influenced

Charles **V** in promulgating the New **Laws of the Indies** which curtailed the worst abuses against the **Indians**. He lies buried in the Convent of San Francisco in **Mexico City**.

PELADO. A slang term with a connotation similar to **Lepero**.

PELAYO. A 3,500 m peak of the Sierra **Nevada**.

PEMEX (Petróleos Mexicanos). Government corporation created by Lázaro **Cárdenas** in 1938 to explore, drill, transport, refine, and market **petroleum**—everything from subsoil rights to retailing. It also enjoys a monopoly in all aspects of conserving, developing, producing, and marketing **natural gas**. No private oil company, domestic or foreign, may operate in Mexico, although in the 1990s concessions for retail service stations began to be available for lease. For its first 36 years, **Pemex** struggled to produce enough petroleum to meet Mexico's own needs, but since 1974 Mexico has become a major oil exporter and the world's fifth largest producer. In the 1980s, although Mexico refused to join **OPEC**, Pemex undertook to cooperate with it, while remaining free to vary supplies to meet United States' needs. It planned to produce 2.25 million barrels a day and export 1.1 million.

For 50 years Pemex paid little attention to its shareholders, the people of Mexico, ignoring, for instance, any protests when it tore up land or polluted rivers in its drive for oil. The first change occurred in 1988 when President Carlos **Salinas de Gortari** sent the army to arrest the all-powerful union leader, Joaquín **Hernández**. In 1994 President **Zedillo** appointed Adrian **Lajous** to reform Pemex. Pemex administrators monitor refineries and drilling teams in the field as never before. The oil workers' union can no longer get the backing of the cabinet for demands that prevent Pemex from making a profit. Politicians on the left have complained about private inroads into the monopoly, but a majority of voters and the **Partido Revolucionario Institucional** now support the changes. In 1999 Pemex began behaving more like a private company to avoid being privatized. The cost of production was brought down to US$ 2.50 a barrel, against a world crude price of US$ 13 a barrel, and the Mexican treasury enjoys an all-time high income from Pemex sales and the taxes it pays. *See also* MAGDALENA DE KINO.

PEÑA Y PEÑA, MANUEL DE LA (1789–1850). A distinguished jurist who held many political posts and belonged to various scientific organizations. He served as chief justice of the **Supreme Court** and had two separate terms as **president** of Mexico, during one of which he signed the 1848 Treaty of **Guadalupe-Hidalgo**.

PENAL CODE (*Código Penal*). Only in 1871 did Mexico replace Spanish criminal **law** with its own codification. This was accompanied in 1880 by a code of criminal procedure. The new, revised, code of December 15, 1929, reflected the progressive influence of the **Revolution of 1910**, e.g., in its abolition of the death penalty. The code was amended in the mid-20th century through the work of Carlos **Franco Sodi** and Francisco **González de la Vega**, and was replaced by the current code on January 4, 2000. [L. H.]

PENINSULAR. In colonial times, a Spaniard born in **Spain**, but living in the New World. It's a far less loaded term than the synonymous **Gachupin**.

PENSACOLA, FLORIDA. Founded, as *Panzacola*, by **Viceroy** Gaspar de la **Cerda Sandoval Silva y Mendoza**, Conde de Galve, who named the entrance to the harbor Santa Maria de Galve.

PERALTA, ÁNGELA (1845–1883). One of the most famous Mexican opera singers of the 19th century. She began her professional career at age 15, sang at La Scala in Milan, and became a favorite in Europe. She died at the height of her career in a **cholera** epidemic then sweeping Mexico.

PERALTA, GASTÓN DE, MARQUES DE FALCES (1510–1580). Third **viceroy** of **New Spain**, 1566–1568. His viceroyalty was brief because of his refusal to sign death warrants for the sons of Hernán **Cortés** for their involvement in the **Ávila-Cortés conspiracy**, believing they would receive a more fair trial in Spain. When the **audiencia** protested to **Philip II**, *visitadores* were sent out to investigate. They decided to dismiss the viceroy for his leniency. Later when he returned and justified his conduct, he was absolved. Then the *vistadores* themselves were dismissed, and Peralto was compensated with the post of constable of his native Navarre. [L. H.]

PERALTA, MATÍAS DE. Viceroy of New Spain, 1649–1650.

PÉREZ, IGNACIO. Co-conspirator of Miguel **Hidalgo y Costilla**, who, warned by the wife of the **corregidor** of **Querétaro** that the authorities had become aware of their plot, rode to tell him the die was cast and that they must begin their rebellion immediately.

PÉREZ DE LA SERNA, JUAN (1573?–1631). Archbishop of Mexico, 1613–1627, he actively sought popularity among the **Creoles** by attending plays and other popular functions. For this and for attacking **corruption** he was reprimanded, leading to a quarrel with both the **audiencia** (which sought his deportation) and the new **viceroy**, Diego **Carrillo de Mendoza y Pimentel** (whom he excommunicated). Perhaps his popularity was what led the crown to recall him not long after the viceroy's own recall. He was then given the title of Archbishop of Zamora. [L. H.]

PÉREZ HERNÁNEZ, JUAN JOSÉ (17??–1775). Senior naval officer at **San Blás**, sent in January 1774 in his ship *Santiago* to explore the Pacific coast up to 60°N. He reached 54°40' (which, as almost the furthest Spanish penetration north, eventually became the southern border of Russian Alaska). After trading for furs on **Nootka** Island, he returned August 28, 1774, and became a member of Bruno de **Hezeta y Dudagoitia**'s 1775 expedition, on which he died. [L. H.]

PÉREZ MARTÍNEZ, HÉCTOR (1906–1948). A dentist from **Campeche** who became an influential journalist. A reporter on El **Nacional**, 1929–1931; he became its editor, 1932–1937; then a member of the **Cámara de Diputados Federales**, **governor** of Campeche, 1939–1944, and interior minister, 1946–1948. He was an inner-circle advisor to Presidents **Ávila Camacho** and **Alemán**, 1940–1948.

PERSHING, JOHN JOSEPH (1860–1948). United States general (afterwards commander of U.S. forces in France in **World War I**) who in 1916 led a punitive expedition into Mexico against Pancho **Villa**.

PERSONALISM. The practice, common in Hispanic countries, of following an individual because of his personal traits, and not necessarily because of his ideological or political beliefs. Outstanding

Mexican examples include López de **Santa Anna**, Pancho **Villa**, and Plutarco Elías **Calles**. *See also* CAUDILLO.

PERU, RELATIONS WITH. Many **viceroys** of **New Spain** were subsequently appointed viceroys of Peru, seen as a slightly more prestigious posting.

PESCA, DEPARTAMENTO DE ("Department of Fisheries"). *See* FISHING.

PESO. The traditional Hispanic American, and later, Mexican, unit of **currency**. Literally "weight," the word was first used, in a colonial Spanish America lacking minted coins, for a standard weight of precious metal. Eventually coins of the same value (28.5 g of **gold**) were minted. Under **Charles III**, the *peso duro* became the largest **silver** coin, known in English as the silver **dollar** or "piece of eight," since it could be legally cut into eight wedge-shaped "bits" worth one real each.

The Mexican peso was replaced in 1993 by the **Nuevo Peso**, at NP$1=1,000 old pesos. After the latter were demonetized on January 1, 1996, the "new" qualification became unnecessary. *See also* BANKS AND BANKING; COINAGE; COLUMNARIO; DOLLAR SIGN; EXCHANGE RATE.

PETRÓLEOS MEXICANOS. *See* PEMEX.

PETROLEUM. Mexico began producing petroleum early in the 20th century, thanks to foreign capital, particularly British. Lázaro **Cárdenas**' government expropriated the entire petroleum industry on March 18, 1938. Mexico is now the world's fifth largest producer of petroleum, which accounts for 57 percent of national exports by value, although part of its consumption was still dependent on imports as recently as 1974. The state with the greatest output of petroleum is **Veracruz-Llave**. *See also* BUCARELI CONFERENCE; NATURAL GAS. [L. H.]

PETROLEUM RESERVES. Incomplete geological research indicated in the mid-20th century reserves of up to 11 billion barrels. But with modern geological exploration, estimates had gone up to 30 billion by 1976, and three years later to 60 billion barrels.

PHILIPPINES, RELATIONS WITH. The division of the Globe by Pope Alexander VI between Castile and Portugal, formalized in the 1494 Treaty of Tordesillas, should have confined Spanish colonial expansion to the New World, but after Portugal had secured the displacement westward of the dividing meridian (following its secret discovery of the east coast of **Brazil**), Spain was able to use compensatory exploration across the Pacific to gain entry to South-East Asia from the opposite (westward) direction. Hence its colonization of the Philippines, sustained by the **Manila Galleon**. The islands remained Spanish even after Mexican **independence** but were annexed by the **United States** following victory in its war with Spain over **Cuba** and granted their own independence in 1936.

A few years later, Mexico's **air force** contributed to the liberation of the Philippines from the Japanese at the end of **World War II**. [L. H.]

PIAXTLA. A river of **Durango state**.

PICO. Mountain peak. *See also* ORIZABA VOLCANO.

PICO, ANDRÉS. The Mexican general who surrendered **Alta California** to John **Frémont** on January 13, 1847.

PIEDRAS NEGRAS. Chihuahua border town facing **Eagle Pass** with a municipal population of 127,898 in 2000. It suffered a flash flood April 6, 2004, in which 31 people drowned.

PIMA. A small **Indian** group in **Sonora** and **Sinola**, included with the **Papago** in the 1995 total of 490 for both.

PIMENTEL Y ENRÍQUEZ DE GUZMÁN, DIEGO. Viceroy of **New Spain**, 1621–1624, also known as Diego **Carrillo de Mendoza y Pimentel**.

PINGUIN, MEMIN. A cartoon character of the 1950s celebrated in a series of commemorative stamps in 2005. His being a little Black boy characterized with exaggeratedly Negroid features produced complaints from Americans so vehement as to constitute an international incident. Mexican reaction was to stress the lovable nature of the character, and there was a rush to buy the stamps. [L.H.]

PINO SUÁREZ, JOSÉ MARÍA (1869–1913). Lawyer-politician, vice president of Mexico, November 6, 1911–February 18, 1913, when he was assassinated by agents of Victoriano **Huerta.**

PINOS. A **municipio** of 2,813 km² in **Zacatecas** with 60,000 inhabitants. The **cabecera**, at 2,419 m, has 3,300 inhabitants.

PLAGUE. The European **disease** was a major cause of Indian depopulation following the Spanish conquest, particularly in the epidemics of 1545 and 1576. The traditional assumption that this was the rat-flea carried bubonic variety has recently been challenged and it has even been suggested by Mexican epidemiologist Roldolfo Acuña Soto (perhaps because of the severity of the symptoms in a population wholly lacking immunity) that the two epidemics were of a local Ebola-type hemorrhagic fever. [L. H.]

PLANNING MINISTRY (*Secretaria de Planeamento Y Del Presupuesto*). Created in 1976 to take over such powers of the Ministry of the **Presidencia** as were not transferred back to the **Interior Ministry**. In 1992 this became the *Secretaría de la Controlaria General de la Federación*, and then the *Secretaría de Controlaría y Desarrollo Administrativeo*, SECODAM.

PLURAL. A critical journal started by Octavio **Paz** in October 1971. A supplement to *Excelsior*, it succumbed to government pressure and ceased publication in April 1976, only to be, in effect, resurrected as *Vuelta*. [L. H.]

POBLANO. Inhabiting **Puebla City** or **Puebla State.**

PODER CONSERVADOR. *See* SUPREMO PODER CONSERVADOR.

POETRY. Important poets include: Ignacio Manuel **Altamirano Basilio**, Homero **Arijis**, Bernardo de **Balbuena**, Juan **Bañuleos**, Rosario **Castellanos**, Isabel **Fraire**, Enrique **González Martínez**, Manuel **Gutiérrez Najera**, Sor **Juana Inés de la Cruz**, Héctor **Manjarrez**, Carlos **Montemayor**, Amado **Nervo**, **Nezahualcõyotl**, José

Emilio **Pacheco**, Octavio **Paz**, Guillermo **Prieto**, Andrés **Quintana Roo**, Efrén **Rebolledo**, Alfonso **Reyes**, José María **Roa Barcena**, José Rubén **Romero**, José **Rosas Moreno**, Francisco Manuel **Sánchez de Tagle**, José Manuel **Sartorio**, Justo **Sierra Méndez**, Carlos de **Sigüenza y Góngora**, José Juan **Tablada**, Francisco de **Terrazas**, and Luis Gonzaga **Urbina**. *See also* CORRIDO; MODERNISMO.

POINSETT, JOEL ROBERTS (1779–1851). American diplomat from South Carolina who occupied a number of posts in Latin America and was the first **United States** envoy to Mexico, March 1825–April 1829. Although he supported Guadalupe **Victoria** and opposed the liberals, he is important in Mexican **Freemasonry** for his support of the liberal York rite masons (**Yorkinos**) to counteract British support of the rival, conservative, Scottish rite masons (**Escoceses**). The *flor mexicana de nochebuena* ("Mexican Christmas bloom") is known in English as the poinsettia because it was he who introduced it into the United States.

POK TA POK. Maya name of the ancient Central American and Caribbean ball game.

POLICE. Mexican police forces include federal and state judicial police, the **Policia Federal Preventativa**, the federal highway police, the federal fiscal police, the federal **immigration** police, the municipal police, and various auxiliary forces. While the maintenance of **law** and order falls to state and municipal forces and to the federal highway police, investigative policing is done by the plainclothes judicial police. There seems general agreement that poor rates of pay make **corruption** endemic. *See also* AGENCIA FEDERAL DE INVESTIGACION; PUBLIC SECURITY MINISTRY; RURALES, SANTA HERMANDAD. [L. H.]

POLICIA FEDERAL PREVENTATIVA (P.F.P.). Security intelligence force formed in 2001 with staff transferred from the **police**, from the **army**, and from the **Centro de Investigación y Seguridad Nacional** (which it effectively replaced). In October 2006, 4,500 P.F.P. were sent to **Oaxaca state** in support of embattled Governor Ulises **Ruiz Ortiz**. [L. H.]

POLÍTICA. Former twice-monthly news magazine of the **Partido Comunista Mexicano**. In the late 1960s, when it was vehemently campaigning against the holding of the **Olympics** in Mexico, its paid circulation was 175,000, but a further 125,000 copies were distributed freely, without any explanation of who was paying for this. In 1967 the government halted publication by embargoing the magazine's paper supplies.

POLITICAL PARTIES. Political parties in the Hispanic world can be traced to the division in the **Cortes de Cádiz** between the traditionalists or conservatives (**conservadores**), who were anxious to rid Spain of its French puppet government and their supporters, hated primarily as radical innovators, and the progressives or liberals (*liberales*) who wanted to drive out the French precisely in order to create an independent, radically modernized Spain. When, in the course of the 19th century, the parties acquired a formal organization, governments (in Mexico and elsewhere) could decide, at election time, whether to recognize their legitimacy. The **Porifiato** recognized only the **Unión Liberal**. During the 20th century, such official recognition came to depend largely on the number of a party's registered members. Electoral law under the **Constitution of 1917** required until 1977 only 75,000 members for a party to register. The 1978 Law of Organic Politics and Processes allowed temporary registration for federal elections to any party that had been functioning prior to 1974, but failure to obtain 1.5 percent of the national vote would cancel a party's registration. For decades, Mexico had had just four registered parties, but in the **election of 1979**, there were seven. This number subsequently increased but since 1988 several of the smaller minority parties have lost their official status by failing to earn the required minimum number of votes. Each registered party gets its own symbol and distinctive combination of two colors, so that the illiterate voter may mark a straight party vote.

Each rightwing or centrist party is headed by a president. The leftwing parties have each a secretary general instead.

For years Mexico was effectively ruled by the official "party of the Revolution"—the **Partido Revolucionario Institucional** and its forerunners. Gradually in the 1980s and 1990s the **Partido de Acción Nacional** and the newer **Partido de la Revolución Democrática** began to gain more seats in state and municipal legislatures and in 2000 the PAN candidate was elected president.

Parties formed to fight the **Election of 2006** include the **Nueva Alianza** and the **Partido Alianza Socialdemócrata y Campesina**. [L. H.]

POLK, JAMES KNOX (1795–1849). United States president, 1845–1849. A Jacksonian Democrat from Tennessee, his determination to decide policy without reference to the opposition has been compared to that of George Bush II and accounts for the modest standing of his historical reputation, even though his tenacious pursuit of "Manifest Destiny" contributed more than the efforts of any other president to the physical enlargement of the **United States**, notably through the **United States-Mexican War**. [L. H.]

PONCE, JUAN GARCÍA (1932–2003). Novelist (*Figura de paja*, 1964; *El nombre olvidado*, 1970; *Crónica de la intervención*, 1981); short story writer; essayist; art critic; and translator from Mérida, Yucatán.

PONCE, MANUEL MARÍA (1882–1948). Composer of classical **music**, from **Zacatecas**.

PONIATOWSKA, ELENA (1932–). Novelist (*Hasta no verte Jesús mío*, 1969); short story writer and playwright; and a founder of *La Jornada*, she was born in Paris but migrated to Mexico as a child.

PONTES GIL, EMILIO (1890–1978). President, 1928–1930.

POPOCATÉPETL. Mexican volcano of the Sierra **Nevada**, reaching 5,452 m (17,885 ft.) above sea level, and associated with nearby **Ixtalccíhuatl** in the Aztec legend of Popo and Ixta.

POPULATION. The decimation of the aboriginal population due primarily to the introduction of European **disease** followed close upon the Spanish **conquest of Mexico**. An estimated total of 25,200,000 in 1520 was reduced to 16,800,000 by 1532; only to fall further, to 6,300,000 by 1548; to 3,380,000 by 1570; to 1,375,000 by 1595; and a nadir of 1,075,000 by 1605. The pre-conquest total would not be reached again until the mid-20th century.

A slow recovery began only more than a century after **Cortes'** arrival, reaching 1,713,000 in 1646; 2,477,000 in 1742; 3,800,000 in 1793; and 4,500,000 in 1800.

The increase then speeded up somewhat, to double during the course of the 19th century, reaching 6,122,000 in 1810; 6,204,000 in 1820; 6,382,000 in 1830; 7,016,000 in 1840; 7,660,000 in 1850; 7,860,000 in 1856; 8,210,000 in 1860; 8,743,000 in 1874; 9,580,000 in 1880; 11,500,000 in 1890; and 13,607,000 in 1900.

The 20th century saw a more than sevenfold increase, thanks largely to advances in preventive medicine, particularly after **World War II**. Despite the **Revolution of 1910**, the number of Mexicans grew from 15,160,000 in 1910 to 16,553,000 by 1930. There were 22,000,000 in 1945; 30,000,000 in 1955; 70,000,000 in 1980; 81,250,000 in 1990; 90,000,000 in 1994; 93,700,000 in 1994; and 95,700,000 in 1997. The total for 1998 was estimated as 98,552,776, although the 2000 census recorded only 97,483,412. The July 2006 census total was 107,449,525. The 2006 annual population growth rate was 1.16 percent.

Despite a now falling **birth rate**, half the Mexican population is still under 18 years of age. *See also* CALIFORNIAN INDIANS; CENSUSES; DISEASE; EMIGRATION; IMMIGRATION; URBANIZATION; WOMEN.

POPULATION DENSITY. 48.5 persons per km^2 in 1997; 54.63 in 2005 (107,029,400 on 1,958,201 km^2), ranking it 142nd among the nations, but Mexico's irregular **topography** makes its distribution most uneven. [L. H.]

PORFIRIATO. The period 1872–1910 when Porfirio **Díaz** was President or, during 1880–1884, exercising effective control of Mexican government through a nominee: the longest rule by one individual since **Independence**.

PORTERS. The pre-Hispanic method of transporting freight on human backs persisted long after the Spanish **conquest of Mexico**. It was hardly possible for any alternative to compete with the low cost of using **Indians** as *tamemes*. Even in the mid-19th century foreign visitors were still remarking on the ubiquity of *cargadores* (as these porters were now called). They substituted not only for carts but even for Sedan chairs. [L. H.]

PORTES GIL, EMILIO (1890–1978). Interim president of Mexico, 1928–1930. Born in **Ciudad Victoria**, he was active in the **Revolution of 1910** and subsequently in public life. Although Plutarco **Calles** largely controlled his administration, he played a significant role in settling the **Cristero Rebellion**, made a serious effort at **agrarian reform**, and broke off relations with the **Soviet Union** because of its propaganda attacks on the Mexican government. After leaving the presidency he continued in public life and at one time was ambassador to India. He died in **Mexico City**.

PORTILLO, PEDRO DE LA. A **creole** civil servant who encouraged an uprising to take power away from the *gachupines* (Spaniards). **Viceroy** Miguel José de **Azanza** was seized and Portillo, occupying his position, proclaimed **independence** and declared war on **Spain**. The rebels were soon overpowered and sentenced to long terms of imprisonment.

PORTOCARRERO LASO DE LA VEGA, MELCHOR, CONDE DE LA MONCLOVA (1636–1705). Viceroy of **New Spain**, 1686–1688. A soldier who had fought in Flanders, France, Algeria, and Catalonia, he began his viceroyalty by leading an army to drive the French out of **Louisiana**. He also founded the **villa** of **Monclova**. Bored by the slow pace, routine nature, and ineffectiveness of administration in Mexico, whose capital lacked even well-kept streets, he contrived a transfer to the viceroyalty of **Peru**, where he arrived August 15, 1689, and found greater outlets for his vigor. He fortified Guayaquil, giving it a naval shipyard and driving pirates out of the Juan Fernández Islands. [L. H.]

PORTS AND HARBORS. Mexico has 56 seaports, 27 of which are used by high seas shipping. The chief ones on the Pacific: **Acapulco, Ensenada, Guaymas, Manzanillo,** La **Paz, Salina Cruz,** and **Topolobampo.** On the **Gulf: Altamira, Coatzacoalcos, Lázaro**

Cárdenas, **Progreso**, **Tampico**, **Tuxpan**, and **Veracruz**. Important in the 18th century but since decayed are **San Blas** and **Zihuatanejo**. [L. H.]

POSADAS ESPINOSA, ALEJANDRO (1939–). A certified public accountant, born May 29 in **Mexico City**, who has helped moderate administrative procedures throughout the federal government. He was an administrator for the **agriculture** ministry, 1954–1958; for the **finance ministry**, 1960–1962; for national warehouses; then for the **Compañía Nacional de Subsistencias Populares**, 1963–1973; and director of the national commission for the **corn** industry, 1973–198?; having meanwhile served as president of the national public accountants' association, 1969–1971; and director of financial and social research for the popular sector of the **Partido Revolucionario Institucional**, 1971. He has been one of Mexico's top experts on the cost of basic foods and their relationship to subsidies and government policies.

POSITIVISM. The philosophy of Augusto Comte that society could be improved by the social sciences, provided it were not corrupted by religion, or any other metaphysical influence. This anti-clerical creed had great influence in 19th century Latin America. In Mexico one of its strongest advocates was Gabino **Barreda**. Because it embodied belief in hierarchy and authority, it found favor with the administration of Porfírio **Díaz**, and in particular with the **científicos** (e.g., the influence of Justo **Sierra Méndez** on Mexican **education**). Its influence declined with the **Revolution of 1910** but has not disappeared. Its most prominent spokesman is Leopoldo **Zea**.

POST CODES. Mexico now has a system of five-digit postal address codes. Thus the *Zona Central* **colonia** of Venustiano Carranza (the **delegación** covering downtown **Mexico City**) is 15100.

POSTAL SERVICE (*Servicio Postal Mexicano—SEPOMEX*). Despite its political fragmentation, ancient **Maya** civilization enjoyed an efficient and internationally protected system of mail, carried over specially dedicated 9 m wide *sacbeoob* ("white highways"), and on canoes along the Caribbean coast as far south as Nicaragua, guided at night by a chain of light houses. The comparable messenger system of the **Aztecs** worked so well that Hernán **Cortés** kept it in existence.

During the colonial period, official mail, the *Correo Mayor de Hostas y Postas de la Nueva España*, was carried within Mexico by regular horse relays along each **camino real**, farmed out to local contractors, the *Correos Mayores*, but with robbery by highwaymen a continual problem. It went to and from Spain on the annual **treasure fleet**, supplemented for urgent messages by unescorted *sueltos* (small craft relying on their speed to escape interception). Only with the 18th century **Bourbon reforms** was a public mail service to the **Indies** introduced, put out to private contract. A similar overland post was set up in 1745, giving a weekly service between **Mexico City** and **Oaxaca** and, from 1748, a monthly service to **Guatemala**. Letter carriers (*carteros*) to provide home delivery of mail were introduced in 1762.

The crown took over the operation of all postal services in 1764–1765, and by 1802 the Spanish **navy** had increased the frequency of its transatlantic post to once a month. Much of the imperial *Ordenanzas de Correos* of 1794 continued to regulate Mexico's postal service until the Republic's own *Código Postal* was promulgated in 1884. From 1765 to 1897, Mexico's postmaster general bore the title *Administrador del Correo*.

By 1801 Mexico's 401 post offices had 901 employees and was moving 1,100,000 items a year. In 1812, the **viceroy**, faced with a growing movement for **independence** began having all suspicious letters opened and read, which led the patriots to develop their own rival postal service. With independence the British and French began packet services between their home countries and **Veracruz** which continued until 1914 and 1939, respectively, while the new Mexican government established its own postal service November 8, 1821. This was reorganized in December 1824 as the *Administración General de Correos* under the **Finance Ministry**. In 1897 it was transferred to the new *Secretaría de Comunicaciones y Obras Públicas*. Meanwhile, in 1879, Mexico had joined the Universal Postal Union.

Mexico began the issue of postage stamps in August, 1856, and the chief post office in the capital, the *Edificio de Correos*, was magnificently rebuilt in 1902–1907 by Adamo **Boari**. This was a direct consequence of the 1901 reorganization of the *Administración General de Correos* as the *Dirección General de Correos*, consequent upon the growth of the service which had by then reached a volume of 135 million items a year, served by 9,784 employees in 1,972 post offices.

Airmail began in the late 1920s, and the first international airmail to other American republics and to Europe followed in 1930–1931, but the efficiency of surface mail had begun to decline. By mid-century letters were taking several days to arrive even within Mexico City and up to two weeks for provincial delivery. From February 1933 the telegraph and postal services were combined in the *Dirección General de Correos y Telégrafos*, only to be separated again in March 1942. The service was restructured in 1979 and again in 1983.

In line with current international fashion, the Mexican post office was then turned into a business corporation, largely independent of government control, August 20, 1986. By 2002 its contracts with private industry were providing 80 percent of its income, with an equal proportion of its deliveries made up of bank statements, telephone bills, and advertising, while the collection and delivery of private correspondence has been increasingly neglected. [L. H.]

POVERTY. *See* INCOME DISTRIBUTION.

POZA, AGAPITO (1899–1976). Jurist and politician, born April 21 in **Querétaro**. A law graduate of the Colegio de Querétaro, he served as a senator, 1940–1943 and **governor** of his home state, 1943–1949, before becoming a justice of the **Supreme Court**, 1950–1952, and chief justice, 1958, and in 1964–1968.

PREHISTORY. *See* ARCHAEOLOGY.

PRENSA, LA. Daily newspaper, founded 1928. A lurid tabloid, it is currently the daily with the largest circulation (300,000 copies).

PRESCOTT, WILLIAM HICKLING (1796–1859). America's first scientific historian of the Hispanic World. This Salem, Massachusetts, born author's *The Conquest of Mexico* (1843) has gone through countless editions in many languages and is still being reprinted.

PRESIDENCY, MINISTRY OF THE (*Secretaría de la Presidencia*). Developed in 1958, in an attempt to reduce the power of the **Interior Ministry** (*Gobernación*), but during the **Echeverría** administration more and more authority was returned back to *Gobernación* and when **López Portillo** became president, in December 1976, he abolished the Presidency Ministry altogether, assigning some of its functions to a new Ministry of **Planning** and the Budget.

PRESIDENT. (1). *Presidente de la República*. Any candidate for this supreme office must not only be a native-born Mexican, but has also to have had native-born parents. He is currently elected by universal adult **suffrage** (*See* PRESIDENTIAL SUCCESSION). Like a colonial **viceroy**, he serves a six-year term. Since 1934 this has begun on December 1st. **Law** forbids his immediate **reelection**.

(2). *Presidente de la Audiencia*. This position of colonial chief justice was usually exercised in the case of the **Mexico City** by the viceroy. Elsewhere, the office, the court, and its jurisidiction was often called the *presidencia* ("presidency").

(3). The head of a university (**United States** "president," England and Wales "vice chancellor") is in the Hispanic world, the *rector*.

(4). The *presidente* of a right-of-center political party, opposed to a *secretario general* heading a left-wing party. [L. H.]

PRESIDENTIAL SUCCESSION. An immediate **reelection** of the chief **executive** has been excluded since the **Constitution of 1917**. The popular conception among the Mexican electorate since 1927 has been that the incumbent president choose his successor, by the "**dedazo**." Anyone (such as Miguel **Henríquez Guzmán** or Carlos A. **Madrazo**) who dared challenge this method received short shrift. The alternative, "**Great Electors**" theory, would seem to have applied only to the unusual circumstances of the **election of 1994**. On March 4, 1999, President **Zedillo**, on **television** and in an address to the **Partido Revolucionario Institucional**, called for an end of 60 years of inner-circle selection of presidential candidates, and proposed a presidential primary election for the selection of the candidate for the **election of 2000**. On May 20, 1999, the PRI's **Comité Ejecutivo Nacional**, after conferring with 31 state party chairmen, announced that Don Fernando **Gutiérrez Barrios** would plan the details of the new **primary elections**.

When the election was won by the opposition, **Partido de Acción Nacional** candidate, the victor, Vicente **Fox Quesada,** certainly had a hand in choosing his party's successful 2006 candidate, Felipe **Calderón Hinojosa.** *See also* ELECTION OF 2006.

PRESIDENTS OF MEXICO.

Chairmen of the **Junta de Gobierno**

Pedro Celestino **Negrete**, April, 1823

José Mariano de **Michelena**, May 1823

Nicolás **Bravo de México**, June 1823

José Mariano de Michelena, again, July 1823

Miguel **Domínguez**, August 1823

Vicente Ramón **Guerrero**, September 1823

José Mariano de Michelena, again, October 1823

José Miguel Domínguez, again, November 1823

Vicente Ramón Guerrero, again, December 1–8, 1823

José Miguel Domínguez, again, December 8–31, 1823

José Mariano de Michelena, again, January 1824

José Miguel Domínguez, again, February 1824

Vicente Ramón Guerrero, again, March 1824

Nicolás Bravo de México, again, April 1824

José Miguel Domínguez, again, May 1824

Vicente Ramón Guerrero, again, June 1824

Constitutional Presidents

Guadalupe **Victoria**, July 1824

Nicolás Bravo de México, again, August 1824

José Miguel Domínguez, again, September 1824

Guadalupe Victoria, again, October 1824–January 1828

Manuel **Gómez Pedraza**, January 7–December 4, 1828

Vicente Ramón Guerrero, again, December 7, 1828–December 12, 1829

José María **Bocanegra**, December 18–23, 1829

Chairman of a Junta de Gobierno

Pedro **Vález**, December 23, 1829–January 1, 1830

Constitutional Presidents

Anastacio **Bustamante**, January 1, 1830–August 1832

Melchor **Múzquiz** (interim), August 14–December 24, 1832
Manuel Gómez Pedraza, again (interim), January 3–April 4, 1833
Valtentín **Gómez Farias**, April 4–May 16, 1833
Antonio López de **Santa Anna**, May 16–June 3,1833
Valentín Gómez Farías, again, June 3–June 18, 1833
Antonio López de Santa Anna, again, June 18–July 5, 1833
Valentín Gómez Farías, again, July 5–September 27, 1833
Antonio López de Santa Anna, again, October 28–December 4, 1833
Valentín Gómez Farías, again, December 16, 1833–April 24, 1834
Antonio López de Santa Anna, again, April 24, 1834–January 27, 1835
Miguel **Barragán**, January 28, 1835–February 27, 1836
José Justo **Corro**, February 27, 1836–April 19, 1837
Anastacio Bustamante, again, January 1, 1837–March 18, 1839
Antonio López de Santa Anna, again, March 18–July 9, 1839
Anastacio Bustamente, again, July 19, 1839–September 22, 1840
Nicolás Bravo, again, September 1840–September 22, 1841
Javier **Echeverría**, September 22–28, 1841
Antonio López de Santa Anna, again, October 4, 1841–October 25, 1842
Nicolás Bravo, October 10, 1842–March 4, 1843
Antonio López de Santa Anna, again, March 5–October 3,1843
Valentín **Canalizo** (interim), October 4, 1843–June 4, 1844
Antonio López de Santa Anna, again, June 4–September 11, 1844
José Joaquín de **Herrera**, September 12–21, 1844
Valentín Canalizo, again, September 21–December 6, 1844
J. J. de Herrera, again (interim), December 6, 1844–December 30, 1845
Mariano **Paredes y Arrillaga**, January 4–July 28, 1846
Nicolás Bravo, again, July 28–August 4, 1846
Mariano **Sales**, August 5–December 12, 1846
Antonio López de Santa Anna, again, December 12, 1846
Mariano Sales, again, December 13–23, 1846
Valentín Gómez Farías, again, December 23, 1846–March 21, 1847
Antonio López de Santa Anna, again, March 21–31, 1847
Pedro María **Anaya**, April 2–May 20, 1847
Antonio López de Santa Anna, again, May 20–September 15, 1847

Manuel de la **Peña y Peña**, September 26–November 13, 1847
Pedro María Anaya, again, November 13, 1847–January 8, 1848
Manuel de la Peña y Peña, again, January 8–June 3. 1848
José Joaquín de Herrera, again, June 3, 1848–January 15, 1851
Mariano **Arista**, January 15, 1851–January 5, 1853
Juan Bautista **Ceballos** (interim), January 6–February 8, 1853
Manuel María **Lombardini**, February 8–April 20, 1853
Antonio López de Santa Anna, again, April 20, 1853–August 8, 1855
Rómulo **Díaz de la Vega**, August 13–15, 1855
Martín **Carrera Sabat** (interim), August 15–September 12, 1855
Rómulo Diaz de la Vega, again, September 12–October 4, 1855
Juan **Álvarez Hurtado**, October 4–December 11, 1855
Ignacio **Comonfort**, December 11, 1855–January 21,1858

[The Wars of the **Reform** led to rival Liberal and Conservative governments in Mexico, 1857–1867:]

Conservative Regime
  Félix **Zuloaga**, January 23–December 23, 1858
  Manuel **Robles Pezuela**, December, 1858–January, 1859
  Félix Zuloaga, again, January–February 2, 1859
  Miguel **Miramón**, February 2, 1859–August 13,1860
  José Ignacio **Pavón**, August 13–15, 1860
  Miguel Miramón, again, August 15–December 24, 1860
  Félix Zuloaga, again, December 28, 1860–April 18, 1862
  Juan Nepomuceno **Almonte**, April 18, 1862–January 12, 1863

Liberal Regime
  Benito Pablo **Juárez García**, January, 1861–July 18, 1863 (having been pretender to the presidency in **Guanajuato** since January 19, 1858, and withdrawing from **Mexico City** to **Chihuahua**, July 1863–July, 1867)

[**Second Empire**, 1863–1867]

Liberal Regime
  Benito Juárez (restored), July 15, 1867–July 18, 1872

Sebastián **Lerdo de Tejada**, July 19, 1872–November 20, 1876
[José María Laglesias (pretender in Salamanca), November, 1876–January 17, 1877]
Juan N. **Méndez**, November 11, 1876–February 17, 1877
Porfírio **Díaz**, February 17, 1877–November 30, 1880
Manuel **González**, December 1, 1880–November 30, 1884
Porfirio Diaz, again, December 1, 1884–May 25, 1911
Francisco **León de la Barra** (provisional), May 25–November 6, 1911

Revolutionary Regime
Francisco I. **Madero**, November 6, 1911–February 19, 1913
Pedro **Lascuraín Paredes**, February 19, 1913
Victoriano **Huerta**, February 19, 1913–July 15, 1914
Francisco S. **Carvajal y Graal**, July 15–August 13, 1914
Venustiano **Carranza**, August 20–October 31, 1914 (but continuing to exercise his office in Veracruz through 1915)
Antonio I. **Villarreal González**, October 31–November 6, 1914
[Pancho **Villa** and Emilio **Zapata** (in Mexico City), November 26, 1914–April, 1915]
[Eulalio **Gutiérrez** (in Aguascalientes), January 17–June 2, 1915]
[Roque **González Garza** (in Querétaro), January 16–June 9, 1915]
Venustiano Carranza, again, August 20, 1915–November 1915
Franciso **Lagos Cházaro**, November 1915–April, 1916 (in Querétaro from June 9, 1915)
Venustiano Carranza (back in Mexico City), April 1916–May 6, 1920
Adolfo de la **Huerta**, (provisional), June 1–November 30, 1920
Álvaro **Obregón**, December 1, 1920–November 30, 1924
Plutarco Elias **Calles**, December 1, 1924–November 30, 1928
Emilio **Pontes Gil**, December 1, 1928–February 4, 1930
Pascual **Ortiz Rubio**, February 5, 1930–September 3, 1932
Abelardo Luján **Rodríguez**, September 4, 1932–November 30, 1934
Lazaro **Cárdenas del Rio**, December 1, 1934–November 30, 1940
Manuel **Ávila Camacho**, December 1, 1940–November 30, 1946
Miguel **Alemán Valdés**, December 1, 1946–November 30, 1952
Adolfo, **Ruiz Cortines**, December 1, 1952–November 30, 1958

Adolfo **López Mateos**, December 1, 1958–November 30, 1964
Gustavo **Dias Ordaz**, December 1, 1964–November 30, 1970
Luis **Echevarría Álvarez**, December 1, 1970–November 30, 1976
Jose **López Portillo y Pacheco**, December 1, 1976–1982
Miguel de La **Madrid Hurtado**, December 1, 1982–1988
Carlos **Salinas de Gortari**, December 1, 1988–1994
Ernesto **Zedillo Ponce de León**, December 1, 1994–2000
Vicente **Fox Quesada**, December 1, 2000–2006
Felipe **Calderón Hinojosa**, December 1, 2006–2012

PRESIDIO. (1) Garrison, and hence, garrison town, fortress. (2) A river of **Durango state**.

PRI. Acronym of the **Partido Revolucionario Institucional**.

PRICKLY PEAR CACTUS (*Nopal*). National symbol of Mexico, home to 83 of the 120 known species, and part of the "**eagle and serpent**" emblem, and often the basis of the ecosystem of desert regions. It is currently threatened by the **cactus moth**. [L. H.]

PRIETO, GUILLERMO (1818–1897). Liberal politician, man of letters, and close supporter of Benito **Juárez**. He backed the Plan of **Ayutla** and was a delegate to the **Constituent Assembly of 1856**, served as a senator, and held cabinet posts in various liberal governments. He was also an accomplished poet, one of his most famous works being *La Musa callejera* on popular poetry, a valuable contribution to establishing Mexican folklore as a significant literary genre.

PRIMARY ELECTIONS. In 1998, the **Partido Revolucionario Institucional**, at President **Zedillo**'s urging, experimented with primary party elections to choose several candidates for state governorships, which seemed to restore party popularity. New rules for primaries were adopted almost unanimously by the PRI's national convention and announced on **television** by José Antonio **González Fernández** on May 18, 1999. Those who wished to be on the primary ballot were to resign their government posts by June 15 of the year before the general election and register as pre-candidates by July 15, but not to begin campaigning for votes before August 1. All registered Mexican voters could vote in the new primaries.

PRIME MINISTER. Title of the head of government under the **Second Empire**, a position held successively by José María de Lacuna (June 13, 1864–October 6, 1866), Teodosio Lares (October 6, 1866–March 19, 1867), and Santiago Vidaurri (March 19–May 15, 1867). [L. H.]

PRINTING. The Spanish printer Juan Pablos was sent to **Mexico City** in the 1530s to install a printing press on behalf of the Seville printer Cromberger. The first known work is dated 1537. *See also* PUBLISHING AND THE BOOK TRADE. [L. H.]

PRISONS. Mexico's penal system includes five federal penitentiaries, eight **federal district** prisons, 336 state prisons, and 99 municipal jails, with an official capacity for 147,809 but in fact holding in 2004 some 182,430 inmates. The overcrowding prevented separation of convicts from those on remand. **Women** (c.8,000) were kept in conditions inferior to those of the men. There were 54 reformatories for juveniles, with (according to U.S. Country Reports on Human Rights Practices) substandard conditions in many of them. *See also* GARCÍA RAMÍREZ, SERGIO; SAN JUAN DE ULÚA; TELLEZ CRUZES, AGUSTÍN; TRES MARÍAS ISLANDS. [L. H.]

PRIVATEERS. Privately owned vessels, or "corsairs," assisting their country's war effort by attacking enemy shipping (*guerre de course*), under the authorization of letters of marque, and financed by the resulting prize money, a practice recognized in international law until 1854. *See also* COAST GUARD; PIRACY. [L. H.]

PRIVATIZATION. From the 1980s onward Mexico has followed international economic fashion in privatizing most state-owned industries and enterprises. The model followed has been similar to that of Russia, with state monopolies turning into oligopolies owned by a small wealthy elite, **Telemex**, for example. The resultant cronyism has been criticized by some foreign observers as denying Mexico the full potential of the change, particularly in the way it has offered few new economic opportunities to the poorer classes. The associated increase in inequality of **income distribution** is, however, a common feature of most modern economies. *See also* ASPE ARMELLA, PEDRO CARLOS; PACTO DE SOLIDARIDAD ECONÓMICA.

PROCESO. Critical news weekly founded by Julio **Scherer García** after he had been ousted as executive publisher of **Excélsior**, as a center-left critic of the **Partido Revolucionario Institucional** establishment. Scherer worked through a booster group of critics to get subscribers in every major Mexican city.

PROCURADOR DE JUSTICIA. Attorney general at **state** level.

PROCURADOR GENERAL. Federal prosecutor, equivalent to attorney general.

PROCURADURÍA GENERAL DE LA REPÚBLICA (PRG). Office of the **procurador general**.

PROFMEX. Acronym (and legal name) of the Consortium for Research on Mexico (*Consortio Mundial para la Investigación sobre México*), a worldwide, non-profit "network for Mexico public policy" of academics, and specialists in government, private business and NGOs, formed in 1982, based in Los Angeles but with a secretariat general in **Mexico City**. [L. H.]

PROGRAMA INDUSTRIAL FRONTERIZO (Border Industrial Program). A Mexican government program to encourage the establishment of assembly plants (**maquilladoras**) along the **United States border**, from **Tijuana, B.C.N.**, to **Matamoros, Tamaulipas**.

PROGRAMA NACIONAL FRONTERIZO (National Border Program). Mexican government program introduced in 1961 to develop sales of Mexican-made products to compete with American-made products in the Mexican-**United States border** region. *See also* PROGRAMA INDUSTRIAL FRONTERIZO.

PROGRESO. Chief port of **Yucatán state**, city, and tourist center with a direct ferry to Miami. Founded by Juan Miguel Castro in 1840, with the growth of local trade with **Cuba** and **Spain**, to replace the colonial port of Sisal (53 km from **Mérida**) with a closer location (34 km). The custom house was moved there from Sisal in 1870. The railroad to Mérida opened in 1875 (and closed in 1993). [L. H.]

PRONUNCIAMIENTO ("declaration"). A coup d'état or revolt, usually military, accompanied by a declaration of what the new leader will do on assuming power. Usually spelled "pronunciamento" in English, such "pronoucements" were common in Spain and Mexico from the early 19th century until the 1920s, except during the **Porfiriato**. [L. H.]

PROPORTIONAL REPRESENTATION. Under a constitutional revision of 1964, the number of seats in the **Cámara de Diputados Federales** was increased to provide representation for minority parties. As the existing congressional district seats were filled overwhelmingly by the dominant **Partido Revolucionario Institucional**, the other parties were to be given five seats for their first 2.5 percent of the total vote, plus one seat for each additional one-half percent. The result that the leader of the **Partido Popular Socialista** became the first opposition leader, and **Partido de Acción Nacional** gained 20 seats. Thereafter each voter has had to mark a first ballot to choose the single candidate for the congressional district, and a second ballot for the seats distributed on the proportional representation formula, not nationally, but within the voter's region, the republic being divided into five regions for this purpose. This original system never gave the opposition more than 40 seats and in the **election of 1972** the formula was changed, giving five seats for the first 1.5 percent, with additional seats up to 25 for extra half percentages. When the Chamber was again enlarged in 1979, 100 seats were provided for election under the proportional representation system. This number was raised to 200 in 1987.

PROTESTANTISM. The latest **census** listed 5 million Protestants: 5.2 percent of the national **population**. *See also* IGLESIA CATOLICA MEXICANA.

PROVINCIAS INTERNAS, COMANDANCÍA GENERAL DE LAS. Administrative unit, headquartered in Arizpe in present-day

Sonora, decreed in 1769 but not created until 1776, to administer the **Far North** and parts of the **Near North**, viz. Sonora, **Sinaloa**, **Nueva Vizcaya**, **Coahuila**, **Texas**, and the Californias (to which **Nuevo León** and **Nueva Santander** were later added), as a direct dependency of the government in Madrid. The first comandante general was Teodoro de **Croix**. It was divided in 1788 into an Eastern (Coahuila, Texas, Nuevo Léon, and Nuevo Santander) and a Western part (Sinaloa, Nueva Vizcaya, and **New Mexico**. It lasted until 1793. [L. H.]

PUBLIC ADMINISTRATION MINISTRY (*Secretaría de la Función Pública***, S.F.P.).** The former Ministry of the **Comptrollership General (SECODAM)** changed its name on April 11, 2003, while retaining identical functions: even using the same manuals of organization and internal regulations. [L. H.]

PUBLIC FINANCE. *See* BUDGET; FINANCE MINISTRY.

PUBLIC HEALTH. *See* BIRTH RATE; DEATH RATE; DISEASE; HEALTH CARE; HEALTH MINISTRY; INFANT MORTALITY.

PUBLIC SECURITY MINISTRY (*Secretaría de Seguridad Pública***, SSP).** Ministry created in 2001 to take over homeland security responsibilities from the **Interior Ministry**. Its subordinate agencies include the **Policia Federal Preventiva**, and the *Coordinación de Fuerzas de Reacción y Apoyo Inmediato*—CFRAI. [L. H.]

PUBLIC WORKS MINISTRY. From 1891 to 1935 and from 1939 to 1959 the *Secretaría de Comunicaciones y Obras Públicas* was a cabinet entity. In 1959 it was divided into the *Secretaría de Obras Públicas* and the *Secretaría de Comunicaciones y Transportes* (*See* TRANSPORT MINISTRY). In December 1976 the former became the **Human Settlements Ministry**. [L. H.]

PUBLISHING AND THE BOOK TRADE. Publishing began in **Mexico City** in the 1530s, to fulfill the catechizing and proselytizing needs of the **University of Mexico**. **Puebla** had the first provincial publishing in the mid-17th century. The total colonial output in **New Spain** was close to 15,000 titles including a few books from **Guatemala**.

Independent commercial publishing began with Mariano **Galván Rivera** in 1826. José **Vasconcelos** made an important effort to encourage publishing textbooks for Mexican schools and the national publishing of literary classics. Government concern at the paucity of Mexican publishing in the fields of science and economics led to the 1934 establishment of the **Fondo de Cultura Económica**. Two years later the outbreak of the **Spanish Civil War** cut off Mexico's chief source of book imports. The war not only stimulated Mexican publishers to expand to fill the void, but Mexico's welcome of Republican refugees, symbolized by the creation of the **Casa de España**, led to the immigration of many writers, publishers, and members of the book trade generally. The long-term result has been a considerable growth in Mexican publishing, much of which is now exported, although a revived Spanish industry not only exports more books, but has invested heavily in the direct ownership of Latin American publishing. On the other hand, at least one Mexican firm, **Siglo XXI Editores**, has branch houses in both Spain and Argentina.

Contemporary Mexico has only about 600 bookstores, and, as elsewhere, independents find it difficult to compete with chain stores promoting best sellers with heavy discounts. A relatively recent development has been the creation of the regular annual international book fair at **Guadalajara**. *See also* ROCAFUERTE, VICENTE. [L. H.]

PUEBLA, BATTLE OF. A crushing defeat of crack French infantry of the Foreign Legion by poorly-equipped cavalry led by Ignacio **Zaragoza** in 1862. Although not decisive in repelling the **French intervention**, the victory is regarded as one of the most glorious episodes in Mexican history and is regularly commemorated as the **Fifth of May**. The French, who were in the process of securing the territory between **Veracruz** and **Mexico City** for the passage of the emperor-to-be **Maximilian**, closed in on **Puebla City**, expecting no serious resistance, but were forced back to the coast. Their General Laurencez was replaced by the more capable General Forey.

PUEBLA CITY. The capital of **Puebla state**, and an archbishopric, 113 km (70 miles) southeast of **Mexico City**, 2,175 m above sea level at 19°03'N, 98°12'W. Founded October 29, 1531, by Spanish

Franciscans (with the individual credit going to Fray Toribio de **Benavente**) as "Puebla de Los Ángeles," it soon displaced the nearby **Indian** city of **Cholula** as the region's center. The Cathedral and the **Universidad de Puebla** typify its baroque architecture. This major industrial and commercial center, has automobile, steel, and chemical industries, and is famous for its ceramics and Talavera titles.

Mexico's second city until it was overtaken by **Guadalajara** in the 1870s, Puebla is now the fifth largest. Its population has grown from 57,000 in 1793 to 75,000 in 1875; 96,000 in 1910; 211,000 in 1950; and 1,346,916 in 2000.

During the **French intervention** it was the base from which Ignacio **Zaragoza**'s troops won the 1862 battle of **Puebla** for which the city was officially renamed "Puebla de Zaragoza." A year later French General Forey laid siege to the city. The Mexicans held out for three months, only surrendering when their food and ammunition was exhausted. The city's full name has, however, become somewhat of a political football, with many on the right keen for a return to "de los Ángeles."

The namesake **municipio** extends over 524 km².

PUEBLA-PANAMA PLAN. An international program with Inter-American Development Bank sponsorship to foster economic integration, measures to prevent and cope with natural disasters, eco-tourism etc. in the region of Meso-America. Its members are the countries of Central America, including **Belize** and Panama, and the Mexican states of **Campeche**, **Chiapas**, **Guerrero**, **Oaxaca**, **Puebla**, **Quintana Roo**, **Tabasco**, **Veracruz**, and **Yucatán**.

PUEBLA STATE. An inland state of south central Mexico, named for its capital, **Puebla City**. Established as an **intendancy** in 1786 and made a state in 1824, it lost territory to the new state of **Guerrero** in 1861 and is now one of the smallest states, with only 33,929 km². It is bordered by **Hidalgo**, **Veracruz**, **México state**, **Tlaxcala**, **Morelos**, **Oaxaca**, and Guerrero. With 658,609 inhabitants in 1857, and 830,000 in 1869, its 1895 population of 980,000 made it the second most populous state (after **Jalisco**). Since then it has been overtaken by Mexico state, the **Federal District**, and Veracruz, having 1,021,000 people in 1900; 1,102,000 in 1910; 1,025,000 in 1921;

1,150,000 in 1930; 1,295,000 in 1940; 1,626,000 in 1950; 1,974,000 in 1960; 2,508,000 in 1970; 3,348,000 in 1980; 4,126,000 in 1990; 5,076,686 in 2000; and 5,383,133 in 2005. Its mountainous terrain is crossed in the center by an east-west range of volcanoes including the **Orizaba volcano**, **Popocatépetl**, and **Ixlaccíhuatl**, Mexico's highest peaks, rising to over 5,180 m (17,000 ft.). Rivers include the **Orizaba**.

Manufacturing industry produces 80 percent of the state's gross product. Onyx, **silver**, and **lead** are mined. **Agriculture** includes **coffee**, **corn**, and **livestock**.

PUENTES Y CALZADAS. *See* CAMINOS Y PUENTES.

PUERTO VALLARTA. A port and, since the 1950s, a fashionable tourist and **sport fishing** resort well provided with luxury hotels on the Pacific coast of **Jalisco state**. Its Banderas Bay has been a port since early colonial times. The ornate Guadalupe church was built in 1800. The town was hit and severely damaged by Hurricane **Kenna**.

PUGA, MARÍA LUISA (1944–2004). Novelist: (*Las posibilidades del odio*, 1978; *Pánico o peligro*, 1983), short story writer, and children's author. Born in **Mexico City**, she lived abroad 1968–1978, originally to write for the London weekly *The Economist*.

PULQUE. An alcoholic beverage made from the fermented juice of the **agave** cactus, popular since pre-Hispanic times.

PURÉPECHA. *See* TARASCAN.

– Q –

QUEMADA, LA. The pre-Hispanic archaeological site near **Zacatecas City**, with monuments and ruined buildings.

QUERÉTARO CITY. The capital of **Querétaro State**, formally *Santiago de Querétaro*, 217 km (135 miles) northwest of **Mexico City**, at 20°36'N, 100°23'W, and 1800 m (5,904 ft.) above sea level, founded by the **Aztecas** on the site of an **Otomí** town conquered by

Montezuma II in 1440, and conquered by the **conquistador** Fernando **Tapia** July 25, 1531. Its **water** supply is brought from the mountains by an 8 km (5 mile) long aqueduct of 74 arches built in 1735. Its colonial Santa Rosa church and its federal building are of local basalt. It became the "cradle of **independence**" as the starting place of Ignacio **Pérez**'s ride to warn Miguel **Hidalgo y Costilla** that their plot had been discovered and that they must therefore start their revolt immediately. During the **United States-Mexican War** of 1846–1848, the city became the temporary federal capital. In 1867 its **Iturbide** Theater was the scene of the trial of the Emperor **Maximilian**. The **municipio** whose 2000 population was 641,386 has **cotton** and woolen mills, and there are opal mines nearby.

QUERÉTARO CONVENTION. *See* CONSTITUENT ASSEMBLY OF 1916–1917.

QUERÉTARO LITERARY SOCIETY. Ostensibly formed to encourage the fine arts, it was really a cover for activity against the colonial government and it became the prime mover in the uprising of 1810 when it finally convinced Miguel **Hidalgo y Costilla** to accept the leadership of the **independence** movement.

QUERÉTARO STATE. A state in central Mexico of 11,769 km², officially Querétaro de Arteaga, with a population of 165,155 in 1857; 166,643 in 1869; 227,000 in 1895; 232,000 in 1900; 245,000 in 1910; 220,000 in 1921; 234,000 in 1930; 245,000 in 1940; 286,000 in 1950; 355,000 in 1960; 486,000 in 1970; 618,000 in 1976; 740,000 in 1980; 1,051,000 in 1990; 1,200,000 in 1995; 1,404,306 in 2000; and 1,598,139 in 2005. In pre-Hispanic times it was occupied by the **Otomí** and at Independence was a Corregimiento. As such it was the only state created by the **Constitution of 1824** that was neither a province nor an intendancy.

It is divided into 18 *municipios* but 46 percent of its population live in the metropolitan area of the capital, **Querétaro City**.

It produces **cotton, corn**, cattle, and hides. It has a growing area of **manufacturing industry** near the capital (**Querétaro City**) producing automobile parts, and, since 1975, has been the largest producer in Mexico of vehicle gear boxes.

QUETZAL. A tropical bird with long green plumes, native of **Meso-America**.

QUETZAL DANCE. Type of **Indian** folk dance performed in **Veracruz**, **Puebla**, and **Hidalgo** by dancers wearing headdresses of paper and ribbons depicting the **quetzal**.

QUETZALCÓATL. (1) The serpent god of the Toltecs, and later of the **Mayas** and **Aztecs**, bedecked in quetzal feathers. God of air and water, and of the morning and evening star, he also took the form of a fair-haired, light-skinned, bearded hero who ruled the Aztecs, preaching virtue and a high code of ethics. He had suddenly departed, perhaps for having succumbed to temptation by Tezcatlipoca, the god of darkness, but with a promise to return. This legend greatly facilitated the Spanish **Conquest of Mexico**, the fair skinned bearded Hernán **Cortés** being taken, even by **Montezuma** as Quetzalcóatl—**Kukulcán** in Maya—fulfilling his ancient promise to return, and claiming his throne.

(2) The are many legends about a person of this name and although any accuracy is now impossible, the most accepted story is that he was a **Toltec** king ruling in the early 13th century, possessing extraordinary abilities, being scientist, metallurgist, and jewelry artisan, and having introduced the use of chocolate and rubber.

QUETZALCÓATL KUKULKÁN. Chief of the **Itzá** who came to **Yucatán** and founded **Chichén Itzá**.

QUEVEDO MORENO, RODRIGO M. (1889–1967). Politician who fought in the **Revolution of 1910** under Pascual **Orozco** against Francisco **Madero**, and alongside Juan **Almazán** against the **Constitutionalists**. In 1920 he became a key supporter and advisor of President Álvaro **Obregón**. In 1935 he became **governor** of his native **Chihuahua**. As a senator in 1958–1964, he was a leader of those formulating new laws on **agriculture**, **immigration**, **mining**, and national defense.

QUINTANA ROO. Former Federal territory of 50,350 km², including the resort islands of **Mujeres** and **Cozumel**. The **Hondo** River forms its border with **Belize**. It currently produces chicle, lumber, **coffee**, **cotton**, **sisal**, and half of Mexico's **tobacco**.

With the outbreak of the **Caste War of Yucatán**, all *latinos* were driven out and for the next fifty years the area became the **Maya** nation of *Chan Santa Cruz*. Although made a federal territory in 1902, it was briefly returned to **Yucatán** in 1915–1931. Until the last third of the 20th century, it had remained relatively empty. Only in 1955 did President **Rúiz Cortines** end the campaign of **Yucatán** state to annex it. Not until 1958 did modern **highways** adequately connect the two states. It finally became the 31st state on October 10, 1974, and is now divided into 8 *municipios*: **Benito Juárez**, **Cozumel**, Felipe Carillo Puerto, Isla **Mujeres**, José María Morelos, Lázaro Cardenas, Othón P. Blanco, and Solidaridad. The capital is **Chetumal**. Its population was 9,000 in 1910; 11,000 in 1921; 11,000 in 1930; 19,000 in 1940; 27,000 in 1950; 50,000 in 1960; 88,000 in 1970; 134,000 in 1976; 226,000 in 1980; 493,000 in 1990; 874,963 in 2000; and 1,125,309 in 2005—almost doubling at each successive post-**World War II** census. Despite its frequent and often severe hurricanes, the state is a tourist resort.

QUINTANA ROO, ANDRÉS (1787–1851). Politician, literary figure, and **independence** fighter from **Yucatán**. In 1813 he presided over the Congress of **Chilpancingo**. After **independence** he served in various offices, including those of senator and **supreme court** justice. His was noted for his honesty and courage, as when he criticized the government for the murder of Vicente **Guerrero**. He was also an accomplished poet, and his ode on the Sixteenth of September is among his best known works.

QUINTANAR, LUIS. Member of the Triumvirate that ruled Mexico in 1829.

QUINTANILLA DEL VALLE, LUIS (1900–1970). Diplomat and educator. Born in Paris, he graduated in philosophy from the Sorbonne, where he obtained a doctorate in political science. He entered the foreign service and was posted to **Guatemala**, **Brazil**, and the **United States**, before heading the Mexican delegation to the **League of Nations** in 1932. He taught international relations at the **UNAM** and also, in 1937–1942, at Johns Hopkins, Virginia, Kansas, and

George Washington universities. He later served as ambassador to Colombia, the **United Nations**, and the **Organization of American States**, 1945–1958. In 1948–1949 he chaired the Inter-American Peace Commission. In 1958 he became director of the **Instituto Nacional de la Vivienda**. In 1950 he authored the widely read *A Latin American Speaks*.

QUIROGA, VASCO DE (1470–1565). A law graduate of the Universidad de Valladolid, he came to **New Spain** in 1531 as an **oidor**. He was interested in administering to the sick and founded the Hospital of Santa Fe, complete with a church and an orphanage. He then became a priest and in 1538 was made bishop of **Michoacán**, a position he retained until his death. Besides numerous hospitals, he founded the **Colegio de San Nicolás Obispo**, which ultimately became the **Universidad de San Nicolás de Michoacán** He encouraged the development of Michoacán along lines of a kind of "primitive Christianity," which each community developing a different speciality, such as tanning in **Uruapán**. He believed in non-violence and was so loved by the **Tarascan Indians** that they called him "Tata Vasco," as a beloved family father, His death occasioned a long period of deep mourning. His life is the subject of an opera by Miguel Bernal **Jiménez**.

QUIVIRA. Mythical land rich in **gold** sought in 1540–1542 by Francisco **Vásquez de Coronado** in what is now the US state of Kansas. Later maps show it close to the mythical strait of **Arian**.

– R –

RABASA, EMILIO O. (1925–). Lawyer, diplomat. After graduating from **UNAM**, he taught law there for 15 years. He was a legal advisor for, successively, the **finance ministry**, the **health ministry**, the department of agrarian affairs, and the **Banco Nacional de Crédito Ejidal**. He then served as director general of the **Banco Nacional Cinematográfica**, 1964–1970; ambassador to the **United States**, 1970; and foreign minister, 1970–1976. During the **Echeverría** administration, he led those trying to keep the President from applying increasingly negative policies towards the United States.

RACE. *See* ETHNICITY; RAZA.

RACER'S HURRICANE. Hurricane that struck **Matamoros** in October, 1837.

RACISM. *See* BLACKS; ETHNICITY.

RADICAL PARTY. *See* PARTIDO RADICAL.

RADIO. Amateur transmitters paved the way for regular broadcasting in 1919–1922, mainly in the north which was then the calmer part of the country—the last big battles of the **Revolution of 1910** were still being fought. **Mexico City** communication officials issued the first licence for broadcasting to a mass audience on June 1, 1923. By then a few residents of northern Mexico had already acquired radio receivers to listen to stations in the **United States**, where public broadcasting had begun in 1920. Daily radio broadcasting began in **Monterrey** in July 1923 from station RR, for owner Roberto Reyes, a furniture manufacturer (later when Mexico introduced a three or four letter system, RR became CYB, and then XEB). Almost immediately, radio pioneer Constantino de **Tárnava Jr.** turned his amateur station 24-A into a public one, CYP (later XEH). About the same time, Mexico City appliance retailers visited Monterrey to purchase crystal-set receivers, which they then began selling on the availability of free concerts on the air. President Álvaro **Obregón**, still desperate for United States diplomatic recognition, sent a "friendly public relations report" to the US Secretary of Commerce that Mexico too was now pioneering public radio broadcasting. It apparently worked, as, three months later, on August 31, 1923, the United States recognized his regime. Another pioneer station was CYL which closed down in 1930 when Emilio **Azcárraga Vidaurrota** launched XEW. Meanwhile, the first non-commercial daily radio station on the AM dial, XFX, had been started on September 1, 1928, by the education minister as Mexico's first educational station. In 1937 it became XEDP and was transferred to the press office of the Presidency, and given a companion shortwave station, XEXA, able to reach over the mountains into almost all regions of the country.

In 1938 station XEFO and companion shortwave station XEXO were licensed to the **Partido Revolucionario Mexicano** (forerunner of the **Partido Revolucionario Institucional**). When the new opposition party, the **Partido de Acción Nacional** requested similar treatment, the government refused, and closed the PRM station, but allowed daily PRM broadcasts on the federal government station XEFO, on the grounds that such broadcasts were merely factual accounts of the progress of the social revolution.

By the late 1960s, most stations had not only associated shortwave transmitters, but also affiliated FM stations.

As in other countries, the radio audience has been considerably and steadily reduced since the 1950s by the introduction and spread of **television**, although the number of radio receivers (22,500,000 in 1992) was still considerably greater than that of **television** receivers (13,100,000).

Radio was the chief means whereby the **Asamblea Popular de los Pueblos de Oaxaca** coordinated its forces in the **Oaxaca** insurrection of 2006. When the movement's transmitter was smashed by the state **police**, it used that of the local university. When that was destroyed in turn, it took over state **television** channel 9, and then, driven out of there, occupied various commercial radio stations, endeavoring to stay always a step ahead of the authorities. *See also* MEDIA.

RAFFUL, FERNANDO (1935–). Campeche-born economist for the Ministry of the "National Patrimony" (i.e., **natural resource**), 1965–1967; director of federal government decentralized agencies and businesses, 1970–1973; assistant minister of natural resources, 1973–1976; and in December 1976 appointed as the first director of the new Department of **Fishing**, an autonomous agency allied with the **agriculture ministry**.

RAILROAD AND BANKING REVOLT. *See* ESCOBAR REBELLION, 1929.

RAILROADS. The very first railroad in Mexico was built in 1850, but construction in so mountainous a country was never to be easy, and when the Emperor **Maximilian** arrived at **Veracruz**, the railroad to **Mexico City** was only half completed and he had to travel the rest of the way by coach. Renamed the **Ferrocarril Mexicano**, it was finally finished under President Porfirio **Díaz**, connecting the capital with its main port and giving Mexico, in a pre-aircraft, pre-automobile age, its front door to the world. The economic effects of this pioneer line encouraged the construction of lines to the major provincial cities, in partnership from the 1890s with the Southern Pacific and Missouri Pacific Railroads. The first rail link from Mexico City to the **United States border** at **El Paso** was built in the 1880s by the Mexican Central Railroad Company. In 1888 the Mexican National Railroad Company connected the capital with **Laredo**, its 800 miles making it the shortest link to the **United States**, although it was not converted from narrow to standard gauge until the early 1900s. The Sonora Railroad Company linked **Guymas** with **Nogales** but the line from Mexico City through **Sonora state** to the Gulf of **California** shore in **Sinaloa state** was only completed in 1961, after "on-again, off-again" construction through the mountain passes of the Sierra **Madre** Occidental over a period of 25 years. A route across the Isthmus of **Tehuantepec** was completed in 1894, but trains were not running regularly between Puerto Mexico (the present-day **Coatzacoalcos**) on the Gulf and **Salina Cruz** on the Pacific until 1907. By 1911 Mexico had 15,000 route miles (24,000 route kms).

In 1937 President Lázaro **Cárdenas**'s government took over most of the private railroad companies, to form the **Ferrocarriles Nacionales de México**. Many loss-making lines, particularly in the south, were closed in the 1980s and later. The remaining lines were again privatized in the 1990s, with a marked improvement in both passenger and freight services, although passenger movement is now overwhelmingly by road.

There are currently 26,300 route-kms of railroads in Mexico. *Ferrocarril Mexicano S.A.* (Ferromex), the largest company, owns 8,460 route-kms, serving the area north from Mexico City. *Transportación Ferroviaria Mexicana* has 4,251 route-kms between Mexico City and **Nuevo Laredo**. *Ferrocarriles Chiapas-Mayor S.A.* is a 1,805 km line from **Coatzacolas** to **Mérida**. The *Ferrocarril del Sureste* runs 1,564 km between Mexico City, **Puebla**, and **Veracruz City**. The *Linea Coahuila a Durango* is 978 km long, and the *Ferrocarril del Istmo de Tehuautepec* just 207 km. [L. H.]

RAINFALL. The rainy season is from June to October, but only seven percent of the country receives sufficient rain for natural cultivation without **irrigation**. The dry areas of the north and center receive under 600 mm annual precipitation, with the very driest fifth of the country receiving under 300 mm, while the 5 percent where tropical rainforest is the natural vegetation (the **Chiapas** highlands) receive 2,000–4,000 mm. But even in the south, there is a large dry area in the flat **Yucatán** peninsula.

RAMÍREZ, FRANCISCO. Felipe **Calderón Hinojosa**'s interior minister, formerly governor of **Jalisco,** and a strong critic of **United Nations**' human rights policies. [L. H.]

RAMÍREZ, IGNACIO (1781–1879). *El Nigromante* ("the Necromancer") was a liberal writer from **San Miguel Allende**, and a strong anti-clerical who played a major role in drafting the **Constitution of 1857.** He originally supported Benito **Juárez**, but he eventually turned against him and ended up supporting Porfirio **Díaz.** Publications he founded included *El Clamor progresista* and *La Insurreción.* Ignacio de **Altamirano** was among his disciples. He died in **Mexico City.**

RAMÍREZ CUELLAR, HÉCTOR (1947–). Activist in the **Partido Popular Socialista**. Born in **Ciudad Juárez,** he studied political science at **UNAM,** 1968–1974, becoming a professor at the **Instituto Politécnico Nacional** in 1975, and teaching subsequently at the **Universidad de Trabajadores** in **Mexico City** and at UNAM. He was a PPS member of the **Cámara de Diputados Federales** in 1976–1979, 1982–1985, and 1991–1994. In 1970–1990 he was a member of the PPS' Central Committee and its secretary of organization.

RAMÍREZ VÁZQUEZ, MARIANO (1903–19??). A lawyer who in the 1930s, as secretary general of the **Federal Conciliation and Arbitration Board,** set the pattern of government dominating all **labor**-management relations. He was a justice of the **Supreme Court,** 1947–1949 and 1954–1976.

RAMÍREZ VÁZQUEZ, PEDRO (1919–). Architect and city planner, born April 16 in **Mexico City.** In 1944–1947 he directed school construction in **Tabasco** and then directed building construction for the **education ministry**. He was manager for all prefabricated school buildings in Mexico, 1964–1966; director of UNESCO's school construction of Latin America; architect of the **Museo Nacional de Antropología**; and chairman of Mexico's 1968 **Olympics** Committee. In 1973 he was founder and president of the **Universidad Autónoma Metropolitana**. In December 1976 he became head of the **Human Settlements Ministry**.

RAMOS ARIZPE, MIGUEL (1775–1843). Priest, economist, and a prominent liberal politician in the early **independence** period. Elected to the **Cortes of Cádiz**, he was later imprisoned for advocating Mexican **independence** and only released by the Spanish Liberal Revolution of 1820 led by Rafael **Riego y Núñez**. He and Valentín **Gómez Farías** were the chief architects of the **Constitution of 1824**. He was deputy from **Puebla** to the Constitutional Convention of 1832, held the position of justice minister, and was one of the most honest and dedicated politicians of an era when **corruption** was unfortunately the overwhelming norm.

RANA. Mexican children's traditional folksong about a frog and a spider.

RANGEL FRIAS, RAÚL (1913–). Lawyer from **Monterrey** who became a law professor, then rector of the **Universidad de Nuevo León**, 1939–1943; and governor of **Nuevo León**, 1955–1961. He pioneered the offering of civics courses for skilled tradesmen at workers' centers in **Mexico City** and throughout northern Mexico to increase working class leadership in public life.

RAYON, IGNACIO LÓPEZ. *See* LÓPEZ RAYON, IGNACIO.

RAZA, LA. ("The race"). The worldwide Spanish-speaking community, celebrated each year on **Columbus Day** as the *Día de la Raza*.

REAL. Pre-decimalization silver coin, worth one eighth of a **peso**, the origin of the American "bit" (as in "two bits" equalling one fourth of a **dollar**). In colonial times the **coinage** had also included a copper real (*real de vellón*) worth one twentieth of a peso. [L. H.]

REBELIÓN DELAHUERTISTA. *See* HUERTA, ADOLFO DE LA.

REBELLIONS. *See* INSURRECTIONS.

REBOLLEDO, EFRÉN (1877–1929). Poet and diplomat. The various diplomatic posts he held around the world inspired much of his work, including *Rimas japonesas* and the novel *Saga de Sigfrida la blonda* (from an appointment in Norway). His output is characterized by his great care and choice of words. He died in Madrid.

REBOZO. A woman's shawl, often dark blue or purple, used by working class Mexicans, and integral to folk dance costumes. Among rural Indian and **mestizo** women, it is the standard overcoat-raincoat, head covering, and wrap for infants. Urban middle-class and upper-class women wear brightly colored and embroidered *rebozos*.

REDUCCIÓN. An enforced settlement of **Indians** under a colonial *corregidor* in a village to which all white laymen were forbidden entry. It was hoped that such segregation under direct royal or **Church** control would be more humane and effective a way of acculturating the Indians than the private **encomienda** and make their **labor** available while avoiding their excessive exploitation. This worthy purpose best achieved in Paraguay under the benevolent despotism of the **Jesuits**. In **New Spain**, the greatest such resettlement took place, not always peacefully, during the **viceroyalty** of Gaspar de **Zúñiga y Acevedo**.

REELECTION. The "no reelection" principle of Francisco **Madero** at the onset of the **Revolution of 1910** still prevents the holder of any elected position from remaining in office for the immediately consecutive term (and is used as a slogan at the end of many official documents). After that term has elapsed, however, anyone is allowed to then run again. *See also* "EFFECTIVE SUFFRAGE AND NO REELECTION"; PARTIDO ANTIRRELECCIONISTA.

REFORM LAWS (*Leyes de la Reforma*). Laws issued by Benito **Juárez** in 1859. His many reforms included a drastic reduction in the powers of the **Church** (civil registry of births, deaths, and marriages, with marriage becoming a civil contract administered by the state; the nationalization of cemeteries, and the confiscation of all Church properties not used for worship). These changes were bitterly contested and led to the Wars of the **Reforms**.

REFORMA, LA. An independent newspaper begun in the early 1990s and not sold from newsstands. It supported the **Partido de la Revolución Democrática** government of the **Federal District**, even over its suppression of the student riots of 1999, and broke ranks with the rest of the media by detailing **López Obrador**'s allegations of fraud in the **election of 2006**, although attacking his subsequent actions as irresponsible "madness." [L. H.]

REFORMA, PASEO DE LA. Main thoroughfare of downtown **Mexico City**, built during **Maximilian**'s Haussman-inspired rebuilding program, but renamed after his overthrow.

REFORMS, WAR OF THE. A very destructive, three-year civil war, provoked by conservative opposition to the **Reform Laws**, which raged from 1858 to 1860.

REFUGEES. *See* EXILES.

REGENCY. (1) A committee formed at **Independence** while it was decided to whom the crown of the new empire should be given. With no royalty interested, that crown was eventually bestowed on Agustín **Iturbide**.

(2) The government of the conservative controlled parts of Mexico from July 1863 until the arrival of **Maximilian** in April 1864. The individual regents were Juan Nepomuceno **Almonte**, Juan Bautista de Ormaechea, Pelagio Antonio de Labastida, and José Mariano de **Salas**. [L. H.]

REGENERACIÓN, LA. Newspaper founded in 1900 by Ricardo **Flores Magón** to rally support against Porfirio **Díaz**. It was promptly suppressed and its editor imprisoned, but Flores Magón escaped to San Antonio, Texas, where he resumed its publication as the organ of his new **Partido Liberal**.

REGIOMONTANO. Inhabiting or pertaining to **Monterrey**, N.L.

RELLANO. Site, close to the **Chihuahua-Durango** state line, of two 1912 battles: a Pascual **Orozco** victory in April followed by his final defeat there by Victoriano **Huerta** in late May.

RENDÓN, LUCIO. Fisherman who, with his companions Jesús Vidana and Salvador Ordóñez were repatriated August 27, 2006, from the Marshall Islands after their rescue by a Taiwanese fishing vessel from an open boat. Their story was of having run out of fuel on a **shark fishing** expedition, drifting for 9 months, living on fish and seabirds. Despite popular rejoicing at their survival, rumors arose that they had eaten the flesh of three missing comrades and that the shark fishing was an invention to hide the possibility that they had been transporting **narcotics**. [L. H.]

RENDÓN, SERAPIO (1867–1913). Lawyer and politician from **Yucatán** who first gained fame as a writer (as "León **Roch**). A strong supporter of Francisco **Madero** and José M. **Pino Suárez**; when they were killed he turned against their presumed murderer, Victoriano **Huerta**, whose followers surprised Rendón and killed him on August 22.

REPARTIMIENTO. Colonial forced **labor** system, also called the **Cuatequil**, legally distinct from the **encomienda**, although hardly different in practice as far as the affected **Indians** were concerned. *See also* REDUCCION.

REPARTO DE UTILIDADES. Profit sharing, as in **Comité Nacional de Reparto de Utilidades**.

REPÚBLICA, LA. Official newspaper of the **Partido Revolucionario Institucional**.

RESIDENCIA, JUICIO DE. A period of review, during colonial times, applied at the end of a Spanish official's term in office.

RETAILING. *See* INTERNAL TRADE.

REVILLA-GIGEDO, COUNT OF. Title held successively by the **viceroys** Juan Francisco **Güermes y Horcasitas** and his son Juan Vicente de **Güermes Pacheco y Padilla**.

REVILLAGIGEDO ISLANDS. An uninhabited group of three volcanic main islands (San Benedicto, **Socorro,** and the more distant Clarión) and several islets (the 246 m long Roca Partida being the largest). Located in the Pacific, at 18°N, 112°W, and 386 km south of Cape **San Luca**, they are included in the **municipio** of **Manzanillo** (in **Colima state**) whose **cabecera** is 720 km to the east. Discovered by Hernando de Grijalvo in 1533, they were named for **Viceroy** Juan Vicente de **Güermes Pacheco y Padilla**, who ineffectually ordered their occupation in 1790.

They were made a nature reserve in 1994. Destruction of marine life from overfishing led to a total ban in 2002 on **fishing** around the islands, but although this has ended sport fishing, illegal commercial fishing continues.

REVISTA MEXICANA DE LITERATURA. A literary quarterly of 1940 whose cultural significance led to its being reprinted in 1982 by the **Fondo de Cultura Económica**. It had been revived in October 1955 (with irregular periodicity) by Carlos **Fuentes** and others with the financial backing of the **Banco Nacional de Comercio Exterior**, but this second series seems not to have survived beyond the August 1961 number. [L. H.]

REVOLTS AND REBELLIONS. *See* INSURRECTIONS.

REVOLUTION DAY. November 20 is celebrated as the anniversary of the start of the **Revolution of 1910**. It's an official public holiday.

REVOLUTION OF 1910. The "Mexican Revolution" par excellence, launched seven years before the Bolsheviks began changing Russia by violent means, it has been the non-Marxist model for nationalistic social change and the quest for social justice, not only in Latin America, but also in other underdeveloped regions of the world. Although the fighting was virtually over by 1920, the Revolution (with capital

R) has been modernizing for decades through ongoing institutionalized reforms.

No one personality dominated the Revolution. As in an Italian opera, various leaders seemed all to be talking at once. Francisco **Madero** supplied its political articulation with his call for "Effective suffrage and no re-election," a phrase still repeated below the signature on every piece of official correspondence. Emiliano **Zapata** gave vent to the peasants' cry for "Land, bread, and justice." Venustiano **Carranza** oversaw the drafting of the new **Constitution of 1917** protecting **labor** rights and the national ownership of subsoil resources. The voices of Generals Álvaro **Obregón**, Pancho **Villa**, and Plutarco **Calles** added further dimensions.

The fighting phase of the Revolution erupted with attacks on government troops in a dozen different states on November 20, 1910, celebrated every year since as the *Día de la Revolución*. It lasted almost a decade, a civil war in which over a million Mexicans (out of a **population** of only 15 million) lost their lives. The **census** (held a year later, in 1921) reveals the terrible impact on individual localities. **Guanajuato state**, for instance, did not regain its 1895 **population** numbers until the 1940s.

From 1920, what the Revolution had sought politically began to become political reality. The consequent social reform came of age during the presidency of Lázaro **Cárdenas**, but although receiving the public allegiance of every political and government leader for most of the 20th century, entwined in the name of the official **Partido Revolucionario Institucional**, and acknowledged as the goal (albeit with differing emphases) of most minor parties, the Revolution had become little more than self-serving rhetoric long before the PRI finally lost power in 2000.

Apprehension of the violence spreading north during its early period (1910–1917) led the **United States** to mobilize a full half of its army along its Mexican border and even to mount the punitive incursion of 1916, led by General **Pershing**.

REVOLUTIONARY COALITION. From the 1920s the interlocking leadership of the federal government, the dominant **Partido Revolucionario Institucional**, state and local governments, the **trade**

unions, and industry—the so-called Revolutionary Coalition— became self replenishing. Outsiders gained admittance through apprenticeships in coalition cliques. This all began to change when the PRI lost office in 2000.

REVUELTAS, JOSÉ (1914–1976). A communist from **Durango** whose violence in his youth put him in prison. *Los muros del agua*, his 1941 novel based on his experience of the prison on the **Tres Marías** Islands, won him national fame as a writer. An important later novel was *El apando* of 1969. He helped organize the **UNAM student riots of 1968** and associated violence during July–October, publicly proclaiming his aim to force the cancellation of that year's **Olympics** and so discredit the government and the **revolutionary coalition**, replacing it with a Marxist dictatorship. Convicted of sedition, he was imprisoned until 1974. The far left continued to distribute his essays throughout the 1970s.

REVUELTAS, SILVESTRE (1899–1940). One of Mexico's leading composers, he developed an original, uncomplicated style based on Mexico's deep folklore traditions. His most famous works include *Janitzio*, *Ventanas*, *Colorines*, and his *Homenaje a García Lorca*, written for chamber orchestra in 1933.

REYES, ALFONSO (1889–1959). Writer, diplomat, historian, and philosopher. Born in **Monterrey**, this outstanding intellectual helped found the **Ateneo de la Juventud** in 1909 and in 1914 worked in the Madrid Center for Historical Studies under the direction of Ramón Menéndez Pidal. In 1920 he began his diplomatic career as second secretary of the embassy in Madrid. His later posts included those of ambassador to **Argentina** and **Brazil**. He was also a member of many intellectual societies, and was, for a time, president of the **Colegio de México**. In 1945 he won Mexico's national prize for literature and was a candidate for the Nobel Prize for Literature. A most prolific writer, his collected works take up more than ten volumes. *Visión de Anáhuac* (1917) is one of his most famous works.

REYES, BERNARDO (1850–1913). Monterrey-born general and politician of the **Porfirato**. While governor of **Nuevo León**, he passed Mexico's first worker's compensation law. Made war minister in 1903, he aspired to become Porfirio **Díaz**'s successor, but he fell from favor through his inability to get along with the dictator's inner circle, especially José Yves **Limantour**. He remained a strong supporter of Diaz, who sent him to Europe in 1910. On his return he led an abortive rebellion against Francisco **Madero**, attempted another in 1913, and was then killed. Alfonso **Reyes** was his son.

REYES HEROLES, JESÚS (1921–1985). Born April 3 in Tuxpan, **Veracruz**, he graduated in law from **UNAM** and did graduate study at the Universidad de Buenos Aires. An administrator for the **Comité Ejecutivo Nacional** of the **Partido Revolucionario Institucional**, 1940–1961; key adviser to President **Ruíz Cortines**, 1952–1958; director of **Pemex**, 1964–1970; president of the PRI, 1972–1976; and interior minister, 1976–May 1979. At the 1972 PRI National Assembly, he tried to broaden the base of popular participation, but his reforms were more cosmetic than substantive.

REYNOSA. A border city at 26°06'N, 98°28'W, and a commercial center of northeastern **Tamaulipas state**. It lies across the **Rio Grande** from **McAllen**, Texas, connected by two bridges with a third under construction. Its **population** was 207,000 in 1976; 429,463 in 2000; and, thanks largely to its many **maquiladora** enterprises, 750,000 in 2006.

It was founded by José de **Escandón** as *Nuestra Señora de Guadalupe de Reynosa* on April 14, 1749.

RICE. In 1958 Mexico's 240 million *tonne* rice harvest was the fifth largest in Latin America; in 1996 with 455 million t, it had fallen to ninth. Its exports grew in the same period from US$ 756 million, to US$ 96 billion, making it Latin America's biggest rice exporter, selling twice as much as its nearest rival, **Brazil**. Its policy of protecting local production of this important food staple with anti-dumping laws was challenged in 2002 by the **World Trade Organization** on behalf of American exporters and production has halved, to 195,000 t on 50,500 ha—barely more than Costa Rica. [L. H.]

RIEGO Y NÚÑEZ, RAFAEL (1785–1823). Spanish **army** colonel who led the Liberal **Spanish Revolution of 1820**.

RINCÓN, VALENTÍN (1901–1968). An attorney from **Chiapas**, a member of the **Cámara de Diputados Federales**, a judge in **Verzcruz** state and in the **Federal District**, he was known throughout Mexico and **Freemasonry** as the Grand Master of the Mexican Masonic Lodges, 1949–1968.

RIO, ANDRÉS DEL (1765–1849). Spanish-born teacher and mineralogist, who studied mineralogy in Europe under **Humboldt** and others. When almost 30 he obtained a chair at what is today the **Colegio de Ingenieros Civiles de México**.

He discovered vanadium and was a member of several international scientific societies. Identifying closely with Mexico, he became a citizen and died in **Mexico City**.

RIO, DOLORES DEL (Dolores Martínez Asúnsolo López Negrete, 1905–1983). Movie actress, born in **Durango**, she took her professional name from that of her husband Jaime Martínez del Rio. After her 1925 debut in *La Muñequita millonaria*, she went to Hollywood where she soon achieved stardom, and only returned to Mexico in 1941 to appear in Emilio **Fernández Romo**'s *Flor silvestre* of 1943.

RIO DE JANEIRO, TREATY OF, 1947. *See* INTERAMERICAN TREATY OF MUTUAL ASSISTANCE.

RIO GRANDE. The "Big River" of 3,060 km, rising in New Mexico and marking 2,575 km (1,600 miles) of the **United States border** from **Ciudad Juárez** downstream to **Matamoros**, known in Mexico as the *Rio Bravo del Norte*, and the only Mexican river with a course greater than 1,000 km. It was claimed as the new western boundary of Texas in 1836 to include a 150-mile wide stretch of American settlement beyond the **Nueces River** which López de **Santa Anna**'s army had evacuated after the Battle of **San Jacinto**. Mexico's failure to accept the new boundary led to the **United States-Mexican War** in 1846. [L. H.]

RIO GRANDE, REPUBLIC OF. An insurrection to unite **Tamaulipas**, **Coahuila**, and **Nuevo León** in an independent *República del Rio Grande* in opposition to the centralizing tendency of the national government. A **Reynosa** lawyer, Jesús Cárdenas, was declared its president on January 7, 1840. The rebellion ended with the surrender of its **army** commander, Antonio Canales, on November 6, later that year. [L. H.]

RIOTS. *See* AGUILAR TALAMANTES, RAFAEL; CORPUS CHRISTI MASSACRE; ELECTION OF 1946; TLATELOLCO, PLAZA DE; UNAM STUDENT RIOTS OF 1968; UNAM STUDENT RIOTS OF 1975; UNAM STUDENT STRIKE OF 1999; UNIVERSIDAD MICHOACANA DE SAN NICOLÁS DE HIDALGO.

RIPSTEIN, ALFREDO. Producer of over 150 movies, including the *Callejón de los milagros* and the controversial *Crimen del Padre Amaro* based on the Portuguese novelist Eça de Queirós' story of clerical seduction of a parishioner. [L. H.]

RIVA PALACIO, VICENTE (1832–1896). Politician and writer. His liberal tendencies led General Miguel **Miramón** to have him imprisoned, although he continued to support Benito **Juárez**. After the end of the **French intervention** he attained high political positions only to be again imprisoned by Porfirio **Díaz** because of his attacks on President Manuel **González**. During this second incarceration he wrote significant portions of *México a través de los siglos*. His other works include *Los Cuentos del general* and the poem, "Al viento."

RIVAS, GENOVEVO (1886–1947). As a colonel he fought **United States** forces under General John **Pershing** in **Chihuahua** in 1915. As a general he helped suppress the **Cristero rebellion** in 1926–1928. In 1938–1939 he was acting governor of his native **San Luis Potosí**.

RIVERA, DIEGO (1886–1959). A painter—generally considered Mexico's greatest—and communist from **Guanajuato**, who studied at the **Academia de San Carlos** (where he was a pupil of José María **Velasco**, and of which he eventually became director) in Madrid (1907–1908). From 1909 he was in Paris, becoming friends with such artists as Pablo Picasso and George Braque. He began to incorporate some of their Cubism into his work, but abandoned Cubism on his 1921 return to Mexico after a brief stay in Italy, moving closer to a neoclassical style, especially after José **Vasconcelos'** decision to use mural **painting** to popularize the ideals of the **Revolution of 1910**. This gave Rivera (who had studied mural paintings in Russia and Italy) a potential audience of millions. Every blank wall became a potential site for his genius, and murals became the most important development in 20th century Latin American painting. His huge frescoes depicted many aspects of Mexican politics, history, and culture, and in particular, its social turmoil, Indian heritage, and the quest for social justice. Criticism of the **United States** and of capitalism were also recurrent themes.

He painted murals in places as varied as the **Alhóndiga de Granaditas**, the Palacio de **Bellas Artes** in **Mexico City**, the **Universidad Autónoma de Chapingo** (often considered his best work), the Palace of Hernán **Cortés** in **Cuernavaca**, Coyoacán, the Institute of Arts in Detroit, the RCA building in New York City, and the stock exchange in San Francisco. His own opinion was that his best work was the unfinished *Market in Tenochtitlán* in the **National Palace**. He was in the United States in 1931–1934, but some of his works there were later destroyed as politically unacceptable. As of mid-2001, only 12 were still extant, seven in Mexico and five in the United States.

His mural "Sunday Afternoon Dream in the Alameda" (1947) in the Hotel del Prado was salvaged from the ruins in the **earthquake of 1985** and re-erected in a specially-built Rivera Museum in the northwest corner of the **Alameda** Park. On the site of the hotel, a copy was placed on a billboard and laminated.

His "Pan American Unity" mural on the dignity of labor, 6.6 m (22 ft) high by 23 m (75 ft) wide, was painted as part of the Art in Action project of the 1939–1940 Golden Gate International Exposition on Treasure Island. Since it was not finished in time, it was not seen by the public until 1961. The special building that is needed for its permanent display has yet to be built. In 1922 he cofounded *El Machete*, which became the Partido Comunista Mexicano's journal in Mexico City, and although subsequently expelled from the party on two occasions for sympathizing with León Trotsky, he insisted in 1954 that his ex-wife Frida Kahlo's coffin be draped in the Soviet flag. In his private life, however, he acted like a capitalist, demanding more money from the government and his other clients as his fame grew, investing it in the stock market. In the 1950s he painted portraits of Mexico's most beautiful rich women for high fees. His will set up a photo gallery of his career, for which visitors were charged $2 at 1965 prices. He married five times. When he wed María Félix (whom he proclaimed the "most beautiful woman in the world," he managed to kid himself by having the wedding photograph appear with the newspaper caption "the long and the short of a famous couple," he being 5 cm (2 in.) shorter than she. When *Life* asked him to appear "dressed as a painter," for an action shot, he did so in the cap and overalls of a house painter. Less than three years before his death he painted over the atheist slogan "Dios no existe" which had occasioned damage to the Del Prado mural by religious fanatics, and then announced he was a Catholic, admitting he had been "politically naive in some ways." *See also* MURALISTS.

RIVERS. *See* HYDROGRAPHY.

ROA BARCENA, JOSÉ MARÍA (1827–1908). Poet and writer whose support of **Maximilian** led to some months' imprisonment when the **empire** fell. In 1875 he became treasurer of the new **Academia Mexicana de la Lengua Castellana**. His works include *Leyendas mexicanas* and *Recuerdos de la invasión norteamericana, 1846–1848*. [L. H.]

ROADS. *See* HIGHWAYS.

ROBLES, ROCIO. Rosario Robles, a founding member of the **Partido de la Revolución Democrática** and successor (1999–2000) to the **Mexico City** mayoralty when Cuauhtemoc **Cárdeans** resigned to run for president.

ROBLES GARNICA, ROBERTO. President of the **Partido de la Revolución Democrática** in 1993.

ROBLES PEZUELA, [GENERAL] MANUEL (1817–1862). President of the conservative faction in Mexico for a month in 1858–1859. He fought in the **United States-Mexican War** and was highly respected as one of the most refined individuals ever to occupy the presidency. He was captured by the liberals and shot as a traitor by General Ignacio **Zaragoza** on March 23.

ROCABRUNA, JOSÉ (1879–1957). Barcelona-born violinist and composer who migrated to Mexico as a young man. His abilities won him many honors, and he held a chair at the **Conservatorio Nacional** for over 50 years. He died in **Mexico City**.

ROCAFUERTE, VICENTE (1788–1847). Ecuadoran diplomat and book publisher who, although holding important political positions in his own country, headed Mexico's legation in London in 1826 and acted in other official capacities for Mexico. Perhaps his most important contribution laid in the books he published, including a reprint of Bartolomé de las **Casas**' *Destrucción de las Indias*.

ROCAS ALIJOS. *See* ALIJOS ROCKS.

ROCH, LEÓN. Pen name of Serapio **Rendón**.

ROCHA, [GENERAL] JUAN NEPOMUCENO (1810–1859). Soldier who fought against López de **Santa Anna**, supported the Plan of **Ayutla**, commanded a division in Jalisco, and was assassinated while retreating after the Battle of La **Albarrada**.

ROCHA, [BRIGADIER GENERAL] SOSTENES (1831–1897). Soldier and writer on military affairs, originally a conservative, who became a strong supporter of Benito **Juárez**. When Porfirio **Díaz** came to power, he sent Rocha to Europe, ostensibly to study military matters, but probably because he had inflicted military defeats on Díaz years earlier. His remains rest in the **Rotonda de los Hombres Ilustres**.

RODRIGO, ISABEL. *See* RODRÍGUEZ, ISABEL.

RODRÍGUEZ, [GENERAL] ABELARDO LUJÁN (1889–1967). Interim president of Mexico, 1932–1934, after **Calles** had forced Pascual **Ortiz Rubio** to resign. He fought in the **Revolution of 1910**, was a close associate of Álvaro **Obregón**, governed the then territory of **Baja California del Norte** and held several other important posts. His otherwise uneventful administration introduced Mexico's first **minimum wage** legislation, created Mexico's modern civil service (both in 1934), and was notable for having Lázaro **Cárdenas del Río** as a cabinet minister.

RODRÍGUEZ, [FRAY] AGUSTIN. Franciscan priest who opened up the territory through El **Paso del Norte** (now **El Paso**, Texas, and **Ciudad Juárez**).

RODRÍGUEZ, AGUSTÍN (1842–1919). One of Mexico's most outstanding jurists, and first rector of the **Escuela Libre de Derecho**.

RODRÍGUEZ, ANTONIO L. A founder of the **Partido de Acción Nacional**, and father-in-law of Octaviano **Longoría Penn**.

RODRÍGUEZ, DIONISIO (1810–1877). A lawyer, educator, and philanthropist. He founded various hospitals and started the *Escuela de Artes y Oficios* in his native **Guadalajara**.

RODRÍGUEZ, ISABEL. "Doña Isabel" (whose surname may have been Rodrigo) accompanied Hernán **Cortés** during his conquest of Mexico, bearing a sword and serving as a nurse.

RODRÍGUEZ, JOSÉ GUADALUPE (18??–1929). Rural schoolteacher, campaigner for **agrarian reform**, and soldier in the **Revolution of 1910**, who organized farmers as a bulwark of government support, but was executed for insubordination.

RODRÍGUEZ, MARIANO (fl.1851–????). Famous 19th century bullfighter, known as *La Monja* ("the nun").

RODRÍGUEZ, PEDRO L. (1841–1918). Born in **Mexico State**, he became a political boss and eventual governor of **Hidalgo**, but lost office in the **Revolution of 1910**.

RODRÍGUEZ AGUILAR, MANUEL (1909–1956). An engineer who founded **Pemex**'s Department of Exploration, managing it until he retired. He died in **Mexico City**.

RODRÍGUEZ ALCONCEDO, JOSÉ LUIS (1762–1815). Silversmith and painter who was shot for having fought alongside **Morelos**. One of his most famous works is a **silver** medallion with a portrait of King **Charles IV**, on display in **Chapultepec Castle**.

RODRÍGUEZ ARANGOITY, EMILIO (1833–1891). Soldier who occupied important posts in Mexico's Corps of Engineers and built the fortifications in **Puebla** which led to the May 5, 1862 victory over the French. President **Juárez** officially recognized Rodríguez for his valuable support of the Republic.

RODRÍGUEZ CABRILLO, JUAN. *See* CABRILLO, JUAN RODRÍGUEZ DE.

RODRÍGUEZ CANO, ENRIQUE (1912–1955). Mayor of **Tuxpan** in 1936 and minister of the presidency under Adolfo **Ruiz Cortines**. [L. H.]

RODRÍGUEZ DE VELASCO Y OSORIO BARBA, MARÍA IGNACIA (1778–1850). Supporter of **Hidalgo** and a close friend of **Iturbide**. The extraordinary beauty of *Güera Rodríguez* ("the Blond Rodríguez") was commented on by the great naturalist Alexander von **Humboldt**.

ROEL GARCÍA, SANTIAGO (1919–). **Monterrey**-born law professor at the **Universidad de Nuevo León** who became speaker of the **Cámara de Diputados Federales** and then a senator. He was assistant secretary general of the **Partido Revolucionario Institucional**; ambassador to India; and then foreign minister, December 1976–May 1979. He was the key presidential adviser working for resumption of diplomatic relations with Spain after the 1975 death of Francisco Franco.

ROJAS, LUIS MANUEL (1871–1949). Supporter of Francisco **Madero** who publicly accused **United States** Ambassador Henry L.

Wilson of responsibility for his death. He was imprisoned for his opposition to Victoriano **Huerta**, but was freed in time to head the **Constituent Assembly of 1916–1917**. He occupied various political posts afterwards and for a brief while headed the *El Universal* newspaper.

ROJO GÓMEZ, JAVIER (1896–1970). Lawyer who helped found the **Confederación Nacional Campesina** in 1936, becoming its secretary general, governor of his home state of **Hidalgo** 1937–1940; governor of the **Federal District** (when he was charged, in 1947, with illegal land sales, which cost him any serious consideration by the **Partido Revolucionario Institucional** as its presidential candidate); ambassador to Indonesia, 1952–1955; ambassador to Japan, 1956–1958; and governor of **Quintana Roo**, 1967–1970.

ROMERO, JOSÉ RUBEN (1890–1952). Poet, novelist, and diplomat. He supported **Madero**, and later governed his native **Michoacán**. His later positions included those of rector of the **Universidad de Michoacán** and ambassador to Brazil and Cuba. But his fame came mainly from his writings such as the anthology *Tacámbro* and, especially, the picaresque novel *La Vida inútil de Pito Pérez* (published in 1938, but still quite popular).

ROMERO RUBIO, MANUEL (1828–1895). Liberal politician, father-in-law of Porfirio **Diaz**.

ROSAL, MARTA DEL. *See* ANDRADE DE DEL ROSAL, MARTA.

ROSAS, JUVENTINO (1868–1894). Violinist and composer, from a family of musicians, who earned much of his livelihood by playing in the family orchestra. His most famous work was *Over the waves*, a waltz frequently attributed to other composers. His early death from tuberculosis prevented his attaining the fame or prosperity that he justly deserved.

ROSAS MORENO, JOSÉ (1838–1863). Poet, dramatist, journalist, and politician, regarded in his time as an outstanding lyric poet and teller of fables. A supporter of **Juárez**, he served in various political posts and in the legislature.

ROTONDA DE LOS HOMBRES ILUSTRES. Mexico's pantheon for its illustrious dead.

ROYAL TENTH. The 10 percent colonial levy on the mining of precious metals.

RUBIO, CARMEN. The second wife of Porfirio **Díaz**, whom he married in 1883. She succeeded in moderating his feelings toward the **Church**.

RUIZ CORTINES, ADOLFO (1890–1973). President of Mexico, 1952–1958. An accountant before embarking on a political career, he supported **Madero** and fought against Victoriano **Huerta**. He served as interior minister in the administration of his close friend Miguel **Alemán**, who helped him become governor of his native **Veracruz State** and later, president. As president he set about to reestablish credibility in government and largely succeeded. He was by no means a flamboyant leader, but this was not resented: Mexicans felt the time was appropriate for a more paternal image. His administration stressed industrialization and the development of hydroelectric power, which decreased the danger of floods and provided **irrigation** to increase food production. **Female suffrage** was enacted, a strike threat from the **Bloque de Unidad Obrera** averted, and the **peso** devalued to resolve the balance of payments deficit. He reacted to public criticism of **United States** involvement in the overthrow of the **Arbenz** regime in **Guatemala** by inviting President Eisenhower to the inauguration of the **Falcón Dam**. He also escorted Vice President Nixon on a tour of **Mexico City**, which led to a joint press conference in which bi-national aid was suggested as a way to tackle the city's widespread poverty and unemployment.

His political gamble of publicly denouncing the **mordida** won him widespread public support, although the effect was more cosmetic than substantive. He personalized his attitude as a moralist by publicly praising the policeman who had given him a speeding ticket when he was using his own car instead of the official limousine.

RUIZ DE ALARCÓN Y MENDOZA, JUAN. *See* ALARCÓN Y MENDOZA, JUAN RUIZ.

RUIZ DE APODACA, JUAN, CONDE DE VENADITO (1754–1835). Governor and captain general of **Cuba**, April 14, 1814–July 18, 1816, and then **viceroy** of **New Spain**, 1816–1821. In 1809 the **Junta Central** had made him its minister in London, whence he was appointed to Havana, where he promoted **sugar** cultivation and the building of ships for the Spanish **navy**. In Mexico he suppressed the revolt of Francisco Javier **Mina**, for which he received his county, but in July 1821 an army junta led by **Iturbide** decided to withdraw support from the new regime imposed by the **Spanish revolution of 1820** and forced the viceroy to abdicate and return to Spain. With the restoration of the *ancien régime* in Madrid, Apodaca was made viceroy of Navarre. [L. H.]

RUIZ MASSIEU, JOSÉ FRANCISCO (1945–1994). Born July 22, elder brother of assistant attorney general Mario **Ruiz Massieu**, he served as governor of **Guerrero State** in 1987–1993 and then as director general of the **Instituto del Fondo Nacional de la Vivienda para los Trabajadores**. He was assassinated September 28, seven months after the murder of Luis Donaldo **Colosio**, following news reports linking the two men, who were seen as dangerous reformers likely to weaken the close links between the **Partido Revolucionario Institucional** and the federal bureaucracy.

RUIZ MASSIEU, MARIO (1950–1999). Law graduate from **UNAM** who rose in the **Procuraduría General de la República** to become assistant **procurador general** (deputy attorney general). Invited by President-elect Ernesto **Zedillo** to investigate the murder of his younger brother José Francisco **Ruiz Massieu**, he suddenly resigned in November 1994, claiming that high-ranking **Partido Revolucionario Institucional** members had sabotaged his investigation.

In March 1997 his unexplained cash balance of US$ 9 million in Houston's Texas Commerce Bank led to his July 1998 appearance before a federal grand jury on money laundering charges. President Zedillo allowed former national police director Adrián Carrera to appear before the grand jury and report that in 1993–1994 he had handed over some US$ 2 million to Ruiz in drug bribes. Ruiz was alleged to have killed himself while being held under house arrest in New Jersey.

RUIZ ORTIZ, ULISES (c.1958–). Former **Partido Revolucionario Institucional** senator selected by Roberto **Madrazo Pintado** to run for governor of **Oaxaca state** in return for his having promoted Madrazo to be the party's leader. Having won, despite widespread irregularities, his vigorous reaction to the schoolteachers' strike of May 2006 provoked a virtual insurrection calling for his resignation for being "repressive" and "corrupt," led by the **Asamblea Popular de los Pueblos de Oaxaca**. [L. H.]

RULFO, JUAN (1918–1986). Juan Nepomuceno Pérez Rulfo, a writer from Sayula, **Jalisco**, who went from the *Centro de Escritores Mexicanos* to become Mexico's leading short story writer with the 1952 collection of 15 stories, *El Llano en llamas*, depicting the violence of life in rural Mexico and the peasants' attitude of resignation. He is also noteworthy for his 1955 novel, *Pedro Páramo*. Less successful was *El gallo de oro* (1980). *See also* JUAN RULFO PRIZE.

RURALES. Popular name for members of the *Guardia Rural*, a kind of highway patrol during the **Porfirato**. Many members were common criminals, but people could now boast of being able to leave their doors unlocked, for it was widely known that law breakers would be dealt with great harshness. This was a great change from the lawless state of rural **highways** in the early 19th century. The photographic archives of the **Colegio de México**, however, show the gruesome methods used by the *Rurales,* all too often employed for political oppression of peasants protesting such injustices as illegal land confiscation. Such atrocities as tying down a naked victim to enable ants to eat him alive, or forcing another with a noose round his neck to keep up with a horse around whose saddle horn the rope was looped explain the ferocity of peasant participation in the **Revolution of 1910**.

RUSSIA, RELATIONS WITH. Russia began to occupy Alaska in the late 18th century. Further expansion along the Pacific coast led José de **Gálvez** to extend the limits of **New Spain** northward in 1767 as far as **San Francisco**. In 1789 **Nootka** was also occupied for the same reason. The boundary eventually established between Russian and Spanish claims is now the southern boundary of the **United States** state of Alaska.

Mexico's 20th-century relations with what became the **Soviet Union** included the offer of asylum to the ousted communist leader Leon **Trotsky** and his subsequent murder in Mexico on Stalin's orders. [L. H.]

RUSSIANS IN MEXICO. These include the film director Sergei **Eisenstein** and the political fugitive Leon **Trotsky**. In the 19th century there was also a presence of Russian fishermen, sealers, and whalers along the Pacific seaboard, with bases on some Mexican **islands**. [L. H.]

– S –

SÁENZ GARZA, AARON (1891–1983). **Sugar** planter and a key adviser to President Plutarco Elías **Calles**, who lost his chance to succeed when interim President **Portes Gil** decided that he was too independent-minded and that Pascual **Ortiz Rubio** would be more reliable as a Calles front-man.

SÁENZ GARZA, MOISES (1888–1941). Educator and diplomat, who served as director of the **Escuela Nacional Preparatoria**, organizer of the first Inter-American Indigenous Congress, and president of the Committee on Indigenous Research. He was a principal figure in developing **secondary education**. He died while ambassador to **Peru**.

SAHAGUÍN DE FOX, MARTA. Wife of President Vicente **Fox Quesada**, apparently implicated in the influence peddling accusations against her sons from her first marriage, Manuel, Jorge, and Fernando **Bribiesca**.

SAHAGUN, BERNARDINO DE (1500?–1590). A Franciscan priest, born Bernardino Ribeira in the Kingdom of **León**, he arrived in **New Spain** in 1529 where he preached to the **Indians** in their own languages and taught Latin at the **Colegio de Santa Cruz de Tlatelolco**. Despite his great reputation as a missionary and teacher, he is best known for his historical writings, particularly *Historia general de las cosas de la Nueva España* dealing with all aspects of life in the New

World, which he constantly revised and amplified to produce three editions.

SAINT PATRICK BATTALION (*Batallón de San Patricio*). A unit recruited from Irish prisoners of war who fought on the Mexican side in the **United States-Mexican War** of 1846–1848. At the end of hostilities they were executed by the U.S. authorities for treason, but Mexicans regard them as heroes.

SAINZ, GUSTAVO (1940–). Novelist: *Gazapo*, 1965; *La princesa del Palacio de hierro*, 1974; and the literary editor of the publishing houses Joaquín Moritz, 1960–1970; and Grijalbo, 1980–1990; and currently a professor at the Univeristy of Indiana, Bloomington.

SAINZ DE BARANDA, PEDRO (1787–1845). Sailor, born in **Campeche** of wealthy **creole** parents, who studied in Spain to become a naval officer, and was wounded at the Battle of Trafalgar (1805). In newly independent Mexico he took charge of its **navy** and dislodged the Spaniards from the island of **San Juan de Ulúa**. Subsequently he became lieutenant governor of **Yucatán** and held other political posts in the region. He died in **Mérida**.

SALAS, JOSÉ MARIANO (1797–1867). Briefly achieved the presidency of Mexico in late 1846, after a long military career, only to give it up to López de **Santa Anna** that December. A staunch conservative, he became part of the **Regency** governing Mexico pending the installation of the **Emperor Maximilian**. He died in **Mexico City**.

SALAZAR MALLÉN, RUBÉN (1905–1986). A popular author from **Veracruz** who became nationally known with *La Democracia y el comunismo* (1947) but whose fame rests on his 1968 novel *Viva México* exposing police brutality and incompetence among journalists.

SALES, [JOSÉ] MARIANO DE (1797–1867). President of Mexico, August 5–December 12, 1846, after a long military career, only to give it up to José Antonio López de **Santa Anna**. A staunch conservative, he became part of the **Regency** governing Mexico pending the installation of Emperor **Maximilian**, July 11, 1863–May 20, 1864. He died in **Mexico City**.

SALES TAX. *See* ALCABALA; IMPUESTO ESPECIAL SOBRE PRODUCCIÓN Y SERVICIOS; VALUE-ADDED TAX.

SALIGNY, DUBOIS. French minister in **Mexico City** who conspired with the **Junta of Notables**, but did not tell them until 1863 that an Austrian archduke (**Maximilian**) would be persuaded that the Mexican people wanted him to accept a Mexican crown.

SALINA CRUZ. Mexico's "port on the **Pacific** that is nearest to the Atlantic," in **Oaxaca** at 16°10'N, 95°11'W, with a direct rail connexion to **Coatzacoalcos**. Conceived by Pedro **Martínez Tornel**, its main export is **corn** but it also handles much container traffic. [L. H.]

SALINAS. River of **Nuevo León**, tributary of the **Rio Grande**.

SALINAS DE GORTARI, CARLOS (1948–). President of Mexico, 1988–1994. Born in **Mexico City**, April 3, he had an economics degree from **UNAM** and a PhD in economics and government from Harvard. He was minister of programming and the budget in 1982–1988. His election as president aroused widespread accusations of ballot stuffing and "creative" arithmetic in the vote count, and even so, he received a majority of barely 10 percent. During the earlier part of his term he won considerable praise at home and abroad in the media and among political analysts for his social and economic leadership. By getting congress to amend article 103 of the **Constitution of 1917** he made peace with the **Church** which recovered its judicial status and full internal autonomy, winning praise from around the world. He undid the nationalization of banks, improving the flow of credit to business, and through this and other economic policies unemployment began to fall. But widespread **corruption** and allegations of money laundering on behalf of the **narcotics** cartels tarnished his image. He was blamed by all three main parties for delaying a needed devaluation of the **peso** (which his successor had to implement) and the consequent recession. He became the most vilified ex-president since Porfirio **Díaz**. He left Mexico in disgrace when his term ended, fleeing, via Cuba to a luxurious exile in Ireland. In February 2000, he was reported to be leaving Ireland to return to **Cuba**, but by 2004 was back as a force within the **Partido Revolucionario Institucional**, accused of plotting to outlaw **López Obrador**'s run for the Presidency.

SALINAS DE GORTARI, RAÚL (1946–). Brother of Carlos **Salinas de Gortari**, born in **Mexico City**. He was director general of public works (within the **Human Settlements Ministry**) in 1977–1978. Already under suspicion of laundering money for the **narcotics** cartels, he became an unofficial suspect in the drawn-out investigation of the murder of Luis Donaldo **Colosio**. In 1999 he was sentenced to 50 years imprisonment for ordering the murder of a critic of the Salinas administration, thanks in part to the testimony of a former associate, Carlos **Cabal Peniche**.

SALINAS PLIEGO, RICARDO BENJAMÍN (1956–). Board chairman of **Azteca TV** (but no kin to the **Salinas de Gortari** brothers).

SALT PRODUCTION. In the mid-1990s Mexico's **Trade Ministry** began developing a large salt plant close to a protected breeding area of grey **whales**, near San Ignacio, **Baja California del Sur**. In March 1999 the Mitsubishi Corporation bought land nearby to develop their own salt plant. This brought the ministry and its perception of the needs of Mexico's economy into conflict with the Natural Resources Defense Council, a San Francisco-based N.G.O. After both sides had involved public opinion to an unprecedented degree, a compromise was reached that, it was hoped, would adequately reduce the environmental impact of the salt processing. [L. H.]

SALTILLO. State capital of **Coahuila**, founded as Santiago del Saltillo by Alberto del **Canto** in 1557 at 101°00'W, 25°25'W. Thanks to its 1,600 m altitude and dry climate, Saltillo is a popular summer resort. Golf, tennis, swimming, and scenic horseback riding are popular recreational pursuits for Mexican and American tourists, as well as for residents. It has a tradition of polo, with championship teams coached by cavalry officers from **Mexico City**. Its **Alameda** Park has an equestrian statue of cavalry hero Ignacio **Zaragoza**.

Its **municipio** had 223,000 inhabitants in 1976; 512,000 in 1986; and 642,367 in 2000; and an extension of 6,837 km². The Battle of Saltillo was fought on February 22–23, 1847.

SALVADOR, RIVER. Tributary of the **Rio Grande**, flowing through **Nuevo León**.

SALVATIERRA. Municipio of 603 km² in the Guatzindeo Valley in the **Bajio** region, which claims the oldest working **irrigation** system in Latin America. The **cabecera**, which was the first settlement in **Guanajuato** state to be made a **city** (in 1644) lies on the **Lerma** at 1749 m above sea-level and has 300 historic buildings recognized as having architectural importance. Founded on the site of the pre-Hispanic Huatzindeo, it was named to honor **Viceroy** García **Sarmiento y Sotomayor**, count of Salvatierra.

SAN ANTONIO. The Texan city, known under Mexican rule as San Antonio de Béjar, was founded in 1718. [L. H.]

SAN BLAS. Small town in **Nayarit**, 62 km northwest of **Tepic**, 120 km north of **Puerto Vallarta**, named for Saint Blaise, now a small rustic tourist resort but an important late-18th century Pacific coast naval base inaugurated February 22, 1768. On a tidal river, it gradually silted up and was closed as a shipping port in 1873. Hurricane **Kenna** destroyed or badly damaged most buildings in the town and fishing boats were toppled at their docks.

SAN BLAS BATTALION (*Batallón de San Blas*). The most valiant among the defenders of the castle in the Battle of **Chapultepec**. They included the fabled **Niños héroes**.

SAN CARLOS ACADEMY. *See* ACADEMIA DE SAN CARLOS.

SAN CRISTÓBAL DE LAS CASAS. City of **Chiapas**. The **municipio** had a population in 2000 of 132,421.

SAN DIEGO. When Juan Rodríguez de **Cabrillo** landed at what he called the *Bahía de San Miguel*, he was the first European to set foot in **Alta California**. Although only 22 km (14 miles) from the border, the modern city shows surprisingly little Hispanic influence, even though Hispanics accounted in 1990 for almost 21 percent of both the city's 1,110,549 inhabitants and the county's 2,498,016. The San Diego region is regarded as forming part of a single San Diego-**Tijuana** regional economy, indeed the largest and fastest growing economy of the whole **United States border** region.

SAN FRANCISCO. Founded at 37°46'N, 122°26'W by Junípero **Serra** in 1776, as part of the occupation of **Alta California**. In 1847 on the eve of the **United States** conquest it still had a population of only 800, but expanded out of all recognition within a few months of the start of the 1849 **gold** rush. Its 2006 population was 798,680. [L. H.]

SAN GERÓNIMO DE ACULCO. *See* ACULCO.

SAN JACINTO. Plains on the outskirts of modern metropolitan Houston, Texas, site on April 21, 1836, of the decisive battle of the Texan War of Independence, when José Antonio López de **Santa Anna**'s force of c.1,500 was crushed by a similar sized force of Texans. Thanks to the carelessness of the Mexicans, the Texans under Sam Houston, fired by memories of the massacre at El **Alamo** seven weeks earlier, surprised their enemy, killing several hundreds and taking prisoner the rest, including Santa Anna, who talked his captors out of killing him and negotiated an end to the war. The subsequent withdrawal of his troops across the **Rio Grande** gave the new republic the opportunity to push its western boundary beyond the **Nueces River**.

SAN JOSÉ, CALIFORNIA. Founded by Junípero **Serra** in 1777.

SAN JUAN, RIVER. (1) **Nuevo León** tributary of the **Rio Grande**. (2) Name for part of the upper reaches of the **Pánuco**.

SAN JUAN DE ULÚA. Fortress on a small island one mile offshore protecting the harbor of **Veracruz City** but also used for loading and unloading ships, and as a custom house. Built in the 16th century, Spain continued to hold it after Mexican **independence** and thereby block the commerce of Mexico's largest port. It was eventually liberated by Miguel **Barragán**, 1825. It was briefly occupied by the French in the **Pastry War** of 1838. At one time it was used as the presidential mansion. Until 1914 it served as a prison. It is now preserved as a national historic monument.

SAN LUCAS. Cruise ship port-of-call with a marina, popular with tourists, at Cabo San Lucas, the southern tip of **Baja California**.

SAN LUIS POTOSÍ, PLAN OF. The manifesto of Francisco **Madero** issued in **San Antonio**, Texas, October 1910, declaring the recent election invalid, listing the changes demanded of Porfirio **Díaz** and, in default, calling on the Mexican people to rise up against him: in effect, the rallying cry for the **Revolution of 1910**, "**effective suffrage and no reelection**," **agrarian reform**, and the reinstatement of the **Constitution of 1857**.

SAN LUIS POTOSÍ CITY. Founded in 1583 as a Franciscan mission, it became a **ciudad** November 4, 1592. Located 360 km (225 miles) northwest of **Mexico City** at 22°16'N, 100°98'W, 1860 m (6,157 ft.) above sea level it is now the capital of its namesake state.

Gold was discovered here in 1590 and **silver** in 1620, whence the *Potosí* in allusion to the great Bolivian **mining** center. The "San Luis" honors France's canonized crusader king Louis IX. The city's government buildings (state and municipal, including the governor's palace) are colonial baroque, of rose-colored stone. The many towers are roofed with colored tiles. During the Period of **Maximilian**'s empire, the city was for a while the provisional capital of his rival, Benito **Juárez**, and gave its name to the 1910 Plan of **San Luis Potosí**. The city population has grown from 294,000 in 1976 to 610,000 in 1995; 670,532 in 2000; 715,000 in 2005 (when that of the whole conurbation reached 1,075,000).

SAN LUIS POTOSÍ STATE. First established as an **intendancy** in 1786, it is now a state of 63,670 km^2 in northcentral Mexico, named for its capital city, with an average elevation of 1830 m (6,000 ft.) and crossed by the Sierra **Madre** Oriental in its southeastern portion. Its **Pánuco** River flows eastward to the Gulf of **Mexico** at **Tampico**. Its neighbor states are **Jalisco**, **Guanajuato**, **Querétaro**, **Hidalgo**, **Veracruz**, **Tamaulipas**, **Nuevo León**, **Coahuila**, and **Zacatecas**.

Its economy includes **silver**, **lead**, mercury, and **copper mining**, and the production of **coffee**, **sugar**, **fruit**, and fiber plants such as **sisal**.

Its population grew from 397,189 in 1857; and 397,735 in 1869; to 588,000 in 1895; fell to 575,000 by 1900; recovered to 628,000 by 1910; fell to 446,000 by 1921 but since then has grown to 580,000 in 1930; 679,000 in 1940; 856,000 in 1950; 1,048,000 in 1960; 1,282,000 in 1970; 1,500,000 in 1976; 1,674,000 in 1980; 2,003,000 in 1990; 2,299,360 in 2000; 2,353,000 in 2003; and 2,410,414 in 2005; divided among 58 *municipios*.

SAN MIGUEL CALPULALPAN, BATTLE OF. Victory of the liberals led by Jesús **González Ortega** which ended the War of the **Reforms**, December 22, 1860.

SAN MIGUEL DE ALLENDE. The first town taken (and pillaged) by the insurgents under Miguel **Hidalgo y Costilla** and Ignacio **Allende**, September 1810.

SAN XAVIER DEL BAC. Mission founded in what is now an Indian reservation south of Tucson, Arizona, by Father Eusebio **Kino**. The splendid baroque mission church, finished in the 1790s, remains in use today.

SAN YSIDRO. The **California** border town facing **Tijuana**.

SANBORNS. A pharmacy chain, originating in **Mexico City**'s Casa de **Tejas**, but expanded in the 1950s (thanks to Walgreens Corporation in partnership with Mexican investors) to a dozen branches throughout the city, and another in **Monterrey**.

SÁNCHEZ, GUADALUPE (1890–????). Revolutionary general from **Veracruz**, a supporter of Alfredo de la **Huerta**, with whom he was exiled after 1923.

SÁNCHEZ DE TAGLE, FRANCISCO MANUEL (1782–1847). Poet who taught at the **Colegio de San Juan de Letrán** and held various political positions after **independence**. His poetic ability was recognized when his "La Lealtad americana" won first place in a contest. *Contrición poética* is representative of his later works.

SÁNCHEZ NAVARRO, MANUEL. Theater actor, a member of a prestigious family descended from the colonial-era aristocracy, and father of Manolo **Fábregas.**

SÁNCHEZ PAREJA Y BELEÑO, EUSEBIO. Viceroy of **New Spain,** 1786–1787.

SÁNCHEZ TABOADA, RODOLFO (1885–1955). A **Puebla**-born long time official of the **Comité Ejecutivo Nacional** of the **Partido Revolucionario Institucional;** budget director for President **Cárdenas,** 1934–1936; president of the PRI, 1946–1952; key adviser to Presidents **Alemán** and **Ruiz Cortinas;** governor of **Baja California del Norte,** 1937–1944; and one of the few civilians to have headed the **naval ministry** (in 1952–1955).

SÁNCHEZ VITE, MANUEL (1915–1996). School teacher, lawyer, member of the **Cámara de Diputados Federales,** and legal adviser to the **Sindicato Nacional de Trabajadores de la Educación.** As governor of his native **Hidalgo,** 1969–1970, he got a leave of absence to be president of the **Partido Revolucionario Institucional,** 1970–1972, and then returned to be governor until 1974.

SANDOVAL, GONZALO DE (1497–1528). Conquistador and close confidant of Hernán **Cortés,** whom he accompanied during the Spanish **conquest of Mexico.** He was the key figure in the defeat of Pánfilo de **Narváez.** After the fall of **Tenochitlán,** Sandoval continued the conquest toward the southeast, reaching **Coatzacoalcos.** On Cortés' orders, he established peace in **Colima** and later accompanied him on his expedition to Honduras. On returning to Spain, he died at the port of Palos after a brief illness.

SANDOVAL SILVA Y MENDOZA, GASPAR DE LA CERDA. *See* CERDA SANDOVAL SILVA Y MENDOZA, GASPAR DE LA.

SANSORES PÉREZ, CARLOS (1918–). Lawyer who served in the **Cámara de Diputados Federales,** 1946–1949, 1955–1958, 1961– 1964, and 1973–1976, and in the **Senate,** 1964–1967. He was governor of his native **Campeche,** 1967–1973, resigning to become majority leader in the *Cámara.* He was president of the **Partido Revolucionario**

Institucional from December 1976 until he resigned in February 1979 in protest at the economic policies of President **López Portillo**.

SANTA. Novel by Federico **Gamboa**, of which four movie versions have been made. The first, in 1918, starring Elena Sánchez Valenzuela, was directed by Luis G. Peredo after a lucky win on the **Lotería Nacional** had given him the wherewithal. The second, adapted by Carlos Noriega Hope, released March 30, 1932, starring Lupita Tovar, directed by the Spaniard Antonio Moreno, and with camera work by Alex Phillips was Mexico's sixth sound film and its first "talkie" with sound recorded directly onto the movie film. The third movie version, directed by Norman Foster and starring Esther Fernández, is often regarded as the best. The most recent version is that of 1968, directed by Emilio Gómez Muriel, and starring Julissa y Enrique Rocha.

SANTA ANNA, [GENERAL] JOSÉ ANTONIO LÓPEZ DE (1794–1876). President of Mexico on eleven occasions, the dominant personality in Mexican politics for 25 years, and as such, largely responsible for the loss to the United States of **Texas** and the **Far North**. Although tending toward conservatism and the **Church**, he was the epitome of political opportunism. Originally a supporter of Spanish rule, he fought against **Hidalgo**, but after **Independence** he played a key role in deposing the conservative Agustín **Iturbide**. In 1829 he supported Vicente **Guerrero**, then turned against him in favor of the conservative Anastacio **Bustamante** only to overthrow him in favor of the liberals, ending up president himself in 1833–1835. As president he alienated the Texans by his treatment of Stephen **Austin** and then, when they revolted, lost the key battle of **San Jacinto** by allowing his troops to take a siesta without bothering to post a guard.

He surrounded himself with sycophants, but whenever he tired of them and of government business he would retire to his ancestral ranch of Manga de Clavo. There he awaited a "recall" by the Mexican people. He used his military prowess for publicity, even sometimes to his detriment, as when he had the leg he lost in the **Pastry War** solemnly buried in a special vault in **Mexico City**. Soon after this he was exiled, and did not return until 1846 when he led his country in the **United States-Mexican War**. He again proved himself on occasion a capable army leader, but he lost the battles of **Buena Vista** and **Cerro Gordo**, and with them, the war. Exiled in consequence, he was recalled and served as president in 1853–1855. Banished by the liberals' Plan of **Ayutla** and their consequent revolt, he remained abroad until the **French intervention** of 1862. With typical duplicity, he offered his services to Benito **Juárez**, and when rebuffed, offered them to **Maximilian**, with the same result. Destitute, ignored, and nearly blind, he lived out his last years in Mexico City, behind the old Basilica of Saint **Mary of Guadalupe**. Mexico does not have a single statue to his memory, evidence of the scorn in which he continues to be held by his fellow countrymen.

SANTA FE. Capital city of **New Mexico** (65,000 inhabitants in 2000), founded by Spanish missionaries in 1609 but only formally established as a **villa** in the 1680s, becoming the mostly northerly administrative center in **New Spain**.

SANTA HERMANDAD ("holy brotherhood"). A rural **police** force created in Spain under **Isabel I** that was introduced into **New Spain** by **Viceroy** Luis de **Velasco**, the elder. [L. H.]

SANTA MARÍA, VICENTE (1775–1813). Franciscan friar involved in the Conspiracy of **Vallalolid**. Caught and imprisoned, he escaped to join José María **Morelos y Pavón**, but died in the assault on Fuerte San Diego, the last royalist hold out in the taking of **Acapulco**.

SANTANTISTA. Relating to or supporting José Antonio López de **Santa Anna**.

SANTIAGO, RIVER. *See* GRANDE DE SANTIAGO, RIO.

SANTIAGO DE QUERÉTARO. Formal name of **Querétaro City**.

SANTIAGO DEL SALTILLO. *See* SALTILLO.

SANTOS, GONZALO N. (1896–1979). A member of the **Cámara de Diputados Federales**; a member of the **Senate**, 1934–1940; and governor of his native **San Luis Potosí state**, 1943–1949. He became the local **cacique**, controlling major policies and government contracts within the state, 1949–1959. In the 1958 campaign President Adolfo **López Mateos** pledged to break the power of such local bosses, and encouraged the protests of the Potosí Civic Union (UCP). In 1959, after businesses owned by UCP members had begun periodic closing, state governor Manuel Álvarez had to resign, and Santos' power was broken.

SARAPE. A brightly colored, striped shawl, folk costume typical of **Jalisco**.

SARDINE. Sardines have replaced anchovies (decimated by overfishing in the late 1990s) as Mexico's chief **fishing** resource by volume (about 36 percent of the total) but this amounts to only 2 percent of the total by value, and the annual catch has been highly variable. [L. H.]

SARMIENTO Y SOTOMAYOR, GARCÍA (c.1595–1659). Comendador of the **villa** de los Santos de Maimona and knight of the Order of St. James, **viceroy** of **New Spain**, 1642–1648. During this time the administration of Mexico was complicated by the quarrel between the partisans of the **Jesuits** and of the order's great antagonist, the recently recalled Bishop-Viceroy Juan de **Palafox y Mendoza**. Also, the coastal areas were under continuous attack by the Dutch and the English. Sarmiento did however work to improve the colony's finances and commerce and to expand missions into **California**. In 1648 he was made viceroy of **Peru**. [L. H.]

SARMIENTO Y VALLADARES, JOSÉ, CONDE DE MOCTE-ZUMA (1643–1708). Viceroy of **New Spain**, 1696–1701, married first to Jerónima Moctezuma y Jofre de Loaisa, granddaughter of **Montezuma II** (whence his title) and then to María Andrea de Guzmán y Dávila, granddaughter of Álvaro **Manrique de Zúñiga** (viceroy, 1585–1590). His viceroyalty saw a famine which he lacked the resources adequately to mitigate, the resumption of **mining**, and the official recognition that **Baja California** was a peninsula and not an island. [L. H.]

SARTORIO, JOSÉ MANUEL (1746–1828). Priest and writer who served on various colonial censorship boards and was president of the

Academy of Moral Sciences of Saint Joachim, but nevertheless favored **independence**.

He also wrote a good deal of (second-rate) poetry (e.g., his "Rasgo en honra de Nuestra Señora de los Dolores").

SCHERER GARCÍA, JULIO (1926–). Journalist. Executive publisher of *Excélsior* until dismissed at President **Echeverría**'s instigation, July 8, 1976, despite his excellent management record. He then founded the news magazine *Proceso*, using his contacts to recruit subscribers in every major city of the Republic.

SCHREITER, HELMUT OSCAR. German resident, who with José Ángel **Urquiza**, organized the **Unión Sinarquista Nacional**.

SCOTT, WINFIELD (1786–1866). **United States** general, supreme commander of the U.S. Army, 1841–1861, and leader of the Southern expedition in the **United States-Mexican War** whose troops captured **Veracruz City** in March 1849.

SCULPTURE. Mexican sculptors with individual entries in this *Dictionary* include Feliciano **Bejar**, Enrique **Carbajal Sebastián**, Felipe **Castañeda**, A. A. **Cencetti**, Jesús F. **Contreras**, José Luis **Cuevas**, Felipe **Ehrenburg**, Mario **Fuentes**, Juan **Soriano**, Rufino **Tamayo**, Manuel **Tolsa**, Francisco **Tresguerras**, and Francisco **Zúñiga**. *See also* CABALLITO, EL; ESMERALDA, LA.

SEA, LAW OF THE. *See* MARITIME SOVEREIGNTY.

SECODAM. Acronym of the *Secretaría de la Contraloría y Desarrollo Administrativo*: Ministry of Government Comptrollership and Administrative Development, replaced in April 2003 by the **Public Administration Ministry**. [L. H.]

SECOND EMPIRE. (1) In Mexico, the Conservative regime imposed as a result of the **French Intervention**. This was headed by the **Junta Superior de Gobierno y Regencia de México**, June 18, 1863–May 20, 1864; by Juan Nepomuceno **Almonte** as *lugarteniente del emperador*, May 29–June 12, 1864; and by Archduke Ferdinand Maximilian of Habsburg (as the Emperor **Maximilian**), June 12, 1864–May

15, 1867, although its rule never quite extended to the entire country. *See also* PRIME MINISTER.

(2) In France, the December 2, 1852–September 4, 1870 regime of Prince Louis Napoleon Bonaparte (as the Emperor **Napoleon III**), responsible for the French Intervention in Mexico and Maximilian's chief foreign support. [L. H.]

SECONDARY EDUCATION. The demand for and promotion of secondary education increased markedly in the last quarter of the 20th century, especially after it became compulsory in 1993. By 2000 it was being claimed that in the more important metropolitan areas, such as **Guadalajara**, the percentage of young people continuing their education into their 18th year was approaching 65. A reform announced for 2006 would reduce the number of subjects studied from ten to eight, with emphasis on Spanish and mathematics. *See also* COLEGIO DE LETRAN; ESCUELA NACIONAL PREPARATORIA. [L. H.]

SECRETARIATS (*secretarías*). *See* MINISTRIES.

SECRETARIO DE ESTADO ("**secretary of state**"). In a Mexican state administration, the chief officer below the governor. Under the **Constitution of 1917**, Mexican states no longer have an office of lieutenant governor. *See also* MINISTER.

SECURITY, PUBLIC. *See* PUBLIC SECURITY.

SENATE (*Senado*). The establishment of an upper chamber, the *Cámara de Senadores*, dates from 1822. Abolished in 1857, it was reestablished November 13, 1874. **The Constitution of 1917** provided that the 31 states and the **Federal District** should each elect two federal senators: a total of 64. Those numbers were doubled in 1997 to provide an additional party-list representation on the **proportional representation** system already adopted by the **Cámara de Diputados Federales**.

SENTIES GÓMEZ, OCTAVIO (1915–1996). A lawyer from **Veracruz** and member of the **Cámara de Diputados Federales**, Mexico's chief spokesman on automobile and truck transportation at international conferences in the 1950s–1960s, and governor of the **Federal District**, 1970–1976.

SEPANAL. Acronym for the **Natural Resources** ministry.

SERDAN, AQUILES (1876–1910). Soldier-politician, co-founder of the **Partido de Anti-reelección** in his native **Puebla**, killed November 18, when his house was surrounded and stormed by government troops.

SERI. Indian group of coastal **Sonora** and (formerly) the island of **Tiburón**, descendants of the pre-Columbian **Guaymas**. In 1995 they numbered a mere 500 individuals.

SERNA, ENRIQUE (1959–). Novelist (*Uno soñaba que era rey*, 1989; *El miedo de los animales*, 1995), short story writer (*Amores de segundo mano*, 1991; *Orgasmógrafo*, 2002), and screen writer, born in **Mexico City**. [L. H.]

SERRA, [FRAY] JUNÍPERO (1713–1784). Religious name of the Spanish-born Franciscan missionary Miguel José Serra who came to Mexico in 1749, was sent to **Baja California** in 1767 and to **Alta California** in 1769, where he spent the rest of his life, building nine missions.

SERRANO, [GENERAL] FRANCISCO (1889–1927). Soldier-politician who fought against Victoriano **Huerta**, was Álvaro **Obregón**'s war minister, and held other posts. As a presidential candidate of the opposition, he was arrested and shot in **Cuernavaca**, along with several of his supporters.

SERVICIO METEOROLÓGICO NACIONAL (S.M.N.). The National Weather Service, a federal government agency that began March 6, 1877, as the *Observatorio Metereológico y Astronómico*, was established in 1878 in **Chapultepec Castle**, received its present designation in 1901, and has been since 1995 part of the **Comisión Nacional del Água**. Its headquarters are now in the old Archbishop's Palace in **Tacubaya**.

SERVICIOS MARÍTIMOS DE TURISMO (SEMATUR). A company formed by the 1989 **privatization** of the state-owned *Caminos y Puentes Federales de Ingresos y Conexos*, the ferryboat division of the former **Ferrocarriles Nacionales de Mexico** (Mexican State Railways).

SEVEN YEARS' WAR. Worldwide conflict, 1754–1763, combining dynastic quarrels in central Europe with colonial rivalries elsewhere, known in North America as the last "French and Indian War." Spain, which was not involved until 1762, suffered the temporary loss of **Cuba**, but acquired **Louisiana** from the French, whose loss of Canada ended their ambitions for an empire on the North American mainland. [L. H.]

SEXENNIUM (*sexenio*). The six-year maximum term of a Mexican **president** (or of a colonial **viceroy** of **New Spain**).

SEXUAL ATTITUDES. *See* MACHISMO, WOMEN.

SHANTY TOWNS. Known in Mexico as *colonias proletarias*.

SHARK. Annual catches have been steadily falling since a record 35,000 t were taken (mainly by artesanal fishermen) in the mid-1990s. The current level is around 28,000 t. Ecological concerns and the desire to reserve some fishing grounds for **sport fishing** have so far prevented any agreement on regulation. [L. H.]

SHEEP FARMING. The Spaniards introduced sheep into the New World, raising them, as in Spain, for wool much more than for meat, and, as in Spain, with a deleterious impact on the environment.

SHEFFIELD, JAMES ROCKWELL. United States ambassador to Mexico, September 9, 1924–1927.

SHIPPING. *See* FERRIES; GALLEON; PIRATES; PORTS AND HARBORS; TREASURE FLEET; U-BOATS.

SHRIMP. The most important sector of Mexico's **fishing** industry, with natural and cultured shrimp together contributing 42 percent of the total harvest by value, 50 percent of fish **exports**, and 82 percent of the industrial fishing fleet. Although a closed season was introduced in 1938, stocks have been severely depleted, with catches in the Gulf of Mexico falling by six percent annually since 1997. Fishing gear and methods are regulated, but enforcement is lax, and the chief official reaction to declining income in the artesanal fishing sector has been to use subsidies to lower fuel prices. [L. H.]

"SICK FAMILY, THE." Derisive name applied to Benito **Juárez** and his inner circle, Melchor **Ocampo** and Guillermo **Prieto** in 1863–1865, as they retreated across México in a black carriage with the curtains drawn, seemingly always one step ahead of the French invaders.

SIDERÚRGICA LÁZARO CÁRDENAS LAS TRUCHAS (SICARTSA). An **iron and steel** complex established by the government in **Michoacán**, under a decree of President **Díaz Ortiz** of October 1969, which Lázaro **Cárdenas** had persuaded him to promulgate. It was built in 1970–1976 on the Balsas River near the Pacific Ocean. With its creation, the federal government became the dominant public sector factor in the then expanding **iron and steel industry**. Within three years of its **privatization** in 1992, productivity doubled.

SIEGE, STATE OF (*estado de sitio*). A legal fiction in Roman Law countries whereby a large area, usually the entire country, is deemed to be a besieged city, a pretext for giving the executive dictatorial rights regardless of any constitutional limitations. [L. H.]

SIEMPRE. Left-wing magazine founded in 1951 by Francisco **Martínez de La Vega** and others. It tends to support both the **Partido Revolucionario Institucional** and the **Partido Popular Socialista**.

SIERRA MADRE. *See* MADRE, SIERRA.

SIERRA MÉNDEZ, JUSTO (1848–1912). **Campeche**-born politician, writer, journalist, and diplomat, son of novelist Justo Sierra O'Reily. An enthusiast of **Postivism** and an outstanding member of the **Porfiriato** as education ministry, responsible for reopening the **University of Mexico**. His prodigious literary achievements included poetry, essays, and history including *La Evolución política del pueblo mexicano, 1900–1902*, translated by Charles Ramsdell as *The Political Evolution of the Mexican People* (1969); *Juárez, su obra y su tiempo* (1906); and *História política de México* (1917). In 1910 he fled to exile in **Spain**, where he entered the diplomatic service.

SIETE LEYES ("Seven Laws"). Thanks to the Conservative's recovery of power, this Constitution of 1836 (with a name suggestive of Spain's medieval *Siete Partidas*) created a unitary (centralized) republic in which states' rights were abolished, a prime motive for American settlers in **Texas** to seek independence. The states were replaced by departments (with governors named by the president), divided into prefectures, and these into districts, under prefects, and sub-prefects, all dependent on the national government. This highly conservative constitution also created an all-powerful fourth branch of government, the **Supremo Poder Conservador**, while imposing high-income qualifications for elective office ($1,500 p.a. for deputies; $2,500 p.a. for senators; and $4,000 p.a. for the president).

SIGLO XXI EDITORES. **Mexico City**'s outstanding independent publisher of social science and humanities titles, founded in 1965. The military regime forced its Argentine subsidiary to close in 1974, but it was reestablished in 2000. Its Spanish subsidiary was founded in 1967 and had to battle the censorship of the Franco years.

SIGÜENZA Y GÓNGORA, CARLOS DE (1645–1700). A Jesuit priest who was born and died in **Mexico City**, a recognized authority in many fields of the arts and sciences and a close friend of *Sor* **Juana Inés de la Cruz**. Although also a poet, he is remembered more for such prose works as *Mercurio volante* and his 28 volumes of history.

SILVA HERZOG, JESÚS (1892–1985). A leading economist, born in **San Luis Potosí**, he graduated in economics from **UNAM** and did graduate studies in New York, 1912–1914. A UNAM professor, 1924–1960, he helped found its School of Economics and was its dean from 1940–1942. He also served as ambassador to the **Soviet**

Union, 1928–1930; assistant education minister, 1932–1934; general manager of **Pemex**, 1939–1940; and assistant finance minister, 1944–1946. He was economics adviser for the ministries of finance and national patrimony, for the customs department, and for six Mexican presidents, and also the editor of *Cuadernos americanos*, 1948–1971. He died March 13.

His works include *La Revolución mexicana en crisis* (1944).

SILVA HERZOG FLORES, JESÚS (1935–). Economist. Son of Jesús **Silva Herzog**, born May 8 in **Mexico City**, he graduated in economics from **UNAM** in 1959 with an honors thesis on the Mexican **petroleum** industry. He also earned a master's in economics from Yale in 1962. He was a senior economist with the **Inter-American Development Bank** and taught economics at UNAM, 1963–1969, and the **Colegio de México**, 1964–1969. He served as coordinator of the **Banco de México**, 1969–1970; director of credit for the Finance Ministry, 1970–1972; director of the **Instituto del Fondo Nacional de la Vivienda para los Trabajadores**, 1972–1976; general manager of the Banco de México, 1977–1978; finance minister, 1982–1986; ambassador to Spain, 1991–1993; minister for **tourism**, 1994; and ambassador to the **United States**, 1994–1998.

SILVER. Mexico has the world's largest output of silver. A pioneer in its colonial extraction was Juan de **Tolosa** in **Zacatecas**, but **San Luis Potosí** became its most important center after 1620. Production was encouraged by the **Bourbon Reforms**, growing threefold in 1740–1803.

SINALOA. A river and **municipio** of their namesake state. The latter had a population of 88,160 in 1990 and 85,100 in 2000. Its **cabecera**, Sinaloa de Leyva, at 25°36'N, 107°33'W, is the former capital of **Sinaloa state**.

SINALOA STATE. A state of northwestern Mexico of 58,480 km² whose long, narrow shape extends 560 km (350 miles) along the Gulf of **California** and the Pacific Ocean. It was formed in 1830 by separation from the Estado de **Occidente**. On its east, the Sierra **Madre**

Occidental separates it from **Chihuahua** and **Durango**. Drained by the **Sinaloa, Culiacán**, and **Fuerte** Rivers, it has iron ore, **lead, silver**, hardwoods, textile plants, **sugar** refineries, and cereals. It produces sugar cane, **coffee, cotton, rice**, and fruit. It is the major supplier of winter vegetables for Canada and of winter tomatoes for the **United States**. It is also the chief route for the smuggling of **narcotics** over the **United States border**.

Its chief towns are **Culiacán**, the capital, and **Mazatlán**. The state's population was 160,000 in 1857; 161,157 in 1869; 259,000 in 1895; 297,000 in 1900; 324,000 in 1910; 341,000 in 1921; 396,000 in 1930; 493,000 in 1940; 636,000 in 1950; 838,000 in 1960; 1,267,000 in 1970; 1,700,000 in 1976; 1,850,000 in 1980; 2,204,054 in 1990; 2,536,844 in 2000; and 2,608,442 in 2005. In 1993 its 18 *municipios* were, in descending order of **population**: Culiacán, Mazatlán, **Ahome**, Guasave, Navolato, **Sinaloa**, El **Fuerte**, Salvador Alvarado, Mocorito, El Rosario, Angostura, Escuinapa, Badiraguato, Elota, Concordia, Choix, San Ignacio, and **Cosalá**.

SINARQUISMO. Mexico's home-grown fascism, organized in 1937 as the **Unión Sinarquista Nacional**. It was of great concern to liberal and conservative politicians, in part because of the mystery surrounding it, but it played no significant role in the **election of 1940**.

SINDICATO NACIONAL DE TRABAJADORES DE LA EDUCACIÓN (S.N.T.E.). The National Union of Workers in Education, the school teachers' trade union with 1.4 million members, led since 1989 by Elba Esther **Gordillo Morales**.

SIQUEIROS, DAVID ALFARO (1889–1974). Painter, revolutionary, and political activist. His speciality was mural **painting** (*See* MURALISTS), with man's progress through the ages and his struggle for social justice as his recurrent theme. He considered his major work to be "The March of Humanity," which covers an 18-sided building in the Hotel de Mexico complex. Other major works include those in the **Escuela Nacional Preparatoria** and the **Instituto Nacional de Bellas Artes**. It is impossible to separate his professional life from his political activities. He fought in the **Revolution of 1910**. He took part in the **Spanish Civil War** as an officer in the

Loyalist (Republican) army. He led 20 gunmen in a failed attempt to kill Leon **Trotsky** in his **Mexico City** home.

As secretary general of the **Partido Comunista Mexicano** in the 1950s–1960s, he was held responsible for PCM support of the 1959 railroad strikes and imprisoned. In 1960 he was awarded a government commission for a mural in **Chapultepec Park**, despite his being involved in anti-United States demonstrations for which he was arrested and imprisoned—an illustration of Mexican ability to recognize genius in its citizens at the same time as it punishes them for acts considered dangerous to the country.

SISAL *(henequén).* A fiber made from the leaves of the **agave**. A full half of Mexico's sisal is grown in **Yucatán**. [L. H.]

SISTEMA PÚBLICA DE SALUD DE MÉXICO. Mexico's national health service. Proposals by the **Fox** administration for its reform are believed to have accounted for much of the increase of voter support for the **Partido Revolucionario Institucional** in the **election of 2004**, due to a widespread fear of its **privatization**. [L. H.]

SLAVERY, AFRICAN. *See* AFRICAN SLAVERY.

SLIM HELIÚ, CARLOS (1940–). Controlling stockholder of **Telemex** and second largest stockholder of **Televisa**.

SMALLPOX. The deadliest of the diseases introduced by the invading Spaniards, often spreading so rapidly as to arrive before the *conquisadores* themselves. One of its first notable victims was the **Cuitláujiac**. Further outbreaks accompanied the **measles** epidemics of 1563–1564 and 1615–1617, and another (again, with high mortality) in 1780. Vaccination eventually defeated the disease, declared eliminated from Mexico in 1951. [L. H.]

SMUGGLING. See CONTRABAND.

SOCCER. A few teams at major universities play American football but for many decades British style "association **football**" (*fútbol*) or soccer has been the leading **sport** in Mexico for amateur and professional athletes alike. Among notable players is Jesús Antonio **Carbajal Rodríguez**. *See also* WORLD SOCCER CUP.

SOCIAL CLASSES. At the end of the 20th century, **UNAM**'s National School of Economics classified five percent of the population as wealthy, 35 percent as middle class (by Latin American rather than North American or European standards), and 60 percent as working class—with many of the lower middle class having incomes barely above those of the working class.

SOCIAL DEVELOPMENT MINISTRY (*Secretaría de Desarrollo Social*, **SEDESOL**). Successor to the **Human Settlements Ministry**.

SOCIAL SECURITY. Since 1940 a remit of the **Labor Ministry**, which in 1943, under a law authored by Adolfo **Zamora**, instituted the **Instituto Mexicano del Seguro Social (IMSS)** for workers in the private sector and the **Instituto de Seguridad y Servicios Sociales de los Trabajadores del Estado (ISSSTE)** for those in the government sector. Under Benito **Coquet** as director general of the IMSS in 1958–1964, social security benefits were extended to medium and small towns not previously covered; but, even in the 1970s, less than a fourth of the total work force was under either IMSS or ISSSTE provision. In the 1980s coverage increased within the full-time employed. In 1984 **Congress** changed an administrative law to give the director general of IMSS more flexibility in determining eligibility. An agency of the Labor Ministry, the *Dirección General de Bienestar* implemented a plan written by Coquet (now retired) to allow IMSS hospitals to admit chronically ill workers even if they were too young to qualify under existing rules.

SOCIALISM. *See* PARTIDO SOCIALISTA DE LOS TRABA-JADORES; PARTIDO SOCIALISTA UNIFICADO DE MÉXICO.

SOCIALIST EDUCATION. A term used in the 1930s to refer nebulously to the supposed Marxist orientation of Mexican **education**. No attempt was ever made to make this a reality, and the appellation "socialist" was replaced in 1940 with "scientific."

SOCIALIST WORKERS' PARTY. *See* PARTIDO SOCIALISTA DE LOS TRABAJADORES.

SOCIEDAD MEXICANA DE CRÉDITO INDUSTRIAL. Government investment corporation which owns stock in **newspapers**, **television** stations, and several manufacturing industries.

SOCIETY OF JESUS (*Compañía de Jesús*). *See* JESUITS.

SOCORRO. The largest of the **Revillagigedo Islands**, measuring 37 km x 14 km (24 miles by 9), and rising to a height of almost 1,200 m (4,000 ft.). John Smith and a party of Australians and Canadians established a brief-lived settlement (with Mexican permission) in 1869. The descendants of the sheep they brought now number 2,000 and threaten the unique native **flora**. A naval base has been on the island since 1957 to assert Mexican sovereignty. [L. H.]

SOLDADERAS. The (mostly Indian) **women** who accompanied their men in the barracks and battles of the **Revolution of 1910**, cooking and otherwise caring for them wherever they might go. Clemente **Orozco** vividly portrays such "women soliders" in his painting of *Las Soldaderas*.

SOLEDAD, CONVENCIÓN DE. February 1862 agreement with **Spain** and the **United Kingdom** (now unwilling to support the wider ambitions of **Napoleon III**), whereby Benito **Juárez** negotiated the end of these countries' intervention provoked by his moratorium on their debts.

SONOMA. Locality north of **San Francisco**, colonial capital of **Alta California** and scene of the coup whereby American settlers proclaimed the "**Bear Flag Republic**" in June 1846. [L. H.]

SONORA. Established as the Northern Province (*Provincia del Poniente*) in 1732 by separation from **Nueva Vizcaya**, it was made an **intendancy** in 1786 and granted statehood at **independence**. It was then made briefly part of the Estado de **Occidente**, 1824–1830. The

Treaty of **Guadalupe Hidalgo** made it a **United States border** state, neighbored on the north by **Arizona** and **New Mexico**, and on the west by the Gulf of **California**. In 1853 William **Walker** led a failed attempt to make it an "independent" state run by American fili-busters, followed in 1854 by a similar try by Raousset **Boulbon**.

Sonora's 184,000 km^2 make it Mexico's second largest state, and it has the third highest state income. It has had **mining** of **copper**, **coal**, and iron ore since colonial times. Alamos is a historic mining town. Eastern Sonora is mountainous. The west is flat with a rocky coastline. The island of **Tiburón** is the former home of the **Seri** Indi-ans, now living on the mainland.

Although much of the state's area is occupied by the Sonoarn Desert (North America's largest), nine hydroelectric dams built since the 1940s have brought extensive **irrigation**. Sonora has **cotton**, cere-als—it supplies 70 percent of Mexico's **wheat**—cattle, commerical **fishing**, and frozen **shrimp** processing. There are **maquilladoras** in **Nogales**. The capital is **Hermo-sillo**, and **Guaymas** is a major port.

The **population** was 139,374 in 1857 and 147,133 in 1869. At suc-cessive **censuses** since then it has been: 191,000 in 1895; 222,000 in 1900; 265,000 in 1910; 275,000 in 1921; 316,000 in 1930; 364,000 in 1940; 511,000 in 1950; 783,000 in 1960; 1,094,000 in 1970; 1,514,731 in 1980; 1,824,000 in 1990; 2,216,969 in 2000; and 2,294,861 in 2005.

Sonora is active in the two-state **Arizona-Sonora Commission** and in the 1980s became the first Mexican state to sign a bi-national agreement to bring Arizona teachers of special **education** into its sec-ondary schools to work with students who are learning disabled.

In 1966 Sonora became the first Mexican state to devote more than half of its annual state budget (53 percent) to public **education**. With this example, by the late 1970s, five other states were devoting half of their state budgets to public education, instead of depending wholly on federal funds.

Sonora was the scene of many important battles in the **Revolution of 1910** and is the home state of four Mexican Presidents: **Obregón**, **Calles**, Abelardo L. **Rodríguez**, and Adolfo de la **Huerta**.

Following the **election of 1997**, Sonora's governor faced a uni-cameral state legislature where **PRI**'s customary dominance had been reduced to a bare majority dependent on cooperation with the opposition. He had to negotiate some budgetary matters with both opposition parties.

SORIANO, JUAN (1920–2006). Guadelajara-born painter, potter, sculptor in **silver** and bronze, and stage and costume designer, awarded Spain's Velazquez prize for his life's work in 2005.

SOTO Y GAMA, ANTONIO DIAZ (1880–1967). Politician, educator, and agrarian leader. He was a close adviser of Emiliano **Zapata**, succeeding him as leader of his movement after his assassination, and organizing the **Confederación Nacional Campesina**. He wrote statements for the barely literate Zapata to read when reporters asked him for his views as acting president: "I do not want to be the conscience of the world. We fight for freedom for ourselves, and to regain land that was taken from us."

SOUTHERN MEXICO. Mexico's tropical, and still largely forested, southern lands have 15 percent of the national **population**, but provide only seven percent of the gross domestic product.

SOVIET UNION. The Union of Soviet Socialist Republics (U.S.S.R.): official name of **Russia** and its Asian colonial possessions, 1922–1991.

SPAIN, RELATIONS WITH. Spain's colonial rule in Mexico lasted from 1520 to the surrender of **San Juan de Ulúa** in 1825. It was followed in 1833 by a general expulsion of all **Peninsular** Spaniards.

Spain, together with the **United Kingdom** and **France**, threatened military intervention in response to the **Foreign Debt Moratorium** of 1861, but, like the United Kingdom, desisted as soon as it became clear that France was intent on imposing a regime change.

Relations were also broken off in 1939 when the Nationalists triumphed in the **Spanish Civil War** and were not renewed until after the death of the *Caudillo* Francisco Franco.

A state visit by King **Juan Carlos** was welcomed in 1978.

Spanish **immigration**, fostered by cultural and linguistic ties, has led to the establishment of charitable foundations such as **Puebla**'s **Beneficiencia Española** hospital. *See also* BUCARELI Y URSUA, ANTONIO MARIA.

SPANISH CIVIL WAR. An attempted **army pronunciamiento** of July 14, 1936, was frustrated when Spain's left-wing republican government issued arms to the general population. The result was a three-year war in which the nationalist insurgents owed their eventual victory to direct intervention by Italy, logistical support by Germany, and an Anglo-French blockade. The doomed republican cause was clamorously supported by progressives throughout Europe and the Americas, who saw it as the first stage in the coming struggle against fascism. The few friendly foreign governments included **Mexico**, **Chile** (at the end of the war), and the **Soviet Union**, which did its utmost to ensure that the Communists would dominate in the bitterly divided Republic.

After the war, Chile welcomed largely proletarian Loyalist (Republican) refugees, while Mexico took in mostly the fallen Republic's intelligentsia, and established the **Casa de España**, now the **Colegio de México**, to cater to their needs. [L. H.]

SPANISH CONQUEST. *See* CONQUEST OF MEXICO, SPANISH.

SPANISH CONSTITUTION OF 1812. Spain's first constitution, drawn up by the **Cortes of Cadiz** in which New World delegates participated. Establishing a limited monarchy, with the major power residing in the **Cortes**, it gave equal rights to all free citizens in Spain and her colonies. New World representatives would make up one half of the Cortes and a minimum of 12 members of the **Council of State**. A very advanced document for its time, it faced strong opposition from conservatives, both Spanish and American. Many of the latter began to plot separation from Spain for fear that a liberal constitutional monarchy would not protect their privileges. Liberals in the Americas, for their part, used the document as a quarry for their own constitution making (whence its influence on the **Constitution of 1824**). When **Ferdinand VII** was restored in 1814, he abrogated the constitution and imprisoned supporters of constitutionalism. It was briefly re-enacted by the **Spanish Revolution of 1820**, and again when liberals took power in Spain in 1836. [L. H.]

SPANISH CORTES OF 1810–1814. *See* CORTES OF CADIZ.

SPANISH FLU (*gripe española*). The **World War I** pandemic seems to have originated in the **United States** and was reputedly brought to **Tampico** in the summer of 1918 by the SS *Harold Walker*, although Mexican folklore explains the name by blaming ships of the Spanish line for supposedly having brought it to **Veracruz**. With a mortality rate of around one third, it produced 500,000 deaths in Mexico (one in 30 of the then population), out of a world total of 20 million deaths. *See also* INFLUENZA. [L. H.]

SPANISH LANGUAGE. Its almost 110 million **population** makes Mexico easily the world's largest Spanish-speaking country. The Mexican variety of the Spanish (and that of adjacent regions of Central America) is a relatively conservative form of the language, although like all forms of American Spanish it practices *seseo* (pronunciation of *z* as *s*) and, like most of them, *yeismo* (pronouncing *ll* as *y*). Although phonetic simplifications such as the loss of syllable-final *s* are much less in evidence than in circum-Caribbean Spanish, the reduction of *j* to the sound of an Anglo-American *h*—whence English "marihuana" for *marijuana*—is quite widespread. The second person pronoun remains current as the familiar form in the singular (*tu*, not *vos*), but *ustedes* always does duty for *vosotros* in the plural. *See also* CASTILLIAN. [L. H.]

SPANISH MAIN (*Tierra firme*). The northern (Caribbean) coast of South America and its hinterland.

SPANISH REVOLUTION OF 1820. Rebellion, led by Colonel Rafael **Riego y Núñez**, of the expeditionary force that had been gathered by **Ferdinand VIII** in order to restore Spanish authority in the Americas and was awaiting embarkation by a promised Russian fleet. The rebels forced the king to restore the 1812 constitution along with other liberal reforms such as the dissolution of the smaller convents. News reached North America in April. The revolution ended in 1823 when France, supported by the "Holy Alliance" of conservative European monarchies, sent her "hundred thousand sons of Saint Louis" into Spain to impose a restoration of the old order, but by then the conservatives in Mexico had united behind

Iturbide, preferring independence to the threat of a liberalism imposed by Spain. [L. H.]

SPANISH SUCCESSION, WAR OF (1700–1713). General European and American conflict with Austria (and Catalonia) allied to what became the **United Kingdom** against Spain (i.e., Castile) allied to France, to determine who would succeed **Charles II**. It resulted in the Treaty of **Utrecht**.

SPANISH TREASURE FLEET. *See* TREASURE FLEET.

SPORT. Since the mid-20th century decline of popularity in **bullfighting**, the chief sports in Mexico, in both spectator attendance and participation, have been **soccer**, **basketball**, **baseball**, track athletics, tennis—since the 1950s there have been some world class players at the professional level—**jai alai**, and volleyball. Since the 1960s, there has also been an increased number of bowling alleys in every metropolitan area. *See also* OLYMPICS; POK TA POK; WRESTLING.

SPORT FISHING. Mexico offers excellent opportunities for fishing its lakes and rivers but tourists have traditionally been most attracted by sea fishing for **tuna** etc. off the coast of **Baja California** and over the Campeche bank of the Gulf of **Mexico**. *See also* HADAS, LAS.

SQUID. Giant squid has an important place in the Mexican **fishing** industry, but the catch has varied according to oceanic conditions that are not yet well understood. [L. H.]

STAN, HURRICANE. This hit Tapachula in **Chiapas** October 4, 2005, just two weeks before Hurricane **Wilma** struck **Yucatán**. [L. H.]

STATE OF SIEGE. *See* SIEGE, STATE OF.

STATES. The adoption of **federalism** by the new Republic transformed the existing colonial provinces, on the American model, into "states" and "**territories**," and a "**Federal District**." Since the 1974 elevation of the two remaining territories, the Mexican union has consisted of the Federal District and the following states: **Aguascalientes State, Baja California del Norte, Baja California del Sur, Campeche State, Chiapas, Chihuahua State, Coahuila, Colima State, Durango State, Guanajuato State, Guerrero, Hidalgo State, Jalisco, México State, Michoacán, Morelos State, Nayarit, Nuevo León, Oaxaca State, Puebla State, Querétaro State, Quintana Roo, San Luis Potosí State, Sinaloa State, Sonora, Tabasco, Tamaulipas, Tlaxcala State, Veracruz State, Yucatán State,** and **Zacatecas State.** Former states include **Alta California** and **Texas,** while **Arizona, Nevada,** and **New Mexico** have become U.S. states subsequent to their loss by Mexico. The constituent provinces of the former captaincy general of **Guatemala** (viz. Costa Rica, Guatemala, Honduras, Nicaragua, and El Salvador) were briefly included in Mexico's **First Empire,** but reorganized, not as states, but as the *comandancias generales* of Chiapas (which remained with Mexico after the break up), Guatemala, and **León.** [L. H.]

STEEL INDUSTRY. *See* IRON AND STEEL.

STEPHENS, JOHN LLOYD (1805–1852). New Jersey lawyer and explorer whose two visits to Central America and the **Yucatán** peninsula, accompanied by the artist Frederick **Catherwood,** in 1839–1842 pioneered Mayan archaeology.

STEPHENS GARCÍA, MANUEL (1925–). Secondary school teacher born in Bellavista, **Nayarit,** who became a leader of the **Partido Popular Socialista**; a member of the **Cámara de Diputados Federales,** 1961–1964 and 1970–1973; a regional secretary of the **Sindicato Nacional de Trabajadores de la Educación**; and in 1975, PPS candidate for the governorship of **Nayarit,** the state that is the PPS's stronghold. He was defeated but charged fraudulent vote counting. The controversy ended a year later when the PPS elected its first federal senator from **Oaxaca,** Jorge **Cruickshank García,** which Stevens claimed was recompense from the **Partido Revolucionario Institucional** for having deprived the PPS of its victory in Nayarit.

STOCK EXCHANGE. *See* BOLSA MEXICANA DE VALORES.

STRAIT OF . . . *See* ARIÁN, STRAIT OF.

STREET OF ALI BABA AND THE FORTY THIEVES. A derisive term for the street in **Cuernavaca** where President **Calles** and his followers lived in ostentatious luxury in huge mansions.

STUDENT FEDERATIONS. Since the 1930s, most public university and preparatory school student unions in Mexico have been led by communists or other leftists, using strikes to protest over national political issues, as in the case of the **UNAM Student Riots of 1968**.

STUDENT RIOTS. *See* UNAM STUDENT RIOTS OF 1968; UNAM STUDENT RIOTS OF 1975; UNAM STUDENT STRIKE OF 1999.

SUÁREZ, VICENTE (1833–1847). One of the "**Niños heroes.**" He has a street named in his honor in the Colonia Condesa neighborhood of **Mexico City**.

SUÁREZ DE MENDOZA, LORENZO, CONDE DE LA CORUÑA, VIZCONDE DE TORIJA (1518–1583). Fifth **viceroy** of **New Spain**, 1580–1583. In his early manhood he had fought in Flanders, Italy, and Tunisia, but when appointed viceroy in his sixties he no longer had the energy to deal with corrupt officials and an administration that was no longer under the effective control of the **Council of the Indies**. He died in office.

SUBSECRETARIO. In Mexican government, not "undersecretary," but "deputy minister," second-in-charge of a major department of state.

SUBWAY. *See* METRO.

SUCCESIÓN PRESIDENCIAL DE 1910, LA. Book by Francisco **Madero**, which, although criticized in some quarters for its implied hostility to Porfirio **Díaz**, merely made the modest proposal that should the president choose to run again in 1910, the citizenry should have a hand in selecting the **vice president**.

SUFFRAGE. The **Spanish constitution of 1812** left voting rights to be, in effect, determined by individual colonial governments, most of which introduced property and literacy qualifications. These were incompatible with the **Revolution of 1910** and a universal right to vote from 18 years of age has existed in Mexico since 1958. *See also* FEMALE SUFFRAGE. [L. H.]

SUFRAGIO EFECTIVO: NO REELECIÓN. *See* "EFFECTIVE SUFFRAGE AND NO RE-ELECTION."

SUGAR. Mexico is the world's fifth largest producer of sugar from cane. Its best sugar plantations are found along the Pacific coastlands of Central Mexico. To protect the industry, soft drinks containing artificial sweetener are currently taxed at a higher rate than those using sugar, giving rise to a dispute with the **United States** over World Trade Organization rules on differential **taxation**. [L. H.]

SULFUR. Mexico is the world's second largest producer of sulfur.

SUN STONE. The **Aztec** calendar now in the **Museo Nacional de Antropología**, the sacred almanac of their polytheism, is a huge disk, 12 ft in diameter, weighing 20 t. At its center is the sun. The twenty day names encircle the central symbols. It contains the concepts of chronometric and cosmological systems handed down by the **Toltec Indians** which the Aztecs expanded and refined.

SUPLENTE. Each congressional candidate runs for election with a *suplente* to replace him in the event of his subsequently vacating the seat (from death, resignation, or disqualification).

SUPREME COURT (*Suprema Corte de Justicia de la Nación*). A *Tribunal Supremo de Justicia* replaced the colonial *audiencias* from March 1825, but this title was changed to *Supreme Corte de Justicia* whenever the liberals were in power. Under the **Second Empire** it was the *Tribunal Superior del Imperio*. Until 1882 the chief justice was *ex-officio* vice president of the Republic. A reform of 1994 reduced the number of supreme court justices to eleven, each to serve a 15-year term (instead of permanency until their 70th birthday). [L. H.]

SUPREMO PODER CONSERVADOR. Five member body, 1837–1841; a creation of the **Siete Leyes**.

SWITZERLAND, RELATIONS WITH. *See* JECKER, JUAN B.

SYMPHONY ORCHESTRAS. The national orchestra in **Mexico City** is the **Orquesta Sinfónica Nacional de México**. **Guadalajara** and **Monterrey** maintain locally funded symphonic orchestras.

– T –

TABASCO. Town of 5,500 inhabitants, 1,600 m above sea level, **cabecera** of a **municipio** of 320 km^2 with 15,600 inhabitants in 2000.

TABASCO STATE. A state of southeastern Mexico, part of the **Maya** empire in pre-Hispanic times and sometimes called *Tobasco*. Its 24,661 km^2 are bordered by the Gulf of **Mexico** to the north, **Campeche** and the Guatemalan department of Petén to the east, **Veracruz** to the west, and **Chiapas** to the south. Its hot humid climate produces **sugar** cane. The population, in its 17 *municipios* has grown from 70,628 in 1857 to 83,707 in 1869; 135,000 in 1895; 160,000 in 1900; 187,000 in 1910; 210,000 in 1921; 224,000 in 1930; 286,000 in 1940; 363,000 in 1950; 496,000 in 1960; 768,000 in 1970; 1,063,000 in 1980; 1,501,744 in 1990; 1,891,829 in 2000; and 1,989,969 in 2005. The capital is **Villahermosa**.

TABLADA, JOSÉ JUAN (1871–1945). An extremely prolific poet, political writer, and satirist. His satires appeared in many **newspapers** and magazines, including *Excelsior* and *El Mundo ilustrado*. "Onix" is one of his best known poems. He was also active in New York, publicizing and disseminating information about Mexican life and culture.

TACUBAYA. Suburb of **Mexico City**; site of the archbishop's palace, built by **Viceroy Vizarrón y Eguiarreta** in 1737 and, as the **exarzobispado**, now used by the **Pan American Institute of Geography and History** and the **Servicio Meteorologico Nacional**. It was itself the site of a battle on April 11, 1858, during the **Wars of the Reforms** when General Leonardo **Márquez** defeated the Liberals, retaining conservative and clerical control of **Mexico City**. The locality was also chosen for a Pan American conference to follow the 1826 **Congress of Panama**, but this second meeting never took place.

TACUBAYA, PLAN OF. An 1857 proposal, with **Radical Party** support, to annul the **Constitution of 1857**, which President **Comonfort** had only accepted with reluctance.

TAIBO, PACO IGNACIO II (1949–). Spanish novelist who has lived in Mexico since 1958. He wrote *Días de combate* (1976) and *La vida misma* (1987), which won an award as best detective novel in Spanish. He has also written a biography of Che Guevara.

TALAMANTES, GUSTAVO L. (1880–1958). Senator from **Chihuahua**, and then its governor, 1935–1940, he was a key policymaker for the federal government's **Banco Nacional de Crédito Ejidal**, 1935–1950.

TALLER. Left-wing literary journal lasting from December 1938 to February 1941. [L. H.]

TAMAULIPAS ("Tamps"). A northeastern state of 79,600 km² bordering the Gulf of **Mexico** and the U.S. state of **Texas**, and named for the pre-Hispanic Tamaulipas **Indians**. It was colonized by Spain in 1746 as **Nuevo Santander**. It has an extensive coastal plain, but a mountainous center crossed by the Sierra **Madre** Oriental. With large **petroleum** and **natural gas** reserves, it was Mexico's first oil producing state in the early 1900s, but now its natural gas is more important, carried by pipeline south to **Veracruz** and southwestward to **Monterrey**. **Irrigation** from the **Rio Grande** fosters cotton, **sugar** cane, and citrus. The **population**, which was 109,673 in 1857, has since been recorded at successive censuses as 208,000 in 1895; 219,000 in 1900; 250,000 in 1910; 287,000 in 1921; 344,000 in 1930; 459,000 in 1940; 718,000 in 1950; 1,024,000 in 1960; 1,457,000 in 1970; 1,924,000 in 1980 (when its inhabitants enjoyed Mexico's second highest per capita income, after **Baja California del Norte**); 2,250,000 in 1990; 2,753,222 in 2000; and 3,024,238 in 2005. The capital is **Ciudad Victoria**. Other cities are the port of **Tampico** and the border cities of **Nuevo Laredo**, **Reynosa**, and **Matamoros**.

TAMAYO, RUFINO (1899–1991). Painter, sculptor, draftsman, print-maker, and the most influential forerunner of modern art in Latin America. He is represented in the Museum of Modern Art in New York and in other major museum collections worldwide, with murals in Latin America and the **United States**. His work, together with that of **Orozco**, **Rivera**, and **Siqueiros**, represents a level of achievement in painting rarely achieved by one nation in so short a period. In contrast to the others, Tamayo is known for his reflective spirit and for expressing great contrasts in his art form. Among his most famous paintings are *Homage to the race* and *Birth of our nationality*, both in the Palacio de **Bellas Artes**. His best artistic qualities are the use of color and his ability to bring out suggestion.

TAMENES. *See* PORTERS.

TAMESÍ. River of eastern Mexico sharing its estuary with the **Pánuco**.

TAMPICO. City of **Tamaulipas**, Mexico's second largest port, and a major oil refining center, at 22°16'N, 97°47'W, just north of the mouths of the **Pánuco** and **Tamesí**, and close to the border with **Veracruz state**. Its pipelines carry **petroleum** and **natural gas** to **Monterrey**, **Mexico City**, and **Veracruz City**. Its population grew from 232,000 in 1976 to 295,442 in 2000.

TAMPICO INCIDENT. In April 1914 the crew of the USS *Dolphin* was arrested in **Tampico** and when, after their release, President Victoriano **Huerta**, protesting **United States** non-recognition of his regime, refused to honor the U.S. flag with a 21-gun salute, President Woodrow **Wilson** sent U.S. ships into the Gulf of **Mexico**, and eventually used these ships to occupy **Veracruz City**.

TANDA LAW. Law promulgated by **Viceroy** Martín **Enríquez de Almanza** to regulate the employment of **Indians** in **mining**.

TAPACHULA. The largest city in **Chiapas**, near the **Guatemalan border**, at 14°51'N, 92°27'W, 118 m above sea level, with 85,000 inhabitants in 1976, and 131,000 in 1995. In 2000 the city **population** had grown to 179,839, and there was a total of 271,674 in the **municipio**.

TAPIA, ENGUERRANDO. A reporter in the 1950s for the dailies *El Imparcial* and *El Regional* of his native **Hermosillo**. In the 1960s–70s he was an adviser on public relations for leaders in **Sonora** of the **Partido Revolucionario Institucional** and of the state government and built up the rival daily *El Sonorense* as publisher-editor.

TAPIA, FERNANDO. Conquistador who conquered **Querétaro City**.

TAPIA, RAFAEL (1858–1913). Army general in the **Revolution of 1910** who was imprisoned after the death of Francisco **Madero** and then killed.

TAPIA CAMACHO, MANLIO (1928–). Lawyer, judge, briefly a senator, and in 1964–1967 mayor of his native **Veracruz City**. Since the 1960s he also has been a journalist and public relations adviser for the **Partido Revolucionario Institucional** in **Mexico City**.

TARAHUMARA. An **Indian** nation of 62,000 (1995 estimate) in **Chihuahua** and also in **Durango** and other parts of the Sierra **Madre** Occidental. The Tarahumaras are particularly noted for their physical stamina as long-distance foot racers.

TARASCAN. An **Indian** nation, also known as the Purépecha, in **Michoacán**, numbering in 1995 about 93,000. Noted fishermen, they have lived for centuries around Lakes **Chapala** and **Pátzcuaro**.

TÁRNAVA, CONSTANTINO DE, JR. (1899–1974). Radio pioneer. He attended high school at St. Edward's University in Austin, Texas, in 1913–1917, and then studied electrical engineering at the University of Notre Dame in South Bend, Indiana, 1918–1923. In 1921 he got instruction in constructing a radio transmitter for an experimental station which he erected in his home town of **Monterrey** as 24-A. In 1923 this amateur station became commercial station CYP, later changed to XEH, today one of Mexico's oldest broadcasting stations.

TARRAGO, LETICIA (1940–). A painter and engraver from **Orizaba, Veracruz state**, she first won international recognition in 1957 for winning a 12-nation KLM Airlines competition entitled "This is My Country." She has studied engraving in Warsaw, and also studied with Dr. Atl. She now has several permanent exhibitions in Europe and the United States. *Burbujas* and *8:45 A.M.* are representative of her color etchings.

TAXATION. *See* ALCABALA; ALMOJARIFAZGO; ESTANCO; IMPESTO ESPECIAL SOBRE PRODUCCIÓN Y SERVICIOS; INCOME TAX; ROYAL TENTH; TELEPHONES; TITHES; VALUE-ADDED TAX.

TAXCO. A tourist resort in **Guerrero state** which has preserved most of the colonial buildings and cobblestone streets of its downtown and commercial areas. It is famed for its artisan **silver**smiths who turn out the most elaborate jewelry in Mexico.

TECPÁN. Municipio on the coastal plain of **Gorier** whose capital, Tecpan de Galeana, had 8,000 inhabitants in 1970. In June 1813 José Maria **Morelos** rewarded the locality's contribution to the struggle for **independence** by giving its name to a new province he was instituting, which extended as far inland as the River Bolsas. Although its existence was confirmed by the **Apatzingán Congress** as Mexico's fourteenth province, it did not last, but it was virtually recreated in 1848 as the current state of **Gorier**.

TEENEK INDIANS. A long isolated **Maya** group of **Indians**, known in Spanish as the *Huastecos*. Numbering some 100,000 in the mid-1990s, they are concentrated along the Pánuco River in **Veracruz-Llave** and **San Luis Potosí** states, but are also found in **Hidalgo** and **Tamaulipas**. They are noted for their folk dances and **huapango** music. Like the **Totonaca** Indians, they perform the flying pole dance, in which they descend a high pole suspended by a whirling rope tied to one ankle.

TEHUANA. The mixed **Zapotec**, **Mixtec**, and **mestizo** population and culture for which **Tehuantec** is named. Its people are noted for their **marimba** folk music and dances. The women carry huge baskets of fruit, flowers, vegetables, or other goods balanced on their heads.

TEHUANTEPEC. GULF OF. The bay on the Pacific immediately to the south of the **Tehuantepec Isthmus.**

TEHUANTEPEC, RIVER. Westward flowing river of **Oaxaca state.**

TEHUANTEPEC ISTHMUS. The narrowest part of Mexico, 193 km (120 miles) across southern Mexico from the Gulf of **Mexico** south-southwest through **Veracruz** and **Oaxaca** states to the Pacific Ocean. The highway and railroad linking the port of **Coatzacoalocos** on the Gulf with **Salina Cruz** on the Pacific run more in a north-south direction than east-west.

[In 1858 the **United States** used the **Juárez** regime's desperate need of recognition to exact the **McLane-Ocampo** Treaty that would have given it sovereign rights of transit across the Isthmus. Fortunately a U.S. Senate, bitterly divided over slavery, failed to ratify and the treaty lapsed. L. H.]

TEJADA, LERDO DE. *See* LERDO DE TEJADA, MIGUEL; LERDO DE TEJADA, SEBASTIAN.

TEJAS, CASA DE ("House of Tiles"). Mansion built in 1596 as the residence of the Count of Orizaba, named for the blue mosaic tiles lining some of its outside walls. Situated one block east of the **Alameda**, it was restored in 1940, and became **Mexico City**'s first **Sanborns** pharmacy, gift shop, and restaurant.

TELECOMMUNICATIONS. *See* RADIO; TELEPHONES; TELE-VISION.

TELEMUNDO. Distribution subsidiary of **Azteca T.V.**

TELEPHONES. *Telefonos de México* (**COFETEL**), the government telephone monopoly, was privatized in 1997, most of it being sold to **Telemex**. In 1993 the country had 11,890,868 telephones, and, in 2000, 15 million, or less than 200 per 1,000 inhabitants. (This compares with 238 in Brazil, 366 in Uruguay, 993 in the **United States**.) In the negotiations for the 2000 **budget**, the **Partido de Acción Nacional** secured the exemption of telephone calls from **taxation**.

TELEVISA. Latin America's largest media conglomerate, and the world's largest producer of **Spanish**-language **television** programs. The number of programs available for lease or rent from Televisa is greater than the total output of **Spain**, **Argentina**, Central America, and Venezuela combined. (**Rede Globo** in Brazil has a larger television network but operates in Portuguese and is less strong in other media). Founded by the Azcárraga family, presently represented by Emilio **Azcárraga Jean**, Televisa owns and operates the three largest TV networks in Mexico (channels 2, 4, and 5) and their affiliated stations throughout Mexico. It also owns cable television networks and holds majority stock in the XEW **radio** stations (AM, FM, and shortwave) and their networks. Although retaining corporate ownership, Televisa encourages each channel to compete for advertising revenue and audiences, and each outlet feeds its own network of provincial affiliates. Televisa also produces feature films for both television and the **cinema**. Its subsidiary Univisión supplies videotaped programs to Spanish language television stations in the **United States** and syndicates Mexican programs to networks in other Spanish-speaking countries.

Purchase pressures from creditors in February 1999 was met with a careful debt restructuring which more than halved its US\$ 1.3 billion debt burden. Azcárraga Jean transferred some shares to a group of institutional lenders, but it was still holding 40 percent and the option for Televicentro (the subsidiary owning the network's physical plant) to repurchase in 2003. He also announced a US\$ 50,000,000 stock-repurchasing program, while paying US\$ 230,000,000 to acquire all the assets of Grupo Alameda, one of Televisa's debtors. Televisa's American depositary stocks are listed on the New York Stock Exchange.

TELEVISION. Latin America's first scheduled program began on the morning of September 1, 1950, with Miguel **Alemán** reading the annual State of the Union Message (*Informe Presidencial*) on station XHTV, channel 4. This was just ahead of **Cuba** which began on October 20.

Currently, **Televisa** provides 65 percent of television programs aired in Mexico, while its rival, **Azteca T.V.**, controls the rest through its own network for syndication, **Telemundo**. Mexico's Federal Broadcasting Law of January 19, 1960, allows corporate control of more than one television network, so Azteca and Televisa each control and manage three separate nationwide networks. Mexicans owned a total of 13,100,000 television receivers by 1992.

TELLEZ BENOIT, MARÍA EMILIA (1921–). A lawyer born December 27, in Washington, DC, she became a pioneer woman foreign service officer in 1946. She rose to director of the **United States** section of the Mexican **foreign ministry**, then of the Europe-Asia-Africa section before becoming successively third secretary of the embassy in Washington, and second secretary in that of Havana. In 1970 she became the foreign ministry's director general of international organizations.

TELLEZ CRUZES, AGUSTÍN (1918–). Jurist. Born November 15, in **Guajanajuato City**, he graduated in law from **UNAM**, served as district court judge in the states of **Hidalgo, Puebla, Chiapas, Sonora,** and **México**, and in the **Federal District**. Appointed to the Federal **Supreme Court**, he was elected its chief justice in 1977, 1978, and 1979. He toured all federal **prisons**, and got improved medical care and vocational rehabilitation for their inmates. He originated the treaty with the **United States** whereby those convicted of **narcotics** crimes in either country may serve their prison terms in the other.

TELLO BARRAUD, MANUEL J. (1898–1971). Career diplomat. A lawyer from **Zacatecas**, he served at the **United Nations** and in Belgium, West Germany, and Japan, before becoming foreign minister, 1951–1952 and 1958–1964. In the intervening years (1952–1958) he was Mexican ambassador in Washington. In 1962 he resisted **Organization of American States** pressure on Mexico to break off diplomatic relations with **Cuba**.

TELLO MACIAS, CARLOS (1938–). Economist son of Manuel J. **Tello** with an economics MA from Cambridge University, England, and an MSc from Columbia. He worked successively for **Nacional Financiera**, the National Patrimony Ministry, and President **Díaz Ordaz**. In December 1976–November 1977 he was the first minister of planning and the budget, an office converted from the defunct Ministry of the **Presidency**.

TELMEX. Private corporation, the most profitable in Latin America, which since the 1991 **privatization** of *Telefonos de México* (whence the acronym by which it is known) has dominated Mexico's US\$ 12 billion telecommunications market, with a net profit in 2001 of 25 percent. This made it 13th in *Business Week*'s list of the top tech firms worldwide, controlling 97 percent of local **telephones**, 68 percent of the long distance market, and 58 percent of international calls. Its controlling shareholder is Carlos **Slim Heliú**. [L. H.]

TENOCH ("prickly pear"). The first known **tlatoani** of the **Aztec** nation, reigning 1325–1375, whence the gentilic **Tenochca**.

TENOCHCA. The people of **Tenoch**: the **Aztec** nation.

TENOCHTITLÁN ("prickly pear over rocks"—but perhaps just "city of the Tenochca"). The **Aztec** capital, founded in 1325 on an island in Lake **Texcoco** at 19°N, 99°W, renamed **Mexico City** after the conquest in 1521: the Spanish city was in effect built over the ruins of its predecessor, preserving much of its street layout. An unbelievably beautiful city which spread over 13 km^2 and attained an eventual population of 250,000. Situated in the center of Lake **Texcoco**, it could only be entered along four broad causeways. Anyone visiting the floating gardens of **Xochimilco** today will have an idea of what Tenochtitlán was like. It was a very clean city and enjoyed a high division of **labor** among its artisans. One of the more exotic handicrafts was the art of feather weaving, long since lost. An abundant **water** supply was brought in by ducts. This proved to be the city's undoing when the Spaniards cut off the water supply.

TEOCALLI. A pre-hispanic **Aztec** temple or shrine.

TEOTIHUACÁN. A pre-Hispanic city, 40 km (25 miles) northeast of **Mexico City**, which flourished 100 BC–750 AD. and whose remains draw foreign tourists from around the world. A religious and political center for a people descended from the **Olmec** Indians, who influenced succeeding **Toltec** and **Aztec** cultures. Its area covered 220 km^2 (85 square miles) and had a population of 50,000 (some sources suggest 200,000 at its apogee c.500 AD). Its north-south axis, called the Street of the Dead, is crossed at its center by an east-west axis. Its temple of **Quetzalcóatl** is known as *La Ciudadela* ("the citadel"). The largest structure is the Pyramid of the Sun, 60 m (200 ft.) high, with five concentric terraces to a top platform. Nearby is the smaller Pyramid of the Moon. The site has 4,000 apartment-like lime-plastered rooms.

TEPANEC. Indian group whose capital was **Azcapotzalco** until this was taken and destroyed by the **Aztecs** in 1428.

TEPEJUAN. Indian group in **Durango**, **Chihuahua**, and **Zacatecas**, whose early 17th century revolt was suppressed by **Viceroy** Diego **Fernández de Córdoba**. In the mid-1990s the group numbered about 17,600 people.

TEPIC. Capital city of **Nayarit** state, which before 1917 was the Territory of Tepic, badly damaged by Hurricane **Kenna**, October 25, 2002. Its municipal population in 2000 was 305,176.

TEPOZÓN, SIERRA DE. Branch of the Sierra **Madre** Oriental rising to the immediate northwest of **Mexico City**.

TEQUILA. A strong clear-colored alcoholic drink made by fermenting certain plants, especially **agave** (*maguey*) cactus, and traditionally drunk after squeezing lemon juice onto the tongue and then a little salt. It is named after a town in **Jalisco**, its supposed origin. It is the symbolic national drink of Mexico, and is closely related to the drinks **pulque** and **mezcal**.

TERCERMUNDISMO. In Mexican foreign policy terms, expressing sympathy and finding common cause with other countries of the "Third World," originally those developing countries not allied militarily with either any of the NATO countries or any of those of the Warsaw Pact.

TERRAZAS, EDUARDO (1936–). A painter born in **Guadalajara** who was a professor of architectonic design at Columbia University, 1963–1966, and has had many one-man exhibitions in Europe and the Americas. His works include *Danzantes* and *Arco iris*.

TERRAZAS, FRANCISCO DE (15??–????). The first poet born in **New Spain**. Most of his works are lost, but the epic poem *Nuevo mundo y conquista* ("New World and conquest") survives, as does the poem "Dejad las hebras de oro ensorijado" ("Leave behind the strands of woven gold").

TERREROS, PEDRO. Mine owner who reopened the Vizcaína vein in **San Luis Potosí** in 1762 and eventually made a multi-million dollar profit and was granted the title of Conde de Regla.

TERRITORIAL WATERS. *See* MARITIME SOVEREIGNTY.

TEXAS. The territory which eventually became known as Texas was sparsely populated when Spanish colonization of *La Provincia de los Tejas* began in 1716, to counter French penetration westward from **Louisiana**. The founding of **San Antonio** (de Béjar) followed in 1718. After Mexican **independence**, American Catholics were encouraged to settle there, but many who arrived were Protestants prepared to lie about their religion, and the Mexican government became apprehensive. In 1829 President Vicente **Guerrero** decreed the abolition of **African slavery**, a move specifically aimed at Texas, since slavery had disappeared from the rest of Mexico some time earlier. But this decree was as unenforceable as the religious requirement. By 1830 there were 25,000–30,000 Americans living in Texas, with their slaves. The government responded by forbidding further immigration and incorporating Texas into the state of **Coahuila**. Relations steadily worsened until, on March 3, 1838, a settlers' convention proclaimed Texan independence and war followed. Before the week was out, 300 Texans had died at the **Alamo**, but victory at **San Jacinto** not only secured Texan independence (which lasted until annexation by the United States in 1846 led to the **United States-Mexican War** of 1846–1848) but pushed the boundary westward beyond the **Nueces River** to the **Rio Grande**.

TEXCOCO (*Tezcoco,* or *Tetzcoco*). One of Mexico's oldest cities, founded c.1000. **Netzahualcóyotl** restored its importance in 1430, when its population reached 300,000. In **Mexico State**, it is the site of the **Universidad Autónoma Chapingo**. *See also* TRIPLE ALLIANCE.

TEXCOCO, LAKE. Home of the **Acolhuas** (or Texcocans) and the site of **Tenochtitlán** (now **Mexico City**), built on an island in its center. With the growth of the city, the lake has dried out and been wholly built over.

TEXTILES. Textile, particularly **cotton**, manufacture has been a feature of the Mexican **manufacturing industry** since the conquest **obraje**. [L. H.]

TEZOZÓMOC (13??–1427). Ruler of Azcapotzalco, 1348–1427, who in 1413 conquered **Texcoco**. Further conquests and the marriage of a daughter to **Huitzilíhuitl** gave him effective control over almost the whole of the Valley of Mexico.

THEATER. *See* DRAMA.

THIRD WORLD. *See* TERCERMUNDISMO.

THREE CULTURES PLAZA. *See* TLATELOLCO.

THREE YEARS' WAR. *See* REFORMS, WAR OF THE.

TIBURÓN. Mexico's largest island, in **Sonora** state, separated from the mainland at Punta Chueca by the Canal del Infiernillo. Discovered in 1540 by Fernando de Alarcón, it measures 50 km x 30 km: 1,208 km^2 and was made a nature reserve in 1963 and its indigenous **Seri Indians** removed. A breeding program, including mule deer, white-tailed deer and pronghorn antelopes, has been most successful with bighorn sheep (*borrego cimarón*), now numbering 650.

TIEMPO, EL. News magazine founded in 1942 by Martín Luis **Guzmán**, modelled on the American *Time*. The resemblance led to legal action which forced *Tiempo* to substitute the title *Hispano-Americano* for copies intended for circulation within the United States.

TIERRA BLANCA. Locality in **Chihuahua**, scene of a battle fought by Pancho **Villa** on January 11, 1914.

"TIERRA Y LIBERTAD" (**"land and freedom"**). The rallying cry of the forces of Emiliano **Zapata**.

TIJUANA. City of **Baja California del Norte**, isolated on the **United States** border, south of **San Diego**, **California**, to which it is closely tied economically. This explains the growth in the population of the **municipio** from 11,000 in 1930 to 22,000 in 1940; 65,000 in 1950; 166,000 in 1960; 341,000 in 1970; 462,000 in 1980; 747,000 in 1990; 1,045,415 in 1995; and 1,210,820 in 2000; accompanying a rise in San Diego County's population from 210,000 in 1930 to 2,690,255 in 1995. Tijuana's immediate cross-border neighbor is **San Ysidro**.

TIME ZONES. Mexican official time is 6 hours behind Greenwich Mean Time (i.e., it corresponds to North American Central Time) except in **Campeche**, **Quintana Roo**, and **Yucatán**, which are 5 hours behind GMT (= Eastern Time), and **Sonora** and **Baja California del Norte** which are 8 hours behind GMT (= Pacific Time). All zones advance an hour during Daylight Saving Time (*hora de verano*). [L. H.]

TITHES (*diezmos*). The Biblical levy of 10 percent on agricultural incomes was collected by the Spanish crown on the **Church**'s behalf as part of the **Patronato Real**. **Indians** were exempt in respect of traditional native crops, and lax enforcement often allowed them to escape any levy on any introduced crops, such as **wheat**, silk, or cattle. The annual collection in **New Spain** has been estimated at 1.8 million pesos.

TIZOC (**"wounded shin"**). Aztec "emperor" (**tlatoani**), 1481–1486 in succession to his brother **Axayácatl**, but supposedly poisoned for his cowardice by his chief general, **Tlacaélel**, and succeeded by **Ahuitzotl**.

TL. Digraph used when **Nahuatl** is written in Latin letters, for the voiceless surd consonant also found in Welsh, where it is spelled *ll*. [L. H.]

TLACAÉLEL. Aztec army commander through the reigns of **Axayácatl**, **Tizoc**, and **Ahítzotl**.

TLACOPAN. Municipio of **Veracruz** with 15,000 inhabitants in 1995, conquered by the Aztecs in 1475. It was occupied by the French, 1862–1865. In 1998 Unesco declared it a cultural patrimony of humanity.

TLÁLOC. Toltec god of rain and water, absorbed into the **Aztec** religion and surviving among some Indians under the guise of a Christian saint. It is also the name of a peak in the Sierra **Nevada**. His **Maya** equivalent was *Chac*.

TLATELOLCO, BATTLE OF. A small plaque commemorating the battle translates roughly as "What happened here was not a defeat, but the painful birth of what is today the Mexican nation."

TLATELOLCO, PLAZA DE ("Three Powers' Square"). Scene of riots led by Eduardo **Valle** in which several hundred students were killed in clashes with the police in October 2, 1968. The deaths were a great propaganda victory for the Left, especially when Octavio **Paz** resigned from his post as ambassador to India in protest. Foreign academics in particular have continued to portray the students (many as young as 16) as martyrs to government "brutality." Future President Miguel De La **Madrid**, then an **UNAM** law professor had detailed documentary proof that Mexican radicals had been assisted by 26 agents from **Cuba** in fomenting the riot. Marxists had helped enrage students into firing at the **police**, even, it was claimed, placing snipers on roof tops. It cannot be proved who attacked first, but snipers did kill police and troops in the front rank of those confronting the students, so triggering a massacre. The rioters' object had been to force a cancellation of the **Olympics**, but the sad affair ended just in time for the games to open.

De La Madrid tried several times to raise the question of outside provocation of the riot within the **Partido Revolucionario Institucional**, but the party preferred to hush it up for the good of harmony between political opponents. *See also* DIRTY WAR.

TLATELOLCO, TREATY OF. Nuclear Non-Proliferation Treaty of 1967, signed originally by Bolivia, **Brazil**, **Chile**, Ecuador, and Mexico, and later also by Colombia, Costa Rica, El Salvador,

Guatemala, Haiti, Honduras, Paraguay, **Peru**, Uruguay, Venezuela, Nicaragua, Trinidad, and Tobago.

TLATOANI ("he who speaks"). Supreme ruler of the **Aztec** nation, a title traditionally translated as "**emperor**." *See also* AZTEC EMPERORS.

TLAXCALÁ CITY. A picturesque small city at 19°31'N, 98°24'W, capital of **Tlaxcalá state**, famous for **textiles**, with a Church of St. Francis, built in 1521, claimed to be the oldest in Mexico. *Tlaxcala* is **Nahuatl** for "rocky place." Its population was 73,230 in 2000. It was the origin of what became the bishopric of **Mexico City**.

TLAXCALÁ STATE. An inland state of only 3,914 km², the smallest in the Republic, and one of the most densely populated and having 60 *municipios*, lying on the central Mexican plateau, east of the **Federal District**, with an average elevation of 2,500 m (7,000 ft). In its southern rim is the dormant Malinche volcano. Its **population** was 90,158 in 1857 and later 117,941. At successive **censuses** since then it has been 167,000 (1895); 172,000 (1900); 184,000 (1910); 179,000 (1921); 205,000 (1930); 224,000 (1940); 285,000 (1950); 347,000 (1960); 421,000 (1970); 557,000 (1980); 761,000 (1990); 962,646 (2000); and 1,068,027 (2005).

TLAXCALAN (*Tlaxcalteca*). Indian nation located east of the mountains around the Valley of **Mexico**, sometime allies of the **Aztec**, whose territory completely surrounded theirs. By the time of Hernán **Cortes'** arrival the Tlaxcalans had become enemies of the Aztec, and their leader, **Xicoténcatl**, allied them with the Spaniards, to whom their help proved crucial.

TLCAN. Acronym of *Tratado de Libre Comercio para América del Norte*, i.e., the **North American Free Trade Association**.

TOBACCO. Cultivation and consumption of the plant began in pre-Hispanic times. As a state monopoly, the colonial **estanco**, its sale became an important source of revenue. In present-day Mexico the industry is a duopoly of *La Moderna* (owned by British American

Tobacco) and *Cigatam* (jointly owned by Philip Morris and the Mexican Grupo Carso).

Government efforts to discourage smoking have included raising the **Impuesto Especial sobre Producción y Servicios** on cigarettes from 85 percent to 100 percent in 1999 and proposing a further increase in 2007 to 110 percent. [L. H.]

TOJOLABAL. Indian group of 22,000 in the mid-1990s, living in **Chiapas.**

TOLEDO, ANTONIO SEBASTIÁN DE, MARQUIS OF MANCERA (1608–1715). Viceroy of New Spain, 1663–1673. After diplomatic service in Venice and Vienna, Toledo was appointed viceroy in December 1662 and arrived in October 1664. The increase in Caribbean **piracy** made its suppression his primary task and obliged him to reorganize the **Windward Fleet.** Nine years later he was appointed viceroy of **Peru.** He then entered the service of the Queen Mother, Mariana of Austria. When it became clear that **Charles II** would die childless, he supported the Austrian candidate for the succession. At the last minute he changed his mind in 1700, convinced that the French candidate would better secure the continued unity of the Spanish empire, and played a decisive role in securing the throne for the Bourbon dynasty. [L. H.]

TOLOSA, JUAN DE. Spanish explorer who founded **Zacatecas City** and, with another explorer, Cristóbal de Oñate, discovered and developed the rich **silver** mines of the Zacatec Indians, making themselves the richest men in **New Spain.**

TOLSA, MANUEL (1755–1816). Spanish architect, sculptor, and dominant figure of his period. In 1790 he was named director of the recently formed **Academia de San Carlos,** and contributed his genius to the near completion of the façade of **Mexico City** cathedral. His most famous work is the equestrian statue of **Charles IV,** known as *El Caballito.*

TOLTEC INDIANS. Nahua-speaking creators in the 9th century of a pre-Hispanic civilization, radiating out from **Tula,** north of the Valley of Mexico. They worshiped **Quetzalcóatl.**

TOLUCA. Capital city of **Mexico state**. An industrial corridor runs from its suburbs to **Mexico City** (60 km away), with automobile and truck factories and related auto part plants, and, nearby, Almoloya de Juárez Maximum Security Prison. The city population was 149,000 in 1976; 415,000 in 1995; and 666,596 in 2000.

TONATIUH. Aztec god of the sun.

TOPOGRAPHY. Mexico was famously compared by Hernán **Cortes** to the Emperor **Charles V** with a crumpled piece of paper. Half of modern Mexico rises to over 975 m (3,200 feet) above sea level, with the terrain ranging from deserts to swamps. Much of central Mexico is the vast hilly Central Plateau between the coastal ranges of the Sierras **Madre** Oriental and Madre Occidental. (There is an obvious comparison with **Spain** itself, the highest country in Europe after Switzerland, with its own central plateau, the Castillian *meseta*.)

A consequence is demographic disequilibrium, significantly increased by **urbanization**, so that by the late 1970s, over half the **population** was living in less than 14 percent of the national territory. [L. H.]

TOPOLOBAMPO. Pacific coast port of **Sinaloa** at 25°35'N, 109°03'W.

TOPONYMS. Replacement of indigenous by Hispanic place names, and the contrary, has been irregular and subject to the vagaries of political fashion. Spelling has also varied (*See* J, X). Most places include a dedicatee in their full official form, e.g., **Cholula** "de Riva-davia" honoring the Argentine statesman. Geographical adjectives and gentilics are not always obvious: e.g., **Regiomontano** for an inhabitant of **Monterrey**. [L. H.]

TORRE, GERARDO DE LA (1938–). Novelist, journalist (and former baseball player) from **Oaxaca**: *Muertes de Aurora* (1980); *Los muchachos locos de aquel verano* (1994). [L. H.]

TORRE LATINOAMERICANO. The 45-story Latin American Tower in **Mexico City** was built in 1950 on innovative floating foundations for protection against **earthquakes**.

TORREÓN. Coahuila's second most populous city, 1,120 m above sea level, at 106°26'W, 25°32'N, and 265 km from **Saltillo**. It began in 1850 as the watchtower (*torreón*) of the Carrizal dam, was reached by a railroad in 1883, became a **villa** in 1893 and a **ciudad** in 1907. It has flour mills, **cotton** gins, chemical plants, **copper** smelters and the medical school of the **Universidad de Coahuila**. It serves as an industrial and trade center for the Laguna region of northern Mexico, including the state of **Durango**. Hydroelectric dams on the Nazas River allow **irrigation** of cotton and grapes. In the 1950s–1960s, 900 families from its **ejidos** were relocated in **Campeche state** following a lengthy drought.

The **municipio**, of 1,948 km², bordered by **Matamoros** and Durango state, had a population of 415,000 in 1995 and 529,093 in 2000.

TORRES BODET, JAIME (1902–1974). Diplomat, scholar, and statesman, born in **Mexico City**. In the 1920s he was professor of French literature at **UNAM**. He was education minister during the Manuel **Ávila Camacho** and Adolfo **López Mateos** presidencies, when he made successful efforts to focus attention on Mexico's educational shortcomings, particularly illiteracy and low teacher wages. He is regarded as one of Mexico's outstanding educators of the 20th century. Under Miguel **Alemán** he was foreign minister, and in 1948–52 he was director general of UNESCO.

TORRES MANZO, CARLOS (1923–). Economics graduate from **UNAM** who did graduate studies in the University of London and became economics professor at UNAM, 1955–1970. In 1964–1970 he was also director of the **Compañía Nacional de Subsistencias Populares**, formulating the policies for selling work clothes and non-food consumer goods to the poor in CONASUPO stores. In 1970–1974 he served as trade and industry minister, and in 1974–1980 as governor of his native **Michoacán**.

TORRES Y RUEDA, MARCOS DE (1588–1649). Viceroy of **New Spain**, 1648–1649. Already Bishop of **Yucatán**, he took up residence in **Tacubaya** on being informed of his appointment as the new viceroy. When, however, he entered **Mexico City** without informing the **audiencia** and before the **bastón** had been formally handed over to him, the *oidores* obliged him to go back to Tacubaya. Some months elapsed before he could take over. Then, less than a year later, he died in office.

TORTILLA. The traditional "bread" of Mexico and Central America, a thin pancake of **corn** meal, the food staple of **Indians** and **mestizo** peasants, eaten plain, or folded and filled with vegetables or chopped meat.

TOSCANA, DAVID (1961–). An industrial engineer turned novelist, from **Monterrey**, inspired by the classical Russians, the Chilean José Donoso, and Uruguayan Juan Carlos Onetti. His dark themes reflect the violence of northern Mexico but are never directly political. *Último lector* relates the death of a girl in a north Mexican ghost town. Among other works are *Las bicicletas* (1992), *Estación Tula* (1995), and *Duelo por Miguel Pruenda* (2002). [L. H.]

TOTONAC. An **Indian** group noted like the **Huastec** Indians for the flying pole dance (dancers descend from a pole whirling from ropes tied to their ankles. Found in **Veracruz** and **Puebla** states, they numbered 186,000 in 1995.

TOURISM. The tourist industry is Mexico's third largest source of foreign earnings (after **petroleum** and **manufacturing industry**) and it accounted in the early 1990s for 16 percent of all **foreign investment** (Mexico's 10,400 hotels now give it the world's seventh largest hotel industry). But although foreign tourism has been growing almost constantly, from US$ 6.3 billion in 1995 to US$ 10 billion in 2005, its relative share of world tourism declined from 1.7 percent in 1985 to 1.4 percent in 1994. In 2004 it had the world's 13th largest tourist industry. It is also overly dependent on economic conditions in the **United States** which supplies 70 percent of its visitors, declining markedly in the two years when American air travel dropped in the wake of the terrorist acts of September 11, 2001. It is also highly concentrated in a few preferred resorts: **Acapulco**, **Cancún**, **Puerta Vallarta**, and Los Cabos, plus a few towns on the border or near to it (**Tijuana**, **Ensenada**), the attractions being sand, surf, shopping, **sport fishing**, and archaeological sites. *See also* BULLFIGHTING. [L. H.]

TOURISM MINISTRY (*Secretaría de Turismo*). Charged with formulating a national tourist policy and supporting private business in the sector, it was created in 1975 when Julio Hirschfield Almada, then director of airports, was appointed the first tourism minister. [L. H.]

TOVAR [GARCÍA], RIGO (1946–2005). Popular singer and composer who combined rock with traditional Mexican music. Born in **Matamorros**, he achieved fame in Houston, Texas. [L. H.]

TOWNS AND CITIES. Mexico's most populous cities are currently **Mexico City, Nezhualcóyoti, Guadalajara, Monterrey, Puebla, León, Ciudad Juárez, Tijuana, Acapulco, Mérida,** and **Chihuahua.** *See also* CABILDO; CIUDAD; MUNICIPIO; URBANIZATION; VILLA.

TRADE. See CONTRABAND; FOREIGN TRADE; INTERNAL TRADE.

TRADE MINISTRY (*Secretaría de Comercio y Fomento Industrial*). A government reorganization of 1853 created a ministry of development, settlement, industry, and trade. Industry and trade were given their own separate ministry in 1917. In 1982 this became the *Secretaría de Comercio y Fomento Industrial*. It is now part of the **Economics Ministry.** [L. H.]

TRADE UNIONS. In Mexico, hundreds of unions federate within a pluralist system. There is a federation for federal government unions (**Federación de Sindicatos de los Trabajadores en Servicio del Estado, F.S.T.S.E.**) and one for state and municipal civil servants' unions (**Federación de Sindicatos de Trabajadores al Servicio de los Gobiernos de los Estados, Municipios y Instituciones Descentralizados de Caráter Estatal de la R.M.**). In the private sector, a majority of unions belong to the **Confederación de Trabajadores Mexicanos (CTM)**, but some belong to the **Confederación Revolucionario de Obreros y Campesinos (CROC)**, some to the **Confederación Regional Obrera Mexicana (CROM)**, and some are autonomous (e.g., the National Federation of Sugar Cane Workers).

In 1958 the CTM joined with some autonomous unions, such as those of the railroad and electricity workers into a **Bloque de Unidad Obrera**. A rival Mexican Workers' Bloc grouped together most electrical workers' unions, the CROC and the sugar cane workers' union. Since 1960 these two blocs have loosely cooperated through the annual conference of the **Congreso de Trabajo (Congress of Labor)**.

The influence of organized **labor** within Mexican government circles was weakened by the death of long time CTM leader Fidel **Velázquez Sánchez** in 1999. After some months of negotiations among labor leaders, the **Partido Revolucionario Institucional** expected that its labor sector would help the party retain its control of **Congress**, but even a parliamentary alliance with the **Partido de la Revolución Democrática** did not suffice.

TRANSPORT MINISTRY (*Secretaría de Comunicaciones y Transportes, S.C.T.*). A *Secretaría de Fomento, Colonización e Industria y Comercio* was set up in 1857. The **Second Empire** gave responsibility for navigation, **postal services**, and **railroads** to the *Departamento Ministerial de Fomento,* whose *Dirección de Puentes y Calzadas* looked after **highways** and bridges. From 1881 all these activities were passed to a new *Secteraría de Comunicaciones y Obras Públicas* (SCOP). This was briefly abolished by President Francisco **Madero** (who entrusted them to the *Secretaría de Gobernación*) but was revived by Victoriano **Huerta**. In 1958 SCOP was divided into a *Secretaría de Obras Públicas* and a *Secretaría de Comunicaciones y Transportes*. From 1976 to 1982 highways, bridges, harbor improvements, and airport construction were briefly entrusted to a separate ministry, the **Human Settlements Ministry**, *Secretaría de Asentamientos Humanos y Obras Públicas*, SAHOP. [L. H.]

TRANSPORTATION. *See* AIR TRANSPORT; FERRIES; GALLEON; HIGHWAYS; PORTERS; PORTS AND HARBORS; POSTAL SERVICE; RAILROADS; TREASURE FLEET.

TRANSPORTES AÉREOS EJECUTIVOS S.A. (TAESA). Mexico's third largest airline, founded in 1991 by **Air Force** veteran and airline captain Alberto Abad, as a small, but full-service airline, with some financing by Carlos **Hank Rohn**. It carried 1,980,000 passengers in its first year, and 2.6 million by 1994. Its non-union crews kept expenses down. The entire airline was grounded on November 25, 1999, following a crash two weeks earlier in which all those aboard died.

TRAVEN, B. (1882–1969). Principal pseudonym of Herman Otto Albrecht Max Feige, a leftist agitator and writer from Swiebodzin, the former Schwiebus in German Poland, who settled in Mexico in 1924, first in **Tampico**, then in **Acapulco**. A man of mystery whose colorful career included brushes with the police in **Germany**, **England**, and the **United States**, he wrote in German, English, and **Spanish**. He became most at home in the last, and his work is most appropriately classed in Mexican literature, especially as it is in Mexico that his quite enormous output has achieved the greatest popularity. For Americans he will be best remembered as Hal Croves, the name under which he befriended John Huston and helped him film *The Treasure of the Sierra Madre*. [L. H.]

TREASURE FLEET. The depredations of French **privateers** forced Spain, in 1543, to adopt the Venetian convoy system for all its transatlantic shipping. From 1561 the convoy to **Veracruz**, the *Flota de Nueva España*, left Seville regularly each August, and took a southerly route, to use the northeast trade winds and the north equatorial current. The following spring the returning fleet from Mexico would be joined at **Havana** by the fleet from Portobelo (Puerto Bello) to make the journey back through the **Florida Strait**, aided by the **Gulf Stream**. Although sailings in both directions were timed to avoid **hurricanes**, such disasters did occur, particularly in the Gulf of **Mexico**: in September 1552 (12 ships lost); in July 1574 (5 ships lost); September 1600 (17 ships lost); and October 1631 (19 ships lost). There was also an annual **Manila galleon**. The system ceased to be obligatory in 1765, but was not finally abandoned until 1789. [L. H.]

TREASURE OF THE SIERRA MADRE. Motion picture directed by John Huston, starring Humphrey Bogart, based on the novel by B. **Traven**.

TREASURY. *See* FINANCE MINISTRY.

TREATIES. *See* BRACERO TREATY; CHAPULTEPEC, ACT OF; GADESDEN PURCHASE; GUADALUPE-HIDALGO; INTER-AMERICAN TREATY OF MUTUAL ASSISTANCE; LIMITS, TREATY OF, 1820; MADRID; MCLANE-OCAMPO; NOOTKA; NORTH AMERICAN FREE TRADE ASSOCIATION; TLATE-LOLCO; TRIPLE ALLIANCE; UTRECHT; WARD, H. G.

TREES. The national tree is the cypress (*ahuehuete*). *See also* DEFOR-ESTATION; FLORA; FORESTS.

TRESGUERRAS, FRANCISCO (1758–1833). A renaissance man who excelled in many fields but was regarded as an outstanding sculptor and architect. His most famous buildings, in his favored neo-classical style, are the Church of Our Lady of Carmen in **Celaya** (1807) and the Alarcón Theater in **San Luis Potosí**.

TRES MARÍAS ISLANDS. Group of four (sic) islands of **Nayarit** state, lying in a northwest to southeast chain between 21°–22°N and 106°–107°W, some 100 km (60 miles) off the coast. Most are still uninhabited, but they provided a pirates' lair in colonial times. Maria Madre is used as a federal penitentiary, described in José **Revueltas'** *Los muros del agua*. Their vegetation is tropical dry deciduous and moist forest, home to the Tres Marias rabbit, abundant a century ago but now in serious decline from habitat loss, introduced predators (mainly rats), and rival herbivores (goats and deer). [L. H.]

TREVI, GLORIA (1970–). Mexican pop diva. In early December 2002 she lost her final appeal against extradition from Brazil to Mex-ico to face charges of kidnapping and corruption of minors. [L. H.]

TREVIÑO, [GENERAL] JACINTO B. (1883–1971). General of the **Revolution of 1910** who supported Álvaro **Obregón** and fought Pan-cho **Villa**. In 1918 he was trade, industry, and labor minister. For sup-porting the unsuccessful **Escobar rebellion**, he went into temporary exile in **Texas**. In 1940 he supported Juan **Almazán** for president. In 1954 he and General Juan **Barragán** founded the **Partido Auténtico de la Revolución Mexicana**.

TRIPLE ALLIANCE (*Triple Alianza*). The alliance forged by **Aztec** *tlatoani* **Itzcóatl** with **Tlacopan** and the **Acolhuas**, definitively from 1428, which came, under Aztec leadership, to dominate central Mexico until the arrival of the Spaniards almost a century later.

TRIQUE INDIANS. A "tribe" originating in the **Oaxaca** highlands and renowned for their **textiles**, but found as itinerant farm workers all over Mexico. One group is settled near **Hermosillo, Sonora**. [L. H.]

TRIUMVIRATE. The brief joint executive of Pedro Vélez, Luis Quintanr, and Luis **Alemán** that exercised power in 1829, prior to the installation of Anastacio **Bustamante**.

TROTSKY, LEON (1879–1940). The former Bolshevik leader, expelled from the **Soviet Union** in 1927, had difficulty in finding political asylum until General Francisco José **Múgica** helped him settle in Mexico, where he stayed with Diego **Rivera** and Frida **Kahlo**, 1937–1939. Soon after moving into a house of his own, he was murdered by a Soviet agent. Russian responsibility for this was finally conceded in late 2006. Trotsky's relationship with **Kahlo** is the theme of a novel.

TRUEBA URBINA, ALBERTO (1903?–1984). Law professor at **UNAM**, 1937–1945; a member of the **Cámara de Diputados Federales**; governor of his native **Campeche**, 1955–1961; and attorney general of **Yucatán**. He became nationally known as author of the leading textbook on constitutional law and was for many years legal adviser to Mexican presidents, **labor** leaders, and cabinet ministers.

TUBOS DE ACERO DE MÉXICO (TAMSA). An **iron and steel** producer, established at **Veracruz** in 1955 by private investors (Mexican at first, subsequently joined by Italians and French) to manufacture steel tubes. It was then Mexico's fourth largest steel corporation, and in 1958 began ingot steel production.

TULA. Archaeological site of **Hidalgo state**, ancient capital of the **Toltec Indians** in pre-Aztec Mexico, until its fall in 1168.

TULANCINGO. City of **Hidalgo state** at 20°14'N, 98°13'W, 2,180 m above sea level, with truck and railroad boxcar manufacturing, officially Tulancingo de Bravo. The **municipio**, created in 1869, is the second city of its state, with an area of 290 km² and a population in 2000 of 122,274.

TUNA. Economically, the second most important sector of the Mexican **fishing** industry. Following the replacement of baitboats with purse seiners using nets in the late 20th century, annual catches in the eastern tropic Pacific grew from 40,000 t to 120,000 t and are currently around 140,000 t. They are hampered by the **United States** embargo on Mexican tuna, ostensibly introduced to protect dolphins from being caught in unsuitable nets, which the Mexican government has outlawed and is seeking to eradicate. *See also* SPORT FISHING. [L. H.]

TUXLA GUTIÉRREZ. Capital city of **Chiapas**, and agricultural and commercial center with a population of 74,887 in 1976; 120,887 in 1995; and 424,579 (of a municipal total of 434,143) in 2000.

TUXPAN. River of **Veracruz-Llave** and city, 11 km from its mouth, at 20°57'N, 97°24'W, a **Huastec** settlement of 1500 B.C., conquered by Hernán **Cortes** in 1522. It became a **villa** in 1830, was transferred from **Puebla** to Veracruz in 1853 and made a city (**ciudad**) in 1881. In 1955 it became officially Tuxpan de **Rodríguez Cano**. The municipal population in 2000 was 126,616 and that of the city, 93,531. It is the nearest major port to **Mexico City**, the nation's 11th biggest overall in cargo handled, but its fourth largest **petroleum** port. [L. H.]

TUXTEPEC, PLAN OF. Porfirio **Díaz**'s proclamation of January 1, 1876, signalling the start of a revolt against President Sebastián **Lerdo de Tejada** by calling for his resignation ("**Effective Suffrage and no re-election**"). Díaz was finally successful toward the end of 1876 and was installed as constitutional president in 1877.

T.V. AZTECA. *See* AZTECA T.V.

TWELTH NIGHT. Epiphany, known as the *Dia de los Reyes*, is a widely, but unofficially, observed public holiday. It is the subject of an essay by Octavio **Paz** and the theme of several English-language novels. [L. H.]

TWENTIETH OF NOVEMBER. *See* REVOLUTION DAY.

TYPHUS. This louse- or flea-borne fever was the probable cause of the Mexican epidemic of the so-called **matlazáhuatl** in 1545–1547, whose death toll among an already weakened Indian population may have been the highest of all early post-conquest afflictions. There were subsequent outbreaks in 1576, in **Guatemala** in 1607–1608, in Central Mexico in 1631–1632, and in Mexico in 1736–1739. [L. H.]

TZELTAL. Mexico's sixth largest **Indian** nation, numbering 212,000 (1995 estimate) in **Chiapas**.

– U –

U-BOATS. Shipping losses to German submarines in the Gulf of Mexico were a major factor in Mexican entry into **World War II**. In 1942–1943 a fleet of 24 U-boats sank some 70 ships. During May 1942 before the convoy system was generally adopted, almost one ship a day was lost. Mexico contributed a squadron of aircraft for anti-submarine patrol. [L. H.]

UGARTE Y LOYOLA, JACOBO DE (17??–1798). Commandant general of the Western Provinces (the future Estado del **Occidente**), with direct control of **Arizona**, **New Mexico**, both **Californias**, and **Sonora**, 1786–1789, who led a punitive expedition against the **Apache Indians** in 1788–1789. [L. H.]

ULÚA. *See* SAN JUAN DE ULÚA.

UNAM. Acronym of the *Universidade Nacional Autónoma de México,* (National Autonomous University of Mexico), the post-1929 successor of the Papal **University of Mexico**. In 1952 it moved from its crowded colonial buildings scattered in downtown **Mexico City** to a vast new campus, **Ciudad Universitaria**, 11 miles to the south, adjacent to the suburb of Pedregal. It is noted for its modern architecture, colorful murals across high-rise buildings, and Olympic-sized swimming and track facilities. Since about that time however, radical leftist-led **student federations** and **trade unions** of both teaching and non-teaching staff have plagued UNAM with many serious strikes. By the 1960s, enrollment exceeded 100,000, making its administration unwieldy. In 1975 the rectorship of medical professor Dr. Guillermo Soberón was notable for its success in reducing tensions and work stoppages. In the late 1970s, **women**, for the first time, made up 10 percent of its faculty. These included four deans, the directors of the National School of Economics, the Hospital Administration Institute of the medical school, and the Graphic Design Institute. Until the 1982–1988 presidency of Miguel de la **Madrid**, it was almost unknown for someone not a UNAM graduate to rise high enough in government office to reach cabinet rank, Guillermo **Grimm González** from the **Universidad Iberoamericana** being one of the first.

[The London *Times* world list of research universities ranked UNAM at 95th position in 2005 and 74th in 2006 and as first in Latin America in both years. L. H.]

UNAM STUDENT RIOTS OF 1968. A large group of leftist students encouraged by José **Revueltas** tried unsuccessfully to force the government to postpone holding the 1968 **Olympic Games** in **Mexico City**. The demonstrations and riots lasted from July 26 until October 2, when at least 200 were gunned down in **Tlatelolco Square**, allegedly after roof-top snipers had first fired on the **police**.

UNAM STUDENT RIOTS OF 1975. During a violent demonstration over policy matters, a Marxist student group leader hit President **Echeverría** on the head with a stone. [L. H.]

UNAM STUDENT STRIKE OF 1999. A university administration plan announced in February 1999 to introduce tuition fees led to a long student strike, culminating in the Mumia **Abu-Jamal** riots, and resolved when the **police** stormed the University, February 7, 2000. [L. H.]

UNDERGROUND ECONOMY. *See* INFORMAL ECONOMY.

UNEMPLOYMENT. *See* EMPLOYMENT.

UNIÓN GENERAL DE OBREROS Y CAMPESINOS DE MÉXICO (UGOCM). General Union of Mexican Workers and Peasants formed by Vicente **Lombardo Toledano** and other members of the **Partido Popular Socialista** and led by Jacinto **López**.

UNIÓN LIBERAL. A political party formed in 1892 for the purpose of legitimizing the **Porfiriato** and dispelling the belief that it was a one-man regime. No other **political parties**, however, were tolerated.

UNIÓN NACIONAL DE TRABAJADORES. The "National Workers' Union," a confederation of **trade unions** formed November 28, 1997.

UNIÓN SINARQUISTA NACIONAL. A fascist movement founded in 1937 by Helmut Oscar **Schreiter** and José Ángel **Urquista**, whose title "without anarchy" indicates its strong right-wing law and order program. Its rise paralleled Nazi success in Europe, 1939–1943. Although it had by the end of **World War II** ceased to pose any serious threat to Mexican institutions and had too few members to register as a recognized political party, its Director General Ignacio **González Gollaz**, ran in the presidential **election of 1982**.

UNIONS. *See* TRADE UNIONS.

UNITED KINGDOM, RELATIONS WITH. Great Britain used its *Asiento de negros* privilege to supply slaves to the **Indies** (granted by the Treaty of **Utrecht**), to engage in **contraband**, at the same time as it permitted logging along the Caribbean coast of Central America. The **American Revolutionary War** proved only a temporary check to its power. Its refusal (from fear of the consequent interruption of its Latin American trade) to back the post-1815 "Holy Alliance" of European monarchies' plans to intervene in the Americas on behalf of **Ferdinand VII** was, however, a key factor in the success of the continent's struggle for **independence**. Later, it mediated, unfavorably to

Mexico, to end the **Pastry War**, and then, like **Spain**, it took aggressive action in support of **French intervention** following the **Foreign Debt Moratorium** of 1861. It desisted as soon as it became clear that **France** was intent on imposing a regime change on Mexico. Thenceforward, however, it permitted the **United States** to achieve preeminence in the Western Caribbean and Central America. Relations with Mexico deteriorated again when the 1938 nationalization of the **petroleum industry** involved the seizure of Britain's principal investments in Mexico. *See also* CAMACHO, SEBASTIAN; ENGLAND. [L. H.]

UNITED NATIONS. Participation on the winning side in **World War II** gave Mexico, a member of the pre-war **League of Nations**, foundation membership in its replacement organization, whose agencies include the **Economic Commission for Latin America** and the **International Labour Organisation**.

UNITED STATES, DIPLOMATIC RELATIONS WITH. Joel Roberts Poinsett was appointed first U.S. envoy to Mexico in 1825 (*See* UNITED STATES AMBASSADORS). The Conservative regime broke off diplomatic relations in 1858, and U.S. envoy Robert **McLane** advised supporting Benito **Juárez** (*See* TEHUANTEPEC ISTHMUS). This meant that the United States would withhold recognition from the **Second Empire**. Later, President Woodrow **Wilson** actively intervened to topple Victoriano **Huerta** (*See* TAMPICO INCIDENT). The U.S. government's sending aircraft to assist in suppressing the **Escobar rebellion** in 1929 is taken as marking the renewal of friendly relations after the **Revolution of 1910**. The signing of the 1993 agreement to establish the **North American Free Trade Association** has been seen as the first step toward the greater economic integration of the Americas. [L. H.]

UNITED STATES, ECONOMIC RELATIONS WITH. American capital supplanted British as Mexico's chief source of foreign investment toward the end of the 19th century. At the end of the 20th century, the United States was buying 85 percent of Mexico's exports and supplying 74.5 percent of her imports. Since 1994 the two countries' economies have been linked in the **North American Free Trade Association (NAFTA/TLCAN)**. [L. H.]

UNITED STATES, POLITICAL RELATIONS WITH. New Spain was involved in the liberation of Florida during the **American Revolutionary War**, was forced by Napoleon I to surrender Louisiana, which he then sold to the **United States**, and was involved in a long subsequent struggle over what is now the American Southwest, leading to the separation of Texas from Mexico and culminating in the **United-States Mexican War** and the **Gadsden Purchase**. U.S. support for Benito **Juárez** played a key role in the overthrow of the **Second Empire**. Intervention during the **Revolution of 1910** (*See* EMBASSY PACT; NIAGARA CONFERENCE; PERSHING, JOHN JOSEPH; VERACRUZ CITY; WILSON, WOODROW) was ultimately ineffective except in increasing Mexico's traditional fear of U.S. foreign policy. Nationalization of the foreign owned **petroleum** industry was a bone of contention in the 1930s.

Mexican **labor** has become essential to the U.S. economy, particularly in **agriculture**, but it has led to long-standing problems over illegal **migration**. There are also chronic problems over **contraband**, especially of **narcotics**. Mexico's idealistic approach to foreign relations has also produced friction: in relation to the **Spanish Civil War**, the Cuban revolution, and the overthrow of governments seen as unfavorable to U.S. interests (e.g., those of Arbenz in **Guatemala**, Allende in **Chile**, Ortega in Nicaragua), or their ostracism (Castro's **Cuba**). [L.H.]

UNITED STATES AMBASSADORS.
Envoy Extraordinary and Minister Plenipoteniary
Joel Roberts **Poinsett**, March 8, 1825–1829

Chargés d'affaires
Anthony Butler, October 12, 1829–1836
Powhatan Ellis, January 5, 1836–1839

Envoys Extraordinary and Ministers Plenipoteniary
Powhattan Ellis, February 15, 1839–1842
Waddy Thompson, February 2, 1842–1844
Wilson Shannon, April 9, 1844–1845
John Slidell, November 19, 1845–1848
Nathan Clifford, July 28, 1848–1849
Robert P. Letcher, August 9, 1849–1852

Alfred Conkling, August 6, 1852–1853
James **Gadsden**, May 24, 1853–1856
John Forsyth, July 21, 1856–1859
Robert M. McLane, March 7, 1859–1860
John B. Weller, November 17, 1860–1861
Thomas Corwin, March 22, 1861–1866
Lewis D. Campbell, May 4, 1866–1867
Marcus Otterbourg, April 1, 1867–1868
William S. Rosecrans, July 27, 1868–1869
Thomas H. Nelson, April 16, 1869–1873
John Watson Foster, March 17, 1873–1880
Philip H. Morgan, January 26, 1880–1885
Thomas C. Manning, August 30, 1886–1888
Edward S. Bragg, January 16, 1888–1889
Thomas Ryan, March 30, 1889–1893
Isaac P. Gray, March 20, 1893–1895
Matt W. Ranson, February 28, 1895–1897
Powell Clayton, March 22, 1897–1898

Ambassadors
Powell Clayton, December 8, 1898–1905
Edwin H. Conger, March 8, 1905–1906
David E. Thompson, January 24, 1906–1909
Henry Lane **Wilson**, December 21, 1909–February 18, 1913

Chargé d'affaires
Nelson O'Shaughnessy

Special Representatives of the U.S. President
John R. Silliman
James Lynn Rogers
Duval West
George Caruthers
León Canova
John Lind

Ambassadors
Henry P. Fletcher, February 25, 1916–1924
Charles Beecher Warren, February 29–September, 1924

James Rockwell **Sheffield**, September 9, 1924–1927
Dwight W. **Morrow**, September 21, 1927–1930
J. Reuben Clark Jr., October 3, 1930–1933
Josephus **Daniels**, March 17, 1933–1941
George S. Messersmith, December 4, 1941–1946
Walter Thurston, May 4, 1946–1950
William O'Dwyer, September 20, 1950–1952
Francis White, May 11, 1953–1957
Robert C. Hill, May 20, 1957–1960
Thomas C. Mann, April 18, 1961
Fulton Freeman, May 4, 1964–1969
Robert H. McBride, June 13, 1969–January 19, 1974
Joseph J. Jova, December 19, 1973–February 21, 1977
Patrick J. Lucey, May 26, 1977–October 31, 1979
Julian Nava, April 3, 1980–April 3, 1981
John A. Gavin, May 7, 1981–June 10, 1986
Charles J. Pilliod Jr., October 16, 1986–April 7, 1989
John D. Negroponte, June 15, 1989–September 5, 1993
James Robert Jones, August 9, 1993–June 25, 1997

Chargé d'Affaires
Charles Ray, June 1997–August 1998

Ambassadors
Jeffrey Davidow, June 29, 1998–September 14, 2002
Antonio O. Garza Jr., November 12, 2002–

UNITED STATES BORDER. The current border totals 3,118 km, whereof 2,575 km are marked by the **Rio Grande**. U.S. concern at increasing illegal border crossing led Congress in late 2005 to propose the building of a 1,130 km long fence, dubbed a "high tech border surveillance structure," signed into law by President Bush in October 2006. *See also* EMIGRATION; MEXICO SEGURO; PROGRAMA NACIONAL FRONTERIZO. [L. H.]

UNITED STATES INTERVENTION. The United States gave arms and other help to Benito **Juárez** well beyond that strictly permitted by law, so ensuring the downfall of the **Second Empire**. *See also*

DOLPHIN, USS; EMBASSY PACT; ESCOBAR REBELLION, 1929; PERSHING, JOHN JOSEPH; VERACRUZ CITY; WILSON, WOODROW. [L. H.]

UNITED STATES–MEXICAN WAR (1846–1848). The *Guerra Mexicano-Norteamericana*, the most disastrous foreign war in Mexican history, resulting in humiliating peace terms that included the loss of the **Far North**, amounting to over half the national territory (albeit the least populated part). Nationalist fervor was a key factor in both countries: "Manifest Destiny" was a popular conception in the United States, while some Mexicans fondly believed that their troops could soon be in Washington, DC. President **Polk** reacted to Mexican protests at the US annexation of **Texas** by dispatching troops to the area between the Nueces and **Rio Grande** Rivers. Mutual declarations of war followed. The United States army conquered northern Mexico as far as **Saltillo**, and also invaded the interior of Mexico through the port of **Veracruz City**. *See also* CHAPULTEPEC, BATTLE OF; SANTA ANNA AND ANTONIO LÓPEZ DE.

UNIVERSAL, El. **Mexico City** daily newspaper, in the mid-20th century second only to *Excélsior* as Mexico's prestige daily, it was owned by the heirs of the Lanz Duret family, who epitomized editorial neutrality. It was acquired in February 1976 by the Organización Editorial Mexicana, immediately after President **Echeverría** had acquired a major stockholding in the latter. Founded in 1916, it is Mexico City's oldest existing daily.

UNIVERSIDAD AUTÓNOMA CHIPANGO (UACh). Established in **Texcoco** on the former **hacienda** of Chipango in 1978. It took over the *Escuela Nacional de Agricultura* of 1916 which had moved there in 1923 and had been founded originally in 1853 as the *Colegio Nacional de Agricultura*—National Agriculture College.

UNIVERSIDAD AUTÓNOMA DE AGUASCALIENTES (UAA). The Autonomous University of **Aguascalientes** created June 1973 by transformation of the *Instituto Autónomo de Ciencias y Tecnología,* a secondary and pre-university institution originally established in 1867 as the state government's *Escuela de Agricultura.*

UNIVERSIDAD AUTÓNOMA DE CAMPECHE (UAC; UACAM). The intended *Universidad de Campeche* was inaugurated by the state government, August 7, 1964, as the *Universidad del Sudeste*. It received its current name October 20, 1989.

UNIVERSIDAD AUTÓNOMA DE GUADALAJARA (UAG). The Autonomous (private) University of **Guadalajara** was founded in 1935 and is reputed academically superior to the older **Universidad de Guadalajara**.

UNIVERSIDAD AUTÓNOMA DE NUEVO LEÓN (UANL). The **Church** established chairs of philosophy and grammar in **Nuevo León** in 1703 but secular higher education in the state began with the 1859 foundation of a *Colegio Civil*. The present institution derives from the 1933 establishment of a *Universidad de* **Monterrey**, soon renamed the *Universidad de Nuevo León*, with 218 staff teaching 1,864 students. A university city was constructed for it in 1958 in the Monterrey suburb of San Nicolás de la Garza. Agitation against state government interference secured its autonomy as the UANL in 1971. It currently has 13 departments, and 8 branch campuses outside the state capital, and its 56,500 students account for nearly 95 percent of all higher education students in Nuevo León. *See also* LIVAS VILLARREAL, EDUARDO. [L. H.]

UNIVERSIDAD AUTÓNOMA DE SAN LUIS POTOSÍ (UASLP). Formerly the *Instituto Científico y Literario*, itself based on a Jesuit College established in 1624. It received its present title in 1923.

UNIVERSIDAD AUTÓNOMA DE YUCATÁN (UADY). A *Colegio de San Francisco Javier*, established by Jesuits in **Mérida** in 1611, became in 1624 the *Real y Pontificia Universidad de San Javier*, only to almost disappear when its staff of eight all died of the **plague** in 1648. When the Jesuits were expelled in 1767, higher education in **Yucatán** became the responsibility of the *Seminario Cibcukuar de San Ildefonso*, founded in 1751, to which was added a *Universidad Literaria* in 1824. Secularization produced the *Colegio Civil Universitario* in 1862, and in 1867 the *Instituto Literario del Estado*, forerunner of the *Universidad Nacional del Sureste* of 1922, which in 1938 became the *Universidad de Yucatán*. The present title was granted in September 1984. [L. H.]

UNIVERSIDAD AUTÓNOMA DEL ESTADO DE HIDALGO. Originating in **Pachuca** 1725 as a **Church** foundation, it became the *Instituto Científico y Literario* in the 1860s, and achieved its current status in 1961. [L. H.]

UNIVERSIDAD AUTÓNOMA METROPOLITANA (UAM). A self-governing, federally financed university established in **Mexico City** in the 1970s to relieve the pressure on **UNAM** of its enormous enrollment.

UNIVERSIDAD DE GUADALAJARA (UDG). Founded 1792, it is now a foundation of the State of **Jalisco**.

UNIVERSIDAD DE LAS AMÉRICAS (UDLA). *See* UNIVERSITY OF THE AMERICAS.

UNIVERSIDAD DE MICHOACÁN. *See* UNIVERSIDAD MICHOACANA DE SAN NICOLÁS DE HIDALGO.

UNIVERSIDAD DE MONTERREY (UDEM). (1) Previous name of the **Universidad Autónoma de Nuevo León**.
(2) A Catholic university established in the city of **Monterrey**, June 8, 1968.

UNIVERSIDAD DE PUEBLA. The origins of what is now the *Benemérita Universidad Autónoma de Puebla* (BUAP) go back to the Jesuit *Colegio del Espíritu Santo* of April 15, 1587, abolished when the order was expelled in 1767 but resurrected in 1790 as the *Colegio Carolino* (named for King **Charles III**). The order's return in 1820 led to a brief name change back to *Real Colegio del Espíritu Santo*, but it was expelled again in 1821 and the college renamed *Imperial Colegio del Espíritu Santo*. On the downfall of the **First Empire**, it became the

Colegio del Estado, a title retained until 1937 when it became the *Universidad de Puebla*. Its autonomy was granted in 1956 and the honorific *"benemérito"* bestowed in 1987. Until the 1960s it was Puebla's only institution of higher education. It currently has 40,600 students (including 1,770 graduate students), a teaching staff of 3,260 (including 140 full-time professors), and 120 departments. [L. H.]

UNIVERSIDAD DE SAN NICOLÁS DE MICHOACÁN. *See* UNIVERSIDAD MICHOACANA DE SAN NICOLÁS DE HIDALGO.

UNIVERSIDAD DE SONORA (UNISON). The committee to form the state university in **Hermosillo** was set up in August 1938, and the first rector appointed from 1942. There are now six faculties and four local campuses.

UNIVERSIDAD DE TRABAJADORES. Workers' University, established in **Mexico City** by Vicente **Lombardo Toledano**.

UNIVERSIDAD IBEROAMERICANA (UIA). Name of several institutions in Mexico and elsewhere of which the most important is a **Jesuit** university, founded in **Mexico City**.

UNIVERSIDAD JUÁREZ DEL ESTADO DE DURANGO (U.J.E.D.). The former *Seminario Conciliar* was secularized in the 1850s as the *Colegio Civil del Estado* and renamed on the death of Benito Juárez, the *Instituto Juárez*. In 1938 it became a branch campus of the **Universidad de México**, but was reestablished as an independent institution under its present name in 1957 by Francisco **González de la Vega**.

UNIVERSIDAD MICHOACANA DE SAN NICOLÁS DE HIDALGO. State university founded in what is now **Morelia** in 1538 as the **Colegio de San Nicolás Obispo**, which thus predates the **University of Mexico** and was already a prestigious institution in colonial times.

On October 2, 1966, a student from **Guerrero** was briefly arrested for leading a large group protesting the administration's increase in tuition fees from a token two pesos to 50 pesos per semester. The city then raised bus fares on all routes leading to the university and a demonstration led by the same student closed down the campus. This student was then shot dead by the police, provoking a riot in which dozens of police and students were wounded. President **Díaz Ordaz** had his interior minister send in troops to occupy the university and to announce the rector's resignation. The state governor, Agustín Arriága Rivera, claimed he learned of this over the radio when paratroopers had already been sent in to assist the police, but he got no media attention until all was a fait accompli.

UNIVERSIDAD NACIONAL AUTÓNOMA DE MÉXICO (**"National Autonomous University of Mexico"**). The full name of **UNAM**.

UNIVERSIDAD PEDAGÓGICA NACIONAL (**"national university of pedagogy,"** UPN). Created in **Mexico City** by presidential decree in 1978 to train primary school teachers. There are institutions with the same title in Bogotá (Colombia), and in Honduras.

UNIVERSIDAD VERACRUZANA (UV). A major Mexican university, created by the state of **Veracruz-Llave** in **Jalapa** in 1944. It has branch campuses in **Veracruz City**, **Oatzacoalcos**. **Orizaba**, and Poza Rica. [L. H.]

UNIVERSITIES. *See* HIGHER EDUCATION.

UNIVERSITY OF MEXICO. Founded 1553 as the *Real y Ponticia Universidad de México* following a royal decree of 1551 which also authorized the *Universidad de San Marcos* in Lima. Ever since, the two universities have disputed their primacy as the first university in the New World. Despite its **Church** origins, the University of Mexico was distrusted during the 1800s by most conservative regimes and suffered closure in 1833, 1857, 1861, and 1865. During the **Porfiriato**, the now "National" institution (*Universidad Nacional de México*) suspended most operations, but it was reopened in 1910 by education minister Justo **Sierra Méndez**. On May 1, 1917, it was revived by President Venustiano **Carranza** who appointed lawyer-educator Natividad Macías as rector to expand all professional courses. In the 1920s, José **Vasconcelos** helped upgrade the programs. On July 10, 1929, President Emilio **Portes Gil** had Congress pass a law separating the University from the **Education Ministry**, so creating the present autonomous **UNAM**.

UNIVERSITY OF THE AMERICAS (*Universidad de las Americas*). The name of two independent, privately owned universities, both of which teach in English as well as in Spanish.

(1) That in **Mexico City** has some American professors, a few Canadians, but mostly Mexicans. It offers courses in English and Spanish to mostly Mexican students.

(2) The older establishment (also *Americarum Universitas*), originally opened in Mexico City in 1940 by Professor Paul Murray as the Mexico City College, acquired in 1968 the extensive Hacienda Santa Catarina Mártir in San Andrés Cholua (just outside the town of **Cholula**, 11 km north of **Puebla** City) where it now functions. Although it increased its proportion of Mexican students in the 1970s, it still draws hundreds of students from the **United States**, Canada, and elsewhere abroad. Its programs follow the semester-hour or quarter-hour concept of North American institutions.

UNO MÁS UNO. Newspaper established by staffers purged by Luis **Echeverría** in July 1976 from *Excelsior*, in order to preserve an editorial voice independent of the Echeverristas. By late 1979 it had built a circulation among readers seeking news from a moderate liberal reform viewpoint.

UPPER CALIFORNIA. Usual English translation of **Alta California**.

URAGA, [GENERAL] JOSÉ L. Chosen in 1853 by President Mariano **Arista** to defend the government, he switched his support to López de **Santa Anna**. In 1860 his rebel forces were defeated by conservatives led by Miguel **Miramón**. In 1864 he assumed command of an army supporting Benito **Juárez**, but when faced in western Mexico with superior numbers of French troops, he defected to support **Maximilian**, ending his career in disgrace when Juárez eventually triumphed.

URBANIZATION. More than half of all Mexicans live in less than 14 percent of the national territory—the Valley of **Mexico**, with industrial payrolls overwhelmingly bunched in the metropolitan areas of **Mexico City**, **Monterrey**, and **Guadalajara**, despite government programs to encourage the decentralization of **manufacturing industry**. Central Mexico alone has 10 cities with populations of 300,000 or more.

In 1900, 80 percent of the **population** were rural or small-town residents; in 1910, 71 percent; in 1930, 67 percent; in 1980, 34 percent; and in 2000, only 20 percent. Of the urban majority, 25 percent now crowd into the three great conurbations just cited. *See also* INTERNAL MIGRATION; TOWNS AND CITIES.

URBINA, LUIS GONZAGA (1864–1934). Poet and journalist, a close friend of **Gutiérrez Nájera** and admirer of Justo **Sierra Méndez**. His 2-volume *Antología del centenario* (1910), planned in cooperation with Sierra, is still regarded as a masterpiece of literary research. Exiled by the **Revolution of 1910**—he did not return until 1920—he continued to write and publish. His more famous poems are "Lámparas en agonía," and "El Poema de Mariel."

URBINA, [GENERAL] TOMÁS (1877–1915). A cattle rustler in **Chihuahua** who in 1914 became executive officer for his **compadre** Pancho **Villa's División del Norte**. In late 1915 he deserted, taking the army payroll, which was never recovered although he himself was captured and executed.

URBINA Y FRIAS, SALVADOR (1885–1963). Lawyer who became attorney general for **Carranza** in 1914, and a justice of the **Supreme Court**, 1923–1935 and 1940–1951, serving as chief justice, 1941–1951.

URDIÑOLA, FRANCISCO DE (1532–1618). Spanish colonizer who had extensive holdings in Parras, **Coahuila**, and was one of the first to develop a wine industry in **New Spain**.

URQUIZA, JOSÉ ÁNGEL. One of the two organizers of the **Unión Sinarquista Nacional.**

URROZ, ELOY (1967–). Novelist born in New York City and currently professor of Spanish and Latin American literature at James Madison University, Virginia, claiming García Márquez and Juan Rulfo as his chief influences: *Las Remoras* (1996), *Herir tu fiera* (1997), *Las almas abatidas* (2000). [L. H.]

URUAPÁN. Town and second most populous **municipio** of **Michoacán** with 265,699 inhabitants in 2000.

URUCHURTU, ERNESTO P. (1906–1997). Lawyer from **Hermosilla** who became a justice of the **Sonora** supreme court, then legal adviser to the agriculture ministry and the **Banco Nacional de Crédito Ejidal**; assistant interior minister, 1946–1951; and interior minister, 1951–1952. In 1952 he became **governor** of the **Federal District**. He remained in office until 1966, when, largely thanks to Gonzalo **Martínez Corbala**, he was forced to resign for an overly extensive slum clearance and street-widening project which yielded high profits for the powerful élite, but left thousands of slum dwellers homeless. He was officially charged with maladministration and failing to rehouse those whose homes were demolished.

USIGLI, RODOLFO (1905–1979). Mexico's leading 20th-century playwright, born November 17. His more than 40 plays included *Medio tono* (1937), *La Mujer no hace milagros* (1939), and *La Familia cena en casa* (1942). His *El Gesticulador* (1937) was the first satirical play about the leaders of the **Revolution of 1910**. His *Corona de sombras*, translated as *Crown of Shadows* (1947) dealt with the tragedy of the Empress **Carlota**, his *Corona de fuego* (1661) with **Aztec** rulers, and his *Corona de luz* (1965) with Saint **Mary of Guadalupe**. His *El Niño y la niebla*, *A dónde van nuestras hijas*, and *Obras primaveras* were also made into films. His novel *Ensayo de un crimen* appeared in 1944. Between 1944 and 1973 he held intermittent diplomatic posts, including ambassadorships to Norway, Lebanon, and Belgium, and other posts in **France** and the **United Kingdom**. He died in his native **Mexico City** on June 18.

U.S.S.R. *See* SOVIET UNION.

USUMACINTA, RIVER. River of 800 km formed in **Guatemala**'s *Sierra de los Cuchumatanes* by the confluence of the Salinas and Pasión. It forms part of the **Guatemalan border** and its watershed was the original home of Mayan culture. The lower reaches, navigable for 300 km, divide just before emptying into the Pacific Ocean. They separate into the Usumacinta proper which flows into the **Grijalva**, which then spills into the Palizada channel, which flows into Términos lagoon and the San Pedro y San Pablo (SS. Peter and Paul) channel, which empties directly into the ocean.

UTRECHT, TREATY OF, 1713. Ending the War of the **Spanish Succession**, the treaty gave international recognition to the new Bourbon dynasty in **Spain**, thereby replacing two centuries of Franco-Spanish conflict with the "family compact" (a Franco-Spanish alliance lasting until 1808). Austria was compensated with the transfer to it from Spain of sovereignty over what is now Belgium, and the **United Kingdom** received the concession of the *asiento de negros* (the right to trade in African slaves), greatly facilitating its economic penetration into Spanish America.

UXMAL. Mayan archaeological site, 88 km (55 miles) south of **Mérida**. The city was founded between 980 and 1007 by Hun Uitzil Chac. Its architecture reflects the high civilization of the Mayans. Its governor's house, the largest building, is one of Mexico's most important pre-Hispanic monuments. Some 90 m (300 ft) long, it rests on a terrace 150 m (500 ft.) north and south, and 180 m (590 ft.) east and west, and is decorated with complex designs telling about Mayan history. Masks, dates, and historical incidents are carved into cornices and doorways. Adjacent is the House of Turtles. There is a 35 m (115 ft.) long court for the ball game of **pok ta pok**. Four buildings comprise the Houses of the Nuns, where Mayan girls lived cloistered lives dedicated to their religion. A pyramid called the House of the Sorcerer is 32 m (102 ft) high and decorated with ornamented carved stones and detailed symbols, including snakes and a rain god. There are interior rooms and an inside stairway as well as a steep exterior stairway. Artifacts from Uxmal have revealed much about Mayan rulers, priests, and their beliefs and philosophy.

– V –

V. A letter whose sound has been confused in Spain with that of **b** since Roman times, producing many alternate spellings (*Carbajal/Carvajal*) and distinguished in dictation as *v de vino* versus *b de burro*.

VALÁDEZ, BALTASAR IGNACIO. First president of the **Partido Demócrata Mexicano**.

VALENCIA, [FRAY] MARTÍN DE (1453–1534). Spanish missionary who was very active in **New Spain**, arriving with the first Franciscans to come to **Mexico City**, where he established the first monastery and the first school dedicated to Indian **education**. He never stopped fighting to obtain better living conditions for the **Indians** and won their respect and cooperation.

VALENZUELA ESQUEERO, GILBERTO (1922–). Civil engineer and assistant director of construction for the **Public Works ministry**, 1952–1959. He directed public works in his native **Federal District**, 1959–1964, when he was a key consulting engineer for the city's expanding system of express **highways** in the 1950s–1960s, and he served as public works minister, 1964–1970.

VALLADOLID. Colonial name of the city of **Morelia** and the name of the 1808–1809 **independence** conspiracy involving José Mariano **Michelena**, his brother Ruperto Mier, and Friar Vicente de **Santa María**.

VALLADOLID DE MICHOACÁN. Colonial **intendancy**, formed in 1787, and which became the post-**independence** state of **Michoacán**.

VALLE, EDUARDO (1947–). Radical student leader known as *El Buho* ("the Owl"). In 1968, using a 5 percent tuition hike as a pretext, he organized students from the preparatory schools of **UNAM** and from the **Instituto Politécnico Nacional** into anti-government protests whose objective rapidly became that of preventing the holding of the **Olympics** in Mexico. It is alleged that he and his student strike committee placed snipers at the top of the towers facing the Plaza de **Tlatelolco** and that, by firing into **police** ranks, deliberately provoked the massacre. Afterwards, Valle thanked all those who had taken part in fighting in the Plaza and expressed regret that the Olympics had not been cancelled, "to bring discredit on President **Díaz Ordaz**, the **Partido Revolucionario Institucional**, and the establishment." He also declared that the blame attributed to President **Díaz Ordaz** for his handling of the riot should also have been aimed at his interior minister, Luis **Echeverría**.

VALLE DE ALLENDE. Former precious metal **mining** center in **Allende municipio, Chihuahua** at 26°58'N, 105°30'W (3,680 inhabitants in 1990), notable for a carbonaceous chondrite meteorite that fell on February 9, 1969. The oldest object man has ever touched, it was formed 4.5 billion years ago making it of exceptional scientific interest.

VALLE DE MÉXICO, ESTADO DEL. Status and title which the **Constitution** decrees will be automatically bestowed upon the **Federal District** should the federal government ever be moved away to a new capital city.

VALLEJO, DEMETRIO (1910–1985). The Communist head of the Railroad Workers' Union (*Sindicato de Trabajadores Ferrocarrileros de la República Mexicana*, STFRM), 1950–1958, who clashed head on with newly elected President Adolfo **López Mateos**, over a pay dispute. Vallejo was imprisoned for the treason of sabotaging the national economy; and when the party's secretary general, David Álfaro **Siqueiros**, supported him he was also imprisoned. The strike was promptly countermanded and both men were eventually released, although Vallejo remained in prison for some years, until various leftist groups petitioned for his release. As a result of these petitions, article 145 of the Penal Code was changed to make such convictions more difficult in the future.

VALLEY OF MEXICO. *See* MEXICO, VALLEY OF.

VALUE-ADDED TAX (*impuesto sobre el valor agregado,* **IVA**). Introduced as part of the taxation reforms of the later 20th century, Mexican V.A.T. was originally 15 percent, subsequently reduced to 10 percent, then put back up to 15 percent in December 1994. In some areas adjoining the **United States border** it is only 6 percent.

VANCOUVER ISLAND. *See* NOOTKA.

VAQUERO. Someone involved in raising cattle, whether a cattleman rancher or a cowboy. *See also* CHARRO.

VASCONCELOS, JOSÉ (**1882–1959**). Philosopher, educator, and politician from **Oaxaca**. A member of the **Ateneo de la Juventud**, he supported Francisco **Madero** at the outbreak of the **Revolution of 1910**, before going into exile in 1915. Upon his return in 1920, he was appointed rector of the **University of Mexico** and in 1920–1924 was education minister. Dedicating himself totally to his work, he was the driving force behind the renewed emphasis on rural **education** and the general raising of the **literacy** level. Devising a new type of basic education extension, he sent 50 traveling missionary teams of a dozen teachers to small towns in various states to teach reading and basis craft skills. The teams became famous as lay missionaries, carrying, not Bibles, but basic books for adult beginning readers and simplified manuals in craftsmanship. Some towns learned to make leather purses, belts, briefcases, and even saddles. Other towns received instruction in woodwork, turning out handcrafted chairs which sold in big-city stores. He also encouraged artists like **Rivera** and **Orozco** to paint on empty walls all over the country, creating a new world-famous school of **muralists**. In 1929 he ran unsuccessfully for president.

A prolific writer, his most famous work, *La Raza cósmica* (1925—translated as *The Cosmic Race*), envisions a new, dynamic people, formed from the union of **Indians** and Europeans. His autobiography, *Ulises criollo* (1935—translated by William Rex Crawford as *A Mexican Ulysses,* 1958), is still widely read in Mexico. His other works include *Ateneo de la juventud* (1911) and *En el ocaso de mi vida* (1957).

VÁZQUEZ DE CORONADO Y VALDÉS, FRANCISCO (1510– 1554). Spanish explorer born in **Salamanca** who arrived in **New Spain** in 1535, married Beatriz Estrada, daughter of the treasurer royal of New Spain, and held various political posts before becoming governor of **Nueva Galicia**. On February 23, 1540, he led an expedition beyond **Sonora** into Arizona, Oklahoma, and as far north as Kansas in a search for the legendary wealth of the fabled Seven Cities of **Cíbola** and the kingdom of **Quivira**. He made important geographical discoveries and left missionaries in the upper Rio Grande valley, who began the conversion pacification of the local **Indians**. After a disabling fall from his horse he returned to **Mexico City** in 1542, a disappointed man. A monument to him was erected near Bisbee, Arizona, in 1952. References to him as just "Francisco Coronado" are said to have originated in the ignorance of British and American historians of the 19th century. His name also appears as Vásquez.

VÁZQUEZ ROJAS, GENARO (1931–1972). School teacher in San Luis, **Guerrero**, who organized the anti-government **Confederación Campesina Independiente** and a Civic Committee in 1961, to organize student strikes throughout **Guerrero**. This led the federal government to remove the state governor, Caballero Abuto, for not stopping a breakdown of law and order. In 1967 Vázquez was captured, along with other Marxist guerrillas at the headquarters of the **Movimiento de Liberación Nacional**, but escaped in 1968 and kidnapped Jaime Castrejón Díaz, rector of the **Universidad de Guerrero**. He died February 2 in a car accident in **Morelia** while fleeing the **police**.

VEGA DOMÍNGUEZ, JORGE DE LA (1931–). Trade Minister, born March 14 in **Chiapas**. An economic graduate from **UNAM**, he became professor of finance at the **Instituto Politécnico Nacional**, and in 1962–1964, dean of its School of Economics. In 1968–1970 he was the **Partido Revolucionario Institucional**'s director of economic, political, and social studies. He was an economist for the Trade and Industry Ministry, the Small Business Bank and assistant director of **Diesel Nacional**. He then served in turn as director general of the **Compañía Nacional de Subsistencias Populares**, governor of **Chiapas**, and trade minister.

VEGETATION. *See* FLORA.

VELASCO, JOSÉ MARÍA (1840–1912). Landscape painter from Tematzcalcingo, **Mexico State** (*Cascada de Rincón Grande,* 1874; *Pirámide del Sol en Teotihuacan,* 1878; *The Bridge of Metlac,* 1881; *Valley of Oaxaca,* 1888; *Bahía de La Habana,* 1889; *Valley of Mexico,* 1894) who trained Diego **Rivera**. He entered the **Academia de San Carlos** in 1858, where he was taught by Eugenio Landesio. Although his rejection of academic traditions lost him his art professorship, he won first prize at the Paris Exhibition of 1889 and was given a large retrospective exhibition in Mexico in 1942. [L. H.]

VELASCO, LUIS DE, THE ELDER (1511–1564). Luis de Velasco y Alarcón, second **viceroy** of **New Spain**, 1550–1564, appointed when Antonio de **Mendoza** decided he wished to become viceroy of **Peru**. With royal backing, Velasco began a policy of humane treatment of the **Indians**, freeing many from the **encomienda** and other situations tantamount to slavery. In 1553 he complied with the royal decree to establish the **University of Mexico**. He established the **Santa Hermandad** (rural **police** force) to reduce **banditry**. He extended Spanish power into **Durango** and opened up vast **silver** mines. His huge accumulation of power and authority partly explains why subsequent viceroys were limited to six-year terms, although he personally had a reputation for honesty, kindness, and generosity, and was truly mourned by the poor at his death. His son was Luis de **Velasco** the younger.

VELASCO, LUIS DE, THE YOUNGER (1539–1616). Luis de Velasco y de Castilla, marqués de Salinas, **viceroy** of **New Spain**, 1590–1595 and 1607–1611. He made yet another attempt at pacifying the **Chichimec Indians**, founded San Luis de la Paz, and settled colonies of Tlaxaltecs in **Jalisco, Guanajuato, Zacatecas**, and **San Luis Potosí**. After serving as viceroy in Lima, he returned to New Spain, where he began the drainage of the Valley of **Mexico**. He quashed a rising of **blacks** in Tierra Caliente and organized Sebastián

Vizcaino's expedition to Japan. In 1611 he became president of the **Council of the Indies**. [L. H.]

VELÁSQUEZ SÁNCHEZ, FIDEL (1900–1999). The best known, most powerful, and longest tenured **labor** leader in Mexican history, born April 24, in Villa Romero. In 1921 he became secretary of the Union of Milk Industry Workers, then head of that union in the **Federal District**. In 1936 he helped found the **Confederación de Trabajadores Mexicanos**, serving on its executive committee until 1940. In 1946 he was elected its secretary general, and was elected to successive six-year terms, to become in 1979 the only head of a labor federation in Latin America to hold office for 33 years. He was an inner-circle adviser on labor for the **Partido Revolucionario Institucional**, the **Labor Ministry**, and successive Mexican presidents.

His death temporarily weakened organized labor as a dominant entity within the PRI (*See* TRADE UNIONS).

VELÁZQUEZ, CONSUELO (1916–2005). Singer from Ciudad Guzmán, **Jalisco**, who trained as a classical pianist but came to fame in the 1940s with such romantic songs as *No me pides nunca*, *Pasional*, and the internationally known ***Besame mucho***. [L. H.]

VELÁZQUEZ CÁRDENAS Y LEÓN, JOAQUÍN (1732–1786). Scientist who traveled to **California** to observe a transit of Venus (the planet passing across the sun). He also founded a school for **mining** engineers.

VELÁZQUEZ DE CUÉLLAR, DIEGO (1465–1524). Conqueror and first governor of **Cuba**. In 1517 he sent Fernando **Hernández de Córdoba** on an unsuccessful attempt to explore **Yucatán**. In 1518 another expedition of his, under the command of his nephew Juan de **Grijalva**, discovered **Mexico**. He obtained the title of **adelantado** over this new land. But he was no match for the cunning of his former secretary Hernán **Cortés** who stole away in the governor's own ships to exploit the new discovery on his own account.

VÉLEZ, PEDRO (1787–1848). Leader of the triumvirate **junta de gobierno** ruling Mexico in late December 1829, the others being Lucas Alemán and Luis Quintanar.

VENEGAS DE SAAVEDRA, FRANCISCO JAVIER DE, MAR-QUÉS DE LA REUNIÓN DE NUEVA ESPAÑA (1760–1838). **Viceroy** of **New Spain**, 1810–1813, a soldier who fought in the Peninsular War until sent to Mexico where he had little success against the patriot rebels and was replaced. [L. H.]

VENTA, LA. Impressive **Olmec** ceremonial site in **Tabasco** with a large pyramid, violently destroyed c.400 B.C.

VERACRUZ, [FRAY] ALONSO DE LA (1504–1584). Augustinian priest, born near Toledo, who received a doctorate in scholastic philosophy and theology from the University of Salamanca. He arrived in **New Spain** (specifically in **Mexico City**) in 1536, and in 1540 began a long career as an educator in **Michoacán**. When the **University of Mexico** was founded, this polymath occupied various chairs there and became one of the most respected educators and learned authors of his time. His writings on the geography of **California** proved particularly useful for Father **Kino**'s explorations there.

VERACRUZ CITY. The largest port in Mexico, on the Gulf of **Mexico**, 320 km (200 miles) by air from **Mexico City**, at 19°11'N, 96°08'W. Its harbor is protected by breakwaters built on reefs and small islands and by the colonial fortresses of **San Juan de Ulúa** and Santiago. Before air travel, it was Mexico's front door, where visitors disembarked to then travel inland by horse or wagon. It is the terminal of Mexico's first railroad. It remains Mexico's chief naval base on the Caribbean.

The site of the first Spanish colonial headquarters in Mexico, it was built in 1519 by Hernán **Cortés** as his base for the conquest. He called it the *Villa de la Vera Cruz* ("town of the True Cross"). The original settlement was moved down the coast but reestablished in 1599. Pillaged by **pirates** in 1653 and 1712, on March 29, 1847, it fell to **United States** troops under General Winfield **Scott**, and in 1861 to soldiers of the **French intervention**.

In 1914 US marines occupied the city for several months, leading to the downfall of President Vitoriano **Huerta**, who had challenged the right of US naval forces to be offshore (*See DOLPHIN*, USS.).

Veracruz's population has grown from 278,000 in 1976 to 457,377 in 2000. It has Mexico's major manufacturers of cigars, liquors, and chocolate.

VERACRUZ-LLAVE ("Ver."). Official name of Veracruz state and previously the **intendancy** of Veracruz, created in 1786. The present state occupies 72,815 km² in eastern Mexico, with a 650 km (400 mile) coastline on the Gulf of **Mexico**, from the **Tamesí river** to the Isthmus of **Tehuantepec**. It extends inland some 160 km (100 miles), but access beyond the narrow coastal plain is made difficult by the Sierra **Madre** Occidental, which includes the 5700 m (18,700 foot) high (but dormant) **Orizaba volcano**, which is Mexico's highest peak. Several of its rivers are navigable, the chief of these being the **Coatzacoalcos** in the southeast. Also flowing across the state into the Gulf is the **Papaloapan**. Heavy rainfall produces tropical vegetation, and the state produces rubber, chicle, **sugar** cane, **coffee**, **tobacco**, rum, bananas, chocolate, liquors, cattle, leather, and timber. Its many oil wells produce more **petroleum** than any other state, making it the basis for the state's petrochemical industry. It is the site of the pre-Hispanic civilization of the **Olmec** Indians and is the present home of the **Totonac** Indians and "La **Bamba**" folksong. The state's inhabitants bear the nickname **Jarocho**. Although **Veracruz City** is the state's largest city, the state capital is **Jalapa**.

Veracruz-Llave had only 349,125 inhabitants in 1857 and 380,169 in 1869, but its 856,000 inhabitants in 1895 and 981,000 in 1900 made it the third most populous state. By 1910, with 1,133,000, it had overtaken **Puebla** to become second (after **Jalisco**) with 1,160,000 in 1921 and first with 1,377,000 in 1930. Although the **Federal District** surpassed it in the 1930s, it stayed the most populous state, with 1,619,000 in 1940; 2,040,000 in 1950; and 2,728,00 in 1960. In the late 1960s, the spread of Mexico City suburbs into **Mexico State** then pushed that state's population above that of Veracruz. However, with 3,815,000 people in 1970; 5,388,000 in 1980; 6,228,000 in 1990; 6,908,975 in 2000; and 7,110,214 in 2005; Veracruz remains in third position among the states proper, just below Jalisco.

VERACRUZ STATE. Officially known as **Veracruz-Llave**.

VICARIO, LEONA (1789–1842). A heroine of the **independence** struggle, for which she donated all her jewelry. After independence she worked closely with her husband, Andrés **Quintana Roo**, in various political and intellectual pursuits.

VICENCIO TOVAR, ABEL (1925–). An attorney from **Mexico City** who has been a leader in the **Partido de Acción Nacional** since the 1950s. He served in the **Cámara de Diputados Federales**, 1963–1967 and 1973–1976. He was successively a party district chairman, a regional chairman, its secretary general, and in 1978–1982 its president.

VICENS, JOSEFINA. Novelist: *El libro vacío* (1952).

VICE PRESIDENT. Office abolished by the **Constitution of 1858**, restored in 1904 (when Porfirio **Díaz** ceased at last to fear its incumbent would use it as the base for rebellion), and again abolished by the **Constitution of 1917**. [L. H.]

VICEROY (*virrey*). Spanish colonial governor general, subordinate to the king alone. Possessed in theory of all the powers of the king himself, his authority was severely limited over captaincies general such as those of **Cuba** and **Guatemala** whose rulers had their own direct access to Madrid. The **Spanish Revolution of 1820** changed the title to *Jefe político superior*. [L. H.]

VICEROYALTY (*virreinato*). A major administrative division of Spain's New World territories. There were originally two, that of **New Spain**, covering all North America, administered from **Mexico City**, and that of **Peru**, administered from Lima and including the Isthmus of Panamá and all lands to its south. In the 18th century new viceroyalties, administered from Bogotá and Buenos Aires, were separated from that of Peru. [L. H.]

VICEROYS OF NEW SPAIN.
Antonio de **Mendoza**, 1535–1550
Luis de **Velasco**, the elder, 1551–1564
Gastón de **Peralta**, 1566–1568
Martín **Enríquez de Almanza**, 1568–1580
Lorenzo **Suárez de Mendoza**, 1580–1582
Luis de **Villanueva y Zapata**, 1582–1583
Pedro de **Moya y Contreras**, 1584–1585
Álvaro **Manrique de Zúñiga**, 1585–1590

Luis de **Velasco**, the younger, 1590–1595
Gaspar de **Zúñiga y Acevedo**, 1595–1603
Juan Manuel **Mendoza y Luna**, 1603–1607
Luis de Velasco, the younger, again, 1607–1611
Fray Francisco **García Guerra**, 1611–1612
Diego **Fernández de Córdoba**, 1612–1621
Diego **Carrillo de Mendoza y Pimentel**, 1621–1624
Rodrigo **Pacheco y Osorio**, 1624–1635
Lope **Díaz de Armendáriz**, 1635–1640
Diego **López Pacheco [Cabrera y Bobadilla]**, 1640–1642
Juan de **Palafox y Mendoza**, 1642
García **Sarmiento de Sotomayor**, 1642–1648
Marcos de **Torres y Rueda**, 1648–1649
Matías de **Peralta**, 1649–1650
Luis **Enríquez y Guzmán**, 1650–1653
Francisco **Fernández de la Cueva**, 1653–1660
Juan de **Leiva**, 1660–1664
Diego **Osorio de Escobar y Llamas**, 1664
Antonio Sebastián de **Toledo**, 1664–1673
Pedro Nuño **Colón de Portugal**, 1673
Fray Payo **Enríquez de Rivera Manrique**, 1673–1680
Tomás Antonio Manrique de la **Cerda y Aragón**, 1680–1686
Melchor **Portocarrero Lasso de la Vega**, 1686–1688
Gaspar de la **Cerda Sandoval Silva y Mendoza**, 1688–1696
Juan de **Ortega Cano Montáñez y Patiño**, 1696
José **Sarmiento y Valladares**, 1696–1701
Juan de Ortega Montáñez, again, 1701
Francisco **Fernández de la Cueva Enríquez**, 1702–1711
Fernando de **Láncaster Noroña y Silva**, 1711–1716
Baltasar de **Zúñiga y Guzmán**, 1716–1722
Juan de **Acuña [y Bejarano]**, 1722–1734
Juan Antonio de **Vizarrón y Eguiarreta**, 1734–1740
Pedro de **Castro y Figueroa**, 1740–1741
Pedro **Cebrián y Agustín**, 1742–1746
Juan Francisco de **Güermes y Horcasitas [Arguayo]**, 1746–1755
Agustín de **Ahumada** (*or* Ahumadas) **y Villalón**, 1755–1760
Don Francisco **Cagigal de la Vega** (*acting*), 1760
Joaquín de **Monserrat y Ciurana**, 1760–1766

Carlos Francisco de **Croix**, 1766–1771
Antonio María de **Bucareli y Urzúa**, 1771–1779
Martín de **Mayorga**, 1779–1783
Matías de **Gálvez**, 1783–1784
Vicente de **Herrera y Rivero**, 1784–1785
Don Bernardo de **Gálvez**, Conde de Gálvez, 1785–1786
Eusebio **Sánchez Pareja y Beleño**, 1786–1787
Ildefonso **Núñez de Haro y Peralta**, 1787
Manuel Antonio **Florez Martínez de Ángulo**, 1787–1789
Juan Vicente de **Güermes Pacheco y Padilla**, 2nd Conde de
 Revilla-Gigedo, 1789–1794
Miguel de la **Grúa Talamanca y Branciforte**, 1794–1798
Miguel José de **Azanza**, 1798–1800
Félix **Berenguer [de Marquina]**, 1800–1803
José de **Iturrigaray**, 1803–1808
Pedro **Garibay**, 1808–1809
Francisco Javier de **Lizana y Beaumont**, 1809–1810
Francisco Javier de **Venegas**, 1810–1813
Félix María **Calleja del Rey**, Conde de Calderón, 1813–1816
Juan **Ruiz de Apocada**, 1816–1821

Jefes Políticos Superiores
 Pedro Francisco **Novella**, 1821
 Juan **O'Donojú** (appointed 1821, but never assumed office)

VICTORIA, GUADALUPE (1786–1843). President of Mexico, 1824–1828. Born Juan Manuel Félix Fernández, he changed his name to show his dedication to the cause of **independence**. After the death of José María **Morales y Pavón**, he waged a **guerrilla** campaign for several years in the mountains around **Veracruz**, even after most of his men had abandoned him. He worked briefly with **Iturbide**, but became disillusioned and joined **Santa Anna**'s successful revolt against him in 1823. He became more conservative during the last years of his presidency, but was the only Mexican president in many years to serve out his full term. Even so, he was shot in Cuilapam.

VILLA ("town"). Status granted to an urban settlement below that of **ciudad** ("city").

VILLA, PANCHO (1877–1923). Francisco Villa, leader in the **Revolution of 1910**, whose real name was Doroteo Arango. As a child he worked as a peon on a **hacienda** in northern Mexico, but he had to flee for his life when he defended his sister against the advances of one of its owners. He turned to **banditry**, showing skill as a soldier, organizer, and administrator. Bereft of formal education, he taught himself to read and write. His strongest trait was his ability to cast fear into his opponents: when necessary he could practice extreme cruelty.

He supported **Madero** and later fought against **Huerta** and **Carranza**, reaching his high point in 1914, when for five months he and **Zapata** occupied **Mexico City**, taking turns sitting in the presidential chair. Subsequently he lost out to **Carranza**, and his **División del Norte** began to melt away, although he was able to raid **Columbus**, New Mexico, in 1916. This led to the United States sending a punitive expedition after him, led by General John J. **Pershing**.

He retired to a *hacienda* in 1920 and was assassinated in **Parral**, June 20, 1923.

VILLAHERMOSA. City of **Tabasco** state, founded in June 1596, at 17°59'N, 92°55'W. Its population has grown from 153,000 in 1976; 261,231 in 1990; and 263,000 in 1995 to 520,308 in 2000.

VILLALPANDO, CRISTÓBAL DE (1649–1714). Painter.

VILLANUEVA Y ZAPATA, LUIS DE. Viceroy of New Spain, 1582–1583.

VILLAREAL, ANTONIO J. (1879–1944). Professor at a teacher training college who acted as president, October 31–November 6, 1914, and thrice received serious consideration as a potential presidential candidate. The last time was in 1934, when what was then the **Partido Nacional Revolucionario** chose Lázaro **Cárdenas** instead. In **United States** exile in 1906, Villareal had headed the **Partido Liberal**. In 1912, as a general, he was governor of his native **Nuevo León**. In 1914 he opened the Casa del Obrero to revive Mexican **trade unions**. He then became a key envoy of Francisco **Madero** in Europe and served as agriculture minister in 1929.

VILLAURRUTIA, XAVIER. Man of letters commemorated in the Xavier Villaurrutia literary award.

VILLORO, JUAN. Novelist: *El disparo de Argón* (1991), and *El testigo* (2004), which won him the Spanish publisher Anagrama's international *Premio Herralde*, from among 264 entrants, for the year's best novel in Spanish.

VIRGIN OF GUADALUPE. *See* MARY OF GUADALUPE, SAINT.

VISITA. An investigation during a colonial official's term of office, as opposed to a *residencia*, carried at the end of his term.

VISITADOR. The investigator performing a **visita**.

VIZARRÓN Y EGUIARRETA, JUAN ANTONIO DE (1695?–1747). **Viceroy** of **New Spain**, 1734–1740, having become a priest in 1715 and becoming archbishop in 1730. As such, he was responsible for building the former Archbishop's Palace in **Tacubaya** in the Calle del Ex-Arcebispado. As viceroy he defeated British Admiral Edward Vernon's attack on Cartagena de las Indias during the War of the **Austrian Succession**. [L. H.]

VIZCAÍNO, SEBASTIÁN (1548–1628). Spanish sailor who came to **New Spain** in 1583, went on to Manila, and returned in 1589. In the 1590s he was sent by **Viceroy** Luis de **Velasco** to take up Juan Rodríguez **Cabrillo**'s search for the Strait of **Anián**. In 1596 he discovered **Baja California** ("New Andalucia"), and, on a second expedition, in 1602, went further along the coast to Mendocino Cape in Upper **California**.

VIZCAÍNO MURRAY, FRANCISCO (1935–). A certified public accountant from **Guaymas, Sonora**, he obtained a doctorate from the **Instituto Politécnico Nacional** and served as secretary general of the **Instituto Mexicano del Seguro Social**, 1970–1972. As assistant health minister, 1972–1976, he became Latin America's first director of environmental protection, formulating and administering pioneer regulations against pollution of air, water, and other resources.

He initiated emission control testing for trucks and **automobiles** and for factories.

VOLKSWAGEN. The German company began manufacturing in Mexico in 1964. It continued making the original "Beetle" long after the model had been phased out in the company's other plants. In 1999 its **Puebla** plant was producing 6,000 **automobiles** a month, primarily for the domestic market, where the Volkswagen had become Mexico's most popular make of automobile.

VOLPI, JORGE. Novelist and university professor from **Puebla**. *In Search of Klingsor* translates his 2002 spy thriller set in Hilter's Germany.

VOTÁN. An early **Mayan** ruler who founded the Kingdom of **Xibablá**.

VOTING. *See* SUFFRAGE.

VUELTA. Literary magazine founded by Octavio **Paz**, to replace *Plural*. It began November 15, 1976, with the December 1 issue, and ended in 1998, soon after Paz's death. [L. H.]

– W –

WAGES. *See* INCOME DISTRIBUTION; MINIMUM WAGE.

WALKER, WILLIAM (1824–1860). Although this filibuster (soldier of fortune) from Nashville, Tennessee, is mainly remembered for his incursions into Central America, he did invade **Baja California** in 1853, proclaiming it and **Sonora** an independent nation. He was soon driven out, however.

WAL-MART. Prominent in Mexican retailing since 1991 when it introduced Sam's Club. It had 67 "supercenters" in 1992. In 2000 it merged its local operation with Cifra (dating from 1977, and which already controlled Bodegas Aurrerá, dating from 1958), to form Wal-Mart de México. In 2004 it was allowed to build a new Aurrerá store in the archaeological zone of **Teotihuacan** despite strong local protest. By 2005, with 884 stores in 136 cities, it employed 141,517 and had sales of 187,508 million pesos. [L. H.]

WARD, H. G. United Kingdom chargé d'affaires in Mexico in the 1820s. His greatest accomplishment was negotiating a trade treaty in 1827, years before the **United States** achieved one. He also supported the Scottish Rite masons (the **Escoceses**), who won out in influence over the more liberal York Rite masons (**Yorkinos**) championed by Joel **Poinsett**.

WAR MINISTRY. *See* DEFENSE MINISTRY.

WARS. *See* AMERICAN REVOLUTIONARY WAR; AUSTRIAN SUCCESSION, WAR OF; CHICHIMES, WAR OF; CIVIL WARS; FRENCH INTERVENTION; INDEPENDENCE, WAR OF; INDIAN WARS; INSURRECTIONS; PASTRY WAR; SEVEN YEARS' WAR; SPANISH SUCCESSION, WAR OF; UNITED STATES-MEXICAN WAR; WORLD WAR I; WORLD WAR II.

WATER. *See* COMISIÓN NACIONAL DE AGUA; GONZÁLEZ COSIO, MANUEL; HYDROGRAPHY; IRRIGATION; RAINFALL.

WEIGHTS AND MEASURES. Although Spanish legislation at the beginning of the 19th century attempted to standardize weights and measures through the empire, some local anomalies remained in various parts of Latin America. All traditional measures were abolished in the early 1880s by **metrification**, except that some use of Anglo-American measures continued, particularly in the **petroleum** industry. [L. H.]

WELFARE. The *Secretaría de Salubridad y Asistencia* (Health and Welfare Ministry) became the **Health Ministry** (*Secretaría de Salud*) in 1982. *See also* SOCIAL SECURITY.

WET BACK. Pejorative term in English for any undocumented Mexican immigrant into the southwestern **United States** (but particularly a **bracero**), from his having, presumably, swum across the **Rio Grande**.

WHALES. Coastal waters near Laguna San Ignacio off the **Baja California del Sur** provide the chief breeding site for the grey whale. In 1994 American environmentalists commended Mexican efforts to protect the area and had felt able to remove the animal from their endangered species list. Five years later the situation was threatened by the Mitsubishi Corporation's plans to develop **salt production** here. Soon the corporation, aided by Mexico's **Trade Ministry**, and the (American) National Resources Defense Council were involved in a public relations battle to defend their respective positions. Mexican students of marine biology wrote to the press on the importance to Mexico of the grey whale. By 1999 it seemed a compromise had been reached. The new salt mines would lessen their environmental impact by reducing their territorial requirements and redesigning their processing equipment. Local fisherfolk might continue to fish for mollusks, but they would police the beaches to clear them of rubbish left by tourists, aided by the sanitation department of **Guerrero Negro** (population 13,000), an effort which would be funded by the **Junta Federal de Mejoramiento**. *Excelsior* cited the case as exemplifying the possibility of collaboration between federal agencies and private industry when conditions were favorable for everyone involved. [L. H.]

WHEAT. A dietary impact of the introduction of Christianity was the need for wheat bread. Long imported, wheat is now grown by **irrigation** in northeastern Mexico. In 2003, 3 million *t* was grown on 626,517 ha, a quite respectable yield of 4.8 t/ha. [L. H.]

WILDLIFE. *See* FAUNA; FLORA.

WILL, BRADLEY RONALD (1980–2006). American freelance journalist caught in the crossfire when government supporters in **Oaxaca** tried to remove a strikers' street barrier by force in October 2006. He died in a hospital of gunshot wounds. The opposition claimed that an American had been murdered deliberately so as to force federal intervention, which the **Fox** administration had been avoiding ever since trouble broke out in May.

La Jornada and Reuters both claimed the murderers were local **police** in plainclothes, but, significantly, the **United States** State

Department merely "requested" (i.e., did not demand) an official Mexican inquiry into the death. [L. H.]

WILMA. Hurricane that killed 13 in Haiti and Jamaica before hitting **Cozumel** and **Cancún**, October 22, 2005. With a 800 km diameter it was half as wide as Katrina, which had hit New Orleans in September 2005. [L. H.]

WILSON, HENRY LANE (1857–1932). United States diplomat from Indiana, ambassdor to Mexico, 1910–1913, and strong defender of American business interests. Formerly an enthusiastic supporter of Porfirio **Díaz**, he was appalled by the property destruction of the **Decena Trágica**. Convinced that **Madero**'s government could not control the situation, he negotiated the "**Embassy Pact**" whereby the rebel leader Félix **Díaz** agreed to support a coup d'état by Victoriano **Huerta**. Woodrow Wilson, the newly elected US president, was outraged at the way Huerta had come to power and assumed his complicity in Madero's murder. Rejecting his ambassador's advice, he refused diplomatic recognition to the new government, which automatically entailed Henry Wilson's recall, July 1913. The unhappy ambassador was blamed for not trying to prevent Madero's fate, and as the **Revolution of 1910** progressed, he became castigated as the uninformed ambassador who had failed to recognize how 35 years of injustice had been about to explode in battles all over Mexico.

WILSON, THOMAS WOODROW (1856–1924). First **United States** president from the Democratic Party in the 20th century (1912–1920). In July 1913 he obliged his namesake ambassador to Mexico, Henry L. **Wilson**, to resign for failing to support Francisco **Madero**. In 1914 he authorized the occupation of **Veracruz City** by U.S. marines in an ultimately successful effort to topple President Victoriano **Huerta**. In 1916 he sent a punitive expedition into Mexico under **Pershing**, in a futile attempt to capture Pancho **Villa**. Wilson's Mexican policy was largely based on the concept that if a foreign government acted immorally, then it should be punished. It culminated in U.S. entry into **World War I** in 1917, following the **Zimmerman telegram**.

WINDWARD FLEET (*Armada de Barlovento*). The naval force established by Spain in the Caribbean to control 17th century **piracy**.

WINE. Introduced as needed for both Spanish cuisine and Catholic liturgy, its distribution was already a primary concern of 16th century **Viceroy** Álvaro **Manrique de Zúñiga**. Local grape cultivation was pioneered by Francisco de **Urdiñola**, although this was subsequently discouraged as contrary to the interests of the Spanish wine industry. The present center of Mexican viticulture is the state of **Coahuila**. **French immigration** in the late 1820s pioneered the industry in **Alta California**, but this was then lost to Mexico through the **United States-Mexican War**. [L. H.]

WITCHCRAFT. *See* FOLK MEDICINE.

WOMEN. Mexico's 17th century **Juana Inés de la Cruz** and 20th century Frida **Kahlo** have become icons of international feminism. The period since the **Revolution of 1910** has been notable for the many women prominent in literature and **art**. María Marcos **Cedillo** was a pioneer aviator of the 1920s. The first female cabinet minister was Amalia **Castillo León** in 1958. Julia **Carabias Lillo** in 1994 was the first woman to be appointed to a key cabinet post. In 1998, Rocio **Robles** became **Mexico City**'s first woman mayor and Rosario **Green Macias** Latin America's first foreign minister. Patricia **Mercado Castro** was among the candidates running for **president** in the **election of 2006**.

The first world conference on the status of women met in **Mexico City** in 1975, International Women's Year, and produced a world action plan for equal access to **education**, employment, **health** services, food and housing, and political participation. Since then Mexico's federal election legislation has been amended to require **political parties** to establish quotas to ensure that at least 30 percent of candidates are female. State and **federal district** criminal codes are being modernized in regard to acts of violence against women.

Important fighters for women's rights include Hilda Josefina **Anderson Nevárez**, Martha **Andrade de Del Rosal**, and María **Cervantes Hernández**. [L. H.]

It was regarded as highly significant that presidential advisor José Antonio **González Fernández**, speaking on **television** about electoral reform, May 18, 1999, referred to "the man *or woman*" who would be the **Partido Revolucionario Institucional**'s presidential candidate. On his January 1999 visit, however, Pope **John Paul II** rejected a petition of Mexican women asking for ordination, and traditional views on women's role in society were still being voiced publicly both by the **Church** and by President **Fox**. Rape was still widely regarded primarily as a threat to any future offspring's legitimacy and therefore resolvable by enforcing matrimony between the assailant and his victim.

The 2000 census counted 49,891,159 women to only 47,592,253 men. *See also* CIUDAD JUAREZ; DIVORCE; FAMILIES; FAMILY PLANNING; FEMALE SUFFRAGE; MACHISMO; SOLDADERAS.

WORKS, MINISTRY OF. *See* PUBLIC WORKS MINISTRY.

WORLD SOCCER CUP (*Campeonato Mundial de Fútbol*). Mexico hosted the 1970 and 1986 **soccer** championship contests. Its national team reached the quarterfinals in 1970 and 1986, and the second round in 1994, in 1998, and in 2006 in Germany, where it was defeated 2–1 in a fiercely contested match by quarterfinalists **Argentina** in overtime.

WORLD TRADE ORGANIZATION (W.T.O.). Successor to the **General Agreement on Trade and Tariffs**.

WORLD WAR I. The **United States'** entry into the "Great War," although ostensibly occasioned by Germany's adoption of unrestricted attacks by its **U-boats** against neutral shipping in European waters, was undoubtedly influenced by German attempts to persuade Mexico to attack the United States, revealed when British counterespionage deciphered the **Zimmerman telegram**.

WORLD WAR II. Mexico broke off diplomatic relations with the Axis Powers (Germany, Italy, and Japan) in February 1942 and declared war on them on May 28, 1942, after German **U-boats** had sunk two Mexican oil tankers. A treaty with the **United States** allowed the recruitment of **braceros** to harvest American crops. The Mexican **Air Force** was directly involved in combat in the Far Eastern theater. Many Mexicans also enlisted voluntarily in the armed forces of other countries, usually those of the United States. *See also* IRON AND STEEL.

WORNAT, OLGA. Argentine journalist whose accusation, in her *Crónicas malditas*, that Manuel **Bribiesca**, son of Mexico's First Lady Marta **Sahaguín de Fox**, had been guilty of influence peddling, resulted in his suing her successfully for defamation and slander, October 3, 2006. The verdict and damages awarded are currently being appealed. [L. H.]

WRESTLING (*lucha libre*). Mexico's second most popular spectator **sport** (after **soccer**), a free-for-all between "good" and "bad" tag-teams of professional *luchadores*. Since Rodolfo Guzmán Huerta in 1942 was inspired by comic book hero *The Phantom* and Dumas' *Man in the Iron Mask* to don a silver face mask and matching costume as "El Santo," anonymity behind a mask has become *de rigueur*. Any contestant whose identity becomes known is permanently banned.

– X –

X. This letter formerly indicated the sound "sh" of *Sherry* (**wine** from the medieval Jerez de la Frontera), but phonetic change in 16th century Spanish made it identical in sound with *j*. It was therefore abolished in the orthographic reform of the 1720s, except in Latinisms where it has the Latin (and English) value of "KS." This reform changed *Mexico* into *Magic*, but it soon became a matter of national pride for Mexicans to conserve the traditional spelling in this and many other place-names. The letter's original *sh* value persists in **Nahuatl**. **Oaxaca** invariably retains the *x* and **Jalapa** is officially Jalapa. The change not only explains the alternations *Baser* with *Badger, Texas* with *Teas*, *Xalisco* with *Jalisco,* but also the purely Castilian *Caxigal* with *Cajigal* and *Cagigal*, *Xavier* with *Javier*, *Ximénez* with *Jiménez* and *Giménez*, etc. [L. H.]

XALAPA DE ENRÍQUEZ. Mexican official name of **Jalapa**.

XALISCO. Official spelling of **Jalisco**.

XIBABLÁ. A Mayan kingdom founded by **Votán**, and which comprised parts of what are today the Mexican states of **Tabasco, Campeche**, and **Yucatán**.

XICALANCAS. A tribe of pre-Hispanic **Indians** who roamed central Mexico before the coming of the **Aztecs** in 1200.

XICAPEXLI. A painted gourd bowl used by peasants and **Indians** throughout Mexico.

XICOTÉNACATL, FELIPE SANTIAGO (1805–1847). Commander of the *Batallón de San Blas* at the Battle of Chapultepec. (He had been named for **Jicoténcal**). It is popularly believed that he was killed wearing the flag he had wrapped around him to avoid its seizure by the enemy. The flag is on show in **Chapultepec Castle**.

XICOTÉNCATL. Tlaxcaltecan leader of resistance to the Spanish, made the hero of a novel, *Jicotencal* by Cuban poet José María Heredia.

XOCHIMILCO. Pre-hispanic tribe, vassals of the **Aztecs**. They filled huge wicker baskets with earth and tied them together to make tiny floating farms on the Xochimilco Lake bed, some 25 km (15 miles) southeast of **Mexico City**. There they grew vegetables and flowers which they traded and also used to pay their tribute to the Aztecs. Over the centuries these "floating gardens of Xochimilco" became permanently rooted in the lake bottom, with canals between them. They are now a tourist attraction. Flat-bottomed launches with vendors of flowers, food, and souvenirs, now follow the boatloads of visitors up and down the canals, especially on weekends. At certain hours, **mariachi** folk bands serenade from their own launches for a fee.

– Y –

Y. This letter is a frequent alternative to *i* in diphthongs and when pronounced as a consonant. It is therefore really superfluous and many words exist in two versions, with *y* and with *i*. The Venezuelan (and later, by adoption, Chilean) scholar Andrés **Bello** proposed a mid-19th century spelling reform (widely adopted for a time) that would have replaced all *y*s. [L. H.]

YÁÑEZ, AGUSTÍN (1904–1980). Educator and novelist. Born May 4, he graduated in law from the **Universidad de Guadalajara** and a PhD in literature from **UNAM**. He became a professor at preparatory schools and teacher training colleges in his native **Guadalajara**; governor of **Jalisco**, 1953–1958; and **education** minister, 1964–1970. His *Al filo de agua* (1947) depicting small town life just before the **Revolution of 1910** became a classic throughout Spanish America, and his 1959 novel *La Creación* (1959) was also widely read. His *Las Tierras flacas* (1962) is the classic portrayal of regional life styles in **Jalisco**.

YÁÑEZ, JOSÉ MARÍA (1803–1880). Soldier who fought the Spaniards at **Tampico** in 1829 and the French in defending **Veracruz** in the **Pastry War**. His most notable achievement was in defeating Raousset de **Boulbon** in **Sonora**.

YÁÑEZ PINZÓN, VICENTE (c.1460–1523). Spanish navigator who sailed along the coast of **Central America** as far as **Yucatán**, 1507.

YAQUI. Indian group of **Sonora** who through the centuries have refused to assimilate. A revolt that began in 1887 led to a fierce repression led by Ramón **Corral** (who had almost half their population transported to **Yucatán**) and also to the survivors' support of **Obregón** during the **Revolution of 1910**. Even as late as the 1920s the Yaqui were battling Mexican troops to keep their villages outside federal jurisdiction. Famous as deer hunters, their folk dances celebrate wild game hunting. They still numbered 30,000 in 1900 but only 9,700 in the mid-1990s.

YAQUI RIVER. River, 680 km long, rising as the Papigóchic in the Sierra de Molinares, draining 16,000 km^2 of **Sonora** and emptying into the Gulf of **California**. [L. H.]

YELLOW FEVER. The urban form of this mosquito-borne disease reached the Caribbean and the eastern shore of the Gulf of **Mexico** in the late 1640s, probably carried from Africa by the transatlantic slave trade. It is possible, however, that the wilderness variety of the disease is endemic in the Americas. [L. H.]

YORKINOS. Members of the York Rite, the liberal wing of **Freemasonry**, which the U.S. Minister Joel **Poinsett** brought to Mexico, in opposition to the Scottish Rite, the **Escoceses**. Led by Miguel **Ramos**

Arizpe, they were active in **Mexico City** and in national politics, 1824–1835, but internal dissensions nullified any chance of the Yorkinos (disparaged as the "Jacobin Society") having any important political influence.

YUCATÁN. A peninsula of southeastern Mexico between the Gulf of **Campeche** on the west, the Gulf of **Mexico** on the north, and the Caribbean Sea on the east. Its 180,000 km^2 (70,000 sq. mile) area comprises three Mexican states (**Yucatán state** taking up a triangular northern third, **Campeche state** the southwestern third, **Quintana Roo** most of the southeast) and, in the far southeast, the neighboring country of **Belize**.

The first Europeans to land in this part of Mesoamerica were Spaniards shipwrecked here in 1512. Its coast was explored by Francisco de Córdoba in 1517 and Juan de **Grijalva** in 1518. Their contacts with the **Maya** soon spread the tale that white gods were coming from the east in fulfilment of the **Aztec** legend. Hernán **Cortés** touched the Yucatán coast in 1519 before launching his conquest of Mexico from **Veracruz**. The conquest of Yucatán, begun by Francisco **Montejo** in 1530 was completed by his son Francisco **Montejo** the younger in 1540. It was made an **intendancy** in 1787, but within the **Captaincy General** of **Guatemala**. The peninsula has been traditionally isolationist and somewhat independent of **Mexico City**. This is particularly true of the north, the eventual state of Yucatán. *See also* CASTE WAR OF YUCATAN.

YUCATAN CHANNEL. The 210 km (130 mile) wide strait separating Cape San Antonio in Cuba from Cabo Catoche, near Puerto Juárez on Mexico's Yucatán Peninsula, and providing the Gulf of **Mexico**'s southern outlet to the Caribbean Sea.

YUCATÁN STATE. Established as an **intendancy** in 1786, it had a **population** of 333,382 at the census of 1789. It became a state at independence, but the 1857 separation of **Campeche** reduced its area to 39,340 km^2, occupying the northern third of the **Yucatan** Peninsula, with a coastline on the Gulf of **Mexico**. Mostly a dry plain, it has a range of hills under 150 m (500 ft) high run along the border with **Campeche state**. A meager rainfall concentrated in May–September seeps through the surface and collects in *cenotes* (underground rivers and wells), pumped out by windmills for the **irrigation** of **sisal, corn,** and **sugar.** Sisal provides the raw material for the state's main industries of rope, cord, bag, and hat making. Tourism depends on the **Maya** ruins of **Chichen Itzá, Uxmal, Izamal,** and **Labná.** In 1858 it lost territory to the newly created **Campeche State,** reducing its **population** from 668,623 then to only 282,634 in 1869. At successive **censuses** since then it has been 298,000 in 1895; 310,000 in 1900; 340,000 in 1910; 358,000 in 1921; 386,000 in 1930; 418,000 in 1940; 517,000 in 1950; 614,000 in 1960; 758,000 in 1970; 1,064,000 in 1980; 1,363,000 in 1990; 1,658,210 in 2000; and 1,818,948 in 2005. The chief port is **Progreso.**

YUREN AGUILAR, JESÚS (1901–1973). One of Mexico's most influential modern labor leaders, born January 1. He headed the **Mexico City** sanitation workers' union in 1922, and in the 1920s organized drivers of federal government and government agency vehicles into a Union of Chauffeurs in State Service. He was one of the founders of the **Confederación de Trabajadores Mexicanos (CTM)** in 1936 and chief Mexican delegate to the International Labour Conference in Geneva in 1938. After working in his earlier years with the anti-establishment Vicente **Lombardo Toledano,** in 1941 he became a close associate of Fidel **Velásquez Sánchez,** attracted by his pro-government position. In 1941–1948 he kept many key labor leaders solidly in the CTM and away from smaller anti-establishment unions and trade union federations. He served as secretary general of the CTM for the **Federal District,** 1949–1973; as secretary for labor action of the **Partido Revolucionario Institucional,** 1958–1964; and was a longtime member of the **Comité Ejecutivo Nacional** of the PRI. He served in the **Cámara de Diputados Federales,** 1943–1946, and in the Senate (where he was the voice of organized labor), 1952–1958 and 1964–1970. He died in his native **Mexico City,** September 22.

– Z –

ZABLUDOVSKY, JACOBO (1928–). Formerly the most prominent news anchorman in Mexico, having served **Televisa's** primetime news broadcasts as managing editor and on-the-air news announcer. While Televisa's Emilio **Azcárraga Jean** insisted on his getting the largest news staff in Mexican TV, Mexican law allowed him to edit news on more than one network. He has now, however, moved to cable **television**.

ZABLUDOWSKY, MOISES (1959–). Painter. His first one-man show in 1977 showed him to be one of Mexico's most promising young artists. His representative works include *Bicicleta* and *Muro de los lamentos*.

ZACATEC INDIANS. The original inhabitants of **Zacatecas state**.

ZACATECAS CITY. Capital of **Zacatecas state**, at 22°48'N, 102°33'W, 2,455 m (8,050 ft.) above sea level in the Sierra **Madre** Occidental, with steep, narrow streets, and surrounded by six peaks, including El Grillo and La **Bufa**. It was founded in 1548 by Juan de **Tolosa**. Colonial buildings include the cathedral (built in 1612) and the town hall. By 1832 its rich **silver** mines had produced bullion valued at US$ 667 million, but their activity decreased in the 1900s. The population grew from 98,000 in 1976 to 123,899 in 2000.

ZACATECAS MARCH (*Marcha de Zacatecas*). Composed by Genaro **Codina**, celebrating a 1914 victory of Pancho **Villa** at Zacatecas, it became the official song of the Mexican **army** when a native of **Zacatecas** on the general staff got it legally adopted. In every parade of élite troops passing in review before the president or other high dignitary, the band plays *Zacatecas*.

ZACATECAS STATE. Established as an **intendancy** in 1786, it is now a state of 75,040 km^2 in the central plateau of Mexico bounded on the north by **Coahuila**, on the east by **San Luis Potosí**, on the south by **Aguascalientes**, and on the west by **Jalisco** and **Durango**. It has 58 *municipios*.

The Sierra **Madre** Occidental runs northwest to southeast across the state. There are valleys with temperate climate and even **rainfall** and deserts with cactus and mesquite. The rivers are tributaries of the Rio **Grande de Santiago** which flows into the Pacific. **Mining** (of **silver**, gold, copper, and lead) is centered on **Zacatecas city**, Mazapil, Fresnillo, Concepción, Sombrerete, and Ojocaliente. The state raises cattle, sheep, and mules. The **population** was 296,789 in 1857 and 398,977 in 1869. In successive **censuses** since then it has been 453,000 (1895); 462,000 (1900); 477,000 (1910); 379,000 (1921); 459,000 (1930); 565,000 (1940); 665,000 (1950); 818,000 (1960): 952,000 (1970); 1,137,000 (1980); 1,276,000 (1990); 1,353,610 (2000); and 1,367,692 (2005).

ZAMBO. A person of mixed African and Indian descent. *See also* BLACKS; MESTIZO; MULATTO.

ZAMNA. One of the very earliest known **Maya** leaders. He probably lived in the latter seventh century. Legend has it he was a priest and a scientist who specialized in plants and medicine, but his greatest surviving work was the naming of many lakes, plains, forests, etc. on the **Yucatán** Peninsula.

ZAMORA, ADOLFO (1902–). A Nicaraguan-born law graduate of **UNAM** who studied at the Paris Sorbonne, 1926–1930, and became professor of social welfare at UNAM and of administration at the **Instituto Politécnico Nacional**. He authored the 1943 law that began Mexico's **social security** system.

ZAPATA, EMILIANO (1877–1919). Indian leader and revolutionary, a native of San Miguel, **Morelos**, who sponsored the Plan of **Ayala**, and was probably the most idealistic of all the leaders of the **Revolution of 1910**. He originally supported Francisco **Madero**, but turned against him when he failed to redistribute any land. He and Pancho **Villa** captured **Mexico City** in 1914 and shared the presidential chair. At one time Zapata controlled most of southern Mexico and was staunchly supported and idealized by his men. He was murdered by agents of **Carranza** who led him into an ambush where he never suspected foul play, April 10, 1919.

Zapata had only three years' schooling in his Indian village before getting a job at age 12 as a stable boy on a nearby **hacienda**. At 15 he had become an expert horse trainer, a useful skill in his fighting career. Antonio **Soto y Gama** acted as his mentor.

ZAPATA, LUIS. Novelist: *El vampiro de la colonia Roma* (1978).

ZAPATA LOREDO, FAUSTO (1940–). Journalist from **San Luis Potosí.** A reporter, then an editor for *La Prensa*, then assistant minister of the **presidency** from 1970–1976, press secretary for the **Confederación Nacional Campesina**, in 1968, and then, from 1970, press secretary for, in turn, Presidents Luis **Echeverría** and José **López Portillo.**

ZAPATISTA. Originally, a supporter of Emiliano **Zapata**, but in the 1970s the word was appropriated by the Marxist **Frente Urbana Zapatista.** Much more significantly, in the 1990s it was appropriated by Rafael Sebastián **Guillén Vicente** and his **Ejército Zapatista de Liberación Nacional**, in furtherance of their claim that their **agrarian reform** proposals continued those of the **Morelos** revolutionary.

ZAPOTEC INDIANS. This **Oaxaca** group, related to the **Mixtec Indians** of the same region, built a civilization in the 14th century with pictograph writing and huge temples at **Monte Albán**, and **Mitla**. Now they are Mexico's third largest Indian group, numbering 347,000 persons in 1995.

ZARAGOZA, [GENERAL] IGNACIO (1829–1862). National hero, born in **Texas** (when still part of Mexico). A strong supporter of Benito **Juárez**, whom he served briefly as war minister before resigning to return to his army career. As victor of the Battle of **Puebla** in 1862, he is commemorated by an equestrian statue in **Saltillo**'s **Alameda** Park and by the official renaming of Puebla as "Puebla de Zaragoza." Shortly after the battle he died of typhoid fever.

ZAVALA, LORENZO DE (1788–1836). Politician from **Yucatán** who held several high posts in various governments after **Independence**. After falling out with Antonio López de **Santa Anna**, he settled in **Texas** and fought for its freedom from Mexico, becoming the new nation's first vice president. Mexicans generally regard him as a traitor.

ZEA, LEOPOLDO (1912–). A leading philosopher, author, advocate of **positivism**, and a long-term dean of philosophy and letters at

UNAM, His *El Positivismo en México* (1943) won the annual Book Fair award and is still widely read. In his 1955 *América en la conciencia de Europa* he stressed the future role of Latin America as a bridge between Old World and New World cultures.

ZEDILLO PONCE DE LEÓN, ERNESTO (1951–). President of Mexico, 1994–2000. An economist whose Yale doctoral dissertation was on the Mexican **petroleum** industry. Having been campaign manager for the assassinated Luis **Colosio,** Zedillo was officially nominated in his place. He symbolized law and order, ran a high-minded campaign, and most observers of the **election of 1994** tended to see the healthy vote for Zedillo as, in part, a vote against violence in political life. From the autumn of 1997, however, Zedillo had to contend with an opposition majority in the **Cámara de Diputados Federales.** A cliffhanger situation dragged on until late December before he could convince the **Partido de Acción Nacional** to desert temporarily its coalition with the **Partido de la Revolución Democrática** and agree to a budget he could live with. A similar situation followed in 1998, with the budget enacted on December 31, with only two days before it had to be in place, and two weeks after the normal end of the congressional session. The new situation impacted on the choice of Zedillo's successor. He suggested that the **Partio Revolucioario Institucional** hold a primary election, without specifying when it should be.

ZEMPALTEPETL. The highest mountain peak in **Oaxaca state,** reaching 3,398 m (11,148 ft.).

ZEPEDA, ERACLIO (1937–). Short story writer from **Chiapas** who studied and taught literature at the **Universidad de Veracruz** and became known nationally in the 1950s for his contributions in magazines ranging from *Situaciones* to the *Revista mexicana de literatura.*

ZEPEDA, RAFAEL (1938–). Engraver and lithographer. Born in **Mexico City,** he studied at the **Instituto Nacional de Bellas Artes** and the Fine Arts Academy of Cracow, Poland. His work has gradually become more abstract.

ZERMEÑO ARAICO, MANUEL (1901–1986). Naval officer, born in **Guadalajara**, who graduated from the naval academy (**Escuela Naval Militar**) at **Veracruz** and rose through officer ranks to admiral, to become the commander of the fleet, 1952–1955, and **navy** minister, 1958–1964. He modernized Mexico's warships, equipping them with missiles.

ZETA. Weekly investigative magazine founded in 1980 by Jesús **Blancornelas** and Felix Miranda, and particularly interested in the **Tijuana narcotics** cartel, blamed for the murder of Miranda in 1980. [L. H.]

ZIHUATANEJO (*Chihuatlán*—**"place of women"**). A Pacific Ocean **fishing** port in **Guerrero state**, at 17°38'N, 101°33'W about 240 km (145 miles) northwest of **Acapulco**, and **cabecera** of José Azueta **municipio**. A pre-conquest matrilineal settlement, it became of naval importance in the 17th century. In 1976, it was struck by Hurricane **Madeleine**.

Since the early 1970s, government has developed Ixtapa, 5 km away, as a fashionable tourist resort.

ZIMMERMAN TELEGRAM. Faced with threatened **United States** entry into **World War I** against the Central Powers, the German foreign ministry considered persuading Mexico to make active response to the various assaults by President **Wilson** on its sovereignty (*See DOLPHIN,* USS; PERSHING, JOHN JOSEPH). This backfired completely when the **United Kingdom** supplied the US administration with the text of messages between Berlin and Zimmerman, its minister in Mexico, which British naval intelligence had intercepted and deciphered. [L. H.]

ZIP CODES. *See* POST CODES.

ZÓCALO. The central square of many **Aztec** cities (e.g., **Cholula**), but in particular, that of **México City**, officially the *Plaza de la Constitución*, one of the world's largest city squares. It contains the **National Palace** (housing the presidential and some cabinet offices) and the **Cathedral of Mexico City**.

In cities first established under Spanish rule, such as **Guadalajara**, the main square tends to be called, Spanish fashion, the *Plaza de Armas*.

ZORRILLA MARTÍNEZ, PEDRO (1933–). Politician from **Monterrey**. A graduate of the **UNAM** *Escuela de Derecho* (Law School), 1995, he obtained an economics PhD from the Paris Sorbonne, 1958, and became professor at UNAM and then at the **Universidad Iberoamericana**. In the 1960s he developed the **Partido Revolucionario Institucional**'s **Instituto de Estudios Políticos, Económicos y Sociales (IEPES)**. In 1972–1973 he served as **procurador de justicia** (attorney general) of the **Federal District**. As governor of **Nuevo León**, 1973–1979, he helped develop the **Programa Industrial Fronterizo**.

ZULOAGA, [GENERAL] FÉLIX [MARÍA] (1813–1876). President of the conservative government, 1858–1962, during the **War of the Reforms**. Born in **Sonora**, he was originally a liberal who supported **Comonfort** but then replaced him as president, January–December 1858. He repealed the **Reform Laws** and served again as president, January 1859–August 1860 and December 1860–April 1862. He was then forced into exile by Miguel **Miramón**. This may have saved his life, for he lived out the **French intervention** in Cuba and returned to Mexico afterward.

ZUMÁRRAGA, JUAN DE (1468–1548). The first bishop of **Mexico City**, and one of the greatest ever to occupy this key post. He was appointed bishop of **Tlaxcalá City**, September 2, 1530; renamed bishop of Mexico, August 11, 1536; and elevated to archbishop, February 12, 1546. **Charles V** came to know him personally, spending Holy Week in the same Spanish monastery where the future bishop then lived, and when Spaniards in **New Spain** sought a bishop the emperor asked the Vatican to appoint Zumárraga. He was also authorized to use the title *Protector de los Indios* and was known as a great benefactor of the **Indians**. His accomplishments included the Cathedral of Mexico City, the introduction of **printing** into Mexico, and the founding of the **Colegio de Santa Cruz de Tlatelolco**. The most dramatic event of his episcopate was the appearance of Saint **Mary**

of Guadalupe to Juan **Diego**. He lies buried in his own cathedral. *See also* INQUISITION.

ZÚÑIGA, ARMANDO (1948–). Painter, known primarily in Mexico, who studied at the *Escuela Nacional de Arquitectura* of **UNAM**.

ZÚÑIGA, FRANCISCO (1912–1998). Costa Rican-born sculptor, painter, draftsman, and lithographer, who moved to Mexico City in 1936 and became a naturalized Mexican. Most of his many public monuments and sculptures are in Mexico. One of his best known works is the painting *Desnudo*.

ZÚÑIGA, JUANA DE. Second wife of Hernán **Cortés**.

ZÚÑIGA Y ACEVEDO, GASPAR DE, CONDE DE MONTER-REY (1560–1606). Viceroy of **New Spain**, 1595–1603, previously a courtier and a soldier fighting in Portugal. He pacified the **Chichimec Indians** and **was** responsible for large-scale resettlement of **Indians** through the **reducción** system, for which a new agency, the *Sala de Congregaciones*, was created. He sent an expedition into **California** and founded **Monterrey**, named for his birthplace in Spain. He was subsequently made viceroy of Peru.

ZÚÑIGA Y GUZMÁN, BALTASAR DE, DUQUE DE ARIÓN, MARQUÉS DE VALERO Y DE ALMONTE (1668–1727?). Viceroy of **New Spain**, 1716–1722. He encouraged the settlement of **Texas** and strengthened the northern frontier and that of **Florida** against French and British incursions. In 1718 a person with schizophrenia tried to assassinate him and was placed in a hospital. He gave up his office to become president of the **Council of the Indies**. [L. H.]

Bibliography

CONTENTS

I. INTRODUCTION

Up-to-date references on Mexico that combine historical perspective and current trends are difficult to find in English. Even readers fluent in Spanish find that their quest for impartial analyses and objective, succinct entries on the historical milestones of Mexico's public life are outnumbered by Mexican publications by authors who are politically committed to one or more entities within Mexico, a natural and understandable circumstance, and one that even, on occasion, insures the accuracy of a chronicler who lives the day-to-day realities inside Mexico.

Yet we know that some of the most balanced and objective overviews of the United States, for example, were written by British scholars, such as the historian and diplomat James Bryce, whose *American Commonwealth* of 1888 guided decades of those seeking to fathom the complexity of American politics and culture. Certainly British historian Paul Johnson captured the real cultural and political aspects of the US in his widely acclaimed *A History of the American People* in 1997. And Henry Albinski, political science professor at Pennsylvania State University, who served with distinction with the Georgetown University Center for Strategic Studies, after visiting professorships in Canada and Australia, produced in 1973 the monumental *Canadian and Australian Politics in Comparative Perspectives*, which evoked praise from top scholars in both those nations for his "balanced perspective on our parliamentary system."

The list that follows conforms to the subject arrangement used in the more recent volumes in this series of "Latin American Historical Dictionaries" and is completed by an index of authors, editors, and illustrators. An attempt has been made to indicate both the earliest and latest editions, together with the original in the case of translations. The selection emphasizes material in English and Spanish but occasionally includes untranslated items in other Western European languages. Individual items have often been included, not to endorse their content, but rather to indicate the range of opinion on a topic. Lack of a collation (pagination, etc.) statement indicates that, although the item is believed to exist, no copy has been traced in any major library.

The penultimate section, on foreign fiction with a Mexican setting, is far longer than the equivalent section in the other historical dictionaries in this series. This does not result from any change of policy, but from the simple circumstance that American writers in particular have been more attracted to their immediate neighbor as a setting for their narratives, if only in relation to cross-border smuggling (whether of cattle, narcotics, or people). [L. H.]

An index to its authors, editors, translators, and illustrators follows this section. The dictionary proper does duty for a subject index as it contains references to the sections and individual items of the bibliography, but the outline arrangement is as follows:

II. BIBLIOGRAPHIES

A. Bibliographies of Bibliographies

Barberena Blásquez, Elvia. "Las fuentes de información y servicios bibliotecarios que uliliza el Banco de México," in *Latin American Economic Issues: Information News and Sources. Papers of the XXVIth Seminar on the Acquisition of Latin American Library Materials, New Orleans, 1981.* Madison: SALALM, 1984: 9–15.

Hallewell, Laurence. "Latin American Area Librarianship: A Guide for Collection Development." *Choice: Current Reviews for Academic Libraries* 33(10):1593–1605 (June 1996).

B. General Bibliographies

1. Multilingual

a. Current

Handbook of Latin American Studies. Washington, DC: Library of Congress, 1936– (annual).

b. Retrospective

Cambridge History of Latin America, ed. Leslie Bethell. *Vol. XI: Bibliographical Essays.* Cambridge, UK: Cambridge University Press, 1995. xix, 1,043 p.

Inter-American Review of Bibliography = Revista interamericana de bibliografía. Washington, DC: Dept. of Cultural Affairs, Pan American Union, v1–49, 1950–1999.

Latin America and the Caribbean: A Critical Guide to Research Sources, ed. Paula H. Covington, et al. Westport, CT: Greenwood Press, 1992. xix, 925 p.

Palau y Dulcet, Antonio. *Manuel del librero hispano-americano: inventario bibliográfico de la producción científica y literaria de España y de la América Latina desde la invención de la imprenta hasta nuestros dias, con el valor comercial de todos los artículo descritos.* Madrid: 1823. 7 v.; 2a. ed., Julio Ollero, 1990.

2. English

Bayitch, S. A. "Mexico" in his *Latin America and the Caribbean: A Bibliography of Works in English.* Coral Gables: Univerisity of Miami Press; Dobbs Ferry: Oceana, 1967. 943 p.

Robbins, Naomi C. *Mexico.* ("World Bibliography Series"). Oxford: Clio Press, 1984. xii, 167 p.

C. Mexican National Bibliographies

Andrade, Vicente Paula de. *Ensayo bibliográfico mexicano del siglo xvii.* 2a. ed., Mexico City: Imprenta del Museo Nacional, 1899. [viii], 804 p.

Anuario bibliográfico mexicano, 1931–1933. Felipe Teixidor, ed. Mexico City: 1932–1934. 3 v.

Beristain y Sousa, José Mariano. *Biblioteca hispano-americano septentrional.* Mexico City: 1816–1819. 6 v.; 2a. ed., Amecameca: 1883. 4 v in 3.

García Icabalceta, Joaquín. *Bibliografía mexicana del siglo xvi. Primera parte: catálogo razonado de libros impresos en México de 1539 á 1600* . . . Mexico City: 1886. Nueva ed. por Agustín Millares Carlo. Mexico City: Fondo de Cultura Económica, 1954. 581 p.

González de Cossío, Francisco. *La imprenta en México, 1594–1820: cien adiciones a la obra de don José Toribio Medina.* Mexico City: Porrúa y Hijos, 1947. 205 p.

Medina, José Toribio. *La imprenta en la Puebla de los Ángeles, 1640–1821.* Santiago de Chile: Imprenta Cervantes, 1908. L, 823 p.

———. *La imprenta en México, 1539–1821.* Santiago de Chile: Medina, 1907–1912. 8 v.

D. Bibliographies of Special Material

1. National Government Publications (Chronologically, in Order of Period of Coverage)

Carpenter, Edwin Hager. "Government Publication in Late Eighteenth-century Mexico," *Bibliographical Society of America Papers* 46: 121–138 (April–June 1952).

Costeloe, Michael P. *Mexico State Papers, 1744–1843: A Descriptive Catalogue of the G. R. G. Conway Collection in the Institute of Historical Research, University of London.* London: Athlone Press, 1976. [v], 153 p.

Ker (afterwards Johnston), Annita Melville. *Mexican Government Publications: A Guide to the Most Important Publications of the National*

Government of Mexico, 1821–1936. Washington, DC: Library of Congress, 1940. xxi, 333 p.

Fernández de Zamora, Rosa Maria. *Las publicaciones oficiales de México: guía de publicaciones periódicas y seriadas, 1937–1970.* Mexico City: UNAM, 1977. 238 p.

Mesa, Rosa Quintero. Latin American Serial Documents. Vol 4: Mexico. Ann Arbor, MI: University Microfilms, 1970. xxi, 355 p.

Hartness, Ann. "Governments as Publishers of Reference Materials: Mexico and Brazil, 1970–1980," *Latin American Research Review* 17(2): 145–49 (1982), and as offprint, Austin: University of Texas, 1982.

González, Nelly L. "Acquisition of Official Publications from Argentina, Brazil and Mexico," *Library Resources on Latin America: New Perspectives for the 1980s. Final Report and Working Papers of the XXVth Seminar on the Acquisition of Latin American Library Materials, Albuquerque, NM, 1980.* Madison, WI: SALALM Secretariat, 1981: 203–22.

———. "Las publicaciones oficiales en América Latina, en especial el caso de México," *SALALM and the Area Studies Community: Papers of the XXVIIth Seminar on the Acquisition of Latin American Library Materials, Austin, TX, May 30–June 4, 1992.* Albuquerque, NM: SALALM Secretariat, 1994: 155–65.

2. Government Publications: Subnational Level

Elmendorf, George and Quinlan, Joan A. "Serials and Government Documents from the States of Mexico," *Latin American Studies into the Twenty-First Century: New Focus, New Formats, New Challenges. Papers of the XXXVIth Annual Meeting of the Seminar on the Acquisition of Latin American Library Materials, San Diego, CA, June 1–6, 1991.* Albuquerque NM: SALALM Secretariat, 1993: 425–31.

Van Patten, Nathan. "Public Documents of the Mexican States and Federal District," in *Public Documents: State, Municipal, Federal, Foreign . . . Papers Presented at the 1933 Conference of the American Library Association.* Ed. A. F. Kuhlman. Chicago: ALA, 1934: 221–27.

3. Journals, Newspapers, and the Press

Garner, Mary A. *The Press of Latin America: A Tentative and Selective Bibliography.* Austin: Institute of Latin American Studies, University of Texas at Austin, 1973. 34 p.

Williams, Gayle, et al. *Index Guide to Latin American Journals.* Austin, TX: SALALM Secretariat, 1999, ix, 170 p.

4. Journal Articles

Hispanic American Periodicals Index, 1970– . Los Angeles: University of California Latin American Center, 1974– (annual).

www.latindex.unam.mx (Sistema Regional de Información en Línea para Revistas Científicas de América Latina, el Caribe, España y Portugal).

III. ARCHIVAL SOURCES AND LIBRARY COLLECTIONS

A. General and Foreign

Abad, Diego José. *Documentos del siglo xvi*. Monterrey: Biblioteca de la Universidad de Nuevo León, 1980.

Burrus, Ernest J. and Zubillaga, Félix. *Misiones mexicanas de la Companía de Jesús, 1618–1745: cartas e informes conservados en la Colección Mateu*. Madrid: J. Porrúa Turanzas, 1982. xviii, 340 p.

Carrera Stampa, Manuel. *Misiones mexicanas en archivos europeos*. Mexico City: Instituto Panamericano de Geografía e Historia, 1949. x, 120 p.

Documentos inéditos o muy raros para la historia de México. Genaro García and Carlos Pereyra, eds. Mexico City: 1905–1911. 36 v. Continued by their *Nuevos documentos*. Mexico City: 1913–1930. ?v.

A Guide to Manuscript Sources for the History of Latin America and the Caribbean in the British Isles. Ed. Peter Walne. London: Oxford University Press, 1973. 580 p.

Hilton, Sylvia L. and González Casanovas, Ignacio. *Fuentes manuscritos para la historia de Iberoamérica: guía de instrumentos de investigación*. Madrid: Instituto Histórico Tavera, 1995. 617 p.

West, Geoffrey, et al. "Colecciones latinoamericanas especiales: colecciones desconocidas del Reino Unido," *Anuario americanista europeo* 2: 118–98 (2004).

Wolf, Gregor. "Legados y colecciones especiales del Instituto Ibero-Americano de Berlín," *Anuario americanista europeo* 2: 199–211 (2004).

B. In North America

Catholic Church, Mexico. *Documents and Acts relating to the first, second, and third Mexican Provincial Councils: MS and printed, 1555–1773*. Berkeley: Bancroft Library of the University of California, 4 v.

Dean, Warren. "Sources for the Study of Latin American Economic History: The Records of North American Private Enterprise," *Latin American Research Review* 3(3):79–86 (1968).

Handbook of Hispanic Source Materials and Research Organizations in the United States. Ronald Hilton, ed., 1942. 2nd ed. Stanford, CA: Stanford University Press, 1956. xiv, 488 p.

C. In Mexico

Concilios Provinciales Mexicanos. Época colonial. Ed. Francisco J. Cervantes Bello and Pilar Martínez López-Cano. (Serie Instrumentos de Consulta, 4). Instituto de Investigaciones Históricas del UNAM: Mexico City, 2004. CD.

Hill, Roscoe R. *The National Archives of Latin America.* Cambridge, MA: Harvard University Press, 1945. ix, 163 p.

Iguiniz, Juan B. "Las bibliotecas mexicanas," pp.190–214 of his *El libro.* Mexico City: Porrua, 1946.

Lindvall, Karen. *Research in Mexico City: A Guide to Selected Libraries and Research Centers.* San Diego: University of California, Instructional Services Department, 1977. 45 p.

Mathes, W. Michael. "Mexico" in *Encyclopedia of Library History*, ed. Wayne A. Wiegand and Donald G. Davis Jr. New York: Garland, 1994: 432–34.

Nauman, Ann Keith. *Handbook of Latin American and Caribbean National Archives . . .* Detroit: Blain-Ethridge Books, 1984. ix, 127 p.

Rubio Mañé, Jorge Ignacio. "El Archivo General de la Nación, México, D.F.," in *Revista de historia de América* 9:63–169 (August, 1940).

1. The National Library

Biblioteca Virtual Miguel de Cervantes, at www.cervantesvirtual.com

Jackson, William Vernon, "National Library of Mexico," in *International Dictionary of Library Histories*, ed. David H. Stam. Chicago: Fitzroy Dearborn, 2001: 532–35.

2. Photographic Archives

Davidson, Martha, et al. *Picture Collections, Mexico: A Guide to Picture Sources in the United Mexican States.* Metuchen, NJ: Scarecrow Press, 1988. xix, 292 p., 32 pls.

D. Virtual Libraries and Internet Resources

1. Gateways

http://kib.nmsu.edu/subject/bord/laguia (La Guía, a guide to internet resources for Latin America at the University of New Mexico, ed. Molly Molloy).

http://lanic.utexas.edu (The University of Texas Latin American Network Information Center).

2. Online Library Catalogs

Many major library catalogs can now be consulted on the Internet, not only by author or title but in many cases also under subject.
www.biblional.bibliog.unam.mx (The National Library, Mexico City).
www.bne.es (The National Library of Spain, Madrid).
www.catalog.loc.gov (United States Library of Congress, Washington, DC).
www.catnyp.nypl.org (The New York Public Library, New York).
www.cibera.de (Biblioteca Virtual Iberoamérica/España/Portugal of the Latin American institutes of Berlin, Hamburg, and Bremen, and of the University of Munster and the Hamburg State Library).
www.copac.ac.uk (The merged online catalogues of 24 of the largest university libraries in the British Isles, plus the British Library and the National Library of Scotland).
www.humbul.uk/latin-american (The Oxford University, England, access service to online resources for humanities teaching and research on Latin America).
www.lalweb1.lai.spk-berlin.de (The Latin American Library of the Prussian Cultural Institute, Berlin: one of the world's largest collections on the region. It includes individual journal articles as well as books).
www.lib.utexas.edu (The Library of the University of Texas at Austin, including its Nettie Lee Benson Latin American Library).

3. Online Indexes

www.oclc.org/support/documentation/firstserarch/databases/details/Clase Periodica.htm (subscription service).

4. Documents Accessible Online

LAGDA (*Latin American Government Documents Archive*), Austin, TX: Benson Latin American Collection at the University of Texas, 2005. www.lanic.utexas.edu/project/arhcives/lagda.
LAGRA (*Latin American Government Reports Archive*), Austin: Benson Latin American Collection at the University of Texas, 2005—. www.lanic.utexas.edu/benson/lagovdocs/index1.html.

IV. HISTORIOGRAPHY

Ensayando la historia. Ed. Clara García Ayluardo. Mexico City: Centro de Investigación y Docencia Económicas. 2003. 194 p.

A. Latin America

Latin America: A Guide to the Historical Literature, ed. Charles Carroll Griffin. Austin, TX: University of Texas Press, 1971. xxx, 700 p.

Stein, Stanley J. "Latin American Historiography, 1965–1976," in *Social Sciences Research on Latin America*, ed. Charles Wagley. (Seminar on Latin American Studies in the United States, 1963). New York: Columbia University Press, 1964. xiv, 338 p.

Wilgus, Alva Curtis. *The Historiography of Latin America: A Guide to Historical Writing, 1500–1800.* Metuchen, NJ: Scarecrow Press, 1975. xv, 333 p.

———. *Histories and Historians of Hispanic America: A Bibliographic Essay.* Washington, DC: Inter-American Bibliographical and Library Association, 1936. xiii, 113 p. 2nd ed., New York: H. W. Wilson, 1942. 144 p. Reprinted, Cooper Square Publishers, 1965. xii, 144 p.

B. Mexico

Hale, Charles A. and Meyer, Michael C. "Mexico: The National Period," in *Latin American Scholarship Since World War II: Trends in History, Political Science, Literature, Geography, and Economics.* Edited by Roberto Esquenazi-Mayo and Michael C. Meyer. Lincoln, NE: University of Nebraska Press, 1971.

Jiménez Marce, Rogelio. *La pasión por la polémica: el debate sobre la historia en la época de Francisco Bulnes.* Mexico City: Instituto Mora, 2003. 306 p.

Knight, Alan. "Patterns and Prescriptions in Mexican Historiography," *Bulletin of Latin American Research* 25(3):340–66 (July 2006).

Potash, Robert A. "History of Mexican Studies since 1821," in *Hispanic American Historical Review* 40:383–424 (August 1960).

V. GENERAL WORKS ON MEXICO
(IN ORDER OF FIRST EDITION)

Hamilton, Leonidas Le Cenci. *Hamilton's Mexican Handbook: A Complete Description of the Republic of Mexico, its Mineral and Agricultural Resources, Cities and Towns of every State, Factories, Trade, Imports and*

Exports . . . Tariff Regulations, Duties, &c., &c., and a Commercial Directory of the Principal Business Men. . . . Boston: D. Lothrop, 1883. 281, xiii p.

Enock, C. Reginald. *Mexico: Its Ancient and Modern Civilization, History and Political Conditions, Topography and Natural Resources, Industry and General Development.* London, Leipzig: T. Fisher Unwin, 1909. Reprinted 1914. xxxvi, 362 p.

Turner, John Kenneth. *Barbarous Mexico.* Chicago: C. H. Kerr, 1911. 340 p.; New ed., Introduction by Sinclair Snow. Austin, TX: University of Texas Press, 1969. xxix, 322 p.

Spence, Lewis. *Mexico of the Mexicans.* New York: Scribner, 1918. vii, 232 p.

Gruening, Ernest. *Mexico and Its Heritage.* New York: The Century Co. [c.1928]. xix, 728 p. Reprinted Appleton-Century, 1940; Greenwood Press, 1968. xi, 692 p.

Chase, Stuart and Chase, Marion Tyler. *Mexico: A Study of Two Americas.* New York: Macmillan, 1931. xii, 338 p.

Simpson, Lesley B. *Many Mexicos.* New York: Putnam, 1941; 3rd ed., revised, with maps. Berkeley, CA: University of California Press, 1952. 349 p.; 4th ed., 1966. xiii, 389 p.

Paz, Octavio, *El laberinto de la soledad*: México City: Cuadernos Americanos, 1950, c.1947. 195 p. Translated by Lysander Kemp, Yara Milos, and Rachel Phillips Belash as *The Labyrinth of Solitude: Life and Thought in Mexico.* New York: Grove Press [1962, c.1961]. 212 p.

México: realización y esperanza. Por José Alcazar Arias et al. Mexico City: Editorial Superación, 1952. xiv, 783 p.

Swan, Michael. *Temples of the Sun and Moon: A Mexican Journey.* London: Cape, 1954. 288 p.

Crow, John A. *Mexico Today.* New York: Harper & Brothers, 1957. xv, 336 p.

Johnson, William Weber. *Mexico.* ("Life World Library.") New York, Time, 1961. 160 p. Reprinted 1967 as *Mexico: The Land, the People, the Spirit,* 1967. 190 p. Revised English ed., London: Sunday Times, 1963. 160 p.

Six Faces of Mexico: History, People, Geography, Government, Economy, Literature & Art. Ed. R. C. Ewing. Tucson, AZ: University of Arizona Press, 1966. 320 p.

Mexico: A Country Study, 4th ed., edited by Tim L. Merrill and Ramón Miró. Washington, DC: GPO for the Federal Research Division, Library of Congress, 1997. xlix, 414 p.

Wide-ranging general survey of Mexico, its government, economy, culture, history etc. Third ed. by James D. Rudolph, 1985; Earlier editions published for the U.S. Army as *Area Handbook for Mexico,* in 1974 by John Morris Ryan et al., and in 1975 by Thomas E. Weil.

Sanders, Sol W. *Mexico: Chaos on our Doorstep.* Lanham, MD: 1986, xiii, 222 p.

Eadie, Peter McGregor. *Essential Mexico.* ("Essential Travel Guides.") Basingstoke, UK: Automobile Association, 1991. 128 p. New ed., by Fiona Dunlop, entitled *AA Essential Mexico* 1999. 126 p.; revised 2004.

———. *Mexico: A Traveller's Cultural History.* London: Batsford, 1991, 189 p.

Mexico Handbook, ed. Joe Cummings and Chicki Mallan. Chico, CA: Moon Publications, 1996. (annual?)

Ross, John B. *Mexico in Focus: A Guide to the People, Politics and Culture.* London: Latin America Bureau, 1996. 75 p.; 2nd ed., with additional accounts and updates by Gregory Gransden. 2003. 102 p.

The Mexico Reader: History, Culture, Politics, ed. Gilbert M. Joseph and Timothy J. Henderson. Durham, NC: Duke University Press, 2002. xiv, 792 p.

A. Illustrations

Conger, Amy. *Edward Weston in Mexico, 1923–1926.* Albuquerque, NM: University of New Mexico Press for the San Francisco Museum of Modern Art, 1983. xx, 127 p.

Rivera, Diego. *Portrait of Mexico; paintings by Diego Rivera and text by Bertram D. Wolfe.* New York, Covici, Friede Press [c.1937]. 211 p., 1 l. 249 p.

VI. ENCYCLOPEDIAS

A. General and Latin American Encyclopedias

Cambridge Encyclopedia of Latin America and the Caribbean, ed. Simon Collier et al. Cambridge: Cambridge University Press, 1985. 2nd ed. 1992. 479 p.

Enciclopedia universal ilustrada europeo-americana. Barcelona: España-Calpe, 1905–1933. 70 v and 10 v *Apéndice.* Continued by 32 (initially annual) supplements from *1934*, published from 1935. [Nueva ed., reestructurada], 2003. 90 v.

Encyclopedia of Latin American History and Culture. Editor in chief Barbara Tenenbaum, New York: Scribner, 1995. 4 v.

1. Electronic

Enciclopedia Universal Micronet, Madrid: Micronet S.A., 1995. CD-ROM; 9a ed., 1999; revised as Versión 2006, also available in DVD.

B. Encyclopedias of Mexico

Aguayo Quezada, Sergio. *México a la mano.* Mexico City: Grialbo, 2003. 263 p.

Diccionario Porrua de historia, biografia y geografia de Mexico. 1a. ed. Mexico City: Editorial Porrúa, 1964. xxxii, 1,723 p. ; 6a ed., corr. y aum., 1995. 4 v.

Enciclopedia de México. Mexico City: Instituto de la Enciclopedia de Mexico, 1966–1977. 12 v.; 4a ed. Director: José Rogelio Álvarez. 1978. 12 v.; Ed. especial, Secretaría de la Educación Pública, 1987–1988. 14 v.

Enciclopedia de México. ("Enciclopedias de paises de América Latina"). Miami: Editorial Oceano, [2002?]. 6 v.

García Cubas, Antonio. *Diccionario geográfico, histórico y biográ-fico de los Estados Unidos Mexicanos.* Mexico City: 1888–1891. 5 v.

López de Escalera, Juan. *Diccionario biográfico y de historia de México.* Mexico City: Editorial del Magisterio, 1964. 1,200 p.

Musacchio, Humberto. *Milenios de Mexico: [diccionario enciclopédica de México].* Mexico City: Hoja Casa Editorial, 1999. 3 v.

Nelson, George E. and Nelson, Mary B. *Mexico, A-Z: An Encyclopedic Dictionary of Mexico.* Cuenravaca: Centro para Retirados, 1975. 832 p.

Todo México, 1985- Mexico City: Enciclopedia de México, 1985- .

VII. GEOGRAPHY AND GEOLOGY

A. Economic Geography and Environment

Elmendorf, George. "Ecology in Central and North Mexico," *Technology, the Environment and Social Change: Papers of the XXXVIIIth Annual Meeting of the Seminar on the Acquisition of Latin American Library Materials, Guadalajara, May, 1993.* Albuquerque, NM: SALALM Secretariat, 1995: 108–12.

Elmendorf, George and Quinlan, Joan A. "Mexico's Environmental and Ecological Organizations and Movements," *Latin American Studies into the Twenty-First Century: New Focus, New Formats, New Challenges. Papers of the XXXVIth Annual Meeting of the Seminar on the Acquisition of Latin American Library Materials, San Diego, CA, June 1–6, 1991.* Albuquerque, NM: SALALM Secretariat, 1993: 123–29.

Simon, Joel. *Endangered Mexico: An Environment on the Edge.* San Francisco: Sierra Club, 1997. x, 275 p.

B. Geology

Garfias, Valentín R. and Chapin, Theodore C. *Geología de México.* Mexico City: Jus, 1949. 202 p.

López Ramos, Ernesto. *Geología general.* 4a ed. Mexico City: 1976–79. 3 v.

C. Seismology

García Acosta, Virginia and Suárez, Gerardo. *Los sismos en la historia de México*. Mexico City: Fondo de Cultura Económica, 1966-? 3v? [New ed. by García Acosta alone], 2001. 3 v.

D. Climate

Vivo, Jorge Abilio and Gómez, José C. *Climatología de México*. Mexico City: Instituto Panamericano de Geografía e Historia, 1946.

E. Flora and Fauna

Biological Diversity of Mexico: Origins and Distribution. Ed. T. P. Ramamoorthy. Oxford: Oxford University Press, xxxix, 812 p.
Wallace, David Rains. *The Monkey's Bridge: Mysteries of Evolution in Central America*. San Francisco, CA: Sierra Club, 1997. xxii, 277 p.

1. Flora

Pesman, Michiel Walter. *Meet Flora Mexicana: An Easy Way to Recognize Some of the More Frequently Met Plants of Mexico as Seen from the Main Highways*. Globe, AZ: D. S. King, 1962. 278 p.

2. Fauna

Leopold, Starker. *Wildlife in Mexico: The Game Birds and Mammals*. Berkeley, CA: University of California Press. 1959.
Wauer, Roland H. *Naturalist's Mexico*. c.1992. Revised edition published as *Birder's Mexico*. College Station, TX: Texas A&M University Press, c.1999. xxvi, 304 p.

a. Mammals

Diversidad y conservación de los mamíferos neotropicales. Ed. Gerardo Ceballos. Mexico City: Comisión Nacional de Conservación y Uso de la Biodiversidad. 2002. 582 p.
Hall, Eugene Raymond and Kelson, Keith R. *The Mammals of North America*. Lawrence KS: Allan Press; New York, Ronald Press, 1959. 2 v.; Second ed., New York: Wiley, 1981. 2v.

b. Birds

Blake, E. R. *Birds of Mexico: A Guide for Field Identification.* Chicago: University of Chicago Press, 1953. ix, 644 p.

Howell, Steve N. G. and Webb, Sophie. *A Guide to the Birds of Mexico and Northern Central America.* Oxford: Oxford University Press, 1995. xvi, 851 p.

Puebla Olivares, Fernando. *Guía de aves del ajusco medio.* Mexico City: Comisión Nacional para el Conocimiento y Uso de la Biodiversidad, 2003. 52 p.

Sutton, George Miksch. *Mexican Birds.* Norman, OK: University of Oklahoma Press, 1951. xv, 282 p.

c. Fish

Stillwell, Hart. *Fishing in Mexico.* New York: Knopf, 1948. xii, 296, iv p.

VIII. MAPS AND ATLASES

Arbingast, Stanley. *Atlas of Mexico.* Austin, TX: Bureau of Business Research, University of Texas, 1974. 165 p.

Aztec, Olmec, and Mesopotamian Maps on GradSchools.com History Link at www.historylink.101.com/1/aztec/aztec_maps.

Crab, Raymond B. *Cartographic Mexico: A History of State Fixations and Fugitive Landscapes.* Durham, NC: Duke University Press, 2004. xviii, 300 p.

Jáuregui O., Ernesto. *Mapas y planos contemporáneos de México.* Mexico City: Instituto de Investigacione Sociales de UNAM, 1968. 132 p.

Mapas Antiguos de México. Comentarios de Joost Depuydt. Mexico City: Fondo de Cultura Económica, 2004. 85 p.

Mexico. Instituto Nacional de Estadística, Geografía e Informática. *Catálogo de publicaciones.* Mexico City: INEGI. 145 p.

Montanus, Arnoldus. "Nova Hispania, Nova Galicia, Gvatimala" in his *De nieuwe en onbekende weerld . . .* Amsterdam: Jacob Meurs, 1671. Translated by John Ogilby as *America: Being the Latest, and Most Accurate Description of the New World . . .* London UK: Ogilby, 1671. 674 p.

Monteiro, Palmyra V. M. *A Catalogue of Latin America Flat Maps, 1926–1964.* Vol. 1: "Mexico, Central America, West Indies." Austin, TX: Institute of Latin American Studies of the University of Texas at Austin, 1967. xvi, 395 p.

Orozco y Berra, Manuel. *Materiales para una cartografía mexicana.* Mexico City: Imprento del Gobierno, 1871. 337 p.

Pick, James B., et al. *Atlas of Mexico.* Boulder: Westview, 1989. 367 p. Revised as *Mexico Handbook: Economic and Demographic Maps and Statistics.* 1994. xxvi, 422 p.

Torres Lanza, Pedro. *Relación descriptiva de los mapas, planos . . . de México y Florida.* Seville: El Mercantil, 1900. Reprinted as *Catálogo de mapas y planos de México.* Madrid: Dirección General de Bellas Artes y Archivos, for Archivo General de Indias, 1985. 2v.

A. Gazeteers

División territorial de los Estados Unidos Mexicanos de 1810 a 1995. Mexico City: INEGI, 1997. 152 p.

Gazeteer of Mexico: Names Approved by the United States Board on Geographic Names. 3rd ed. Washington, DC: US Defense Mapping Agency, 1992. 3v.

IX. TRAVEL GUIDES (IN CHRONOLOGICAL ORDER OF FIRST EDITION)

Janvier, Thomas Alibone. *The Mexican Guide.* New York: Scribner, 1886. ix, 310 p.; 4th ed., 1890. xvi, 531 p.; 5th ed., 1891. xvi, 531 p.

Muirhead, James Fullarton. *The United States, with an Excursion into Mexico: Handbook for Travellers* Leipsic: Karl Baedeker; London: Dulau and Co., 1893. c, 516 p. Mexican section revised and updated by Bleyleben, Anita, et al. as *Mexico.* Stuttgart: Baedecker, 1998. Translated by Wendy Bell, et al. 3rd ed., entitled *Baedeker's Mexico* London: Automobile Association. 2000. 624 p.

Campbell's Guide and Descriptive Book of Mexico. Laredo, TX: Sonora News Co., [before 1908]. 350 p.

South American Handbook, 1923– . Bath: Footprint Handbooks (formerly Trade & Travel), 1924– . Mexican section now published separately (item no. 0162 below).

Terry, Thomas Philip. *Terry's Guide to Mexico: The New Standard Guidebook to the Mexican Republic, with Chapters on the Railways, the Airways, and the Ocean Routes to Mexico . . .* Revised ed., Boston: Houghton Mifflin, 1930. ccxlix, 597 p.

Toor, Frances A. *Frances Toor's Guide to Mexico.* Mexico City: [The Author], 1933, 160 p.; *Guide to Mexico.* Mexico City, 1935. xiv, 264 p.; *New Guide to Mexico.* New York: Crown, 1948. 270 p.

May, Jutta. *Mexiko: Reiseführer und Wegweiser durch die alten Kulturen des Landes mit Sprachführer.* (Goldstadt-Reiseführer, Bd. 205). Pforzheim: Goldstadtverlag, 1967. 304 p.

Fodor's Mexico. New York: Random House for Fodor's Travel Publications, 1972– . 896 p. (annually, in August)

Franz, Carl. *The People's Guide to Mexico*. Santa Fe, NM: John Muir Publications, 1972; 4th ed., 1976; 5th ed., 1979. [xv], 592 p.; 12th ed., edited by Lorena Haven and Steve Rogers. Emeryville, CA: Avalon Travel. 2002. [xiv], 585 p.

Bradt, Hilary and Bradt, George. *Backpacking in Mexico & Central America*. Chalfont St. Peter UK, Boston MA: Bradt, 1978. 134 p.; 2nd ed., by Hilary Bradt and Rob Rachowiecki, subtitled *A Guide for Walkers and Naturalists*. Cambridge, MA: 1982. 247 p. Rewritten by Tim Burford Burford as *Backpacking in Mexico*. Chalfont St. Peter: Bradt; Old Saybrook, CT: Globe Pequot, 1997. vii, 248 p.

Frommer's Mexico. New York: Macmillan Travel, 1996– . Annual, published since 2003 by Wiley of Hoboken, NJ. 2000, ed. David Baird and Lynne Bairstow. Continues *Frommer's Mexico and Guatemala on $10 a day*. Ed. Tom Brisnahan and Jane Kretchman. New York: Pasmatier, 1981– .

Noble, John, et al. *Mexico: A Travel Survival Guide*. Hawthorne, Victoria: Lonely Planet, 1982. 3rd ed., 1989. 940 p., 9th ed. (entitled *Lonely Planet, Mexico*), 2004. 1028 pp. 8 col. pls.

Fisher, John. *The Rough Guide to Mexico*. New York: Penguin Books, 1985. 4th ed., 2004. xxiv, 912 p.

Let's Go: The Budget Guide to Mexico. Kenneth Hale-Wehmann, ed.; written by Harvard Student Agencies, Inc. New York: St. Martin's Press, 1985 and subsequent annual (?) revisions with frequent change of editor. Retitled from 2002 as *Let's Go Mexico ["on a budget"]*, Angle K. Chen et al., editors. 1st ed. Cambridge MA: Let's Go Publications; Bastingstoke, UK: Macmillan, 2002. xx, 666 p.; [5th? annual? ed.], Kavita Shishir Shah, ed. 2006, xvi, 720 p.

Mexico & Central American Handbook. Bath: Trade & Travel. 1991 (annual). Editions 7–11, 1997–2001, ed. Peter Hutchinson, entitled *Mexico & Central America Handbook*. Edition 12, 2002, entitled *Central America and Mexico*, published by Footprint Handbooks. Edition 13, 2003, ed. Sarah Cameron and Ben Box, 1,264 p., entitled *Footprint: Mexico & Central America Handbook*. (annual).

Collis, John and Jones, David Michael. *Blue Guide Mexico*. Atlas, maps, and plans by John Fowler. London, UK: A. & C. Black, 1997. 948 p.

Mexico. (DK Eyewitness Travel Guides). London: Dorling Kindersley, 1999; 4th ed., 2003. 284 p.

"Portrait of Mexico," 26pp; "History," 17pp. Mexico City, 67pp., "Region by region," 159pp., "Travelers' Needs," 43pp., "Survival Guide," 21pp.; Index, and Phrase Book (4pp). Printed on glossy paper with a wealth of colored illustrations and endpaper maps.

Egelkraut, Ortrun. *Mexiko*. Cologne: Vista Point, 2000. 296 p. Updated 2nd ed., 2004.

Nichols, Fiona. *Mexico.* ("Globetrotter Travel Guides.") London: New Holland, 2000. 128 p.

Mallan, Chicki and Mallan, Oz. *Colonial Mexico: A Traveler's Guide to Historic Districts and Towns.* 2nd ed. Emeryville, CA: Avalon Travel, 2001. [xiv], 361 p.

Onstott, Jane. *"National Geographic" Traveler: Mexico.* Washington, DC: National Geographic Society; Basingstoke UK: A.A. [Automobile Association] Publishing, 2001. 400p.

King, Mona. *Mexico.* Peterborough UK: Thomas Cook Publishing, 2002. 192 p.

Zee, Foo Mei and Kastelein, Barbara. *Mexicochic: Hotels, Haciendas, Spas.* London: Bolding Books; Singapore: Editions Didiet Millet, 2003. 232 p.

Mexique, Guatemala & Belize, 2005. ("Guides du Routard"). Paris: Hachette Tourisme, 2004.

Hermann, Helmut. *Mexiko.* 5. Auflage. Bielefeld: Reise Know-How Verlag Peter Rump, 2006. 900 p.

A. Guides for Settlers

Albright, Richard and Montgomery, Alan W. *Mexico The Bargain Paradise; a Practical Guide to Carefree Living, Vacationing and Investing in Mexico.* Los Angeles: Almo Co. [1967]. 128 p.

Sannebeck, Norvelle. *Everything You Ever Needed to Know about Living in Mexico.* Andersen, SC: Droke House, 1970. 251 p.

B. Travelers' and Visitors' Accounts (Chronologically)

1. Individual Accounts

a. Sixteenth Century

Hawkins, [Sir] John. *A True Declaration of the Troublesome Voyadge of M. John Hawkins to the Parties of Guynea and the West Indies, in . . . 1567 and 1568.* London: Lucas Harrison, 1569. 30 p. Reprinted as *Declaration of the Troublesome Voyadge.* Amsterdam: Theatrum Orbis Terrarum, 1973. 33 p.

Hortop, Job. *The Rare Travailes of Iob Hortop, an Englishman, who was not Heard of in Three and Twentie Yeeres' Space.* London, Printed for William Wright, 1591. 23 l.

Ciudad Real, Antonio de. *Relación breve y verdadera de algunas cosas de las muchas que sudidieron al padre fray Alonso Ponce en las provincias de la Nueva Espana . . .* Madrid: Vidua de Caller, 1873. 2 v.

Champlain, Samuel de. *Brief discord des choses plus remarcables*. Translated from the original and unpublished manuscript as *Narrative of a Voyage to the West Indies and Mexico in the Years 1599–1602*, with a biographical notice and notes by Alice Wilmere; edited by Norton Shaw. London: Printed for the Hakluyt Society, 1859.vi, xcix, 48 p.

b. Seventeenth Century

Mota y Escobar, Alonso de la. *Memoriales del obispo de Tlaxcala: un recorrido por el centro de México a principios del siglo xvii,* Mexico City: Secretaría de Educación Pública, 1987. 180 p.

Nieto, Pedro. *Relazione sulla Nuova Spagna*. Ed. Pietro Colletta. Palermo: Facoltà di Lettere e Filosofia, 2004. 191 p.

Gage, Thomas. *The English-American: His Travail by Land and Sea; or, A New Survey of the West Indies*. London: Cotes, 1648. Reprinted as *Thomas Gage's Travels in the New World*, edited and with an introduction by J. Eric S. Thompson. Norman, OK: University of Oklahoma Press [1958] li, 379 p.

Newton, Norman. *Thomas Gage in Spanish America*. London: Faber & Faber, 1969. 214 p.

Vázquez de Espinosa, Antonio *Descripción de la Nueva España en el siglo XVII, por el padre fray Antonio Vázquez de Espinosa, y otros documentos del siglo XVII*. México: Editorial Patria, 1944. 254 p.

Gemelli Careri, Giovanni Francisco. *Le Mexique à la fin du xviie siècle, vu par un voyageur italien*: a translated selection from his *Giro del mondo*. Paris: Calman Lévy, 1968. 277 p.

c. Eighteenth Century

Gerhard, Peter. *México en 1742*. México City: Porrúa, 1962. 47 p.

Francisco, de Ajofrín, fray. *Diario del viaje que hicimos a México fray Francisco de Ajofrín y fray Fermín de Olite, capuchinos*. Mexico City: Porrúa Hnos., 1936. 32 p. Reprinted as *Diario del viaje a la Nueva Espana*. Mexico City: Secretaría de Educación Pública, 1986. 220 p.

O'Crouley, Pedro Alonso. *Idea compendiosa del reyno de Nueva Espana*. Unpublished MS of 1774, translated and edited by Seán Galvin as *A Description of the Kingdom of New Spain*. San Francisco: J. Howell, 1972. xviii, 148 p.

Ilarione da Bergamo, [*Fra*] *Viaggio al Messico*. Bergamo: Secomandi, 1976. 125 p. Translated by William J. Orr as *Daily Life in Colonial Mexico*. Edited by Robert Ryal Miller and William J. Orr. Norman, OK: University of Oklahoma Press, 2000. xi, 240 p.

Chappe d'Auteroche, abbé. *Voyage en Californie pur l'observation du passage de Venus sur le disque du soleil*. Translated as *A Voyage to California*.

London: Dilly, 1778. Reprinted with an introduction by Kenneth L. Holmes. Richmond: Richmond Publishing, 1973. 105 p.

d. Early Nineteenth Century

Humboldt, Alexander von. *Essai politique sur le royaume de la Nouvelle-Espagna.* Paris: F. Schoell, 1811. 5 v. Translated by John Black as *Political Essay on the Kingdom of New Spain.* 3rd ed. London: Longman, 1822. 4 v.; ed. and abridged by Mary Maples Dunn, New York:Knopf, 1972. 242 p.

Hardy, Robert William Hale. *Travels in the Interior of Mexico, in 1825, 1826, 1827, and 1828.* London: H. Colburn and R. Bentley, 1829. xiii, 540 p.

Taylor, Edward Thornton. *Mexico, 1825–1828: The Journal and Correspondence.* Ed. C. Harvey Gardiner. Chapel Hill, NC: University of North Carolina Press, 1959. xii, 212 p.

Becher, Carl Christian. *Mexico in den ereignissvollen Jahren 1832 und 1833 und die Reise hin und zurück . . . nebst mercantilischen und statistischen Notizen.* Hamburg: Perthes & Besser, 1834. xii, 269 p.

Stephens, John Lloyd. *Incidents of Travel in Central America, Chiapas, and Yucatan.* New York: Harper & Brothers, 1841. 2v. [and numerous later editions].

Brantz, Mayer. *Mexico As it Was and As it is Now.* New York: J. Winchester, 1844. xii, 390 p.

Ruxton, George Frederick Augustus. *Adventures in Mexico and the Rocky Mountains.* London: John Murray, 1847. viii, 332 p.

e. Late Nineteenth Century

Sartorius, Carl Christian. *Mexiko: Landschaftsbilder und Skizzen aus dem Volkleban.* Translated as *Mexico: Landscapes and Popular Sketches.* Ed. Dr. [Thomas William] Gaspey, with 8 steel engravings . . . from original sketches by [Johann] Moritz Rugendas. Darmstadt: Lange, 1858. vi, 202, 16 plates. Reprinted as *Mexico About 1850.* Stutgart: Brockhaus, 1961. viii, 202 p.

Robertson, William Parish. *A Visit to Mexico, by the West India Islands, Yucatan and United States: With Observations and Adventures on the Way.* London: Simpkin Marshall, 1853. 2v.

Wilson, Robert A. *Mexico: Its Peasants and its Priests; or, Adventures and Historical Researches in Mexico and its Silver Mines During . . . 1851–1854.* New ed. New York: Harper & Brothers, 1856. 418 p.

Fossey, Mathieu de. *Le Mexique.* Paris: H. Plon, 1857. viii, 581 p.

Fröbel, Julius. *Aus Amerika.* Leipzig: 1857–1858. Translated in part as *Seven Years' Travel in Central America, Northern Mexico, and the Far West of the United States.* London: R. Bentley, 1859. xiv, 587 p.

Hill, S. S. *Travels in Peru and Mexico.* London: Longman, 1860. 2v.

Gray, Albert Zabriskie. *Mexico as it is: Being Notes of a Recent Tour in that Country, with some Practical Information for Travellers in that Direction, as also Some Study on the Church Question.* New York: E. P. Dutton, 1878. 148 p.

Finerty, John Frederick. *John F. Finerty Reports Porfirian Mexico, 1879,* ed. Wilbert H. Timmons. El Paso, TX: Texas Western Press, 1974 xviii, 334 p.

Brocklehurst, Thomas Unett. *Mexico Today: A Country with a Great Future. And a Glance at the Prehistoric Remains and Antiquities of the Montezumas* . . . London UK: John Murray, 1883. xvi, 259 p.

Conkling, Howard. *Mexico and the Mexicans; or, Notes of Travel in the Winter and Spring of 1883.* New York: Taintor brothers, Merrill and Co., 1883. x, 298 p.

Leclercq, Jules Joseph. *Voyage au Méxique, de New York à Vera-Cruz, en suivant les routes de terre.* Paris: Hachette, 1885. 446 p.

Bertie-Marriott, Clément. *Un Parisien au Méxique.* 2e éd. Paris: E. Dentu, 1886. 384 p.

Griffin, Solomon Bulkley. *Mexico of Today.* New York: Harper & Brothers, 1886. 267 p.

Smith, Francis Hopkinson. *A White Umbrella in Mexico.* Boston: Houghton Mifflin, 1889. viii, 227 p.

Ballow, Maturin Murray. *Aztec Land.* Boston, New York: Houghton, Mifflin, 1890. x, 355 p.

f. Early Twentieth Century

Barton, Mary. *Impressions of Mexico with Brush and Pen.* London: Methuen, 1911. xi, 161 p.

Cameron, Charlotte. *Mexico in Revolution: An Account of an Englishwoman's Experiences & Adventures in the Land of Revolution, with a Description of the People, the Beauties of the Country & the Highly Interesting Remains of Aztec Civilisation.* London: Seeley, Service, 1925. 278 p.

Lawrence, David Herbert. *Mornings in Mexico.* London: Martin Secker, 1927. 177 p. Reissued as *Mornings in Mexico and Etruscan Places.* London: Heinemann, 1956. vii, 115 p.

Chase, Stuart. *Mexico: A Study of Two Americas.* Illustrated by Diego Rivera. London: Bodley Head, 1932. vii, 336 p.

Huxley, Aldous. *Beyond the Mexique Bay.* London: 1934: New York: Vintage Books, 1960. 262 p.

Bowman, Heath and Dickinson, Stirling. *Mexican Odyssey* . . . Chicago: Willett, Clark & Co., 1935. x, 294 p.

King, Rosa Eleanor. *Tempest over Mexico: A Personal Chronicle.* Boston, MA: Little, Brown, 1935, 319 p.

Greene, Graham. *The Lawless Roads*. London, 1939; published in New York as *Another Mexico*. viii, 279 p. Reprinted Harmonsworth: Penguin Books, 1971.

Marett, [*Sir*] Robert Hugh Kirk. *An Eye-Witness of Mexico*. London: Oxford University Press, 1939. xi, 268 p.

Cerwin, Herbert. *These are the Mexicans*. New York: Reynal & Hitchcock, 1947. 384 p.

Spratling, William. *Little Mexico*. New York: Peter Smith, 1947. 198 p.

Royer, Fanchón. *The Mexico we found*. Milwaukee, WI: Bruce Publishing, 1948. ix, 210 p.

g. Late Twentieth Century and After

Bedford, Sybille. *The Sudden View: A Mexican Journey*. London: Gollancz, 1953. 288 p. New ed., entitled *A Visit to Don Otavio: A Traveller's Tale from Mexico*. London: Collins, 1960. 318 p. Reprinted with an introduction by Bruce Chatwin as *A Visit to Don Otavio: A Mexican Journey*. New York: Dutton, 1986. 288 p.

Fergusson, Erna. *Mexico Revisited*. New York: Knopf, 1955. [xii], 346, vi p.

Verríssimo, Érico. *México: história duma viagem*. Porto Alegre: Globo, 1957. Translated by Linton Barrett as *Mexico*. New York: Orion Press, 1961. vii, 342 p.

Lincoln, John. *One Man's Mexico: A Record of Travels and Encounters*. London: Bodley Head, 1967; New York: Harcourt, Brace & World, 1968. 238 p.

Annaheim, Hans and Leuenberger, Hans. *Mexiko*. Berne: Kümmerly & Frey, 1967. Color photographs by Henri-Maurice Barney and H. Leuenberger. Translated by Ewald Osers as *Mexico*. London: Harrap, 1968. 124 p.

Pride, Nigel. *A Butterfly Sings to Pacaya: Travels in Mexico, Guatemala and Belize*. London: Constable, 1978. 367 p.

Marnham, Patrick. *So Far from God: A Journey to Central America*. New York: Viking, 1985. 253 p.

Hickman, Katie. *A Trip to the Light Fantastic: Travels with a Mexican Circus*. London: Harper Collins, 1993. 301 p., 16 pls.

Egelkraut, Ortrun. *Reise durch Mexiko*. Würzburg, Germany: Stürtz, 1997. 128 p.

Becker. Kavan. *Mexiko: Land der Geheimnisse und Mythen*. Bad Honnet: Horlemann, 2004. 198 p.

2. Anthologies of Travelers' Accounts

Diadiuk, Alicia. *Viajeras anglosajonas en México: memorias*. Mexico City: Secretaría de Educación Pública, 1973. 205 p.

Iturriaga de la Fuente, José N. *Anecdotario de viajeros extranjeros en México, siglos xvi-xx.* Mexico City: Fondo de Cultura Económica, 1988–1989. 4v.

Mexico. Edited by James O'Reilly and Larry Habegger. ("Travelers' Tales.") San Francisco: Publishers Group West, 1995. New ed., 2001.xviii, 442 p.

México visto por algunos de sus viajeros, siglo XVI y XVII. Berta Flores Sallinas, compiladora. [México, 1964] iv, 156 leaves.

Reisende in Mexiko: ein Kulturhistorisches Lesebuch. Ed. Ulrike Keller. Vienna: Promedia, 2003. 229 p.

Richardson, William Harrison. Mexico through Russian Eyes, 1806–1940. Pittsbugh, PA: University of Pittsburgh Press, 1988. xi, 287 p.

Stories of Popular Voyages and Travels; with Illustrations. Containing Abridged Narratives of Recent Travels of Some of the Most Popular Writers on South America. With a Preliminary Sketch of the Geography of that Country. [Compiled by the publisher?]. London: Charles Tilt, 1829. [iv] 1,278 p.

Testimonios de viaje, 1823–1873. [Editor, Mario de la Torre; investigación histórica y textos, Elena Horz de Vía]. México City: Smurfit Cartón y Papel de México, 1989. 227 p.

Viajes en México: crónicas extranjeras Selección, traducción e introducción de Margo Glantz. México City: Fondo de Cultura Económica, 1980. Reprinted 1982. 2 v. 680 p.

3. Bibliography

"Mexico" in Thomas L. Welch and Myriam Figueras, *Travel Accounts and Descriptions of Latin America and the Caribbean, 1800–1920: A Selected Bibliography.* Washington, DC: Columbus Memorial Library, 1982: 150–74.

C. Accounts by Foreign Residents (Chronologically)

Poinsett, Joel Roberts. *Notes on Mexico Made in the Autumn of 1822.* Philadelphia: Carey & Kea; London: J. Miller, 1825. viii, 298 p. Reprinted. by Alva Curtis Wilgus, New York: Praeger, 1969. viii, vi, 359 p.

Bullock, William. *Six Months' Residence and Travels in Mexico, Containing Remarks on the Present State of New Spain, its Natural Productions, State of Society, Manufactures, Trade, Agriculture, and Antiquities, etc.* London: 1824; Reprinted Washington, NY: Kennikat Press, 1971. xiv, 532 p.

Ward, Henry George. *Mexico in 1827.* London: H. Colburn, 1828.

———. *Mexico: His Majesty's Chargé d'Affairs in that Country During the Years 1825, 1826, and Part of 1827, with an Account of the Mining Companies, and of the Political Events in that Republic to the Present Day.* 1829. 2v.

Lyon, [Capt.] George Francis, R. N. *Journal of a Residence and Tour in the Republic of Mexico in the Year 1826, with some Account of the Mines of that Country,* London: John Murray, 1828. 2v., illus. Reprinted Port Washington, NY: Kennikat Press, 1971. 2v.

Calderón de la Barca, Frances Erskine. *Life in Mexico.* With a preface by W. H. Prescott. London: Chapman & Hall; Boston, MA: 1843. xii, 436 p. Reprinted as *Life in Mexico. The Letters of Fanny Calderón de la Barca with new material from the author's private journals.* Ed. and annotated by Harvard T. Fisher and Marion Hall Fisher. Garden City, NY: Doubleday, 1966. xxix, 834 p.

Aguilar, Federico Cornelio. *Último año de residencia en México.* Bogotá: 1885: Impr.de I. Borda. 263 pp. Reprinted Mexico City: Siquisiri, 1995.

Gooch, Fanny Chambers. *Face to Face with the Mexicans: The Domestic Life, Educational, Social and Business Ways, Statesmanship and Literature, Legendary and General History of the Mexican People, as Seen and Studied by an American Woman During Seven Years of Intercourse with Them.* New York: Fords, Howard & Hulbert; London: Sampson Low, 1887. 584 p., 17 pl. Reprinted with an introduction by C. Harvey Gardiner. Carbondale, IL: Southern Illinois University Press, 1966. xx, 248 p.

Lindbergh, Reeve. *No More Words: A Journal of My Mother.* New York: Simon & Schuster, 2001. 224 p.

Bennett, Bernard. *Mexico From Within: A Memoir.* Houston, TX: Panam Association, 1999. [xi], 287 p.

Cohan, Tony. *On Mexican Time: A New Life in San Miguel.* New York: Broadway Books, 2000. 289 p.

X. MEXICAN NATIONAL CHARACTER

Alba, Victor. *The Mexicans: The Making of a Nation.* London: Pall Mall Press; New York: Praeger, 1967. vii, 268 p.

Bartra, Roger. *Jaula de la melancolía.* Mexico City: Grijalbo, 1987. Translated by Christopher J. Hall as *The Cage of Melancholy: Identity and Metamorphosis in the Mexican Character.* New Brunswick, NJ: Rutgers University Press, 1992. xi, 199 p.

Cramer, Mark. *Culture Smart! Mexico.* Portland, OR: Graphic Arts Center; London: Kuperad, 1998. 222p. New edition by Guy Mavor, 2005. 168 p.

Doremus, Anne T. *Culture, Politics and National Identity in Mexican Literature and Film, 1929–1952.* New York, Oxford: P. Lang, 2001. xi, 206 p.

Flandrau, Charles Macomb. *¡Viva Mexico!* New York: Appleton, 1908. 293 p. Reprinted Harper, 1955. 218 p.

Lafaye, Jacques. *Quetzalcóatl et Guadalupe*. Paris: Éditions Gallimard, 1974. Translated by Benjamin Keen as *Quetzalcoatl and Guadalupe: The Formation of Mexican National Consciousness, 1513–1813*. Chicago: University of Chicago Press, 1976. xxx, 336 p.

Lawrence, David Herbert. *The Plumed Serpent*. London: Martin Secker, 1926. 476 p.; American ed. entitled *The Plumed Serpent: Quetzalcoatl* New York: A. A. Knopf, 1926. 445 p.

Paz, Octavio. *Posdata*. Mexico City: Siglo Veintiuno Editores [1970]. 148 p. Translated by Lysander Kemp as *The Other Mexico: Critique of the Pyramid*. New York: Grove Press [1972]. xii, 148 p.

Ramos, Samuel. *El perfil del hombre y la cultura en México*. 2a ed. Mexico City: P. Robredo, 1938. 182 p.

Romanell, Patrick. *Making of the Mexican Mind: A Study in Recent Mexican Thought*. Lincoln, NE: University of Nebraska Press, 1952. ix, 213 p.

Turner, Fred[erick] C., *The Dynamic of Mexican Nationalism*. Chapel Hill, NC: University of North Carolina Press, 1968. xii, 350 p.

A. Foreign Interpretations

Cooper Alarcón, Daniel. *The Aztec Palimpsest: Mexico in the Modern Imagination*. Tucson, AZ: University of Arizona Press, 1997. xx, 224 p.

B. Cuisine

Bayless, Rick. *Rick Bayless' Mexican Kitchen: Capturing the Vibrant Flavors of a World-Class Cuisine*. Photographs by Maria Robledo; illustrations by John Sanford. New York. Scribner, 1996. 448 p.

Bayless, Rick, and Bayless, Deann Groen, *Authentic Mexican Cooking: Regional Cooking from the Heart of Mexico*. New York: Morrow; London: Headline, 1987. 384 p.

Kennedy, Diana Southwood. *The Cuisines of Mexico*. New York: Harper & Row, 1971. xx, 378 p. Revised and updated as *The Essential Cuisines of Mexico*. New York: Clarkson Potter, 2000. xviii, 526 p.

Milton, Jane. *Classic Mexican Kitchen: Mexico's Culinary Heritage: Ingredients, Techniques, Recipes*. London: Southwater, 2001. 128 p.

———. *The Practical Encyclopedia of Mexican Cooking*. London: Lorenz, 2000. 256 p.

Pilcher, Jeffrey M. *¡Que Vivan los Tamales! Mexican Cuisine and National Identity*. Albuquerque, NM: University of New Mexico Press, 1998. x, 234 p.

XI. COLLECTIVE BIOGRAPHY AND GENEALOGY

A. General

Magner, James Aloysius. *Men of Mexico*. Milwaukee: Bruce Publishing, 1942. x, 615 p.

Mundo Lo, Sara de. *Index to Spanish-American Collective Biography. Volume 2: Mexico*. Boston: G. K. Hall, [1981?].

B. Colonial Period

Burkholder, Mark A. and Chandler, D. S. *Biographical Dictionary of Audiencia Ministers in the Americas, 1687–1821*. Westport, CT: Greenwood Press, 1982. xxv, 493 p.

Mañueco Baranda, Tello. *Diccionario del Nuevo Mundo*. Valladolid: Ámbito Ediciones. 2006. 384 p.

C. Republican Period to 1910

Camp, Roderic Ai. *Mexican Political Biographies, 1884–1935*. Austin TX: University of Texas Press, 1991. xxix, 458 p.

Lansing, Marion Florence. *Liberators and Heroes of Mexico and Central America*. Boston: L. C. Page, 1941. xviii, 299 p.

Sosa, Francisco. *Biografías de mexicanos distinguidos*. Mexico City: Secretaría de Fomento, 1884. xii, 1,123 p.

D. Contemporary Period

Alisky, Marvin. *Who's Who in Mexican Government*. Tempe: Arizona State University Center for Latin American Studies, 1969. 64 p.

Camp, Roderic Ai. *The Making of a Government: Political Leaders in Modern Mexico*. Tucson, AZ: University of Arizona, 1984. x, 237 p.

———. *Mexican Political Biographies, 1935–1993*. Austin, TX: University of Texas Press, 1995. xxvii, 468p. Earlier editions: *Mexican Political Biographies, 1935–1975*. Tucson, AZ: University of Arizona Press, 1976; *Mexican Political Biographies, 1935–1981*. Tucson, AZ: University of Arizona Press, 1982. xxiv, 447 p.

———. "Mexican Governors since Cárdenas," *Journal of Inter-American Studies and World Affairs*. (November 1974): 454–81.

————. *Who's Who in Mexico Today.* Boulder, CO: Westview, 1988. 183 p.

Quin es quin en la administration Pública de México. Mexico City: Presidencia de la Republic, 1982. 552 p.

XII. STATISTICS

A. General Statistics

Bibliography mexicana de estadística. Mexico City: Dirección General de Estadística, 1941. 2v.

Estadísticas históricas de México. Mexico City: INEGI, 1985. 2v.

García y Cubas, Antonio. *Noticias geográficas y estadísticas de la Republic Mexicana.* Mexico City: Imp. de J. M. Lara, 1857. 27 p.

Mexico. Dirección General de Estadística. *México en cifras.* 3a. ed. Mexico City: 1959. 56 p.

Mitchell, Brian R. *International Historical Statistics: The Americas and Australasia.* London: Macmillan, 1983. vii, 949 p.

Nacional Financiera S.A. *La economía mexicana en cifras,* Mexico City: 1966. 378 p.

Ortiz de Ayala, Tadeo. *Resúmen de la estadística del imperio mexicano, siglo xix.* Mexico City: UNAM, 1968. 105p.

Romeo, Marís. *Geographical and Statistical Notes on Mexico.* New York: Putnam, 1898. 231 p.

Statistical Abstract of Latin America. Ed. James W. Wilkie and José Guadalupe Ortega. Vol. 38. Los Angeles: Latin American Center Publications, University of California, 2002. 1094 p.

West, Robert A. "Wanted, Preferably Alive: Reliable Information on Mexico," *Planning Review* 7(4):18–19 (July 1979).

B. Census Publications

Goyer, Doreen Suzanne and Domschke, Eliane. *The Handbook of National Populations Censuses: Latin America and the Caribbean, North America and Oceania.* Westport, CT: Greenwood, 1983. xv, 713 p.

Gleason Galicia, Rubén. *Las estadísticas y censos de México: su organización y estado actual.* Mexico City: Instituto de Investigaciones Sociales de la UNAM, 1968. 129 p. Reprinted, 1969.

Instituto Nacional de Estadística, Geografía e Informática. *XIV Censo Industrial, XI Censo Comercial y XI Censo de Servicios.* Mexico City (?): INEGI, 1995. 32 v.

―――. *Conteo de población y vivienda, 1995: Resultados definitivos. Tabulados básicos.* Mexico City (?): 1996. 37v in 47, by state.

Koberstein, Gerhard. *Comparabilidad de los censos mexicanos.* Mexico City: Instituto de Investigaciones Sociales de la UNAM, 1972. 325 p.

Mexico. Dirección general de estadística. *Censo General de la Republic Mexicana verificado el 20 de octubre de 1895.* Mexico City: 1899. 502 p.

―――. *Censo general de la Republic Mexicana verifcada el 28 de octubre de 1900.* Mexico City: 1901–1907. 30 v.

―――. *Tercer censo de población de los Estados Unidos Mexicanos verificado el 27 de octubre de 1910.* Mexico City: 1918–1920. 3v.

Mexico. Departamento de la estadística nacional. *Censo general de habitantes, [1921].* Mexico City: 1925–1928. 31v.

Mexico. Dirección general de estadística. *Quinto censo de población. 15 de mayo de 1930.* Mexico City: 1932–1926. 8v in 6.

―――. *Sexto censo de población, 1940.* Mexico City: 1943–48. 30v.

―――. *Séptimo censo general, 6 de junio de 1950.* Mexico City: 1953– .

―――. *Octavo censo general de población, 8 de junio de 1960.* Mexico City: 1963. 31v in 34.

―――. *Noveno censo general de población, 28 de enero de 1970.* Mexico City: 1971–72. 33v in 23.

―――. *Décimo censo general de población, 1980.* Mexico City: 1985–1990. 32v in 21.

Instituto Nacional de Estadística, Geografía e Informática. *XI censo general de población y vivienda, 1990. Resultados definitivos.* Aguascalientes: 1990― . 127v.

―――. *XII censo general de población y vivienda, 2000. Tabulados básicos.* Aguascalientes, 2001. 33v.

XIII. HISTORY

A. General

1. Latin America

The Cambridge History of Latin America. Edited by Leslie Bethel. Cambridge: Cambridge University Press, 1984. 11v in 12.

Henderson, James D. *A Reference Guide to Latin American History.* Armonk, NY: M. E. Sharpe, 2000. ix, 615 p.

Herring, Hubert. *A History of Latin America from the Beginnings to the Present.* New York: Knopf, 1955. xx, 796 p.; 3rd ed., revised, with the assistance of Helen Baldwin Herring, 1968. xxii, 1002, xxv p.

Werlich, David. *Research Tools for Latin American Historians: A Select Annotated Bibliography.* New York: Garland, 1980. xvi, 269 p.

Williamson, Edwin. *The Penguin History of Latin America.* London: Penguin, 1992. viii, 631 p.

2. Mexico (Chronologically by First Edition)

Alamán y Escalada, Lucas. *Historia de México desde los primeros movimientos que prepararon su independencia en el año de 1808, hasta la época presente.* Mexico City, 1849–1852. Reprinted Mexico City: Librería Universitaria, 1957, and Instituto Cultural Helénico: Fondo de Cultura Económica, c.1985. 5 v.

Brantz, Mayer. *Mexico: Aztec, Spanish and Republican: A Historical, Geographical, Political, Statistical and Social Account of that Country from the Period of the Invasion by the Spaniards to the Present Time, with a View of the Ancient Aztec Empire and Civilization, a Historical Sketch of the Late War, and Notices of New Mexico and California.* Hartford: S. Drake, 1852. 2 v.

Bancroft, Hubert H. *History of México.* San Francisco: The History Company, 1883–1888. 6 v.

México a través de los siglos: historia general y completa del desenvolvimento social, político, religioso, militar, artístico, científico y literario de México desde la antigüedad más remotas hasta la época actual. Dirección de Vicente Riva Palacio. Mexico City: 1884–1889. 5 v. Reprinted, Editorial Cumbre, 1984. 16 v.

Hale, Susan. *The Story of Mexico.* ("Story of the Nations.") London: Unwin; New York, Putnam, 1889. xx, 428 p. Reprinted 1890, 1891, 1897, as *Mexico.*

Pereyra. Carlos. *Historia del pueblo mexicano.* Mexico City: J. Ballescá, 1909. 2 v.

Rabasa, Emilio. *La evolución histórica de México.* Mexico City: Impr. Franco-Mexicana, 1920. 349 p. New ed., Porrúa, 1972.

Priestley, Herbert Ingram. *The Mexican Nation: A History.* New York: 1923. Reprinted New York: Cooper Square Publishers, 1969. xv, 511 p.

Chávez Orozco, Luis. *Historia de México.* Mexico City: 1934– ? v.

Teja Zabre, Alfonso. *Historia de México: una moderna interpretación.* Mexico City: Secretaría de Relaciones Exteriores, 1935. 399p.

Parkes, Henry Bamford. *A History of Mexico.* Revised ed. Boston: Houghton Mifflin: 1938. Reprinted 1969. xii, 460 p. Translated by Sylvia López de Sarmiento as *La historia de México.* Mexico City: Editorial Diana, 1979. 475 p.

Cuevas, Mariano. *Historia de la nación mexicana.* Mexico City: 1940.

Bravo Ugarte, José. *Historia de México.* Mexico City: 1941–1944. 4 v.

Palavicini, Félix F. *México, historia de su evolución constructiva*. Mexico City: 1945. 4 v.

Jiménez Moreno, Wigberto, and García Ruiz, Alfonso. *Historia de México: una síntesis*. Mexico City: INAH, 1962. 132 p.

Rodman, Saldes. *The Mexico Traveler: A Concise History and Guide*. New York: Meredith Press, 1969. xix, 264 p. Reprinted 1981 as *A Short History of Mexico*.

Quirk, Robert E. *Mexico*. ("The Modern Nations in Historical Perspective.") Englewood Cliffs, NJ: Prentice-Hall, 1971 viii, 152 p.

Meyer, Michael C., and Sherman, William L. *The Course of Mexican History*. 1st ed., New York: Oxford University Press, 1979. xv, 696, xxxiii p.; 2nd ed., 1983; 3rd ed., 1987. xiii, 711, xxxiii p.; 6th ed., 1999.

Historia de México. Coordinación general: Miguel León-Portilla, Mexico City: Salvat, 1986. 6 v.

Ruiz, Ramón Eduardo. *Triumphs and Tragedy: A History of the Mexican People*. New York: 1992. 512 p.

Hamnett, Brian Roger. *A Concise History of Mexico*. Cambridge: Cambridge University Press, 1999. xv, 336 p.

Oxford History of Mexico [by Helen Nader et al.]. Ed. Michael C. Meyer and William H. Beezley. Oxford: Oxford University Press, 2000. ix, 709 p.

Pearce, Kenneth. *A Traveller's History of Mexico*. Northampton, MA: Interlink Publishing, 2002. xii, 388 p.

a. Illustrations

Historia gráfica de México. Enrique Florescan, coordinador general. Mexico City: Instituto Nacional de Antropología e Historia, and Editorial Patria, 1998. 10 v.

B. Pre-Hispanic Era and Archaeology

Aveleyra Arroyo de Anda, Luis. *Prehistoria de México: "revisión de prehistoria mexicana: el hombre de Tepexpan y sus problemas*. Mexico City: Ediciones Mexicanas, 1950. 167 p.

Benevente, Toribio de ("Motolinia"). *Memoriales e historia de los indios de la Nueva Espana*. Mexico City: Chávez Hayhoe, 1941. xlviii, 320 p. Trans. and ed. Elizabeth Andros Foster as *Motolinia's History of the Indians of New Spain*. Berkeley, CA: Cortés Society, 1950. x, 294 p.

Bernal, Ignacio. *A History of Mexican Archaeology: The Vanished Civilization of Middle America*. London: Thames & Hudson, 1980. 208 p.

———. *Tenochtitlán en una isla*. Mexico City: INAH, 1959. 147 p.; revised ed., 1972. 159 p. Translated by Willis Barnstone as *Mexico Before Cortez:*

Art, History and Legend. Garden City, NY: Doubleday, 1963; revised ed., 1975. 140 p.

Carrasco, Pedro, et al. *Estratificación social en la Mesoamérica Prehispánica.* Mexico City: Centro de Investigaciones Superiores del Instituto Nacional de Antropología e Historia, 1976. 300 p.

Ciudad Ruiz, Andrés. *Las culturas del antiguo México.* Madrid: Alhambra, 1989. 231 p.

Clavijero, Francisco Javier. *Storia antica del Messico, cavata da' migliori storici spagnuoli . . .* Cesena: Biasini, 1780–1781. 4 v. Translated by Charles Cullen as *The History of Mexico.* London: Robinson, 1787. 2 v. Translated into Spanish as *Historia antigua de México y de su conquista.* Mexico City: Lara, 1844. 2v in 1. Reprinted Porrúa, 1958, 1962. xxxvii, 631 p.

Coe, Michael D. *America's First Civilization.* New York: American Heritage, 1968. 159 p.

————. *The Jaguar's Children: Pre-Classic Central Mexico.* New York: The Museum of Primitive Art, 1965. 126 p.

————. *Mexico, from the Olmecs to the Aztecs.* ("Ancient Peoples and Places"). London: Thames & Hudson; New York: Praeger, 1962. 244 p. 5th ed., revised and expanded, with Rex Koontz as coauthor. London: Thames & Hudson, 2002. 248 p.

———— et al. *Atlas of Ancient America.* New York: Facts on File, 1986.

Davies, Nigel. *The Ancient Kingdoms of Mexico.* London: A. Lane, 1982. 272 p.

Gorenstein, Shirley. *Not Forever on Earth: Prehistory of Mexico.* Photos. by Lee Boltin. New York, Scribner [1974, c.1975]. xvi, 153 p.

Helfritz, Hans. *Götterburgen Mexikos.* Cologne: DuMont Schauberg, [1968]. 180 p. Translated as *Mexican Cities of the Gods: An Archaeological Guide.* New York: Praeger, 1970. 180 p.

Humboldt, Alexander von. *Histoire des nations civilisées du Méxique et de l'Amérique Centrale pendant les siècles antérieurs à Christophe Colomb.* Paris: 1857–1859. 4 v.

Hunter, C. Bruce. *A Guide to Anciente Mexican Ruins.* Norman, OK: University of Oklahoma Press, 1977. xix, 261 p.

James, N. *Aztecs & Maya: The Ancient Peoples of Middle America.* Stroud (Gloucs.); Charleston, NC: Tempus Publishing, 2001. 162 p.

Longhena, Maria. *Antico Messico: storie e cultura dei maya, degli aztechi e di altri popoli precolombiani.* Milan: Edizioni White Star, 1998. 292 p. Translated by Neil Frazer Davenport as *Splendours of Ancient Mexico.* London: Thames & Hudson, 1998. 292 p., and into Spanish as *México Antiguo: historia y cultura de los pueblos precolombinos.* Barcelona: Editorial Optima, 2002. 291 p.

Martínez del Río, Pablo. *Los orígenes mexicanos*. Mexico City: Porrua, 1936. xiii, 277 p.

Miller, Mary Ellen and Taube, Karl. *The Gods and Symbols of Ancient Mexico and the Maya: An Illustrated Dictionary of Meso-american Religion*. London: Thames & Hudson, 1993. 216 p. Reprinted as *An Illustrated Dictionary of the Gods and Symbols of Ancient Mexico and the Maya*. 1997. 216 p.

Peterson, Frederick A. *Ancient Mexico: An Introduction to the Pre-Hispanic Cultures*. London: Allen & Unwin; New York, Putnam, 1959. 313 p.

Piña Chan, Román. *Ciudades arqueológicas de México*. Mexico City: Instituto Nacional de Antropología e Historia, 1963. viii, 152 p.

———. *Una visión del México prehispánico*. Mexico City: Instituto de Investigaciones Históricas de UNAM, 1967. 339 p.

Porter, Muriel Noe, *afterwards* Weaver, Muriel. *Tlatilco and the Pre-Classic Cultures of the New World*. New York: Wenner-Gren Foundation for Anthropological Research, 1953. 104 p.

———. *The Aztecs, Mayas, and Their Predecessors: Archaeology of Mesoamerica*. New York: Seminar Press, 1972. 3rd ed., San Diego: Academic Press, 1993. xix, 567 p.

Reed. Alma M. *The Ancient Past of Mexico*. New York: Crown, 1966. xi, 388 p.

Sabloff, Jeremy A. *The Cities of Ancient Mexico: Reconstructing a Lost World*. New York, London: Thames & Hudson, 1989. Revised ed., 1997. 224 p.

Sahagún, [Fray] Bernardino de. *Historia general de las cosas de Nueva Espana* . . . Mexico City: A. Valdés, 1829–1830. 3 v. Translated by Arthur J. O. Anderson and Charles E. Ibble as *General History of the Things of New Spain*. Santa Fe, NM: School of American Research and the University of Utah, 1950–1957. 13 v in 12.

Verrill, Alpheus Hyatt, and Verrill, Ruth. *America's Ancient Civilization*. New York: Putnam, 1953. xvii, 334 p.

Wauchope, Robert. *The Indian Background of Latin American History: The Maya, Aztec, Inca, and Their Predecessors*. New York: Alfred A. Knopf, 1970. viii, 211 p.

Wolf, Eric Robert. *Sons of the Shaking Earth*. Chicago: University of Chicago Press, 1959. ix, 303 p.

1. Aztecs

Alcocer, Ignacio F. *Apuntes sobre la antigua México-Tenochtitlán*. Tacubaya, DF: Instituto Panamericana de Geografía e Historia, 1935. 110 p.

Bray, Warwick. *Everyday Life of the Aztecs*. London: Batsford, 1968. 208 p.

Brundage, Burr Cartwright. *A Rain of Darts: The Mexican Aztecs*. Austin, TX: University of Texas Press, 1972. xvii, 354 p.

————. *The Jade Steps: A Ritual Life of the Aztecs*. Salt Lake City: University of Utah Press, 1985. xv, 280 p.

Burland, Cottie Arthur and Forman, Werner. *Feathered Serpent and Smoking Mirror*. New York: Putnam, 1975. 128 p.

Caso, Antonio. *Pueblo del Sol*. Mexico City: 1953. 125 p. Translated by Lowell Dunham as *The Aztec: People of the Sun*. Norman, OK: University of Oklahoma Press, 1958. 125 p.

Clendinnen, Inga. *Aztecs: An Interpretation*. Cambridge UK: Cambridge University Press, 1991. xiv, 398 p.

Davies, Nigel. *The Aztec Empire: The Toltec Resurgence*. Norman, OK: Oklahoma University Press, 1987. xiv, 431 p.

————. *The Aztecs: A History*. New York: Putnam; London: Macmillan, 1973. xvii, 363 p.

Durán, [Fray] Diego. *Historia de las Indias de Nueva Espana y Islas de Tierra Firme*. Translated by Doris Heyden and Fernando Horcasitas as *The Aztecs: The History of the Indies of New Spain*. New York: Orion Press, 1964. Reprinted Norman, OK: University of Oklahoma Press, 1994. xxxvi, 642 p.

Gibson, Charles. *The Aztecs under Spanish Rule: A History of the Indians of the Valley of Mexico*. Stanford: Stanford University Press, 1964. xii, 657 p.

Gruzinski, Serge. *Le destin brisé de l'empire aztèque* Paris: Gallimard, 1988. Translated as *The Aztecs: Rise and Fall of an Empire*. London: Thames & Hudson, 1992. 191 p.

Hassig, Ross. *Aztec Warfare: Imperial Expansion and Political Control*. Norman, OK: University of Oklahoma Press, 1988. xx, 404 p.

The Inca and Aztec States, 1400–1800: Anthropology and History. Ed. George A. Collier et al. New York: Academic Press, 1982. xx, 475 p.

León Portilla, Miguel. *Filosofía nahuatl, estudiada en sus fuentes*. Mexico City: Instituto Indigenista Interamericano, 1956. xv, 344 p. Translated by Jack Emory Davis as *Aztec Thought and Culture: A Study of the Ancient Nahuatl Mind*. Norman, OK: University of Oklahoma Press, 1963. 241 p.

Matos Moctezuma, Eduardo. *The Aztecs*. New York: Rizzoli, 1989; and in Spanish, *Los Aztecas*. Madrid: CONACULTA, 2000. 239 p.

Pasztory, Esther. *Aztec Art*. New York: H.N. Abrams, 1983. 335 p.

Prem, Hanns J. *Die Azteken: Geschichte, Kultur, Religion*. Munich, Beck, 1996; 2. Aufl., 1999. 143 p. Translated by Jesús Lamba as *Los aztecas: historia, cultura, religión*. Madrid: Acento, [2002]. 140 p.

Smith, Michael E. *The Aztecs*. Oxford UK: Blackwell, 1996. xix, 361 p.

Soustelle, Jacques. *La vie quotidienne des aztèques à la veille de la conquête*. Paris: Hachette, 1955. 318 p. Translated by Patrick O'Brien as *The Daily Life of the Aztecs on the Eve of the Spanish Conquest*. London: Weidenfeld &

Nicholson, 1955. 302 p. Reprinted, Stanford CA: Stanford University Press, 1970. 321 p.

Stuart, Gene S. *The Mighty Aztecs*. Washington: National Geographic Society, 1981. 199 p.

Vaillant, George Clapp. *Aztecs of Mexico*. Garden City, NY: Doubleday, 1941. xxii, 340 p. Revised by Susannah B. Vaillant as *Aztecs of Mexico: Origin, Rise, and Fall of the Aztec Nation*. 1962. xxii, 312 p.

Von Hagen, Victor Wolfgang. *The Aztec, Man and Tribe: An Archaeological History of a People who Created a Rich and Intricate Culture in the Heart of Primitive Mexico*. New York: The North American Library, Mentor Books, 1958. 222 p.

Zorita, Alonso de. *Breve y sumaria relación de los señores de la Nueva Espana*. Prólogo y notas de Joaquín Ramírez Canabanas. 2a ed. Mexico City: UNAM, 1963. xxi, 205 p. Translated by Benjamin Keen as *Life and Labor in Ancient Mexico: The Brief and Summary Relation of the Lords of New Spain*. New Brunswick, NJ: Rutgers University Press, 1963. 328 p.

a. Montezuma

Burland, Cottie Arthur. *Montezuma, Lord of the Aztecs*. New York: Putnam; London: Weidenfeld and Nicolson, 1973. 269 p.

b. Quetzalcoatl

Carrasco, David. *Quetzalcoatl and the Irony of Empire: Myths and Prophecies in the Aztec Tradition*. Chicago: University of Chicago Press, 1982. xii, 233 p.

2. Maya

Adams, Richard E. W. *Prehistoric Mesoamerica*. Boston: 1977. Rev. ed., Norman, OK: University of Oklahoma Press, 1991. xviii, 354 p.

Andrews, George F. *Maya Cities: Placemaking and Urbanization*. Norman, OK: University of Oklahoma Press, 1975. xviii, 468 p.

Benson, Elizabeth P. *The Maya World*. New York: Crowell, 1967. ix, 172 p.

Brunhouse, Robert Levere. *Sylvanus G. Morley and the World of the Ancient Mayas*. Norman, OK: University of Oklahoma Press, 1971. x, 353 p.

Coe, Michael D. *The Maya*. New York: Praeger, 1966; 6th ed., London: Thames & Hudson, 1999. 256 p.

Drew, David. *The Lost Chronicles of the Maya Kings*. London: Wiedenfeld & Nicholson, 1999. xiv, 450 p.

Gallenkamp, Charles. *Maya: The Riddle and Rediscovery of a Lost Civilization*. New York: David McKay, 1959. 3rd ed., Viking Penguin, 1985. xiii, 235 p.

Gann, Thomas William Francis and Thompson, J. Eric. *History of the Mayas from the Earliest Times to the Present Day.* New York: Scribner, 1931. x, 264 p.

Hammond, Norman. *Ancient Maya Civilization.* New Brunswick, NJ: Rutgers University Press, 1982. Updated ed., 1988. xii, 337 p.

Hunter, C. Bruce. *A Guide to Ancient Maya Ruins.* Norman, OK: University of Oklahoma Press, 1974. xvii, 332 p.

Ivanoff, Pierre. *Città Maya.* Presentazione di Miguel Ángel Asturias. Milan: Mondadori, 1970. 191 p. Translated as *Maya.* London: Cassell; New York: Madison Square Press, 1973. 191 p.

Miller, Mary Ellen. *Maya Art and Architecture.* London: Thames & Hudson, 1999. 240 p.

Morley, Sylvanus Griswold. *The Ancient Maya.* Stanford CA: Stanford University Press, 1946. xxxii, 520 p.; 2nd ed., 1947. 520 p. 3rd. ed., revised by George W. Brainerd. 1956, x, 494 p. Reprinted 1972. x, 307 p. 4th ed., revised by Robert J. Sharer, 1983. xviii, 708 p.; 5th ed., 1994. xxxii, 892 p.

Rivet, Paul. *Cités maya.* 2e éd. Paris: Guillot, 1962. 195 p. Translated by Miriam and Lionel Kochan as *Maya Cities.* London: Putnam; New York, Elek Books, 1960. 234 p.

Roys, Ralph L. *The Book of Chilam Balam of Chumayel.* Washington, DC: Carnegie Institution, 1933. Reprinted with introduction by J. Eric S. Thompson. Norman, OK: University of Oklahoma Press, 1967. xvi, 229 p.

Ruz Lhuillier, Alberto. *La civilización de los antiguos mayas.* Santiago de Chile: Universidad de Oriente, 1957. 191 p.; 3a ed., Mexico City: Fondo de Cultura Económica, 1991. 97 p.

Schele, Linda and Friedel, David. *A Forest of Kings: The Untold Story of the Ancient Maya.* New York: Quill, 1990. 542 p.

Stuart, George E. and Stuart, Gene S. *The Mysterious Maya.* Washington: National Geographic Society, 1977. 199 p.

Thompson, [*Sir*] John Eric Sidney. *Maya Archaeologist.* London: 1962; Norman, OK: University of Oklahoma Press, 1963. xvii, 284 p. Reprinted with a foreword by Norman Hammond. 1994. xvii, 284 p.

———. *Maya History and Religion.* Norman, OK: University of Oklahoma Press, 1970. xxx, 415 p.

———. *The Rise and Fall of Maya Civilization.* Norman, OK: University of Oklahoma Press, 1954. xii, 287 p.; 2nd ed., 1966. xv, 328 p.

Tozzer, Alfred Marston. *A Comparative Study of the Mayas and Lacandrones.* New York: MacMillan, 1907. xx, 195 p. Reprinted AMS Press, 1978.

Von Hagen, Victor W. *World of the Maya.* New York, New American Library, Mentor Books, 1960. 224 p.

Webster, Edna Robb. *Early Exploring in the Lands of the Maya . . . : A Collection of Adventures and Research . . . , 1928–1940 . . .* Sherman Oaks, CA: Wilmar Publishers, 1973. xiv, 247 p.

a. Bibliography

Valle, Rafael Helidoro. *Bibliography maya.* Mexico City: Instituto Panamericano de Geografía e Historia, [1946?]. 2 v.

3. Mixtecs

Caso, Alfonso. *Culturas mixteca y zapoteca.* Mexico City: Nacional, 1942. 118 p.
Spores, Ronald. *The Mixtec Kings and Their People.* Norman, OK: University of Oklahoma Press, 1967. xvii, 269 p.
———. *The Mixtecs in Ancient and Colonial Times.* Norman, OK: University of Oklahoma Press, 1984. xiv, 264 p.

4. Olmecs

Bernal, Ignacio. *El mundo olmeca.* Mexico City: 1968. xxxii, 155 p., translated by Doris Heyden and Fernando Horcasitas as *The Olmec World.* Berkeley, CA: University of California Press, 1969. xiv, 273 p.
The Olmecs and Their Neighbors: Essays in Memory of Matthew W. Stirling. Ed. Elizabeth P. Benson. Washington, DC: Dumbarton Oaks: 1981. xii, 346 p.
Piña Chan, Román and Covarrubias, Luis. *El pueblo del jaguar: los olmecas arqueológicos.* Mexico City: Museo Nacional de Antropología, 1964. 68 p.

5. Tarascans

Pollard, Helen Perlstein. *Taríacuri's Legacy: The Prehistoric Tarascan State.* Norman, OK: University of Oklahoma Press, 1993. xx, 266 p.
Warren, J. Benedict. *The Conquest of Michoacán: The Spanish Domination of the Tarascan Kingdom in Western Mexico, 1521–1530.* Norman, OK: University of Oklahoma Press, 1985. xv, 352 p.

6. Toltecs

Davies, Nigel. *Toltec Heritage: From the Fall of Tula to the Rise of Tenochtitlán.* Norman, OK: University of Oklahoma Press, 1980. xii, 401 p.
———. *The Toltecs, Until the Fall of Tula.* Norman, OK: University of Oklahoma Press, 1977. xviii, 533 p.

7. Zapotecs

Whitecotton, Joseph W. *The Zapotecs: Princes, Priests and Peasants*. Norman, OK: University of Oklahoma Press, 1977. xvi, 338 p.

C. History since 1519

Altman, Ida, et al. *The Early History of Greater Mexico*. Upper Saddle River, NJ: Prentice-Hall, 2003. xi, 394 p.

Chávez Ordozco, Luis. *Historia de México*. 4? v. Mexico City: Secretaría de Educación Pública, 1931–4.

Orozco y Berra, Manuel. *Historia antigua y de la conquista de Mexico*. Mexico City: Esteva, 1880–81. 4 v. Reprinted, with an introduction by Ángel Maria Garibay K. Porrúa, 1960.

Suchlicki, Jaime. *Mexico, From Montezuma to NAFTA and Beyond*. Washington, DC: Brassy's, 1996. Paperback edition with a new introduction. New Brunswick, NJ: Transaction Publishers, 2003. xiv, 228 p.

1. Colonial Period: General

Gibson, Charles. *Spain in America*. New York: Harper & Row [1966]. xiv, 239 p.

Jiménez Rueda, Julio. *Historia de la cultura en México: el virreinato*. Mexico City: Editorial Cultura, 1960. 336 p.

Rubio Mañé, Jorge Ignacio. *El virreinato*. Mexico City: Fondo de Cultura Económica, for Instituto de Investigaciones Históricas de la UNAM, 1983. 4 v. Reprinted 1992.

2. Bibliography

López Cervantes, Gonzalo and García García, Rosa. *Ensayo bibliográfico del período colonial de México*. Mexico City: Instituto Nacional de Antropología e Historia, 1989. 237 p.

3. Fifteenth to Seventeenth Centuries

Weckmann, Luis. *La Herencia medieval de México*. Mexico City: Colegio de México, 1984. 2 v. Translated by Frances M. López Morillas as *The Medieval Heritage of Mexico*. New York: Fordham University Press, 1992. vii, 692 p.

a. Exploration

Brebner, John Bartlet. *The Explorers of North America, 1492–1806*. London: Black, 1933. xv, 502 p.; Garden City, NY: Doubleday, 1955. 431 p.

b. The Spanish Conquest

Bannon, John F. *The Spanish Conquistadores: Men or Devils?* New York: Holt, Rinehart and Winston, 1960. 43 p.

Díaz del Castillo, Bernal. *Historia verdadera de la conquista de la Nueva Espana, escrita por . . . uno de sus conquistadores.* Madrid: Impr. del Reyno, 1632. Translated by A. P. Maudslay as *The Discovery and Conquest of Mexico, 1517–1521.* Edited from the original manuscript . . . New York: Harper, 1928. Reprinted New York: Farrar, Straus, and Cudahy, 1956. xxxi, 478 p.

Gardiner, Clinton Harvey. *The Constant Captain, Gonzalo de Sandoval.* Carbondale, IL: Southern Illinois University Press, 1961. 221 p.

Horgan, Paul. *Conquistadors in North American History.* New York: Farrar, Straus, 1963. 303 p.

Innes, Hammond. *The Conquistadors.* London: Collings; New York: Knopf, 1969. 336 p.

Martínez Rodríguez, José Luis. *Motecuhzoma y Cuauhtémoc: los últimos emperadores aztecas.* Madrid: Anaya, 1988 127 p.

Prescott, William Hickling. *History of the Conquest of Mexico.* Philadelphia: Lippincott; Chicago: Hooper, Clarke, 1843. 3 v.

Thomas, Hugh. *Conquest: Montezuma, Cortés, and the Fall of Old Mexico.* New York: Simon & Schuster, 1993. xx, 812 p.

Visión de los vencidos. Ed. Miguel León Portilla. Traducido del Nahuatl por Ángel María Garibay K. Mexico City: UNAM, 1959. 211 p. Translated from Spanish into English by Lysander Kemp as *The Broken Spears: The Aztec Account of the Conquest of Mexico.* Boston MA: Beacon Press, 1962. xxxi, 168 p., Expanded and updated ed., 1992. xliv, 196 p.

c. Hernán Cortés

Cantu, Caesar C. *Cortés and the Fall of the Aztec Empire.* Los Angeles: Modern World Publishing, 1966. 384 p.

Cortés, Hernán. *Cartas de relación.* Madrid: Castalia, 1993. 687 p. Translated by J. Bayard Morris as *Five Letters of Cortés to his Emperor, 1519–1526.* London: Routledge, 1927; xlvii, 388 p. Reprinted. New York: W. W. Norton, 1962.

López de Gómara, Francisco. *Crónica de la Nueva Espana.* Published as *La conquista de México.* Edición de José Luis de Rojas Cortés. Madrid: Historia 16, 1987. 502 p. English version by Lesley Byrd Simpson issued as *The Life of the Conqueror, by his Secretary.* Berkeley: University of California Press, 1964. xxvi, 425 p.

Madariaga, Salvador de, *Hernán Cortés: Conqueror of Mexico.* New York: Macmillan, 1941. ix, 554 p. Also issued in Spanish as *Hernán Cortés.* Buenos Aires, Sudamericana, 1941. 739 p.

White, Jon Ewbank Manchip. *Cortés and the Downfall of the Aztec Empire: A Study in a Conflict of Cultures.* London: Hamilton; New York: St. Martin's Press, 1971. 352 p.

d. Mexico under the Spanish Habsburgs

Benítez, Fernando. *Vida Criolla en el siglo xvi.* Mexico City: Colegio de México. 1953. 322 p. Translated by Joan MacLean as *The Century after Cortés.* Chicago, IL: University of Chicago Press, 1965. 296 p.

Beyond the Codices: The Nahua View of Colonial Mexico. Trans. and ed. Arthur J. O. Anderson et al. Berkeley, CA: University of California Press, 1976. ix, 235 p.

Arteaga, [*Sor*] Cristina de la Cruz de. *Una mitra sobre dos mundos: la vida venerable de Don Juan de Palafox y Mendoza,* Puebla: El Claustro, 1985. Reprinted 1995.

Dávila y Padilla, Agustín. *Historia de la provincia de Santiago de la Nueva Espana del Orden de Santo Domingo.* Madrid: 1596.

Leonard, Irving A. *Baroque Times in Old Mexico: Seventeenth-Century Persons, Places, and Practices.* Ann Arbor, MI: University of Michigan Press, 1959. 260 p. Reprinted in paperback, 1966.

Liss, Peggy K. *Mexico under Spain, 1521–1556: Society and the Origins of Nationality.* Chicago: University of Chicago Press, 1975. xvi, 229 p.

Martínez Vega, María Luisa. *La crisis barroca en el virreinato de la Nueva Espana: el Marqués de Gálves.* Madrid: Editorial de la Universidad Complutense, 1990. iv, 1,261 p. in 2 v.

e. Núñez Cabeza de Vaca

Long, Haniel. *The Marvelous Adventure of Cabeza de Vaca.* With introduction by Henry Miller. Clearage, CA: Dawn Horse, 1992. 63 p.

f. Bartolomé de las Casas and the Black Legend

Carbie, Roomily D. *Historia de la leyenda negra hispano-americana.* Buenos Aires: Patagonia Press, 1943; Madrid: Consejo de la Hispanidad, 1944. 261 p.

Menéndez Pidal, Ramón. *El Padre Las Casas: su doble personalidad.* Madrid: Espasa Calpe, 1963.

Wagner, Henry Raup. *The Life and Writings of Barolomé de las Casas.* Albuquerque, NM: University of New Mexico Press, 1967. xiv, 310 p.

4. Eighteenth Century

Nunn, Charles F. *Foreign Immigrants in Early Bourbon Mexico, 1700–1760.* Cambridge: Cambridge University Press, 1979. xii, 244 p.

a. Mexico under Charles III and Charles IV

The Birth of Modern Mexico, 1780–1824. Ed. Christian L. Archer. Wilmington DE: Scholarly Resources Books, 2005. 257 p.

Bobb, Bernard E. *The Viceregency of Antonio María Bucareli in New Spain, 1771–1779.* Austin: University of Texas Press, 1962. 313 p.

The Expulsion of the Jesuits from Latin America, ed. Magnus Mörner. New York: Knopf, 1965. 207 p.

Hamnett, Brian R. *Roots of Insurgency: Mexican Regions, 1750–1824.* Cambridge: Cambridge University Press, 1986. ix, 276 p.

La independencia de México y el proceso autonomista novo-hispano, 1808–1824. Mexico City: Instituto Mora, 2001. 456 p.

Mexico in the Age of Democratic Revolutions, 1750–1824. Ed. Jaime E. Rodríguez. Boulder, CO: Lynne Rienner, 1994. xiii, 330 p.

b. Independence Struggle

Anna, Timothy A. *The Fall of the Royal Government in Mexico City.* Lincoln, NE: University of Nebraska Press, 1978. xix, 289 p.

Flores Caballero, Romeo R. *La contrarrevolución en la independencia.* Mexico City: Colegio de México, 1969. 201 p. Translated by Jaime E. Rodríguez O. as *Counterrevolution: The Role of the Spaniards in the Independence of Mexico, 1804–1838.* Lincoln, NE: University of Nebraska Press, 1974. xiii, 186 p.

Mexico and the Spanish Cortes, 1810–1822: Eight Essays. Ed. Nettie Lee Benson. Austin, TX: University of Texas Press, 1966. 243 p.

Van Young, Eric. *The Other Rebellion: Popular Violence, Ideology and the Mexican Struggle for Independence, 1810–1821.* Stanford, CA: Stanford University Press, 2001. xvii, 702 p.

Warren, Harris Gaylord. *The Sword Was Their Passport: A History of American Filibustering in the Mexican Revolution.* Baton Rouge, LA: Louisiana State University Press, 1943. ix, 286 p.

i. Hidalgo

Hamill, Hugh M. *The Hidalgo Revolt: Prelude to Mexican Independence.* Gainesville, FL: University of Florida Press, 1966. xi, 284 p.

Lieberman, Mark. *Hidalgo: Mexican Revolutionary.* New York: Praeger, 1970. vi, 161 p.

ii. Morelos

Timmons, Wilbert H. *Morelos: Priest, Soldier, Statesman of Mexico.* El Paso, TX: Texas Western College Press, 1963. 184 p.

c. Independent Mexico

Baant, Jan. *A Concise History of Mexico: From Hidalgo to Cárdenas.* Cambridge: Cambridge University Press, 1977. ix, 222 p.

Brandenburg, Frank Ralph. *The Making of Modern Mexico.* Introduction by Frank Tannenbaum. Englewood Cliffs, NJ: Prentice-Hall, 1964. xv, 379 p.

Call, Tomine Clark. *The Mexican Venture: From Political to Industrial Revolution in Mexico.* New York: Oxford University Press, 1953. xii, 273 p.

Calvert, Peter. *Mexico.* (Nations of the Modern World.) Tonbridge, UK: Ernest Benn, 1973. 361 p.

Gutiérrez de Lara, L. and Pinchon, Edgcumb. *The Mexican People: Their Struggle for Freedom.* Garden City, NY: Doubleday, 1914. xi, 360 p.

Historia moderna de México, ed. Daniel Cosío Villegas. Mexico City: Editorial Hermes, 1948–1965. 8 v.

Junco, Alfonso. *Un siglo de México: de Hidalgo a Carranza.* Mexico City: Ediciones Botas, 1937. 332 p.

Krauze, Enrique. *Mexico, Biography of Power: History of Modern Mexico, 1810–1996.* Translated from the Spanish by Hank Heifetz. New York: HarperCollins, 1997. xxii, 872.

5. Mid-Nineteenth Century

Anna, Timothy E. *Forging Mexico, 1821–1835.* Lincoln, NE: University of Nebraska Press, 1998. xv, 330 p.

Callcott, Wilfrid Hardy. *Liberalism in Mexico, 1857–1929.* Leland Stanford Junior University, 1931. Reprinted New York: Archon Books, 1965. xv, 410 p.

Essays on Mexican History: The Charles William Hackett Memorial Volume. Ed. Thomas E. Cother. Austin: Institute of Latin American Studies, 1958. xv, 309 p.

Green, Stanley C. *The Mexican Republic: The First Decade, 1823–1832.* Pittsburgh, PA: University of Pittsburgh Press, 1987. x, 314 p.

Hale, Charles A. *Mexican Liberalism in the Age of Mora, 1821–1853.* New Haven, CT: Yale University Press, 1968. xi, 347 p.

Krauze, Enrique. *Siglo de caudillos: biografía políitca de México, 1810–1910.* Barcelona: Tusquets, 1994. 349 p.

Mexico from Independence to Revolution, 1810–1910. [By Victor Alba et al.] Ed. with a commentary by W. Dirk Raat. Lincoln, NE: University of Nebraska Press, 1982. xiv, 308 p.

a. Iturbide

Anna, Timothy E. *The Mexican Empire of Iturbide.* Lincoln, NE: University of Nebraska Press, 1990. xii, 286 p.

Robertson, William Spence. *Iturbide of Mexico.* Durham, NC: University of North Carolina Press, 1952. ix, 361 p. Reprinted New York: Greenwood, 1968.

b. Guerrero

Vincent, Theodore G. *The Legacy of Vicente Guerrero, Mexico's First Black Indian President.* Gainesville, FL: University Press of Florida, 2001. 336 p.

c. Santa Anna

Callcott, Wilfrid Hardy. *Santa Anna, the Story of an Enigma Whose Race Was Mexico.* Norman, OK: University of Oklahoma Press, 1936. xiv, 392 p.

Jones, Oakah L., Jr. *Santa Anna.* New York: Twayne Publishers, 1968. 211 p.

Olivera, Ruth and Crété, Liliane. *Life in Mexico under Santa Anna, 1822–1855.* Norman: University of Oklahoma Press, 1991. xv, 264 p.

Santa Anna, Antonio López de. *The Eagle: The Autobiography of Santa Anna.* Ed. Ann Fears Crawford. Austin, TX: Penherton Press, 1967. xix, 299 p. Reprinted. Austin, TX: State House Press, 1988.

6. The United States–Mexican War

Bauer, Karl Jack. *The Mexican War, 1846–1848.* New York: Macmillan, 1974. xxi, 454 p. Reprinted with an introduction by Robert W. Johannsen. Lincoln, NE: University of Nebraska Press, 1993. xxvii, 454 p.

The Mexican War: Changing Interpretations. Ed. Odie B. Faulk and Joseph A. Stout. Chicago: The Swallow Press, 1973. 244 p.

Price, Glenn W. *Origins of the War with Mexico: The Polk-Stockton Intrigue.* Austin, TX: University of Texas Press, 1967. x, 189 p.

Ramírez Gómez, José Fernando. *Mexico durante su guerra con los Estados Unidos.* Mexico City: Bouret, 1905. viii, 322 p.; translated by Elliott B. Scherr as *Mexico During the War with the United States.* Ed. Walter V. Scholes. Columbia, MO: University of Missouri, 1950. 165 p.

Ripley, Roswell Sabine. *The War with Mexico.* New York: Harper, 1849. 2 v. Reprinted New York: Franklin, 1970. 2 v.

Ruiz, Ramón Eduardo. *The Mexican War: Was It Manifest Destiny?* New York: Holt, Rinehart and Winston, 1963. 118 p.

Smith, Justin H. *The War with Mexico.* Gloucester, MA: Peter Smith, 1963. 2 v.

To Mexico with Taylor and Scott, 1845–1847. Ed. Grady McWhiney and Sue McWhiney. Waltham, MA: Blaisdell, 1969. x, 214 p.

Wilcox, [*General*] Cadmus Marcellus. *History of the Mexican War.* Washington, DC: Church News, 1892. x, 711 p.

7. Reform

Molina Enríquez, Andrés. *Juárez y la Reforma.* Mexico City: Libro-Mex, 1956. 156 p. Reprinted Costa-Amic, 1972. 153 p.

a. Mariano Arista

Arista, Mariano. *A Mexican President's Diary, 1845–1849,* translated by Edwina Lagos. Mexico City: Librería Universitaria, 1955.

b. Juárez

Blancke, W. Wendell, *Juárez of Mexico.* New York: Praeger, 1971. 152 p.

Burke, Ulick Ralph. *A Life of Benito Juárez, Constitutional President of Mexico.* London: Remington, 1894. x, 384 p.

Cadenhead, Ivie Edward, Jr. *Benito Juárez.* New York: Twayne, 1973. 199 p.

Hamnett, Brian Roger. *Juárez.* ("Profiles in Power.") London: Longman, 1994. xix, 301 p.

Roeder, Ralph. *Juárez and His Mexico: A Biographical History.* New York. The Viking Press, 1947. 2v.; repinted Greenwood, 1968.

Scholes, Walter V. *Mexican Politics During the Juárez Regime, 1855–1872.* Columbia, MO: University of Missouri, 1957. 190 p.

Smart, Charles Allen. *Viva Juárez! A Biography.* Philadelphia, Lippincott, 1963. Reprinted Westport, CT: Greenwood, 1975. 444 p.

Weeks, Charles A. *The Juárez Myth in Mexico.* University, AL: University of Alabama Press, 1987. ix, 204 p. Reprinted, 2005. 224 p.

i. Juárez: Bibliography

Avilés, René. *Bibliography de Benito Juárez.* Mexico City: Sociedad Mexicana de Geografía y Estadística, 1972. 345 p.

8. The Second Empire

Anderson, William Marshall. *An American in Maximilian's Mexico, 1865–1866: The Diaries of William Marshall Anderson.* Ed. Ramón Eduardo Ruiz. San Marino, CA: The Huntington Library, 1959. xxxii, 132 p.

Basch, Samuel, *Erinnerungen aus Mexico: Geschichte der letzen zehn Monate des Kaiserreichs.* Leipzig: Dunker & Humbolt, 1868. 2 v. Edited and translated by Fred D. Ullman as *Recollections of Mexico: The Last Ten Months of Maximillian's Empire.* Delaware: Scholarly Resources, 2001. xxiv, 288 p.

Blasio, José Luis. *Maximiliano íntimo: el emperador Maximiliano y su corte.* Paris: Bouret, 1905. [iv], 478 p. Translated by Robert Hammond Murray as *Maximillian, Emperor of Mexico: Memoirs of his Private Secretary.* 2nd ed. New Haven: Yale University Press, 1941. xx, 235 p.

Blumberg, Arnold. *The Diplomacy of the Mexican Empire, 1863–1867.* Philadelphia: American Philosophical Society, 1971. 152 p.

Corti, [*Conte*] Egon Caesar. *Maximilian und Charlotte von Mexico: nach den bisher unveroffentlichen Geheimarchiv.* Zurich: Amalthea, 1924. Translated from the German by Catherine Alion Philips as *Maximilian and Charlotte of Mexico.* New York: Knopf, 1928. Reprinted Archon Books, 1968. xxiii, 976 p.

Hanna, Alfred Jackson and Abbey, Kathryn. *Napoleon III and Mexico: American Triumph over Monarchy.* Chapel Hill: University of North Carolina Press, 1971. xxii, 350 p.

Harding, Bertita. *Phantom Crown: The Story of Maximilian and Carlotta of Mexico.* Indianapolis, IN: Bobbs-Merrill, 1934. 381 p. Reprinted New York: Blue Ribbon Books, 1939.

Haslip, Joan. *The Crown of Mexico: Maximilian and his Empress Carlotta.* New York: Holt, Rinehart and Winston, 1971. xi, 531 p.

Hyde, Harford Montgomery. *Mexican Empire: The History of Maximilian and Carlota of Mexico.* London: Macmillan, 1946. ix, 349 p.

Kératy, [*Count*] Émile de. *L'empereur Maximilien, son élévation et sa chute . . .* Leipzig: Duncker & Humbolt, 1867. 323 p. Translated by G. H. Venables as *The Rise and Fall of the Emperor Maximilian, 1861–1867 . . . with the Imperial Corresponsence.* London: S. Low, Son & Marston, 1868. viii, 312 p.

O'Connor, Richard. *The Cactus Throne: The Tragedy of Maximilian and Carlota.* New York: Putnam, 1971. 375 p.

Pani, Erika. *Para mexicanizar el Segundo Imperio: el imaginario político de los imperialistas.* Mexico City: Colegio de México, 2001. 444 p.

Ridley, Jasper. *Maximilian and Juárez.* London: Phoenix Press, 1993. [ix], 353 p.

Smith, Gene. *Maximilian and Carlotta: A Tale of Romance and Tragedy.* New York: William Morrow, 1973. ix, 318 p.

Villalpando César, José Manuel. *Maximiliano.* ("Trilogía del Im-perio," v 3.) Mexico City: Clio, 1999. 285 p.

9. The Restored Republic

Ceballos, Ciro B. *Aurora y ocaso, 1867–1906: gobierno de Lerdo.* Mexico City: Talleres Tipográficos, 1912. 980 p.

Noll, Arthur Howard. *From Empire to Republic.* Chicago: McClurg, 1903. x, 336 p.

Perry, Laurens Ballard. *Juárez and Díaz: Machine Politics in Mexico.* DeKalb, IL: Northern Illinois University Press, 1978. xx, 468 p.

10. The Porfiriato

Beals, Carleton. *Porfirio Díaz, Dictator of Mexico*. Philadelphia: J. B. Lippincott, 1932. 436 p. Reprinted Westport, CT: Greenwood Press, 1971.

Brown, Lyle C. *The Mexican Liberals and their Struggle against the Díaz Dictatorship*. Mexico City: Mexico City College Press, 1956. Translated as "Los liberales mexicanos y su lucha en contra de la dictadura de Porfirio Diaz, 1900–1906," in *Antologia M.C.C.* Mexico City, 1956: 89–136.

Bryan, Susan E. "Teatro popular y sociedad durante el Porfiriato," *Historia mexicana* 33:130–69 (1983).

Creelman, James, *Díaz: Master of Mexico*. New York: Appleton, 1911. vii, 441 p.

Garner, Paul H. *Porfirio Díaz*. ("Profiles in Power.") London: Longman, 2001. x, 269 p.

Navarro, Juan N. "Mexico of Today," *National Geographic Magazine* 12(4): 152–57, (5):176–79, (6):235–38 (April–June, 1901).

a. Bernardo Reyes

Bryan, Anthony. "El Papel del General Bernardo Reyes en la política nacional y regional de México," *Humanitas* 13:331–40 (1972).

Niemeyer, Eberhardt Victor, Jr. *The Public Career of General Bernardo Reyes*. Translated by Juan Antonio Ayala as *El General Bernardo Reyes*. Monterrey, NL: Nuevo León, 1966. 261 p.

11. Modern Mexico

Is the Mexican Revolution Dead? Ed. Stanley Robert Ross. Philadelphia, PA: Temple University Press, 1966; 2nd ed, 1975. xxxviii, 339 p.

Johnson, William Weber, *Heroic Mexico: The Violent Emergence of a Modern Nation*. [1st ed.] Garden City NY: Doubleday, 1968. x, 463 p. Reissued as *Heroic Mexico: The Narrative History of a Twentieth Century Revolution*. Doubleday, 1968. Revised, paperback ed., San Diego: Harcourt Brace Jovanovich, 1984. x, 463 p.

Twentieth Century Mexico [by John M. Hart et al.]. Ed. W. Dirk Raat and William H. Beezley. Lincoln, NE: University of Nebraska Press, 1986. xvii, 318 p.

Wilkie, James Wallace. *The Mexican Revolution: Federal Expenditure and Social Change since 1910*. Berkeley, CA: University of California Press, 1967. xxix, 337 p., 2nd ed., revised, 1970, xxi, 337 p.

a. Early Twentieth Century

Tannenbaum, Frank. *Mexico: The Struggle for Peace and Bread*. New York: Knopf, 1950. xiv, 293, xiii.

————. *Peace by Revolution, an Interpretation of Mexico*. New York: Columbia University Press, 1966. 316 p.

i. Oral History

Wilkie, James Wallace and Monzón de Wilkie, Edna. *Mexico visto en el siglo XX: entrevistas de historia oral [con] Ramón Beteta, Marte R. Gómez, Manuel Gómez Mórin, Vicente Lombardo Toledano, Miguel Palomar y Vizcarra, Emilio Portes Gil, [y] Jesús Silva Herzog.* México City: Instituto Mexicano de Investigaciones Económicas, 1969. x, 770 p.

b. The Mexican Revolution

Aguilar, Manuel G. *La Derrota de un régimen*. Hermosillo, Sonora: Imprenta Regional, 1971.

Alessio Robles, Miguel. *Historia política de la revolución*, Mexico City: Botas, 1938. 473 p.; 3a ed. 1946. 393 p. Reprinted Comisión Nacional para las Celebraciones del 175 Aniversario de la Independencia Nacional y 75 Aniversario de la Revolución Mexicana, 1985.

Amaya, Juan Gualberto. *Madero y los auténticos revolucionarios de 1910*. Mexico City: Editorial Fernando, 1946.

Beals, Carleton. *Mexican Maze*. Illustrations by Diego Rivera. Philadelphia, PA: Lippincott, 1931. 369 p. Reprinted Westport, CT: Greenwood, 1971.

————. *Mexico: An Interpretation*. New York: Huebsch, 1923. 280 p.

Beteta, Ramón. *Pensamiento y dinámica de la Revolución Mexicana: antología de documentos politicosociales*. Mexico City: Editorial México Nuevo, 1950. 579 p.

Britten, John A. *Revolution and Ideology: Images of the Mexican Revolution in the United States*. Lexington, KY: University Press of Kentucky, 1995. viii, 271 p.

Calvert, Peter. *The Mexican Revolution. 1910–1914: The Diplomacy of the Anglo-American Conflict*. Cambridge: Cambridge University Press, 1968. x, 331 p.

Cockcroft, James D. *Intellectual Precursors of the Mexican Revolution, 1900–1913*. Austin, TX: University of Texas Press, 1968. x, 329 p.

Cosío Villegas, Daniel. *Change in Latin America: The Mexican and Cuban Revolutions*. Lincoln, NE: University of Nebraska Press, 1961. 54 p.

Cumberland, Charles Curtis. *The Meaning of the Mexican Revolution*, Boston: D. C. Heath, 1967. xvi, 110 p.

————. *Mexican Revolution: Genesis under Madero*. Austin, TX: University of Texas Press, 1952. ix, 298 p.

————. *Mexican Revolution: The Constitutionalist Years*. Austin, TX: University of Texas Press, 1972. xix, 449 p.

Dulles, John W. F. *Yesterday in Mexico: A Chronicle of the Revolution, 1919–1936.* Austin: University of Texas Press, 1961. 805 p.

García Rivas, Heriberto. *Breve historia de la revolución mexicana; contiene la relación cronológica de los hechos, las biografías de los gobernantes y principales revolucionarios, los documentos más importantes. . . .* Mexico City: Editorial Diana, 1964. 246 p.

Guerra, François-Xavier. *Le Mexique: de l'ancien régime à la Révolution.* Paris: Éditions L'Harmattan, 1983. 542 p.

Kautsky, John H. *Patterns of Modernizing Revolutions: Mexico and the Soviet Union.* Beverly Hills, CA: Sage Publications, 1975. 59 p.

Knight, Alan. *The Mexican Revolution.* Cambridge: Cambridge University Press, 1986. 2 v.

Rutherford, John. *Mexican Society During the Revolution: A Literary Approach,* Oxford, Clarendon Press, 1971. xii, 347 p.

Silva Herzog, Jesús. *Breve historia de la Revolución mexicana.* Mexico City: Fondo de Cultura Económico, 1972. 2 v.

i. Madero

Beezley, William H. *Insurgent Governor: Abraham Gonzales and the Mexican Revolution in Chihuahua.* Lincoln, NE: University of Nebraska Press, 1973. xiv, 195 p.

Francisco I. Madero: Apostle of Mexican Democracy. ed. Stanley R. Ross. New York: Columbia University Press, 1955. 378 p.

Henderson, Peter V. N. *Félix Díaz, the Porfirianos and the Mexican Revolution.* Lincoln, NE: University of Nebraska Press, 1981. xiii, 239 p.

ii. Orozco

Meyer, Michael C. *Mexican Rebel: Pascual Orozco and the Mexican Revolution.* Lincoln, NE: University of Nebraska Press, 1967. x, 172 p.

iii. Victoriano Huerta

Bulnes, Francisco. *La responsabilidad de Wilson.* 1916. Reprinted as *Toda la verdad acerca de la Revolución Mexicana: la responsa-bilidad criminal del Presidente Wilson en el desastre mexicano.* Mexico City: Los Insurgentes, 1960. 354 p. Authorized translation by Dora Scott entitled *The Whole Truth about Mexico: The Mexican Revolution and President Wilson's Part Therein, as Seen by a Científico.* New York: M. Bulnes, 1916. x, 395 p. Reprinted Detroit, MI: Blaine Ethridge, 1972, xi, 359 p.

Meyer, Michael C. *Huerta: A Political Portrait.* Lincoln, NE: University of Nebraska Press, 1972. xvii, 272 p.

iv. Aguascalientes

Quirk, Robert E. *The Mexican Revolution, 1914–1915: The Convention of Aguascalientes.* Bloomington, IN: Indiana University Press, 1960. 325 p. Reprinted Westport, CT: Greenwood, 1981.

v. Pancho Villa

Brady, Haldeen. *Pershing's Mission in Mexico.* El Paso, TX: Texas Western Press, 1966. xvii, 82 p.

Clendenen, Clarence Clemens. *The United States and Pancho Villa: A Study in Unconventional Diplomacy.* Ithaca, NY: Cornell University Press, 1961. 352 p. Reprinted Port Washington, NY: Kennikat Press, 1972.

Guzmán, Martín Luis. *El águila y la serpiente.* Madrid: Aguilar, 1928. 402 p. Translated by Harriet de Onís as *The Eagle and the Serpent*, with an intro. by Federico de Onís. Garden City, N.Y., Dolphin Books [1965]. xiv, 386 p.

———. *Memorias de Pancho Villa; según el texto establecido y ordenado por Martín Luis Guzmán.* México City: Ediciones Botas, 1938–1940. 4 v. Condensed and translated by Virginia H. Taylor as *Memoirs of Pancho Villa.* Austin, TX: University of Texas Press, 1965. xii, 512 p.

Katz, Friedrich. *The Life and Times of Pancho Villa.* Stanford: Stanford University Press, 1998. xv, 985 p.

McLynn, Frank. *Villa and Zapata: A Biography of the Mexican Revolution.* London: Cape, 2000. [xv], 459 p.

Plana, Miguel. *Pancho Villa and the Mexican Revolution.* Translated by Arthur Figliola. New York: Interlink Books, 2002. 124 p.

vi. Emiliano Zapata

Womack, John, Jr. *Zapata and the Mexican Revolution.* New York: Alfred Knopf, 1969. xi, 435, xxi p.

vii. De la Huerta

Meyer, Michael C. *Huerta: A Political Portrait.* Lincoln, NE: University of Nebraska Press, 1967. xvi, 272 p.

viii. Obregón

Dillon, Emile Joseph. *President Obregon: A World Reformer.* London: Hutchinson, 1923. vi, 351 p.; Boston: Small, Maynard, 1923. 350 p.

c. Mid-Twentieth Century (1920–1946)

Cline, Howard. *Mexico: Revolution to Evolution, 1940–1960.* New York: Oxford University Press, 1962. xiv, 375 p.

O'Malley, Ilene V. *The Myth of the Revolution: Hero Cults and the Institutionalization of the Mexican State, 1920–1940.* New York: Greenwood Press, 1986. xii, 659 p.

i. Calles

Camp, Roderic Ai. "La Campaña presidencial de 1929 y el liderazgo político en México," *Historia mexicana* 27(2):231–59 (1977).
Matute Aguirre, Álvaro. "La encrucijada de 1929: caudillismo versus institucionalización," in Jaime E. Rodríguez O. *The Evolution of the Mexican Political System.* Wilmington, DE: SR Books, 1993: 187–202.

ii. Cristeros Rebellion

Bailey, David C. *Viva Cristo Rey: The Cristero Rebellion and the Church-State Conflict in Mexico.* Austin, TX: University of Texas Press, 1974. xiii, 346 p.
Butler, Matthew. *Popular Piety and Political Identity in Mexico's Cristero Rebellion: Michoacán, 1927–1929.* Oxford: Oxford University Press, 2004. 272 p.
Gulisano, Paolo. *Cristeros! L'insorgenza cattolica e popolare del Messico, 1926–1929.* Rimini: Il Cerchio, 1996. 135 p.
Meyer, Jean A. *La Christiade: société et idéologie dans le Mexique contemporain.* 3e éd. Paris: Payot, 1975. 411 p.; translated by Aurelio Garzón del Camino as. *La cristiada: conflicto entre la iglesia y el estado, 1926–1929.* 2a ed. Mexico City: Siglo Veintiuno, 1974. 2v.; and translated by Richard Southern as *The Cristero Rebellion: The Mexican People between Church and State, 1926–1929.* Cambridge: Cambridge University Press, 1976. xii, 260 p.
Tierra de cristeros. Colotlán: Campus Norte, Universidad de Guadalajara, 2002. 320 p.
Tuck, Jim. *The Holy War in Los Altos: A Regional Analysis of Mexico's Cristero Rebellion.* Tucson: University of Arizona Press, 1982. xiv, 230 p.

iii. Lázaro Cárdenas

Millán, Verna Carleton. *Mexico Reborn.* Boston, MA: Houghton Mifflin, 1939. 312 p.
Múñoz, Hilda. *Lázaro Cárdenas, sintesis ideológica de su campaña presidencial.* Mexico City: Fondo de Cultura Económica, 1976. 162 p.
Novo, Salvador. *La vida en México en el período presidencial de Lázaro Cárdenas.* Mexico City: Empresas Editoriales, 1964. Reprinted Instituto Nacional de Antropología e Historia, 1994. 746 p.

Silva Herzog, Jesús. *Lázaro Cárdenas: su pensamiento económico, social y político.* Mexico City: Nuevo Tiempo, 1975. 137 p.

Townsend, William Cameron. *Lázaro Cárdenas: Mexican Democrat.* Ann Arbor, MI: George Wahr, 1952. xvii, 380 p. 2nd ed., Waxhaw, NC: International Friendship, 1979. viii, 408 p.

Weyl, Nathaniel and Weyl, Sylvia. *Reconquest of Mexico: The Years of Lázaro Cárdenas.* London: Oxford University Press, 1939. 394 p.

iv. Manuel Ávila Camacho

Novo, Salvador. *La vida en México en el período presidencial de Manuel Ávila Camacho.* Mexico City: Empresas Editoriales, 1965. 825 p.

d. Late Twentieth Century

Cumberland, Charles Curtis. *Mexico: The Struggle for Modernity.* London: Oxford University Press, 1968. xi, 394 p.

Helman, Judith A. *Mexico in Crisis.* New York: Holmes and Meier, 1978. vi, 229 p.; 2nd ed., 1983. xiii, 345 p.

Latell, Brian. *Mexico at the Crossroads: The Many Crises of the Political System.* Stanford: Hoover Institution, 1986. 34 p.

i. Miguel Alemán Valdés, 1946–1952

Norton, J. A. *Las entrevistas con Presidente Miguel Alemán.* Mexico City: Editorial Norton, 1950.

Novo, Salvador. *La vida en México en el período presidencial de Miguel Alemán.* Mexico City: Porrúa, 1967. 666 p.

ii. Adolfo Ruiz Cortines, 1952–1958

Novo, Salvador. *La vida en México en el período presidencial de Adolfo Ruiz Cortines.* Mexico City: Consejo Nacional para la Cultura y las Artes, 1996–7. 2 v.

iii. Adolfo López Mateos, 1958–1964

Novo, Salvador. *La vida en México en el período presidencial de Adolfo López Mateos,* Mexico City: Instituto Nacional de Antropología e Historia, 1998. 2 v.

Taylor, Philip B. "The Mexican Elections of 1958," *Western Political Quarterly* (September 1960): 722–44.

iv. Gustavo Díaz Ordaz, 1964–1970

Cochrane, James D. "Mexico's New Cienfícios: The Díaz Ordaz Cabinet," *Inter-American Economic Affairs* (Summer 1967): 67–72.

Michaels, Albert L. "The Crisis of Cardenismo," *Journal of Latin American Studies* 2(1):51–79 (1970).

Novo, Salvador. *La vida en México en el período presidencial de Gustavo Diaz Ordaz*. Mexico City: CONACULTA, 1998. 2 v.

Poniatowska, Elena. *La noche de Tlatelolco: testimonios de historia oral*. Mexico: Era, 1971. 282 p. Translated by Helen R. Lane as *Massacre in Mexico*. New York: Viking, 1975. xvii, 333 p. Reprinted Columbia, MO: University of Missouri Press, 1991.

Valadés, José C. *El Presidente de México en 1970*. Mexico City: Editores Mexicanos Unidos, 1969. 184 p.

v. Luis Echeverría Álvarez, 1970–1976

Alisky, Marvin. "Mix of Many Ministries," *Mexican-American Review*. (June 1976): 10–16.

Novo, Salvador. *La vida en México en el período presidencial de Luis Echeverría*. Mexico City: CONACULTA, 2000. xxv, 521 p.

Pellicer de Brody, Olga. "Mexico in the 1970s," in *Latin America and the United States: The Changing Political Realities*. By Heraclio Bonilla et al., edited by Julio Cotler and Richard R. Fagen. Stanford, CA: Stanford University Press, 1974.

Rosales, José Natividad. *La muerte (?) de Lucio Cabañas*. Mexico City: Editorial Posada, 1974. 190 p.

Sierra, Carlos Justo. *Luis Echeverría: raíz y dinámica de su pensa-miento*. Mexico City: Editorial Nacional, 1969. 124 p.

vi. José López Portillo y Pacheco, 1976–1982

Hernández Rodríguez, Rogelio. *Empresarios, banca y estado: el conflicto durante el gobierno de José López Portillo, 1976–1982*. Mexico City: Facultad Latinoamericana de Ciencias Sociales, 1988. 302 p.

López Portillo y Pacheco, José. *Mis tiempos: biografía y testimonio político*. Mexico City: Fernández, 1988. 2 v. (xxiv, 1293 p.).

Mirón, Rosa María and Pérez Fernández, Germán. *López Portillo: auge y crisis de un sexenio*. Mexico: Plaza y Valdés, 1988. 196 p.

vii. Miguel de La Madrid Hurtado, 1982–1988

Alisky, Marvin. "Response of the Mexican Media to the de la Madrid Case for Reform and Austerity," *The Mexican Forum=El Foro Mexicano* (July 1983): 8–9.

viii. Carlos Salinas de Gortari, 1988–1994

Ayala Anguiano, Armando. *Salinas y su México*. Mexico City: Grijalbo, 1995. 189 p.

Russell, Philip L. *Mexico under Salinas*. Austin: Mexico Resource Center, 1994. x, 489 p.

ix. Ernesto Zedillo Ponce de León, 1994–2000

Changing Structure of Mexico: Political, Social, and Economic Prospects. Ed. Laura Randall. Amonk, NY: M. E. Sharpe, 1996. xv, 413 p.; 2nd. ed., 2006. 512 p.

Una historia contemporánea de México. Ed. Ilán Bizberg et al. Mexico City: Oceano, 2003– . v1– .

Mexico Under Zedillo. Ed. Susan Kaufman Purcell and Luis Rubio. Boulder, CO: Lynne Riemer, 1998. xv, 151 p.

e. Mexico in the New Century

i. Vicente Fox Quesada, 2000–2006

México Under Fox. Ed. Luis Rubio and Susan Kaufmann Purcell. Boulder, CO: Lynne Rienner, 2004. xii, 178 p.

D. Local History

1. General

The Provinces of Early Mexico: Variants of Spanish American Regional Evolution. Ed. Ida Altman and James Lockhart. Los Angeles, CA: Latin American Center, University of California, 1976. x, 291 p.

Sánchez Gutiérrez, Arturo. "La política en el México rural de los años cincuenta," in Jaime E. Rodríguez O. *The Evolution of the Mexican Political System.* Wilmington, DE: SR Books, 1993: 215–44.

2. Mexico City

a. General

Kandall, Jonathan. *La Capital: The Biography of Mexico City.* New Haven, CT: Yale University Press, 1988. [ix], 643 p.

b. Seventeenth Century

Maza, Francisco de la. *La Ciudad de México en el siglo xvii.* Mexico City: Fondo de Cultura Económica, 1968. 135 p.

Rubial García, Antonio. *La plaza, el palacio y el convento: la ciudad de México en el siglo XVII.* Mexico City: Consejo Nacional para la Cultura y las Artes, 1998. 168 p.

c. Eighteenth Century

Viqueira Albán, Juan Pedro. *¿Relajados o reprimidos? Diversiones públicas y vida social en la ciudad de México durante el siglo de las Luces.* Mexico City:

Fondo de Cultura Económica, 1987. 302 p. Translated by Sonya Lipsett-Rivera and Sergio Rivera Ayala as *Property and permissiveness in Bourbon Mexico*. Wilmington, DE: Scholarly Resources, 1999. xxii, 280 p.

d. Nineteenth Century

Fernández Christlieb, Federico. "Géomètre urbaine et progrès à Mexico au XIXème siècle: le "Paseo de la Reforma," in *Histoire et sociétés de l'Amérique Latine*. 5:167–81 (1997).

Guedea, Virginia, "First Popular Elections in Mexico City, 1812–1813," translated by Jaime E. Rodríguez O. in his *The Evolution of the Mexican Political System*. Wilmington, DE: SR Books, 1993: 45–69.

e. Early Twentieth Century

Simpich, Frederick. "North America's Oldest Metropolis: Through 600 Melodramatic Years Mexico City has Grown in Splendor and Achievement," *National Geographic Magazine* 58(1):45–84 (July 1930).

f. Modern

Bataillon, Claude and Panabière, Louis. *Mexico aujourd'hui: la plus grande ville du monde*. Paris: Publisud, 1988. 245 p.

Cornelius, Wayne A. *Politics and the Migrant Poor in Mexico City*. Stanford, CA: Stanford University Press, 1975. xii, 319 p.

Davis, C. L. "Mobilization of Public Support: The Lower Class in Mexico City," *American Journal of Political Science* (November 1976): 653–70.

Hernández Jiménez, Dalmasio. *La marginalidad: el comportamiento de las familias marginales en la Colonia Santa Anita, Delegación Iztacalco, México, D.F.* Mexico City: UNAM, 1984. 140 p.

Lewis, Oscar. *The Children of Sánchez: Autobiography of a Mexican Family*. New York: Random House, 1961. 499 p.

Yañez Reyes, Sergio. *Industria y pobreza urbana en la ciudad de México: antropología social de los pobres de Álvaro Obregón*. Mexico City: Porrúa, 2003. 194 p.

3. The Far North (of Pre-1848 Mexico)

Benavides, Adán. "The Borderlands, Then and Now: Manuscript and Archival Sources at the University of Texas at Austin," *Latin American Identities: Race, Ethnicity, Gender, and Sexuality: Papers of the XLVIth Annual Meeting of the Seminar on the Acquisition of Latin American Library Materials, Tempe AZ, May 26–29, 2001*. Austin, TX: SALALM Secretariat, 2005: 167–73.

Bolton, Herbert Eugene. *The Spanish Borderlands: A Chronicle of Old Florida and the Southwest.* New Haven, CT: Yale University Press, 1921. xiv, 320 p.

————. *Rim of Christendom: A Biography of Eusebio Francisco King, Pacific Coast Pioneer.* New York: Macmillan, 1936. xiv, 644. Reprinted Russell and Russell, 1960.

Cook, Warren L. *Flood Tide of Empire: Spain and the Pacific Northwest, 1543–1819.* New Haven: Yale University Press, 1973. xiv, 620 p.

Day, A[rthur] Grove. *Coronado's Quest.* Berkeley: University of California Press, 1965. xvi, 419 p. Reprinted Westport, CT: Greenwood, 1981.

Geiger, Maynard J. *The Life and Times of Fray Junípero Serra, O.F.M.; or, The Man who Never Turned Back, 1713–1784, a Biography.* Washington, DC: Academy of American Franciscan History, 1959. 2 v.

Moorhead, Max L. *The Apache Frontier: Jacobo Ugarte and Spanish-Indian Relations in Northern New Spain, 1769–1791.* Nebraska: University of Oklahoma Press, 1968. xiv, 309 p.

Powell, Philip Wayne. *Soldiers, Indians & Silver: The Northward Advance of New Spain.* Berkeley, Los Angeles: University of California Press, 1952. xi, 317 p.

Sepúlveda, César. *La frontera norte de México: historia, conflicts, 1762–1975.* Mexico City: Porrúa, 1976. 171 p.

Tenenbaum, Barbara A. "The Making of a Fait Accompli: Mexico and the Provincias Internas, 1776–1846," in Jaime E. Rodríguez O. *The Evolution of the Mexican Political System.* Wilmington, DE: SR Books, 1993: 91–115.

Thurman, Michael E. *The Naval Department of San Blas: New Spain's Bastion for Alta California and Nootka, 1767 to 1798.* Glendale, CA: Arthur H. Clark Co., 1967. 382 p.

a. Alta California

Chapman, Charles E. *A History of California: The Spanish Period.* New York: Macmillan, 1921. xi, 527 p.

Heizer, Robert F. *The Destruction of the California Indians.* Lincoln, NE: University of Nebraska Press, 1974. xxi, 321 p.

b. Texas

The Mexican Side of the Texas Revolution by the Chief Mexican Participants, ed. and translated by Carlos E. Castaneda. Dallas, TX: P. L. Turner Company, 1928. vii, 391 p. Reprinted 1956.

4. The Near North

Across the Chichimec Sea: Papers in Honor of J. Charles Kelly. Ed. Carroll L. Riley and Basil C. Hendrick. Carbondale: Southern Illinois University Press, 1978, xviii, 318 p.

Jones, Oakah L., Jr. *Nueva Vizcaya: Heartland of the Spanish Frontier*. Albuquerque, NM: University of New Mexico Press, 1988. xx, 342 p.

Dobie, James Frank. *Tongues of the Monte*. Garden City, NY: Doubleday, Doran, 1935. ix, 301 p.

Lumholtz, Carl. *Unknown Mexico*. New York: Scribner's, 1902. 2 v.

a. Baja California

Blaisdell, Lowell. *The Desert Revolution: Baja California, 1911*. Madison, WI: University of Wisconsin Press, 1962. xiii, 268 p. Reprinted Westport, CT: Greenwood, 1986.

Maldonado Sánchez, Braulio. *Baja California: comentarios políticos*. Mexico City: Costa-Amic, 1960. 136 p.; S.E.P., 1993. 169 p.

Price, John A. *Tijuana: Urbanization in a Border Culture*. South Bend, IN: University of Notre Dame Press, 1973. xvi, 195 p.

b. Sonora

Alisky, Marvin. *Guide to the Government of the Mexican State of Sonora*. Tempe, AZ: Arizona State University Center for Latin American Studies, 1971. 48 p.

———. *State and Local Government in Sonora, Mexico*. 2nd ed. Tempe, AZ: Arizona State University Center for Latin American Studies, 1962. 20 p.

———. "Surging Sonora," *Arizona Highways* (November 1964): 17–37.

Borrero Silva, María del Valle. *Fundación y primeros años de la gobernación de Sonora y Sinaloa, 1732–1750*. Hermosillo: Colegio de Sonora, 2004. 245 p.

Voss, Stuart F. *On the Periphery of Nineteenth-Century Mexico: Sonora and Sinaloa, 1810–1877*. Tucson, AZ: University of Arizona Press, 1982. xv, 318 p.

c. Sinaloa

Cruz-Torres, María Luz. *Lives of Dust and Water: An Anthropology of Change and Resistance in Northwestern Mexico*. Tucson, AZ: University of Arizona Press, 2004. xvi, 325 p.

Ortega Noriega, Sergio. *Breve historia de Sinaloa*. Mexico City: Fondo de Cultura Económica, 1999. 332 p.

Robertson, Thomas A. *A Southwestern Utopia*. Los Angeles: Ward Ritchie Press, 1964. xiii, 266 p.

d. Chihuahua

Martínez, Oscar. *Border Town: Ciudad Juarez since 1848*. Austin, TX: University of Texas Press, 1975. 231 p.

Wasserman, Mark. *Capitalists, Caciques and Revolution: The Native Elite and Foreign Enterprise in Chihuahua, Mexico, 1854–1911*. Chapel Hill, NC: University of North Carolina.

e. Coahuila

Falcón, Romana. "Poderes y razones de las jefaturas políticas: Coahuila en el primer siglo de vida independiente" in Jaime E. Rodríguez O. *The Evolution of the Mexican Political System*. Wilmington: SR Books, 1993: 137–86.

f. Durango

Anaya, Samuel. *El Estado de Durango*. Durango: Prensa Félix, 1946.

Maza, Francisco de la. *Ciudad de Durango: notas de arte*. 2a ed., 1999. 62 p.

g. Nuevo León

Balan, Jorge. *Man in a Developing Society: Geographic and Social Mobility in Monterrey, Mexico*. Austin, TX: Institute for Latin American Studies, University of Texas, 1973. 184 p.

Alisky, Marvin. *Government of the Mexican State of Nuevo León*. Tempe, AZ: Arizona State University Center for Latin American Studies, 1971. 50 p.

Garza, Gustavo. *Políticas urbanas en grandes metrópolis: Detroit, Monterrey y Toronto*. Mexico City: Colegio de México, 2003. 402 p.

Saragoza, Alexander M. *The Monterrey Elite and the Mexican State, 1880–1940*. Austin, TX: University of Texas Press, 1988. x, 258 p.

h. Tamaulipas

Alvarado Mendoza, Arturo. *Historia regional de Tamaulipas,* Mexico City: Limusa Noriega, 2000. 130 p.

i. Zacatecas

Bakewell, Peter John. *Silver Mining and Society in Colonial Mexico: Zacatecas, 1546–1700*. Cambridge: Cambridge University Press, 1971. xiii, 294 p.

Flores Olague, Jesús, et al. *Breve historia de Zacatecas*. Mexico City: Fondo de Cultura Económica, 1996. 231 p.

5. Central Mexico

Mallon, Florencia E. *Peasant and Nation: The Making of Post-Colonial Mexico and Peru*. Berkeley, CA: University of California Press, 1995. xxiv, 472 p.

a. Nayarit

Coyle, Philip Edward. *Nyari History, Politics, and Violence: From Flowers to Ash*. Tucson, AZ: Univeristy of Arizona Press, 2001. xiv, 263 p.

Stager, Kenneth R. "The Avifauna of the Tres Marias Islands, Mexico," *The Auk: Quarterly Journal of Ornithology* 74(4):413–32 (October, 1957).

b. Jalisco

Riojas López, Carlos. *Industria y estrategia económica en México, 1877–1992: el caso de Jalisco.* Guadalajara: Centro Universitario de Ciencias Económico-administrativas, 1999. 133 p.

Valerio Ulloa, Sergio. *Historia rural jalisciense: economía agrícola e innovación tecnológica durante el siglo xix.* Guadalajara: Universidad de Guadalajara, 2003. 351 p.

c. San Luis Potosí

Iturriaga de la Fuente, José N. *Viajeros extranjeros en San Luis Potosi.* San Luis Potosi: Editorial Ponciano Arriaga, 2000. 403 p.

Kaiser Schlitter, Arnaldo. *Breve historia de la ciudad de San Luis Polosí.* San Luis Potosí: Al Libro Mayor, 1992. 76 p.

d. Aguascalientes

Gómez Serrano, Jesús. *La guerra chichimeca, la fundición de Aguascalientes y el extermino de la población aborigen, 1548–1620: un ensayo de reinterpretación.* Zapopan: El Colegio de Jalisco, 2001. 129 p.

e. Guanajuato

Chowning, Margaret. *Rebellious Nuns: The Troubled History of a Mexican Convent, 1752–1863.* Oxford: Oxford University Press, 2006. x, 246 p.

Ferry, Elizabeth Emma. *Not Ours Alone: Patrimony, Value, and Collectivity in Contemporary Mexico.* New York: Columbia University Press, 2005. xix, 273 p.

f. Querétaro

Daville Landero, Selva L. *Querétaro: sociedad, economía, política y cultural.* Mexico City: Centro de Investigaciones Interdisciplinarias en Ciencias y Humanidades de la UNAM, 2000. 234 p.

González Gómez, Carmen Imelda. *El tabaco virrenal: monopolio de un costumbre.* Santiago de Querétaro: Fundo Editorial de Querétaro, 2002. 250 p.

g. Hidalgo

Ballesteros G., Victor M. *Bibliografía general del estado de Hidalgo, con una selección de hemeografia.* Pachuca: Universidad Autónoma del Estado de Hidalgo, 1994. 394 p.

h. Veracruz-Llave

Blázquez Domínguez, Carmen. *Breve historia de Veracruz*. Mexico City: Fondo de Cultura Ecnómica, 2000. 203 p.

Carroll, Patrick James. *Blacks in Colonial Veracruz: Race, Ethnicity, and Regional Development*. 2nd ed. Austin, TX: University of Texas Press, 1991. 244 p.

Siemens, Alfred H. *Between the Summit and the Sea: Central Veracruz in the Nineteenth Century*. Vancouver: University of British Columbia Press, 1990. xx, 234 p.

i. Jalapa

Fagen, Richard R. and Tuohy, William S. *Politics and Privilege in a Mexican City*. Stanford: Stanford University Press, 1972. xii, 209 p.

Spratling, William. *More Human than Divine: An Intimate and Lively Self-portrait in Clay of a Smiling People from Ancient Vera Cruz*. Mexico City: Universidad Nacional Autónoma de México, 1960. 29 p.

ii. Veracruz City

Wood, Andrew Grant. *Revolution in the Street: Women, Workers, and Urban Protests in Veracruz, 1870–1922*. Wilmington: SR Books, 2001. xxiii, 239 p.

i. Puebla

Hoekstra, Rik. *Two Worlds Merging: The Transformation of Society in the Valley of Puebla, 1570–1640*. Amsterdam: CEDLA, 1993. 285 p.

Thomson, Guy P. C. *Patriotism, Politics, and Popular Liberalism in Nineteenth-Century Mexico*. Wilmington, DE: Scholarly Resources, 1998. xviii, 420 p.

i. Cholula

Maza, Francisco de la. *Ciudad de Cholula y sus iglesias*. Mexico City: Impr. Universitaria, 1959. 159 p.

ii. Puebla City

Liehr, Reinhard. *Stadtrat und städtische Oberschicht von Puebla am Ende der Kolonialzeit, 1787–1810*. Wiesbaden: Steiner, 1971. viii, 233 p.

Thomson, Guy P. C. *Puebla de los Angeles: Industry and Society in a Mexican City, 1700–1850*. Boulder CO: Westview Press, 1989. xxiv, 396 p.

j. Tlaxcala

Rendón Garcini, Ricardo. *Breve historia de Tlaxcala*. Mexico City: Fondo de Cultura Económica, 1996. 182 p.

k. Michoacán

Ochoa, Álvaro and Sánchez Díaz, Gerardo. *Breve historia de Michoacán*. Mexico City: Fondo de Cultura Económica, 2003. 287 p.

l. Colima

Romero de Solís, José Manuel. *Bibliografía de Colima*. Zamora: Colegio de Michoacán & Colima: Universidad de Colima, 1986– ?

m. Mexico State

Bustamante, Carlos María de. *Viaje a Toluca en 1834*. Mexico City: Bibliotaca Enciclopédica del Estado de México, 1969. 78 p.

Castro Domínguez, Pablo. *Chayotes, burros y machetes*. Zinacantepec: Colegio Mexiquense, 2003. 488 p.

n. Morelos (State)

Hernández Chávez, Alicia. *Breve historia de Morelos*. Mexico City: Fondo de Cultura Económica, 2002. 247 p.

o. Guerrero (State)

Guardino, Peter F. *Peasants, Politics, and the Formation of Mexico's National State: Guerrero, 1800–1857*. Stanford, CA: Stanford University Press, 1996. viii, 319 p.

6. Southern Mexico

a. Isthmus of Tehuantepec

Covarrubias, Miguel. *Mexico South: The Isthmus of Tehuantepec*. New York: Knopf, 1946. xxviii, 437, viii p.

7. Oaxaca

Higgins, Michael James. *Somos Tocayos: Anthropology of Urbanism and Poverty*. Lanham, MD: Univeristy Press of America, 1983. 220 p.

Iturribarría, Jorge Fernando. *Oaxaca en la historia, de la época pre-colombina a los tiempos actuales*. Mexico City: Stylo, 1955. 471 p.

Overmyer Velázquez, Mark. *Visions of the Emerald City: Modernity, Traditions, and the Formation of Porfiran Oaxaca, Mexico*. Durham, NC: Duke University Press, 2006. 256 p.

a. Tabasco

Martínez Assad, Carlos. *Breve historia de Tabasco*. Mexico City: Fondo de Cultura Económica, 1998. 250 p.

b. Chiapas

Ross, John. *Rebellion From the Roots: Indian Uprising in Chiapas.* Monroe, ME: Common Courage Press, 1995. 424 p.

Rovira, Guiomar. *Mujeres de maíz: la voz de las indígenas de Chiapas y la rebellión zapatista.* Barcelona: Virus, 1996. 348 p. Translated by Anna Keene as *Women of Maize: Indigenous Women and the Zapatista Rebellion.* London: Latin America Bureau, 2000. 188 p.

———. *¡Zapata vive! La rebelión indígena de Chiapas contada por sus protaganistas.* Barcelona: Virus, 1994. 320 p.

Weinburg, Bill. *Homage to Chiapas: New Indigenous Struggles in Mexico.* London: Verso, 2000. xxiv, 456 p.

c. Campeche

Sierra, Carlos Justo. *Breve historia de Campeche.* Mexico City: Fondo de Cultura Económica, 1998. 250 p.

8. Yucatán

Chamberlain, Robert S. *The Conquest and Colonization of Yucatán, 1517–1550.* New York: Octagon Books, 1966.

Landa, [Fray] Diego de. *Relación de las cosas de Yucatán.* 1566. Ed. María del Carmen León Cazares. Mexico City: Consejo Nacional para la Cultura y las Artes, 1994. 221 p.; Translated and edited by William Edmond Gates as *Yucatán, Before and After the Conquest.* Baltimore, MD: The Maya Society, 1937. xv, 162 p., and by Alfred M. Tozzer as *Landa's Relación de las Cosas de Yucatán.* Cambridge, MA: Peabody Museum of American Archaeology and Ethnology, 1941. xiii, 394 p.

López de Cogolludo, Diego. *Historia de Yucathán.* Madrid: Juan García Infanzón, 1688. [xxviii], 792 p.; 5a ed. Campeche: Ayuntamiento, 1995–1997. 3 v.

Pérez Martínez, Héctor. *Yucatan: An Annotated Bibliography of Documents and Manuscripts on the Archaeology and History of Yucatan in Archives and Libraries of Mexico, North America and Europe = Catálogo de documentos para la historia de Yucatán y Campeche que se hallen en diversos archivos y bibliotecas de México y del extrangero.* Salisbury, NC: Documentary Publications, 1980. 131 p.

Reed, Nelson. *The Caste War of Yucatán.* Stanford, CA: Stanford University Press, 1964. x, 308 p. Revised ed., 2001. xvi, 428 p.

a. Quintana Roo

Macias Richard, Carlos. *Nueva frontera mexicana: milicia, burocracia y ocupación territorial en Quintana Roo, 1902–1927.* Mexico City: Consejo Nacional de Ciencia y Tecnología, 1997. 347 p.

XIV. SOURCES OF CURRENT INFORMATION

Latin America Monitor: Mexico. London: Latin American Monitor, 1984– .
Latin America Weekly Report. London: Latin American Newsletters, 1979– .
Mexico and Nafta Regional Report. London: Latin American Newsletters, 1979– (monthly).
"Mexico" in *Europa World Yearbook, 1927–* . London: Europa Publications, 1926– (annual).
"Mexico" in *The Statesman's Yearbook, 1865–* . London: Macmillan, 1864– (annual).

A. Electronic

Latin American Newsletters: [an online version of items 0737 and 0738, updated weekly]. At "www.latinnews.com."
Mexico and the World Webjournal, edited James W. Wilkie, 1996– at: "www.isop.ucla.edu/profmex."

XV. SECTORAL HISTORY

A. Church and Religious History and Policy

1. Pre-Hispanic

Duverger, Christian. *La fleur létale: economie du sacrifice aztèque.* Paris: Editions. du Seuil, [1979]. 49 p.

2. Catholicism

Cuevas, Mariano. *Historia de la Iglesia en México.* Mexico City: 1921–1928. 5 v.

a. Sixteenth and Seventeenth Centuries

Braden, Charles Samuel. *Religious Aspects of the Conquest of Mexico.* Durham, NC: Duke University Press, 1930. xv, 344 p.
García Icazbalceta, Joaquín. *Don fray Juan de Zumárraga, primer obispo y arzobispo de México.* Mexico City: 1947.
Greenleaf, Richard E. *Zumárraga and the Mexican Inquisition, 1536–1543.* Washington, DC: Academy of American Franciscan History, 1961.
Grunberg, Bernard. *L'Inquisition apostolique au Mexique: histoire d'une institution et de son impact dans une société coloniale, 1521–1571.* Paris: L'Harmattan, 1998. 236 p.

McAndrew, John. *The Open-Air Churches of Sixteenth-Century Mexico: Atrios, Posas, Open Chapels, and Other Studies.* Cambridge, MA: Harvard University Press, 1965. xxvi, 755 p.

Mendieta, [Fray] Gerónimo de. *Historia eclesiástica indiana.* Edición facsimilar del códice. Mexico City: Porrúa, 1971. xlv, 790 p. A partial translation of this by Felix Jay issued as *Historia Eclesiástica Indiana: a Franciscan's View of the Spanish Conquest, critically reviewed with selected passages translated.* Leviston: Edwin Mellea Press, 1997. 139 p.

Richard, Robert. *Confute spirituelle du Mexique.* Paris: Instituto d'Ethnologie, 1933. xix, 404 p. Translated by Lesley Byrd Simpson as *The Spiritual Conquest of Mexico: An Essay on the Apostolate and the Evangelizing Methods of the Mendicant Orders in New Spain, 1523–1572.* Berkeley, CA: University of California Press, 1966. xii, 423 p.

The Roman Catholic Church in Colonial Latin America. Ed. Richard E. Greenleaf. New York: Alfred Knopf, 1971. xi, 272 p. Reprinted Tempe, AZ: Center for Latin American Studies, Arizona State University, 1977.

Schwaller, John Frederick. *Church and Clergy in Sixteenth Century Mexico.* Albuquerque, NM: University of New Mexico Press, 1987. xvi, 263 p.

b. Eighteenth Century

Connaughton Hanley, Brian Francis. *Ideología y sociedad en Guadalajara, 1788–1853.* Mexico City: Consejo Nacional para la Cultura y las Artes, 1992. 468 p. In English as: *Clerical Ideology in a Revolutionary Age: The Guadalajara Church and the Idea of the Mexican Nation, 1788–1853.* Calgary: University of Calgary Press; Boulder, CO: University Press of Colorado, 2003. ix, 426 p.

Taylor, William B. *Magistrates of the Sacred: Priests and Parishioners in Eighteenth Century Mexico.* Stanford, CA: Stanford University Press, 1996. xiv, 868 p.

c. Nineteenth Century

Callcott, Wilfrid Hardy. *Church and State in Mexico, 1822–1857.* New York: Octagon Books, 1965. ix, 357 p.

Costeloe, Michael P. *Church Wealth in Mexico: A Study of the Juzado de Capellanías in the Archbishopric of Mexico, 1800–1858.* Cambridge: Cambridge University Press, 1967. ix. 139 p.

Estado, iglesia y sociedad en México, siglo xix. Ed. Álvaro Matute, Evelia Rejo, Brian Connaughton. Mexico City: M. A. Porrúa, 1995. 430 p.

Toro, Alfonso. *La Iglesia y el Estado en México: estudio sobre los conflictos entre el clero católico y los gobiernos mexicanos desde la Independencia hasta nuestos dias.* Mexico City: Taller Gráfico de la Nación, 1927. 501 p.

d. Twentieth Century and After

Dooley, Francis Patrick. *Los Cristeros, Calles, y el catolicismo mexicano.* Traducción Maria Emilia Martínez Negrete Deffis. Mexico City: Moderno, 1976. 214 p.

Quirk, Robert E. *The Mexican Revolution and the Catholic Church, 1910–1929.* Bloomington, IN: Indiana University Press, 1973. 276 p.

3. Protestantism

Baldwin, Deborah J. *Protestants and the Mexican Revolution: Missionaries, Ministers, and Social Change.* Urbana, IL: University of Illinois Press, 1990. xii, 203 p.

Bowen, Kurt Derek. *Evangelism and Apostasy: The Evolution and Impact of Evangelicals in Modern Mexico.* Montreal: McGill-Queen's University Press, 1996. xi, 270 p.

Case, Alden Burell. *Thirty Years with the Mexicans: In Peace and Revolution.* New York: Fleming H. Revell, 1917. 285 p.

Moses, Jasper Turner. *Today in the Land of Tomorrow: A Study in the Development of Mexico.* Indianapolis, IN: Christian Women's Board of Missions, 1907. xi, 83 p.

XVI. PHILOSOPHY AND POLITICAL THEORY

A. General

Camp, Roderic Ai. "The National School of Economics and Public Life in Mexico," *Latin American Research Review* (Fall 1975): 137–51.

Krauze, Enrique. *Daniel Cosío Villegas: una biografía intelectual.* Mexico City: Editorial E.K., 1980.

Needler, Martin C. "Daniel Cosío Villegas and the Interpretation of Mexico's Political System," *Journal of Inter-American and World Affairs* 1(1): (1977).

El pensamiento de la reacción mexicana; historia documental 1810–1962. Compilación de Gastón García Cantú. Mexico City: Empresas Editoriales [1965]. 1,022 p.

B. Freemasonry

Davis, Thomas Brabson. *Aspects of Freemasonry in Modern Mexico: An Example of Social Cleavage.* New York: Vantage Press, 1976. xxiv, 421 p.

Freemasonry on Both Sides of the Atlantic: Essays Concerning the Craft in the British Isles, Europe, the United States, and Mexico. Ed. R. William Weisberger, Wallace McLeod, and S. Brent Morris. Boulder: East European Monographs; New York. Colombia University Press. 2002. xxviii, 942 p.

Mateos, José María. *Historia de la masonería en México desde 1806 hasta 1884.* Mexico City: Cardenas, 1884.

C. Positivism

Aziria, Alejandro M. R. *The Impact of Positivism in Mexico, 1867–1910.* Glasgow: Glasgow University, 1977.

Raat, William Dirk. *Positivism in Diaz Mexico.* Translated by Andrés Lira as *El positivismo durante el Porfiriato, 1876–1910.* Mexico City: Secretaría de Educación Pública, 1975. 175 p.

———. "The Antipositivist Movement in Prerevolutionary Mexico, 1892–1911," *Journal of Interamerican Studies* 19(1):83–98 (1977).

Zea, Leopoldo. *El positivismo en México.* Mexico City: Colegio de México, 1943. 254 p. Translated by Josephine H. Schulte as *Positivism in Mexico.* Austin, TX: University of Texas Press, 1974. xxiii, 241 p.

D. Socialism and Communism

García Cantú, Gastón. *El socialismo en México, siglo XIX.* México City: Ediciones Era [1969]. 514 p.

Schmitt, Karl M. *Communism in Mexico.* Austin: University of Texas Press, 1965. xii, 290 p.

XVII. CONSTITUTIONAL, ADMINISTRATIVE, AND LEGAL HISTORY

A. Law

Armstrong, George M. *Law and Market Society in Mexico.* New York: Praeger, 1989. 250 p.

Mayagoitia Garza, Alberto. *A Layman's Guide to Mexican Law.* Albuquerque, NM: University of New Mexico Press, 1977. xviii, 131 p. Revised as *Guide to Mexican Law.* 3rd. English ed. Mexico City: Ediciones Lara, 1979. xviii, 131 p.; new ed., Panorama Editorial, 1981.

1. Human Rights

Hanke, Lewis. *The Spanish Struggle for Justice in the Conquest of America.* Philadelphia: University of Pennsylvania Press, 1949. xi, 217 p. Reprinted with new introduction by Susan Scafidi and Peter Bakewell . . . [and] personal and professional reminiscence by the author. Dallas, TX: Southern Methodist University Press, 2002. xx, 246 p.

2. Courts

Polanco Alcántara, Tomás. *Las reales audiencias en las provincias americanas de España.* Madrid: Mapfre, 1992. 216 p.
www.scjn.gob.mx (website of the Mexican Supreme Court).

3. Crime

Arrom, Silvia Maria. "Crime and Citizen in Modern Mexico," *The Americas* 58(1):162–63 (July 2001).
Mendoza, Salvador. "El nuevo código penal de México," *Hispanic American Historical Review* 10(3):299–312 (August 1930).
Taylor, William B. *Drinking, Homicide and Rebellion in a Colonial Mexican Villages.* Stanford, CA: Stanford University Press, 1979. 242 p.

XVIII. CONSTITUTIONAL LAW AND ADMINISTRATION

Lanz Duret, Miguel. *Derecho constitucional mexicano y consideraciones sobre la realidad política de nuestro regimen.* 4a ed. Mexico City: Editorial L.D., 1947. xxxi, 427 p.
Niemeyer, Eberhardt Victor, Jr., *Revolution at Querétaro: The Mexican Constitutional Convention of 1916–1917.* Austin, TX: University of Texas Press for the Institute of Latin American Studies, 1974. xiii, 297 p.
Rodríguez O., Jaime E. "The Constitution of 1824 and the Formation of the Mexican State," in his *The Evolution of the Mexican Political System.* Wilmington, DE: SR Books, 1993: 71–90.
Sierra, Justo. *Evolución política del pueblo mexicano.* Mexico City: Casa de España, 1940. xxi, 480 p. Reprinted Fondo de Cultura Económica, 1950; Edición de Edmundo O'Gorman. UNAM, 1977. 426 p.

A. Government

1. Colonial

Schäfer, E. *El Consejo real y supremo de las Indias.* Seville: Imp. M. Carmona, 1935–1947. 2 v.

2. Since Independence

Camp, Roderic Ai. "Political Modernization in Mexico: Through a Looking Glass," in Jaime E. Rodríguez O. *The Evolution of the Mexican Political System.* Wilmington, DE: SR Books, 1993: 245–64.

Fernández, Julio A. *Political Administration in Mexico.* Boulder, CO: University of Colorado Bureau of Governmental Research, 1969. xi, 80 p.

Tucker, William Pierce. *The Mexican Government Today.* Minneapolis, MN: University of Minnesota Press, 1957. xii, 484 p.

B. Public Finances

Aguilar Gutiérrez, Genaro. *Nueva reforma fiscal en Mexico.* Mexico City: Porrúa, 2003. 115 p.

Bailey, Norman A. and Cohen, Richard. *The Mexican time bomb.* New York: Priority Press Publications, 1987. vi, 61 p.

Klein, Herbert S. *The American Finances of the Spanish Empire: Royal Income and Expenditure in Colonial Mexico, Peru, and Bolivia, 1680–1809.* Albuquerque, NM: University of New Mexico Press, 1998. xii, 221 p.

1. The Budget

Aguilar, Gustavo F. *Los presupuestos mexicanos desde los tiempos de la colonial hasta nuestros dias.* Mexico City: Secretaría de Hacienda, 1940. ix, 190 p. Reprinted Editorial GFA, 1947.

Coleman, Kenneth M. and Wanant, John. "On Measuring Mexican Presidential Ideology Through Budgets," *Latin American Research Review* (Spring 1975): 77–88

Dahle, José. *Los presupuestos en los tiempos de la colonia.* Mexico City: Librería Ariel, 1944.

C. The Political Process

Camp, D. A., Jr. "Autobiography and Decision-making in Mexican Politics," *Journal of Inter-American Studies and World Affairs.* May 1977: 275–83.

Camp, Roderic Ai. "Education and Political Recruitment in Mexico: The Alemán Generation," *Journal of Inter-American Studies and World Affairs* August 1976: 310–18.

———. *The Education of Mexico's Revolutionary Family.* Tucson, AZ: University of Arizona Press, 1979.

———. *Memoirs of a Mexican Politician.* Albuquerque, NM: University of New Mexico Press, 1988. xvii, 230 p.

――――. "The Middle-Level Technocrat in Mexico," *Journal of Developing Areas*. July 1972: 571–81.

――――. *Mexico's Leaders: Their Education and Recruitment*. Tucson, AZ: Arizona University Press, 1980. xvi, 259 p.

――――. *Political Recruitment across Two Centuries: Mexico, 1884–1991*. Austin, TX: University of Texas Press, 1995. xiv, 289 p.

――――. "A Reexamination of Political Leadership . . . in Mexico, 1934–1973," *Journal of Developing Areas*. January 1976: 193–211.

Córdova, Arnaldo. *La formación del poder político en México*. Mexico City: Ediciones Era, 1978. 99 p.

Cornelius, Wayne A. and Craig, Ann L. *The Mexican Political System in Transition*. La Jolla, CA: Center for U.S.-Mexican Studies, University of California, San Diego, 1991. 124 p.

Cosío Villegas, Daniel. *El sistema político mexicano: las posibilidades de cambio*. 2a ed., corregida. Mexico City: Joaquín Moritz, 1972. 116 p.

González Casanova, Pablo. *La democracia en México*. México City: Ediciones ERA, 1965. 258 p. 2a ed., 1967. Translated by Danielle Salti as *Democracy in Mexico*. New York, London: Oxford University Press, 1970. xvii, 245 p.

Huacuja Routree, Mario and Woldenberg, José. *Estado y lucha política en el México actual*. Mexico City: Ediciones El Caballito, 1976. 281 p.

Johnson, Kenneth F. *Mexican Democracy: A Critical View*. Boston: Allyn and Bacon. 1971. xii, 190 p. Rev. ed., New York: Praeger, 1978. 3rd ed., 1984. xxi, 279 p.

Middlebrook, Kevin. "Political Change and Reform in an Authoritarian Regime: Mexico." Paper presented at the Latin American Studies Association Conference, October 1980; revised as *Political Liberalization in an Authoritarian Regime: The Case of Mexico*. La Jolla, CA: Center for US-Mexican Studies, University of California San Diego, 1985. iv, 36 p.

Needleman, Carolyn and Needleman, Martin. "Who Rules Mexico?" *Journal of Politics* (November 1969): 1011–34.

Needler, Martin C. *Mexican Politics: The Containment of Conflict*. 2nd ed., New York: Praeger, 1990; 3rd ed., Praeger, 1995. xix, 144 p.

――――. *Politics and Society in Mexico*. Albuquerque, NM: University of New Mexico Press [1971]: xii, 143 p.

Padgett, Leon Vincent. *The Mexican Political System*. Boston: Houghton Mifflin, 1966. viii, 244 p.; 2nd ed. 1976. xvii, 332 p.

Scott, Robert Edwin. *Mexican Government in Transition*. Urbana, IL: University of Illinois Press, 1959; rev. ed., 1964. 345 p.

Smith, Peter Hopkinson. *Labyrinths of Power: Political Recruitment in Twentieth-Century Mexico*. Princeton, NJ: Princeton University Press, 1979. xvi, 348 p.

Stevens, Evelyn P. *Protest and Response in Mexico*. Cambridge, MA: M.I.T. Press, 1974. viii, 372 p.

D. The Executive

Cosío Villegas, Daniel. *El estilo personal de gobernar.* 4a ed. Mexico City: Joaquín Moritz, 1974. 128 p.

———. *La sucesión presidencial.* Mexico City: Joaquín Moritz, 1975. 149 p.; 2a ed. entitled *La sucesión: desenlace y perspectivas.* 1976. 118 p.

Gil-Mendieta, Jorge and Schmidt, Samuel. "La carrera por la presidencia de México: militares v. financieros," *Review of Latin American Studies* 3(2): 197–233 (1990).

Mora, Juan Miguel de. *Por la gracia del señor presidente: México, la gran mentira.* Mexico City: Editores Asociados, 1975. 280 p.

1. Office Holders

"Gobiernos de México" in *Diccionario Porrúa de México.* 6a. ed. v 2: 1447–95.

Musacchio, Humberto. *Milenios de Mexico: [diccionario enciclopédica de México].* Mexico City: Hoja Casa Editorial, 1999. 3 v. www.rulers.org/mexstat

E. Government Agencies

1. CONASUPO

Alisky, Marvin. "CONASUPO, A Mexican Agency," *Inter-American Economic Affairs* (Winter 1973): 37–59.

2. Servicio Meteorológico Nacional

http//smn.cna.gob.mx.

F. Political Parties

Garza, David T. "Factionalism on the Mexican Left," *Western Political Quarterly* (September 1966): 447–60.

Guerra Utrilla, José Gabriel. *Los partidos políticos nacionales.* Mexico City: Editorial América, 1970. 246 p.

Madrazo, Carlos A. *Madrazo: voz postrera de la Revolución.* Mexico City: Cruz Zapata Librería, 1971.

Mexican Politics in Transition. Edited by Judith Gentleman. Boulder, CO: Westview Press, 1987. xiii, 320 p.

Political Parties of Latin America and the Caribbean: A Reference Guide. Editors: John Coggins and D. S. Lewis. London: Longman, 1992. vii, 341 p.

Los partidos políticos mexicanos en 1991. Federico Reyes Heroles, comp.; textos de Luis H. Álvarez et al. Mexico City: Fondo de Cultura Económica, 1991. 446 p.

1. The PRI

The Awkward Embrace: One Party Domination and Democracy. Ed. Hermann Buhr Giliomee and Charles Edward Wickens Simkins. Cape Town: Tafelberg, 1999. xxi, 368 p.

Ayala Anguiano, Armando. *El Día que perdió el PRI.* Mexico City: Editorial Contenido, 1976.

————. *México en crisis: el fin del sistema.* 2a ed. Mexico City: Océano, 1982. 166 p.

Bailey, John J. *Governing Mexico: The Statecraft of Crisis Management.* New York: St. Martin's Press, 1988. xvi, 238 p.

Burgess, Katrina. *Parties and Unions in the New Global Economy.* Pittsburgh, PA: University of Pittsburgh Press, 2004. xiii, 209 p.

Coleman, Kenneth M. *Diffuse Support in Mexico: the Potential for Crisis.* Beverly Hills, CA: Sage Publications, 1976. 52 p.

Cornelius, Wayne A. *Mexican Politics in Transition: The Breakdown of a One-Party-Dominent Regime.* (Monograph no. 41). La Jolla, CA: Center for US-Mexican Studies, University of California at San Diego, 1996. viii, 122 p.

Siller Rodríguez, Rodolfo. *La Crisis del Partido Revolucionario Institucional.* Mexico City: Costa-Amic, 1976. 219 p.

2. The PAN

González Luna Morfín, Efraín. *El camino social y el PAN.* Mexico City: Ediciones de Acción Nacional, 1975.

Mabry, Donald J. *Mexico's Acción Nacional: A Catholic Alternative to Revolution.* Syracuse, NY: Syracuse University Press, 1973. xiv, 269 p.

Von Sauer, Franz. *The Alienated "Loyal" Opposition: Mexico's Partido Acción Nacional.* Albuquerque, NM: University of New Mexico Press, [1974]. xx, 197 p.

XIX. FEDERALISM

El Establecimiento del federalismo en México. Ed. Josefina Zoraida Vázquez. Mexico City: Colegio de México, 2003. 682 p.

Federalismos latinoamericanos: México, Brasil, Argentina. Por Germán Bidart Campos, et al. Ed. Marcello Carmagnani. Mexico City: Fondo de Cultura Económica, 1993. 416 p.

XX. LOCAL GOVERNMENT

Alisky, Marvin. "Budgets of State Governments in Mexico," *Public Affairs Bulletin* 5(2):4–8 (1966).
———. *The Governors of Mexico,* (Southwestern Studies Monographs, 12.) El Paso, TX: University of Texas at El Paso, 1965. 31 p.
Hiskey, Jonathan, "The Political Economy of Subnational Economic Recovery in Mexico," *Latin American Research Review* 40(1):30–55 (2005).
Ugalde, Antonio. *Power and Conflict in a Mexican Community: A Study of Political Integration.* Albuquerque, NM: University of New Mexico Press, 1970. xxi, 193 p.

XXI. ART, CULTURE, AND SPORT

Encyclopedia of Contemporary Latin American and Caribbean Culture. Ed. Dan[iel] Baldeston, Mike Gonzalez, and Ana M. López Santos. London: Routledge, 2000. 3 v.
Fragments of a Golden Age: The Politics of Culture in Mexico since 1940. Edited by Gilbert M. Joseph, Anne Rubinstein, and Eric Zolov. Durham NC: Duke University Press, 2001. xvii, 507 p.

A. Architecture and City and Regional Planning

Baird, Joseph Armstrong. *The Churches of Mexico, 1530–1810.* Photos by Hugo Rudinger. Berkeley, CA: University of California Press, 1962. xvii, 126 p.
Bayón, Damón, "Latin American Architecture, c.1920–c.1980 . . ." in *The Cambridge History of Latin America,* ed. Leslie Bethel. Cambridge: Cambridge University Press, 1995.
Katzman, Israel. *La arquitectura contemporánea mexicana: precedentes y desarrollo.* Mexico City: Nuevo Mundo, 1964. 205 p.
Marquina, Ignacio. *Arquitectura prehispánica.* Mexico City: Instituto Nacional de Antropología e Historia, 1951, 2a ed., 1964. xix, 1055 p.
Sanford, Trent Elwood. *The Story of Architecture in Mexico, Including the Work of the Ancient Indian Civilizations and that of the Spanish Colonial Empire*

. . . *together with an Account of the Background in Spain and a Glimpse at the Modern Trend.* New York: Norton, 1947. xviii, 363 p.

Stierlin, Henri. *Ancient Mexico.* ("Architecture of the World.") Cologne: Benedkt Taschen, 1996. 192 p.

B. Painting and Sculpture

Brenner, Anita. *Idols behind Altars.* New York: Payon & Clark, 1929; 359 p. Reprinted as *Idols behind Altars: Modern Mexican Art and its Cultural Roots.* Mineola, NY: Dover, 2002. 359 p.

Charlot, Jean. *Mexican Art and the Academy of San Carlos, 1785–1915.* Austin, TX: University of Texas Press, 1962. 177 p.

Encyclopedia of Latin American and Caribbean Art. Ed. Jane Turner & Diane Fortenberry. London: Macmillan Reference, 1999. 800 p. [New ed.] by Jane Turner. ("Grove Dictionaries.") 2000. xxi, 782 p.

Fernández, Justino. *Arte mexicano, de sus orígenes a nuestros días.* 3a ed. Mexico City: Porrúa, 1968. 206 p.; Translated by Joshua C. Taylor as *A Guide to Mexican Art, from its Beginnings to the Present.* Chicago: University of Chicago Press, 1969. xvii, 398 p.

New York City Museum of Modern Art. *Twenty Centuries of Mexican Art.* New York: The Museum, 1940. 100 p. Reprinted Arno Press, 1972. 198 p.

1. Pre-Hispanic

Anton, Ferdinand. *Alt-Mexico und seine Kunst.* Leipzig: Seeman, 1965. 307 p. Translated by Betty and Peter Ross as *Ancient Mexican Art.* London: Thames & Hudson; New York: Putnam, 1969. 309 p.

Covarrubias, Miguel. *Arte antiguo de México y América Central.* Mexico City: 1961. 2 v.

Enciso, Jorge. *Sellos del antiguo México.* Mexico City: 1947. xx p. 1,521 pl. of illus. Translated as *Design Motifs of Ancient Mexico.* New York: Dover Publications, 1953. 153 p.

Kubler, George. *Art and Architecture of Ancient America, the Mexican, Maya, and Andean Peoples.* Harmondsworth, Baltimore, Penguin Books, 1962. xxxv, 126 p., 168 pls.; 3rd ed, 1984. 572 p.

Miller, Mary Ellen. *The Art of Mesoamerica: From Olmec to Aztec.* ("The World of Art" Library). London: Thames and Hudson, 1986. 240 p., 3rd ed., 2001.

La pintura mural prehispánica en México. Directora del proyecto Beatriz de la Fuente. Coordinadora Leticia Staines Cícero. Mexico City: Instituto de Investiaciones Estéticas de la UNAM, 1998. 4 v.

Soustelle, Jacques. *L'art du Mexique ancien*. Paris: Arthaud, 1967. 181 p. Translated by Elizabeth Carmichael, as *Arts of Ancient Mexico*. London: Thames and Hudson, 1967. 160 p.; and by H. Pardellans as *El arte del Mexico antiguo*. Barcelona: Juventud, 1969. 178 p.

Westheim, Paul. *Die Kunst von Alt-Mexico*. Cologne: DuMont Schauber, 1966. 251 p. Earlier ed. translated by Mariana Frenk as *Arte antiguo de México*. 2a ed., Mexico: Fondo de Cultura Económica, 1963. 348 p.; (rev., Era, 1970. 439 p. Reprinted 1988. 439 p.). Translated from the Spanish, by Ursula Bernard, as *The Art of Ancient Mexico*. Garden City, NY: Doubleday, 1965. xvii, 260 p. Later version, *Kunst Alt-Mexikos*, translated under the direction of Lancelot C. Sheppard as *Prehispanic Mexican Art*. New York: Putnam, 1972. 447 p.

Wicke, Charles R. *Olmec, an Early Art of Precolumbian Mexico*. Tucson, AZ: University of Arizona Press, 1971. xvii, 188 p.

2. Colonial

Kubler, George and Soria, Martin. *Art and Architecture in Spain and Portugal and their American Dominions, 1500 to 1800*. (Pelican History of Art). Harmondsworth: Penguin Books, 1959. xxviii, 445 p.

León Portilla, Miguel, coord. general. *Historia de México. Tomo 8: Arte colonial*. Mexico City: Salvat Mexicana, 1986. pp. 1273–1440.

Pierce, Donna, et al. *Painting a New World: Mexican Art and Life, 1521–1821*. Denver, CO: Denver Art Museum, 2004. 327 p.

Weismann, Elizabeth Wilder. *Art and Time in Mexico: From the Conquest to the Revolution*. Photographs by Judith Hancock Sandoval. New York: Harper and Row, 1985. xix, 284 p.

www.colonialmexico.com.

3. Nineteenth Century

Art and Faith in Mexico: The Nineteenth-Century Retablo Tradition. Ed. Elizabeth Netto Calil Zarur and Charles Muir Lovell. Albuquerque, NM: University of New Mexico Press, 2001. 359 p.

4. Twentieth Century

Aspects of Contemporary Mexican Painting. Organized by the Americas Society, curated by Edward J. Sullivan. New York: Americas Society, 1990. 113 p.

Contemporary Latin American Artists: Exhibitions at the Organization of American States, 1965–1985. Ed. Annick Sanjurjo. Metuchen, NJ: Scarecrow Press, 1993. ix, 71 p.

Myers, Bernard Samuel. *Mexican Painting in Our Time.* New York: 1956. xiv, 283 p.

[Soriano, Juan]. *Juan Soriano: Esculturas.* Guadalajara: Museo Regional, 1992. 34 p.

[———.] *Juan Soriano: Homenaje nacional en su 80 aniversario. Obra grafica 1944–2000.* Mexico City: Museo Nacional de la Estampa, 2000. 45 p.

Stern, Peter A. "Art and the State in Post-Revolutionary Mexico and Cuba," *Artistic Representation of Latin American Diversity: Sources and Collections. Papers of the XXXIVth Annual Meeting of the Seminar on the Acquisition of Latin American Library Materials, Charlottesville VA, May 31–June 5, 1989.* Albuquerque, NM: SALALM Secretariat, 1993: 17–32.

Valdés, Carlos, *José Luis Cuevas.* Mexico City: Bellas Artes, 1966.

5. Mural Painting

Charlot, Jean. *The Mexican Mural Renaissance.* New Haven, CT: Yale University Press, 1967.

Emily, Edward and Álvarez, Bravo. *Painted Walls of Mexico from Prehistoric Times until Today.* Austin, TX: University of Texas Press, 1966.

a. Diego Rivera

Wolfe, Bertram D. *The Fabulous Life of Diego Rivera.* New York: Stein and Day, 1969.

C. Folk Art

Porter, Katherine Anne. *Outline of Mexican Popular Arts and Crafts.* Los Angeles: Young & McCallister, 1922. 56 p.

Taller de grafica popular: Werkstatt für grafische Volkskunst; Plakate und Flugblätter zu Arbeiterbewegung und Gewerkschaften in Mexiko 1937–1986; [eine Ausstellung des Ibero-Amerikanischen Instituts-Stiftung Preussischer Kulturbesitz, Berlin; Berlin, Staatsbibliothek, 23. Oktober–23. November 2002]. Berlin: Ibero-Amerikanisches Instituto, 2002. Richly illustrated (137 pp) with 3 long essays.

D. Folklore

Campos, Ruben M. *El folklore literario de Mexico.* Mexico City: Secretaría de Educación, 1929. Revised as *El folklore literaria y musical de México.* Mexico City: Secretaría de Educación Pública, 1946. 94 p.

Lenguajes de la tradición popular: fiesta, canto, música y represettación. Yvette Jiménez de Báez, editora. Mexico City: Colegio de México, 2002. 529 p.

The Mexican Revolution: Corridos About the Heroes and Events, 1910–1920, and Beyond. Edited by Guillermo E. Hernández. 178 p., 4 CDs.

Simmons, Merle E. *The Mexican Corrido.* Bloomington, IN: Indiana University Press, 1957.

Toor, Frances A. *A Treasury of Mexican Folkways.* [Mexico City?, 1932?]; revised as *A Treasury of Mexican Folkways: The Customs, Myths, Folklore, Traditions, Beliefs, Dances, and Songs of the Mexican People.* New York: Crown, 1947. xxxi, 570 p. Reprinted 1967.

1. Festivals and Holidays

Carmichael, Elizabeth and Sayer, Chloe. *The Skeleton at the Feast: The Day of the Dead in Mexico.* Austin, TX: University of Texas Press, 1992.

E. Literature

1. Spanish American Literature

Cambridge History of Latin American Literature. Ed. Robert González Echevarría and Enrique Pupo-Walker, Cambridge: Cambridge University Press, 2002. 3 v.

Franco, Jean. *An Introduction to Spanish-American Literature.* Cambridge: Cambridge University Press, 1969; 3rd ed., 1994. xii, 390 p.

2. Mexican Literature

Cortés, Eladio. *Dictionary of Mexican Literature.* Westport, CT: Greenwood Press, 1992. xliii, 768 p.

Écrire le Mexique. Claude Fell et al. Paris: Presses de la Sorbonne Nouvelle, 1999. 238 p.

Foster, David William. *Mexican Literature: A History.* Austin, TX: University of Texas Press, 1994. x, 458 p.

García Rivas, Heriberto. *Historia de la literatura mexicana.* Mexico City: Textos Universitarios S.A., 1971–1974. 4 v.

González Peña, Carlos. *Historia de la literatura mexicana.* Mexico City: 1928. 2a ed. rev. *Historia de la literatura mexicana desde los orígenes hasta nuestros días.* Mexico City: Editoriales Cultura y Polis, 1940. xiii, 327 p.; 15a ed., Mexico City: Porrúa, 1984. 362 p.; translated by Gusta Barfield Nance and Florence Johnson Dunstan as *History of Mexican Literature*. 3rd ed. Dallas: Southern Methodist University Press, 1969. xii, 540 p.

Historia de la literatura mexicana, desde sus orígenes hasta nuestros dias. Ed. Beatriz Garza Cuarón, Georges Baudot, and Raquel Chang-Rodríguez. Mexico City: Siglo Veintiuno, 1996–2002. 2 v.

Jiménez Rueda, Julio. *Historia de la literatura mexicana*. 4a ed., puesta al día y aumentada. Mexico City: Ediciones Botas, 1946. 347 p.

Olavarría y Ferrari, Enrique de. *Reseña histórica del teatro en México, 1538–1911*, Prólogo de Salvador Novo. 3a ed., ilustrada y puesto al día de 1911 a 1961. Mexico City: Porrúa, 1961. 5 v.

Urbina, Luis Gonzaga. *La vida literaria de México*. Mexico City: Impr. Hermanos Sáez, 1917. 298 p.

Valenzuela Rodarte, Alberto. *Historia de la literatura en México*. Mexico City: Editorial Jus, 1961. 623 p.

a. Bibliography

Brem, Walter. "Evaluating Mexican Literature: Sources and Uses," *Modernity and Tradition: The New Latin American and Caribbean Literature, 1956–1994: Papers of the XXXIXth Annual Meeting of the Seminar on the Acquisition of Latin American Library Materials, Salt Lake City, May 28–June 2, 1994*. Austin, TX: SALALM Secretariat, 1996: 66–71.

Foster, David William. Mexican Literature: A Bibliography of Secondary Sources. 2nd ed., enlarged and updated. Metuchen, NJ: Scarecrow Press, 1992. 698 p.

Mercader, Yolanda. "Bibliografía sobre revistas literarias en México," *New Writers of Latin Americas: Final Report and Working Papers of the XXth Seminar on the Acquisition of Latin American Library Materials, Bogotá, June 15–20, 1975*. Austin, TX: SALALM Secretariat, 1978: 374–90.

"Mexico" in *Latin American Serials, Vol. 3: Literature with Language, Art and Music*. Ed. Laurence Hallewell. London: Committee on Latin America, 1977: 107–23.

Woodbridge, Hensley C. *Guide to Reference Works for the Study of the Spanish Language and Literature and Spanish American Literature*. New York: Modern Language Association of America, 1987. xvi, 183 p.

b. Bio-Bibliography

Ocampo, Aurora Maura and Prado Velázaquez, Ernesto. *Diccionario de escritores mexicanos*. Mexico City: Centro de Estudios Literarios de la UNAM. 1967. xxviii, 422, xxxix–xlvii p.

3. Pre-Hispanic

Literatura del México antiguo: los textos en lengua nahuatl. Edición, estudios introductorios y versiones de textos de Miguel León Portilla. Caracas: Biblioteca Ayacucho, 1978. xxxii, 492 p.

Nicolson, Irene. *Firefly in the Night: A Study of Ancient Mexican Poetry and Symbolism.* Illustrated by Abel Mendoza. London: Faber and Faber, 1959. 231 p.

————. *Mexican and Central American Mythology.* London: Paul Hamlyn, 1967. 141 p.; New ed., revised by Cottie Burland. Feltham: Newnes, 1983. 144 p.

León Portilla, Miguel. *Literaturas pre-colombinas de México.* Mexico City: Pormaca, 1964. x, 205 p. Translated by Grace Lobanov and the author as *Pre-Columbian Literatures of Mexico.* Norman, OK: University of Oklahoma Press, 1969. xiii, 191 p.

4. Colonial

La Novela del México Colonial. Ed. Antonio Castro Leal. Mexico City: Aguilar, 1969. 2 v.

Pena, Margarita. *Historia de la literatura mexicana: período colonial.* Mexico City: Alhambra Mexicana, 1989. 142 p.

Sampson Vera Tudela, Elisa. *Colonial Angels: Narratives of Gender and Spirituality in Mexico, 1580–1750.* Austin, TX: University of Texas Press, 2000. xv, 202 p.

a. Juana de la Cruz

Flynn, Gerard C. *Sor Juana Inés de la Cruz.* New York: Twayne Publishers, 1971. 123 p.

Paz, Octavio. *Sor Juana Inés de la Cruz, o, Las trampas de la fe.* Barcelona: Seix Barral, 1982. 658 p.; Translated by Margaret Sayers Peden as *Sor Juana; or, The Traps of Faith.* Cambridge, MA: Belknap Press, 1988. x, 547 p.

5. Nineteenth Century

Caballo, Emmanuel. *Historia de las letras mexicanas en el siglo xix.* Guadalajara: Universidad de Guadalajara / Xalli, 1991. 380 p.

La crítica de la literatura mexicana en el siglo xix: 1836–1894. Ed. Fernando Tola de Habich. Mexico City: Coordinación de Difusión Cultural de la UNAM, 1897. 144 p.

García Barragán, María Guadalupe. *El naturalismo en México: reseña y notas biobibliográficas.* Mexico City: Instituto de Investigaciones Filológicas de la UNAM, 1979. 110 p.

Jiménez Rueda, Julio. *Letras mexicanas en el siglo xix.* Mexico City: Fondo de Cultura Económica, 1944. 189 p.

Martínez, José Luis. *La expresión nacional: letras mexicanas del siglo xix.* Mexico City: Imprenta Universitaria, 1955. 306 p.

Múñoz Fernández, Ángel. *Fichero: bio-bibliográfico de la literatura mexicana del siglo xix.* Mexico City: Factoria Ediciones, 1995. 2 v.

6. Early Twentieth Century

Forster, Merlin H. *Los contemporáneos, 1920–1932; perfil de un experimento vanguardista mexicano.* Mexico City: Ediciones de Andrea, 1964. 145 p.

7. Fiction

Braham, Persephone. *Crimes Against the State, Crimes Against Persons: Detective Fiction in Cuba and Mexico.* Minneapolis, MN: University of Minnesota Press, 2004. xv, 169 p.

Brushwood, John Stubbs. *Mexico in its Novel: A Nation's Search for Identity.* Austin, TX: University of Texas Press, 1966. xii, 292 p.

Cabrera López, Patricia. *Una inquietud de amanecer: literatura y política en México, 1963–1987.* Mexico City: Plaza y Valdés for CIICH, 2006.

Langford, Walter M. *The Mexican Novel Comes of Age.* South Bend, IN: University of Notre Dame Press, 1971. x, 229 p.

Pleasants, Ernest Hemingway. *The Caudillo: A Study in Latin-American Dictatorships.* Monmouth IL: Commercial Art Press, 1959. xiii, 143 p.

Raymond, Leslie Williams. *The Twentieth-Century Spanish American Novel.* Austin, TX: University of Texas Press, 2003. xi, 266 p.

Read, John Lloyd. *The Mexican Historical Novel, 1826–1910.* New York: Instituto de España en los Estados Unidos, 1939. xiv, 337 p. Reprinted Russell and Russell, 1973.

Rosser, Harry L. *Conflict and Transition in Rural Mexico: The Fiction of Social Realism.* Waltham, MA: Crossroads Press, 1980. 173 p.

Sommers, Joseph. *After the Storm: Landmarks of the Modern Mexican Novel.* Albuquerque, NM: University of New Mexico Press, 1968. xii, 208 p.

Taylor, Kathy. *The New Narrative of Mexico: Subversions of History in Mexican Fiction.* Lewisburg: Bucknell University Press, 1994. 185 p.

Williams, Raymond L. and Rodríguez, Blanca. *La narrativa posmoderna en México.* Xalapa: Universidad Veracruzana, 2002. 193 p.

a. Bibliography

Carballo, Emmanuel. *Bibliografóa de la novela mexicana del siglo xx.* Mexico City: UNAM, 1988. 233 p.

8. Poetry

Antología de la poesía mexicana moderna. Ed. Jorge Cuesta. Mexico City: Contemporaneos, 1928. 218 p.; 5a ed. Fondo de Cultura Económica, 1998. 276 p.

Paz, Octavio. *Anthology of Mexican Poetry.* Preface by C. M. Bowra; translated by Samuel Beckett. Bloomington, IN: Indiana University Press, 1958. Reprinted London: Calder & Boyars, 1970. 213 p.

Stanton, Anthony. *Inventores de tradición: ensayos sobre poesía mexicana moderna.* Mexico City: Colegio de México, 1998. 238 p.

Vital Diaz, Alberto. *La cama de Procrusto: vanguardias y polémicos, antologías y manifiestos: México, 1910–1980.* Mexico City: Centro de Estudios Literarios de la UNAM, 1996. 124 p.

9. Drama

Burgess, Ronald D. *The New Dramatists of Mexico, 1967–1985.* Lexington KY: University Press of Kentucky, 166 p.

Magaña Esquivel, Antonio. *Medio siglo de teatro mexicano, 1900–1961.* Mexico City, Depto. de Literatura, Instituto Nacional de Bellas Artes, 1964. 173 p.

10. Children's Literature

Rey P., Mario E. *Historia y muestra de la literatura infantil mexicana.* Mexico City: SM de Ediciones: Consejo Nacional para la Cultura y las Artes, 2000. xxiii, 448 p.

Seminar on the Acquisition of Latin American Library Materials, XIX, Austin, TX, 1974. *Final Report and Working Papers, Vol. 3. Papers of the Postconference, the First Symposium on Spanish Language Materials for Children and Young Adults.* Amherst, MA: SALALM Secretariat, 1976. 186 p.

Seminario sobre Edición de Libros Infantiles y Juveniles, Bogotá, 1979. [*Actas*]. Bogotá: Centro Regikonal para el Fomento del Libro en América Latina y el Caribe, 1980. 113 p.

Chon, Isabel. *Mexico and its Literature for Children and Adolescents.* Tempe Center for Latin American Studies, Arizona State University, 1977. 54 p.

11. Modern Indigenous Literature

Words of the True Peoples: Anthology of Contemporary Mexican Indigenous-Language Writers = Palabras de los seres verdaderos . . . Ed. Carlos Montemayor and Donald Frischmann; photography by George O. Jackson Jr. Austin, TX: University of Texas Press, 2004– . v1- .

F. Music

Alisky, Marvin. "Jazz in Mexico City," *Metronome* (April 1955): 26, 44–45.

Brenner, Helmut. *Música ranchera: das mexikanische Äquivalent zur country and western music aus historischer, musikalischer und kommerzieller Sicht.* Tutzing: Schneider, 1996. 691 p.

Estrada, Jesús. *Música y músicos de la época virreinal.* Mexico City: Secretaría de Educación Pública, 1973. 165 p. Reprinted SEP Drama, 1980. 164 p.

The Garland Handbook of Latin American Music. Ed. Dale A. Olsen and Daniel E. Sheehy. New York: Garland, 2000. xviii, 431 p.

Martí, Samuel. *Instrumentos musicales precortesianos.* Mexico City: Instituto Nacional de Antropología, 1955. 227 p.; 2a ed., corregida, 1968. 378 p.

Maulrón Rodríguez, Gustavo. *Música en el virreinato de la Nueva España . . . siglos xvi y xvii.* Puebla: Universidad Iberoamericana Golfo-Centro; Mexico City: Lupus Inquisitor, 1995. 181 p.

Mendoza de Arce, Daniel. *Music in Ibero-America to 1850: A Historical Survey.* Lanham, MD: Scarecrow Press, 2001. xviii, 723 p.

Pareyón, Gabriel. *Diccionario de música en México.* Guadalajara: Secretaría de Cultura de Jalisco, 1995. 606 p.

Slavery and Beyond: The African Impact on Latin America and the Caribbean. Darién J. Davis, editor. Wilmington DE: Scholarly Resources, 1995. xxvi, 301 p.

Soto Millán, Fernando. *Diccionario de compositores de música de concierto, siglo xx.* Mexico City: Fondo de Cultura Económica, 1996–1998. 2 v.

Stevenson, Robert Murrell. *Music in Mexico: A Historical Survey.* New York: Thomas Y. Crowell, 1952. 300 p.

Zolov, Eric. *Refried Elvis: The Rise of Mexican Counterculture.* Berkeley, CA: University of California Press, 1999. 349 p.

G. Sport

1. Baseball

Oleksak, Michael M. and Oleksak, Mary Adams. *Beisbol: Latin Americans and the Grand Old Game.* Grand Rapids: 1991. xv, 303 p.

Treto Cisneros, Pedro. *The Mexican League: Complete Player Statistics, 1937–2001.* Jefferson NC: McFarland & Co., 2002. vii, 504 p.

2. Soccer

Fábregas Puig, Andrés. *Lo sagrado del rebano: el fútbol como integrador de identidades.* Fotografías de Alberto Gómez Barbosa. Zapopan, Jalisco: Colegio de Jalisco, 2001. 117 p.

Mejía Narquera, Fernando. *Fútbol mexicana: glorias y tragedias, 1929–1992.* Mexico City: El Nacional, 1993. 395 p.

Taylor, Chris. *The Beautiful Game: A Journey Through Latin American Football.* London: Gollancz, 1998. 288p.

XXII. THE MEDIA

A. General

World Directory of Moving Image and Sound Archives, ed. Wolfgang Klaue. Munich: Saur, [for] Fédération Internationale des Archives du Film, 1993. 192 p.

World Press Encyclopedia: A Survey of Press Systems Worldwide. 2nd ed. Farmington Hills, MD: 2002. 2 v.

1. Censorship

Alisky, Marvin. "Mexico," in *Censorship: An International Encyclopedia,* ed. Derek Jones. London: Fitzroy Dearborn, 1999.

B. Broadcasting

Fox, Elizabeth. "Latin American Broadcasting," in *The Cambridge History of Latin America,* ed. Leslie Bethel. Vol X. Cambridge: Cambridge University Press, 1995: 501–65.

Mejía Barquera, Fernando. *La industria de la radio y la televisión y la politica del estado mexicano. Vol 1: 1920–1960.* Mexico City: Fundación Manuel Buendia, 1989. 195 p.

Noriega, Luis Antonio de and Leach, Frances. *Broadcasting in Mexico.* London: Routledge & Kegan Paul; Genoa: International Institute of Communications, 1979. xii, 89 p.

1. Radio

Adolar, Emilio. *Anecdotário de radio en México.* Mexico City: Editorial Delgado, 1970.

Alisky, Marvin. "Early Mexican Broadcasting," *Hispanic American Historical Review* (November 1954): 515–26.

————. "Mexico City's Competitive Radio Market," *Inter-American Economic Affairs* (Winter 1953): 19–27.

————. "Mexico's National Hour on Radio," *Nieman Reports* (October 1953): 17–18.

————. "Mexico's Rural Radio," *Quarterly of Film, Radio, and Television* (Summer 1954): 405–17.

————. "Radio's Role in Mexico," *Journalism Quarterly* (Winter 1954): 66–72.

Schwoch, James. *The American Radio Industry and its Latin American Activities, 1900–1939.* Urbana: University of Illinois Press, 1990. viii, 185 p.

2. Television

Apuntes para una historia de la televisión mexicana. By Fernando González et al. Col. Roma, Mexico: Revista Mexicana de Comunicación, 1998. 589 p.

Castellot de Ballin, Laura. *Historia de la televisión en México, narrado por sus protagonistas.* Mexico City: Alpe, 1993.

Esparza Oteo T., Luis. *La política cultural del estado mexicano y el desarrollo de la T.V.* Mexico City: Taller de Investigación para la Comunicación Masiva de la Universidad Autónoma Metropolitana-Xochimilco, 1984. 116 p.

Institute for Communications Research. *Towards the Social Use of Commercial Television: Mexico's Experience with the Reinforcement of Social Values through TV Soap Operas.* Mexico City: Institute for Communications Research, 1981. 54 p.

Pérez Espino, Efraín. *Los motivos de Televisa: el proyecto cultural de XEQ Canal 9.* Mexico City: Instituto de Investigaciones Sociales de la UNAM, 1991. 93 p.

Toussaint Alcaraz, Florence. *Televisión sin fronteras.* Mexico City: Siglo Veintiuno, 1998. 183 p.

Zarur Orego, Antonio E. *El estado y el modelo de televisión adoptado en México, 1950–1988.* Mexico City: Universidad Autónoma Metropolitana—Unidad Azcapotzalco, 1996. 142 p.

3. Motion Pictures

Mexican Cinema. Edited by Paulo Antonio Paranaguá; translated by Ana M. López. London: British Film Institute, 1995. x, 321 p.

Karetnikova, Inga. *Mexico According to Eisenstein.* Albuquerque, NM: University of New Mexico Press, 1991. vii, 200 p.

Quezada, Mario A. *Diccionario del cine mexicano, 1970–2000.* (Colección "Mirando en la Oscuridad"). Mexico City: UNAM, 2005. 906 p.

XXIII. NEWSPAPERS

Aguilar Plata, Blanca. *Publicidad y empresa periodística en México: estudio descriptivo de la publicidad en nueve diarios capitalinos, 1977.* Mexico City: Centro de Estudios de la Comunicación, UNAM, 1986. 67 p.

Alisky, Marvin. "Growth of Newspapers in Mexico's Provinces," *Journalism Quarterly* (Winter 1960): 75–82.

Chilcote, Ronald H. "The Press in Latin America, Spain, and Portugal," *Hispanic American Report* (August 1963).

Independent Mexico in Newspapers, the 19th Century: Guide to the Microfilm Set. Ed. Adán Benavides and Agnes L. McAlester. Austin, TX: The Nettie Lee Benson Latin American Collection, University of Texas at Austin, 2005. xxviii, 96 p.

Loyola Diaz, Rafael. *El Nacional, 1940–1953.* Mexico City: Instituto de Investigaciones Sociales de la UNAM, 1996. 170 p.

Palma, Oscar Edmundo. *Periodismo en crisis.* Mexico City: Ediciones del Ermitano, 1998. 131 p.

Revolutionary Mexico in Newspapers, 1900–1929: Guide to the Microfilm Set. Ed. Adán Benavides and Agnes L. McAlester. Austin, TX: The Nettie Lee Benson Latin American Collection, University of Texas at Austin, 2002. xvi, 65 p.

A. Newspapers Readable Online

www.cronica.com.mx (*La crónica de hoy*).

www.elfinanciero.com.mx (*El financiero*).

www.eluniversal.com.mx (*El universal*).

www.heraldo-adi.com.mx (*El heraldo de México*).

www.jornada.unam.mx (*La jornada*).

www.la-prensa.com.mx (*La prensa*).

www.reforma.com (*La reforma*).

www.unomasuno.com.mx (*Uno más uno*).

XXIV. PUBLISHING

Curiel, Guadalupe and Gómez Camacho, Arturo. "450 años de imprenta en México," *Revista de la Universidad de México* 45(467):36–42 (December 1989).

Iguiniz, Juan B. "El libro en México," pp. 151–90 of his *El libro.* Mexico City: Porrua, 1946.

A. Colonial

De Micheli, Alfredo. "Los libros italianos en la Nueva España del siglo xvii," *Revista de la Universidad de México* 30(11):39–42 (July 1976).

Fernández Castillejo, Federico. *Libros y libreros en el siglo xvi.* Mexico City: 1914.

Peconi, Antonio. "Libri e stampatori italiani nella Nuova Spagna nel secolo xvi," *Quaderni Ibero-Americani* 7(51/52):164–70 (June–December 1978).

Thompson, Lawrence Sidney. *Printing in Colonial Spanish America.* Hamden CT: Shoestring Press, 1962. 108 p.

Torre Villar, Ernesto de la. "El libro belga en México," *Boletín del Instituto de Investigaciones Bibliográficas de la UNAM* 10:9–15 (July–December 1973).

B. Since Independence

Cardoza, Lya de. "¿Que lee México?" *Casa de las Américas* 13(75):152–55 (November–December 1972).

Corona Berkin, Sara. "Los libros para niños en México: las políticas editoriales de 1956 a 1993," *Modernity and Tradition: The New Latin American and Caribbean Literature, 1956–1994: Papers of the XXXIXth Annual Meeting of the Seminar on the Acquisition of Latin American Library Materials, Salt Lake City, May 28–June 2, 1994.* Austin, TX: SALALM Secretariat, 1996: 54–65.

Gamiz, Abel. *La verdad sobre el asunto de los libros de texto; refutacion al folleto "En pro del libro mexicano."* Mexico City: H. Barrales sucs., 1920. 63, [1] p.

Hallewell, Laurence. "Mexico: Growth and Prosperity in the Mexican Publishing Industry," *Bulletin of the Society for Latin American Studies* 17:35–39 (April 1973).

Holt, Patricia. "Publishing in Mexico: Its Time Has Come," *Publishers' Weekly* 217(16):33–46 (April 25, 1980).

Knoop, Astrid et al. "De editores y editoriales: informe sobre un posible perfil del editor y de la industria editorial mexicanos," *Dialogos* 20(2):97–109 (March–April 1984).

"Mexico" in *Selection of Library Materials for Area Studies. Part 1: Asia, Iberia, the Caribbean and Latin America, Eastern Europe and the Soviet Union, and the South Pacific.* Cecily Johns, editor. Chicago: American Library Association, 1990.

Ortega Cuenca, Concepción and Pérez de León, Victoria. "Mexico: A note" in *International Book Publishing, an encyclopedia*, edited by Philip G. Altbach and Edith S. Hoshino. New York: Garland Publishing, 1995: 600–603.

Peñalosa, Fernando. *The Mexican Book Industry.* New York: Scarecrow Press, 1957. 312 p.

Taylor, Sally A. "Mexico: A Brighter Prospect," *Publishers Weekly* 240(20): S7–S13 (May 17, 1993).

XXV. EDUCATION

A. General

Historia de la educación pública en México. Ed. Fernando Solana et al. Mexico City: Fondo de Cultura Económica, 1982. 2 v.

Obedecer, servir y resistir: la educación de las mujeres en la historia de México. Ed. María Adelina Arredondo. Tlalpan DF: Universidad Pedagógica Nacional; Mexico City: Porrúa, 2003. 386 p.

B. Pre-Hispanic Era

Izquierdo, Ana Luisa. *La educación maya en los tiempos prehispánicos.* Mexico City: Centro de Estudios Mayas de la UNAM, 1983. 93 p.

C. Colonial Period

Canedo, Lino Gómez. *La educación de los marginados durante la época colonial: escuelas y colegios para índios y mestizos en la Nueva España.* Mexico City. Porrúa, 1982. xxiii, 425 p.

De maestros y discípulos: México, siglos xvi–xix. Ed. Leticia Pérez Puente. Mexico City: UNAM, 1998. 252 p.

Fox y Fox, Pilar. *La revolución pedagógica en Nueva España, 1754–1820.* Madrid: Instituto Gonzalo Fernández de Oviedo, C.S.I.C., 1981. 2 v.

Gonzalbo Aizpuru, Pilar. *Historia de la educación en la época colonial: el mundo indígena.* Mexico City: El Colegio de México, 1990. 274 p.

———. *Historia de la educación en la época colonial: la educación de los criollos y la vida urbana.* Mexico City: Colegio de México, 1990. 395 p.

Luque Alcaide, Elisa. *La educación en Nueva España en el siglo xviii.* Seville: La Escuela de Estudios Hispano-Americanos de Sevilla, 1970. 403 p.

D. Nineteenth Century

Barreda, Gabino. *La educación positiva en México.* Mexico City: Porrúa, 1978. xxix, 281 p.

Bazant, Milada. *Historia de la educación durante el Porfiriato.* Mexico City: Centro de Estudios Históricos del Colegio de México, 1993. 297 p.

Vaughan, Mary K. *The State, Education, and Social Class in Mexico, 1880–1928.* DeKalb: Northern Illinois University Press, 1981. x, 316 p.

Zapeda-Rast, Beatriz. *Education and the Institutionalisation of Contending Ideas of the Nation in Reforma Mexico.* (PhD diss.). London: University of London, 2002. 242 leaves.

E. Early Twentieth Century

Añorve Aguirre, Carlos Daniel. *La Organización de la Secretaría de Educación Pública, 1921–1994.* Mexico City: Universidad Pedagógica Nacional, 2000. 200 p.

Bremauntz, Alberto. *La educación socialista en México: antecedentes y fundamentos de la reforma de 1934.* Mexico City, 1943. 451 p.

Guevara González, Luis. *La educación en México, siglo xx.* Mexico City: Porrúa, 2002. 139 p.

Johnston, Marjorie Cecil. *Education in Mexico.* Washington, DC: GPO for the Dept. of Health, Education, and Welfare, 1956. vii, 135 p.

Mexico. Secretaría de Educación Pública. *La educación pública en México.* Mexico City: 1926. 300 p.

———. *La educación pública en México.* Mexico City: 1940. 3 v.

Sánchez, George I. *Mexico: A Revolution by Education.* New York: Viking, 1936. xv, 211 p. Reprinted Westport, CT: Greenwood, 1971.

Sanders, Thomas Griffin. *Mexican Education: The Post-Revolutionary Period, 1920–1940.* Hanover: American Universities Field Staff, 1978. 18 p.

Schell, Patience Alexandra. *Church and State Education in Revolutionary Mexico City.* Tucson, AZ: University of Arizona Press, 2003. xxv, 253 p.

Weiss, Edouard. *Scala zwischen Staat und Gesellschaf: Mexiko, 1920–1976.* Munich: Fink, 1983. 790 p.

Zea, Leopoldo. *Del liberalismo a la Revolución en la educación mexicana.* Mexico City: Biblioteca del Instituto Nacional de Estudios Históricos, 1956. 205 p.

1. José Vasconcelos

Crespo, Regina. *Itinerarios intelectuales: Vasconcelos, Lobato y sus proyectos para la nación.* Mexico City: UNAM, 2004. 383 p.

Fell, Claude. *José Vasconcelos: los años del águila, 1920–1925: educación, cultura e iberoamerianismo en el México postrevolucionario.* Mexico City: UNAM, 1989. 742 p.

Galván de Terrazas, Luz Elena. *El proyecto de educación pública de José Vasconcelos: una larga labor de intentos reformadores.* Mexico City: Centro de Investigaciones y Estudios Superiores en Antropología Social, 1982. 244 p.

Guillén, Fedro. *Vasconcelos, "apresurado de Dios."* Mexico City: Novaro, 1975. 245 p.

Haddox, John Herbert. *Vasconcelos of Mexico.* Austin, TX: University of Texas Press, 1967. ix, 103 p.

Piñeda, Hugo. *José Vasconcelos: político mexicano.* Mexico City: Harper & Row Latinoamericana, 1975. xiii, 174 p.

Vasconcelos, José. *Antología de textos sobre educación.* Introducción y selección de Alicia Molina. Mexico City: Fondo de Cultura Económica, 1981. 306 p.

F. Late Twentieth Century

Gill, Clark C. *Education in a Changing Mexico.* Washington, DC: G.P.O. for U.S. Office of Education, 1969. vii, 127 p.

———. *The Educational System of Mexico.* Washington, DC: G.P.O. for U.S. Office of Education, 1977. 19 p.

Kneller, George Frederick. *Education of the Mexican Nation.* New York: Columbia University Press, 1951. xi, 258 p. Reprinted Octagon Books, 1973.

Sales-Gómez, Daniel A. and Torres, Carlos Alberto. *The State, Corporatist Politics, and Educational Policy Making in Mexico.* New York: Praeger, 1990. xxiv, 197 p.

Taylor, Edward and Yúñez Naude, Antonio. *Education, Migration and Productivity: An Analytical Approach and Evidence from Rural Mexico.* Paris. O.E.C.D., 1999. 98 p.

G. Primary

Brooke, Nigel. The Quality of Education in Mexican Rural Primary Schools. Brighton, UK: Institute of Development Studies of the University of Sussex, 1980. iv, 101 p.

Chávez Orozco, Luis. *La educación pública elemental en la ciudad de México durante el siglo xviii.* Mexico City: Biblioteca de la Secretaría de Educación, 1936. 145 p.

Martin, Christopher J. *Schooling in Mexico: Staying in or Dropping out.* Aldershot, UK: Avebury, 1994. xi, 221 p.

Tanck Estrada, Dorothy. *La educación ilustrada, 1786–1836: educación primaria en la Ciudad de México.* Mexico City: Colegio de México, 1977. x, 280 p.

H. Secondary

Ibarrola Nicolion, María de. *La enseñanza media en México, 1900–1968: guía bibliográfica.* Mexico City: Instituto de Investigaciones Sociales de la UNAM, 1970. x, 266 p.

Levison, Bradley A. *We are All Equal: Student Culture and Identity at a Mexican Secondary School, 1988–1998.* Durham, NC: Duke University Press, 2001. xii, 433 p.

Santos del Real, Annette. *La educación secundaria: perspectivas de su demanda.* Aguascalientes: Universidad Autónoma de Aguascalientes, 2001. 302 p. Doctoral dissertation.

I. Higher

Alisky, Marvin. "Tranquility: The Colegio de Mexico," *Intellect* (April 1974): 445–47.

Galván de Terrazas, Luz Elena. *La educación superior de la mujer en México, 1876–1940.* Mexico City: SEP Cultura, 1985. 95 p.

Gräfe, Martin. *Die mexikanische Hochschulexpansion und reform nach 1950 unter Berücksichtigung des gesellschaftlichen Strukturwandels in Mexico.* Cassel: Gesamthochschule Kassel, 1988. iii, 399 p.

Innes, John S. "Universidad Popular Mexicana," *The Americas* 30(1):110–22 (1973).

King, Richard G. *The Provincial Universities of Mexico: An Analysis of Growth and Development.* New York: Praeger, 1971. xxi, 234 p.

Lau, Jesús and Cortés, Jesús. "La divulgación del conocimiento de las universidades públicas mexicanas: la distribución de sus publicaciones," *SALALM in the Age of Multimedia: Technological Challenge and Social Change. Papers of the XLIst Annual Meeting of the Seminar on the Acquisition of Latin American Library Materials, New York, June 1–5, 1996.* Austin TX: SALALM Secretariat, 1998: 178–97.

Levy, Daniel C. *University and Government in Mexico: Autonomy in an Authoritarian System.* New York: Praeger, 1980. xiv, 173 p.

Lorey, David E. *The Rise of the Professions in Twentieth-Century Mexico: University Graduates and Occupational Changes since 1929.* Los Angeles: UCLA Latin American Center, 1992. xvii, 232 p.

———. *The University System and Economic Development in Mexico since 1929.* Stanford, CA: Stanford University Press, 1993. xviii, 260 p.

Mabry, Donald J. *Mexican University and the State: Student Conflicts, 1910–1971.* College Station, TX: Texas A&M University, 1982. xi, 328 p.

Osborn, Thomas Noel. *Higher Education in Mexico: History, Growth and Problems in a Dichotomized Industry.* El Paso: Center for Inter-American Studies, 1976. 150 p.

Soler Vinyes, Marti. *La casa del éxodo: los exilados y su obra en la Casa de España y el Colegio de México, 1938–1947.* Mexico City: Colegio de México. 1999. 165 p.

La universidad novohispana: corporación, gobierno y vida académica. Ed. Clara Inés Ramírez and Armando Pavón. Mexico City: UNAM, 1996. 472 p.

Urquidi, Victor L. and Lajous Vargas, Adrián. *Educación superior, ciéncia y tecnología en el desarrollo económico de México.* Mexico City: Secretaría de Educación Pública, 1967. 86 p.

J. Adult Education

Educación de adultos en México: nuevas direcciones en el sector educativo, ed. María Luisa de Anda. Mexico City: Confederación Nacional de Trabajadores de Educación, 1983. 294 p.

Pieck Gochicoa, Enrique. *The Social Function and Meaning of Nonformal Education: A Study of Official Community Programmes in the State of Mexico.* (PhD diss.). London: University of London Institute of Education, 1993. 420 leaves.

Torres, Carlos Alberto. *La educación de adultos en México, 1976–1981.* Mexico City: Facultad Latinoamericana de Ciencias Sociales, 1984. 51 leaves.

K. Technical and Vocational

Emery, Sarah Snell. *The Push for Industrialization: Mexico's Technical Training and Education: An Annotated Bibliography.* Monticello, IL: Vance Bibliographies, 1984. 40 p.

López Acevedo, Carlos. *An Alternative Technical Education System in Mexico: A Reassessment of CONALEP.* Washington, DC: Poverty Reduction and Economic Management Unit (Latin America) of the World Bank, 2001. 74 p.

XXVI. ECONOMIC HISTORY

A. General

Austin, Ruben Vargas. *The Development of Economic Policy in Mexico, with Special Reference to Economic Doctrines, 1600–1958.* New York: Garland, 1987. 336 p.

Historia económica de México. Ed. Enrique Cárdenas. Mexico City: Fondo de Cultura Económica, 1989–1993. 4 v.; 2 a ed., 2003–2004. 2 v.

López Rosado, Diego G. *Historia y pensamiento económico de México.* Mexico City: UNAM, 441 p.

Randall, Laura. "Mexico:" v 1 of her *A Comparative Economic History of Latin America, 1500–1914.* New York: Columbia University Institute of Latin-American Studies, 1977. 3 v.

B. Sixteenth and Seventeenth Centuries

Barbosa-Ramírez, A. René. *La estrutura económica de la Nueva España, 1519–1810.* Mexico City: Siglo XXI, 1971. v, 259 p.

Calderón, Francisco R. *História económica de la Nueva España en tiempo de los Austrias.* Mexico City: Fondo de Cultura Económica, 1988, 711 p.

Hoberman, Louisa Schell. *Mexico's Merchant Elite, 1590–1660: Silver, State, and Society.* Durham, NC: Duke University Press, 1991. xiv, 352 p.

C. Eighteenth Century

Bitar Letayf, Marcelo. *Economistas españoles del siglo xviii: sus ideas sobre la libertad del comercio con las Indias.* Madrid: Ediciones Cultura Hispánica, 1968. xxvii, 257 p.

Garner, Richard and Stefanou, Spiro E. *Economic Growth and Change in Bourbon Mexico.* Gainesville, FL: University Press of Florida, 1993. xiii, 354 p.

Ilustración española, reformas borbónicas y liberalismo temprano en México. Francisco Javier Rodríguez García and Luciano Gutiérrez Herrera, eds. Azcapotzalco: Universidad Antónoma Metropolitana, 1992. 261 p.

Ouweneel, Arij. *Ciclos interrumpidos: ensayos sobre historia rural mexicana, siglo xviii–xix.* Zinacantán: Colegio Mexiquense, 1998. 444 p.

D. Nineteenth Century

How Latin America Fell Behind: Essays on the Economic Histories of Brazil and Mexico, 1800–1914. Ed. Stephen Haber. Stanford CA: Stanford University Press, 1997. xi, 315 p.

Bernecker, Walther. *Industirie und Außenhandel: zur politischen Ökonomie Mexikos im 19, Jh.* Saarbrücken: Breitenbach, 1987. 301 p. Translated by Perla Chinchilla Pauling as *De agiotistas y empresarios: en torno de la temprana industrializacion.* Mexico City: Siglo XXI, 1979. 377 p.

Howell, Edward J. *Mexico: Its Progress and Commercial Possibilities.* London: Whittingham, 1892. 203 p.

The Mexican Economy, 1870–1930: Essays on the Economic History of Institutions, Revolution, and Growth. Ed. Jeffrey Bortz and Stephen Haber. Stanford, CA: Stanford University Press, 2002. xvii, 348 p.

Pletcher, David M. *Rails, Mines and Progress: Seven American Promoters in Mexico, 1867–1911.* Ithaca, NY: Cornell University Press, 1958. 321 p.

Weiner, Richard. *Race, Nation, and Market: Economic Culture in Porfirian Mexico.* Tucson, AZ: University of Arizona Press, 2004. xi, 167 p.

1. Contraband

Bernecker, Walther. *Schmuggel: Illegalität und Korruption im Mexiko des 19. Jahrhunderts.* Frankfurt am Main: Vervuert, 1989. 158 p., translated by Manuel Emilio Waelti as *Contrabando: ilegalidad y corrupción en el México del siglo xix.* Mexico City: Universidad Iberoamericana, 1994. 163 p.

E. Early Twentieth Century (to 1945)

Babb, Sarah L. *Managing Mexico: Economists from Nationalism to Neoliberalism.* Princeton, NJ: Princeton University Press, 2001. xv, 295 p.

Moreno, Julio. *Yankee Don't Go Home: Mexican Nationalism, American Business Culture, and the Shaping of Modern Mexico, 1920–1950.* Chapel Hill, NC: University of North Carolina Press, 2003. xi, 321 p.

Pilcher, Jeffrey, "Mad Cowmen, Foreign Investors and the Mexican Revolution," *JILAS: Journal of Iberian and Latin American Studies* 4(1):1–16 (Melbourne: La Trobe University, July 1998).

F. Late Twentieth Century and After (since 1945)

Glade, William P., Jr. and Anderson, Charles W. *The Political Economy of Mexico.* Madison, WI: University of Wisconsin Press, 1963. vii, 242 p.

Hansen, Roger D. *The Politics of Mexican Development.* Baltimore, MD: Johns Hopkins Press, 1971. xiii, 267 p.

Hodges, Donald C. and Gandy, Ross. *Mexico: The End of Revolution.* Westport, CT: Praeger, 2002. [vii], 215 p.

King, Timothy. *Mexico: Industrialization and Trade Policies since 1940.* London: Oxford University Press for O.E.C.D. 1970. x, 160 p.

Looney, Robert E. *Economic Policy Making in Mexico: Factors Underlying the 1982 crisis.* Durham, NC: Duke University Press, 1985. xviii, 309 p.

———. *Mexico's Economy: A Policy Analysis with Forecasts to 1990.* Boulder, CO: Westview, 1978. xvii, 250 p.

Mexico's Recent Economic Growth: The Mexican View. Essays by Enrique Pérez López et al., translated by Marjory Urquidi. Austin, TX: University of Texas Press, 1967. xv, 217 p.

Pérez López, Enrique. "El desarrollo económico de México y la estabilidad monetaria," in *El trimestre económico* 25(3):378–86 (1958).

Public Policy and Private Enterprise in Mexico. Studies by Miguel S. Wionczek et al., ed. Raymond Vernon. Cambridge, MA: Harvard University Press, 1964. vii, 324 p.

Reynolds, Clark Winton. *The Mexican Economy: Twentieth-Century Structure and Growth.* New Haven, RI: Yale University Press, 1970. xxiv, 468 p.

Solís, Leopoldo. "La Política económica y el nacionalismo mexicano," *Foro Internacional* 9(2):235–48 (1969).

Vernon, Raymond. *The Dilemma of Mexico's Development The Roles of the Private and Public Sectors.* Cambridge, MA: Harvard University Press, 1963. xi, 226 p.

1. Privatization

Bigger Economies, Smaller Governments: The Role of Privatization in Latin America. Edited by William Glade with Rossana Corona. Boulder, CO: Westview Press, 1996. viii, 407 p.

MacLeod, Dag. *Downsizing the State: Privatization and the Limits of Neoliberal Reform in Mexico.* University Park, PA: Pennsylvania State University Press, c.2004. xiii, 306 p.

2. The Informal Economy

Alisky, Marvin. "Tapping the Resources of Mexico's Underground Economy," *Wall Street Journal* (December 30, 1988): A7.

Pobreza, marginalidad e informalidad: una bibliografía mexicana, 1960–1990. Enrique Contreras Suárez et al., compiladores. Mexico City: UNAM, 1992. 161 p.

Roubaud, François. *L'économie informelle au Mexique: de la sphère domestique à la dynamique macroéconomique.* Paris: Éditions de L'orstom, 1994. 453 p.

Staut, Kathleen. *Free Trade? Informal Economies at the U.S.-Mexico Border.* Philadelphia, PA: Temple University Press, 1998. xii, 211 p.

Tendencias de la estructura económica y el sector informal en México, 1988–1993. Mexico City: Secretaría del Trabajo y Previsión Social, 1995. 186 p.

G. Regional

L'agriculture, la pêche et l'artisanat au Yucatan: prolétarisation de la paysan-nerie au Mexique. Ed. Yvan Breton and Marie-France Labrecque. Quebec: Presses de l'Université Laval, 1981. 384 p.

Hamnett, Brian Roger. *Politics and Trade in Southern Mexico, 1750–1821.* Cambridge: Cambridge University Press, 1971. 210 p.

Producción, ejidos y agua en el noreste de México: la región citrícola de Nuevo León, siglos xix y xx. Mario Cerutti, ed. Monterrey, NL: Facultad de Filosofía y Letras de la Universidad Autónoma, 1994. 179 p.

Ruvalcaba Mercado, Jesús. "Vacas, mulas, azúcar y café: los efectos de su introducción en la Huasteca, México," *Revista española de antropología americana* 26: 121–41 (1996).

El siglo xix en México. Cinco procesos regionales: Morelos, Monterrey, Yucatán, Jalisco y Puebla. Por Domenico Sindico et al.; ed. Mario Cerutti. Mexico City: Claves Latinoamericanas, 1985. 239 p.

Urbanización, cambio tecnológico y costo social: el case de la región centro de México. Ed. Adrián Guillermo Aguilar. Mexico City: Porrúa, 2003. 334 p.

Van Young, Eric. *Hacienda and Market in Eighteenth-Century Mexico: The Rural Economy of the Guadalajara Region, 1675–1820.* Berkeley, CA: University of California Press, 1981. xvi, 388 p. Reprinted Lanham: Rowman & Littlefield, 2006. Translated by Eduardo L. Suárez as *La ciudad y el campo en el México del siglo xviii* . . . Mexico City: Fondo de Cultura Económica, 1989. 392 p.

Yates, Paul Lamartine. *El desarrollo regional de México.* Mexico City: Banco de México, 1961. 405 p.

XXVII. FARMING, FISHERIES, AND NARCOTICS

A. Agriculture: General

Aboites, Jaime. *Industrialización y desarrollo agrícola en México.* Mexico City: Plaza y Valdés, 1989. 201 p.

Carlos, Manuel L. *Politics and Development in Rural Mexico: A Study of Socio-economic Modernization.* New York: Praeger, 1974. xv, 128 p.

Durán, Juan Manuel. *¿Hacia una agricultura industrial? México, 1940–1980.* Guadalajara: Universidad de Guadalajara, 1988. 247 p.

Flores, Edmundo. *Tratado de economía agrícola.* Mexico City: Fondo de Cultura Econòmica, 1961. 442 p.

Fujigaki Cruz, Esperanza. *La agricultura, siglos xvi al xx.* Ed. Enrique Semo. Mexico City: Oceano, 2004. 199 p.

García Zamora, Rodolfo. *Crisis y modernización del agro en México, 1940–1990.* Mexico City: Universidad Autónoma Chapingo, 1993. 335 p.

Institutional Adaptation and Innovation in Rural Mexico. Ed. Richard Snyder. La Jolla, CA: Center for US-Mexican Studies, 1999. viii, 166 p.

Romero Polanco, Emilio. *Un siglo de agricultura en México.* Mexico City: Porrúa, 2002. 101 p.

Tutino, John. *From Insurrection to Revolution in Mexico: Social Bases of Agrarian Violence, 1759–1940.* Princeton: Princeton University Press, 1986. xx, 425 p.

Venezian, Eduardo L. *The Agricultural Development of Mexico: Its Structure and Growth Since 1950.* New York: Praeger, 1969. 281 p.

1. Bibliography

Bibliografía agrícola y agraria de México. Mexico City: Secretaría de Agricultura y Fomento, 1946. 377 p.

B. Land Tenure

McBride, George McCutchen. *The Land Systems of Mexico.* New York: American Geographical Society, 1923. xii, 204 p. Reprinted Octagon Books, 1971.

Phipps, Helen. *Some Aspects of the Agrarian Question in Mexico: A Historical Study.* Austin, TX: The University, 1925. 157 p.

Reformando la reforma agraria mexicana. Ed. Laura Randall. Mexico City: Universidad Autónoma Metropolitiana, 1999. xi, 434 p.

Tannenbaum, Frank. *The Mexican Agrarian Revolution.* New York: Macmillan, 1929. xvi, 543 p. Reprinted Hamden, CT: Archon Books, 1968.

Taylor, William B. *Landlord and Peasant in Colonial Oaxaca.* Stanford, CA: Stanford University Press, 1972. 287 p.

1. Bibliography

Martínez Ríos, Jorge. *Tenencia de la tierra y desarrollo agrario en México: bibliografía selectiva y comentada, 1522–1968,* Mexico City Instituto de Investigaciones Sociales, 1970. ix, 305 p.

(Perhaps based on the earlier bibliography, *Tenecia de la tierra y agricultura en México, 1918–1960*. Mexico City: Banco de México, 1963. 77 p.?)

C. Encomiendas

Simpson, Lesley Byrd. *The Encomienda in New Spain: Forced Native Labor in the Spanish Colonies, 1492–1550*. Berkeley, CA: University of California Press, 1929; Revised as *The Encomienda in New Spain: The Beginning of Spanish Mexico*, 1950. xv, 257 p. Reprinted 1982.

D. Haciendas and Ranches

Brading, David Anthony. *Haciendas and ranchos in the Mexican Bajío: León, 1700–1860*. Cambridge: Cambridge University Press, 1978. xviii, 258 p.

Chevalier, François. *La formation des grands domaines au Mexique: terre et société aux xvie-xviie siècles*. Paris: Institut d'ethnologie, 1952. xxvii, 480 p. Translated by Alvin Eustis as *Land and Society in Colonial Mexico: The Great Hacienda*. Berkeley, CA: University of California Press, 1963. ix, 334 p. Reprinted 1970. Translated by Antonio Alatorre as *La formación de los grandes latifundios en México*. Mexico City: Fondo de Cultura Económica, 1957. 2a ed., aum. as *La formación de los latifundios en México: tierra y sociedad en los siglos xvi y svii.* 1976. xvi, 510 p.; 3a ed. *La formación de los latifundios en México: haciendas y sociedad en los siglos xvi, xvii y xviii.* 1999. 643 p.

Harris, Charles Houston. *A Mexican Family Empire: The Latifundio of the Sánchez Navarros, 1765–1867*. Austin: University of Texas Press, 1975. xvii, 410 p.

Orígen y evolución de la hacienda en México: siglos xvi al xx . . . Ed. María Teresa Jarquín Ortega et al. Toluca: Colegio Mexiquense; Mexico City: Instituto Nacional de Antropología e Historia, 1990. vi, 263 p.

E. Peasantry and Ejidos

Adie, Robert F. "Cooperation, Cooptation, and Conflict in a Mexican Peasant Organization," *Inter-American Economic Affairs* (Winter 1970): 3–25.

Baant, Jan. "Peones, arrendatarios y parceros," *Historia mexicana*. November 19, 1970): 512–35.

DeWalt, Billie R. *Modernization in a Mexican Ejido: A Study in Economic Adaptation*. Cambridge: Cambridge University Press, 1978. 303 p.

Grindle, Merilee Serrill. *Bureaucrats, Politicians, and Peasants in Mexico: A Case Study in Public Policy*. Berkeley, CA: University of California Press, 1977. xix, 220 p.

Hewitt de Alcántara, Cynthia. *La modernización de la agricultura mexicana, 1940–1970*. Mexico City, Siglo XXI, 1978. 319 p., previously published in English translation as *Modernizing Mexican Agriculture: Socioeconomic Implications of Technological Change, 1940–1970*. Geneva: UN Research Institute for Social Development, 1976. 350 p.

Infield, Henrik F. and Freir, Koka. *People in Ejidos: A Visit to the Cooperative Farms of Mexico*. New York: Praeger, 1954. 151 p.

Lewis, Oscar. *Life in a Mexican Village: Tepoztlán Restudied*. Urbana, IL: University of Illinois Press, 1951. xxvii, 512 p.

———. *Pedro Martínez: A Mexican Peasant and his Family*. New York: Random House, 1964. lvii, 597 p.; repinted Vintage Books, 1967.

Simpson, Eyler N. *The Ejido: Mexico's Way Out*. Chapel Hill, NC: University of North Carolina Press, 1937.

Warman, Arturo. *Los Campesinos*. Mexico City: Editorial Nuestro Tiempo, 1972. 138 p.; 4a ed., 1975.

F. Irrigation

Aboites, Luis. *El agua de la nación: una historia política de México, 1888–1946*. Mexico City: Centro de Investigaciones y Estudios Superiores en Antropología Social, 1998. 220 p.

Doolittle, William Emery. *Canal Irrigation in Prehistoric Mexico: The Sequence of Technological Change*. Austin, TX: University of Texas Press, xiv, 205 p.

Greenberg, Martin Harry. *Bureaucracy and Development: A Mexican Case Study*. Lexington, MA: Heath Lexington Books, [1970]. x, 158 p.

Huerta Meza, Joaquín. *Uso del agua en irrigación*. Mexico City: Comisión del Plan Nacional Hidráulico, 1978. 79 p.

Orive Alba, Adolfo. *La política de irrigación en México: historia, realizaciones, resultados agrícolas, económicos y sociales, perspectivas*. Mexico City: Fondo de Cultura Económica, 1960. xiv, 292 p.

Tamayo, Jorge L. *El problema fundamental de la agricultura mexicana*. Mexico City: Instituto Mexicano de Investigaciones Económicas, 1964. 181 p.

G. Agricultural Products

1. Agave and Pulque

Loyola Montemayor, Elías. *La industria del pulque*. Mexico City: Banco de México, 1956. 348 p.

2. Cacao

Cacao: historia, economía y cultura. Mexico City: Nestlé, 1992. 189 p.

Millon, René. *When Money Grew on Trees: A Study of Cacao in Ancient Mesoamerica.* Ann Arbor, MI: UMI Dissertation Service, 2003. viii, 302 p. PhD diss., Columbia University, 1955.

Wood, George Alan Roskruge. *Report on Cocoa Growing in the Dominican Republic, Mexico, Guatemala and Costa Rica.* Bournville, UK: Cadbury Bros., 1957. 40 p.

3. Coffee

Martínez Morales, Aurora Cristina. *El proceso cafetalero mexicano.* Mexico City: Instituto de Investigaciones Económicas de la UNAM, 1997. 190 p.

Sistema agroindustrial café en México: diagnóstico, problemática y perspectivas. Ed. Horacio Santoyo Cortés et al. Chapingo: Centro de Investigación Económica, Sociológica y Tecnológica de la Agricultura y la Agronomía Mundial, 1994. 157 p.

a. Chiapas

Kanzleiter, Boris and Pesara, Dirk. *Die Rebellion der Habennichtse: der Kampf für Land und Freiheit gegen deutsche Kaffeebarone in Chiapas.* Berlin: Ed. ID-Archiv, 1997. 139 p.

Lavín, Mónica. *Café: desde las alturas.* Mexico City: Fondo Nacional de Apoyo a Empresas Sociales, 1999. 98 p.

Mahnken, Winifred. *Mi vida en los cafetales: Tapachula, 1882–1992.* Mexico City: Gobierno del Estado de Chiapas, 1993. 83 p.

Martínez Quezada, Álvaro. *Crisis del café y estategías campesinas: el caso de la Unión de Ejidos Majomut en los Altos de Chiapas.* Mexico City: Universidad Autónoma Chapingo, 1995. 208 p.

b. Oaxaca

Porter, Robert M. *The Coffee Farmers' Revolt in Southern Mexico in the 1980s and 1990s.* Lewiston, NY: Edwin Mellen Press, 2002. viii, 216 p.

c. Veracruz

Escamilla Prado, Esteban, et al. "Los sistemas de producción de café en el centro de Veracruz, México: un análisis tecnológico," *Revista de historia, San José* 30:41–67 (1994).

Hoffmann, Odile, et al. "Urbanizare o migrar: ¿cuales opciones frente a la crisis? El devenir de las comunidades cafetaleras en el centro de Veracruz, México," in *Revista de historia, San José* 30:165–85 (1994).

4. Corn

Florescano, Enrique. *Precios del maíz y crisis agrícolas en México, 1708–1810: ensayo sobre el movimiento de los precios y sus consecuencias económicas y sociales.* Mexico City: Colegio de México, 1969. 254 p.

Florescano, Enrique, and Moreno Toscano, Alejandro. *Bibliografía general del maíz en México.* 3a ed. Mexico City: Instituto Nacional de Antropología e Historia, 1987. 251 p. First ed. entitled *Bibliografía del maíz en México.* Xalapa, 1966. 359 p.

Montañés, Carlos, and Aburto, Horacio. *Maíz, política institucional y crisis agrícola.* Mexico City: Nueva Imagen, 1979. 249 p.

Montañés, Carlos, and Warman, Arturo. *Los productores de maíz en México: restrictions y alternatives.* Mexico City: Centro de Ecodesarrollo, 1985. 226 p.

Solís Algin, Felipe R. *La cultura del maíz.* Mexico City: Clio, 1998. 93 p.

5. Cotton

Plana, Manuel. *Il rego del cotone in Messico: la struttura agraria de La Laguna, 1855–1910.* Milan: Franco Angeli, 1984. 250 p.

Senior, Clarence Ollsion. *Land Reform and Democracy.* Gainesville, FL: University of Florida Press, 1958. xiii, 269 p. Reprinted Westport, CT: Greenwood, 1974.

6. Livestock

Chauvet, Michelle. *La ganadería bovina de carne en México: del auge a la crisis.* Azcapotzalco: Universidad Autónoma Metropolitana-Azcapotzalco, 1999. 206 p.

Machado, Manuel A., Jr. *An Industry in Crisis: Mexican-United States Cooperation in the Control of Foot-and-Mouth Disease.* Berkeley, CA: University of California Press, 1968. viii, 99 p.

———. *The North Mexican Cattle Industry, 1910–1975: Ideology, Conflict and Change.* College Station, TX: Texas A&M University Press, 1980. xiv, 152 p.

Melville, Elinor G. K. *A Plague of Sheep: Environmental Consequences of the Conquest of Mexico.* Cambridge: Cambridge University Press, 1994. xiii, 203 p.

Saucedo Montemayor, Pedro. *Historia de la ganadería en México.* Mexico City: UNAM, 1984– . v 1- .

7. Sisal

Chardon, Roland Emanuel Paul. *Geographic Aspects of Plantation Agriculture in Yucatán.* Washington, DC: National Academy of Sciences, 1961. 200 p.

Manero, Enrique. *La anarquía henequenera de Yucatán.* Mexico City: [The Author], 1966. 28 [xix] p.

8. Sugar

Barrett, Ward Judson. *The Sugar Hacienda of the Marqueses del Valle.* Minneapolis, MN: University of Minnesota Press, 1970. 147 p. History of the plantation of the Marquises of the Valle de Oaxaca in Morelos from its foundation by Hernán Cortés through to the 19th century.

Cardoso, Gerald. *Negro Slavery in the Sugar Plantations of Veracruz and Pernambuco, 1550–1680: A Comparative Study.* Washington, DC: University Press of America, 1983. xi, 211 p.

El estado, los cañeros y la industria azucarera, 1940–1980. Ed. Luis Paré et al. Azcapotzalco: Instituto de Investigaciones Sociales de la UNAM, Universidad Autónoma Metropolitana, 1987. 295 p.

Hernández Palomo, José Jesús. *El agardiente en caña en México, 1724–1810.* Seville: Escuela de Estudios Hispano-Americanos, 1974. 181 p.

Huerta, María Teresa. *Empresarios del azúcar en el siglo xix.* Mexico City: Instituto Nacional de Antropología e Historia, 1993. 192 p.

Melville, Roberto. *Crecimiento y rebelión: el desarrollo económico de las haciendas azucareras en Morelos, 1880–1910.* Mexico City: Centro de Investigaciones del Desarrollo Rural, 1979. 113 p.

Mexican Sugarcane Growers: Economic Restructuring and Political Options. Ed. by Peter Singelmann. La Jolla, CA: Center for U.S.-Mexican Studies, University of California at San Diego, 1985. 85 p.

Naveda Chávez-Hita, Adriana. *Escravos negros en las haciendas azucareras de Córdoba, Veracruz, 1690–1830.* Xalapa: Universidad Veracruzana, 1987. 189 p.

Ruiz de Velasco, Felipe. *Historia y evoluciones del cultivo de la caña y de la industria azucarera en Mexico hasta el año de 1910.* Mexico City: "Azúcar" 1937. 546 p.

Wobeser, Gusela von. *La hacienda azucarera en la época colonial.* Mexico City: Secretaría de Educación Pública; UNAM, 1988. 366 p.

9. Tobacco

Amerlinck, María Concepción. *Historia y cultura del tabaco en México.* Mexico: Tabacos Mexicanos, 1988. 293 p.

Chumacero, Antonio. *Orígen de una empresa pública: el caso de Tabacos Mexicanos.* Tepic: Universidad Autónoma de Nayarit, 1985. xviii, 279 p.

Deans-Smith, Susan. *Bureaucrats, Planters, and Workers: The Making of the Tobacco Monopoly in Bourbon Mexico.* Austin, TX: University of Texas Press, 1992. xxi, 352 p. Based on her Cambridge University PhD thesis of 1984.

González Gómez, Carmen Imelda. *El tabaco virreinal: monopolio de una costumbre.* Santiago de Querétaro: Fondo Editorial de Querétaro, 2002. 250 p.

Robicsek, Francis. *The Smoking Gods: Tobacco in Maya Art, History, and Religion.* Norman, OK: University of Oklahoma Press, 1978. xxv, 233 p.

Ros Torres, María Amparo. *La producción cigarrera a finales de la colonia: la fábrica de México.* Mexico City: INAH, 1984. 97 p.

10. Wheat

Mertens, Hans Günther. *Wirtschaftliche und soziale Strukturen zentralmexikanischer Weizenhaciendas aus dem Tal von Atlixo, 1890–1912.* Wiesbaden: F. Steiner, 1983. 382 p.

H. Food Supply

Barkin, David. *El fin de la autosuficiencia alimentaria.* Mexico City: Océano, 1985. 249 p.

Food Policy in Mexico: The Search for Self-Sufficiency. Ed. James E. Austin and Gustavo Esteva. Ithaca, NY: Cornell University Press, 1987. 383 p.

Gamble, Stephen Holland. *The Despensa System of Food Distribution: A Case Study of Monterrey, Mexico.* New York: Praeger, 1971. 137 p.

Pilcher, Jeffrey M. "Feeding Mexico: The Political Uses of Food Since 1910." *The Americas* 58(1):163–64 (July 2001).

Zubirán, Salvador, et al. *La desnutrición del mexicano: entrevistas de Beatriz Reyes Nevares; testimonios de Salvador Zubirán . . .* Mexico City: Fondo de Cultura Económica, 1974. 63 p.

I. The Drug Trade

Tinajero Medina, Ruben and Hernández Iznaga, María del Rosario. *El narcocorrido: ¿Tradicción o mercado?* Chihuahua: Universidad Autónoma de Chihuahua, 2004. 151 p.

Toro, María Celia. *Mexico's "War" on Drugs: Causes and Consequences.* Boulder: Lynne Reinner, 1995. xi, 105 p.

Velasco, José Luis. *Insurgencey [sic], Authoritarianism, and Drug Trafficking in Mexico's "Democratization,"* New York: Routledge, 2005. xvi, 239 p.

Wald, Elijah. *Narcocorrido: A Journey into the Music of Drugs, Guns, and Guerrillas.* New York: Rayo, 2001. xiii, 333 p.

J. Fisheries

Ochoa, Arnulfo. *A flor de agua: la pesquería de atún en Enseada.* Mexico City: Plaza y Valdés for CONACULTA, 2003. 164 p.

Ortiz, Fernando. *La pesca en México.* Mexico City: Fondo de Cultura Económica, 1975. 63 p.

XXVIII. MANUFACTURING INDUSTRY

Contreras, Ariel José. *Mexico 1940: industrialización y crisis política.* Mexico City: Siglo Veintiuno, 1983. 219 p.

Mosk, Sanford Alexander. *Industrial Revolution in Mexico.* Berkeley, CA: University of California Press, 1950. xii, 331 p. Reprinted New York: Russell & Russell, 1975.

A. Iron and Steel

Alisky, Marvin. "Mexico's Steel Industry," *Intellect* (March 1976): 462–65.

Cole, William E. *Steel and Economic Growth in Mexico.* Austin, TX: University of Texas Press, 1967. xviii, 173 p.

B. Textiles

Keremitsis, Dawn. *The Cotton Textile Industry in Porfiriato Mexico, 1870–1910.* New York: Garland, 1987. 232 p.

Salvucci, Richard J. *Textiles and Capitalism in Mexico: An Economic History of the Obrajes, 1539–1840.* Princeton, NJ: Princeton University Press, 1987. xiv, 249 p.

XXIX. FINANCIAL AND FISCAL

Carstens, Catherine Mansell. *Las finanzas populares en México: el redescubrimiento de un sistema financiero olvidado.* Mexico City: Centro de Estudios Monetarios Latinoamericanos, 1995. xxvii, 306 p.

De colonia a nación: impuestos y política en México, 1750–1860. Essays by Ana Lidia García Pena et al., ed. Carlos Marichal and Daniela Marino. Mexico City: Colegio de México, 2001. 279 p.

Devlin, Robert and French-Davis, Ricardo. "The Great Latin American Debt Crisis: A Decade of Asymmetric Adjustment," *Revista de Economia Política* 15(3) (July 1995).

Fitzgerald, Edmund Valpy Knox. *The Fiscal Deficit and Development Finance: A Note on the Accumulation Balance in Mexico* (Research Report, 35). Cambridge, UK: Center of Latin American Studies, University of Cambridge, 1979. 28 p.

Griffiths, Brian. *Mexican Monetary Policy and Economic Development.* ("Praeger Special Studies in International Economics and Development.") New York: Praeger, 1972. xii, 163 p.

Maurer, Noel. *The Power and the Money: The Mexican Financial System, 1876–1932.* Stanford, CA: Stanford University Press, 2002. xiv, 250 p.

Ortiz Mena, Antonio. *Las finanzas públicas en el desarrollo socioeconómico de Mexico. Vol. 1.* Mexico City: Libros Sela, 1969. xv, 516 p.

Pérez Siller, Javier. *L'hégémonie des financiers au Mexique sous le Porfiriat: l'autre dictature.* Paris: L'Harmattan, 2003. 202 p.

Ygarza, Alberto. "El futura de la política fiscal en México," *Investigación económica* 32(1):13–22 (1971).

A. Foreign Investment and Trade

Bennett, Douglas C. and Sharpe, Kenneth E. *Transnational Corporations and the State: The Political Economy of the Mexican Auto Industry.* Princeton, NJ: Princeton University Press, 1985. xiii, 299 p.

Herrera Canales, Inés. *El comercio exterior de México, 1821–1875.* Mexico City: Colegio de México, 1977. 195 p.

The Second Conquest of Latin America: Coffee, Henequen, and Oil During the Export Boom, 1850–1930. Ed. Steven C. Topik and Allen Wells. Austin, TX: University of Texas Press, 1998. viii, 271 p.

Tardiff, Guillermo. *Historia general del comercio exterior mexicano.* Mexico City: Gráfica Panamericana, 1968. 2 v.

Turlington, Edgar. *Mexico and Her Foreign Creditors.* New York: Columbia University Press, 1930. x, 449 p.

B. Income Distribution

Aspe, Pedro. *The Political Economy of Income Distribution in Mexico.* New York: Holmes and Meier, 1984. 552 p.

Bortz, Jeffrey. "Earning a Living: A History of Real Wage Studies in Twentieth-Century Mexico," *Latin American Research Review* 41(2):113–38 (Spring 2006).

Eckstein, Susan. *The Poverty of Revolution: The State and the Urban Poor in Mexico.* Princeton, NJ: Princeton University Press, 1977. xv, 300 p.

Espinosa de los Reyes, Jorge. *La distribución del ingreso nacional.* Mexico City: Escuela Nacional de Economía, 1958.

C. Banking

Anaya Merchant, Luis. *Colapso y reforma: la integración del sistema bancario en el México revolucionario, 1913–1932.* Mexico City: Miguel Ángel Porrúa, 2002. 337 p.

La banca regional en México, 1870–1930. Ed. Mario Cerutti and Carlos Marichal. Mexico City: Fondo de Cultura Económica, 2003. 350 p.

Boylan, Delia M. *Defusing Democracy: Central Bank Autonomy and the Transition from Authoritarian Rule.* Ann Arbor, MI: University of Michigan Press, 2001. xiii, 295 p.

Brett, Virgil. *Central Banking in Mexico.* Ann Arbor, MI: School of Business Administration, University of Michigan, 1957. 235 p.

Conant, Charles. *Banking Systems of Mexico.* Washington, DC: GPO, 1910. 210 p.

Nacional Financiera, 1934–1884: medio siglo de banca de desarrollo. Testimonio de sus directores generales. Mexico City: Nacional Financiera, 1985. 310 p.

Potash, Robert A. *Mexican Government and Industrial Development in the Early Republic: The Banco de Avio.* Amherst, MA: University of Massachusetts Press, 1983. xii, 251 p. PhD diss., University of Massachusetts, 1953, first published in translation by Ramón Fernández y Fernández as *El Banco de Avío: el fomento de la industria, 1821–1846.* Mexico City: Fondo de Cultura Económica, 1959. 281 p.

D. Businesses and Corporations

Shafer, Robert Jones. *Mexican Business Organizations: History and Analysis.* Syracuse, NY: Syracuse University Press, 1973. xi, 397 p.

1. Small Firms

Shadlen, Kenneth. *Democratization without Representation: The Politics of Small Industry in Mexico.* University Park, PA: Pennsylvania University Press, 2004. xvi, 208 p.

XXX. LABOR

Aguilar, Abel. *La Política obrera.* Mexico City: Atlas, 1970.

Anguiano, Arturo. *El Estado y la política obrera del cardenismo.* Mexico City: Ediciones Era, 1975. 185 p.

Millon, Robert P. *Mexican Marxist: Vicente Lombardo Toledano.* Chapel Hill, NC: University of North Carolina Press, 1966.

Ruiz, Ramón E. *Labor and the Ambivalent Revolution: México, 1911–1923.* Baltimore, MD: Johns Hopkins University Press, 1976. 145 p.

A. Slavery

"The Atlantic Slave Trade and Slave Life in the Americas: A Visual Record," http://hitchcock.itc.virginia.edu/Slavery/index.php.

B. Trade Unions

Alba, Victor. *Politics and the Labor Movement in Latin America.* Stanford, CA: Stanford University Press, 1968. 404 p.

Ashby, Joe C. *Organized Labor and the Mexican Revolution under Cárdenas.* Chapel Hill, NC: University of North Carolina Press, 1967. x, 350 p.

Clark, Marjorie Ruth. *Organized Labor in Mexico.* Chapel Hill, NC: University of North Carolina Press, 1934. 315 p. Reprinted New York: Russell & Russell, 1973.

Guadarrama, Rocío. *Los sindicatos y la política en México: la CROM, 1918–1928.* Mexico City: Era, 1981. 239 p.

López Aparicio, Alfonso, *El movimiento obrero en México.* Mexico City: Editorial Jus, 1952; 2a ed., 1958. 280 p.

Mayer, Jean François and Marier, Patrick. "Unions and Pension Reform in Mexico: The Impact of Democratic Governance," *JLAS; Journal of Iberian and Latin American Studies* 11(2):29–52 (La Trobe: December 2005).

Navarrete, Alfredo. *Alto a la contrarrevolución.* (Testimonios de Atlacomulco). Mexico City: Libros de México, 1971. 402 p.

XXXI. MINING AND EXTRACTIVE INDUSTRIES

Bernstein, Marvin D. *The Mexican Mining Industry, 1890–1950: A Study of the Interaction of Politics, Economics, and Technology.* Albany, NY: State University of New York Press, 1964. xvi, 412 p.

A. Petroleum

Powell, J. R. *The Mexican Petroleum Industry, 1938–1950.* Berkeley, CA: University of California Press, 1956. xiv, 269 p.

Williams, Edward J. "Oil in Mexican-US Relations," *Orbis* (Spring 1978): 210–11.

B. Silver

Couturier, Edith Boorstein. *The Silver King: The Remarkable Life of the Count of Regla in Colonial Mexico.* Albuquerque, NM: University of New Mexico Press. 2003. x, 224 p.

Pérez Herrero, Pedro. *Plata y libranzas: la articulación comercial del México bornónico.* Mexico City: Colegio de México, 1988. 362 p.

Shepherd, Grant. *The Silver Magnet: Fifty Years in a Mexican Silver Mine.* New York: Dutton, 1938. 302 p.

XXXII. SERVICE INDUSTRIES

Mulder, Johan Meindert. *The Economic Performance of the Service Sector in Brazil, Mexico, and the USA: A Comparative Historical Perspective.* Groningen: Rijksuniversiteit, 1999. xvii, 366 p.

A. Telecommunications

O'Grady, Mary Anastasia. "Mexico's Telephone Monopoly Hang-Up," *Wall Street Journal* (June 18, 1999): A21.

B. Transportation

Privatizing Monopolies: Lessons from the Telecommunications and Transport Sectors in Latin America, ed. Ravi Ramamurti. Baltimore, MD: Johns Hopkins University Press, 1996. vi, 401 p.

C. Air Transport

Alisky, Marvin. "Airlines: Makers of Modern Mexico," *Mexican-American Review* (October 1967): 19–22.

Davies, Ronald Edward George. *Airlines of Latin America since 1919.* London: Putnam, 1984. xiv, 698 p.

D. Highways

1. Colonial

Castleman, Bruce A. *Building the King's Highway: Labor, Society, and Family on Mexico's Caminos Reales, 1757–1804*. Tucson, AZ: University of Arizona Press, 2005. xii, 163 p.

Driever, Steven L., "The Veracruz-Mexico City Routes in the Sixteenth Century and the Study of Pre-Industrial Transport in Historical Geography," *Geografía y desarrollo* 6(12):5–18 (Mexico City: 1995).

Pérez González, María Luisa. "Los caminos reales de América en la legislación y en la historia," *Anuario de estudios americanos* 50(1):33–60 (Seville: 2001).

Preston, Douglas and Esquibel, José Antonio. *The Royal Road: El Camino Real from Mexico City to Santa Fe*. Photographs by Christine Preston. Albuquerque, NM: University of New Mexico Press, ix, 170 p.

Sánchez de Tagle, Esteban. *Los dueños de la calle: una historia de la vía pública en la época colonial*. Mexico City: INAH, 1997. 267 p.

Suárez Argüello, Clara Elena. *Camino real y carrera larga: la arrería en la Nueva España durante el siglo xviii*. Mexico City: CIESAS, 1997. 350 p.

2. Modern

Allhoff, Michael. *Traumstraßen Mexiko*. Fotos: Christian Heeb. Munich: Südwest Verlag, 2000. 174 p.

Delgado, Javier. *Ciudad-región y transporte en el México central: un largo camino de rupturas y continuidades*. Mexico City: Plaza y Valdés, 1998. 221 p.

Friske, Thomas. *Die Panamericana: von Alaska bis Feuerland: Traumstaße der Welt für jedermann*. Grafing: Friske, 1999. 367 p.

García Martínez, Bernardo. *Las carreteras de México, 1891–1991*. Mexico City: Secretaría de Comunicaciones y Transportes, 1992. 197 p.

Moreno-Quintero, Eric. *Planner-use Interactions in Road Freight Transport: A Modelling Approach with a Case Study from Mexico*. Leeds: University of Leeds, 2004. xiv, 202 leaves.

E. Railroads

Coatsworth, John H. *Growth Against Development: The Economic Impact of Railroads in Porfirian Mexico*. Mexico City: Editorial Cosmos, 1975. 296 p.

Drury, George H. *The Historical Guide to North American Railroads*. Milwaukee, WI: Kalmbach Books, c.1985. 2nd ed., Waukesha, WI: Kalmbach Books, c2000. 480 p.

Dunn, Archibald Joseph. *The Tehuantepec Railway: A New Through Route to the East*. London: Van Bardun, 1896. 12 p.

Ferrocarriles y vida económica en México, 1850–1950 surgimiento tardío al decaimiento precoz. Ed. Sandra Kuntz Ficker and Paolo Riguzzi. Mexico City: El Colegio Mexiquense, 1996. 383 p.

Gurría Lacroix, Jorge. *Bibliografía mexicana de ferrocarriles*. México City: Ferrocarriles Nacionales, 1956. 499 p.

Kuntz Ficker, Sandra. *Empresa extranjera y mercado interno: el Ferrocarril Central Mexicano, 1880–1907*. Mexico City: Colegio de México, 1955. 391 p.

"Mexico," in *Jane's World Railways, 1997–1998*, ed. James Abbott. Coulsdon, UK: 1997 (and earlier years).

Ortiz Hernán, Sergio. *Los ferrocarriles de México: una visión social y económica*. 2a. ed., [corr. y aumentada]. México City: Secretaría de Comunicaciones y Transportes, 1974. 277 p.

Powell, Fred Wilbur. *The Railroads of Mexico*. Boston: Stratford, 1921. vii, 226 p.

Schmidt, Arthur. *The Social and Economic Effect of the Railroad in Puebla and Veracruz, Mexico, 1867–1911*. New York: Garland, 1987. 297 p.

F. Shipping

Haring, Clarence Henry. *Trade and Navigation between Spain and the Indies in the Time of the Hapsburgs*. Cambridge, MA: Harvard University Press, 1918. xxviii, 371 p.

Hockins, Charles. *Dictionary of Disasters at Sea During the Steam Age, 1824–1962*. London: Lloyd's Register of Shipping, 1969. 2 v.

Horner, Dave. *The Treasure Galleons: Clues to Millions in Sunken Gold and Silver*. London: Hale, 1973. xxviii, 259 p.

Katz, Friedrich. "Hamburger Schiffahrt nach Mexiko, 1870–1914" in *Hansische Geschichtsblätter* 83:94–108 (Cologne: 1965).

Kirsch, Peter. *Die Galeonen: grosse Segelschiffe um 1600*. Coblence: Bernard & Graefe, c.1988. 232 p. Translated as: *The Galleon: The Great Ships of the Armada Era*. Annapolis, MD: Naval Institute Press, c.1990. 214 p.

Marx, Robert F. *Shipwrecks of the Western Hemisphere*. New York: New World Publishing, 1971. xxi, 452 p.

Ships and Shipwrecks of the Americas: A History Based on Underwater Archaeology, Ed. George Fletcher Bass. London: Thames and Hudson, 1988. 272 p.

G. Tourism

Boardman, Andrea. *Destination México: A Foreign Land a Step Away. U.S. Tourism to Mexico, 1880s–1950s*. Dallas, TX: Southern Methodist University, 2001. 101 p.

Clancy, Michael. *Exploring Paradise: Tourism and Development in Mexico.* Amsterdam; London: Pergamon, 2001. vii, 170 p.

Jiménez Martínez, Alfonso de Jesús. *Desarrollo turístico y sustentabilidad: el caso de México.* Mexico City: M. A. Porrúa, 1998. 191 p.

Pattullo, Polly. *Last Resorts: The Cost of Tourism in the Caribbean.* London: Cassell, 1996. viii, 220 p.

H. Retail Distribution

Breña Valle, Gabriel. *Las mil caras de la moneda: comercio en México.* Mexico City: Banco Nacional del Pequeño Comercio, 1991. 115 p.

James, Daniel. "Sears, Roebuck's Mexican Revolution," *Harper's* (June 1959): 1–6.

XXXIII. INTERNATIONAL RELATIONS

A. General

Kirk, Bett. *Covering the Mexican Front: The Battle of Europe versus America.* Norman, OK: University of Oklahoma Press, 1942. xiv, 367 p.

Halperin, Maurice. "Mexico Shifts Her Foreign Policy," *Foreign Affairs* (June 1941): 207–21.

Latin American Foreign Policies: An Analysis. Ed. Harold Eugene Davis and M. C. Wilson. Baltimore, MD: Johns Hopkins University Press, 1975. xiii, 470 p.

Latin American International Politics: Ambitions, Capabilities and the National Interest of Mexico, Brazil, Argentina. By Carlos Alberto Astiz et al., ed. Carlos Alberto Astiz. South Bend, IN: University of Notre Dame Press, 1969. viii, 343 p.

Meyer, Michael C. "Isidro Fabela's documentos históricos," *Hispanic American Historical Review* (February 1972): 123–29.

El reconocimiento de la independencia de México. Ed. María Eugenia López de Roux and Roberto Marín. Mexico City. S.R.E., 1995. 809 p.

B. With Other Spanish-Speaking Countries

1. Spain

Delgado, Jaime. *España y México en el siglo xix.* Madrid: Instituto Gonzalo Fernández de Oviedo, 1950–1953. 3 v.

Flores Torres, Oscar. *Revolución mexicana y diplomacia española: contrarrevolución y oligarquía hispana en México, 1909–1920.* Mexico City: Instituto Nacional de Estudios Históricos de la Revolución Mexicana, 1995. 467 p.

MacGregor, Joselina. *México y España: del porfirato a la revolución.* Mexico City: Instituto Nacional de Estudios Históricos de la Revolución Mexicana, 1992. 243 p.

Pérez Montfort, Ricardo. *Hispanismo y falange: los sueños imperiales de la derecha española y México.* Mexico City: Fondo de Cultura Económica, 1992. 204 p.

El tratado de paz con España (Santa-María-Calatrava). Mexico City. S.R.E., 1927. xxix, 222 p.

2. Central America

Las relaciones de México con los países de América Central. Ed. Mario Ojeda. Mexico City: Colegio de México, 1985. 151 p.

Toussaint Ribot, Mónica. *Vecindad y diplomacia: Centroamérica en la política exterior mexicana, 1821–1988.* Mexico City: Acervo Histórico Diplomático, 2001. 262 p.

La Trinagulación Centroamérica-México-EUA. Por H. Rodrigo Jaubeth Rojas et al. Translated as *The Difficult Triangle: Mexico, Central America and the United States.* Boulder: Westview, 1992. xvi, 192 p.

3. Caribbean Countries

Múñoz Mata, Laura. *Geopolítica, seguridad nacional y política exterior: México y el Caribe en el siglo xix.* Mexico City: Instituto Mora, 2001. 194 p.

4. Cuba

Pellicer de Brody, Olga. *México y la revolución cubana.* Mexico City: Colegio de México, 1972. 131 p.

Smith, Arthur K. *Mexico and the Cuban Revolution: Foreign Policy-Making under President Adoilfo López Mateos, 1958–1964.* ("Dissertation Series.") Ithaca, NY: Cornell University Latin American Studies Program, 1970. ix, 344 p.

5. Hispanophone South America

Borah, Woodrow Wilson. *Early Colonial Trade and Navigation Between Mexico and Peru.* Berkeley: University of California Press, 1954. 170 p.

Cavarozzi, Marcelo, et al. *Asilo diplomático mexicano en el Cono Sur.* Mexico City: Instituto Mora, 1999. 157 p.

Lemoine Villicaña, Ernesto. *México y Hispanoamérica en 1867.* Mexico City: UNAM, 1997. 294 p.

México y América Latina: la nueva política exterior. Mexico City: Colegio de México, 1974. 201 p.

Yankelevich, Pablo. *La revolución mexicana en América Latina: intereses políticos e itinerarios intelectuales.* Mexico City: Instituto Mora, 2003. 175 p.

6. Brazil

Weckman, Luis. "Mexico-Brasil: una correspondencia imperial," *Historia mexicana* 39(1):235–41 (July/September, 1989).

7. The United States

Callahan, James Morton. *American Foreign Policy in Mexican Relations.* New York: Macmillan, 1932. xi, 644 p. Reprinted Cooper Square, 1967.

Cline, Howard Francis. *The United States and Mexico.* Cambridge: Harvard University Press. 1953. xvi, 452 p.; rev. enl. ed., 1963. 484 p.

García Cantú, Gastón. *Las invasiones norteamericanas en México.* Mexico City, 1971. Reprinted Ediciones Era, 1980. 362 p.

Hundley, Norris. *Dividing the Waters: A Century of Controversy Between the United States and Mexico.* Berkeley, CA: University of California Press, 1966. xii, 266 p.

Rippy, James Fred. *The United States and Mexico.* New York: Knopf, 1926. xi, 401 p.; rev. ed., Crofts, 1931. xi, 423 p. Reprinted AMS Press, 1971.

Schmitt, Karl Michael. *Mexico and the United States, 1821–1973: Conflict and Co-existence.* New York: Wiley, 1974. xiii, 288 p.

Vázquez, Josefina Zoraida. *México frente a Estados Unidos: un ensayo histórico, 1776–1980.* Mexico City: Colegio de México, 1982. 235 p.; 4a., aumentada, 2001. 262 p.

a. Early Nineteenth Century

Egan, Feroi. *The El Dorado Trail: The Story of the Gold Rush Route Across Mexico.* New York: McGraw-Hill, 1970. Reprinted Lincoln, NE: University of Nebraska Press, 1984. xiv, 313 p.

Espinosa de los Reyes, Jorge. *Relaciones económicas entre México y Estados Unidos, 1870–1910.* Mexico City: Nacional Financiera, 1951. 189 p.

Gerber, Paul Neff. *The Gadsden Treaty.* Gloucester, MA: P. Smith, 1923.

Nance, Joseph Milton. *After San Jacinto, The Texas-Mexican Frontier, 1836–1841.* Austin, TX: University of Texas Press, 1963. xiv, 642 p.

————. *Attack and Counter-attack: The Texas-Mexican Frontier, 1842.* Austin, TX: University of Texas Press, 1964. xiv, 750 p.

b. During the Porfiriato

Cosío Villegas, Daniel. *Estados Unidos contra Porfirio Diaz.* Mexico City: Hermes, 1956. 344 p. Reprinted Ed. Clio; Colegio Nacional, 1997. 265 p. Translated by Nettie Lee Benson as *The United States versus Porfirio Díaz.* Lincoln, NE: University of Nebraska Press, 1963. xii, 259 p.

Foster, John Watson. *Diplomatic Memoirs.* Boston: Houghton Mifflin, 1909. 2 v.

c. Early Twentieth Century

Moreno, Julio. *Yankee Don't Go Home: Mexican Nationalism, American Business Culture, and the Shaping of Modern Mexico, 1920–1950.* Chapel Hill, NC: University of North Carolina Press, 2003. vi, 321 p.

Wood, Bryce. *The Making of the Good Neighbor Policy.* New York: Macmillan, 1961. 438 p.

d. Occupation of Veracruz

Quirk, Robert E. *An Affair of Honor: Woodrow Wilson and the Occupation of Veracruz.* Lexington, KY: University of Kentucky Press, 1962. vii, 184 p. Reprinted New York: Norton, 1967.

Sweetman, Jack. *The Landing at Veracruz, 1914: The First Complete Chronicle of a Strange Encounter . . .* Annapolis: United States Naval Institute, 1968. xvi, 224 p.

e. Presidency of Calles

Horn, James J. "El embajador Sheffield contra el Presidente Calles," *Historia mexicana* 20(2):265–84 (1970).

f. Since World War II

Agee, Philip. *Inside the Company: CIA Diary.* London: Allen Lane; Harmondsworth: Penguin, 1975. 639 p.; American edition, New York: Stonehill, 1975. 639 p.

Aguayo Quezada, Sergio, et al. *Almanaque Mexico-Estados Unidos.* Mexico City: Fondo de Cultura Económica. Ideas y Palabras, 2005. 326 p.

Alisky, Marvin. "U.S.-Mexican Relations," *Intellect* (February 1978): 292–94.

Baer, M. Delal. "Mexico: Ambivalent Ally," *Washington Quarterly* (Summer 1987): 103–13.

————. "Misreading Mexico," *Foreign Policy* (Fall 1997): 138–49.

————. "The Sting Mexicans Can't Forgive, Forget," *Los Angeles Times* (June 21, 1998).

————. "The U.S. at Odds with Itself on Mexico," *Washington Post* (June 1, 1998): A17.

Brown, Lyle C. and Wilkie, James W. "Recent United States-Mexican Relations," in *Twentieth Century Foreign Policy*, ed. John Braeman. Columbus, OH: Ohio State University Press, 1971.

Dimensions of United States-Mexican Relations: Papers Prepared for the Bilateral Commission on the Future of United States-Mexican Relations. Edited by Rosario Green and Peter H. Smith. [San Diego]: Center for US-Mexican Studies, University of California, San Diego, 1989. 5 v. v 1: Images of Mexico in the United States. Edited by John H. Coatsworth and Carlos Rico. 1989. xi, 137 p.; v 2: The Economics of Interdependence: Mexico and the United States. Edited by William Glade and Cassio Luiselli, translated from La economía de la interdependencia. xi, 183 p.; v 3: Mexican Migration to the United States: Origins, Consequences, and Policy Options. Edited by Wayne A. Cornelius and Jorge A. Bustamante. 1989. xi, 181 p.; v 4: The Drug Connection in U.S.-Mexican relations. Edited by Guadalupe González and Marta Tienda. xi, 137 p.; v 5: Foreign Policy in U.S.-Mexican Relations. Edited by Rosario Green and Peter H. Smith. xi, 244 p.

Fagen, Richard R. "Realities of US-Mexican Relations," *Foreign Affairs* (July 1977): 685–700.

Klein, Dianne. "Mexico Turns to PR to Improve Image in the U.S.," *Houston Chronicle* (April 20, 1986): 20.

Paz, Octavio. "Mexico and the United States, Positions and Counter-positions," in his *Tiempo nublado*. (Biblioteca Breve) Mexico City: Seix Barral, 1983.

g. Since the Creation of NAFTA

United States State Dept. "U.S. Relations with Mexico," *Annual Policy Report.* Washington, DC: GPO for Inter-American Affairs, State Dept., 1998.

h. Migration and the U.S.–Mexican Border

Alisky, Marvin. "U.S.-Mexican Border Conflicts," *South Eastern Latin Americanist* (September 1973): 1–6.

The Border that Joins: Mexican Migrants and U.S. Responsibilities, ed. Peter Brown and Henry Shue. Totowa, NJ: Rowman and Littlefield, 1983. x, 254 p.

Briggs, Vernon Mason and Gordeon, Wendell. "United States Border Policy," *Social Science Quarterly* (December 1975): 476–91.

Bustamante, Jorge A. *Espaldas mojadas: a materia para la expansión del capital norteamericana.* Mexico City: Colegio de México, 1975. 2a ed., 1983. 45 p.

Akers Chacón, Justin and Davis, Mike. *No One is Illegal: Fighting Racism and State Violence on the U.S.-Mexico Border.* Chicago: Haymarket Books: 2006.

Jamail, Milton E. and Gutiérrez, Marzo. *The United States-Mexico Border.* Austin, TX: 1980. Revised and updated as *The Border Guide: Institutions and Organizations of the United States-Mexico Borderlands.* Austin, TX: Center for Mexican-American Studies, 1992. x, 193 p.

Views Across the Border: The United States and Mexico, ed. Stanley Robert Ross. Albuquerque, NM: University of New Mexico Press, 1978. xiv, 456 p.

8. Canada

Natural Allies? Canadian and Mexican Perspectives on International Security. Ed. H. P. Klepak. Ottawa, Ont.: Carlton University Press, 1996. 208 p.

9. Europe

Cruz Miramontes, Rodolfo. *Las relaciones comerciales multilaterales de México y el tratado de comercio con la Unión europea,* Mexico City: Universidad Iberoamericana, 2003. 237 p.

a. The United Kingdom

Johnston, Henry McKenzie. *Missions to Mexico: A Tale of British Diplomacy in the 1820s.* London: British Academic Press, 1992. xv, 301 p.

Meyer, Lorenzo. *Su majestad británica contra la revolución mexicana, 1900–1950: el fin de un imperio informal.* Mexico City: Colegio de México, 1991. 579 p.

Tischendorf, Alfred Paul. *Great Britain and Mexico in the Era of Porfírio Diaz.* Durham, NC: Duke University Press, 1961. xii, 197 p.

———. "Britain's Disastrous Adventure in Mexican Real Estate and Rubber, 1885–1911," *Inter-American Economic Affairs* 13(3):72–86 (1959).

b. France

Fuentes Mares, José. *La emperatriz Eugenia y su aventura mexicana.* Mexico City: Colegio de México, 1976. ix, 243 p.

García Cantú, Gastón. *La intervención francesa en México.* México City: Clío, 1998. 181 p.

Lally, Frank Edward. *French Opposition to the Mexican Policy of the Second Empire.* Baltimore, MD: Johns Hopkins Press, 1931. 163 p.

Maximilien et le Mexique, 1864–1867: histoire et littérature: de l'Empire aux "Nouvelles de l'Empire." Ed. Daniel Meyran. Illus. Leopoldo Flores. Perpignan: Presse de l'Université de Perpignan, 1992. 154 p.

Penot, Jacques. *Méconnaissance, connaissance et reconnaissance de l'independance du Mexique par la France.* Paris: Éditions Hispaniques, 1975, 132 p.

c. The Netherlands

Vuurde, Rob[ert Edouard Maarten] van. *Nederland, olie en de Mexicaanse revolutie, 1900–1950.* Utrecht: Vakgroep Geschiedenis der Universiteit, 1994. Translated by Sonia E. van Nipsen as *Los Paises Bajos, el petroleo y la Revolución mexicana, 1900–1950.* Amsterdam: Thela, 1997. vi, 160 p.

d. Germany and Austria

Katz, Friedrich. *Deutschland, Diaz und die mexikanische Revolution.* East Berlin: 1964. Revised, enlarged, and translated as *The Secret War in Mexico: Europe, the United States, and the Mexican Revolution.* Chicago: University of Chicago Press, 1981. xii, 659 p.

Schuler, Friedrich. "Germany, Mexico, and the United States during the Second World War," *Jahrbuch für Geschichte von Staat, Wirtschaft und Gesellschaft Lateinamerikas* 22:456–78 (1985).

e. Switzerland

Die Schweiz und Lateinamerika im 20. Jahrhundert: Aspekte ihrer Wirtschaft und Finanzbeziehungern. Ed. Walther Bernecker et al. Frankfut am Main: P. Larig, 1997. 261 p.

f. Italy

De Micheli, Alfredo. "Corrientes de cultura entre Italia y la Nueva España," *Revista de la Universidad de México* 31(4/5):89–92 (December 1976–January 1977).

g. Russia and Eastern Europe

Kruszewksi, Zbigniew Anthony and Richardson, William. *Mexico and the Soviet Union: The Foreign Policy of a Middle Power.* Bolder, CO: Westview Press, 1986. 170 p.

Institut Latinskoi Ameriki. *Sovetsko-meksikanskie otnosheniia, 1917–1980: Sbornki dokumentov.* Ed. A. I. Sizonenko and L. Cárdenas. Moscow: Mizhdunarodnye Otnosheniia, 1981. 111 p. Translated as *Relaciones mexicanosoviéticas 1917–1980.* Mexico City: SRE, 1981. 191 p.

Richardson, William Harrison. *Mexico Through Russian Eyes, 1806–1940.* Pittsburgh, PA: University of Pittsburgh Press, 1988. xi, 287 p.

Spencer, Daniela. *The Impossible Triangle: Mexico, Soviet Russia, and the United States in the 1920s.* Durham, NC: Duke University Press, 1999. xiv, 254 p.

10. China

Relaciones diplomáticas entre México y China, 1898–1948. Ed. Felipe Pardinas. Mexico City: Secretaría de Relaciones Exteriores, 1982. 2 v.

11. The Philippines

Yuste López, Carmen. *El Comercio de la Nueva España con Filipinas, 1500–1785.* Mexico City: INAH, 1984. 98 p.

XXXIV. MILITARY HISTORY AND POLICY

A. Colonial

Archer, Christian L. *The Army in Bourbon Mexico, 1760–1810.* Albuquerque, NM: University of New Mexico Press, 1977. xv, 366 p.

———. "Politicization of the Army of New Spain during the War of Independence, 1810–1821," in Jaime E. Rodríguez O. *The Evolution of the Mexican Political System.* Wilmington: SR Books, 1993: 17–44.

López Urruita, Carlos. *El Real Ejército de California.* Madrid: Grupo Medusa, 2000. 317 p.

B. Nineteenth Century

Alexius, Robert M. "The Army and Politics in Porfirian Mexico." PhD diss., University of Texas at Austin, 1976.

C. Twentieth Century

Lieuwen, Edwin. *Mexican Militarism: The Political Rise and Fall of the Revolutionary Army, 1910–1940.* Albuquerque, NM: University of New Mexico Press, 1968. xiii, 194 p. Reprinted Westport, CN: Greenwood, 1981.

Salas, Elizabeth. *"Soldaderas" in the Mexican Military: Myth and History.* Austin, TX: University of Texas Press, 1990. xiii, 163 p.

D. Today's Armed Forces

1. The Army

The Modern Mexican Military: A Reassessment, ed. David F. Ronfeldt. La Jolla: University of California San Diego Center for US-Mexican Studies, 1984, x, 218 p.

2. The Air Force

Frawley, Gerard. *The International Directory of Military Aicraft, 1998/99*. Canberra: Aerospace Publications, 1998. 191 p.

Ragsdale, Kenneth B. *Wings over the Mexican Border: Pioneer Military Aviation in the Big Bend*. Austin, TX: University of Texas Press, 1984. xxv, 266 p.

3. The Navy

"Mexico" in *Jane's Fighting Ships*. 198th ed., *2005–2006*. Coulson, UK: Janes, 2005: 480–91.

E. Guerrilla Warfare

1. The EZN

Ronfeldt, David, et al. *The Zapatista Social Network in Mexico*. Santa Monica: Rand Arroyo Center for the United States Army, 1998. xiii, 168 p.

Weinberg, Bill. *Homage to Chiapas: The New Indigenous Struggles in Mexico*. London: Verso, 2000. xxiv, 456 p.

The Zapatista Reader. By José Saramango et al., ed. Tom Hayden. New York: Thunder's Mouth Press, 2002. vii, 503 p.

XXXV. SOCIAL HISTORY

A. General

Alba, Victor. *Las ideas sociales contemporáneas en México*. ("Historia de las ideas en América.") Mexico City: Fondo de Cultura Económica, 1960. 473 p.

Iturriaga. José E. *La estructura social y cultural de México*. Mexico City: 1951. Reprinted Secretaría de Educación Pública, 1987. 287 p.

Sierra, Justo. *México, su evolución social.* Mexico City: 1900–1902. 3 v.

1. Colonial

Céspedes del Castillo, G. "La sociedad colonial americana en los siglos xvi y xvii," in his *Historia social y económica de España y America.* Barcelona, 1961.

Lewis, Laura. *Hall of Mirrors: Power, Witchcraft, and Caste in Colonial Mexico.* Durham, NC: Duke University Press, 2003. xiv, 280 p.

2. Modern

Wilkie, James Wallace. *The Mexican Revolution: Federal Expenditure and Social Change since 1910.* Berkeley, CA: University of California Press, 1967. xxix, 337 p., 2nd ed., revised, 1970, with a foreword by Howard F. Cline. 2nd rev. ed. 1970. xxxi, 337 p.

B. Rural Life

Malina, Robert. *Patterns of Childhood Mortality and Growth Status in a Rural Zapotec Community [in Oaxaca].* Austin, TX: University of Texas at Austin, 1970. 25 p.

Martin, Cheryl. *Rural Society in Colonial Morelos.* Albuquerque, NM: University of New Mexico Press, 1985. 255 p.

Whetten, Nathan Laselle. *Rural Mexico.* Chicago: University of Chicago Press, 1948. xxv, 671 p.

C. Urban Life

Hayner, Norman Sylvester. *New Patterns in Old Mexico: A Study of Town and Metropolis.* New Haven, CT: College and University Press, 1966. 316 p.

XXXVI. DEMOGRAPHY

Alba [Hernández], Francisco. *La población de México.* Mexico City: Colegio de México, 1976. xiv, 122 p.; revised as *La población de México: evolución y dilemas.* 1977. viii, 189 p.; translated by Marjory Mattingly Urquidi as *The Population of Mexico: Trends, Issues, and Policies.* New Brunswick: Transaction Books, 1982. xii, 127 p.

Alisky, Marvin. "Mexico versus Malthus," *Current History* (May 1974): 200–203, 227–30.

———. "Mexico's Population Pressures," *Current History* (March 1977): 106–10, 131–34.

Brachet de Márquez, Vivane. *La población de los estados mexicanos en el siglo xix, 1824–1895.* Mexico City: INAH, 1976. 141 p.

Cook, Sherburne Friend. *Essays in Population History: Mexico and the Caribbean.* Berkeley, CA: University of California Press, 1971. 450 p.

Turner, Frederick C. *Responsible Parenthood: Politics of Mexico's New Population Policies.* Washington, DC: American Enterprise Institute, 1974. 43 p.

A. Internal Migration

Browning, Harley. *Selectivity of Migrants to a Metropolis in a Developing Country: A Mexican Case Study.* Austin, TX: Institute of Latin American Studies, University of Texas, 1969. 347 p.

Hopgood, James. *Settlers of Bajavista: Social and Economic Adaptation in a Mexican Squatter Settlement.* Athens, OH: Center of International Studies, 1979. 145 p.

Lomnitz, Larissa Adler. *Networks and Marginality: Life in a Mexican Shantytown.* New York: Academic Press, 1977. 230 p.

Silvers, Arthur L. *Rural Development and Urban-Bound Migration in Mexico.* Washington, DC: Resources for the Future, 1980. 150 p.

B. Immigration

Herrera Barreda, María del Socorro. *Inmigrantes hispanocubanos en México durante el porfirato.* Mexico City: M. A. Porrúa, 304 p.

Meyer, Eugenia and Salgado, Eva. *Un refugio en la memoria: la experiencia de los exilios latinoamericanos en México.* Mexico City: Océano, 2002. 361 p.

Wei, Karen T. "Chinese Immigration to Mexico from the Nineteenth Century to 1911," in *Technology, the Environment and Social Change: Papers of the XXXIIIrd Annual Meeting of the Seminar on the Acquisition of Latin American Library Materials, Guadalajara, May, 1993.* Albuquerque, NM: SALALM Secretariat, 1995: 320–27.

1. Bibliography

Extranjeros en México, 1821–1990: bibliografía. Ed. Dolores Pla et al. Mexico City: INAH, 1993. 153 p.

C. Emigration

Ál, Marvin. "Mexican Americans Make Themselves Heard," *The Reporter* (February 9, 1967): 45–48.

———. "Migration and Unemployment in Mexico," *Current History* (December 1983): 429–32.

———. "Population and Migration Problems in Mexico," *Current History* (November 1981): 365–69, 387–88.

1. Bibliography

Meier, Matt S. *Bibliography of Mexican American History.* Westport, CT: Greenwood, 1984. xi, 500 p.

Valdez, Robert Otto Burciaga, et al. *An Annotated Bibliography of Sources on Mexican Immigration.* Santa Monica, CA: RAND, 1987. x, 57 p.

XXXVII. HEALTH, MEDICAL CARE, AND WELFARE

Cooper, Donald B. *Epidemic Disease in Mexico City, 1761–1813: An Administrative, Social, and Medical Study.* Austin, TX: University of Texas Press, 1965. x, 236 p.

Hernández Ramos, Juan Manuel. "Health Care for the Poor in Mexico: Which is More Effective, the Social Security System or the Ministry of Health." PhD diss., University of Liverpool, 2001.

Mazzaferri, Anthony. *Public Health and Social Revolution in Mexico, 1877–1930.* Kent, OH: Kent State University, 1968. 393 p.

National Economic Research Associates. *The Health Care System in Mexico.* London: Pharmaceutical Partners for Better Health Care, 1998. xvii, 249 p.

Newson, Linda A. "Medical Practice in Early Colonial Spanish America: A Prospectus," *Bulletin of Latin American Research* 25(3):367–91 (July 2006).

Reshaping Health Care in Latin America: A Comparative Analysis of Health Care Reform in Argentina, Brazil and Mexico. Ed. Sonia Fleury, Susana Belmarino, and Enis Baris. Ottawa: International Development Research Centre, 2000. x, 279 p.

A. Folk Medicine

Abelar, Taisha. *The Sorcerers' Crossing.* New York: Viking Arkana, 1992. xiii, 252 p. Reprinted London: Penguin, 1993.

Aguirre Beltrán, Gonzalo. *Medicina y magía: proceso de aculturación en la estrutura colonial.* Mexico City: Instituto Nacional Indigenista, 1963. 443 p. Reprinted 1992. 389 p.

XXXVIII. THE WORKING CLASS AND THE POOR

Lewis, Oscar. *Five Families: Mexican Case Studies in the Culture of Poverty.* New York: Basic Books, 1959. 351 p.

Ruiz, Ramón Eduardo. *Mexico: Challenge of Poverty and Illiteracy.* San Marino, CA: Huntington Library, 1963. xiv, 234 p. Translated by María Elena Hope as *México, 1920–1958: el reto de la pobreza y del analfabetismo.* Mexico City: Fond de Cultura Económica, 1977. 263 p.

Serrón, Luis A. *Scarcity, Exploitation, and Poverty: Malthus and Marx in Mexico.* Norman, OK: University of Oklahoma Press, 1980. xxiv, 279 p.

XXXIX. RACE RELATIONS AND ANTHROPOLOGY

Bernal, Ignacio. *Museo Nacional de Antropología; Arqueología.* Mexico City: Aguilar, 1967; translated by Carolyn B. Czitron as *The Mexican National Museum of Anthropology.* London: Thames and Hudson, 1968. 216 p. and as *3000 Years of Art and Life in Mexico.* New York: Abrams, 1968. 2nd ed. of original Spanish, 1969. 418 p.

Cervantec, María Antionata. *National Anthropological Museum.* Barcelona: Grijalbo, 1980; 2a. ed., 1983. 195 p.

Levine, Robert M. *Race and Ethnic Relations in Latin America and the Caribbean: A Historical Dictionary.* Metuchen, NJ: Scarecrow Press, 1980. viii, 252 p.

A. Indians

Aguirre Beltrán, Gonzalo. *El Proceso de aculturación.* Mexico City: Universidad Nacional Autónoma de México, 1957. 269 p.

Aguirre Beltrán, Gonzalo, and Poazas, Ricardo. *Instituciones indígenas en el México actual.* Mexico City: Fondo de Cultura Económica, 1960.

Ariel de Vidas, Anath. *Thunder Doesn't Live Here Any More: The Culture of Marginality Among the Teeneks of Tantoyaca.* Boulder, CO: University Press of Colorado, 2004. xviii, 436 p.

Beals, Ralph L. "Anthropology in Contemporary Mexico," in *Contemporary Mexico Papers* of the IV International Congress of Mexican History, ed.

James W. Wilkie, Michael C. Meyer, and Edna Monzón de Wilkie. Berkeley, CA: Univeristy of California Press, 1975.

Guarisco, Claudia. *Los indios del valle de México y la construcción de una nueva sociabilidad política, 1770–1835.* Zinacantepec: Colegio Mexiquense, 2003. 289 p.

Redfield, Robert. *Tepoztlan, a Mexican Village: A Study of Folk Life.* Chicago: University of Chicago Press, 1930. xi, 247 p.

Serdán, Félix. *Félix Serdán: memorias de un guerrillero.* Ed. Renato Ravelo Lecuoma. Mexico City: Rizoma, 2002. 217 p.

B. Blacks

www.afromex.com

C. Chinese

Mesa, Rosa Q. "Los chinos en México, 1947–1959," *Technology, the Environment and Social Change: Papers of the XXXIIIrd Annual Meeting of the Seminar on the Acquisition of Latin American Library Materials, Guadalajara, May, 1993.* Albuquerque, NM: SALALM Secretariat, 1995: 332–41.

D. Jews

Elkin, Judith Larkin. "Latin America's Jews: A Review of Sources," *Latin American Research Review* 20(2):124–41 (1985).

E. Germans and Austrians

Katz, Friedrich. *Österreicher im Exil: Mexiko 1938–1947: eine Dokumentation,* Vienna: Deuticke, 2002. 704 p.

Zogbaum, Heidi. "Vicente Lombardo Toledano and the German Communist Exile in Mexico, 1940–1947," *JILAS, Journal of Iberian and Latin American Studies* 11(2):1–28 (La Trobe: December 2005).

F. South Americans

Blanck de Cerejildo, Fanny, et al. *El exilio argentino en la Ciudad de México.* Mexico City: Instituto de Culura de la Ciudad, 1999. 41 p.

En México, entre exilios: una experiencia de sudamericanos. Por María Luis Tavares et al.; ed. Pablo Yankelevich. Mexico City: Plaza y Valdés, 1998. 222 p.

G. Spaniards

Smith, Lois Elwyn. "Mexico and the Spanish Republicans," *University of California Publications in Political Science* 4(2):165–315 (1955).

XL. SEX, SEXISM, GENDER, AND SEXUAL ATTITUDES

Bary, Paul. "Sexuality and Gender in Colonial and 19th-Century Mexico: New Uses and Interpretations of Photographs in the Tulane Collection," *Latin American Identities: Race, Ethnicity, Gender, and Sexuality: Papers of the XLVIth Annual Meeting of the Seminar on the Acquisition of Latin American Library Materials, Tempe, AZ, May 26–29, 2001.* Austin, TX: SALALM Secretariat, 2005: 89–97.

Náñez Falcón, Guillermo. "Actos Prohibidos: Documenting Sexuality in Colonial Mexico from Documents in the Latin American Library, Tulane University," *Latin American Identities: Race, Ethnicity, Gender, and Sexuality: Papers of the XLVIth Annual Meeting of the Seminar on the Acquisition of Latin American Library Materials, Tempe, AZ, May 26–29, 2001.* Austin, TX: SALALM Secretariat, 2005: 79–88.

A. Homosexuality

Carrier, Joseph. *De Los Otros: Intimacy and Homosexuality Among Mexican Men.* New York: Columbia University Press, 1995. xxii, 231 p.

Carrillo, Héctor. *The Night is Young: Sexuality in Mexico in the Time of AIDS.* Chicago: University of Chicago Press, 2002. xiii, 371 p.

The Famous 41: Sexuality and Social Control in Mexico, 1901. Ed. Robert McKee Irwin et al. Basingstoke, UK: Palgrave Macmillan, 2003. xii, 311 p.

Guillén, Laura. *Soy homosexual.* Mexico City: Ediciones del Milenio, 1994. 213 p.

B. Women

Confronting Change, Challenging Tradition: Women in Latin American History. Gertude M. Yeager, editor. Wilmington, DE: Scholarly Resources, 1994. xxi, 242 p.

Franco, Jean. *Plotting Women: Gender and Representation in Mexico.* London: Verso, 1989. 235 p.

Gonzalbo, Pilar. *Las mujeres en la Nueva España: educación y vida cotidiana.* Mexico City: Centro de Estudios Históricos del Colegio de México. 1987. 323 p.

Hirsch, Jennifer S. *A Courtship After Marriage: Sexuality and Love in Mexican Transitional Families.* Berkeley, CA: University of California Press, 2003. xxi, 376 p.

Reyes Manzo, Carlos. "The Crosses of Juárez" in *Open Democracy* (February 16, 2006) at www.opendemocracy.net.

Rodríguez, Victoria Elizabeth. *Women in Contemporary Mexican Politics.* Austin, TX: University of Texas Press, 2003. xxi, 322 p.

Schaefer, Claudia. *Textured Lives: Women, Art, and Representation in Modern Mexico.* Tucson, AZ: University of Arizona Press, 1992. xvi, 163 p.

Vallens, Vivian M. *Working Women in Mexico During the Porfiriato, 1880–1910.* San Francisco: R&E Research Associates, 1978. vii, 98 p.

1. Bibliography

Latinas of the Americas: A Source Book, ed. K. Lynn Stoner. New York: Garland, 1989. xix, 692 p.

Lindvall, Karen J. "Women in the Maquilladoras: A Guide to Literature on Female Labor Participation in Mexico's Border Industries," *Latin American Masses and Minorities: Their Images and Realities. Papers of the XXXth Annual Meeting of the Seminar on the Acquisition of Latin American Library Materials, Princeton, NJ, June 19–23, 1985.* Madison WI: SALALM Secretariat, 1987: v 1, 192–214.

2. Statistics

Martínez Fernández, Alicia Inés. *México.* ("Mujeres latino-americans en cifras," coord. Teresa Valdés Echeñique and Enrique Gomáriz Moraga, (v 12). Madrid: Instituto de la Mujer; Santiago de Chile: FLASCO, 1995. 127 p.

XLI. FAMILIES, CHILDREN, AND YOUTH

Byrnes, Dolores M. *Driving the State: Families and Public Policy in Central Mexico.* Ithaca, NY: Cornell University Press, 2003. x, 229 p.

Holt, Pat M. "Mexico's Dramatically Shrinking Families," *The Christian Science Monitor* (June 21, 1999): 9.

Investigation on the Trafficking, Sex Tourism, Pornography and Prostitution of Children in Central America and Mexico: Regional Synthesis. Ed. Gustavo Leal. San José, CR: Casa Alianza Internacional, 2002. 160 p.

Klich, Kent. *El Niño, en berättelse om gautbarn i Mexico City.* [Stockholm?].: 1999. 168 p. Translated as: *El Niño: Children of the Streets, Mexico City . . .* : *Photographs by Kent Klich; Text by Elena Poniatowska.* Syracuse, NY: Syracuse University Press, 1999. 167 p.

Minor Omissions: Children in Latin American History and Society. Ed. Tobias Hecht. Madison, WI: University of Wisconsin Press, 2002. viii, 277 p.

Simonelli, Jeanne. *Two boys, a girl and enough: Reproductive and Economic Decision Making on the Mexican Periphery.* Boulder, CO: Westview, 1986. 230 p.

Stern, Alexandra Minna. "Responsible Mothers and Normal Children: Eugenics, Nationalism, and Welfare in Post-Revolutionary Mexico, 1920–1940," *Journal of Historical Sociology* 12(4):369–97 (1999).

XLII. LANGUAGE

A. Mexican Spanish

1. Bibliographies

A Bibliographical Guide to Materials on American Spanish, ed. Madaline Walls Nicols. Cambridge, MA: Harvard University Press, 1941. xii, 114 p.

Davis, Jack Emory, "The Spanish of Mexico: An Annotated Bibliography for 1940–1969," *Hispania* 54:624–56 (1971).

2. Dictionaries

Company, Concepción. *Léxico histórico del Español de México: régimen, clases funcionales, usos sintácticos, frecuencias y variación gráfica.* Mexico City: Instituto de Investigaciones Filológicas de la UNAM, 2002. 952 p.

Santamaría, Francisco Javier. *Diccionario de mejicanismos.* Mexico City, 1978. 2a ed., corregida y aumentada. Mexico City: Porrúa, 2000. xxiv, 1,207 p.

3. General Works

Unidad y variación léxicas del español de América. Ed. Gerd Wotjak and Klaus Zimmermann. Frankfurt am Main: Vervuert; Madrid: Ibero-americana, 1994. 249 p.

B. Indigenous Languages

Cifuentes, Bárbara. *Letras sobre voces: multilingüismo a través de la historia.* Mexico City: CIESAS: Instituto Indigenista Interamericana, 1998. 340 p.

De Boe de Harris, María and Daly, Margarita H. de. *Bibliografía del Instituto Lingüístico de Verano en México, 1935–1984.* Mexico City: Summer Institute of Linguistics, 1985. xxii, 204 p.

Heath, Shirley Brice. *Telling Tongues: Language Policy in Mexico, colony to nation.* New York: Teachers College Press, 1972. xx, 300 p.

Ligorred Perramón, Francisco de Asis. *Lenguas indígenas de México y Centroamérica: de los jeroglíficos al siglo xxi.* Madird: MAPFRE, 1982. 305 p.

Mariano Flores, Anselmo. *Bibliografía lingüística de la República Mexicana.* Mexico City: Instituto Indigenista Interamericana, 1957. 95 p.

"Mexico" in *Living Languages of the Americas.* Dallas, TX: Summer Institute of Linguistics, 1996.

XLIII. FICTION WITH A MEXICAN SETTING PUBLISHED OUTSIDE MEXICO

A. Individual Novels

1. Originally Written in English (Chronologically)

Titles for children omitted if first published after World War II.

Reid, Mayne. *The Scalp Hunters.* Philadelphia: Lippincott, Grambo, 1851. 204 p. Reprinted as *The Scalp Hunters; or, Romantic Adventures in Northern Mexico.* London: C. J. Skeet, 1852, and as *The Scalp Hunters: A Thrilling Tale of Adventure and Romance in Northern Mexico.* New York: Hurst, 1899. 468 p.

Wallace, Lew. *The Fair God; or, The Last of the 'Tzins: A Tale of the Conquest of Mexico.* Boston: Osgood, 1873. British ed., *The Fair God: A Tale of the Conquest of Mexico.* London: Frederick Warne, [19–?]. xvi, 411 p. Reprinted as *The Fair God; or, The Last of the 'Tzins.* Philadelphia: Polyglot Press, 2005.

Henty, George Alfred. *By Right of Conquest; or, With Cortez in Mexico.* London: Blackie, [1880?]. Reprinted Latimer House, 1957. 223 p. Adventure tale for boys.

Janvier, Thomas Allibone. *The Aztec Treasure House: A Romance of Contemporaneous Antiquity.* New York: Harper, 1890. Reprinted Upper Saddle River, NY: Gregg Press, 1970. viii, 446 p.

Haggard, Henry Rider. *Montezuma's Daughter.* London: Longmans, Green, 1893. 325 p.

Steinbeck, John. "The Pearl of the World," *Women's Home Companion* (1902). Reprinted as *The Pearl.* New York: Viking, 1947. 87 p.

Janvier, Thomas Allibone. *Legends of the City of Mexico.* New York: Harper, 1910. xviii, 164 p.

Tomlinson, Everett Titsworth. *Scouting with General Funston.* Garden City, NY: Doubleday, Page, 1917. xi, 243 p. Reprinted as *Scouting in the Desert.* New York: Appleton, 1927. vii, 243 p.

Cooke, Arthur Owens. *The Luck of Colin Charteris: A Story of Adventure in Modern Mexico.* London: Blackie, [1920?]. 320 p.

Hamby, William Henry. *The Ranch of the Thorn: An Adventure Story.* New York: Chelsea House, 1924. 312 p.

Bellamy, Francis Rufus. *Spanish Faith: A Romance of Old Mexico and the Caribbean.* New York: Harper, 1926. 378 p.

Lawrence, David Herbert. *The Plumed Serpent.* London, Martin Secker, 1926. 426 p. Reissued as *The Plumed Serpent, Quetzalcoatl.* Introduction by William York Tindall. New York, Knopf, 1951. xiv, 445 p.

Treadwell, Sophie. *Lusita.* New York: J. Cape & H. Smith, 1931. 248 p.

Le May, Alan. *Thunder in the Dust.* New York: Farrar & Rinehart, 1934. 301 p.

Beals, Carleton. *The Stones Awake: A Novel of Mexico.* Philadelphia: Lippincott, 1936. 464 p.

Cain, James Mallahan. *Serenade.* New York: Knopf, 1937. 314 p. Reprinted as *Serenade in Mexico.* Amsterdam: Querido, 1938. 183 p.

Grayson, Rupert. *Gun Cotton in Mexico.* London: Grayson & Grayson, 1937. 283 p.

Aiken, Conrad. *A Heart for the Gods of Mexico.* London: Secker, 1939. 156 p. Reprinted Norwood, PA: Norwood Editions, 1976. 146 p.

Greene, Graham. *The Power and the Glory.* London: Heinemann, 1940. Reissued as a Heinemann pocket edition, 1945. 169 p.

Niggli, Josephina. *Mexican Village.* Chapel Hill, NC: University of North Carolina Press, 1945. Reprinted Albuquerque, NM: University of New Mexico Press, 1994. xxxi, 491 p.

Lowry, Malcolm. *Under the Volcano.* London: Cape, 1947. 395 p. Reprinted New York: Lippincott, 1947. 376 p.

Gillmor, Frances. *Flute of the Smoking Mirror: A Portrait of Nezahualcóyotl, Poet-King of the Aztecs.* Albuquerque, NM: University of New Mexico Press, 1949. Reprinted Tucson, AZ: 1968. 183 p.

MacDonald, John Dann. *The Damned.* [New York?]: 1952. 192 p. Reprinted London: Robert Hale, 2005.

Bellow, Saul. *The Adventures of Augie March, a Novel.* New York: Viking, 1953. 536 p.

Orourke, Frank. *High Dive.* New York: Random House, 1954. 205 p.

Kerouac, Jack. *On the Road.* New York: Viking, 1957. 310 p.

———. *Mexico City Blues.* New York: Grove Press, 1959. 244 p.

———. *Tristessa,* New York: Avon, 1960. 126 p.

Stacton, David. *A Signal Victory.* London: Faber & Faber, 1960. 224 p.

Gavin, Catherine Irvine. *The Cactus and the Crown.* London: Hodder & Stoughton, 1962. 384 p.

Gillmor, Frances. *The King Danced in the Market Place.* Illustrated by Carolyn Huff Kinsey. Tucson, AZ: University of Arizona Press, 1964. xvi, 271 p.

Kerouac, Jack. *Desolation Angels: A Novel.* New York: Coward-McCann, 1965. xxviii, 366 p.

Taylor, Robert Lewis. *Two Roads to Guadalupé.* London: Deutsch, 1965. 42 p.

Bagley, Desmond. *The Vivero Letter.* London: Fontana Books, 1968. 238 p.

Lowry, Malcolm. *Dark as the Grave Wherein my Friend is Laid.* Toronto: General Pub. Co., 1968. xxiii, 255 p. Reprinted New York: New American Library, 1968. xxiii, 255 p.

Higgins, Jack. *The Wrath of God,* by James Graham [pseud]. Garden City, NY: Doubleday; 1971. 277 p; London: Macmillan, 223 p.

Wilson, Carter. *A Green Tree and a Dry Tree.* New York: Macmillan, 1972. 300 p.

Oliver, Lange. *Incident at La Junta.* Stein & Day, 1973. 225 p.

Brandt. Jane Lewis. *La Chingada.* London: Cassell, 1979. 463 p.

Highwater, Jamake. *The Sun, He Dies.* New York: Lippinxorr Crowell, 1980. 216 p.

Jennings, Gary. *Aztec.* New York: Atheneum, 1980. 754 p.

Doerr, Harriet. *Stones for Ibarra.* 1978. New York: Viking Press, 1984. 214 p.

Deighton, Len. *Mexico Set.* London: Heinemann, 1984. 280 p. Reprinted New York: Knopf, 1985. 373 p.

Burroughs, William S. *Queer.* New York: Viking, 1985. xxiii, 134 p.

Ford, Richard. *The Ultimate Good Luck.* Boston: Houghton Mifflin, 1981. 201 p. Reprinted London: Collins, 1989. 208 p.

Scofield, Sandra Jean. *Gringa.* Sag Harbor, NY: Permanent Press, 1989. 267 p.

Portis, Charles. *Gringos: A Novel.* New York: Simon Schuster, 1991. 269 p.

Roberts, Nora. *Without Trace.* Richmond: Silhouette, 1991. 249 p.

Silko, Leslie Marmon. *Almanack of the Dead: A Novel.* New York: Simon & Schuster, 1991. 763 p.

Michener, James Albert. *Mexico.* New York: Random House, 1992. xiii, 625 p.

Bignioides. Sandra. *A Place Where the Sea Remembers.* Minneapolis, MN: Coffee House Press, 1993. 151 p.

Doerr, Harriet. *Consider This, Señora.* New York: Harcourt Brace, 1993. 241 p.

Grafton, Sue. *J is for Judgment.* New York: Henry Holt, 1993. 288 p.

Carey, Gabrielle. *The Borrowed Girl.* Sydney, NSW: Picador Australia, 1994. 275 p.

Waller, Robert James. *Puerto Vallarta Squeeze: The Run for El Norte.* New York: Warner Books, 1995. 214 p.

Zollinger, Norman. *Chapultepec.* New York: Forge, 1995. 432 p.

Anderson, Kevin J. *Ruins.* ("The X-Files.") London: Voyager, 1996. 291 p.

Ireland, Ann. *The Instructor.* Toronto, ON: Doubleday Canada, 1996. 208 p.

Masters, Hilary. *Home is the Exile.* Sag Harbor, NY: Permanent Press, 1996. 286 p.

Maw, James. *Year of the Jaguar.* London: Sceptre, 1996. 326 p.

Morgan, Lee. *McMasters: Mexican Standoff.* New York: Jove, 1996. 186 p.

Porter, Alan C. *The Company of Heroes.* London: Robert Hale, 1996. 159 p.

Scofield, Sandra Jean. *A Chance to See Egypt.* New York: Harper Collins, 1996. 252 p.

Trolley, Jack. *Juarez Justice.* New York: Carroll & Graf, 1996. 241 p.

Harrington, Kent A. *Dia de los Muertos: Day of the Dead.* Tucson, AZ: Dennis Mcmillan, 1997. 244 p.; Reprint attributed to Harrington and James Crumley, Santa Barbara: Capra Press, 2003. 250 p.

Preston, Alison. *A Blue and Golden Year.* Winnipeg: Turnstone Press, 1997. 182 p.

Rabassa, George. *Floating Kingdom: A Novel.* Minneapolis, MN: Coffee House Press, 1997. 324 p.

Bannister, Jo. *Unlawful Entry.* Sutton: Severn House, 1998. 192 p.

Brown, Sandra. *A Whole New Light.* London: Warner, 1998. 261 p.

Gifford, Barry. *The Sinaloa Story.* Edinburgh, Scotland: Rebel Inc., 1998. 231 p.

Johansen, Iris. *And Then You Die—.* London: Hodder & Stoughton; New York: Bantam Books, 1998. 344 p.

Mornau. C. G. *Scenes from a Dark Childhood.* London: Minerva Press, 1998. 129 p.

Walker, Alice. *By the Light of My Father's Smile: A Story of Requited Love, Crossing Over, and the Sexual Healing of the Soul.* London: Women's, 1998. 224 p.

Cabot, Angel. *Skipping Stones.* [n/p]: 1999.

Edwards, Dean. *The Valley of Death.* London: Robert Hale, 1999. 158 p.

Escandón, María Amparo. *Esperanza's Book of Saints.* New York: Scribner 1999. 254 p.

Kirwan, Ty. *Railroad Law.* London: Robert Hale, 1999. 159 p.

Orr, Alice. *Heat of Passion.* Richmond: Silhouette Intrigue, 1999. 251 p.

Ortez. Gustavo. *Rambling Rose.* Atlanta, GA: Minerva Press, 1999, 305 p.

Parry, Tom. *The Bandit Trail.* London: Robert Hale, 1999. 158 p.

Tetlow, L. D. *Piquito Trail.* London: Robert Hale, 1999, 160 p.

Thorn, Harry J. *The Far Side of the River.* London: Robert Hale, 1999. 160 p.

Easterman, Daniel. *The Jaguar Mask.* London: Harper Collins, 2000. 419 p.

Farcau, Bruce W. *A Little Empire of Their Own: A Novel of Old Mexico.* Arlington, VA: Vandamere Press, 2000. 344 p.

Lockwood, Glenn. *Ride for the Rio.* London: Robert Hale, 2000.

Major, Ann. *Wild Enough for Willa.* Richmond, VA: Mira, 2000. 379 p.

Runcie, James. *The Discovery of Chocolate.* London: Harper Collins, 2000. 264 p. Reissued, New York, 2001.

Aspinal, John Brian. *Gringo Soup.* London: Sceptre, 2001. 307 p.

Black, Rory. *Spurs of the Spectre.* London: Robert Hale, 2001. 157 p.

Clement, Jennifer. *A True Story Based on Lies.* Edinburgh, Scotland: Canongate, 2001. 164 p.

Gershten, Donna M. *Kissing the Virgin's Mouth: A Novel.* New York: Harper Collins, 2001. 267 p.

McCarthy, Cormac. *All the Pretty Horses.* London: Picador, 2001. 320 p.

Patino, Ernesto. *In the Shadow of a Stranger.* London: Robert Hale, 2001. 224 p.

Braverman, Kate. *The Incantation of Frida K.* New York: Seven Sisters Press, 2002. 235 p.

Delahunt, Meaghan. *In the Blue House.* London: Bloomsbury. Reprinted as *In the Casa Azul: A Novel of Revolution and Betrayal.* New York: St. Martin's Press, 2002. 308 p.

Gallagher, Jack. *Nullo.* London: Robert Hale, 2002. 158 p.

Benítez, Sandra. *Night of the Radishes.* New York: Theia, 2003. viii, 276 p.

Doctorow, Cory. *A Place so Foreign, and Eight More Stories.* New York: Four Walls Eight Windows, 2003. 258 p.

Hambly, Barbara. *Days of the Dead.* New York: Bantam Books, 2003. 314 p.

Patterson, Roy. *Apache Fury.* London: Robert Hale, 2003. 159 p.

Pierre, D. B. C., pseud. [i.e., Peter Finlay]. *Vernon God Little: A 21st Century Comedy in the Presence of Death.* London: Faber, 2003; Orlando, FL: Harcourt, 2004. 279 p.

Reilly, T. James. *Serenading Dionysus.* Peterborough, UK: Upfront Publishing, 2003. 235 p.

Sundeen, Mark. *The Making of the Toro: Bull Fights, Broken Hearts, and one Author's Quest for the Acclaim he Deserves.* New York: Simon & Schuster, 2003. 179 p.

Benke, Richard. *The Ghost Ocean: A Novel.* Albuquerque, NM: University of New Mexico Press, 2004. vii, 280 p.

Desai, Anita. *The Zig-Zag Way.* London: Chatto; Boston: Houghton Mifflin, 2004. 159 p.

Kelton, Elmer. *Jericho's Road.* New York: Forge, 2004. 288 p.

Newman, Robert. *The Fountain at the Centre of the World.* London: Verso; New York: Soft Skull Press, 2004. 334 p.

Bojanowski, Marc. *The Dog Fighter.* London: Duckworth, 2005. 291 p.

Hampson, Anne. *The Night is Ours.* Sutton: Severn House, 2005. 220 p.

Kellerman, Jesse. *Sunstroke.* New York: Putnam, 2005; London: Time Warner, 2006. 370 p.

Levack, Simon. *Shadow of the Lords: An Aztec Mystery.* London: Simon & Schuster, 2005. 392 p.

Spinrad, Norman. *Mexica.* London: Little Brown UK, 2005. 506 p.

Angsten, David. *Dark Gold.* New York: Thomas Dunne Books, 2006. 352 p.

Pollen, Bella. *Midnight Cactus.* London: Pan Macmillan, 2006. 256 p.

Sherwood, Frances. *Night of Sorrows: A Novel.* New York: Norton, 2006. 425 p.

a. Bibliography

Coan, Otis Weston and Lillard, Richard G. *America in Fiction: An Annotated List of Novels That Interpret Aspects of Life in the United States, Canada, and Mexico.* 5th ed. Palo Alto, CA: Pacific Books, 1967. viii, 232 p.

Gunn, Drewey Wayne. *Mexico in American and British Letters: A Bibliography of Fiction and Travel Books, Citing Original Editions.* Metuchen, NJ: Scarecrow Press, 1974. vii, 150 p.

Rutherford, John. *An Annotated Bibliography of the Novels of the Mexican Revolution of 1910–1917: In English and Spanish.* Troy, NY: Whitston, 1972. 180 p.

Walker, Ronald G. *Infernal Paradise: Mexico and the Modern English Novel.* Berkeley, CA: University of California Press, 1978. xvi, 391 p.

2. Originally Written in Spanish Outside of Mexico (by Original Publication Date)

Heredia y Heredia, José María. *Jicotencal.* [New York?]. 1826. Reprinted together with García Baamonde's *Xioténcal*, Mexico City: Instituto de Investigaciones Bibliográficas de la UNAM, 2003. 232 p.

García Baamonde, Salvador. *Xicoténcal, príncipe americano.* [Madrid?:] 1831. Reprinted together with José María Heredia's *Jicotencal*, Mexico City: 2003 (item 1624).

Gómez de Avellaneda y Arteaga, Gertrudis. *Gutimozin, último emperador de Méjico: novela histórica.* Madrid: Espinosa, 1846. 4 v in 1.

Madariaga, Salvador de. *El corazón de piedra verde.* Madrid: Espasa-Calpe, 1942. 644 p. Translated as *The Heart of Jade.* London: Collins, 1944. 547 p.

———. *Guerra en la sangre.* Translated as *War in the Blood.* London: Collins, 1957. 320 p.

Galeano, Eduardo H. *Memoria del fuego,* Madrid, Mexico City: 1982–1986, 3 v. Translated by Cedric Belfrage as *Memory of Fire.* London: Quartet; New

York, Pantheon, 1985–1988. 3 v. Uruguayan author's panorama of Latin American history: v 1. *Los nacimientos (Genesis)*; v 2: *Las caras y las máscaras (Faces and Masks)*: v 3: *El siglo de viento (Century of the Wind)*.

3. Originally Written in Czech

Frýd, Norbert. *Císarovna: román Charloty Mexické*. 3rd ed. Prague: Ceskoslovenský Spisovatel, 1977. 336 p.

4. Originally Written in French (by Original Publication Date)

Aimard, Gustave. *L'eclaireur*. Paris: Amyot, 1859. Translated as *The Indian Scout: A Story of the Aztec City*. London: Ward & Lock, 1861. vi, 429 p.

———. *Valentin Guillois*. Paris: Amyot, 1862. Reprinted Dentu, 1888. ii, 354 p. Translated as *The Red Track: A Story of Social Life in Mexico*. London: 1865. viii, 344 p.

———. *Le montonero*. Paris: Amyot, 1864. Translated as *The Insurgent Chief*. London: C. H. Clarke, 1867. 344 p.

Ferry, Gabriel [*pseud. of* Louis Bellemare]. *Costal l'Indien*. Paris: Hachette, 1891. 296 p.

Bibescu, [Princess] Marthe Lucie Lahovary. *Charlotte et Maximilien*. Paris: Gallimard, 1937. 221 p. Translated by John Ghika as *Carlota*. London: Heinemann, 1956. 214 p.

Cartano, Tony. *Le Conquistador: fiction*. Paris: Buchet-Chastel, 1973. 196 p.

———. *Bocanegra*. Paris. Grasset, 1984. 537 p. Translated by S. Fischman as *After the Conquest*. London: David & Charles, 1988.

Blais, Marie-Claire. *Soifs: roman*. Montreal: Boréal, 1995. 313 p. Translated by Sheila Fischman as *These Festive Nights*. Concord, ON: Anasi, 1997. 293 p.

Le Bris, Michel. *Les filibustiers de la Sonore*. Paris: Flammarion, 1998. 557 p.

5. Originally Written in German (by Original Publication Date)

May, Karl. *Benito Juarez: roman*. Bamberg, Karl-May, 1952.

Stucken, Eduard. *Die weissen Götter: ein Roman*. Berlin: R. Reiss, 1918. 2 v. Translated by Frederick H. Martens as *The Great White Gods: An Epic of the Spanish Invasion of Mexico and the Conquest of the Barbaric Aztec Culture of the New World*. New York: Farrar & Rinehart, 1934. 712 p.

De Cesco, Federica. *Der Prinz von Mexiko*. Düsseldorf: Benziger, 1965. Translated by Frances Lobb as *The Prince of Mexico*. New York: John Day; London: Burke, 1968. 224 p.

Janacs, Christoph. *Der Gesang des Coyotan: mexikanische Geschichten.* Innsbruck: Haymon, 2002. 173 p.

6. Originally Written in Japanese

Oe, Kensaburo. *Jinsei no Shinski.* Tokyo: Shinchosha, 1989. Translated by Margaret Mitsutani as *An Echo of Heaven.* London: Kodansha International, 1996. 204 p.

7. Originally Written in Portuguese

Queirós, Eça de. *O crime do Padre Amaro.* Lisbon: Castro Irmão, 1876. 362 p. New ed., published as: *Scenas da vida devota.* Oporto: 1880. ix, 675 p.; Translated by Nan Flanagan as *The Sin of Father Amaro.* London: Max Reinhardt, 1962. 351 p. Reprinted as *The Crime of Father Amaro,* Manchester: Carcanet Press, 1994.

8. Originally Written in Russian

Gordin, Iakov Arkad'evich. *Krestgny put' pobeditelei: istoriches-kii roman.* St. Petersburg: Pushkinskogo Fonda, 2003. 414 p.

XLIV. DEPICTION OF MEXICO IN FOREIGN LITERATURE AND MOVIES

Wildes Paradies, rote Hölle: das Bild Mexikos in Literatur und Film der Moderne. Friedhelm Schmidt (Hrsg.). Bielefeld: Aisthesis Verlag, 1992. 236 p.

About the Author

Marvin Alisky has been attuned to Mexican public life since his child-hood in San Antonio, Texas. By age six his parents had taken him on two summer vacations in Monterrey, and he had become bilingual, speaking Spanish without an American accent. At age 24 he was a newscaster at WOAI, the NBC radio network affiliate in San Antonio, becoming the network's youngest foreign correspondent in Mexico City. After a stay in Buenos Aires covering Argentina and Uruguay, he completed a PhD in Latin American politics at the University of Texas at Austin.

In academia, he taught Indiana University's first course in Latin American government. He then went to Arizona State University (ASU), where he expanded its single course on Latin American government into several: Inter-American Relations and the Political Systems of Mexico, Central America, and South America. In 1965 he founded ASU's Center for Latin American Studies, directing it until 1972.

Alisky has been a visiting professor at Trinity University in San Antonio. He was also a Fulbright scholar at the Catholic University in Lima and at the National University of Nicaragua, founding the School of Journalism and Political Science in Managua. He has been a visiting scholar at the Woodrow Wilson International Affairs School at Princeton, at the Hoover Institution at Stanford, and, thanks to a World Media Association research grant, at the Latin American Institute in Moscow.

He has done research at the Latin American Center in Beijing and lectured at Oxford University's Latin American Centre. He was associate scholar at the 1975 Inter-Parliamentary Conference of United States and Mexican members of Congress at La Paz, Baja California, and in 1973 an associate at the Colegio de México. In 1984–1989 he served on the 12-member Board of the Fulbright Commission on Foreign Scholarships, a presidential appointment.

Alisky's published works include more than 200 magazine, encyclopedia, and yearbook articles, mostly on Latin America (mainly Mexico), including newspaper articles for the *Wall Street Journal* and *Christian Science Monitor* and on U.S.-Mexican relations for Mexican readers. He has written eight books and has co-authored ten other volumes, mostly collections of studies on Latin American topics.

In 1962 he covered the meeting of Presidents Kennedy and López Mateos for NBC radio. In 1974 he was President Ford's advisor at his meeting with President Echeverría at the Arizona-Sonora border. He has interviewed Presidents Alemán and Ruíz Cortines and several cabinet ministers for NBC radio. Manolo Fábregas twice interviewed him on his Sunday night talk show on Mexican TV Channel 8. He has served four times on the board of the Governor's Arizona-Mexico Commission to promote cultural and trade relations between Arizona and Sonora.

In 1997, in a column written 10 days before Mexico's congressional elections, Alisky correctly forecast that the PRI would lose its majority in the lower house for the first time since 1929. He has been listed in *Who's Who in America* since 1985.